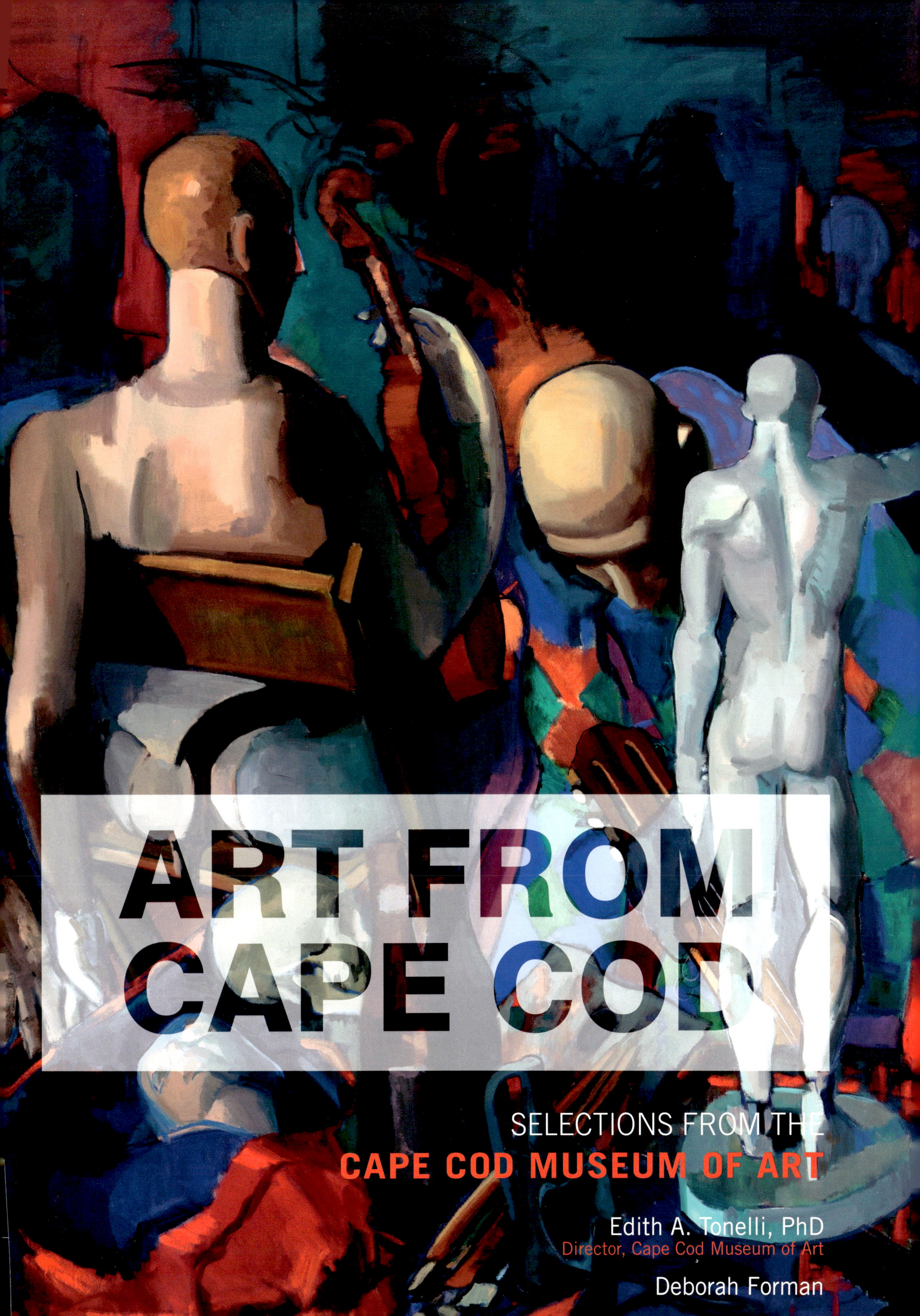

ART FROM CAPE COD

SELECTIONS FROM THE CAPE COD MUSEUM OF ART

Edith A. Tonelli, PhD
Director, Cape Cod Museum of Art

Deborah Forman

Many thanks to the Sidwell Family Trust
for its generous support of this publication.

Other Schiffer Books by Deborah Forman:
Contemporary Cape Cod Artists: Images of Land and Sea, ISBN 978-0-7643-4451-0
Contemporary Cape Cod Artists: On Abstraction, ISBN 978-0-7643-4865-5
Contemporary Cape Cod Artists: People and Places, ISBN 978-0-7643-4722-1
Perspectives on the Provincetown Art Colony, ISBN 978-0-7643-3682-9

Library of Congress Control Number: 2016937528

Designed by John P. Cheek
Cover design by Brenda McCallum

Photography by James Zimmerman.

Front Cover: Romanos Rizk, *Pond #5 Beechwood Forest,* n.d.

Back Cover: Top Left: Exterior, Cape Cod Museum of Art, photo by Christy King. *Top Right:* Hans Hofmann, *Untitled,* 1950. *Bottom:* Ross Moffett, *Blue Heron, Pilgrim Lake*, 1969. Sculpture: Del Filardi, *Heron,* 1996.

Title page: Salvatore Del Deo, *Studio Concept II*, 1992.

Type set in Bauer Bodoni BT/Trade Gothic LT Std

ISBN: 978-0-7643-5134-1
Printed in China

Published by Schiffer Publishing, Ltd.
4880 Lower Valley Road
Atglen, PA 19310
Phone: (610) 593-1777; Fax: (610) 593-2002
E-mail: Info@schifferbooks.com
Web: www.schifferbooks.com

For our complete selection of fine books on this and related subjects, please visit our website at www.schifferbooks.com. You may also write for a free catalog.

Schiffer Publishing's titles are available at special discounts for bulk purchases for sales promotions or premiums. Special editions, including personalized covers, corporate imprints, and excerpts, can be created in large quantities for special needs. For more information, contact the publisher.

We are always looking for people to write books on new and related subjects. If you have an idea for a book, please contact us at proposals@schifferbooks.com.

Contents

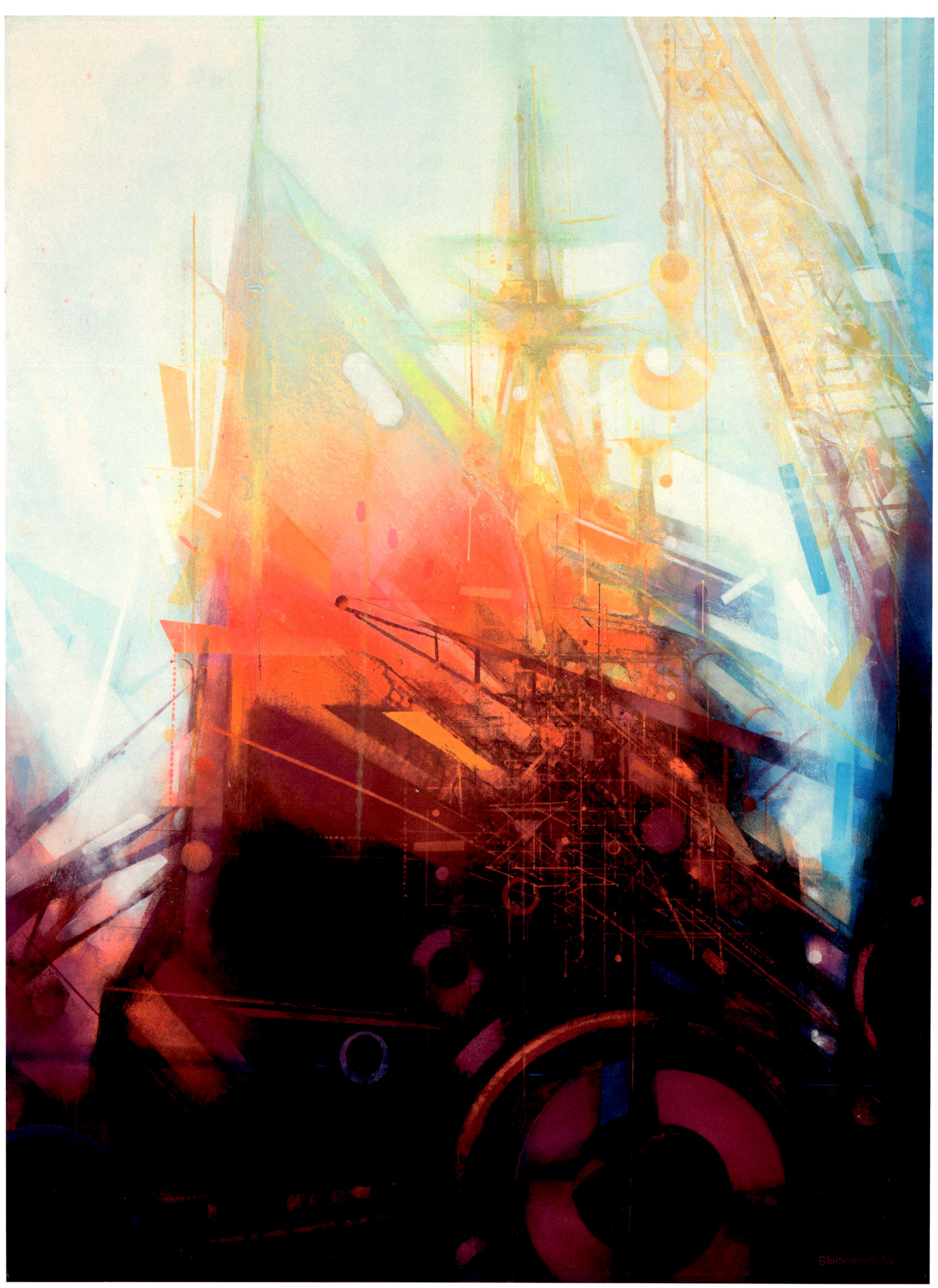

Donald Stoltenberg, *Battleship in Drydock,* 1988.

Acknowledgments

As the relatively new director of the Cape Cod Museum of Art, I am extremely grateful to all of those contributions over the years that have combined to make this publication possible. There are many, many people to thank. Our founders, Harry Holl and Roy Freed, accompanied by supporters Arnold Geissbuhler, Anne Stout, and Margaret Whittlesey, who had the dream of a museum with a comprehensive collection of "Art from Cape Cod," deserve a huge debt of gratitude.

The creative artists and the generous donors who brought this collection into existence gave of themselves and their treasures to make this art available to the public. They can never be thanked enough.

To all the former museum administrators, trustees, and staff who had the vision, as well as the will, throughout the years, to encourage the giving of these gifts, and the commitment to create a place to preserve them for future generations, we are most obliged and indebted. In addition, many thanks to the dedicated members of the Collections/Acquisitions Committee, who, throughout the years, spent countless hours reviewing the works of art offered to the museum, including several of those who helped from the beginning, including Barbara Rockefeller, Robert Douglas Hunter, Dr. Linda Miller, Joyce Johnson, and Ann O'Connell.

Former directors Suzanne Packer, Gregg Harper, and Elizabeth Ives Hunter have been especially generous in contributing their time and reminiscences to help round out this remarkable history.

Steve and Kate Sidwell, of the Sidwell Family Trust, are most heartily thanked for their faith and their generosity. They were first in encouraging and supporting the idea of this publication, and coming forward with the seed money to enable the research, the writing, and the photographing of the art in this book.

The entire staff of the museum, who have given time and taken on extra tasks, so that the work of this book could go forward, are greatly appreciated for their understanding and patience. Within this staff, special thanks must go to Angela Bilski, registrar, who contributed countless hours to the inventory, organization, and processing of every object in this collection of 2,020 objects—and counting. James Doherty, registrarial assistant, arrived on site at just the right moment to aid in the compiling and organizing of the data, and in the physical arranging of the pieces that were needed for photography.

James Zimmerman, photographer par excellence, was invaluable. He made it possible for us to document the highlights of our collection, and have high-quality images, in a record amount of time, with consummate professionalism and flexibility.

I personally must thank Suzanne Packer, first director of the museum, and currently our volunteer archivist, for her diligent, methodical organization of the archives, her lively articulation of the history of the museum, and unfailing support and encouragement.

And to Deborah Forman, I express my sincerest gratitude. Without her, this volume would never have been realized. Her commitment and dedication, her generosity with her time and advice, her wealth of knowledge, her precision and attention to detail, coupled with her patience and good humor, have made this enterprise rewarding and enjoyable for me and everyone involved.

Edith A. Tonelli, PhD
Director

Introduction

From the Beginning

Walking through the Cape Cod Museum of Art and its sculpture garden, you might see impressionistic landscapes, an exhibition of surreal photographs, or abstract sculpture made with found objects, all by artists who work on the Cape, but whose range goes far beyond it. Cape Cod art has always been, and continues to be, diverse and widespread, and the museum has enthusiastically embraced that diversity from its earliest days.

The Cape Cod Museum of Art celebrates its thirty-fifth anniversary in 2016. In 1981, with $100 in its bank account, it was established by a handful of supporters who were concerned that much of the art created locally was being sold and collected outside the Cape Cod region. At that time, the only institution actively collecting on Cape Cod was the Provincetown Art Association and Museum on the Lower Cape, and its focus was on artists in Provincetown and neighboring towns, a focus that continues to the present day. Harry Holl, a sculptor and potter who had a broad-minded vision of art and what this museum should exhibit and collect, and his lawyer-artist friend, Roy Freed, founded the CCMoA with the support of art patrons Anne Stout and Margaret Whittlesey.

CCMoA's first name was The Scargo Lake Museum, a bow to the beautiful, fresh-water lake that was the home base for the sculptor Arnold Geissbuhler, and later, his son-in-law, Harry Holl. Geissbuhler's support and gifts of art were a major impetus for the founding of the museum. In 1982, the nonprofit was renamed, loftily, the Cape Museum of Fine Arts. Suzanne Packer, the first director of the museum and an essential contributor to this catalogue, expressed that even she felt that this name "sounded far too important and well established for an organization that did not have a building, or . . . a single piece of art." However, creating an institution that could live up to the implications of that name was the core dream of its idealistic founders.

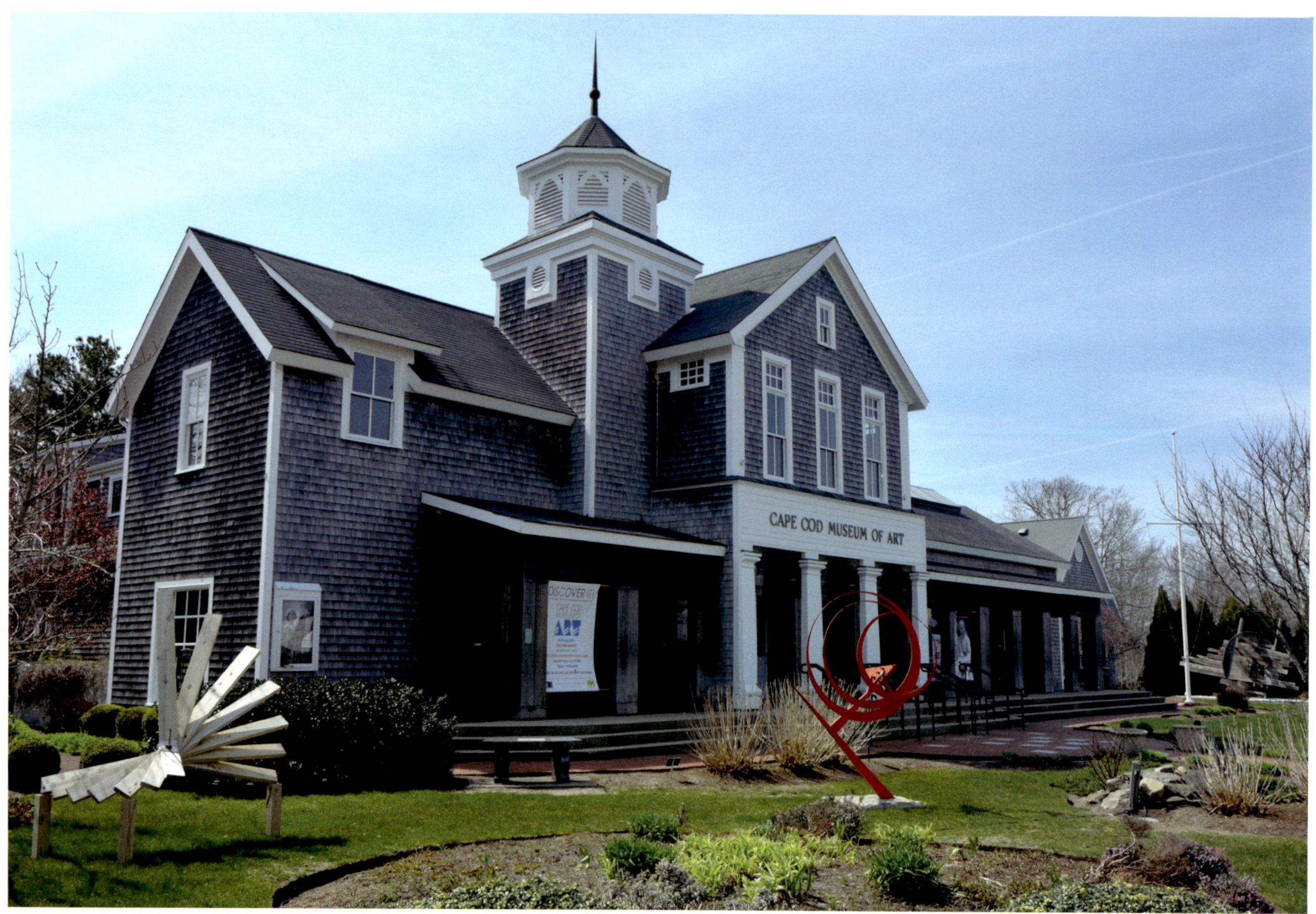

Cape Cod Museum of Art, April 2016. *Photo courtesy of Benton Jones.*

In 1982, a charter membership drive was begun. A rented storefront in Theater Marketplace on Route 6A in Dennis Village provided the first home for the museum. To facilitate growth in a permanent location, the museum trustees signed an agreement with the Raymond Moore Foundation in 1984 to lease an acre of land on the grounds of the historic Cape Playhouse in Dennis Village to "erect a fine arts museum for the Cape." By 1985, there were nearly a thousand members.

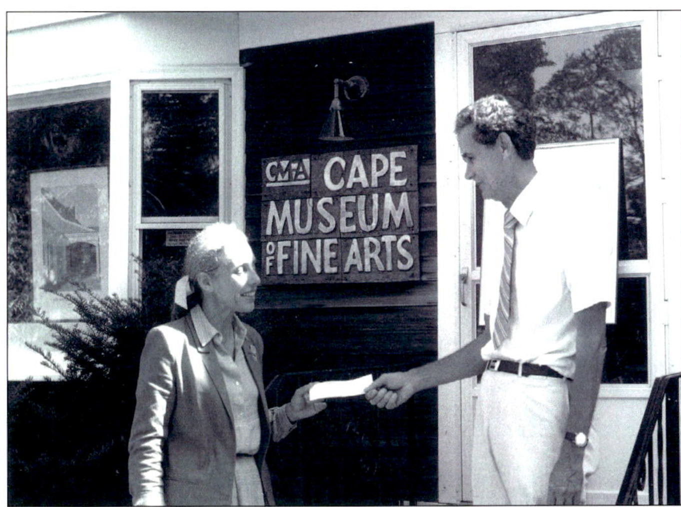

Suzanne Packer, first director of the Cape Museum of Fine Arts, accepting a donation from Bill Saxton of Exxon Corporation, 1987. *Photographer unknown.*

Within two years, the Davenport West family in Harwich had donated a building to permanently house the growing collection of fine art. Holl and his friends were not daunted by the prospect of having to take apart and move this 10,000-square-foot building. They wanted a grand and impressive space that could house and exhibit paintings, large-scale sculpture, furniture, and pottery. A $300,000 campaign, titled "Museum on the Move," was established to fund the construction of a foundation and to move the building from South Harwich to the leased site in Dennis. When the building was moved to Dennis in September of 1987, it was divided into eleven pieces and required seven trucks to make

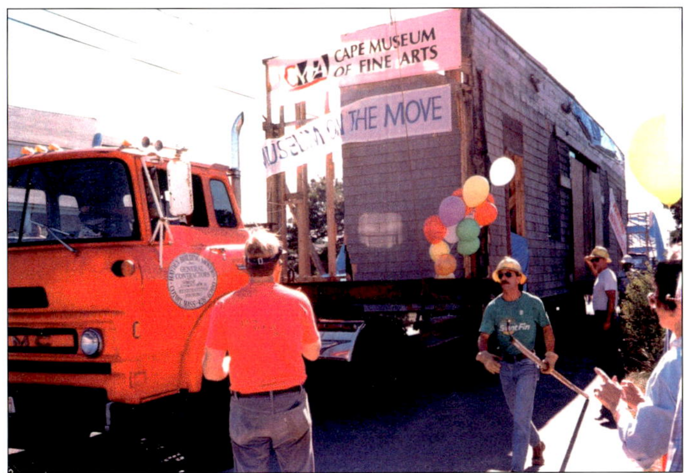

Cape Museum of Fine Arts—A "Museum on the Move," September 1987. *Photographer unknown.*

the journey across the Cape, traveling Route 6 to Old Bass River Road and Route 6A to reach the Raymond Moore grounds.

The founders' continued optimism toward building an important museum was based on the pledge of donations from several local patrons of collections that needed homes. From the very beginning, those gifts were more diverse than most museums initially collect. "Fine Arts," for the museum's founders, donors, and supporters, was broadly defined. The first gift, of the diverse work of Arnold Geissbuhler, a Cape-based sculptor who had studied in Europe with Antoine Bourdelle and Alberto Giacometti, included bronze sculpture, terra cotta busts, bas-reliefs, drawings, and sketches. Other early gifts, from Howard Gibbs's and Vernon Smith's studios, included oil paintings, wood carvings, prints, and drawings.

It took more than twenty years and several changes of administration before the museum changed its "Fine Arts" moniker to just "Art"; hence, the Cape Cod Museum of Art, which signaled a clear-cut mandate—the commitment to a broad definition of art. Intervening years had already brought in collections and exhibitions that spanned the spectrum of craft, design, illustration, photography, printmaking, and mixed media, as well as painting and sculpture. In the earliest years of the museum, under the direction of Ms. Packer, exhibitions were held with titles such as *Circus, 3 Illustrators,* and *The Cape Playhouse and Cinema Connections*.

The two primary directors who followed Suzanne Packer (1986–1992) were Gregg Harper (1993–2001) and Elizabeth Ives Hunter (2003–2012), and they continued in this spirit of diversity in both collecting and programming. Mr. Harper was interested in professionalizing the museum and building the collection around the earlier Cape artists' schools or groups, such as that of Hans Hofmann and the "Punkhorn" group, and also in expanding the concept of "fine art" to include "fine craft." He added large-scale works for the sculpture garden, a carved bas-relief in wood by Vernon Smith, and an oversized mobile by Arthur Bauman, which became a permanent fixture in the large Hope-McClennen Gallery (p. 255). Harper also presented exhibitions of Native American ceramics and metal casting, as well as one titled *Beyond Conventional Expectations: Wood/Fabric/Clay/Glass,* indicating his support for art in many forms.

Elizabeth Ives Hunter inherited a collection that was, in her words, "an interesting but spotty representation of the art of the region." She hoped that the collections would eventually reflect a broad diversity of materials and processes, including, "paintings, sculpture, furniture, jewelry, glass, and other decorative arts made in the region from as early as possible to the present . . . and include work from all over the world, which had influenced regional artists and craftsmen." During her tenure, she acquired objects as diverse as a Peter Hunt furniture hutch, Harry Holl's tea ceremony bowls, many mixed-media constructions, and two Japanese woodblock prints, as well as a classic Hans Hofmann oil painting (p. 51) and a Thomas Hart Benton lithograph (p. 66).

What follows in this volume is a selection of work by 121 of the 511 artists represented in a collection that numbers more

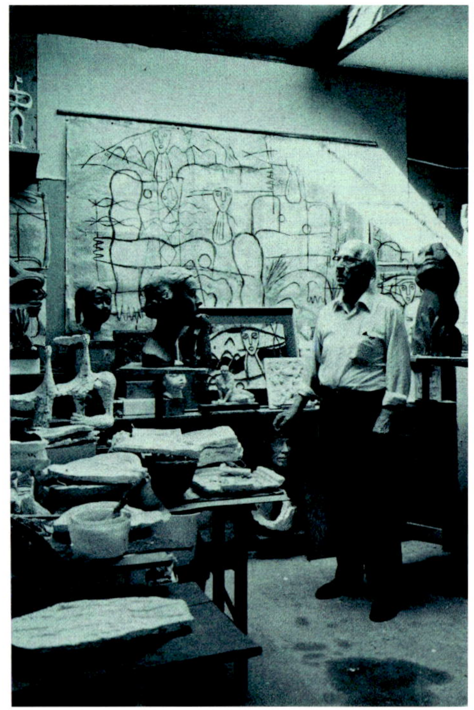

Sculptor Arnold Geissbuhler in his studio, 1982. *Photo courtesy of Paul Giambarba.*

than 2,000 objects. Choices for inclusion were made both on the basis of the importance of the artist historically, nationally, and regionally, and on the quality of the individual works of art that the museum currently houses. Limitations of space meant that many fine contemporary artists could not be included, but may hopefully be part of a subsequent publication.

Cape Cod Art Traditions: A Context for a Collection

Because of the diversity of art making on Cape Cod, the CCMoA has an opportunity to research and present the broad sweep of local creative activity and place it within the context of the region and larger framework of American art history. These are local stories that have not been well documented, except for the importance of the art colony in Provincetown, which has been most recently chronicled in two publications, *A Century of Inspiration* (PAAM, 2015), and the two-volume *Perspectives on the Provincetown Art Colony* (Schiffer Publishing, 2011). One of the missions of our museum is to encourage research into the many long-standing artistic traditions on this peninsula, as well as into the scattered artists' groups and associations that developed over the past decades, including, but also looking beyond, the confines of what the Pilgrims called the "Provincelands," when they stopped here before settling in Plymouth.

The earliest of those creative traditions that has informed local artistic activity is scavenging in nature to produce beautiful objects. This tradition is vibrantly expressed today in the collages and sculptures of artists such as Varujan Boghosian, Mike Wright, and Paul Bowen. Boghosian's title for his whimsical sculptural collage, *Something for Magritte*, (p. 212) alludes to the early-twentieth-century French surrealist movement, and Bowen's found-wood sculptures (p. 287) innovatively reference cubism. The context for these artists' work is not only twentieth-century European and American art movements, but also the creativity of those Wampanoag craftswomen from the sixteenth and seventeenth centuries who gathered grasses to make baskets and collected white and purple shells to create currency (wampum) and decorative beads. Today, following this age-old creative thread, many Cape Cod artists pursue beachcombing, dumpster-diving (Mike Wright, p. 286), and recycling as part of their active artistic process.

There is also an influential, long-standing tradition from Colonial craftsmen-artists of creating hand-worked functional objects from local, natural materials to produce pottery, glass, furniture, and decorative painting. The tradition of glass-making is well documented locally, beginning with the Sandwich Glass Factory and continuing with the many small studio-glass enterprises that now produce both functional and sculptural artifacts. Artist-potters, many of them former students of the museum's founder, Harry Holl (p. 204), have studios and galleries throughout the region. Local woodworkers and furniture-makers have long created one-of-a-kind objects, some with decorative surfaces, and some reusing driftwood and recycled beams, planks, and wood fragments that date back to the colonial period.

Many styles and techniques, which now seem synonymous with Cape Cod landscape painting, were influenced by local artists' exposure to nineteenth-century *plein-air* (outdoor) painting and impressionist responses to light. John Joseph Enneking (p. 18), Charles Hawthorne (p. 42), Henry Hensche (p. 110), John Whorf (p. 128), and Edward Hopper, all of whom lived and worked on Cape Cod, influenced many generations of painters. Adding to those more obvious traditions was the precision of the neoclassical realists and the drama of the eighteenth- and nineteenth-century romantics, which filtered down through American luminist traditions and the Hudson River School to the "Boston School" realism of Robert Douglas Hunter (p. 236), the mysteries of Robert Vickery (p. 220), and the landscape work of Anne Packard (p. 262), William Davis (p. 289), and Joseph McGurl (p. 293).

But Cape Cod art also has been dramatically influenced by twentieth-century modernist traditions. Beginning with cubism and expressionism, lively experimentation was employed by such diverse artists as Blanche Lazzell (p. 46), Lucy L'Engle (p. 70), Karl Knaths (p. 76), Vernon Smith (p. 83), and Thomas Eastwood (p. 114). Surrealism infiltrated the work of George Grosz (p. 82), Lawrence Kupferman (p. 158), Leo Manso (p. 172), and even the current work of Carmen Cicero (p. 216). Precisionism, an outgrowth of cubism, reverberated with many American painters, and found its way to Cape Cod through the work of Xavier Gonzalez (p. 100), Richard Florsheim (p. 182), and Donald Stoltenberg (p. 226).

As a dynamic teacher, Hans Hofmann (p. 50) encouraged experimentation in even the most abstract directions, with many artists crossing into areas of formalism and nonobjective productions. Abstract expressionism became pure abstraction in the work of some of his students and colleagues, such as William Freed (p. 118), William Littlefield (p. 120), Peter Busa (p. 170), Lillian Orlowsky (p. 174), Sam Feinstein (p. 177),

Taro Yamamoto (p. 196), and Boris Margo, as well as developing into the formal geometrics of Haynes Ownby (p. 247), Myron Stout, and Budd Hopkins (p. 257).

Finally, there are debts to Asian aesthetic traditions, dating from the colonial-era sea-trade through nineteenth-century art imports, of asymmetry, simplification of forms and color, and patterning. The Japanese technique of woodcut printmaking directly influenced the work of the American artist and teacher Arthur Wesley Dow, and, in turn, prompted the print experiments in Provincetown. White-line woodcut printing in black-and-white and color produced the local imagery of Agnes Weinrich (p. 44), Blanche Lazzell (p. 47), and Ferol Sibley Worthen (p. 72).

These artistic traditions, intermingled with the unrelenting attraction of the Cape's natural surroundings—water on all sides and light that can mesmerize—have infused and inspired the eclectic mix of past and current techniques and imagery. There is something special and different about living and creating on Cape Cod. Many artists have commented on the "pull" of the natural world and the need to integrate personal aesthetic and artistic training with the "demands" and stimulation of insistent nature. Always evident is the smell of ocean spray; the warm, seductive, reflected light; the strong presence and immediacy of preserved natural beaches, marshes, and meadows; and the distinct "feel" of each season.

The Demand of Cape Cod's Diversity: Building a Museum and a Collection

As the newest director of this institution, I have been thrilled to discover what an invaluable resource the Cape Cod Museum of Art is for education and inspiration. The museum's mandate to preserve and present the Cape's diverse cultural heritage, in order to inspire audiences locally and globally, creates a challenge, but a worthwhile one.

The first part of that challenge is continuing to collect and present the variety of art that has developed out of the local profusion of materials, techniques, and imagery. Some of this diversity has come from local and natural sources, some from external or global influences. The second part of that challenge is to make this diversity of artistic creation understandable and enjoyable to all our audiences, although some of it may not be familiar or expected.

People find value in many ways, and the passion that enlivens our community museum flows from the joy of creating a place of quiet contemplation or riotous laughter, of intense, individual creativity, or cooperative adventure, while constantly encouraging interaction, socialization, and building of community. The museum's diverse offerings can speak to each of us in different ways at different times. It is rewarding to hear someone remark on the quiet, calming energy felt in the galleries, or a grandmother tell her grandchild that she used to swim "right there, right off the dock in that painting!" And it is inspiring to see a young woman taking a "selfie" through a dramatic outdoor installation, or a father showing his son an artwork that had mesmerized him as a student, or an artist demonstrating how one special art exhibition inspired her to create an entirely new series of work. There have been many moments like these.

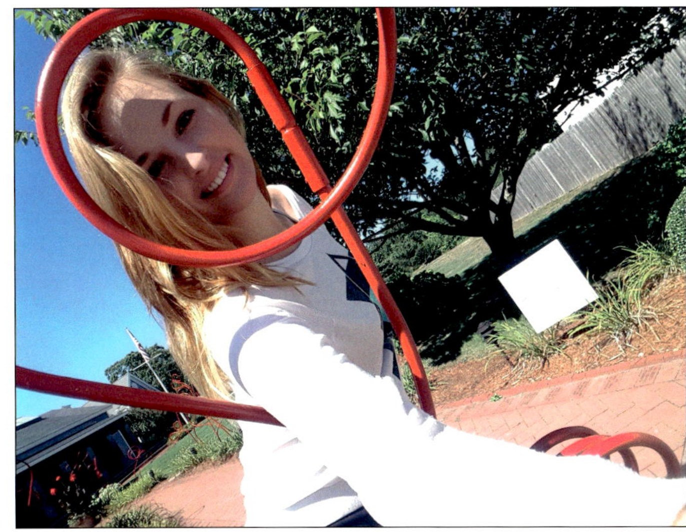

A "selfie" at the CCMoA, August 2015. *#RedLineSelfie* Outdoor Sculpture by Angela Rose. *Photo courtesy of Edith A. Tonelli.*

A collection of artworks, reflecting the feelings and ideas that so many experience, becomes the core from which to build a variety of interactive opportunities. There are clearly some wonderful objects in this collection, and just as clearly, there is consolidation needed and historical gaps that need filling for this museum to fulfill its mission. There is a limited ability to educate and inspire without adding pieces that refer back to those art historical traditions that have informed the Cape's artists. Just as surely as more cubist Karl Knaths and Blanche Lazzell works are needed, the addition of a representative Pablo Picasso or Georges Braque image would visually illuminate those cubist references better than any written text. In the same manner, an Edward Hopper painting, which represents his influence on decades of the Cape's *plein-air* painters, is as essential as acquiring a more typical landscape by Robert Douglas Hunter or Joseph McGurl. In addition, the museum must embrace its responsibility to search continually for significant works by artists who are under-represented and as yet unrecognized.

At thirty-five, we are a very "young" institution in the world of museums. Having no "name" founder with great wealth, and no endowment for operation, we are required to develop a broad community base of support for what already has become a priceless resource. And that support can come from each and every person, whether in the form of encouraging friends to wander through our galleries and sculpture garden; becoming a member; liking us and sharing posts on Facebook; taking a class; volunteering; sponsoring a special event; making a bequest; or giving gifts of art, skills, or funds. This regional museum has a solid base for growth and unlimited potential to become an even more powerful catalyst for inspiring creativity, finding joy, and providing moments to stop, look, and breathe. Its growth is in the hands of each of us.

Edith A. Tonelli
Director

Selections from the Collection of the Cape Cod Museum of Art

JOHN JAMES AUDUBON
(1785–1851)

The Audubon name is essentially synonymous with images of birds. Ornithologist, artist, and naturalist, John James Audubon is known for his study and illustrations of them in their natural habitats.

He was born in Saint Domingue, now Haiti, and raised in France, where he first began drawing birds. When he was eighteen, he came to America, lived on a family-owned estate near Philadelphia, and began his study of North American birds. He later moved to Kentucky, owned a dry-goods store and continued to draw as a hobby. After his business failed in 1819, he set out to document every ornithological species in North America. He was an ardent observer of nature; he

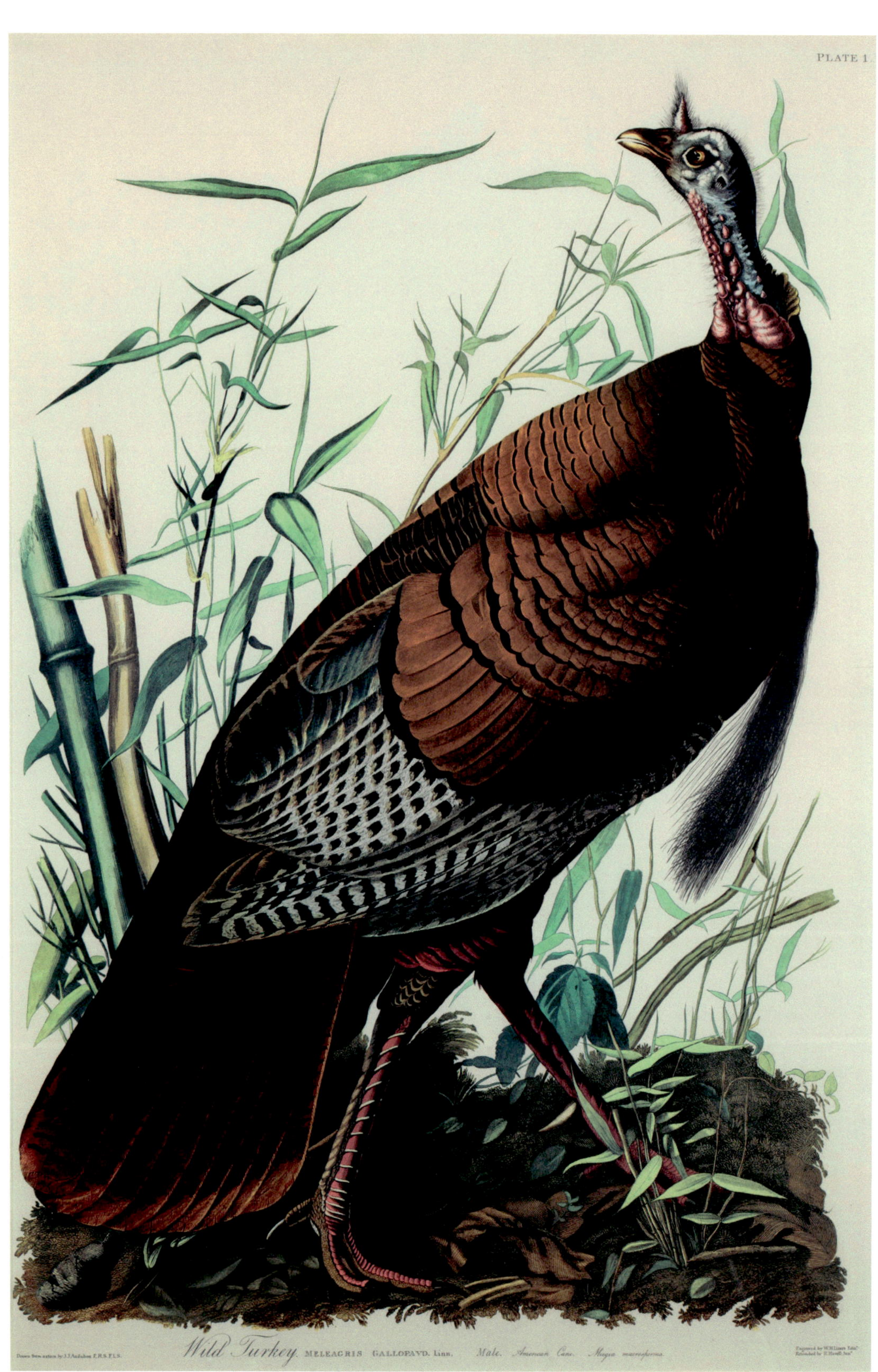

John James Audubon, *Wild Turkey* (Plate 1, Amsterdam Edition), n.d. Engraved print on paper, 38¼ × 25½ inches. *Gift of Richard and Elizabeth Doncaster*, 2005.

made pencil and pastel sketches, and later watercolors, the medium he would most often employ for the rest of his career. The precision and beauty of his work has made Audubon a household name.

By 1824 he was considering publication of his drawings, but was advised to find a publisher in Europe, where there were better engravers. In 1826, he took his collection to England. His life-sized bird portraits found an audience. *Birds of America*, a collection of 435 life-sized prints, was first printed in Edinburgh and later in London. He eventually worked with Scottish ornithologist William MacGillivray on the histories of each of the species in the work. Until 1839, Audubon divided his time between Europe and America, completing illustrations. With his reputation established, he settled in New York City and prepared a smaller edition of his *Birds of America,* and a new work, *Viviparous Quadrupeds of North America*.

In the Cape Cod Museum of Art collection are five Audubon prints. Four—of a turkey, curlew, swan, and whooping crane—are shown within a carefully delineated habitat and have an atmospheric quality. The fifth, of wood ducks, is more like an isolated specimen, a scientific depiction of these beautifully patterned waterfowls.

Audubon's works are in major museum collections, including the Metropolitan Museum of Art in New York, the Museum of Fine Arts in Boston, the Pennsylvania Academy of Fine Arts in Philadelphia, and the National Gallery of Art in Washington, DC.

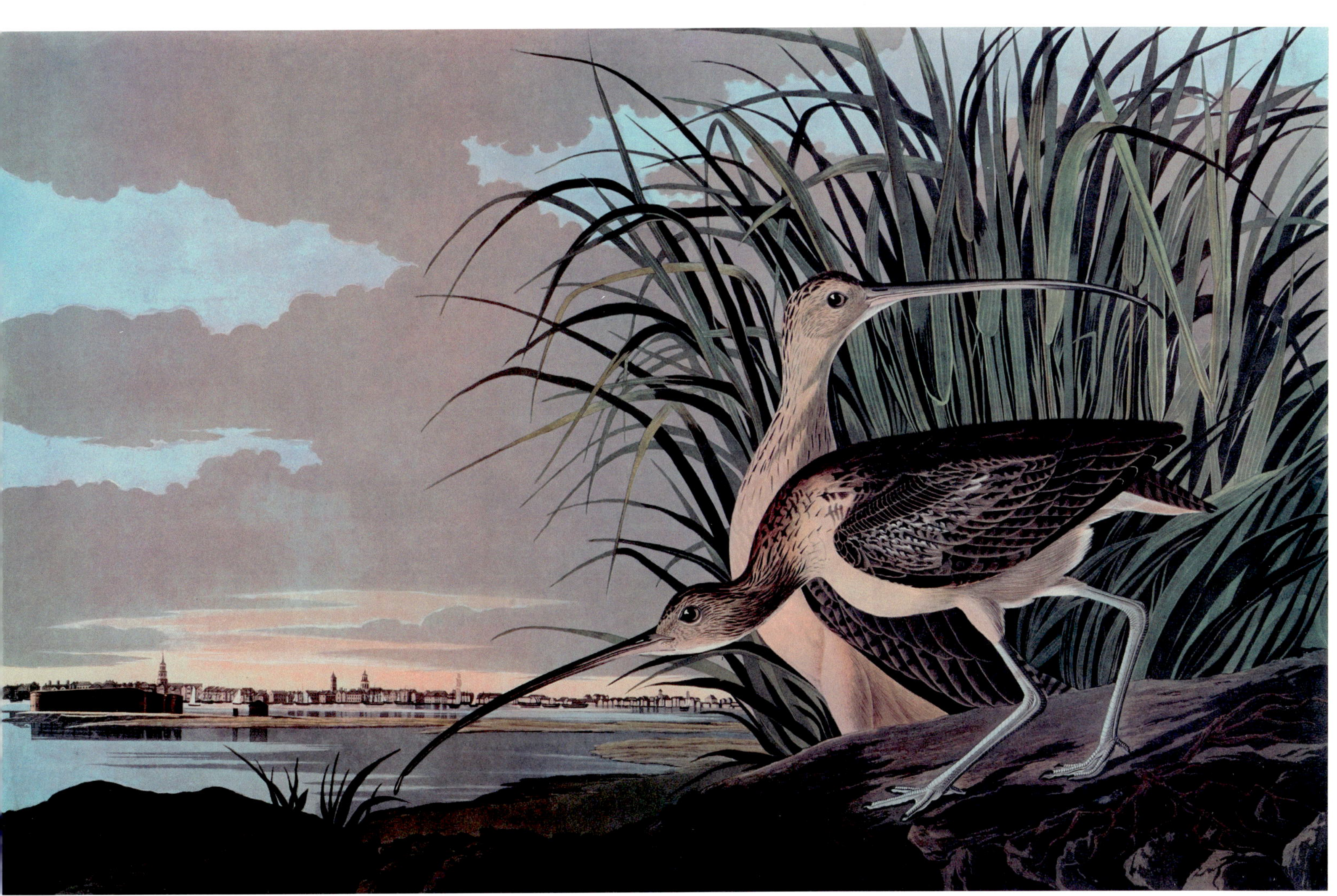

John James Audubon, *Long-Billed Curlew* (Plate CCXXX, Amsterdam Edition), 1834. Engraved print on paper, 22¼ × 35½ inches. *Gift of Richard and Elizabeth Doncaster*, 2007.

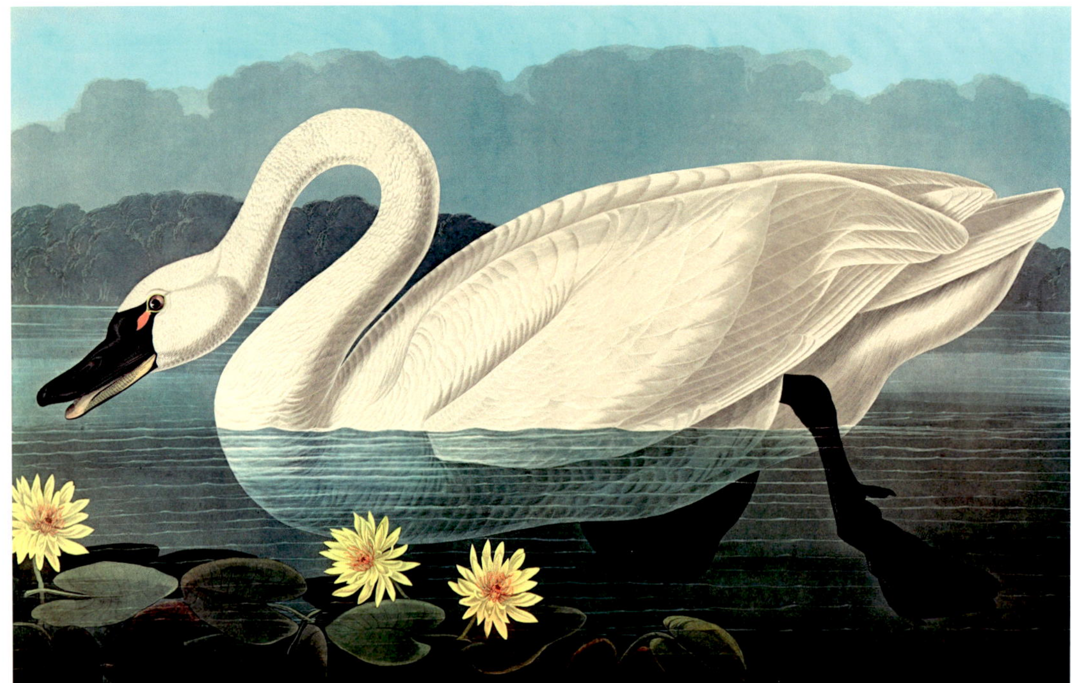

John James Audubon, *Common American Swan* (Plate CCCCXI, Amsterdam Edition), 1834. Engraved print on paper, 33½ × 46 inches. *Gift of Richard and Elizabeth Doncaster*, 2007.

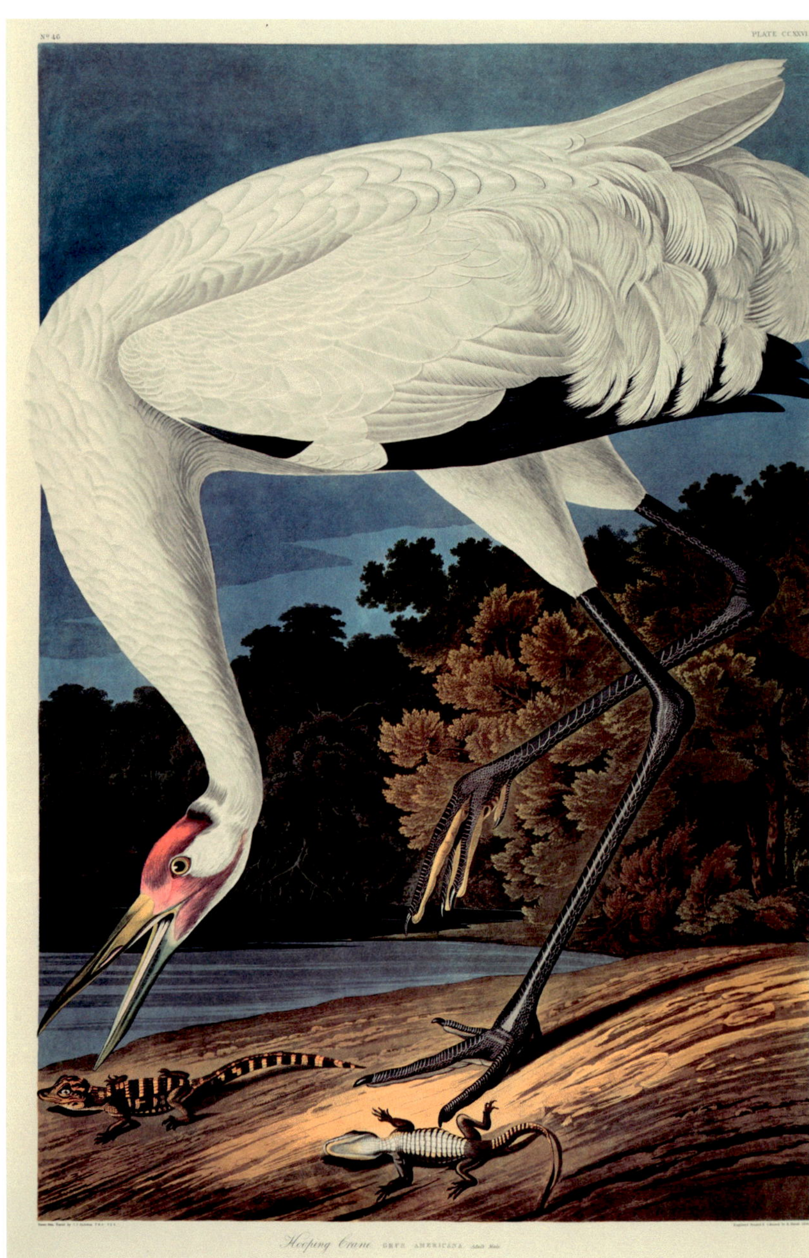

John James Audubon, *Hooping* [sic] *Crane* (Plate CCXXVI, Amsterdam Edition), 1834. Engraved print on paper, 46 × 33½ inches. *Gift of Richard and Elizabeth Doncaster*, 2007.

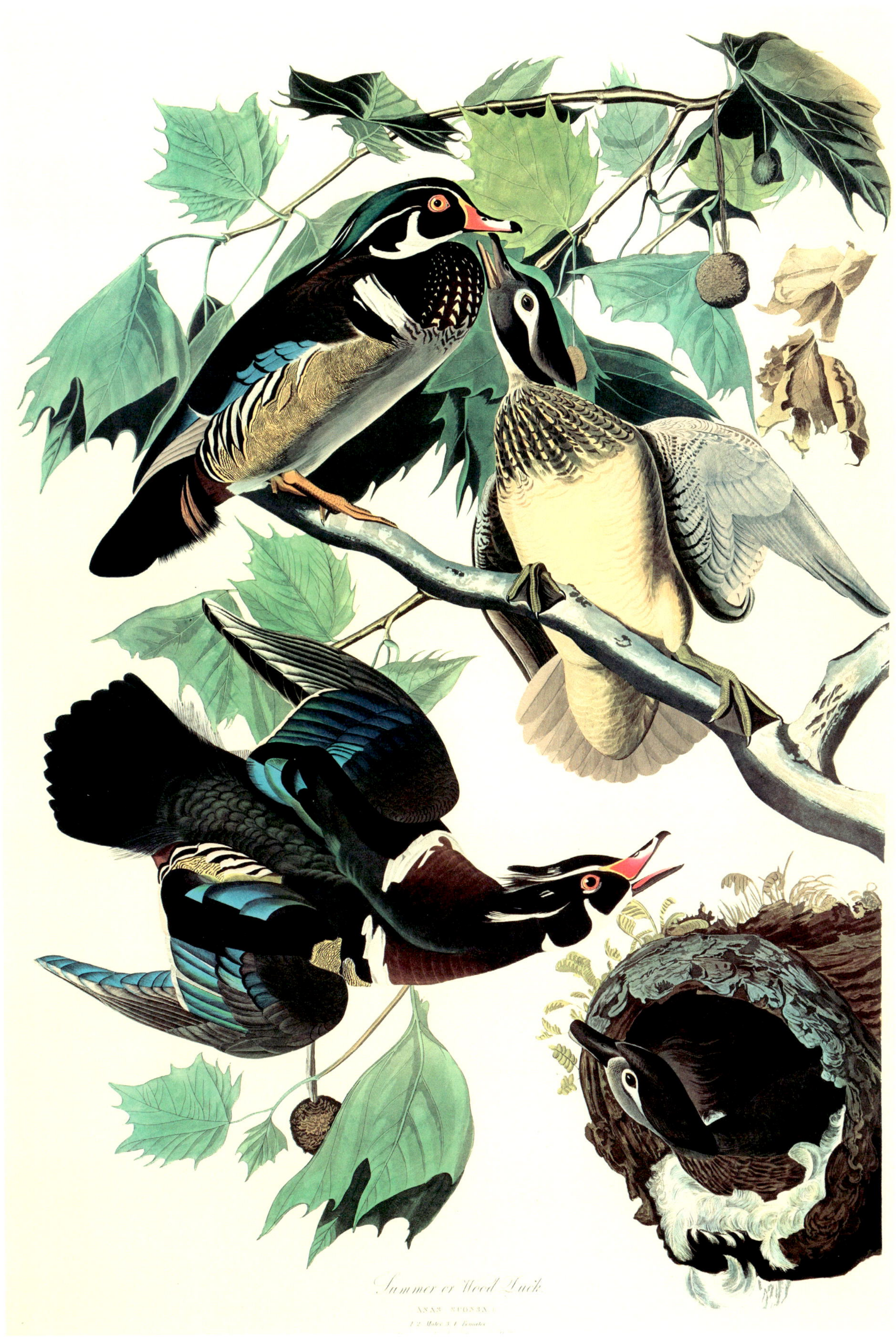

John James Audubon, *Summer or Wood Duck* (Plate CCVI, Amsterdam Edition), 1834.
Engraved print on paper, 46 × 33½ inches. *Gift of Richard and Elizabeth Doncaster*, 2007.

JOHN JOSEPH ENNEKING
(1841–1916)

John Joseph Enneking went to Europe in the 1870s, studied at the Royal Academy in Munich, and spent three years in Paris, where he was influenced by the Barbizon paintings of Charles-Francois Daubigny, Camille Corot, and Jean-Francois Millet. He also met the artists Pierre-Auguste Renoir, Claude Monet, Camille Pissarro, and Édouard Manet, and had the opportunity to paint alongside Monet and Pissarro in Monet's Argenteuil garden in 1873 and 1874. When he returned to Boston in 1876, he brought with him the gift of impressionism.

Born in Minster, Ohio, Enneking grew up on a farm. In 1858 he took drawing lessons at St. Mary's College in Cincinnati. He fought as a Union soldier during the Civil War until he was wounded. He studied art in Boston before his trip abroad. *Raspberries*, in the Cape Cod Museum of Art collection, is an early work painted before his time in Europe.

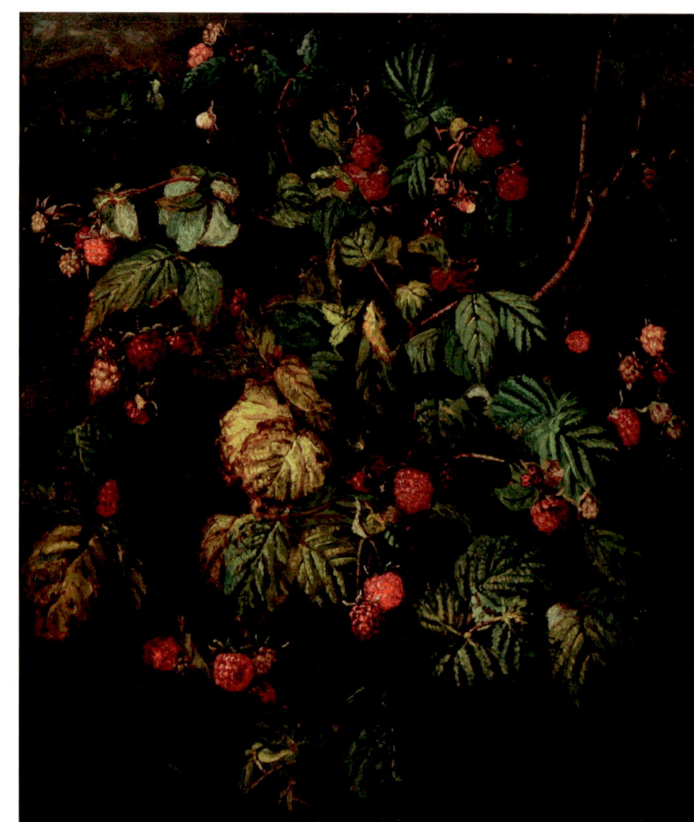

John Joseph Enneking, *Raspberries*, n.d. Oil on canvas, 12 × 14 inches. *Gift of Professor Morris Cohen*, 2006.

John Joseph Enneking, *Fiery Sunset*, n.d. Oil on canvas, 20 × 24 inches. *Gift of Professor Morris Cohen*, 2006.

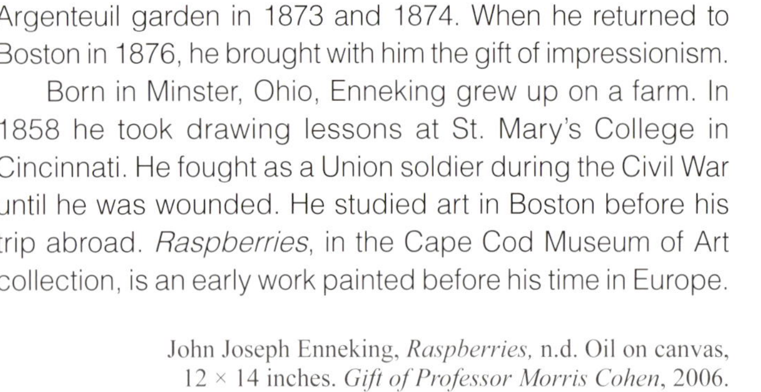

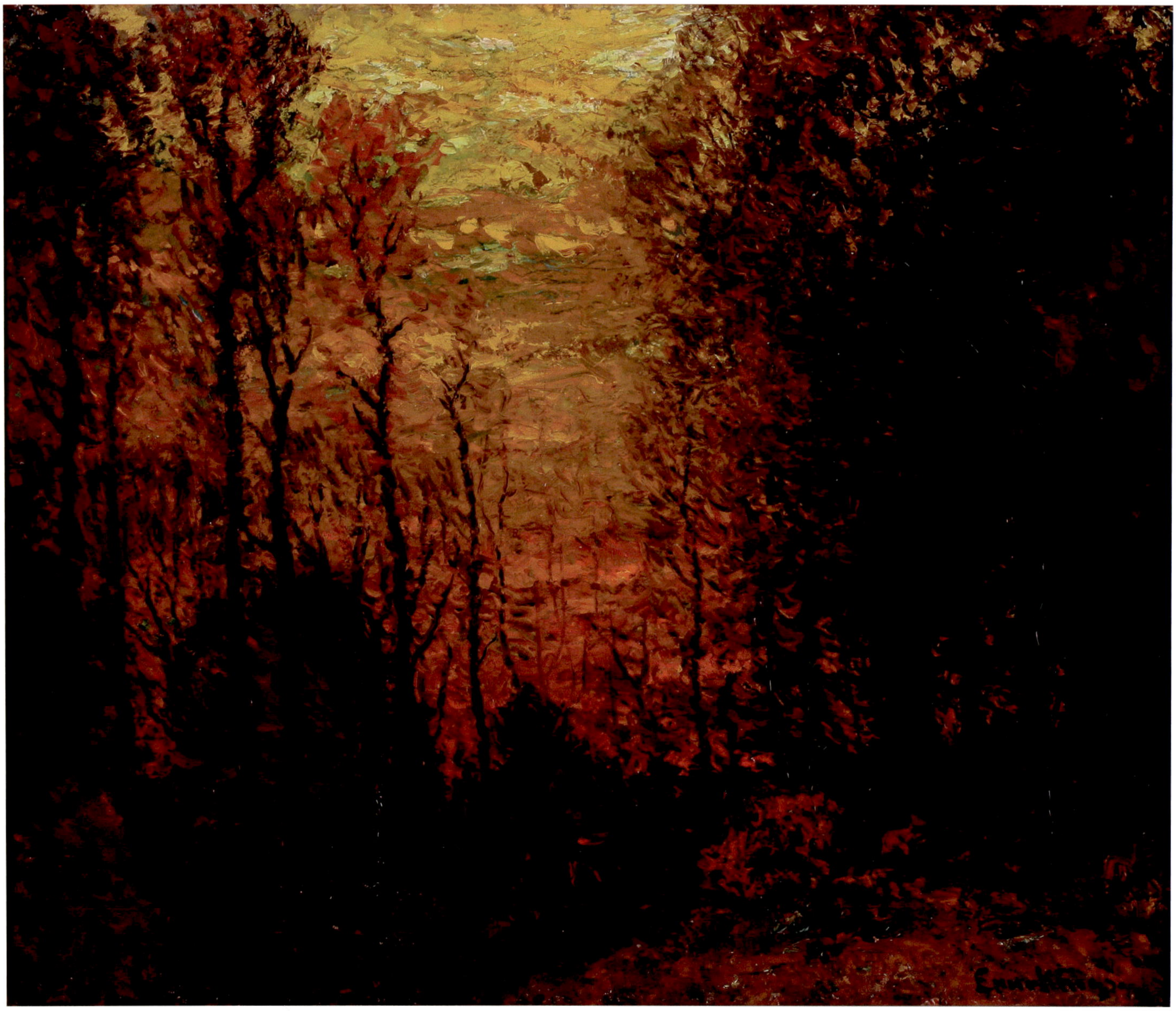

After his years in Paris, Enneking settled in Boston and spent summers painting in Maine and in areas south of Boston, even likely Cape Cod. At first, his palette reflected the tonalities of the Barbizon School, as in *Fiery Sunset*, in the museum collection. Later, his landscapes and figural pieces were known for their vibrant colors and rich impasto, which merged the techniques of the Barbizon and French impressionist painters, as in *Moonlight on the Ocean* and the glorious sunset image, *Obersee*.

Several of his impressionistic works are in the museum collection and include *Grand Canal, Venice* and *Boston Commons and the State House.*

Enneking's paintings are in other museum collections, including the Museum of Fine Arts in Boston, the Indianapolis Museum of Art in Indiana, and the Farnsworth Art Museum in Rockland, Maine.

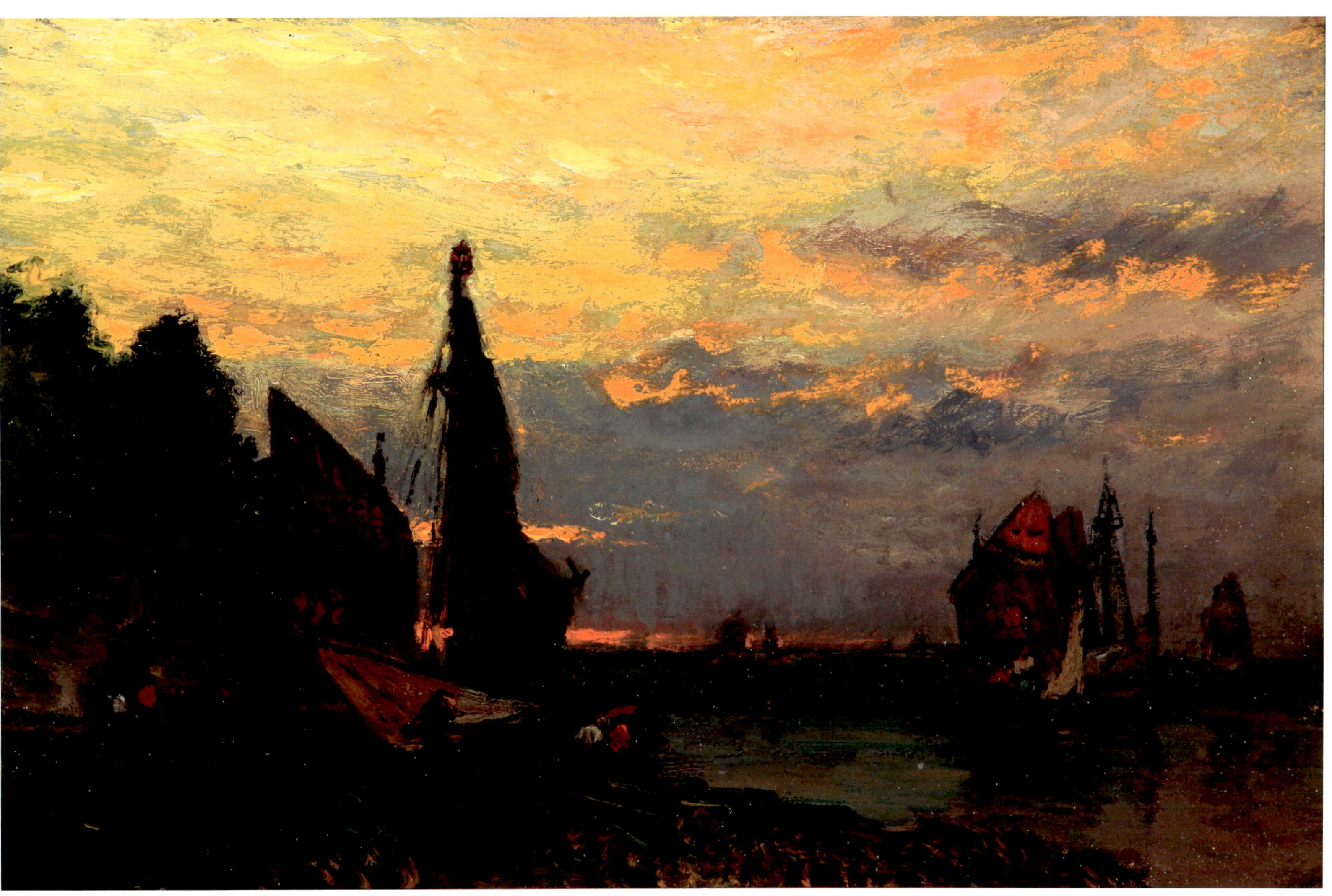

John Joseph Enneking, *Obersee*, n.d. Oil on canvas, 10 × 16 inches. *Gift of Professor Morris Cohen*, 2006.

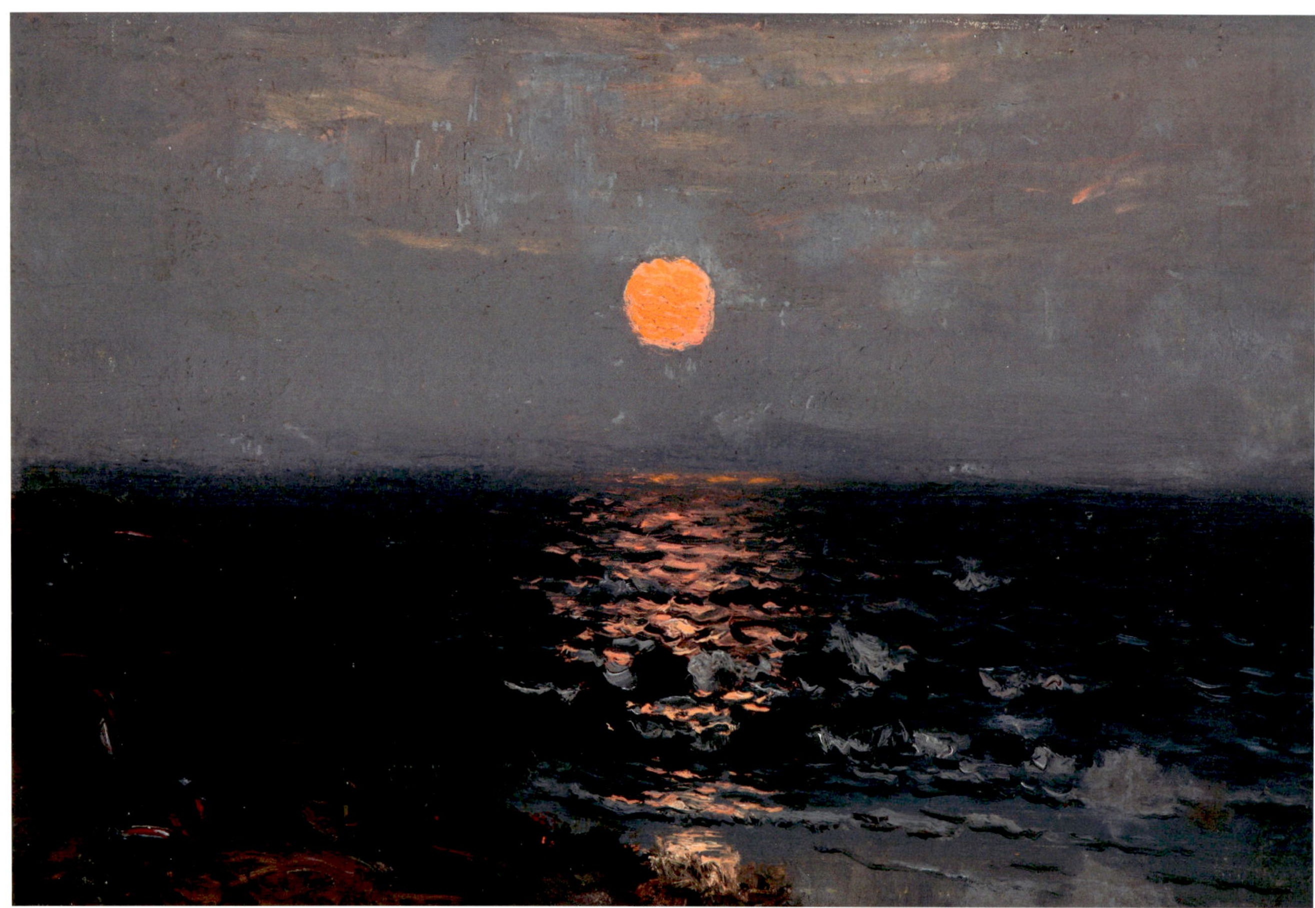

John Joseph Enneking, *Moonlight on the Ocean,* n.d. Oil on board, 8¾ × 13 inches. *Gift of Professor Morris Cohen*, 2006.

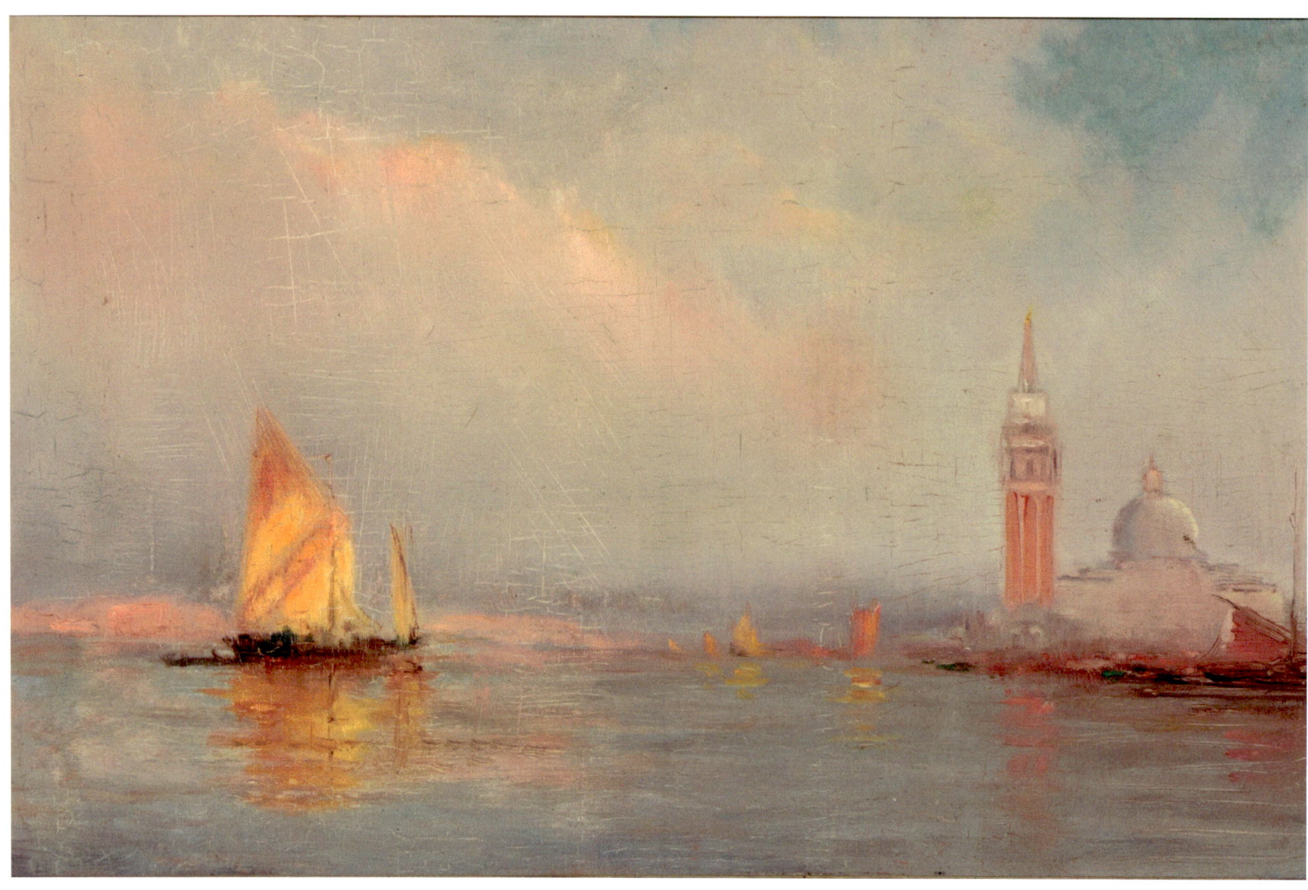

John Joseph Enneking, *Grand Canal, Venice*, n.d. Oil on board, 7 × 11 inches. *Gift of Professor Morris Cohen*, 2006.

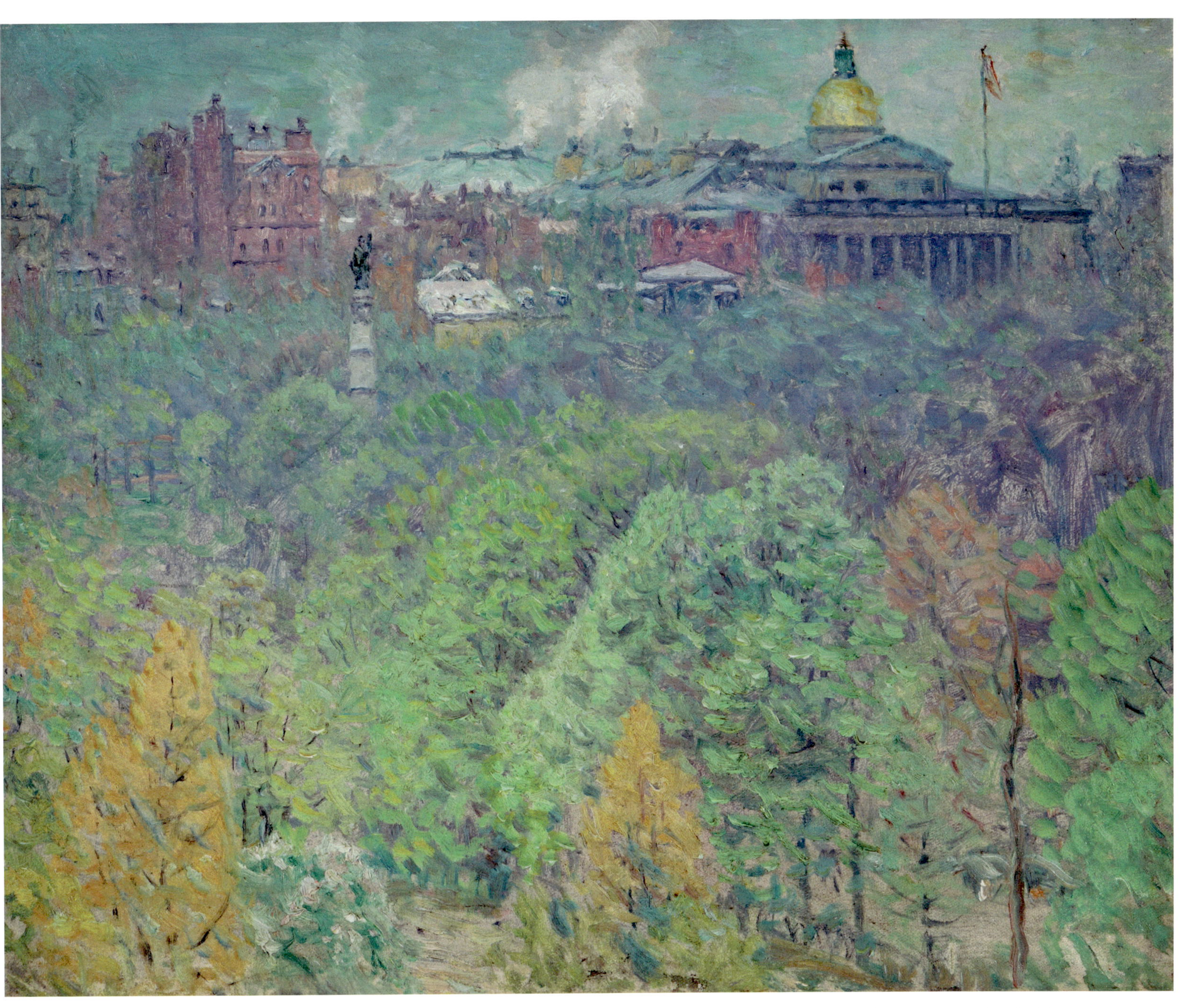

John Joseph Enneking, *Boston Commons and the State House,* n.d. Oil on board, 16 × 20 inches. *Gift of Professor Morris Cohen*, 2006.

CHARLES DREW CAHOON
(1861–1951)

Born in Harwich on Cape Cod, the son of a sea captain and an amateur artist, Charles Cahoon went to sea as a boy. He was drawn to painting from an early age and was essentially self-taught. He worked in a photography studio on the Cape and later in Boston as a photographic retoucher.

By 1903, he had given up photography to become a painter. He maintained a studio in Boston, but also spent time painting on Martha's Vineyard. After returning to Harwich, he painted detailed, peaceful landscapes and seascapes of Cape Cod: marshes, beaches, dunes, harbors, and fishing scenes. He also painted local landmarks, such as the herring run in Brewster, Corn Hill in Truro, Long Pond in Harwich, as well as village scenes, portraits, and still lifes.

Evidence of his commitment to the local area is prominent in several pieces in the Cape Cod Museum of Art collection. In the subtly painted *Eastham House, Sand Dune,* and *Oyster Pond*, you see a serene view of Cape Cod. Although seemingly of another time, some of these views are still happily part of local scenery. In *Ziba Hunt's Workshop*, also in the museum collection, Cahoon takes the viewer indoors, and presents a nostalgic view of a craftsman.

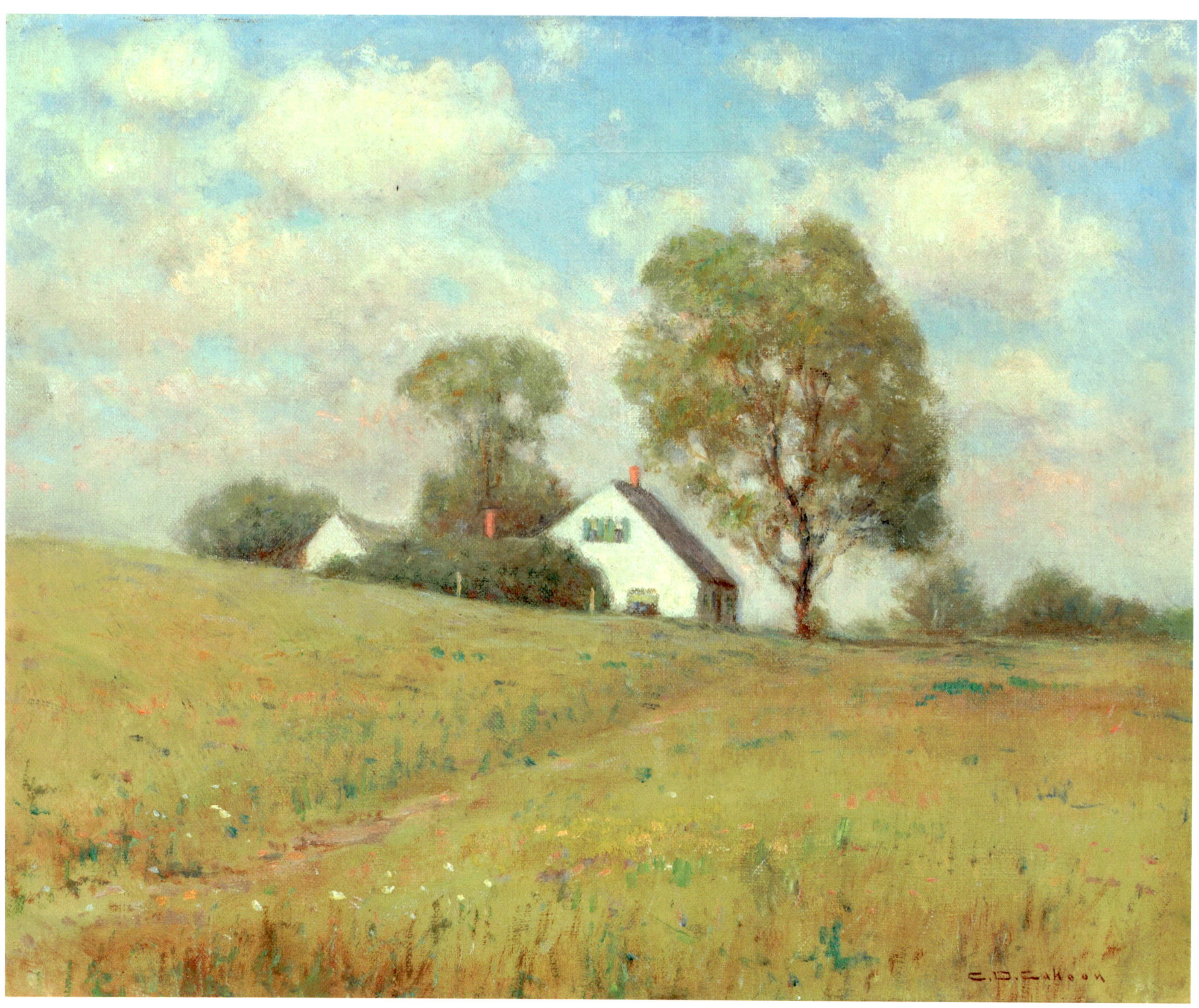

Charles Drew Cahoon, *Eastham House,* n.d. Oil on canvas, 11 × 14 inches.
Gift in honor of Oscar J. Cahoon by his family, 1998.

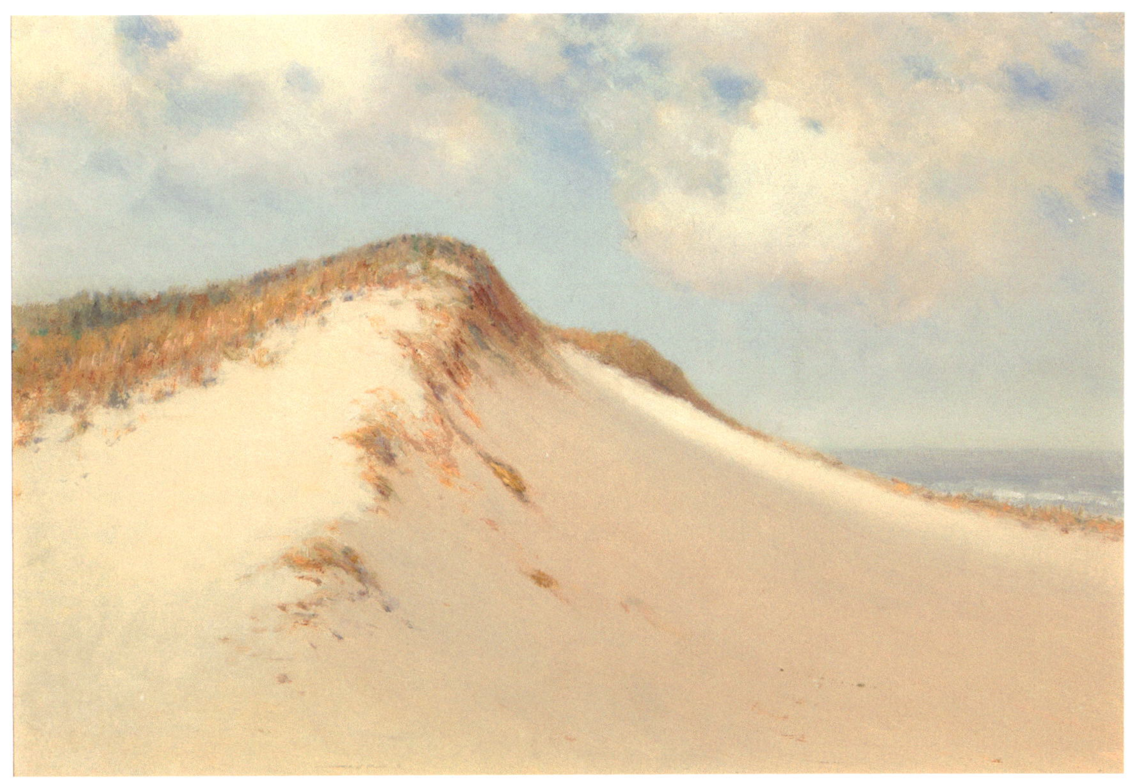

Charles Drew Cahoon, *Sand Dune*, 1939. Oil on canvas, 10 × 15¼ inches.
Gift in honor of Oscar J. Cahoon by his family, 1998.

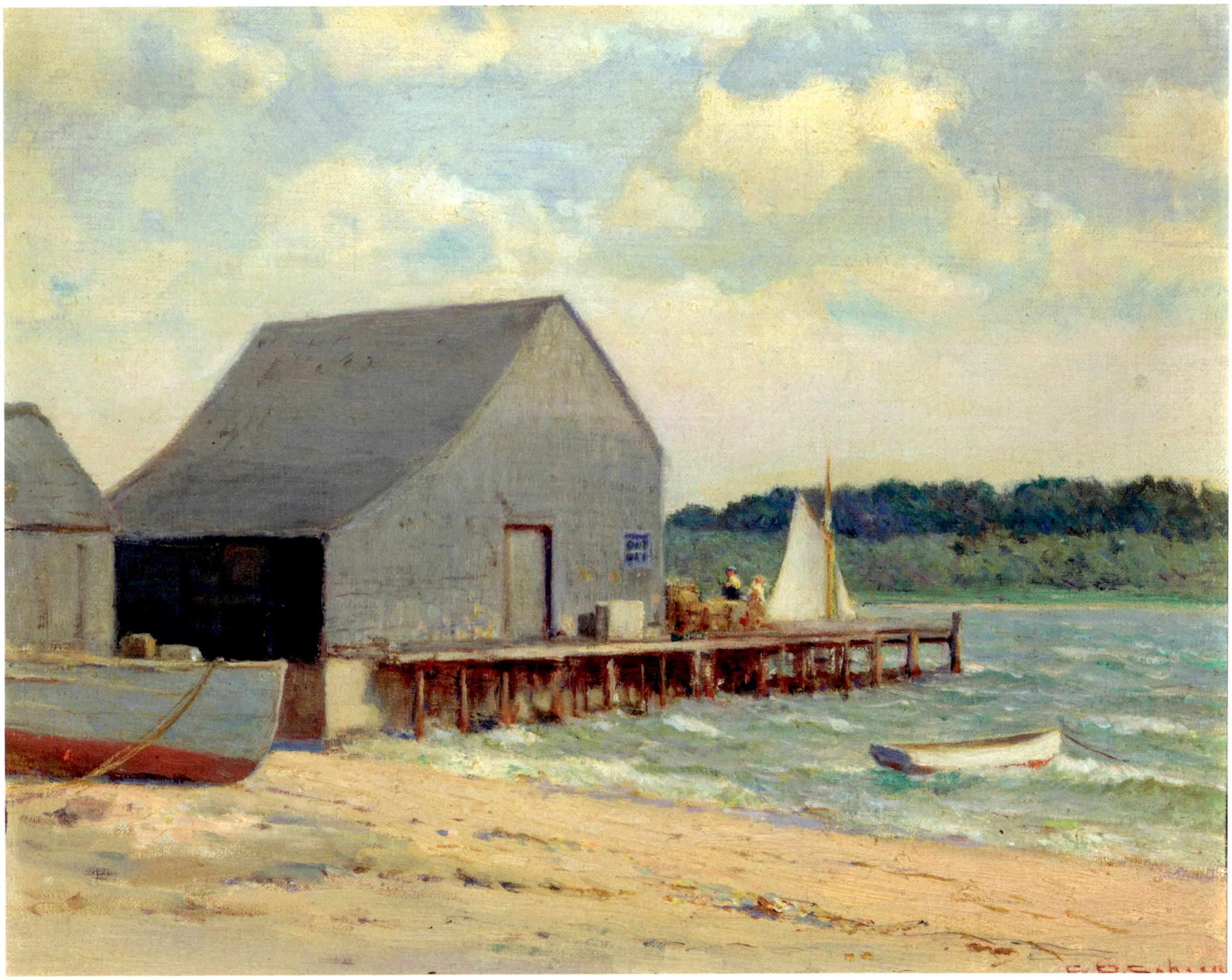

Charles Drew Cahoon, *Oyster Pond,* n.d. Oil on board, 12 × 15⅜ inches. *Gift in honor of Oscar J. Cahoon by his family*, 1998.

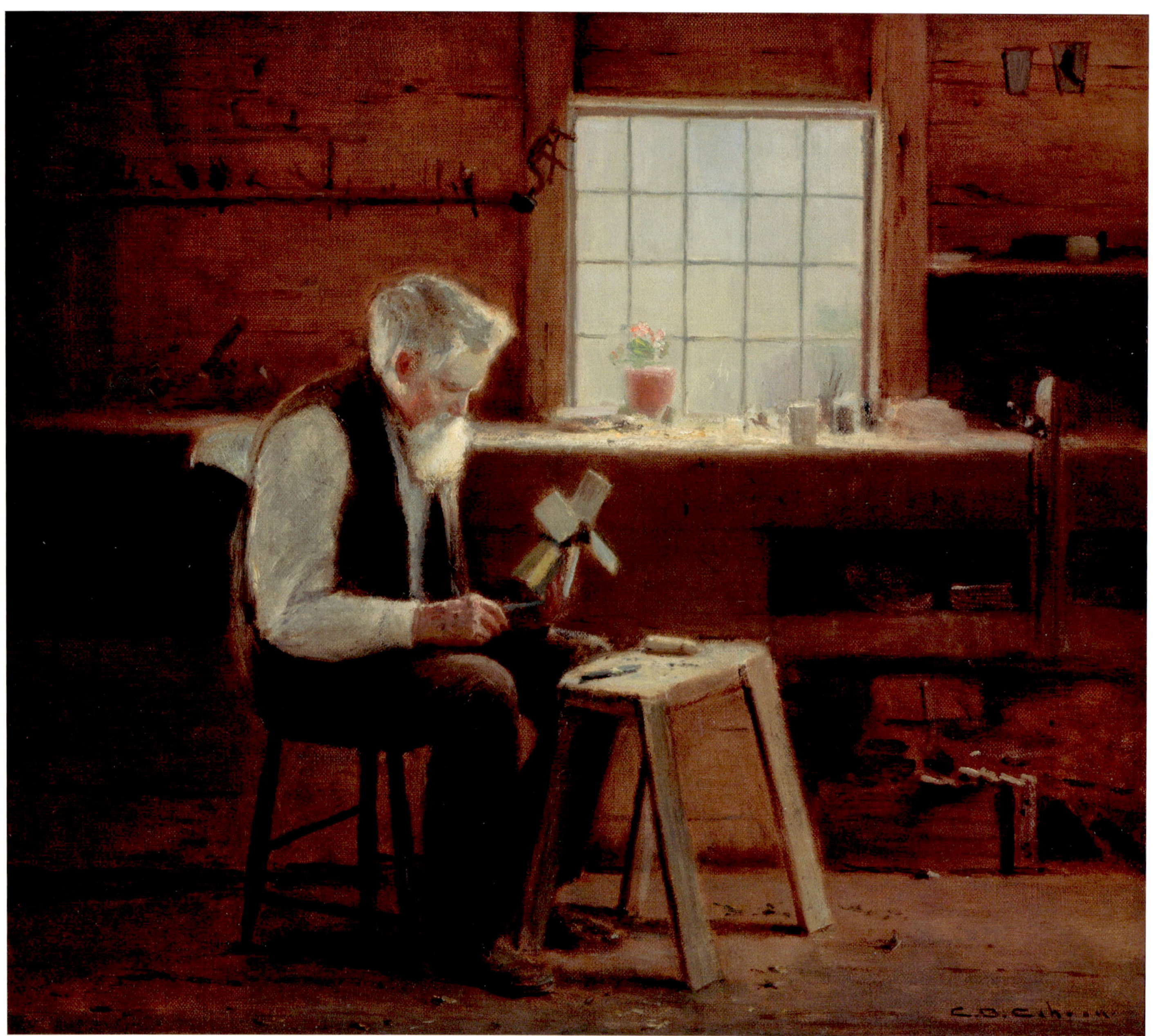

Charles Drew Cahoon, *Ziba Hunt's Workshop*, n.d. Oil on canvas, 14 × 16 inches. *Gift in memory of Mr. & Mrs. Oscar J. Cahoon*, 2003.

FREDERICK JUDD WAUGH
(1861–1940)

The son of Philadelphia portrait painter Samuel Waugh, Frederick Judd Waugh was born in Bordentown, New Jersey. He studied under Thomas Eakins at the Pennsylvania Academy of Fine Arts and at the Académie Julian in Paris. He is celebrated for his marine paintings that vigorously capture waves crashing against rocks. The works are full of drama and capture the powerful forces of the ocean.

Waugh traveled extensively and lived in England for fifteen years. It was during this time that he became enamored with the rocky coastline of England and developed his dramatic approach to marine painting.

In 1928, he arrived in Provincetown and stayed the rest of his life. Surrounded by water, Provincetown offered him great opportunities to paint the ocean, although the shoreline was often calm and smooth, as shown in the serene *Coastal Scene*, a watercolor in the collection of the Cape Cod Museum of Art. Waugh sketched the coastline and then painted from memory, undoubtedly sometimes combining his recollections of the roaring waves dashing against the rocks in Great Britain with local Cape Cod views.

He was also an illustrator, a writer of children's books, a bookplate designer, a designer of silver and copper objects, and a camouflage artist during World War I. In 1945 in a barnlike building that Waugh had built in the West End of Provincetown, Hans Hofmann held his legendary classes.

Waugh's works can be found in other museum collections, including the Art Institute of Chicago, the Brooklyn Museum, and the Los Angeles County Museum of Art.

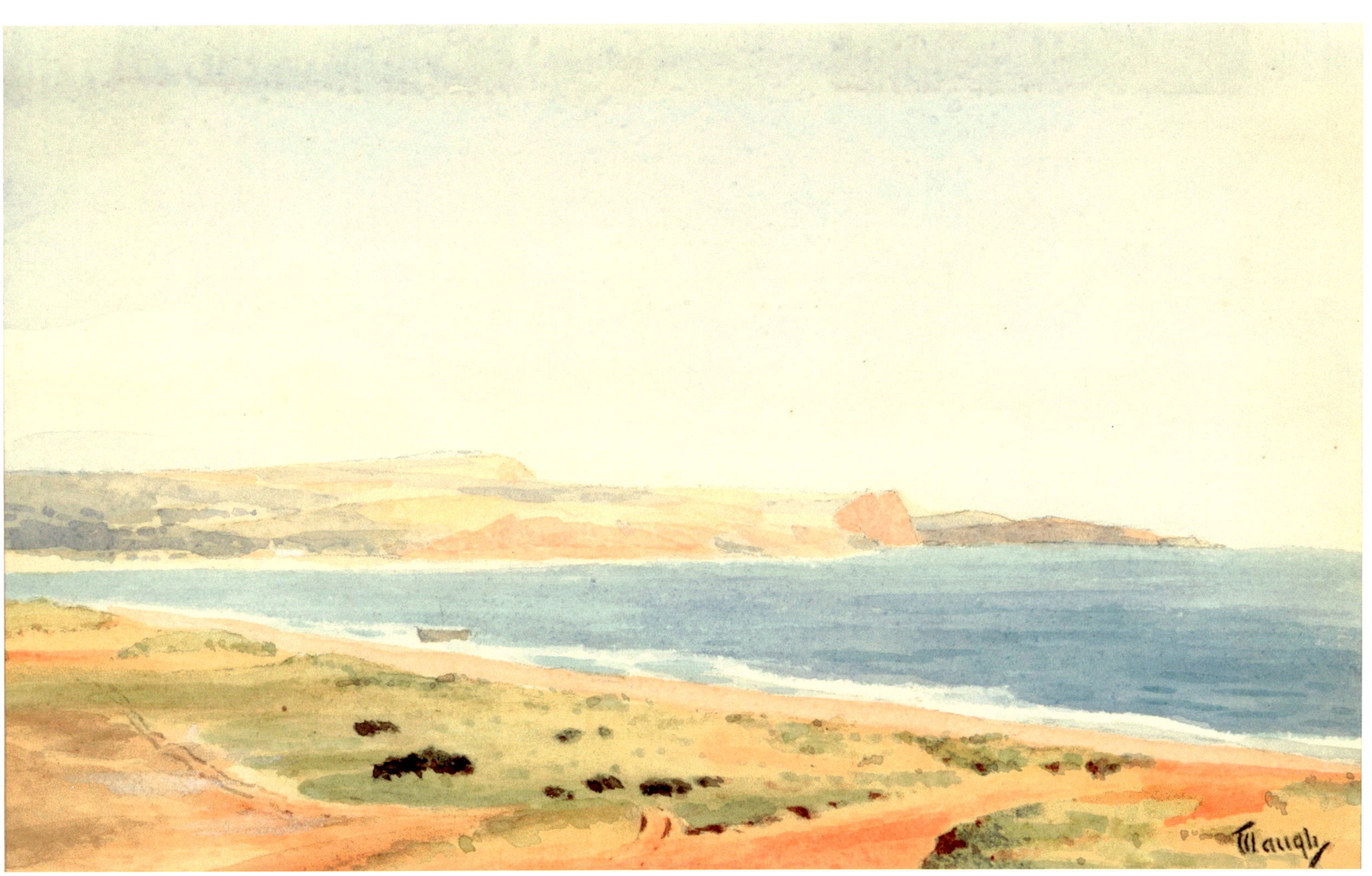

Frederick Judd Waugh, *Coastal Scene*, n.d. Watercolor on paper, 5¼ × 8¾ inches. *Anonymous gift*, 2009.

FRANK WESTON BENSON
(1862–1951)

A native of Salem, Massachusetts, Frank Weston Benson was part of the group of Boston School painters, along with Edmund Tarbell and William McGregor Paxton, who trained at Boston's School of the Museum of Fine Arts and later at the Académie Julian in Paris. They became known as American impressionists, employing a more conservative approach to impressionism than the French.

After studying in Paris, Benson opened a studio in Salem and painted portraits, in which he employed the academic techniques he learned in Paris, along with impressionistic approaches to painting the effects of light, which he would have encountered in France at that period. His portraits and figure paintings during this time were usually set in elegant interiors.

In 1889, Benson was appointed instructor of antique drawing at Boston's School of the Museum of Fine Arts, at a time when Tarbell and Paxton were also teaching there. Also, beginning in 1889, Benson and his family spent summers in Dublin, New Hampshire, a little summer colony at the foot of Mount Monadnock. Benson's outdoor works of the 1890s were mostly landscapes and marine paintings. In the late 1890s, Benson bought a hunting lodge overlooking Cape Cod's Nauset Marsh and he began working with black-and-white wash drawings.

Following that, during the late 1890s, Benson summered in Newcastle, on New Hampshire's short stretch of seacoast, and it was there that his version of impressionism took hold. It was also at this time that Benson became part of the group "Ten American Painters," which was the title of the catalogue for their first exhibition in 1898, The Ten included Benson, Childe Hassam, John Henry Twachtman, J. Alden Weir, Thomas W. Dewing, Joseph De Camp, Willard Leroy Metcalf, Edmund Tarbell, Robert Reid, E. E. Simmons, and later, William Merritt Chase. The group held annual shows in New York City, Boston, and occasionally in other cities.

By the beginning of the twentieth century, impressionism became the focus of Benson's work. His summer home on the island of North Haven in Maine's Penobscot Bay was the setting for some of Benson's best known *plein-air* paintings. He also is known for his lithographs, watercolors, oils, and etchings of wildfowl and sporting subjects. His drawings *Canada Geese Feeding* and *Osprey Hunting* and his etching *Yellowlegs No. 4*, all in the Cape Cod Museum of Art collection, are fine examples of those works, and reflect his life-long interest in ornithology.

Around 1919, he began a series of still lifes, although similar arrangements had often been part of his figure paintings. His meticulous brushwork of intimate settings produced a quiet, reflective mood and a snapshot of a moment in time.

His works are included in numerous public collections, including the Los Angeles County Art Museum, the Metropolitan Museum of Art in New York, the Museum of Fine Arts in Boston, the Pennsylvania Academy of Fine Arts in Philadelphia, and the National Gallery of Art in Washington, DC.

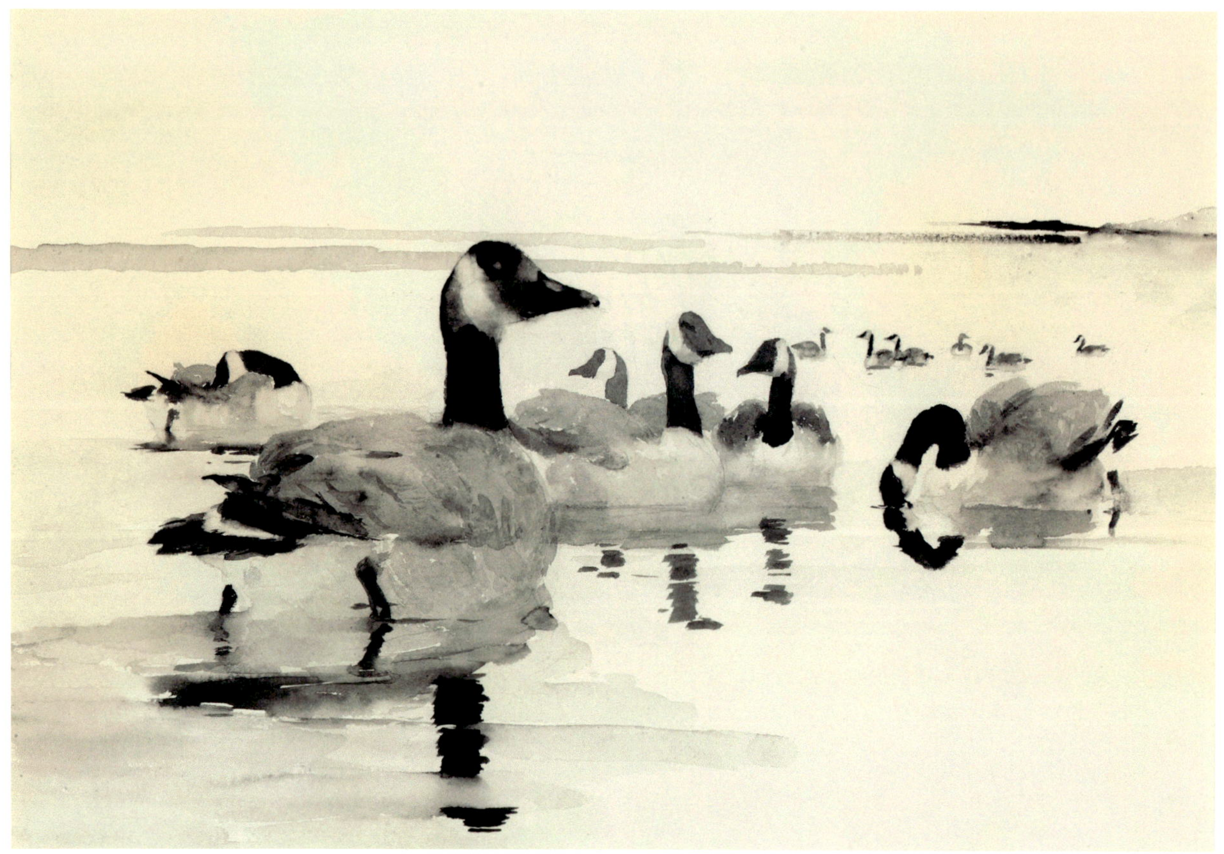

Frank Weston Benson, *Canada Geese Feeding*, n.d. Pencil and ink wash drawing on paper, 12⅝ × 18⅝ inches.
Gift of Corinne Benson Johnson, 2012.

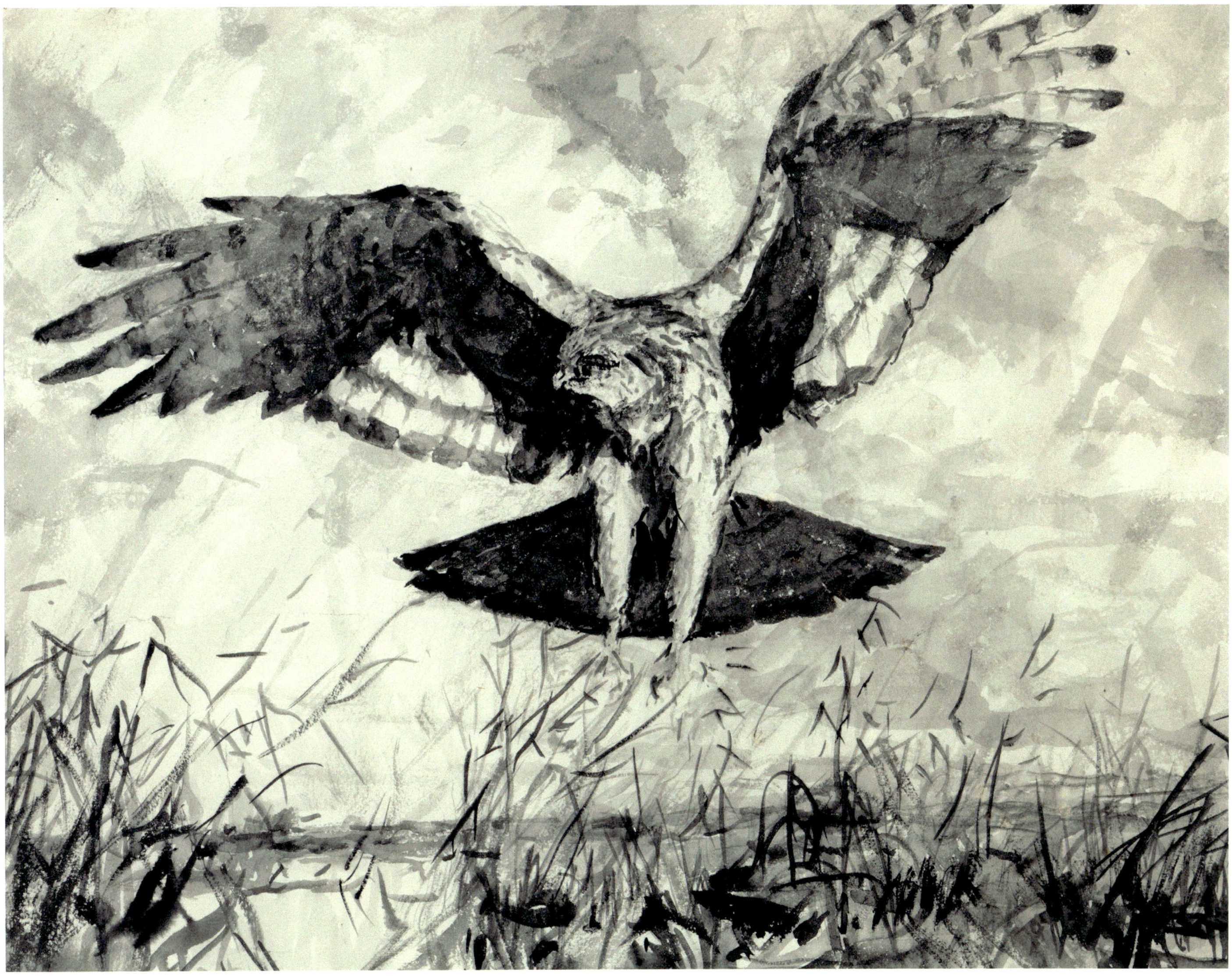

Frank Weston Benson, *Osprey Hunting*, n.d. Ink wash drawing on paper, 16 × 20 inches. *Gift of Corinne Benson Johnson*, 2012.

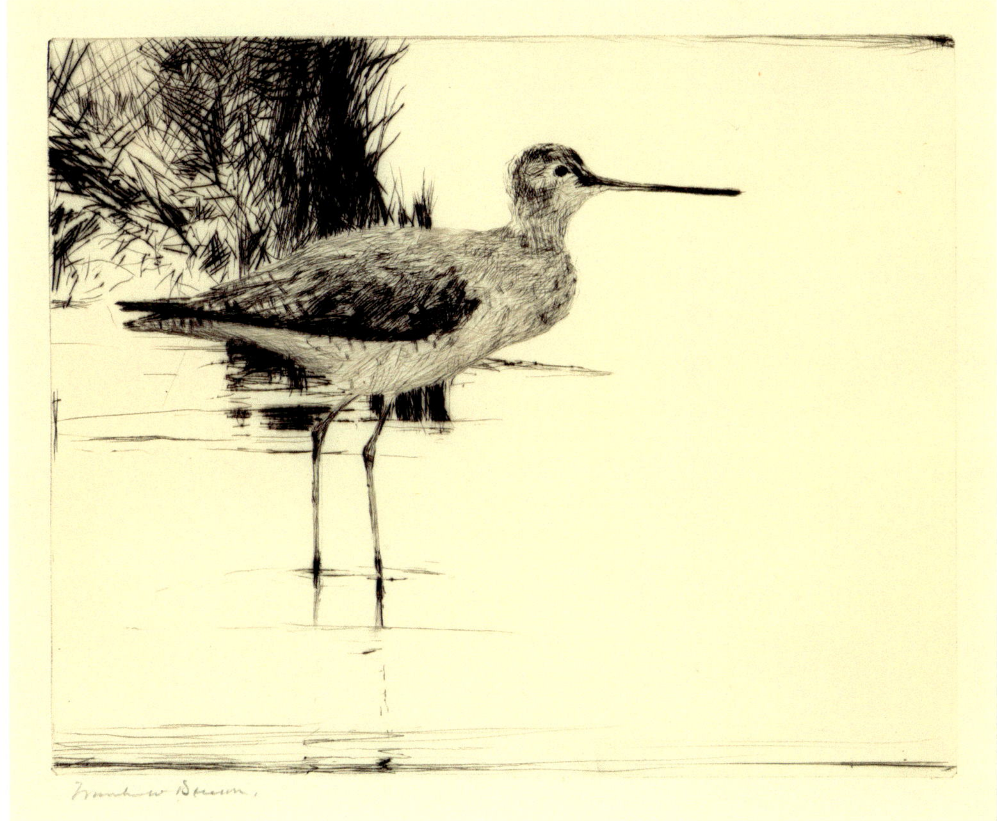

Frank Weston Benson, *Yellowlegs No. 4* (PAFF 284), n.d. Etching on paper, 7¾ × 9¾ inches. *Gift of Ann O'Connell*, 2014.

REYNOLDS BEAL
(1866–1951)

Reynolds Beal, the elder brother of artist Gifford Beal, was born in New York City and became a well-known American impressionist painter.

Although Beal showed early signs of artistic talent, he decided to study naval architecture at Cornell University. By 1890, however, his interest in art was revived and he studied at the artists' communities in Old Lyme and Noank, Connecticut, with Henry Ward Ranger. Later, he visited New York and took classes at the Art Students League and with William Merritt Chase at the Shinnecock School on Long Island.

Enamored of dramatic scenery and colorful characters, he early on painted the Hudson River Valley and the circus and carnival events that were part of the summer season. Beal also painted the New England coastline—particularly Provincetown, Gloucester, and Rockport, where he spent the last twenty years of his life. His subjects included boating events, shipyards, harbors, and lighthouses. In the Cape Cod Museum of Art collection is *The Commodore Morris Whaler of New Bedford*, an aquatint that shows his *plein-air*, naturalist approach.

Beal traveled to Europe, sketching in Paris, Spain, and North Africa, and painted the waterways of Nicaragua, Costa Rica, and Asia. He was one of the founders of the Society of Independent Artists, a group of leading painters of the day, including Childe Hassam, Maurice Prendergast, and John Sloan.

In 1919, he was included in an exhibition of American artists at the Luxembourg Museum in Paris. Beal's interest in the artistic movements of his time marked him as a modernist because he championed not only the ideas of impressionism but also the bold color and patterns of the post-impressionists, including the fauves.

His works are included in museum collections, including the Metropolitan Museum of Art in New York; the Florence Griswold Museum in Old Lyme, Connecticut; the Fogg Art Museum at Harvard University in Cambridge, Massachusetts; and the Phillips Collection in Washington, DC.

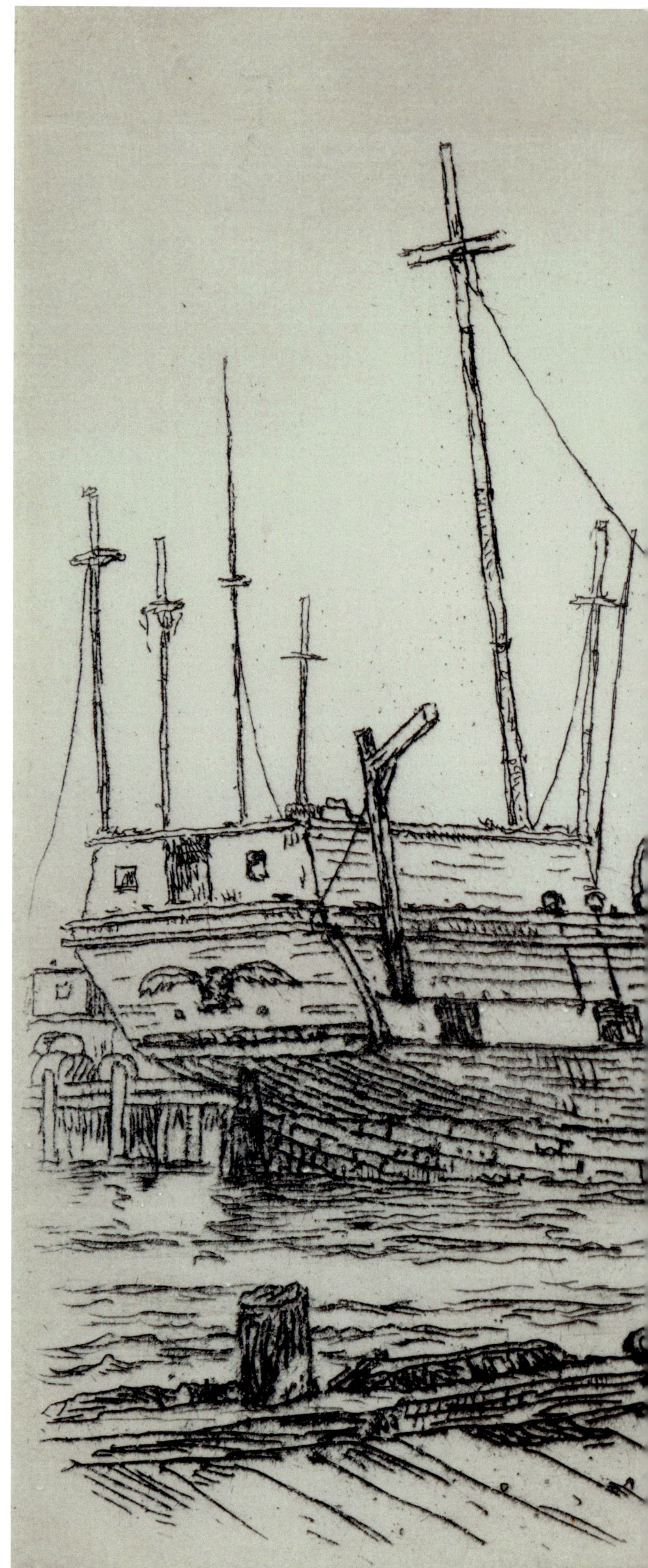

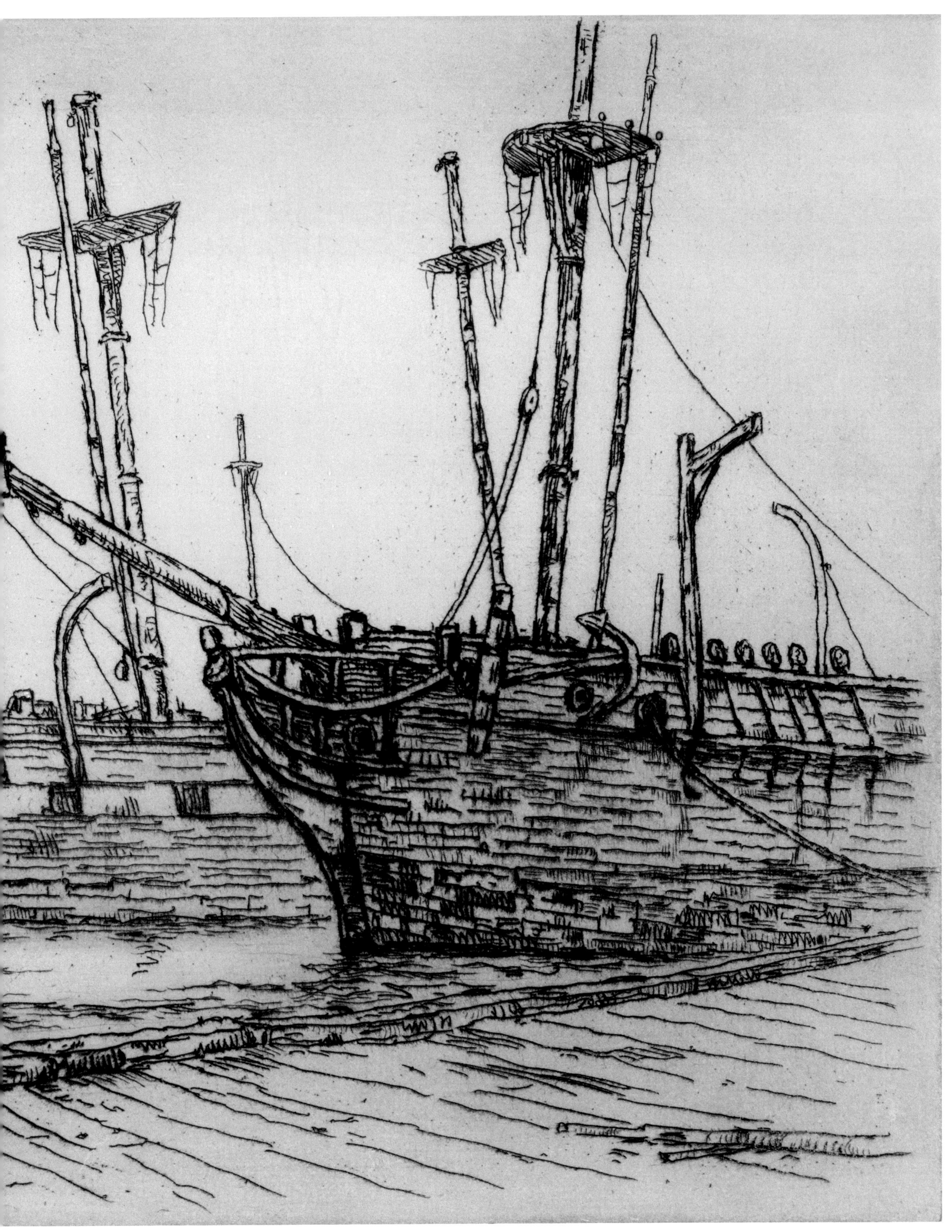

Reynolds Beal, *The Commodore Morris Whaler of New Bedford*, 1995. Aquatint (Monotype), 17½ × 25½ inches. *Anonymous gift*, 2009.

MAX BOHM
(1868–1923)

Born in Cleveland, Ohio, Max Bohm spent many years in Europe, influenced by nineteenth-century romanticism. He attended classes at the Cleveland School of Art before traveling to Europe when he was nineteen. He studied at the Académie Julian in Paris and quickly became successful. He exhibited at the Paris Salon and received a gold medal there in 1898 for his painting *En Mer*. He also exhibited widely in Germany, as well as in America, even though he remained an expatriate for many years. He taught in Étaples on the Brittany coast and later in London.

Bohm traveled back and forth from Europe to America until 1916 when he made America his permanent home, dividing his time between Bronxville, New York, and Provincetown, Massachusetts, where he was active in the growing art colony. His subjects were wide ranging and include pastoral settings, seagoing struggles, idyllic figures, and portraits. Bohn died in Provincetown in 1923. His granddaughter is the artist Anne Packard.

Bohm's romanticism, with its heavy impasto, loose brushstroke, intense palette, and mystical references, is related to the work of Albert Pinkham Ryder. His *Mother and Children*, in the Cape Cod Museum of Art collection, is a truly romantic image, painted in dark colors with soft brushwork and evoking a dreamy mood.

His works are included in the collections of the Metropolitan Museum of Art in New York, the Luxembourg Museum in Paris, and the Smithsonian American Art Museum and the National Gallery of Art in Washington, DC.

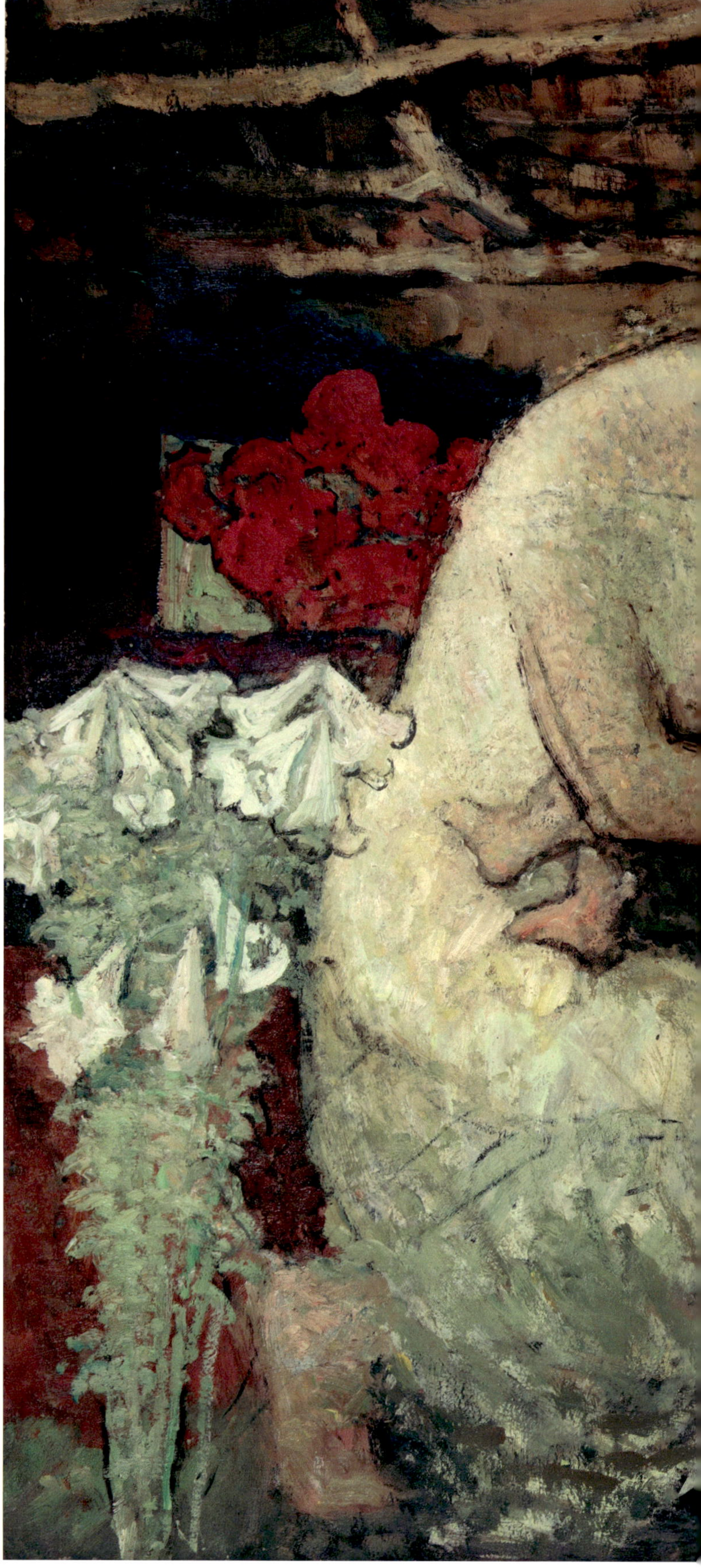

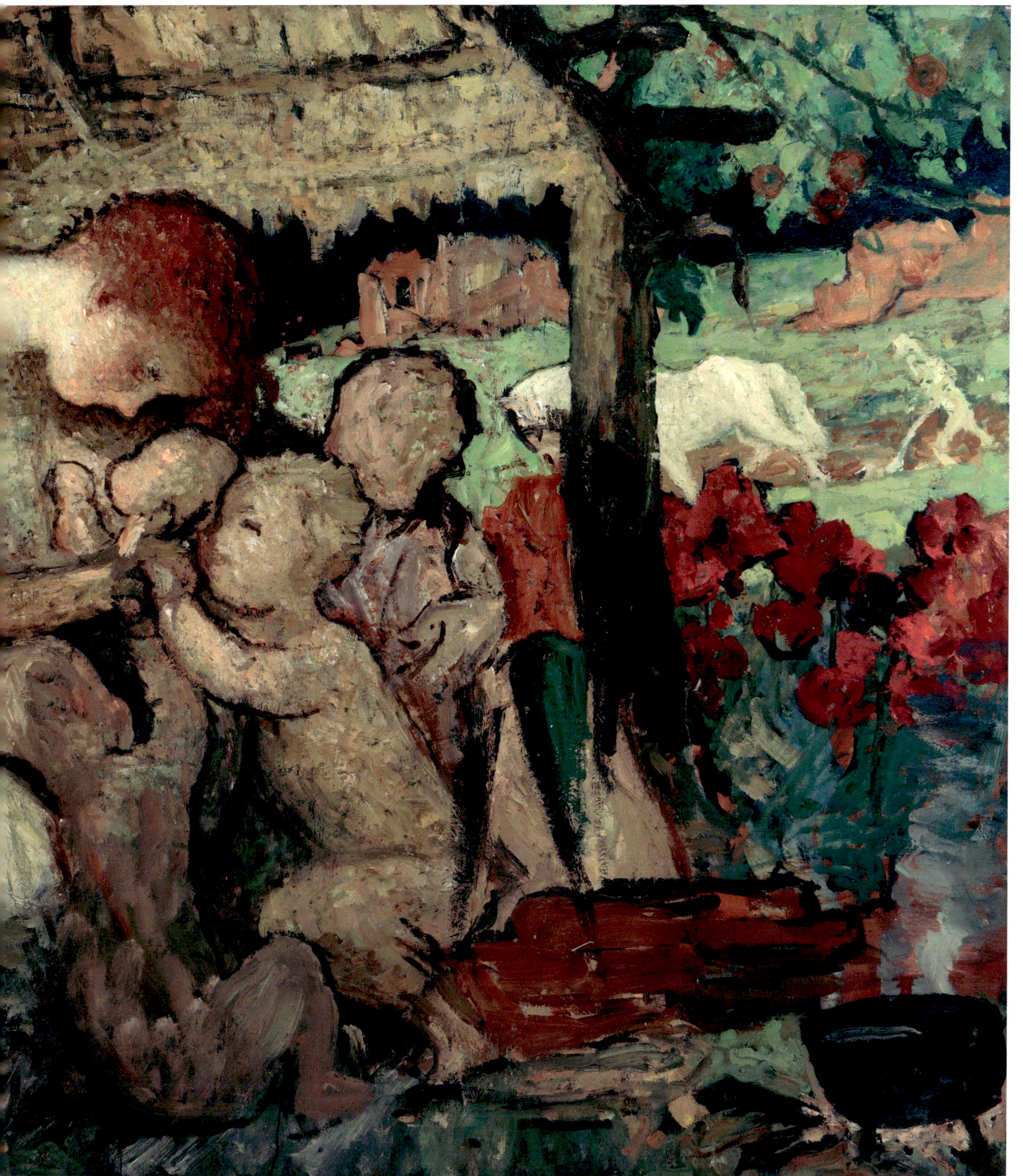

Max Bohm, *Mother and Children*, n.d. Oil on canvas, 57 × 77 inches. *Gift of Anne Packard*, 2010.

WILLIAM MCGREGOR PAXTON
(1869–1941)

William McGregor Paxton, who was born in Baltimore, Maryland, became part of the Boston School of painters along with Edmund C. Tarbell and Frank Weston Benson. He studied with Dennis Miller Bunker at the Cowles Art School in Boston, and in Paris with Jean-Léon Gérôme at École des Beaux-Arts and at Académie Julian. He later taught at the School of the Museum of Fine Arts in Boston.

The Boston School of painters Americanized impressionism, combining some of the elements of French impressionism with a conservative approach to figure painting. Paxton is known for his elegant paintings of stylish women in plush rooms, in which he presented the grace and character of life of the affluent. Some have compared his work to that of Johannes Vermeer.

Although *Dark Hair, Dark Dress*, in the Cape Cod Museum of Art collection, is not an example of his impressionistic style, it is an insightful portrait with intense contrasts of light and shadow, an example of how beautifully he was able to capture the effects of light. He often painted his patrons' daughters and wives, situated in the luxurious comfort of a grandly appointed room, and in these works you feel the presence of a narrative, of perhaps a woman out of a Henry James novel. He also painted models in his studio, setting the scene with appropriate props.

During the early years of the twentieth century, Paxton spent summers in Provincetown. *Cape Inlet*, in the museum collection, is an example of his loose impressionism.

His works are in the collections of major museums, including the Metropolitan Museum of Art in New York, the Museum of Fine Arts in Boston, the Pennsylvania Academy of Fine Arts in Philadelphia, the Brooklyn Museum of Art, the Princeton University Art Museum in New Jersey, and the Smithsonian American Art Museum in Washington, DC.

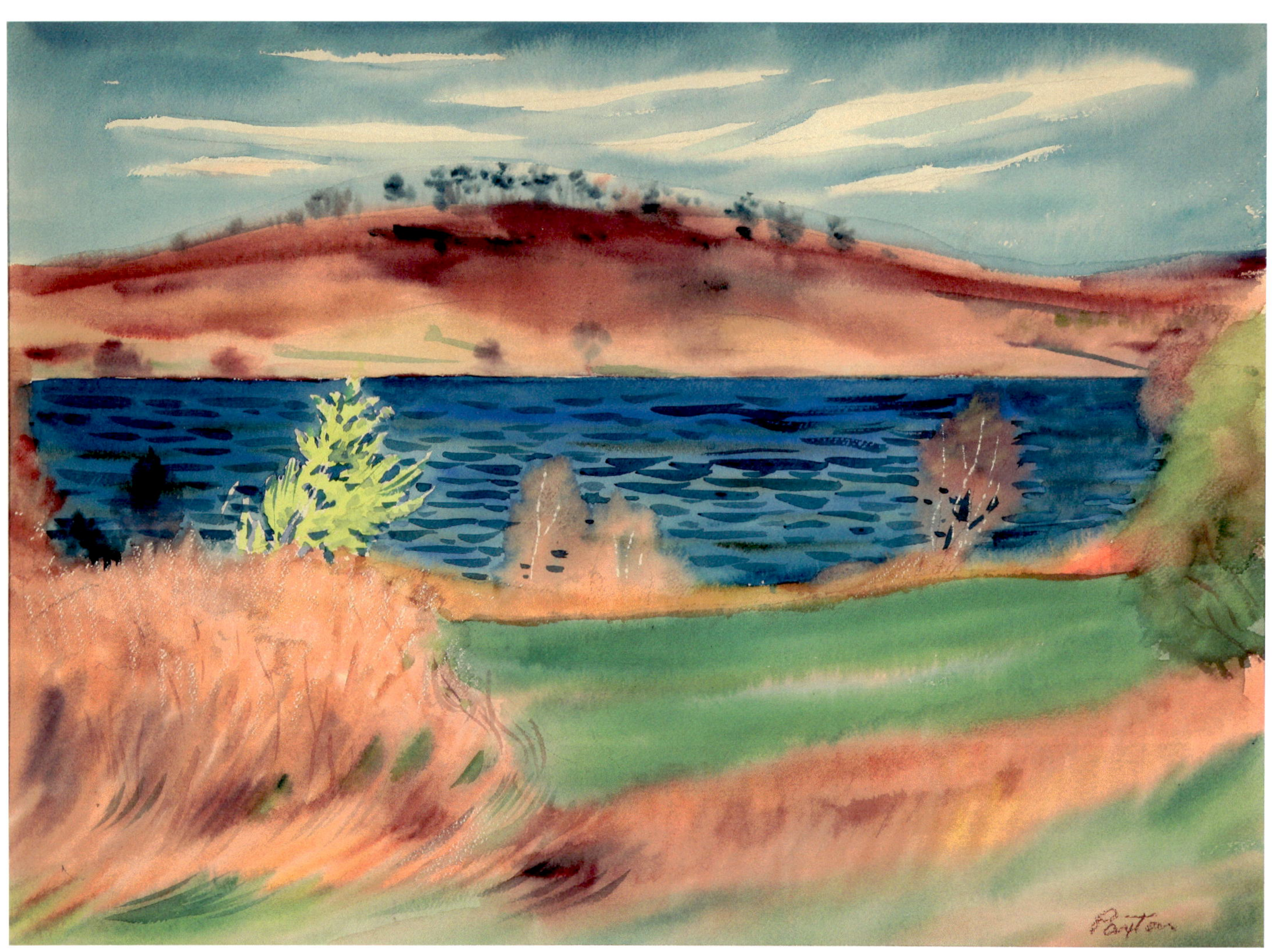

William McGregor Paxton, *Cape Inlet,* n.d. Watercolor on paper, 16½ × 20 inches. *Gift of Robert Douglas Hunter*,1999.

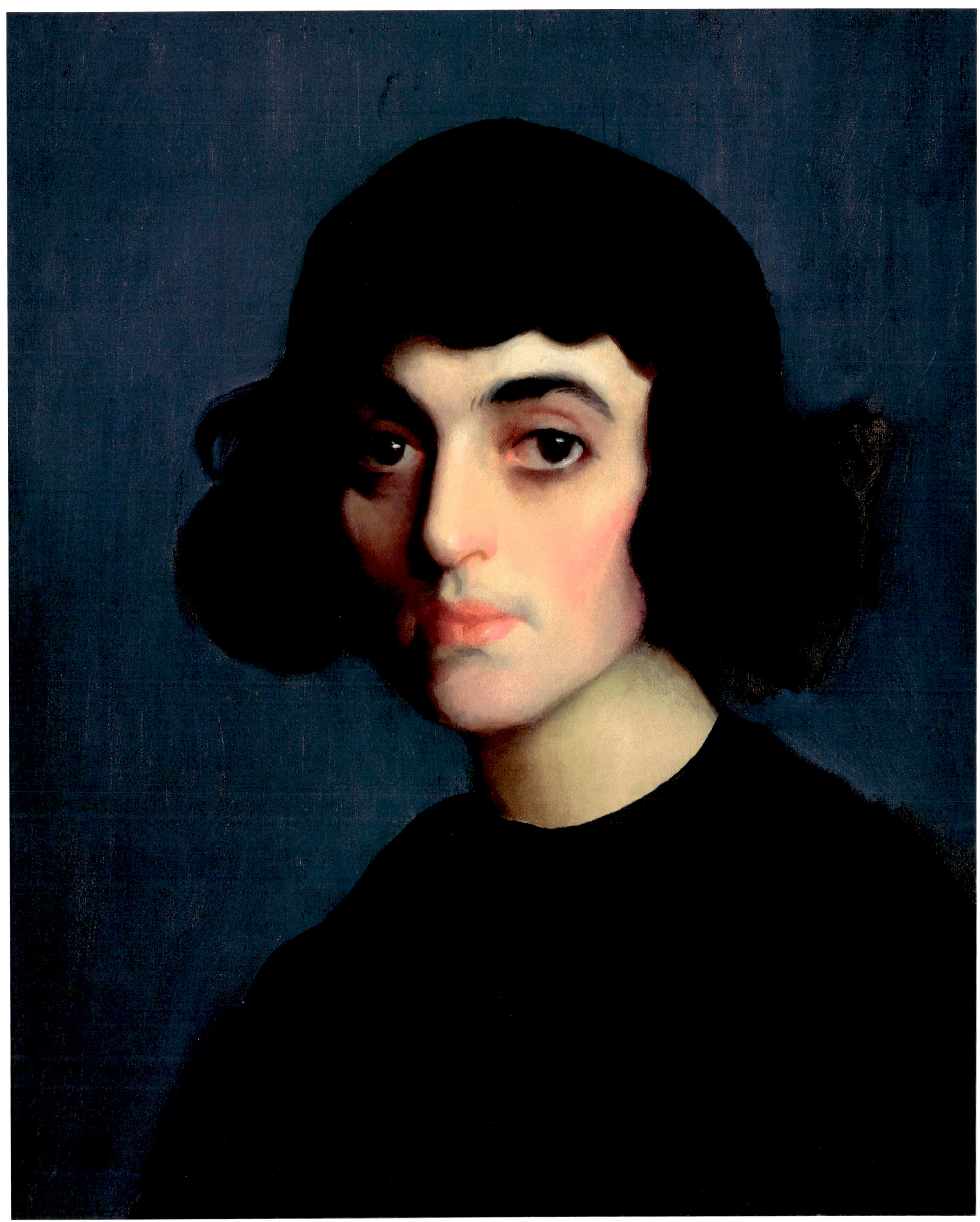

William McGregor Paxton, *Dark Hair, Dark Dress*, 1924. Oil on canvas, 18 × 15 inches. *Gift of Robert Douglas Hunter*, 1989.

ARTHUR VIDAL DIEHL
(1870–1929)

Growing up, London-born Arthur Diehl spent hours copying works at the National Gallery and British Museum, as well as the paintings he saw while visiting museums and studying in Italy. In 1893, he came to America and for a while earned a living copying European paintings. Later he had studios in Asbury Park, Lakewood, and Leonia, in New Jersey.

Diehl and his family first came to Cape Cod for the summer of 1912, renting a cottage at Ballston Beach in Truro, and later renting rooms in Provincetown. He returned the following summer and set up a studio in Provincetown, and the little fishing village became his summer residence for the rest of his life, although he divided his time between there and locations in Sandwich and Monument Beach on Cape Cod.

Diehl's landscapes are mostly of Cape Cod's dunes and wharfs. Figures play only a small role in the scenes. His *Untitled (Blooming Dunes at Dusk)* and *MacMillan Wharf*, in the Cape Cod Museum of Art collection, capture the sparkling light that lured so many artists to Provincetown. He was influenced early on by the French Barbizon painters, but his work became more impressionistic toward the end of his life. The impressionistic landscape *French Scene*, also in the museum collection, is bathed in blue and shows a marked sensitivity to light and atmosphere.

Diehl was known for running an open studio, where people could come and watch him work. Another Cape artist, Ross Moffett, described how Diehl could paint a dune or beach scene quickly even as he continued an entertaining conversation with onlookers.

His works are in the collections of the State Museum of Pennsylvania in Harrisburg and the Lightner Museum in St. Augustine, Florida.

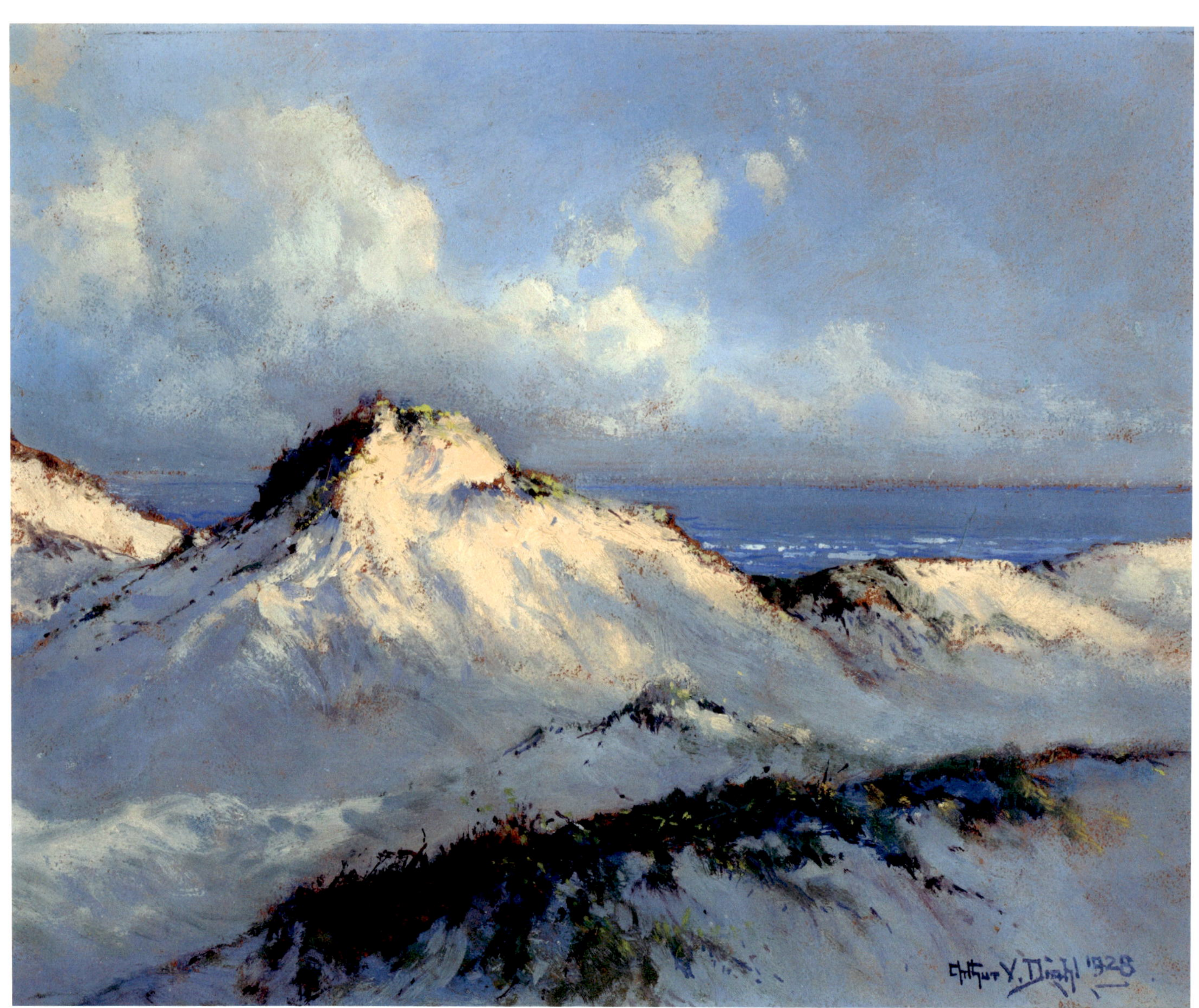

Arthur Vidal Diehl, *Untitled (Blooming Dunes at Dusk)*, 1928. Oil on board, 12 × 15 inches. *Anonymous gift*, 2009.

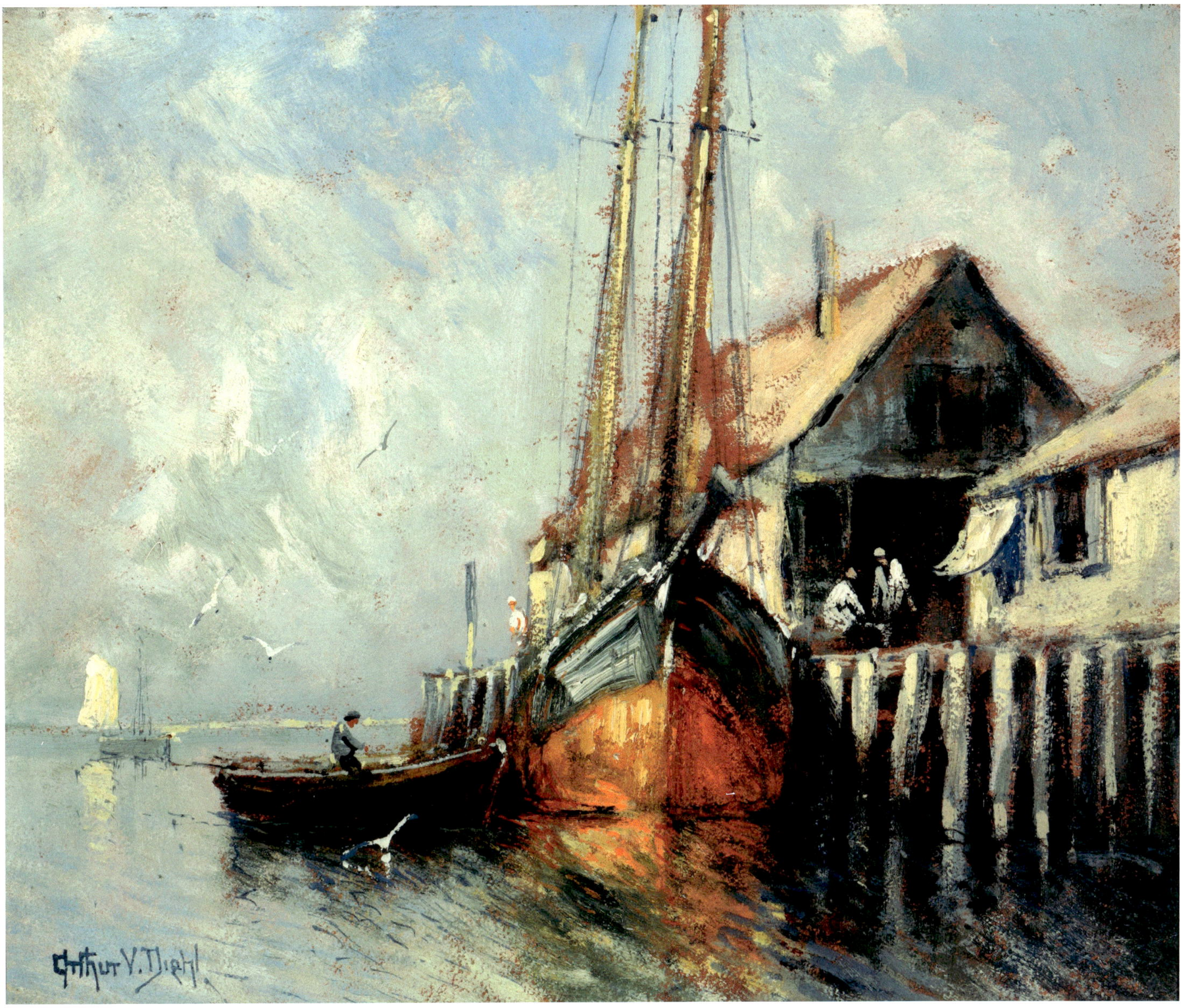

Arthur Vidal Diehl, *MacMillan Wharf*, early 1920s. Oil on board, 18¾ × 6 inches. *Gift of James and Mary T. Couzens*, 1990.

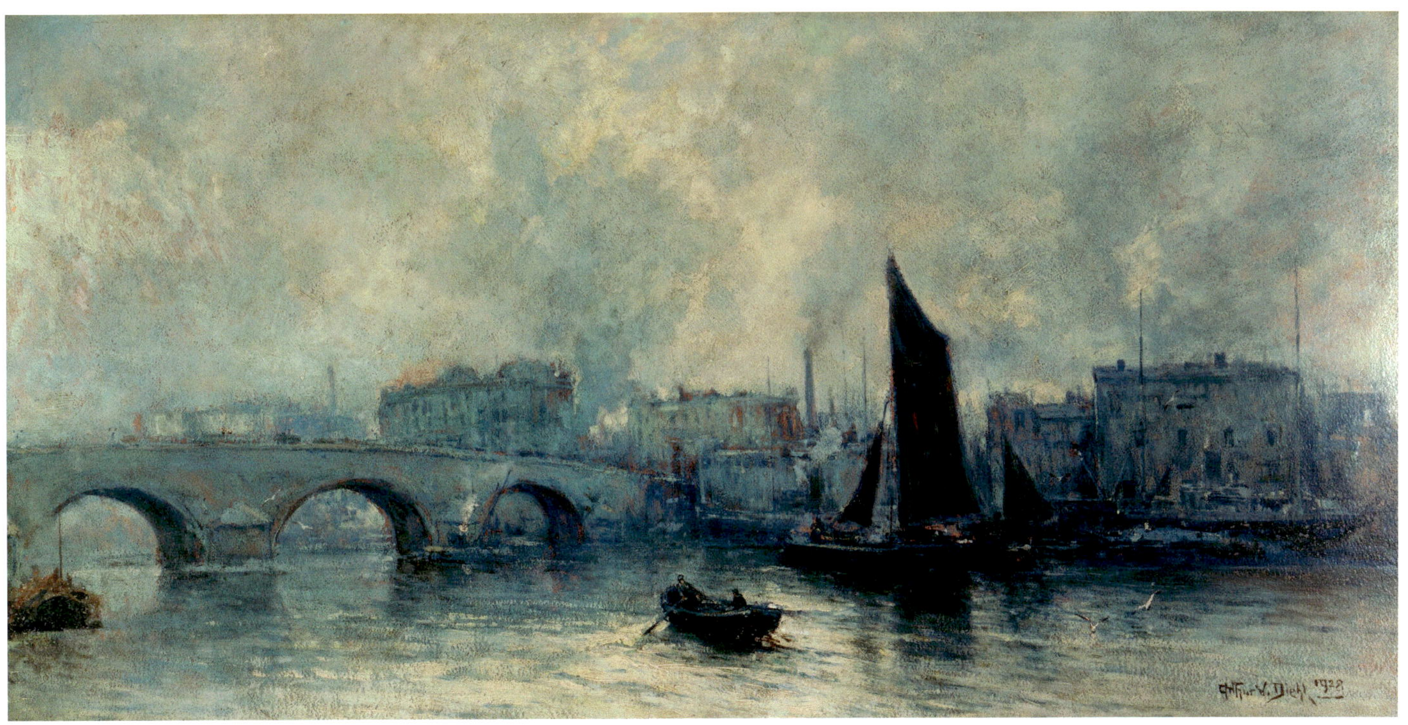

Arthur Vidal Diehl, *French Scene*, 1928. Oil on board, 19 × 39 inches. *Gift of Rosalind Russell,* 1999.

MARION CAMPBELL HAWTHORNE
(1870–1945)

Before Marion Campbell met Charles Hawthorne at William Merritt Chase's art school in Shinnecock, Long Island, she had studied art in Paris and at the School of the Art Institute of Chicago. Charles and Marion were married in 1903, four years after Hawthorne opened his Cape Cod School of Art in Provincetown. Marion was active in the school, working as Charles's assistant. Her *Mudhead/Coastal Scene*, in the Cape Cod Museum of Art collection, represents how her husband posed his subjects with the sun behind so that the facial features were blurred; thus these works became known as "mud heads."

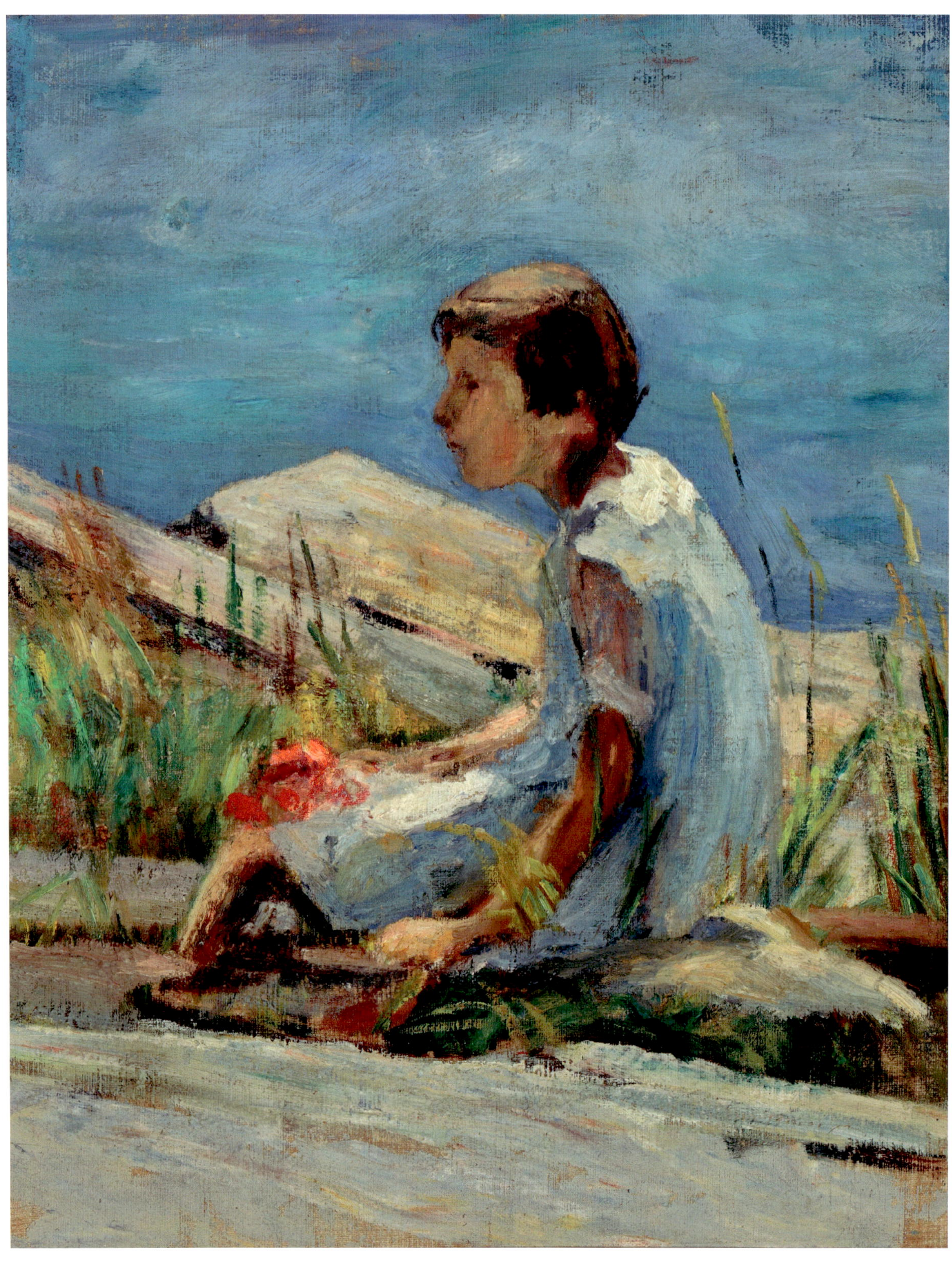

Marion Campbell Hawthorne, *Mudhead/Coastal Scene Verso*, n.d. Oil on board, 20 × 16 inches. *Anonymous gift*, 2009.

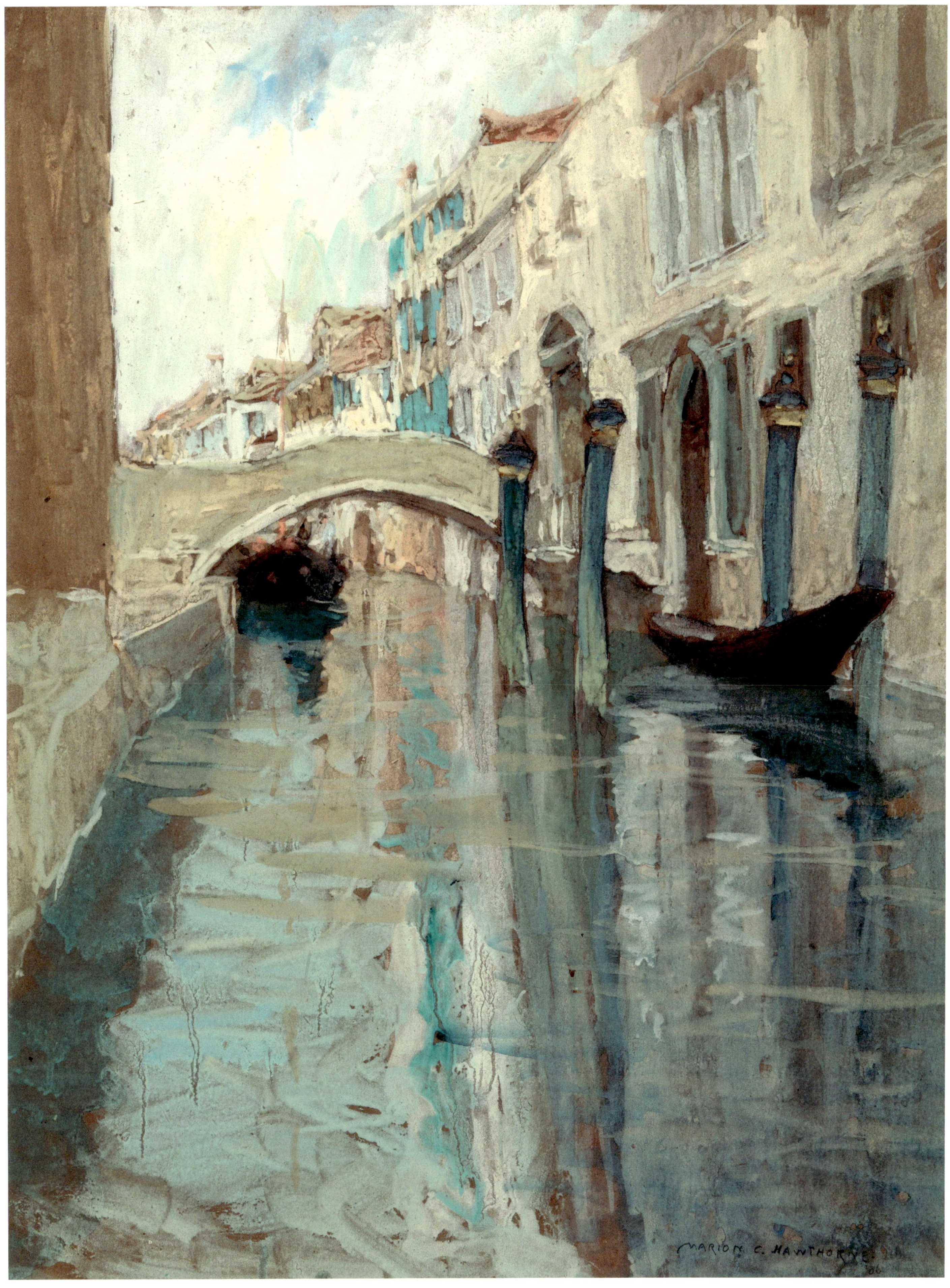

Marion Campbell Hawthorne, *Canal Venice*, 1906. Gouache on paper, 18¾ × 14¼ inches. *Gift of the Estate of Audrey Harris*, 2010.

Marion Hawthorne was known for her watercolor and gouache paintings that have an impressionistic quality, produced by transparent washes of color as in *Canal in Venice*, also in the museum collection. She apparently was influenced by Chase's tonal style of painting as well as her husband's *plein-air* approach, which emphasized the importance of light and color.

After her husband's death, she compiled and published her husband's teaching notes as *Hawthorne on Painting*. Her artwork has been collected by the Butler Institute of American Art in Youngstown, Ohio.

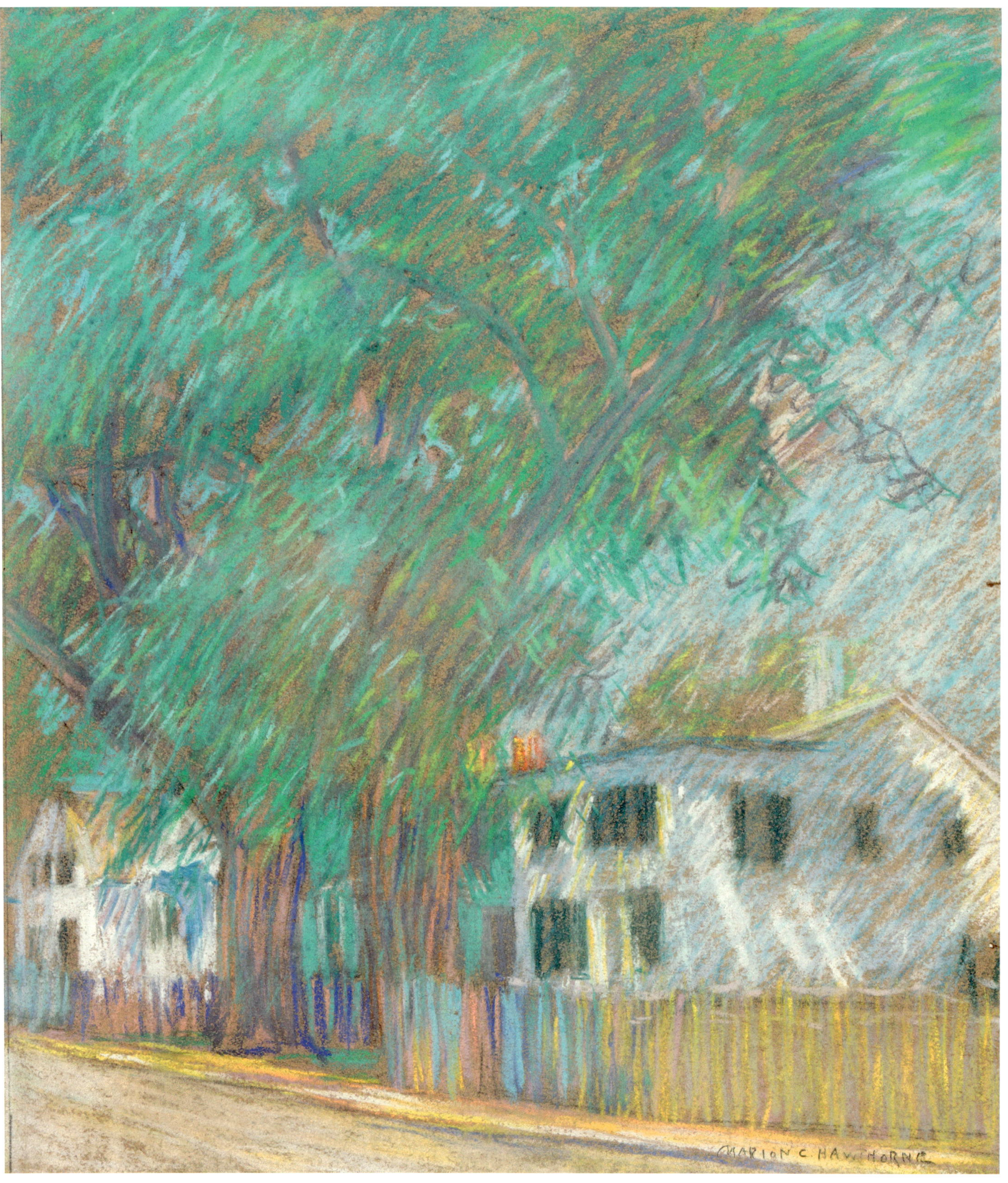

Marion Campbell Hawthorne, *A Street in Provincetown,* 1915. Pastel on paper, 16 × 14 inches. *Anonymous gift in memory of Robert Douglas Hunter*, 2014.

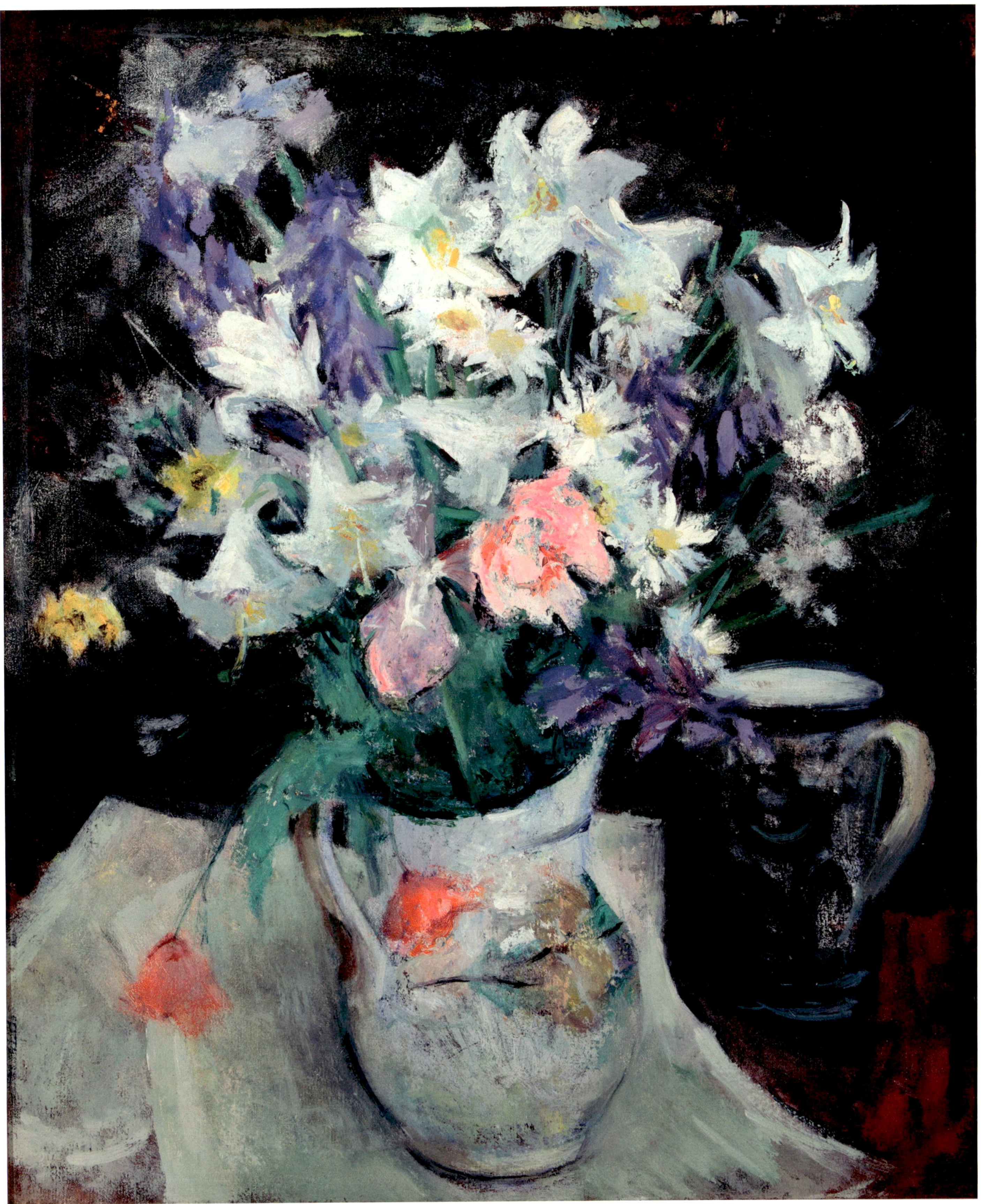

Marion Campbell Hawthorne, *A Floral Still Life with Vase*, n.d. Oil on canvas, 25 × 21¾ inches. *Gift of Mr. and Mrs. Joseph Hawthorne*, 1993.

GEORGE ELMER BROWNE
(1871–1946)

George Elmer Browne was a Massachusetts native and studied in Boston at the School of the Museum of Fine Arts and at the Académie Julian in Paris. While studying in Paris in the early years of the twentieth century, he was introduced to both the Barbizon painters Camille Corot and Jean-François Millet and the French impressionists, and brought these varied approaches home with him.

He founded the West End School of Art in Provincetown in 1916, which was one of five schools in the town at the time the art colony was already making its mark.

He painted landscapes, like his bucolic *Provincetown,* in the Cape Cod Museum of Art's collection, and marine subjects in a loose impressionistic style with an expressionistic brushstroke. His paintings of ships are often vivid night scenes. His marine etchings, *Trawlers* and *Net Menders*, also in the museum collection, show a deftly drawn line and evoke a somber mood.

Browne's subjects related to his travels in Europe, and, of course, Provincetown, where he spent many summers until he died there in 1946. His studio later became the home of another Cape artist, Chaim Gross, who also had a long history in the art colony.

His works are in the collections of major museums, including the Metropolitan Museum of Art in New York, the Los Angeles County Museum of Art, the Art Institute of Chicago, and the Smithsonian American Art Museum in Washington, DC.

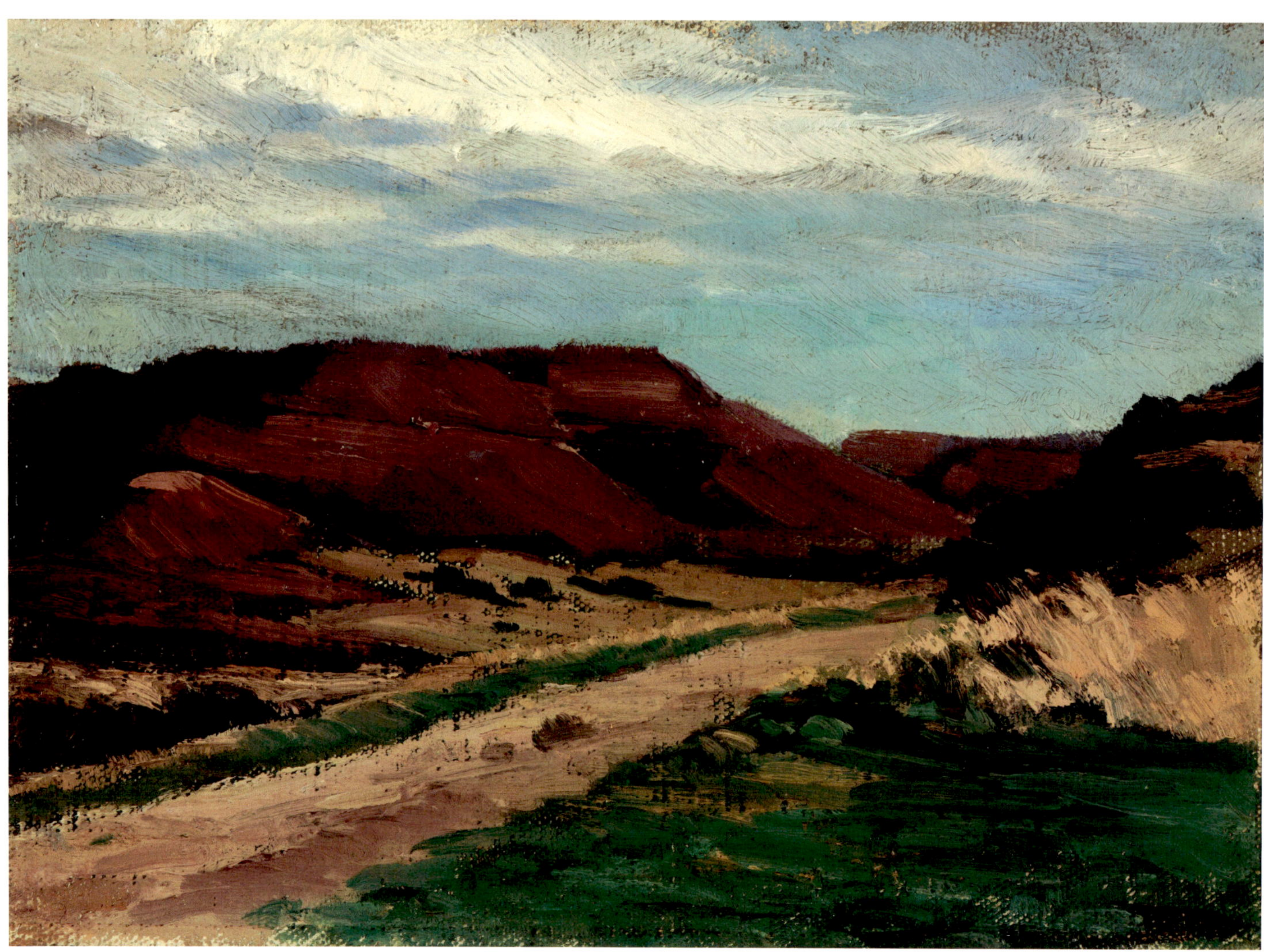

George Elmer Browne, *Provincetown,* 1920. Oil on board, 7 ¾ × 11 inches. *Anonymous gift*, 2009.

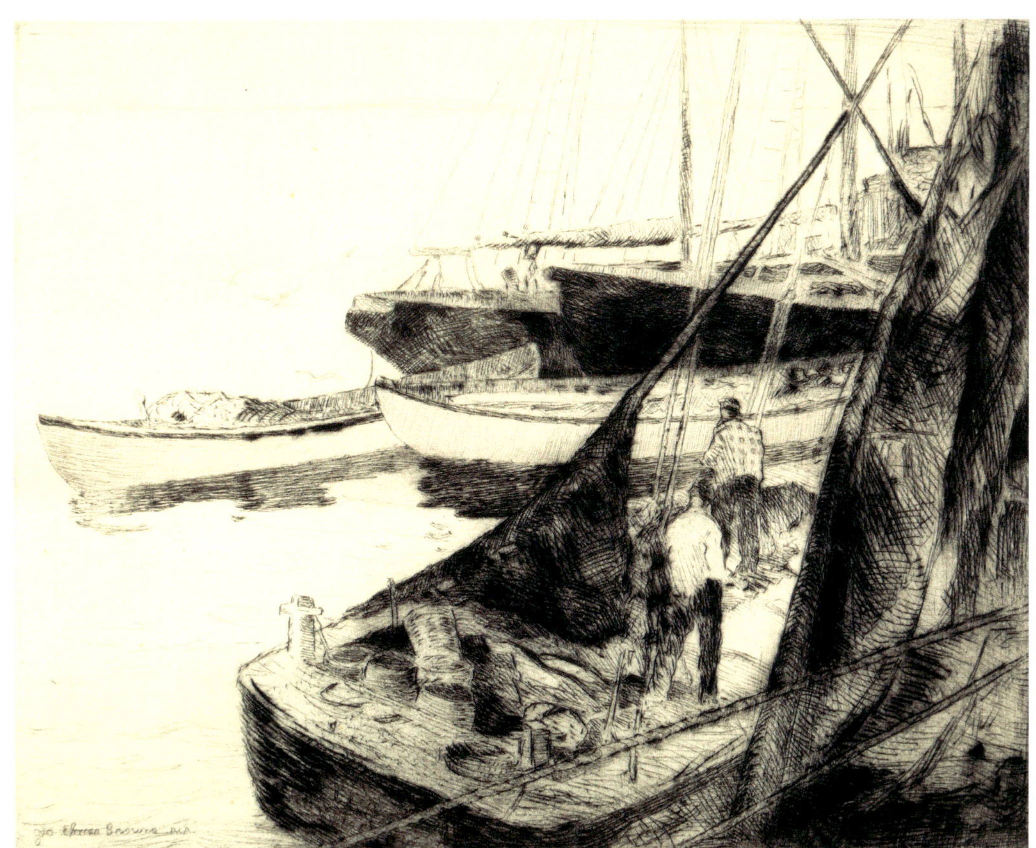

George Elmer Browne, *The Trawlers*, n.d. Etching on paper, 8½ × 10½ inches. *Gift of Robert Douglas and Elizabeth Hunter*, 1995.

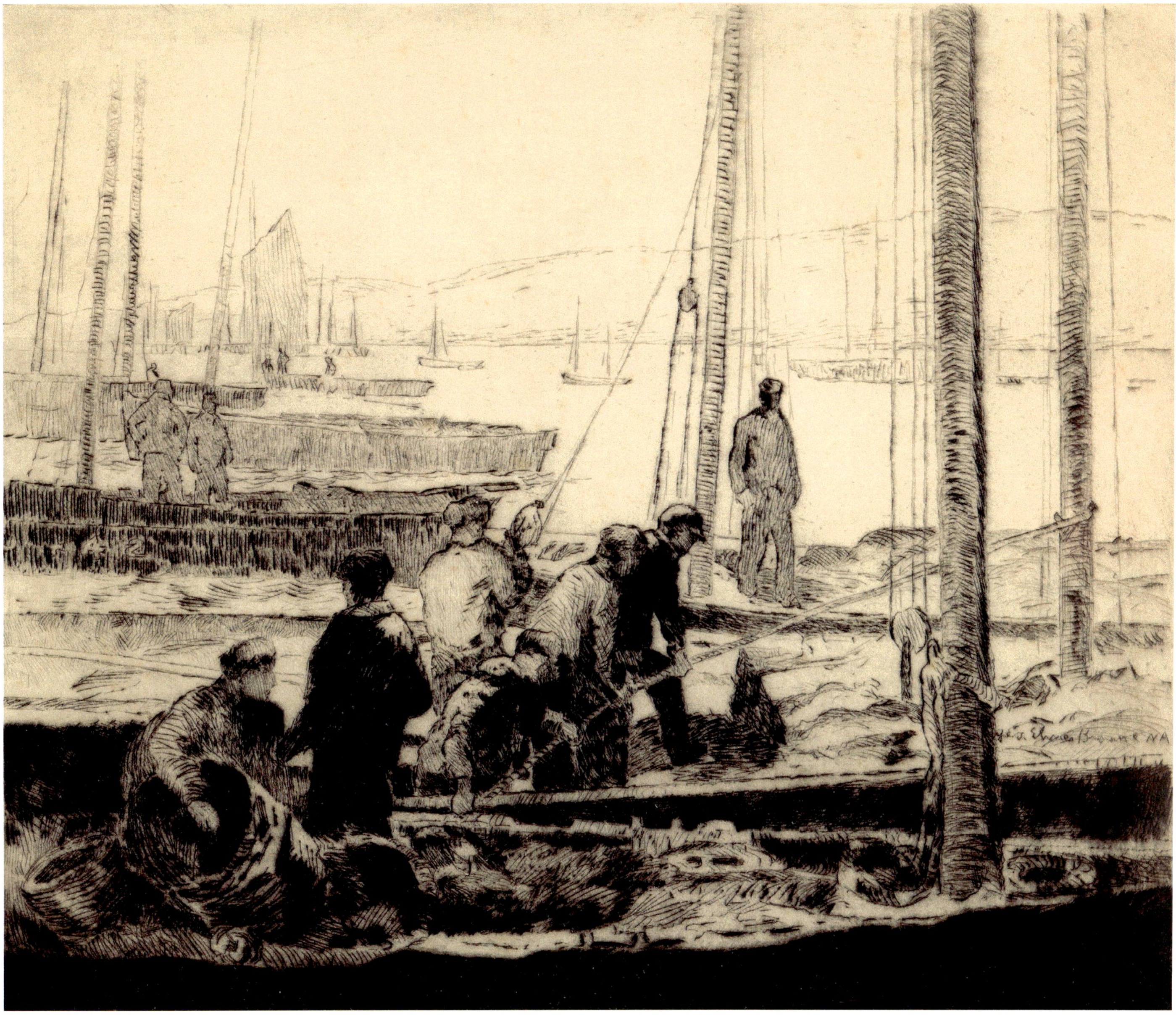

George Elmer Browne, *The Net Menders,* 1920s. Etching on paper, 8¼ × 10¼ inches. *Gift of Robert Douglas and Elizabeth Hunter*, 1996.

CHARLES W. HAWTHORNE
(1872–1930)

Drawn by the light in the little fishing village on the tip of Cape Cod, Charles Hawthorne opened his Cape Cod School of Art in 1899 and launched the Provincetown art colony, which several years ago was designated by the National Trust for Historic Preservation as home of the nation's oldest continually operating art colony.

Hawthorne had studied at the National Academy of Design and the Art Students League, as well as working as an assistant to American impressionist William Merritt Chase at his summer art school in Shinnecock on Long Island in 1897. Although he had come under the spell of *plein-air* painting and an impressionistic approach, his exposure to the academic traditions of Italy, the Netherlands, and France also influenced his style of painting and teaching.

Hawthorne's summer classes drew thousands of students and lasted until he died in 1930. The classes were set on the wharves and beaches in Provincetown and drew artists who became the nucleus of the budding art colony.

Committed to the art colony, Hawthorne was a founding member of the Provincetown Art Association in 1914. Struck by the life of the fishing community, he frequently painted the fishermen and their families. Many of these oil paintings

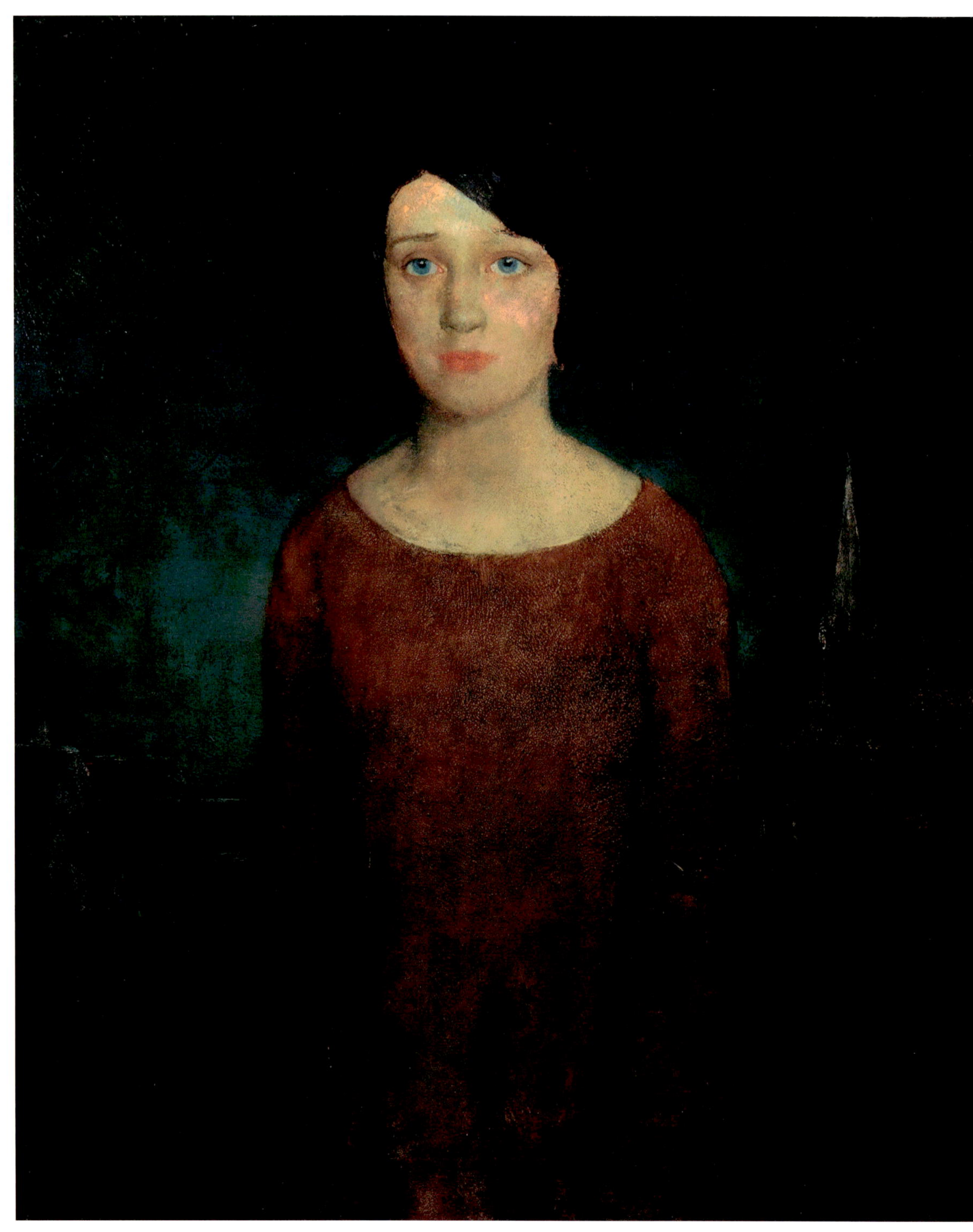

Charles W. Hawthorne, *Portrait of Anita*, n.d. Oil on masonite, 30 × 25 inches. *Gift of Mr. and Mrs. Joseph Hawthorne*, 1993.

are done in a tonal, academic tradition, as are the two portraits in the Cape Cod Museum of Art collection. *Portrait of Anita*, of a young woman, and *Untitled (Portrait),* of an older woman, are typical of these tonal portraits. Other works capture the rugged aspects of the villagers' lives, which were so intricately tied to the sea.

In his *plein-air* classes, Hawthorne directed his students to focus on the effects of light, creating shapes with color, and building a composition not by details but by relating one color to another. In setting up a model, he posed her with the sun behind so that her facial features were blurred, causing these works to be known as "mud heads." In his late watercolors, there is an obvious influence of impressionism with his simplification of the basic elements and focus on color. These works are evocative of a mood, a particular moment, a special light, while some even approach abstraction.

His works are in numerous public collections, including the Metropolitan Museum of Art in New York, the Chicago Art Institute, the Philadelphia Museum of Art, and the Hirshhorn Museum and Sculpture Garden in Washington, DC.

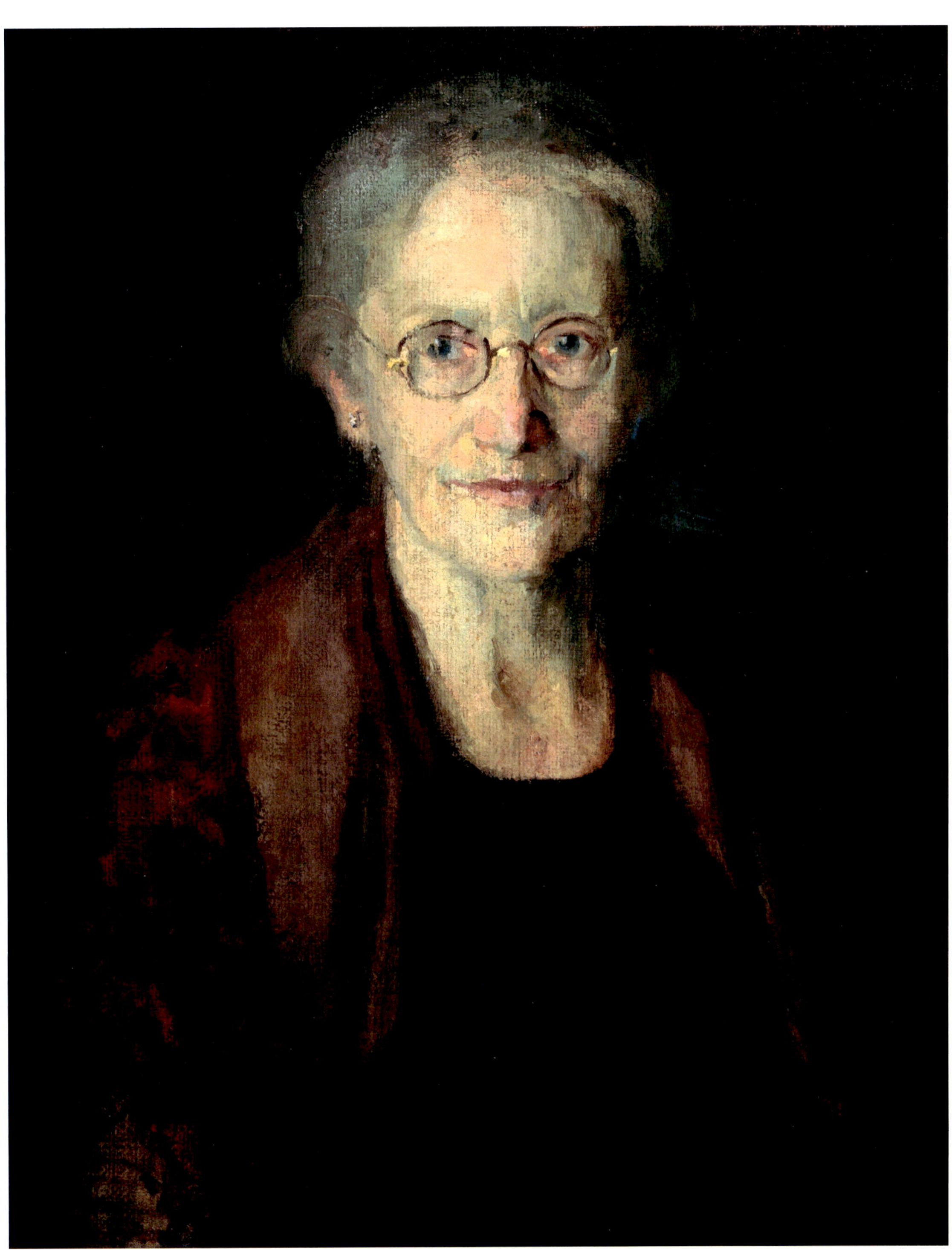

Charles W. Hawthorne, *Untitled*, n.d. Oil on canvas, 17 × 21 inches. *Anonymous gift in Honor of Mr. Robert Duffy*, 2009.

AGNES WEINRICH
(1873–1946)

Agnes Weinrich's inclination toward cubism set her apart from many of the artists working in America in the first half of the twentieth century. She was born on a farm in Iowa, studied at the Art Institute of Chicago, and then traveled to Europe to study in Berlin and Paris.

In 1914 at the outbreak of World War I, Agnes and her sister Helen, along with many other American artists in Paris, came to Provincetown. Agnes took classes with Charles Hawthorne and also studied in New York at the Art Students League, but summers were spent in Provincetown,

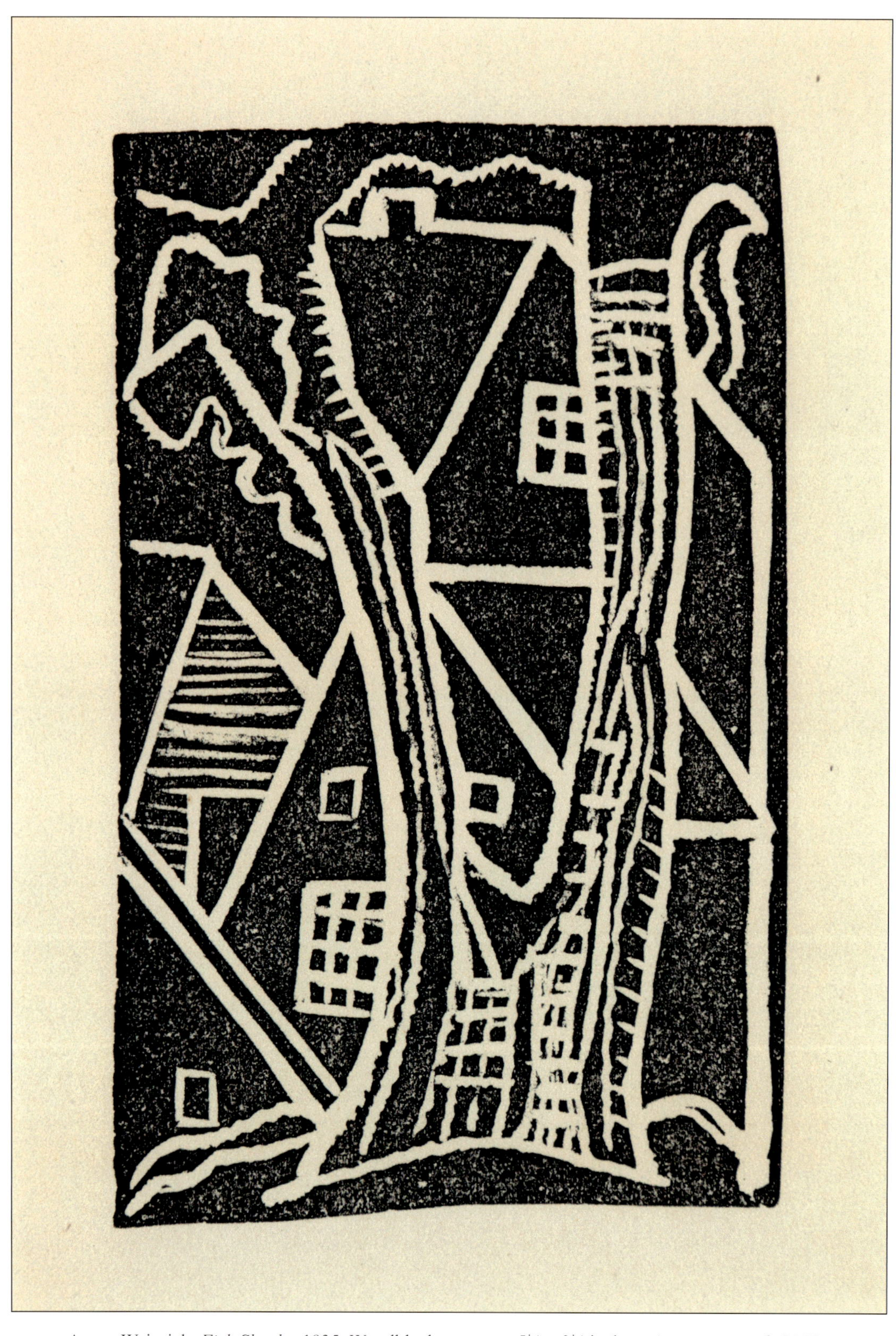

Agnes Weinrich, *Fish Shacks*, 1935. Woodblock on paper, 5½ × 3½ inches. *Anonymous gift*, 2009.

which ultimately became Helen and Agnes's permanent home.

In 1916, Weinrch joined the Provincetown Printers, a group known for the white-line woodcut, a process initiated by artist Ethel Mars and refined by printmaker B. J. O. Nordfeldt. The technique simplified the color woodblock print by using only one block instead of the Japanese approach of a separate block for each color. This method allowed all the colors to be applied to a single block, so the entire image appeared at once.

Weinrich's prints and paintings include fauvist and cubist images of Provincetown life, vibrant florals, still lifes, and bold arrangements of geometric shapes. The black-and-white woodblock print *Fish Shacks,* in the Cape Cod Museum of Art collection, shows her cubist inclinations. Her abstractions, built up with various shapes, sharp angles, and gentle curves, lyrically explore space and color, as does *Clams*, also in the museum collection.

Weinrich organized and directed the New York Society of Women Painters (the first women painters' association in America) in the 1920s, and participated in the first exhibition in 1915 at the Provincetown Art Association. She was part of the modernist group at the Art Association who led the rebellion against the conservatives, also called the "normals," by those inside the group. Following her sister Helen's marriage in 1922 to artist Karl Knaths, Agnes became a major influence on his work, introducing him to a more modern approach. She lived with her sister and brother-in-law in Provincetown until her death in 1946.

Her works are in the collections of several museums including the Brooklyn Museum of Art and the Phillips Collection in Washington, DC.

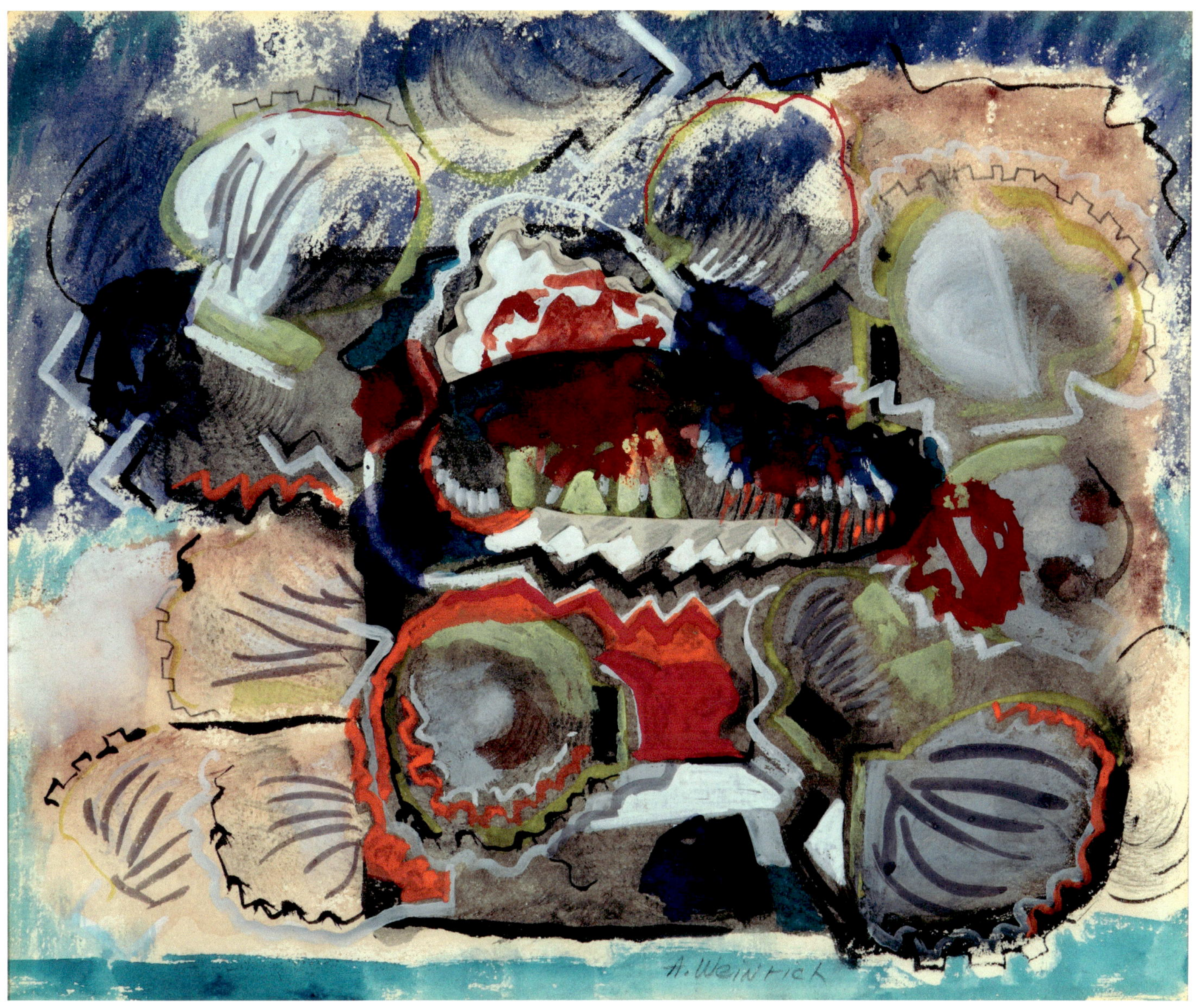

Agnes Weinrich, *Clams,* n.d. Mixed media on paper, 17¼ × 18¼ inches. *Gift of the Penny and Elton Yasuna Collection*, 2000.

BLANCHE LAZZELL
(1878–1956)

Blanche Lazzell was an early advocate of European modernism. Although the cubist influence is what is most notable in Lazzell's work, she did experiment with expressionistic colors and shapes learned from her study of the fauves and advocated by one of her later teachers, Hans Hofmann.

She was born on a farm in West Virginia and earned degrees in fine arts, literature, and liberal arts. In 1907, she moved to New York City and studied at the Art Students League with William Merritt Chase. Chase was a powerhouse as a painter and teacher and was a direct line to Charles Hawthorne, who had assisted him at his Long Island school.

In 1912, Lazzell sailed for Europe. She took classes at the Académie Julian and the Académie Moderne in Paris, where fauvism and the lessons of Paul Cézanne were taught. She had the opportunity to see the works of Cézanne, Pablo Picasso, Georges Braque, and Henri Matisse, and was introduced to Japanese woodblock prints, whose flat planes, asymmetry, and intricate patterns fascinated her.

Lazzell arrived in Provincetown in 1915 and studied with Charles Hawthorne. She returned the following summer, but wanted someone more progressive than Hawthorne, and began to study with Oliver Chaffee, who taught her printmaking. Lazzell became part of the Provincetown Printers, whose trademark was the white-line woodcut. The Provincetown Printers had exhibitions in New York and Provincetown in 1916. Lazzell created more than a hundred woodblocks from 1916 until her death in 1956. The work of the group depicted the scenic charms of this Cape Cod fishing village in bright, fauvist colors, flat planes and expressive patterns that celebrate the vitality of the print. A few, like Lazzell and Agnes Weinrich, moved onto a cubist approach.

Lazzell's rhythmic abstractions are colorful overlappings of various rectilinear shapes, sometimes referencing the houses and roofs of Provincetown, and of elegant curved forms, suggesting bottles or flowers. She filled the contours with patterns and allowed the colors to define spatial relationships, which always remained shallow. Often, she played a still life or vase of flowers against planes of vibrant color. Her tightly packed compositions of Provincetown's

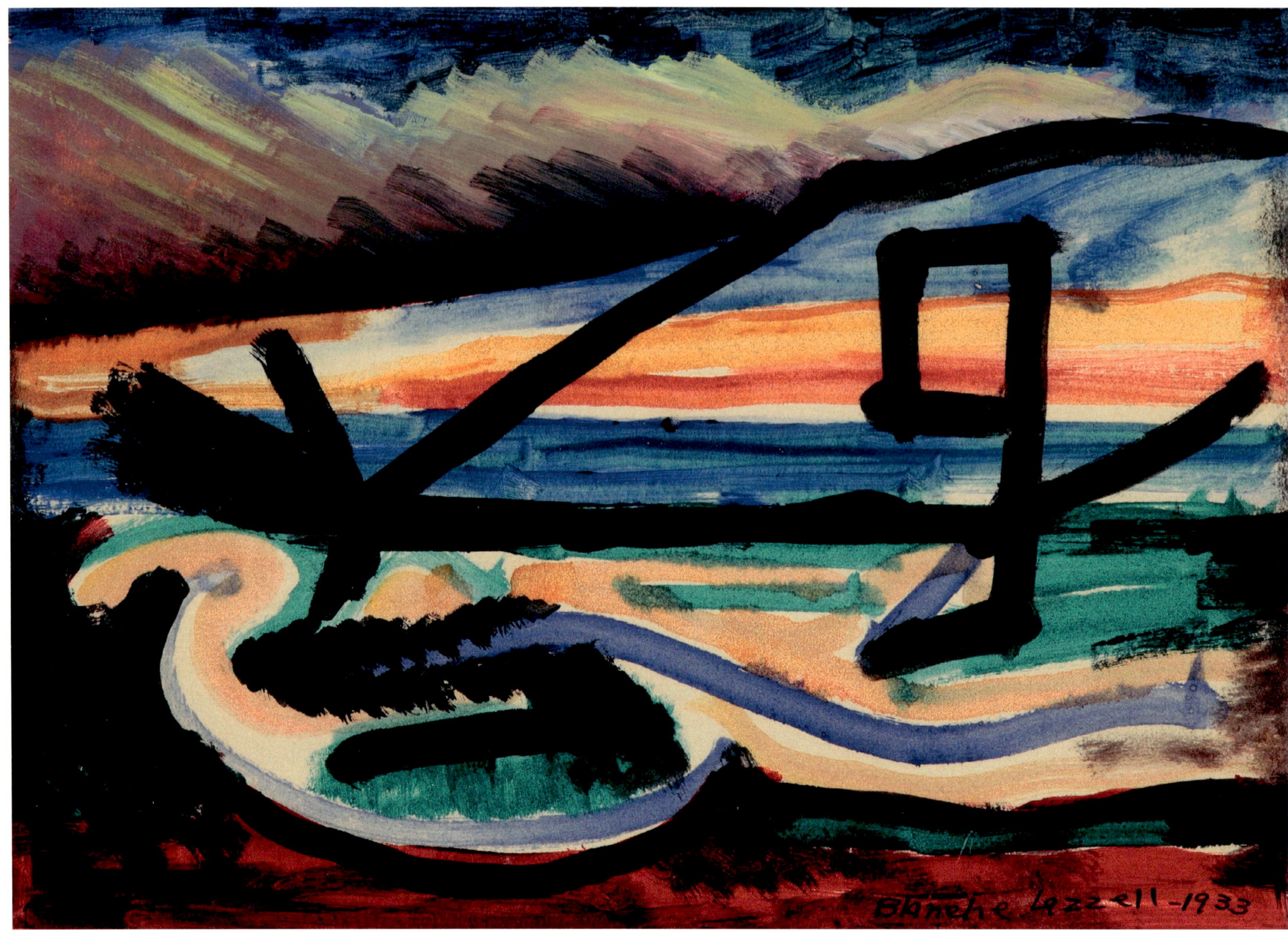

Blanche Lazzell, *Abstract Long Point,* 1933. Watercolor on paper, 8 × 10 inches. *Anonymous gift*, 2009.

houses and boats, her floral still lifes, and abstractions show a brilliant sense of innovative color, a creative arrangement of planes, and a strong sense of dynamic patterns.

In her black-and-white woodblock print *My Studio,* in the Cape Cod Museum of Art collection, her cubist-influenced composition of planes and patterns highlights the simple structure that was her studio in an old fish shack on a Provincetown wharf.

In 1923, Lazzell returned to Paris and settled in Montparnasse, which was still a haven for artists and writers looking to charge their creativity. She studied with cubists Fernand Léger, Andre L'Hote, and Albert Gleizes, and exhibited at the Salon d'Automne. In a few years, however, she was back in New York and Provincetown, experimenting even more with abstraction, color, and asymmetry. In the mid-1930s, she was taking classes with Hans Hofmann, in his Provincetown school, and producing brightly colored geometically abstracted prints for the Federal Art Project of the WPA. The watercolor *Abstract Long Point*, also in the museum collection, demonstrates her modernist approach in a boldly colored, expressive view of a familiar local site.

Her works are in the collections of major museums, including the Metropolitan Museum of Art and the Whitney Museum of American Art in New York, the Art Institute of Chicago, the Fine Arts Museums of San Francisco, the Museum of Fine Arts in Boston, and the Hirshhorn Museum and Sculpture Garden and the Smithsonian American Art Museum in Washington, DC.

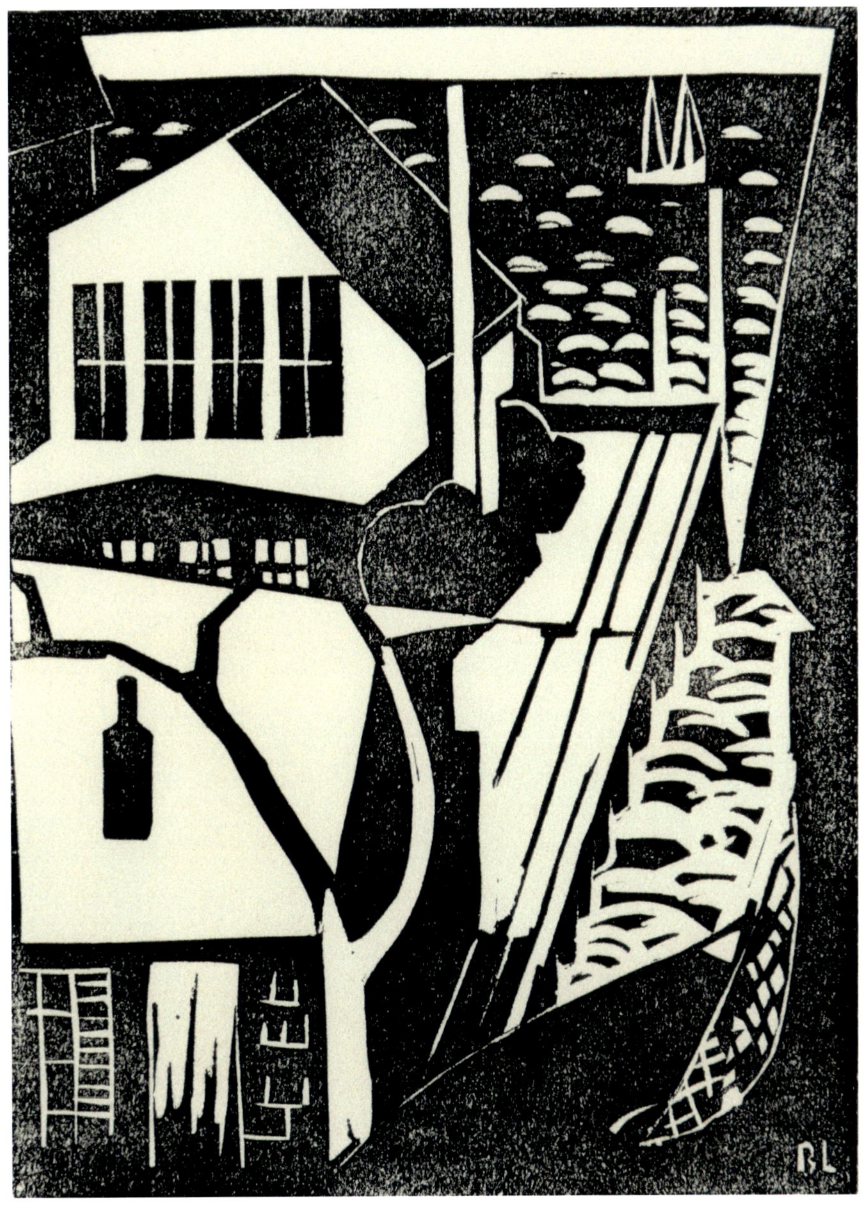

Blanche Lazzell, *My Studio*, 1935. Woodblock on paper, 5⅜ × 4 inches. *Anonymous gift*, 2009.

GIFFORD BEAL
(1879–1956)

Gifford Beal studied with William Merritt Chase at his summer school in Shinnecock Hills, Long Island. After graduating from Princeton University, Beal also studied at the Art Students League in New York.

His early work depicted the leisure life of the affluent, including garden parties and hunting expeditions. Influenced by Chase, these paintings are vibrant with twinkling color and light and quick impressionist brushstrokes. His work during the summers that the New York-born artist spent by the sea is noted for its realistic approach depicting the rugged life of fishermen on the New England coast. Two paintings in the Cape Cod Museum of Art collection are seaside views. *Seagulls No. 3* vibrantly depicts five gulls flying across a big sky of sweeping colors. By drawing a low horizon line in this work and *Twin Lights—Thacher (Walthers) Island*, Beal was able to focus on the spread of colors across the sky, so that in *Twin Lights*, the lighthouses are essentially silhouettes. In both paintings, the sea takes up just a small strip at the bottom of the compositions.

During his mid-career, Beal painted simplified compositions with subdued colors and vigorous brushwork. In the 1940s, he focused on theater and circus scenes, in which he returned to his earlier style of bright colors and impressionistic light effects. Later, his approach became more expressive in subjects garnered from New York life and his travels.

Beal's works are in a number of museum collections, including the Metropolitan Museum of Art and the Whitney Museum of American Art in New York City, the Los Angeles County Museum of Art, the Art Institute of Chicago, and the Phillips Collection in Washington, DC.

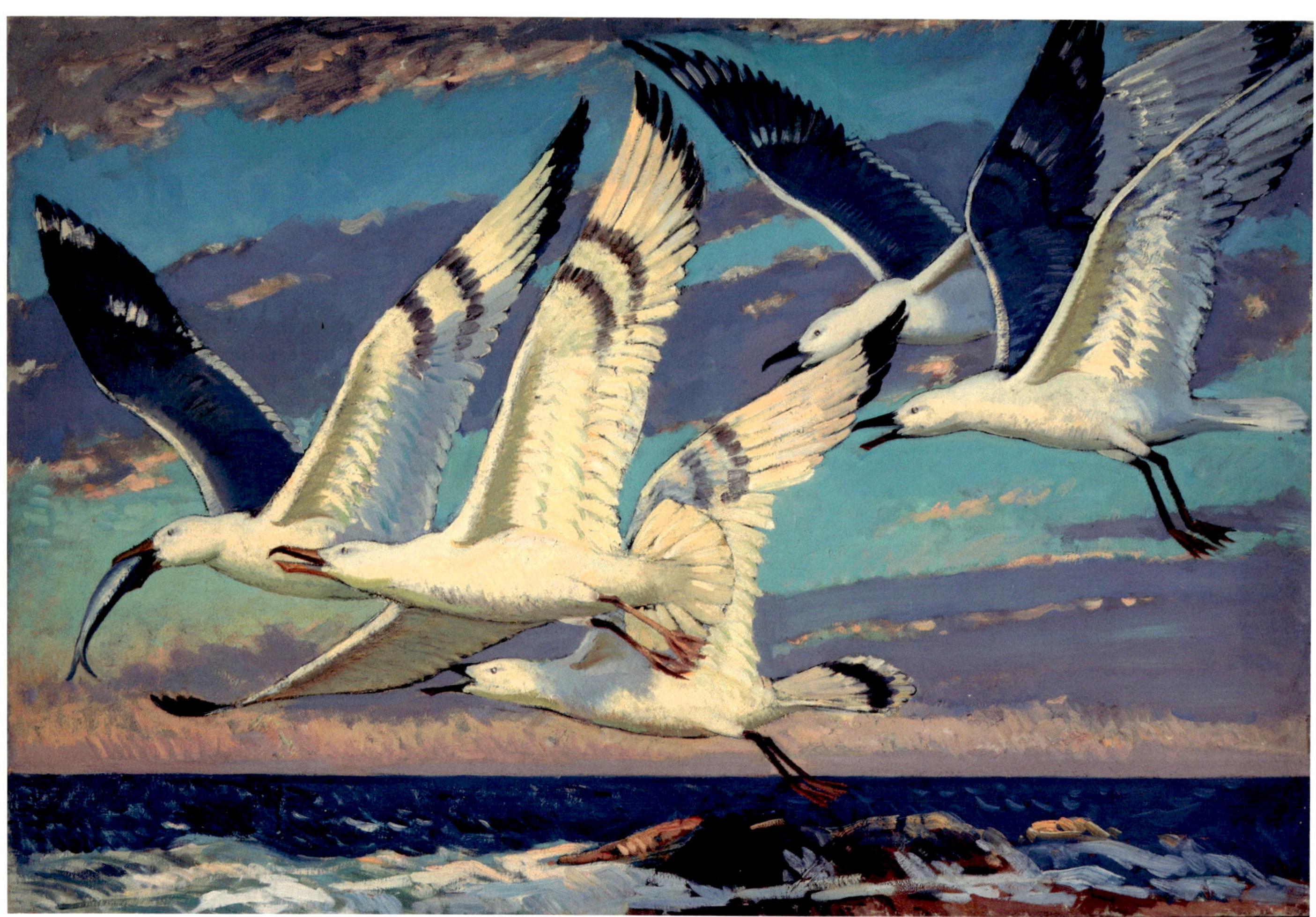

Gifford Beal, *Seagulls No. 3,* circa 1925. Oil on canvas, 36 × 54 inches. *Gift of the Estate of Gifford Beal. Courtesy of Kraushaar Galleries, New York*, 2015.

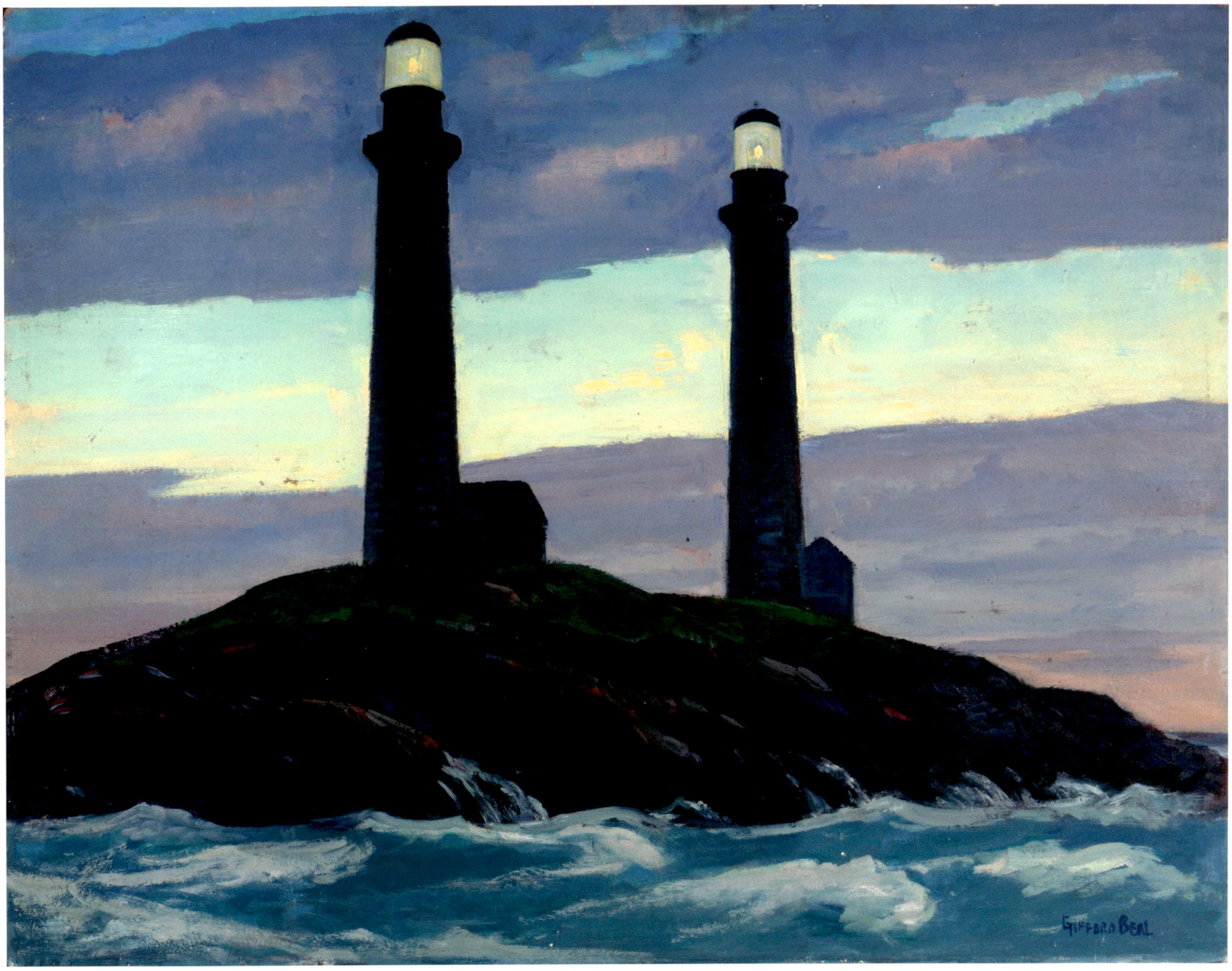

Gifford Beal, *Twin Lights-Thatcher (Walthers) Island,* circa 1933. Oil on masonite, 36 × 48 inches.
Gift of the Estate of Gifford Beal. Courtesy of Kraushaar Galleries, New York, 2015.

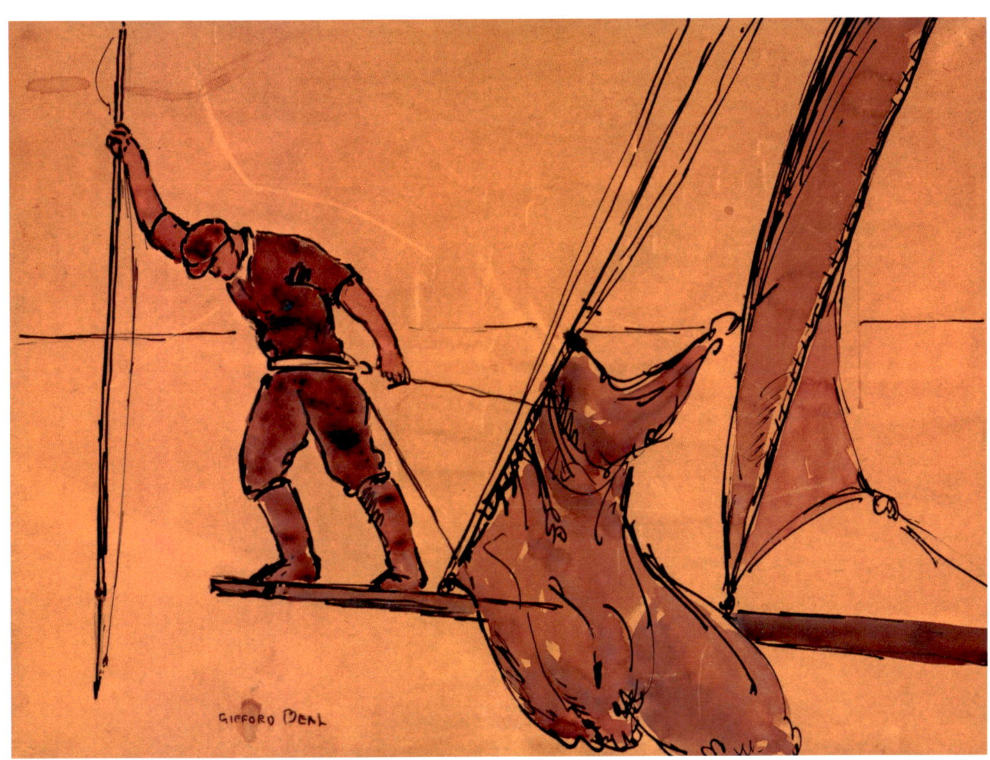

Gifford Beal, *Sword Fisherman*, n.d.
Ink and watercolor on paper,
18¾ × 13¾ inches.
Anonymous gift, 2009.

HANS HOFMANN
(1880–1966)

Hans Hofmann is one of the European artists who brought modernism to America. Although a number of early twentieth-century artists had been influenced by cubism and fauvism, in the 1920s and 1930s the representational images of the Ashcan School, social realism, and regionalism held sway in America.

Born in Weissenburg, Germany, Hofmann began studying art in Munich. In 1904, he went to Paris, which was buzzing with fauvism; a few years later the revolutionary ideas of cubism would enliven the scene. Hofmann was introduced to the work of Paul Cézanne, Pablo Picasso, Georges Braque, Juan Gris, Henri Matisse, and others. He also undoubtedly knew the work of the artists associated with Die Brücke and Blaue Reiter groups, which were active in his native country.

Hofmann returned to Germany in 1914, and when war broke out, Paris became off-limits to him. He opened the School for Modern Art in a Munich suburb in 1915. In 1930, one of his students, Worth Ryder, who was chairman of the art department at the University of California at Berkeley, invited Hofmann to teach there. In 1932 he moved to New York to teach at the Art Students League. By 1933, he had opened the Hans Hofmann School of Fine Arts in Manhattan, and a year later, his classes in Provincetown launched an era that lasted twenty-three years.

During Hofmann's time in Provincetown, hundreds of artists came to the little fishing village to study with him. His reputation as an innovative and exuberant teacher was widespread, and his students celebrated his exceptional teaching style, unbridled optimism, and passion for art. Hofmann brought together the structures of Picasso and Braque's cubism with the evocative power of Matisse's colors, and motivated a generation of American artists to free themselves from the constraints of representational art and to launch an indigenous American art movement. Although at least partly based on European ideas, this new art form was energized with the American spirit that rose with the emergence of the United States as a world power at the end of the Second World War. Hofmann exerted a pivotal influence

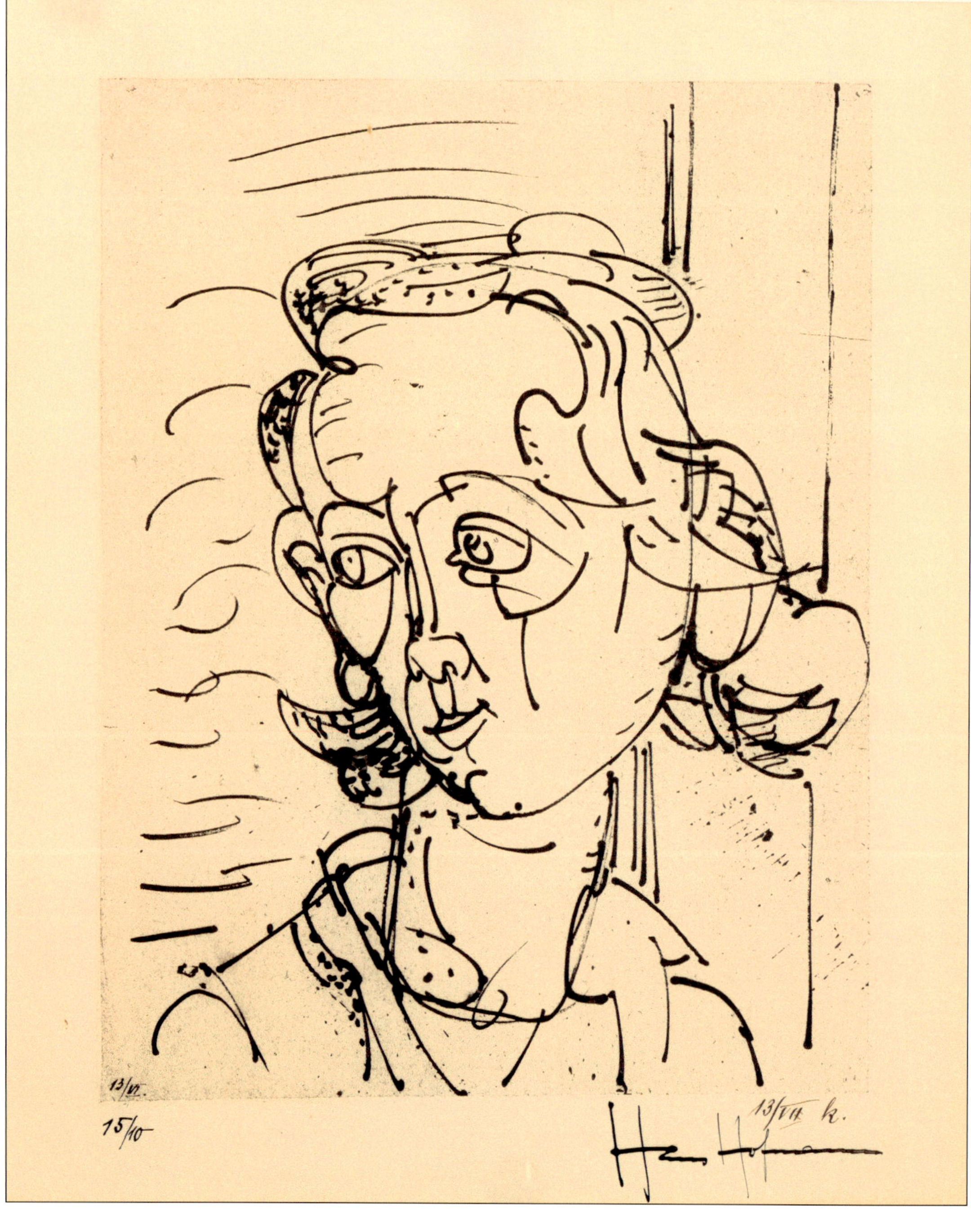

Hans Hofmann, *Portrait of a Young Lady* 15/10 13/VII, n.d. Lithograph on paper, 16 × 13½ inches. *Gift of Lillian Orlowsky and William Freed,* 2004. © *2010 The Renate, Hans & Maria Hofmann Trust/Artists Rights Society (ARS), New York.*

on the rise of abstract expressionism, which transported the center of the art world from Paris to New York.

Hofmann did not expect his students to paint or draw a representation of what they saw; rather, he hoped they would express their personal experiences, as they considered movement, color relationships, planes, and volume. It amounted to placing the elements so that the space was rhythmically activated by a system of forces and counterforces—his "push-and-pull" theory. If one element in an artwork pushed, there would be a response—a pull—from another element. This approach promoted a dynamic relationship between color and form.

Hofmann's expressionistic work of the 1930s and 1940s shows evidence of a landscape, figure, or still life. *Portrait of a Young Lady*, a lithograph in the collection of the Cape Cod Museum of Art, shows his expressionistic approach in the kinetic lines that captured the face.

In the late 1940s and 1950s, he moved into abstraction. He created a whirlwind of meandering lines across ravishing colors. The 1950 oil painting *Untitled*, in the museum collection, shows the dash and vigor of his work. By the early 1950s, he introduced spacious planes that preceded his signature rectangles, which became dominant in the mid-1950s. These works reference cubism and Mondrian's arrangement of geometric forms. The colors hearken back to Matisse.

In 1958, Hofmann closed his schools. He was seventy-eight and wanted to paint full time. Throughout the 1950s and early 1960s he continued his devotion to the rectangle. Toward the end of his life, his compositions took on amorphous shapes soaking up vivacious colors. He continued to summer in Provincetown and painted until his death in 1966, one month before his eighty-sixth birthday. He is buried in Truro, Massachusetts.

His works are in the collections of major museums, including the Metropolitan Museum of Art, the Museum of Modern Art, and the Whitney Museum of American Art in New York; the Los Angeles County Museum of Art; the National Gallery of Art in Washington, DC; the Philadelphia Museum of Art; the San Francisco Museum of Modern Art; Tate Modern in London; and the Israel Museum in Jerusalem.

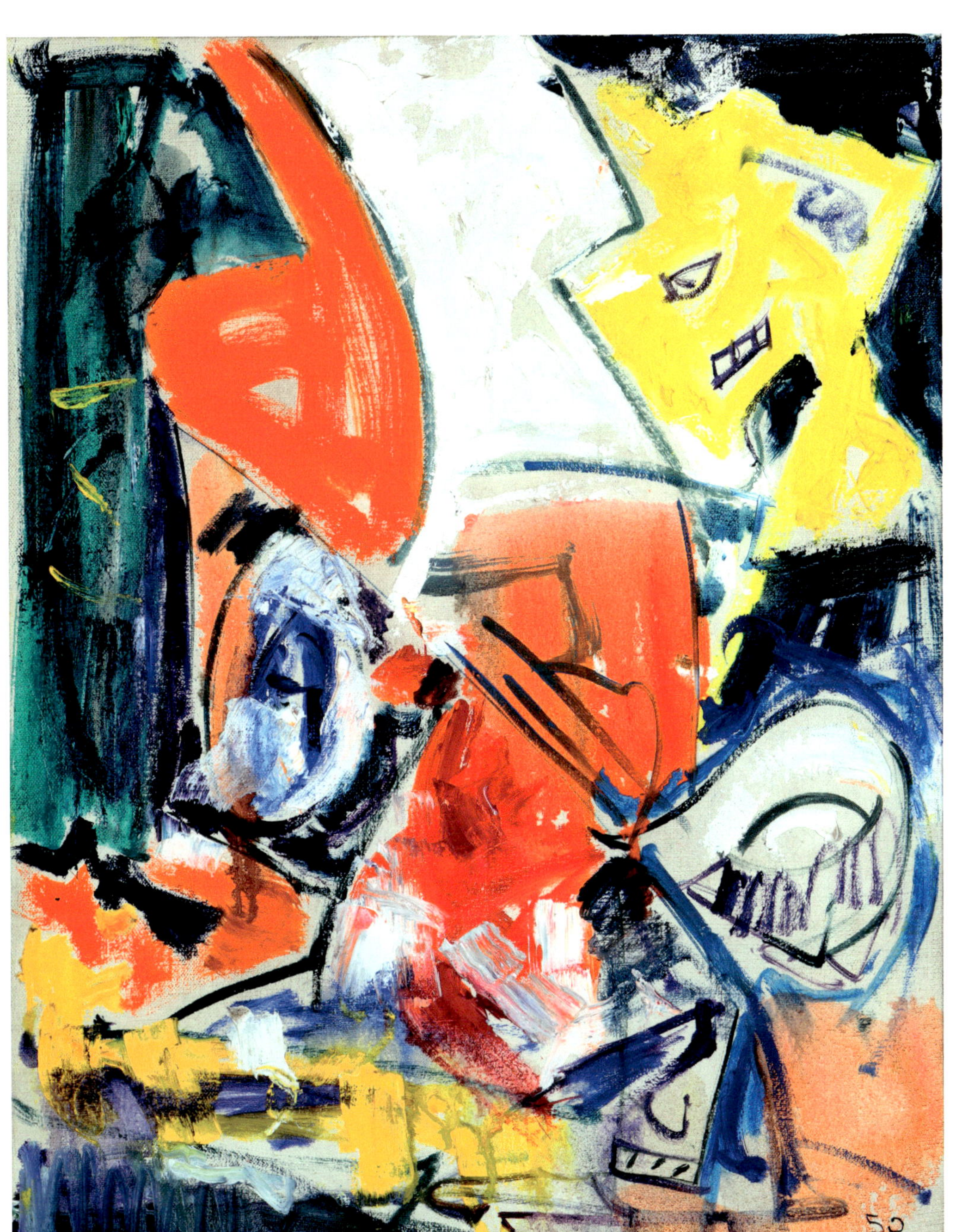

Hans Hofmann, *Untitled*, 1950. Oil on canvas, 19 × 15 inches. *Anonymous gift*, 2005. *© 2010 The Renate, Hans & Maria Hofmann Trust/Artists Rights Society (ARS), New York .*

OLIVER NEWBERRY CHAFFEE
(1881–1944)

Oliver Newberry Chaffee studied in New York with William Merritt Chase and Robert Henri and in 1904 he came to Provincetown to take classes with Charles Hawthorne, who gave him insight into the importance of light and color. Chaffee's early paintings were impressionistic, but after studying in Paris and seeing the work of the fauves and Picasso, his work evolved. He was one of eighteen artists with Provincetown connections who were part of the 1913 Armory Show, where he exhibited three fauvist landscapes.

Forced to abandon Paris during World War I, he returned to Provincetown in 1914, in time to participate in the founding of the Provincetown Art Association as a place where artists could show their work. He traveled again to France in the early 1920s, but soon returned, and in 1925 married Ada Gilmore, one of the original Provincetown Printers.

Chaffee's exuberant works are dominated by simplified forms, sinuous outlines, and passionate colors. His 1928 oil painting *The White Horse*, in the collection of the Cape Cod Museum of Art, is evidence of his modernist approach at a time when few were adventurous enough to tackle it. Like his wife, Chaffee was part of the Provincetown Printers and taught the techniques of the white-line woodcut. *3 Central*, in the museum collection, is an example of one of his woodblock prints. Chaffee remained active in Provincetown until his death in 1944. Ross Moffett wrote of him in *Art in Narrow Streets*: "He was a modern before modernism became popular."

His works are included in the collection of the Smithsonian American Art Museum in Washington, DC.

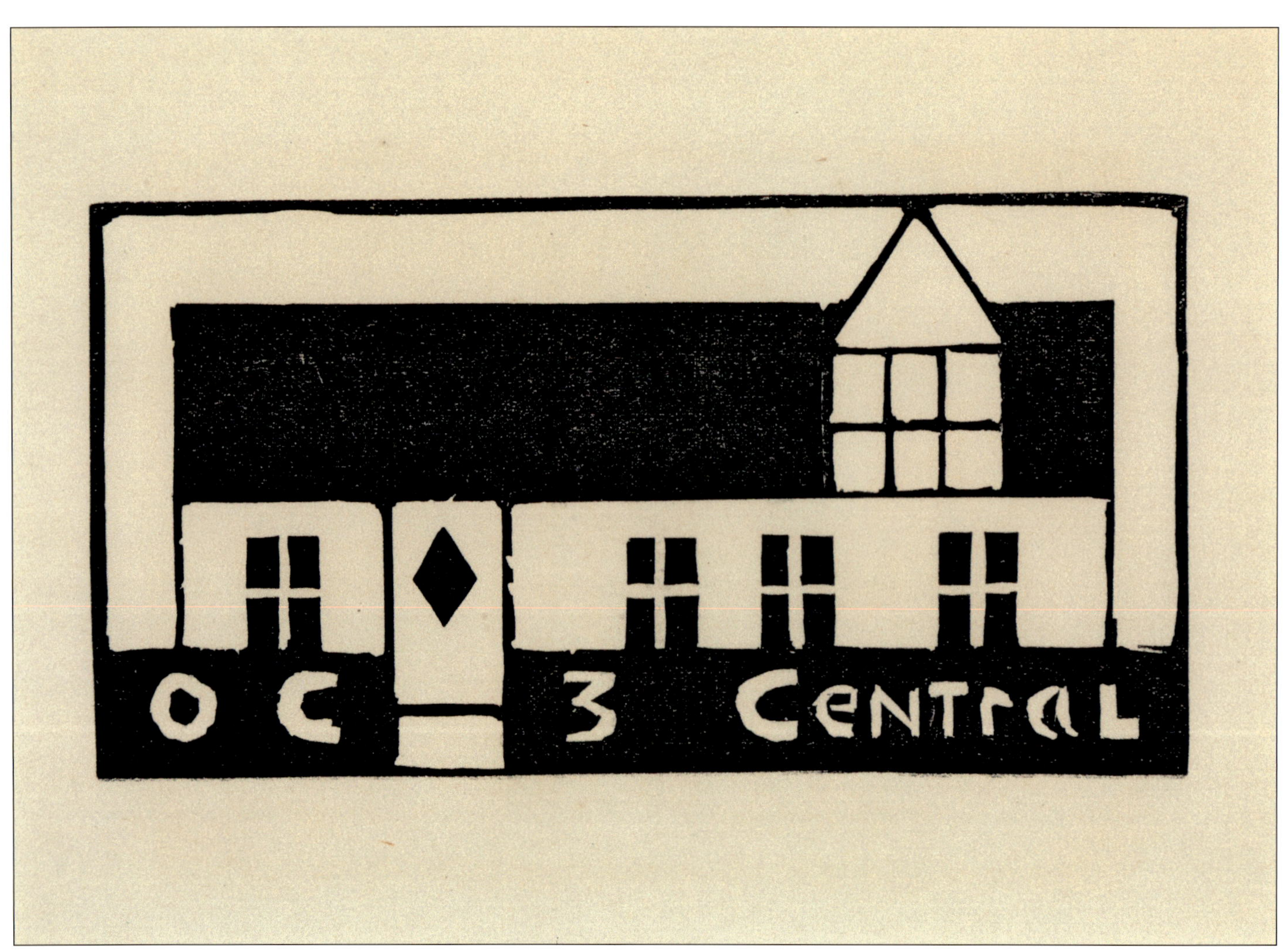

Oliver Newberry Chaffee, *3 Central*, 1935. Woodblock on paper, 19 × 15 inches. *Anonymous gift*, 2009.

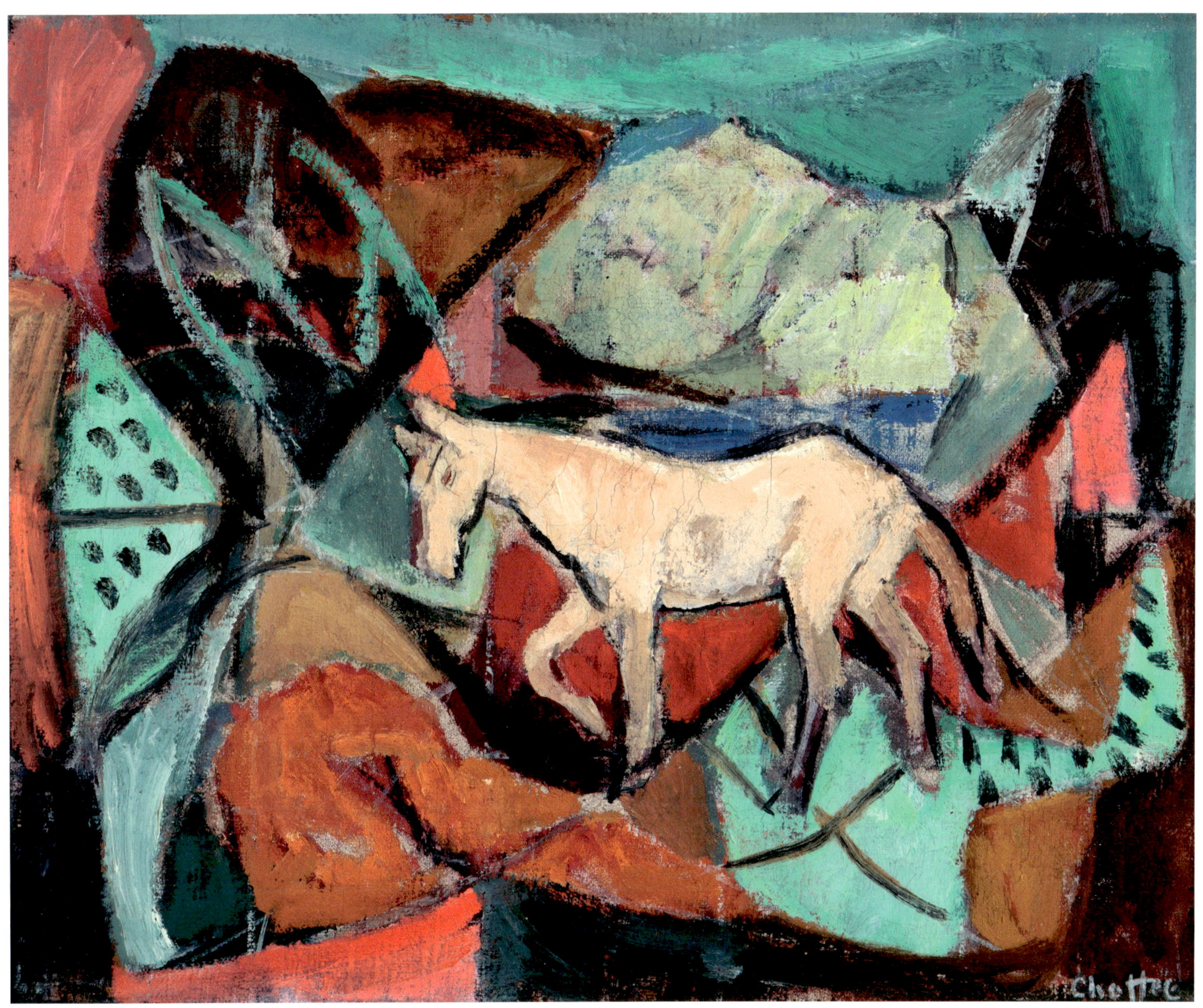

Oliver Newberry Chaffee, *The White Horse*, 1928. Oil on canvas, 16 × 20 inches. *Gift of Mr. William M. Baxter and Mr. Allen J. Ward*, 1992.

ROCKWELL KENT
(1882–1971)

Visitors to Cape Cod who drop in to see a film at the Cape Cinema in Dennis, adjacent to the Cape Cod Museum of Art, will find a very dramatic mural by Rockwell Kent on the ceiling of the theater. Kent was commissioned to do the design in 1930 by Raymond Moore, founder of the Cape Playhouse and Cinema in Dennis. The work of transferring and painting the designs on the 6,400-square-foot span was done by stage designer Jo Mielziner and a crew of stage set painters from New York City. The mural is painted in oil on strips of canvas affixed to the ceiling and captures the heavens with constellations and dancing figures. The signatures of both Kent and Mielziner appear on opposite walls of the cinema.

Born in Tarrytown Heights, New York, Kent began his art training at William Merritt Chase's summer art school at Shinnecock Hills on Long Inland. He went on to study with Kenneth Hayes Miller and Robert Henri at the New York School of Art in 1900. He took classes at the Art Students League and earned a degree in architecture from Columbia University in New York.

In 1905, Kent went to Monhegan, an island off the coast of Maine, to paint. He was attracted by the sharp edges and strong contrasts of the rugged Maine coast and returned the following year and built a house. Kent was inspired by the austerity and stark beauty of the wilderness. He traveled to Newfoundland, Alaska, Greenland, Ireland, Tierra del Fuego, and the Straits of Magellan at the southern tip of South America to locate subject matter. His landscapes and seascapes of these locations capture the mysteries and wonders of the natural world. His work evokes nature's powerful forces.

His style is frequently identified with that of the American social realists. His figure-studies show him as a skilled draftsman with an ability to portray the human form in a

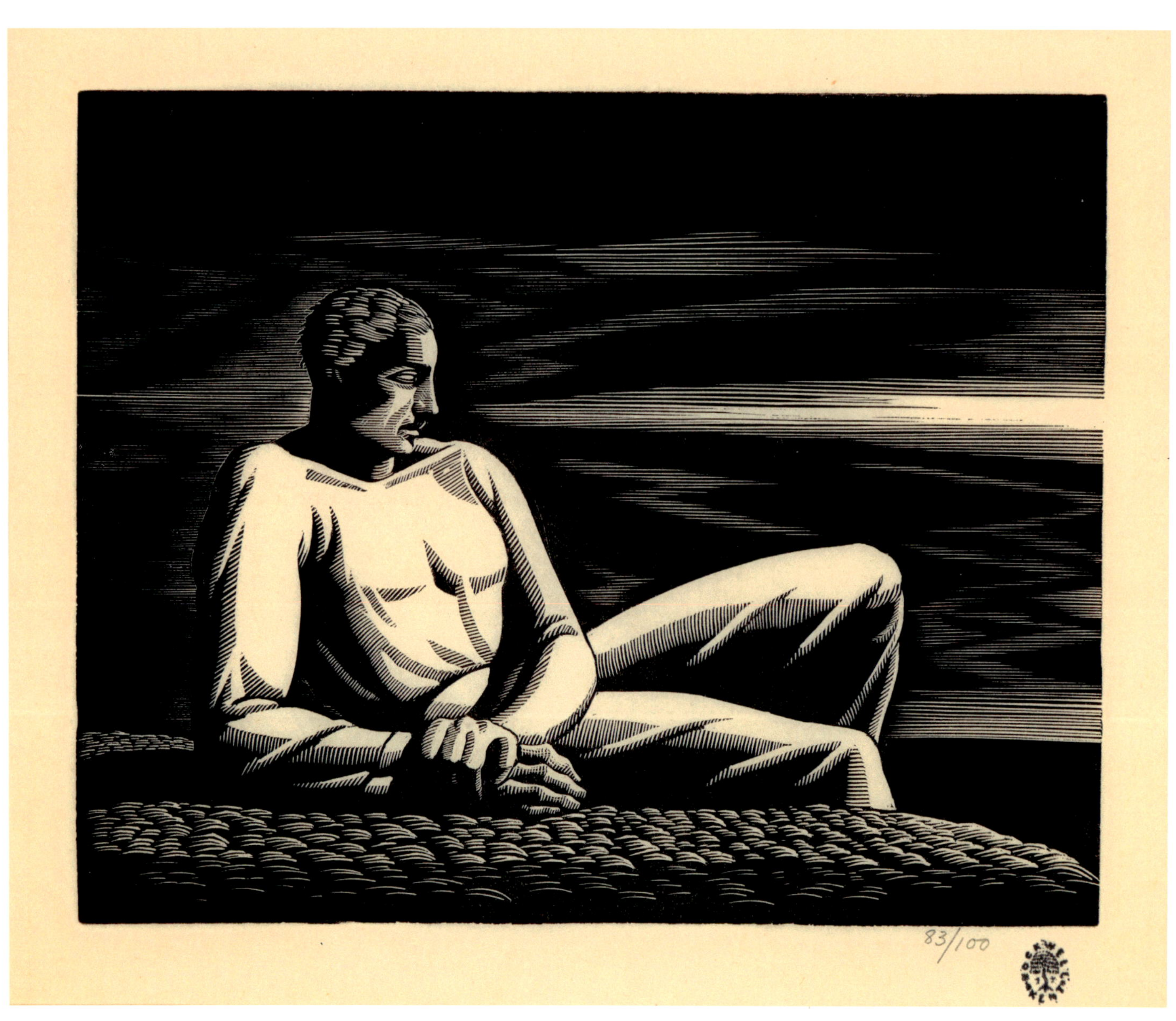

Rockwell Kent, *The Far Horizon 83/100*, n.d. Wood engraving on paper, 6½ × 8 inches. *Gift of Roy N. Freed, Esquire*, 1987.

diversity of ways. The wood engraving *The Far Horizon*, in the Cape Cod Museum of Art collection, portrays a heavily shadowed figure with intense black-and-white contrasts.

His graphic art is in the tradition of British illustrators and the pre-Raphaelites. Kent wrote and illustrated several books: *Wilderness: A Journal of Quiet Adventure in Alaska*; *Voyaging Southward from the Strait of Magellan; Salamina about Greenland*; and two autobiographies. Examples of his graphic works in the museum collection are three record album covers: *Carmina Burana*, *The Wraggle, Taggle Gipsies*, and *Best Loved German Songs*.

A political activist, Kent's support of radical causes contributed to a decline in his artistic popularity during the 1940s and 1950s. The State Department even revoked his passport, which was ultimately reinstated. He was popular in the Soviet Union, and he donated eighty paintings and 800 prints and drawings to Russia. In 1967, he was awarded the Lenin Peace Prize.

His works are included in a number of museums, including the Metropolitan Museum of Art in New York, Seattle Art Museum in Washington, the New Britain Museum of American Art in Connecticut, and the Fine Arts Museums of San Francisco.

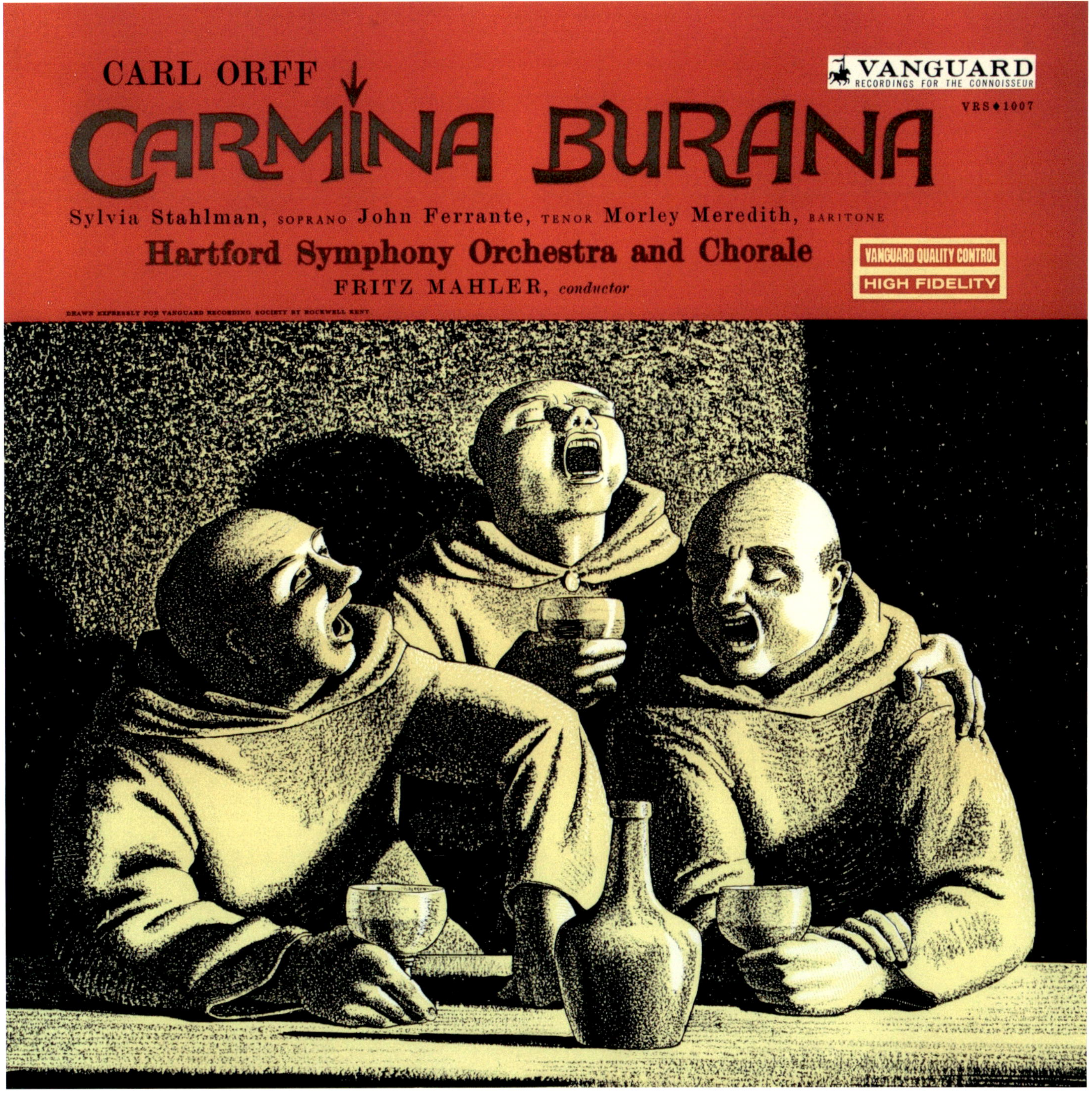

Rockwell Kent, *Carmina Burana* (Printers Proof, Vanguard Record Album Cover), 1950–1961. Silkscreen on paper, 14¾ × 16 inches.
Gift of James T. Valliere, 1995.

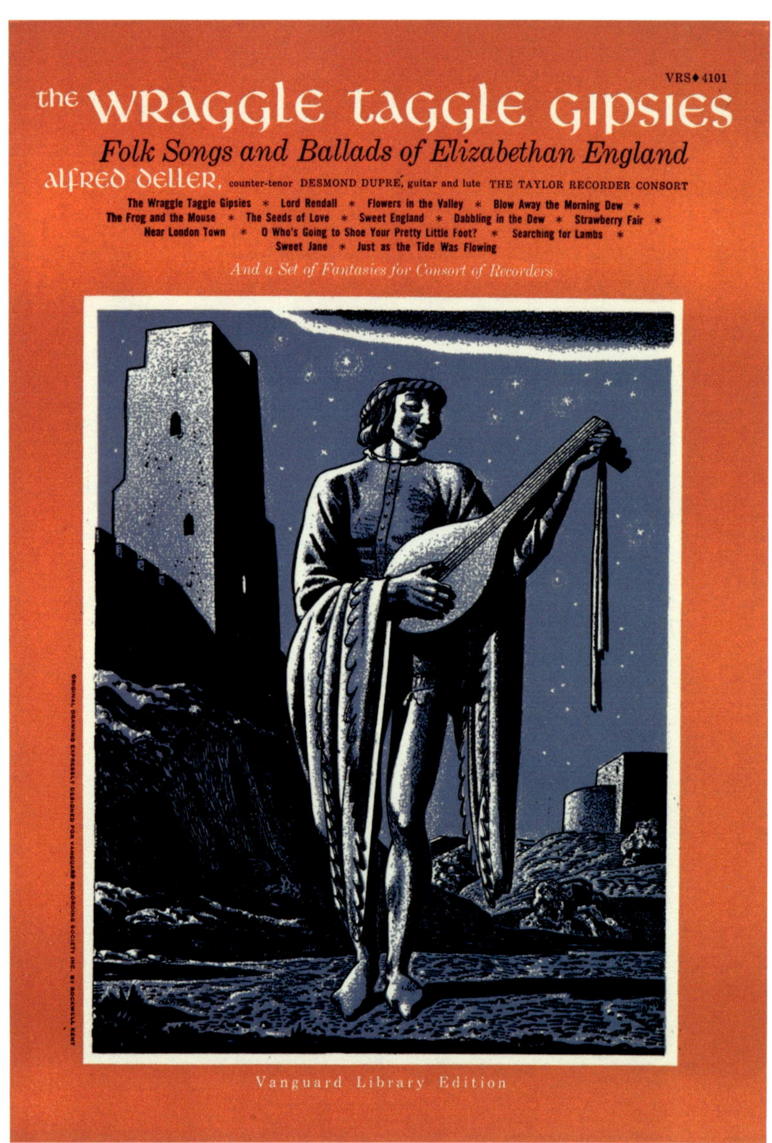

Rockwell Kent, *The Wraggle Taggle Gipsies* (Printers Proof, Vanguard Record Album Cover), 1950–1961. Silkscreen on paper, 15 × 11½ inches. *Gift of James T. Valliere*, 1995.

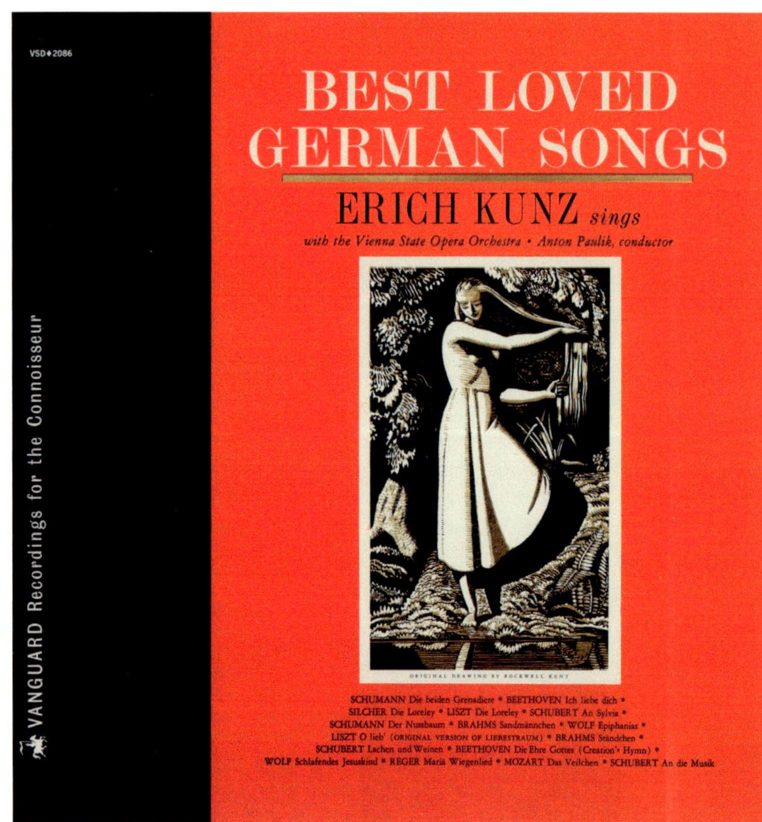

Rockwell Kent, *Best Loved German Songs* (Printers Proof, Vanguard Record Album Cover), 1950–1961. Silkscreen on paper, 15 × 14¾ inches. *Gift of James T. Valliere*, 1995.

ADA GILMORE
(1883–1955)

Ada Gilmore was one of the Provincetown Printers who, in the early years of the art colony, began working in the newly created white-line woodblock print. Along with Blanche Lazzell, B. J. O. Nordfeldt, Ethel Mars, Maud Hunt Squire, Edna Boies Hopkins, and Mildred McMillen, Gilmore made a significant contribution to printmaking in the early twentieth century.

She studied at the School of the Art Institute of Chicago, and a year before the outbreak of World War I, she traveled to Paris, where she learned woodblock printing from the artist Ethel Mars, who taught the traditional method that involved a block cut for each color. Gilmore, along with Mars, Squire, Lazzell, and Hopkins, participated in the Salon d'Automne exhibitions in Paris.

When war broke out, Gilmore, Mars, Hopkins, Squire, and McMillen returned to America, and in 1915 discovered the art colony in Provincetown. Along with two other artists, Nordfeldt and Juliette Nichols, they formed the nucleus of the group of woodcut artists who became known as the Provincetown Printers, and created their own little revolution.

Swedish-born Nordfeldt has long been given credit for the development of the white-line woodcut, the technique of making colorful prints from a single woodblock, which became the trademark of the Provincetown Printers. However, it was Ethel Mars who first experimented with the white-line technique, and suggested it to Nordfeldt. The women artists adopted this approach once Nordfeldt had refined it, and soon they were all making cheerful images of Provincetown's houses and wharves, boats, and townspeople. Gilmore's subjects include village cottages and streets, and scenes of women gardening and doing laundry. The woodblock print *Sandpipers,* in the Cape Cod Museum of Art collection, whimsically captures these birds often seen on the seashore. Similar to other Provincetown prints, Gilmore's woodcuts show the influence of Paris, and especially of Henri Matisse and his fauve colleagues, in the flat planes, expressive patterns, and bold contrasts.

Gilmore also made watercolors of the village architecture, and her woodcuts have the same translucent quality of her watercolor paintings. In 1925, Gilmore married Provincetown artist Oliver Newberry Chaffee. She lived with Chaffee in Provincetown until her death in 1955.

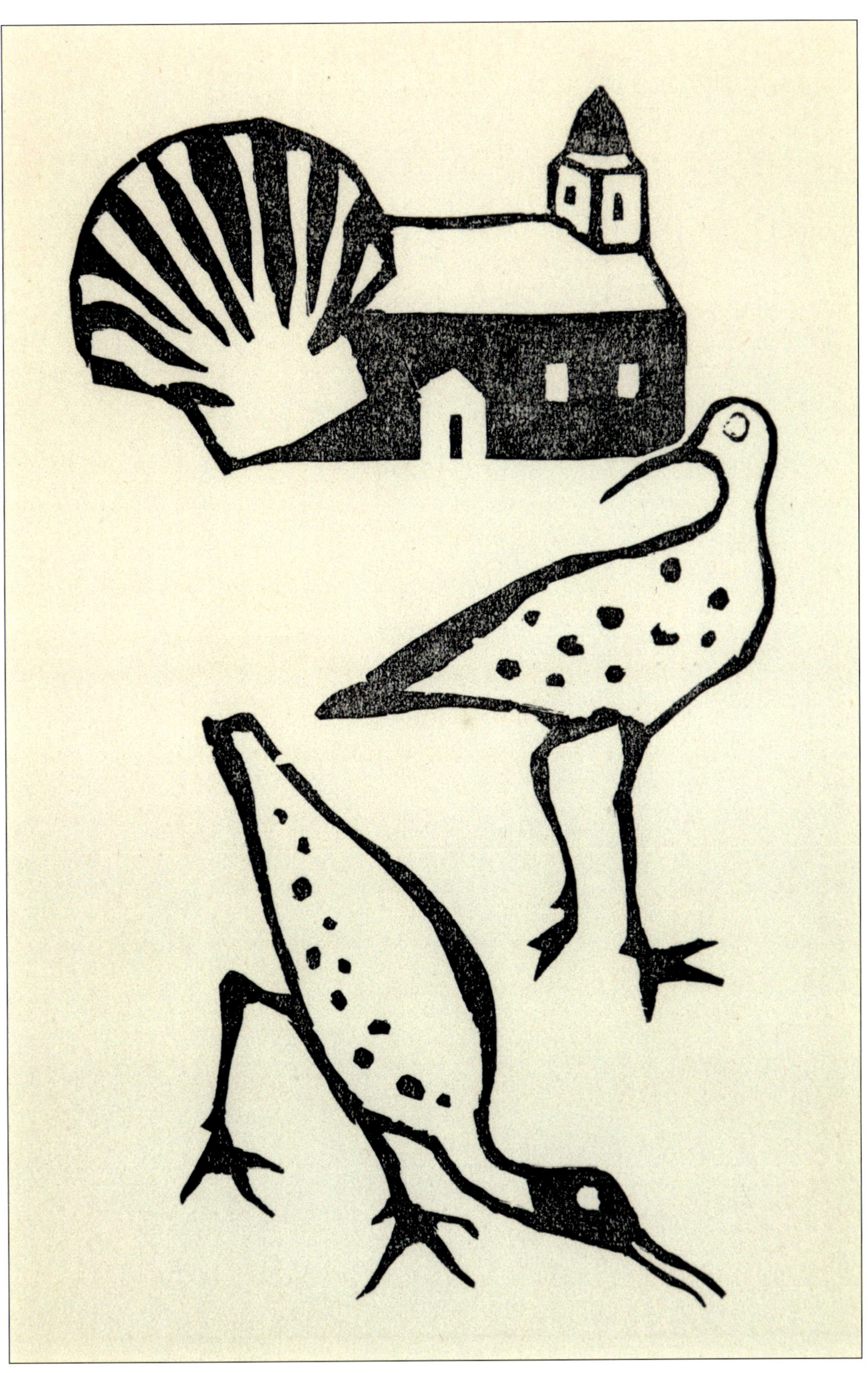

Ada Gilmore, *Sandpipers*, 1935.
Woodblock on paper, 8 × 5½ inches.
Anonymous gift, 2009.

CHARLES LLOYD HEINZ
(1884–1953)

Born in Shelbyville, Illinois, Charles Heinz studied at the Chicago Academy of Fine Arts and St. Louis School of Fine Arts. In 1929 he took classes with Charles Hawthorne in Provincetown, where he eventually decided to settle. Influenced by Hawthorne's impressionism, Heinz went further, adapting the fauvist approach of Henri Matisse with expressionistic color and a dynamic brushstroke.

In the 1930s, Heinz was part of the Massachusetts Federal Art Project of the WPA, and painted mostly watercolors of traditional subject matter with a modernist use of color. His color in these paintings is heavily applied, even lush, and bright in hue. And the application of the color is done rapidly, in thick, quick strokes.

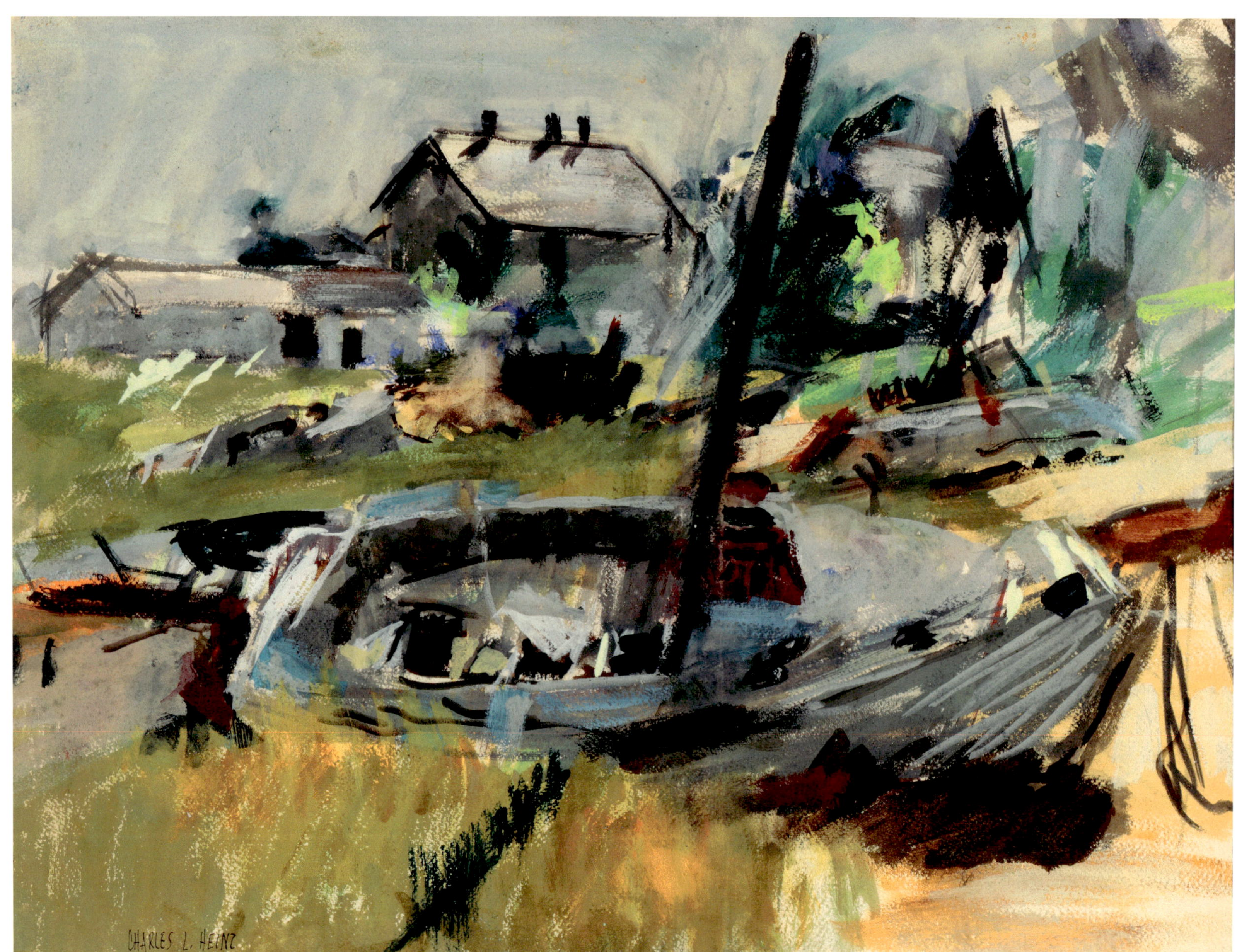

Charles Lloyd Heinz, *Provincetown East End*, n.d. Oil on paper, 19 × 25½ inches. *Anonymous gift*, 2009.

Heinz painted landscapes, village streets, cottages, boats, and wharves with an intense vitality and in vivid colors. His colors are speckled and his brushstroke lively. His scenes of the waterfront are dynamic with diagonal masts cutting through space, as in *Provincetown East End*, in the Cape Cod Museum of Art collection. His views over angled village rooftops provide a perspective that reflects elements of cubism, which can be seen in *Untitled (Blue Roof)*, also in the museum collection.

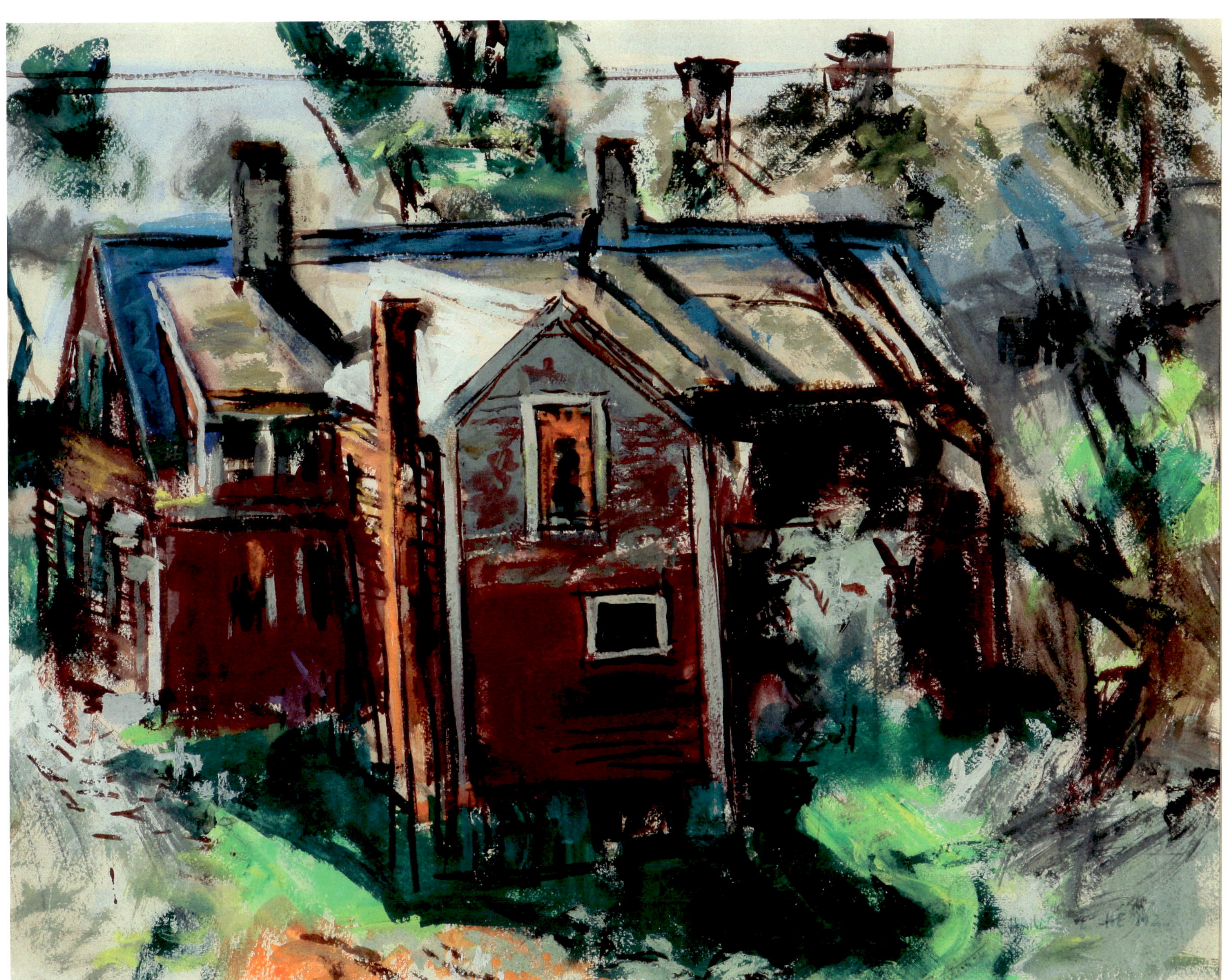

Charles Lloyd Heinz, *Untitled (Blue Roof)*, 1940. Gouache on paper, 19½ × 25 inches. *Gift of Roy and Sheila Mennell*, 1997.

TOD LINDENMUTH
(1885–1976)

A member of the Provincetown Printers, Tod Lindenmuth came to Provincetown in 1915 to study with E. Ambrose Webster and George Elmer Browne. He exhibited in the Provincetown Art Association's first show in 1915 and served on the jury for the Art Association's First Modernistic Exhibition in 1927. Prior to his time in Provincetown, the Pennsylvania native studied with Robert Henri at the New York School of Art in Manhattan.

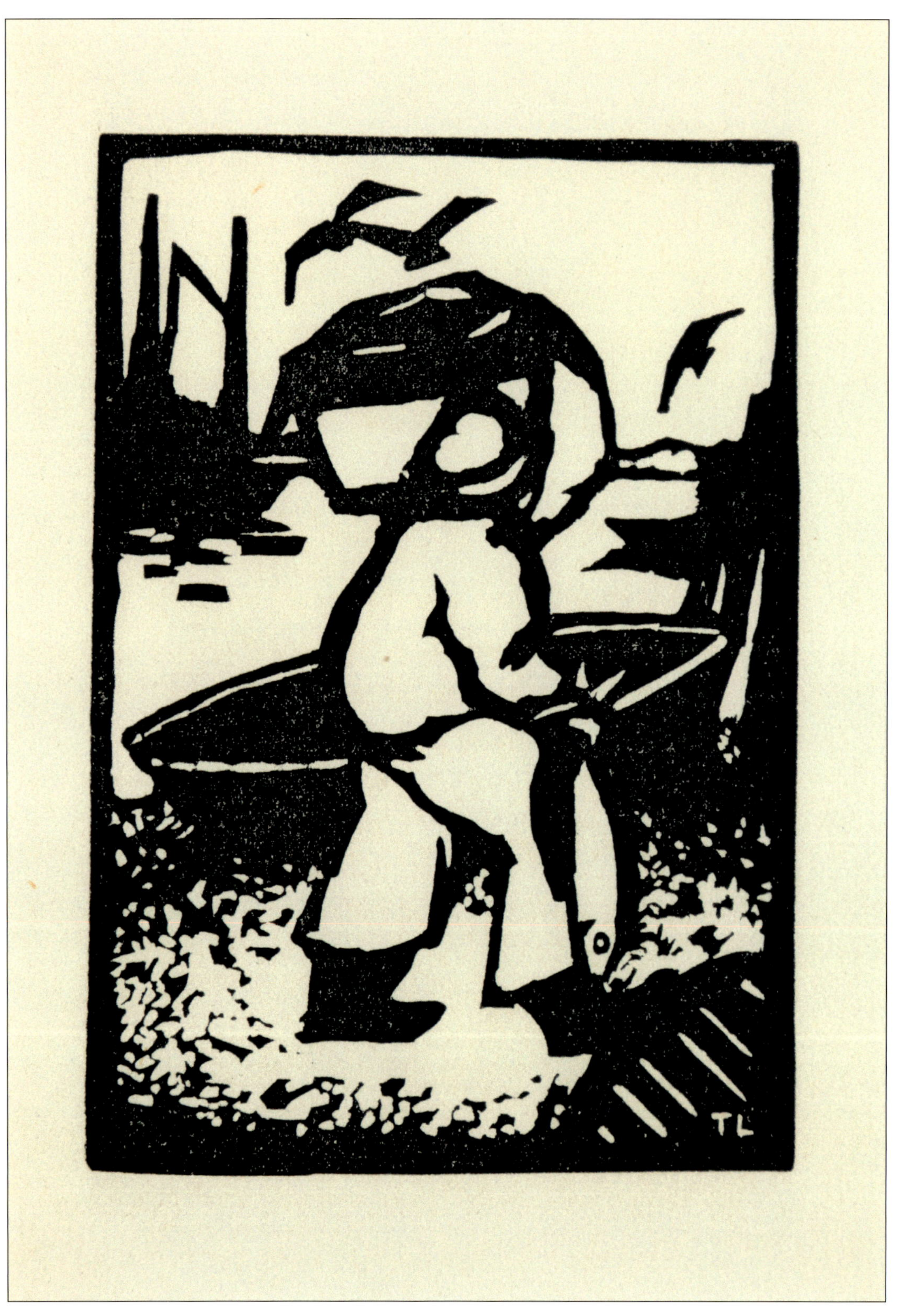

Tod Lindenmuth, *Fisherman*, 1935. Woodblock on paper, 5¼ × 3¾ inches.
Anonymous gift, 2009.

Working with the Provincetown Printers, Lindenmuth was influenced by modernism, in both his woodblock prints and paintings. His 1935 *Fisherman*, in the collection of the Cape Cod Museum of Art, is a robust woodblock print capturing an image that reflects the industry that was so instrumental in the town's economy of that period. By the mid-1930s, Lindenmuth was working under the Emergency Relief Administration (ERA), and subsequently, for the Massachusetts Federal Art Project of the WPA, creating bold woodcuts that show his manipulation of space and abstraction of form.

Although active for many years in the Provincetown art colony, in 1940 he moved his summer studio to Rockport, Massachusetts, and spent winters in St. Augustine, Florida. Around that time he abandoned printmaking and focused on painting. He loved to paint marine subjects of Provincetown and Rockport, as well as landscapes of the South. His painting *Provincetown Coastal Scene*, also in the museum collection, depicts a serene view of the shoreline.

Lindenmuth's works are in a number of museum collections, including the Los Angeles County Museum of Art, the Pennsylvania Academy of Fine Arts, and the Museum of Fine Arts, Houston.

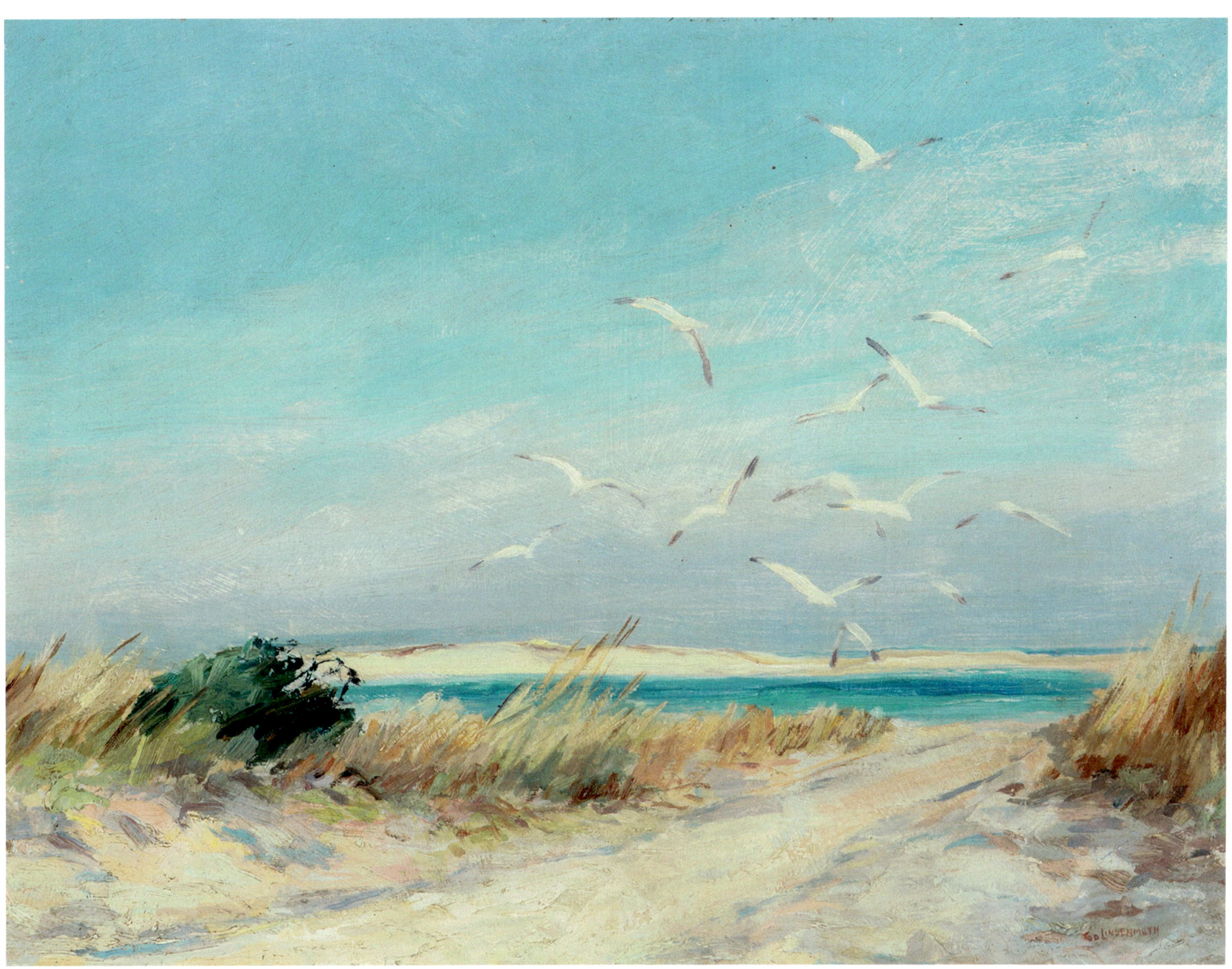

Tod Lindenmuth, *Provincetown Coastal Scene*, n.d. Oil on board, 12 × 16 inches. *Anonymous gift*, 2009.

ROSS MOFFETT
(1888–1971)

Ross Moffett was just one of many artists who came to Provincetown to study with Charles Hawthorne. The year was 1913 and Provincetown was still a cheap place to live. Studios rented for $50 or $60 a season, or for a year if one wanted to risk the winter. Moffett's book, *Art in Narrow Streets*, reveals his love affair with Provincetown, where he lived most of the rest of his life.

He was born in Iowa and studied art in Chicago before he arrived in Provincetown. In the early years there, he rented a studio at Days Lumberyard on Pearl Street, as did Charles Hawthorne and Edwin Dickinson. Many of Moffett's paintings are devoted to depicting Provincetown of that era: the streets and the townspeople, the land and sea, the harbors and beaches, the fishermen and their boats, and the farmers hard at work.

His works, which have a primitive quality and somber mood, are noted for simplified figures and distortions, which express the struggles and toil of the Portuguese fishermen and farmers in the community. In the Cape Cod Museum of Art collection is *Untitled*, one of Moffett's dark views of village life. *Conversation on the Shore*, in the collection, is also typical of his somber view of life in Provincetown. His colors are muted, earthy, like the soil the farmers worked in.

In addition to depicting the harsh aspects of life, he painted serene landscapes, the dunes, marshes, and waters. *Blue Heron, Pilgrim Lake*, in the museum collection, is a fine example. Noteworthy are the swirls across the sky and the rugged curves of the landscape.

Moffett also saw the value of modernism. He had seen the work of European and American modernists at the 1913 Armory Show and was inspired by them. *St. Augustine Rooftops* shows this approach. In some works, you can even see the influence of cubism in his views of the houses and streets of Provincetown.

During the 1930s, Moffett completed several mural projects throughout Massachusetts, and was also a registered studio artist, supported to produce easel paintings under the WPA's Federal Art Project. He later received a commission, with Louis Bouché, from the National Academy of Design for the Eisenhower Memorial Foundation in Abilene, Kansas, which was completed in 1956.

His works are in several museum collections, including the Whitney Museum of American Art in New York, the Pennsylvania Academy of Fine Arts in Philadelphia, and the Smithsonian American Art Museum in Washington, DC.

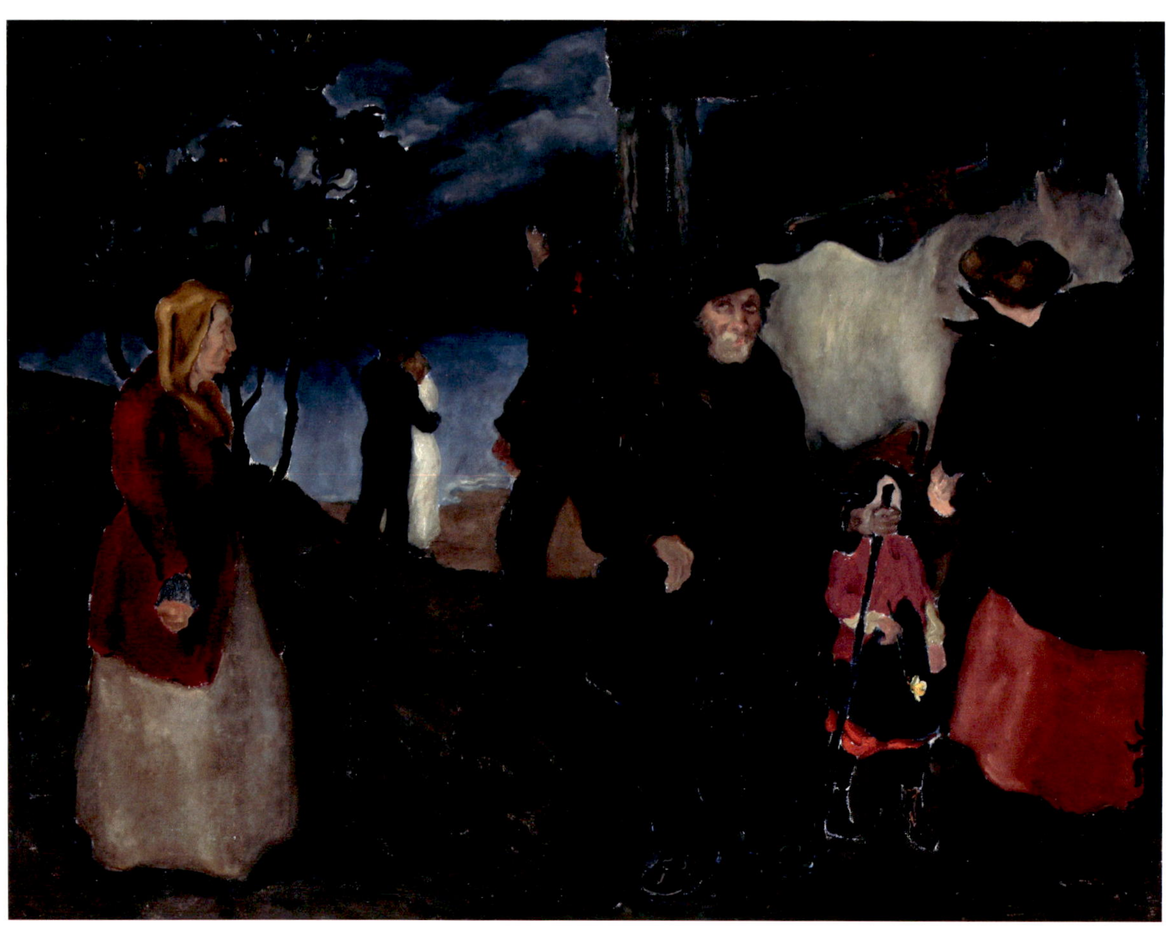

Ross Moffett, *Untitled*, n.d. Oil on canvas, 36 × 45 inches. *Gift of Frank and Ruth Hogan*, 1999.

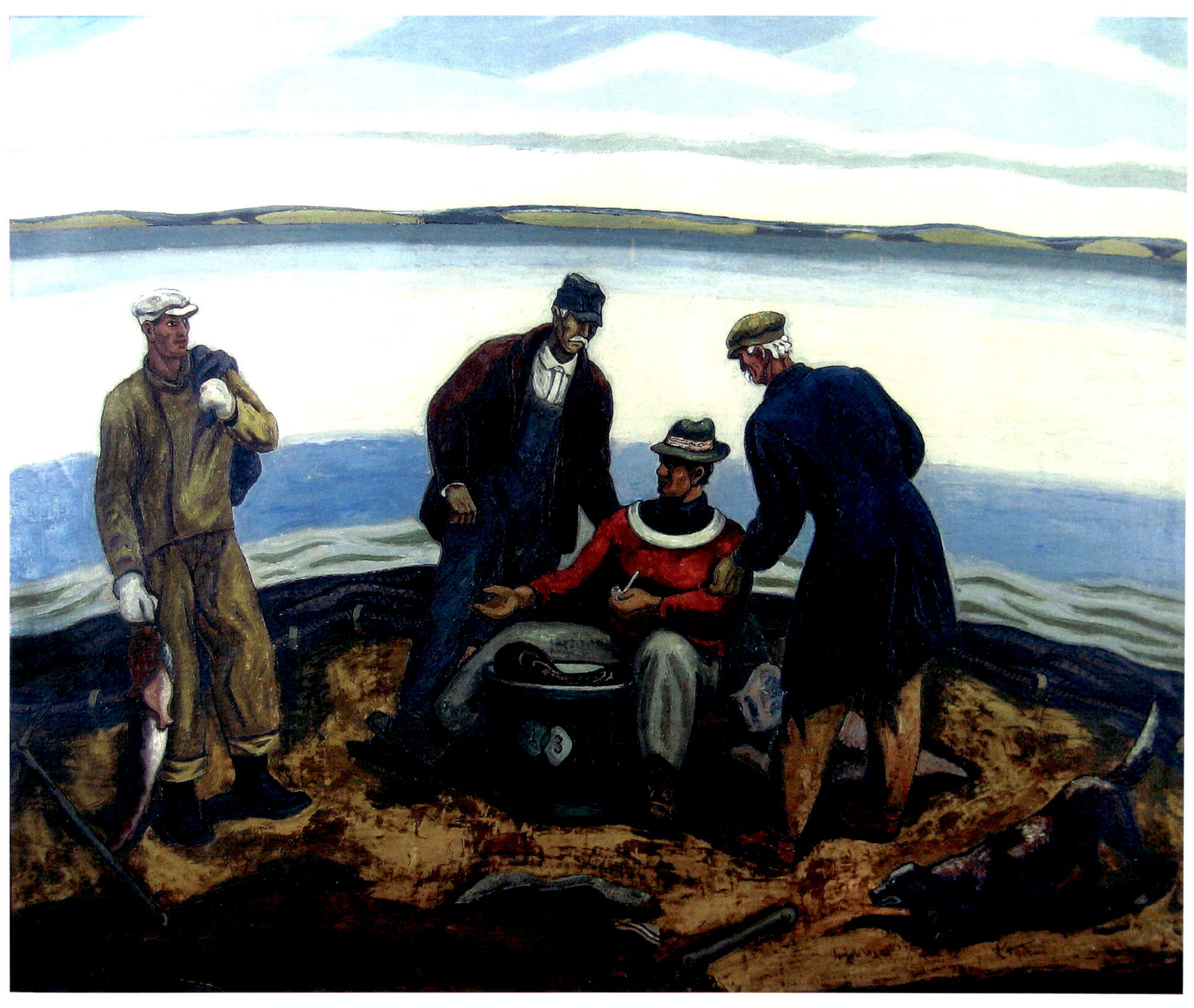

Ross Moffett, *Conversation on the Shore*, 1932. Oil on canvas, 48 × 60 inches. *Gift of Morris B. Abram, Esquire*, 1986. *Photo courtesy of Christy King.*

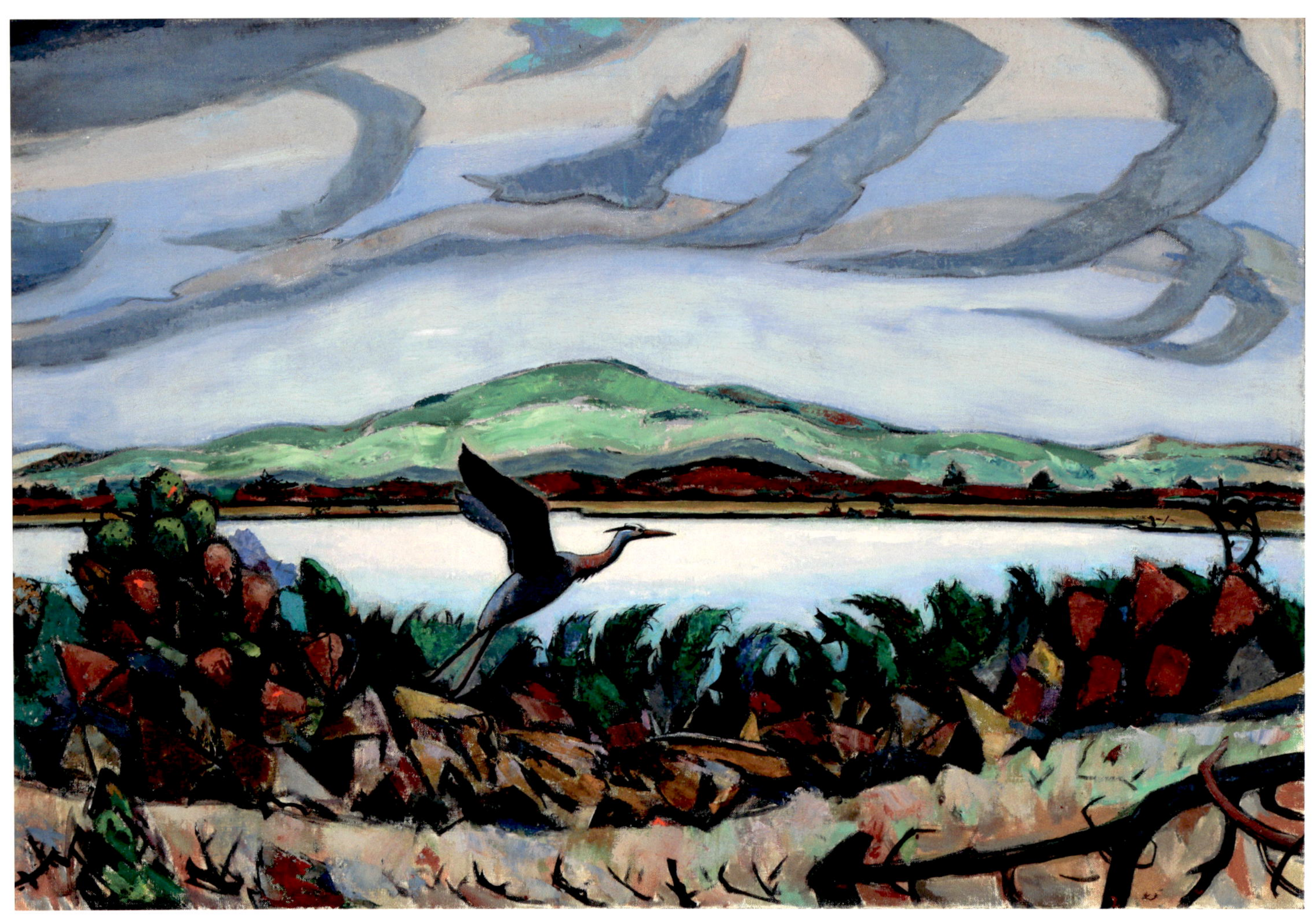

Ross Moffett, *Blue Heron, Pilgrim Lake*, 1969. Oil on canvas, 24 × 36 inches. *Gift of Robert Aron*, 1995.

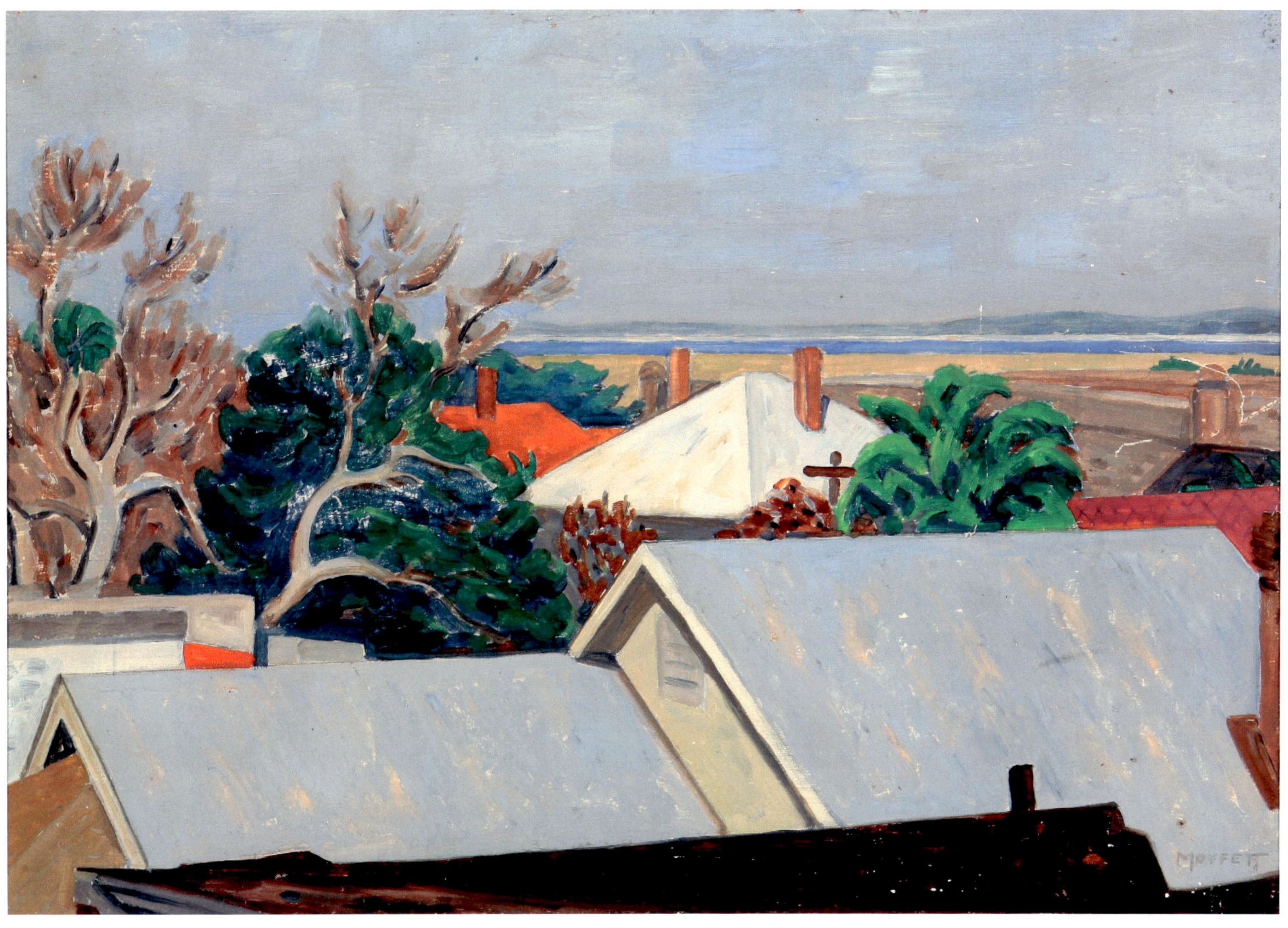

Ross Moffett, *St. Augustine Rooftops*, 1939. Oil on masonite, 14 × 20 inches. *Gift of Joyce G. Aaron*, 1999.

THOMAS HART BENTON
(1889–1975)

Thomas Hart Benton, along with Grant Wood and John Steuart Curry, was part of the regionalist art movement, which flourished in America beginning in the 1920s and was at its height during the Depression years.

Like the other regionalists or American Scene Painters, who were from the rural Midwest, Benton was born in Neosho, Missouri. In 1907, he studied at the Art Institute of Chicago, and two years later, in Paris at the Académie Julian.

In 1912, he moved to New York City. While teaching at the Chelsea Neighborhood Association, he began sculpting, which impacted the style of his painting, giving his figures a sculptural, three-dimensional quality with a well-defined play of light and shadow. Although he had been influenced by modernism and some of his early works were abstract, by the late 1920s he made a commitment to representational art in his desire to depict the American experience.

His paintings and murals portray people in everyday activities. His figures are fluid and show the impact of his foray into sculpture. His distortions of figures show the influence of El Greco's elongated forms. Benton's expressionistic paintings depict Americans employed in strenuous work and express the despair of the workingman's life. His art is noted for its robust details and complex compositions of interwoven figures in free-form arrangements.

Although his paintings focus on the rural experience of farmers and the working class in the Midwest, South, and West, he lived in New York City for twenty years. He taught at the Art Students League in New York from 1926 to 1935 and his most famous student was Jackson Pollock, whose work changed dramatically from Benton's after his liberating experience working under the Federal Art Project of the WPA.

Benton summered on Martha's Vineyard for a half-century, which inspired much of his work of rolling landscapes, farm workers, quiet harbors, and figures at leisure. One of those is *Island Hay*, a lithograph in the Cape Cod Museum of Art collection, which depicts farmers arduously working in the fields. The image has stark contrasts and is typical of Benton's expressionistic qualities.

His murals include 1930s *Indiana Murals* and *The Arts of Life in America*, a set of large works for an early site of the Whitney Museum of American Art. In 1935, he was commissioned to create a mural, *A Social History of Missouri,* for the Missouri State Capitol in Jefferson City. In this work he depicted images of slavery and the Missouri outlaw Jesse James. His *America Today* mural painted for New York's New School for Social Research is now in the collection of the Metropolitan Museum of Art in New York. After World War II, the popularity of regionalism was eclipsed by the rise of abstract expressionism. However, Benton remained active for another thirty years.

His works are included in numerous museums, including the Metropolitan Museum of Art, the Museum of Modern Art, and the Whitney Museum of American Art in New York; the Los Angeles County Museum of Art; the National Gallery of Art, the Hirshhorn Museum and Sculpture Garden and Phillips Collection in Washington, DC.; the Philadelphia Museum of Art; the Pennsylvania Academy of Fine Arts; and the Art Institute of Chicago.

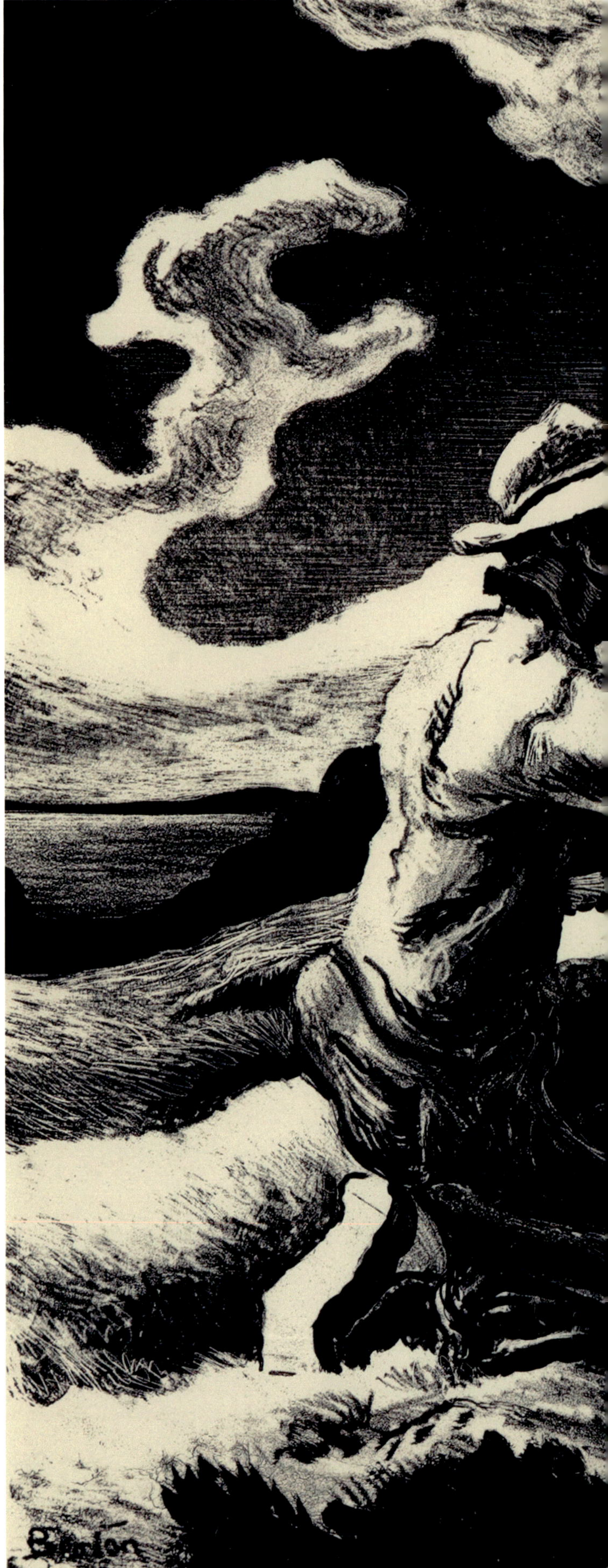

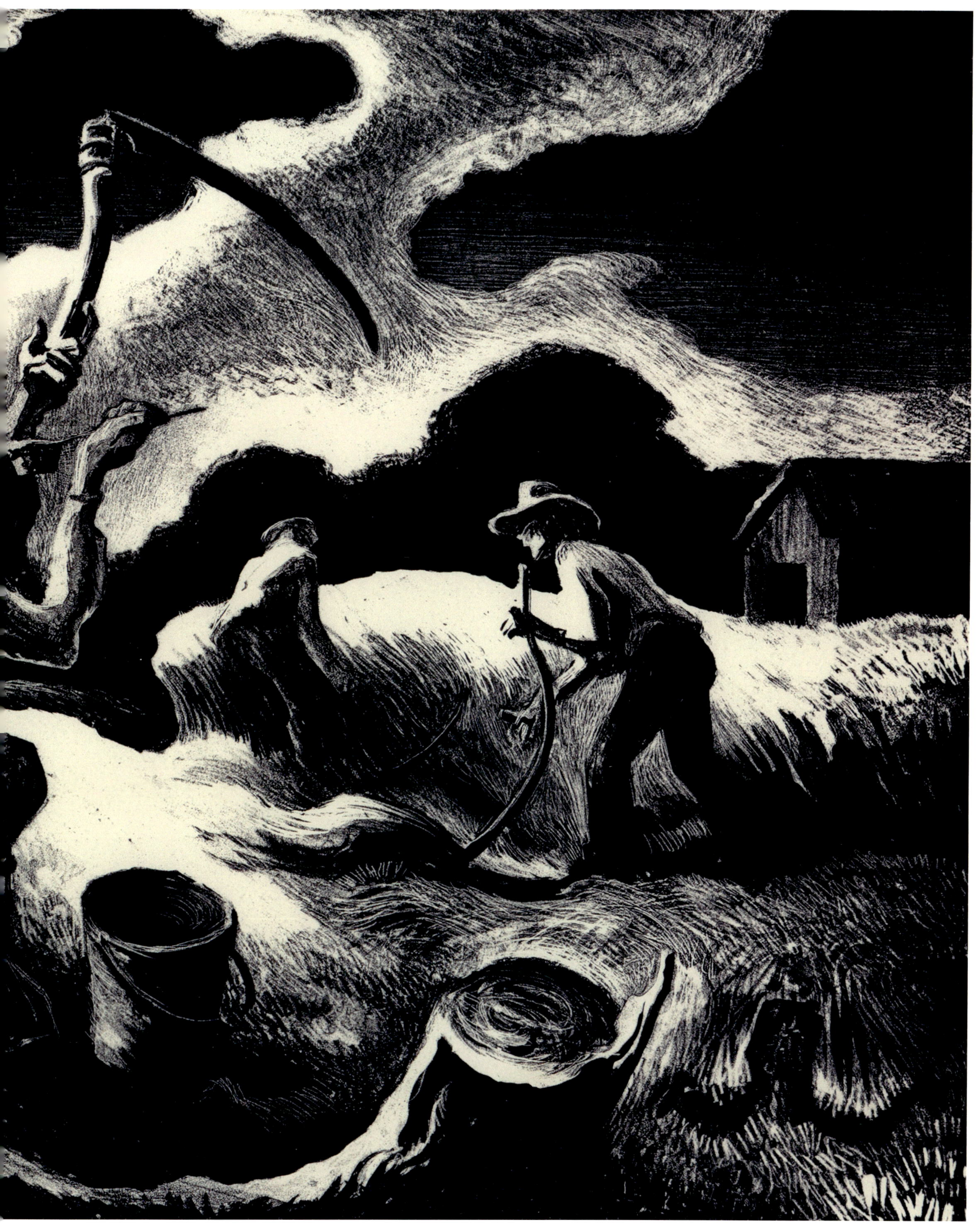

Thomas Hart Benton, *Island Hay* (Edition of 250), 1945. Lithograph on paper, 10 × 12½ inches. *Museum purchase through Eleanor Ferri Jones Fund,* 2010.
© T. H. Benton and R.P. Benton Testamentary Trusts/UMB Bank Trustee/Licensed by VAGA, New York, New York.

CHARLES ANTON KAESELAU
(1889–1972)

Charles Kaeselau was a representational painter and printmaker who had a long history in Provincetown. His landscapes; harbor and village scenes; and paintings of fishermen, boats, and clipper ships are subtly colored, atmospheric, quiet, and moody. His watercolor *Town Center with Boats*, in the collection of the Cape Cod Museum of Art, is a fine example of his draftsmanship and is a nostalgic view of the town. His 1935 woodblock print *Wellfleet Oysterman*, also in the museum collection, is a vigorous image representing an industry still active today.

Born in Stockholm, Sweden, he studied at the Kensington School of Art in London, at the Acadèmie Julian in Paris, and from 1911 to 1915 at the Art Institute of Chicago. He also studied with Jaoquin y Sorolla and Charles Hawthorne.

Beginning in 1922, he made his home in Provincetown, where he also had a painting school. In 1923, he was director of the Provincetown Art Association and was active in the art colony for the rest of his life. During the Depression, Kaeselau was a Works Progress Administration artist for a short time before he was dismissed in 1937 for not having US citizenship. While with the WPA, he produced oil paintings and watercolors, as well as murals commissioned for post offices in Concord, Massachusetts, and Lebanon, New Hampshire.

His works are in the collections of the Museum of Fine Arts in Boston, the Whitney Museum of American Art in New York, and the Phillips Collection in Washington, DC.

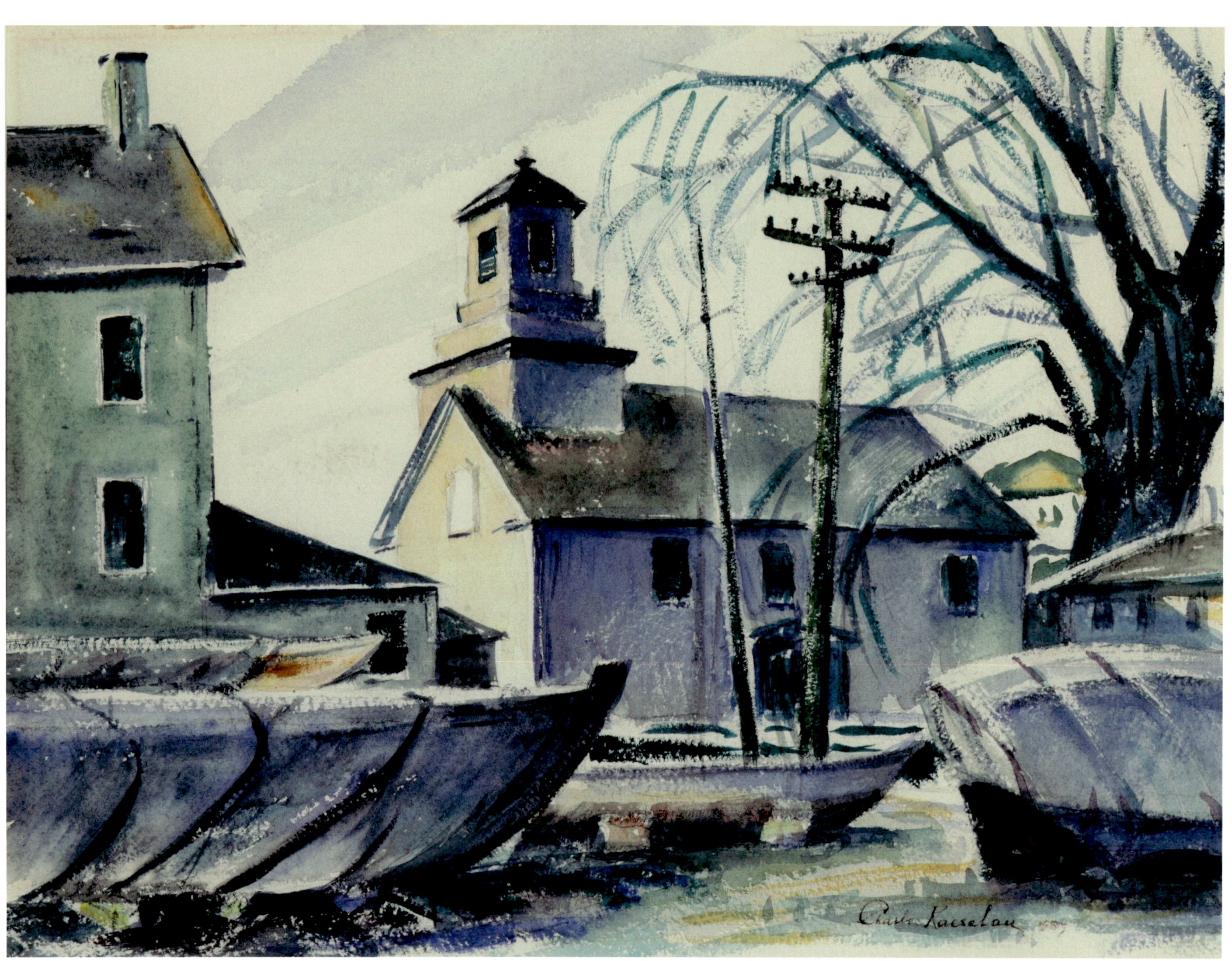

Charles Anton Kaeselau, *Town Center with Boats,* n.d. Watercolor on paper, 15 × 20 inches. *Gift of Roy Mennell,* 1989.

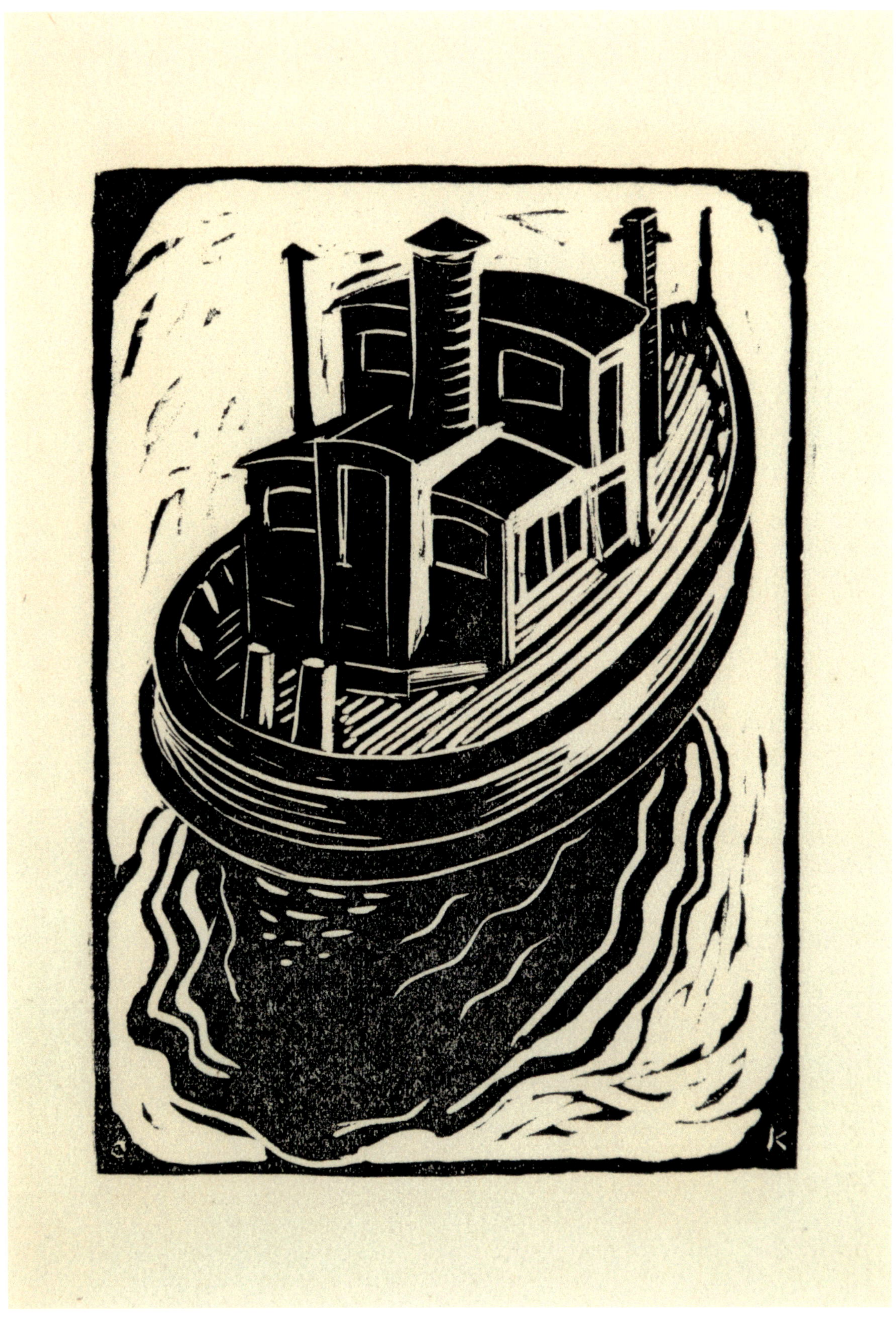

Charles Anton Kaeselau, *Wellfleet Oysterman*, 1935. Woodblock on paper, 5⅛ × 3¾ inches. *Anonymous gift*, 2009.

LUCY BROWN L'ENGLE
(1889–1978)

Lucy L'Engle was born in New York City to an affluent family, headed by Charles Stelle Brown, a very successful real estate broker. Her mother, Lucy Barnes Brown, was the first US Women's Amateur Golf Champion in 1893. L'Engle's brother, former New York congressman Lathrop Brown, was Franklin Delano Roosevelt's roommate at Groton and Harvard.

She studied at the Art Students League, with Charles Hawthorne in Provincetown, and in Paris at the Académie Julian and with the cubist painter Albert Gleizes. In 1914, she married William L'Engle, a fellow art student, also from an affluent family, allowing them the means to be independent artists. In 1916, the couple visited Provincetown, where they spent many seasons and were active in the art colony.

She was attracted to cubism, and her work included abstractions in that manner as well as representational painting. Some of her figures show a reference to the work of Paul Cézanne. Her cubist approach, influenced by Georges Braque, unfolds in her representational work with sharp angles, shallow space, and facets of shaded color. Her colors are buoyant without being bold. *Signals*, in the Cape Cod Museum of Art collection, shows her use of modernist abstraction.

L'Engle first exhibited at the Provincetown Art Association in 1918. She also served as a juror for the association's modernist exhibitions, and was a staunch advocate of modernism there and in New York. She was a founding member of the New York Society of Women Artists.

Her works are in the collections of several museums, including the Lightner Museum in St. Augustine, Florida.

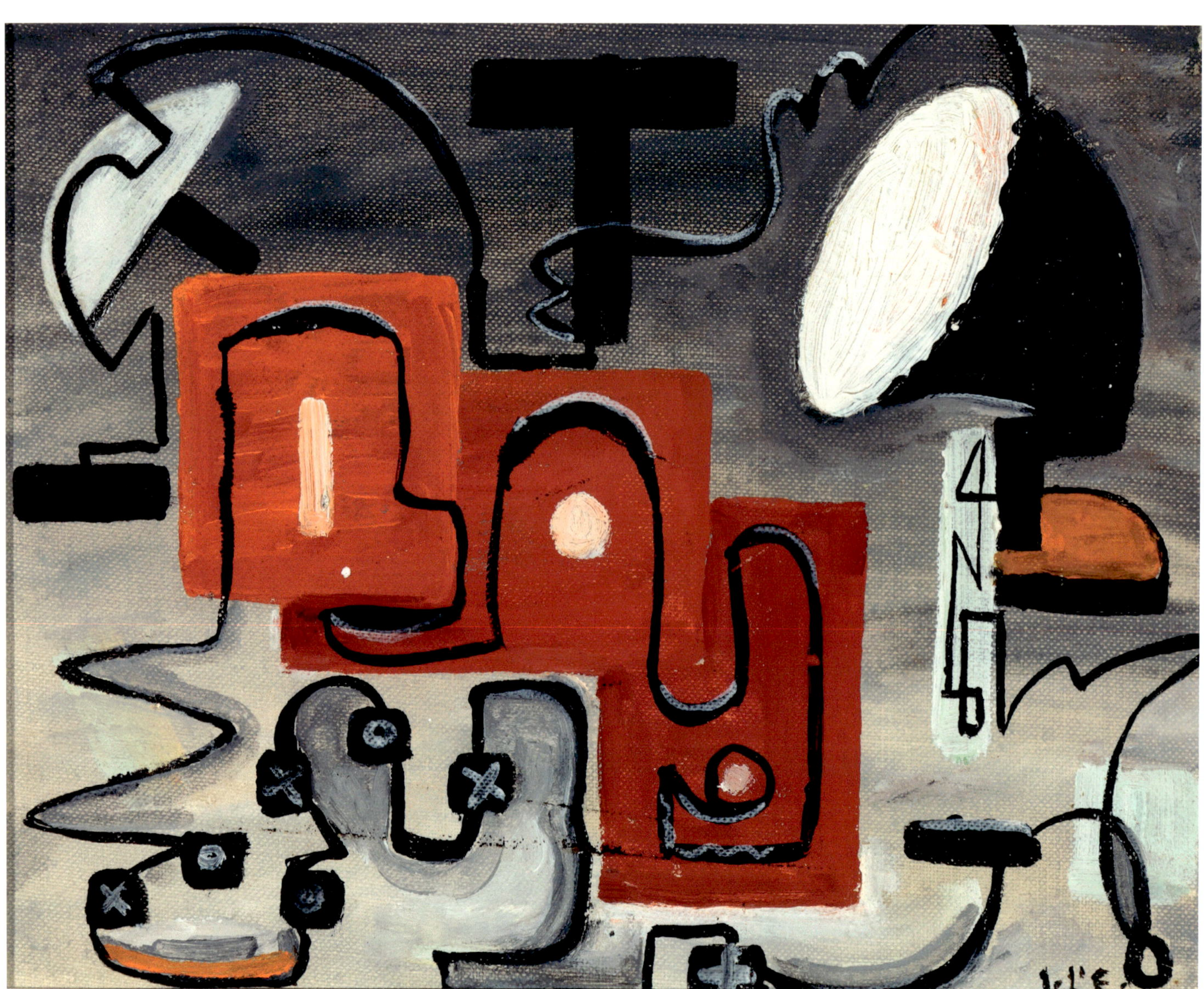

Lucy L'Engle, *Signals*, n.d. Oil on board, 8¼ × 10½ inches. *Gift of the Penny and Elton Yasuna Collection*, 2000.

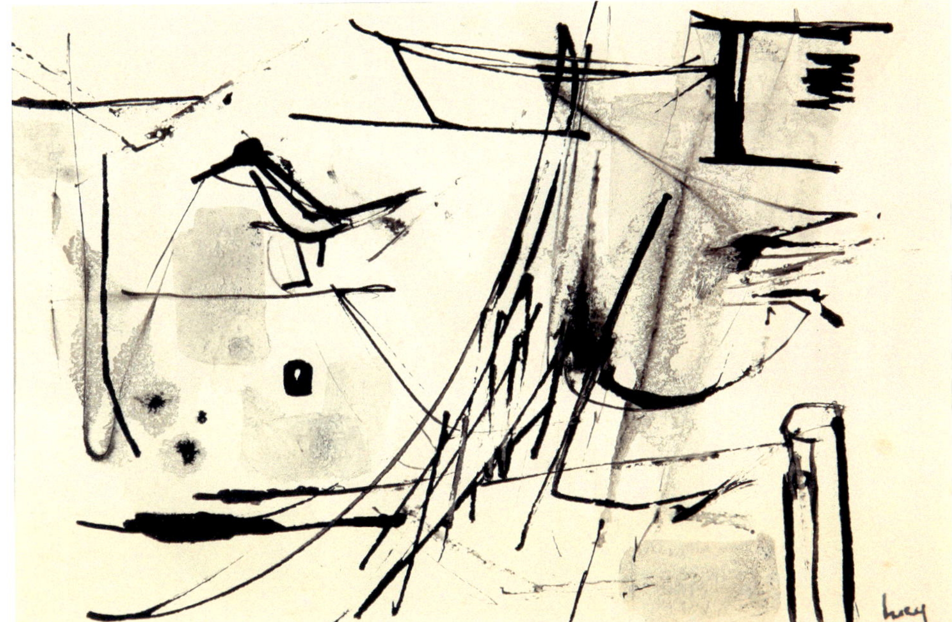

Lucy L'Engle, *The Wharf,* 1959. Pen and ink wash on paper, 7 × 11 inches. *Gift of Lester Heller*, 2000.

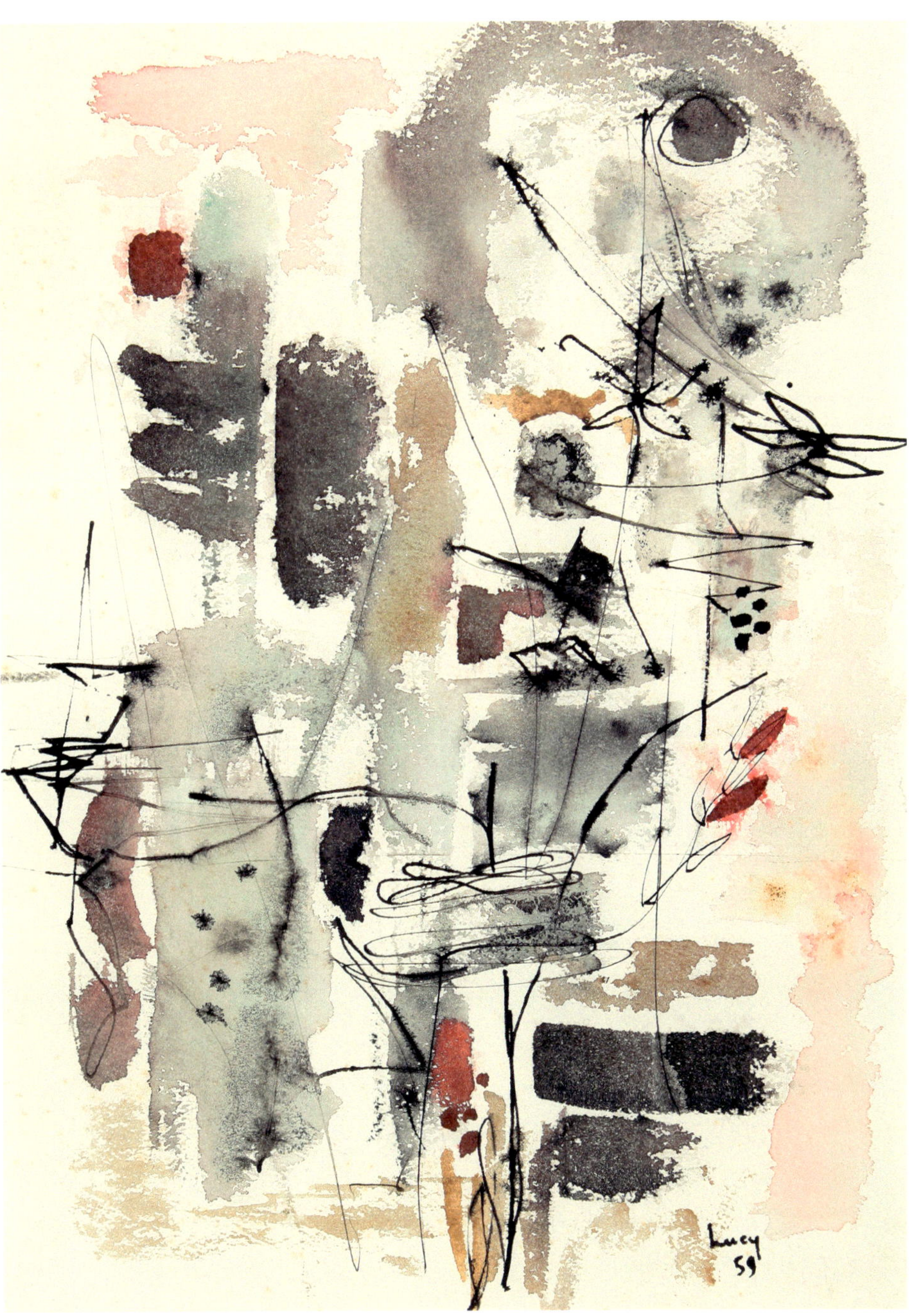

Lucy L'Engle, *Winter Garden,* 1959. Watercolor on paper, 16 × 11½ inches. *Gift of Lester Heller*, 2000.

FEROL SIBLEY WARTHEN
(1890–1986)

Ferol Sibley Warthen was born on a farm in South Dakota and showed an early interest in art, which brought her on a scholarship to New York to the Art Students League, where she studied with William Merritt Chase and Kenneth Hayes Miller.

She did her first woodblock print in 1911, but then, like so many women, she became immersed in the practicalities of life, marriage, and childrearing. She did further her studies at Ohio State University where she earned a bachelor's degree in education in 1917. But her interest in art remained and she studied with modernist Karl Knaths in Washington, DC.

She began spending summers in Provincetown in 1950 and continued there for the rest of her life. She learned about the white-line, one-block woodcut from Blanche Lazzell, who had been doing the process for more than twenty years. Like Lazzell, Warthen was influenced by cubism, as shown in the white-line print *Provincetown Sails* in the Cape Cod Museum of Art collection. Using bright colors and intersecting planes, she depicted Provincetown's wharves and boats, figures, and still lifes with flowers. Her white-line prints have a dynamic energy created with intricately spaced angles and fractured colors.

Her prints are in the collection of a number of museums, including the Museum of Fine Arts in Boston and the Smithsonian American Art Museum in Washington, DC.

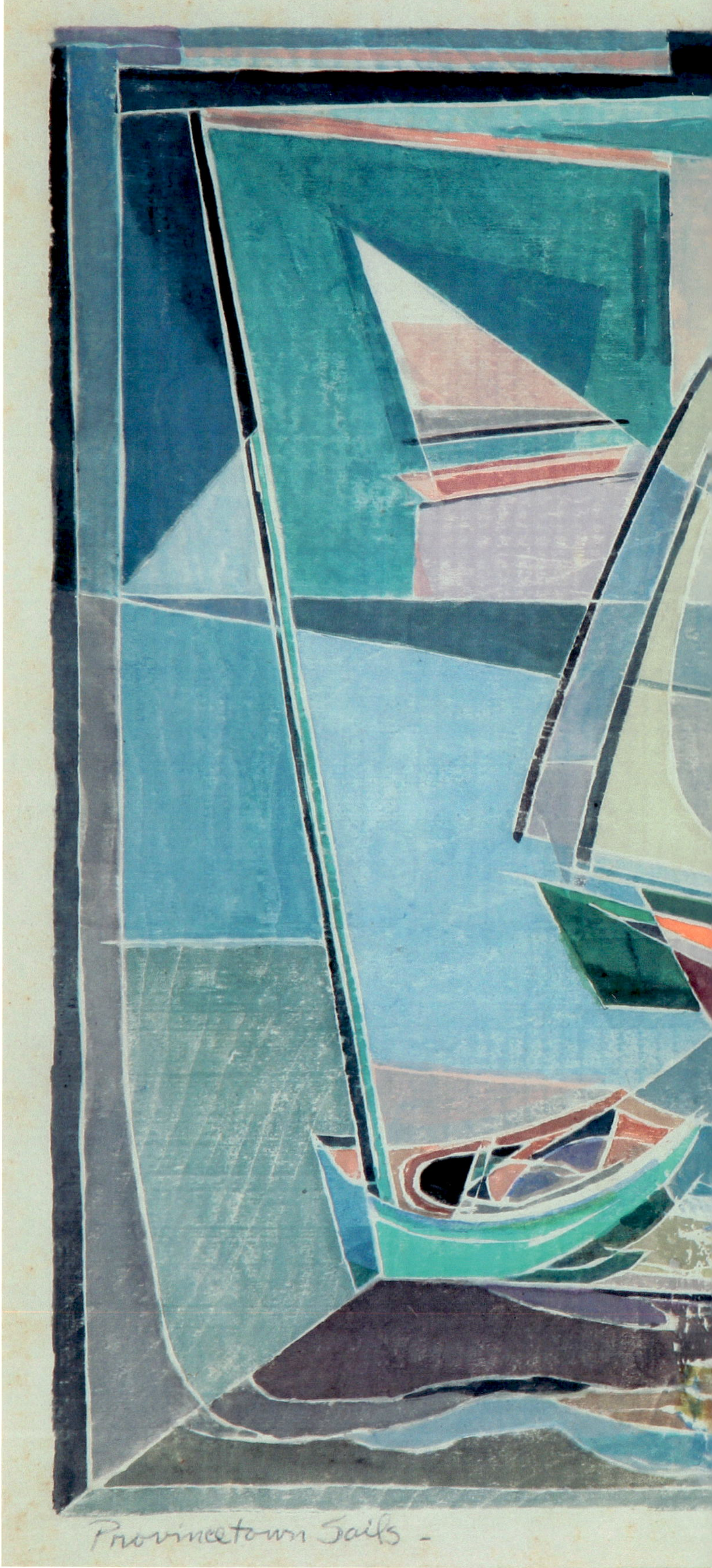

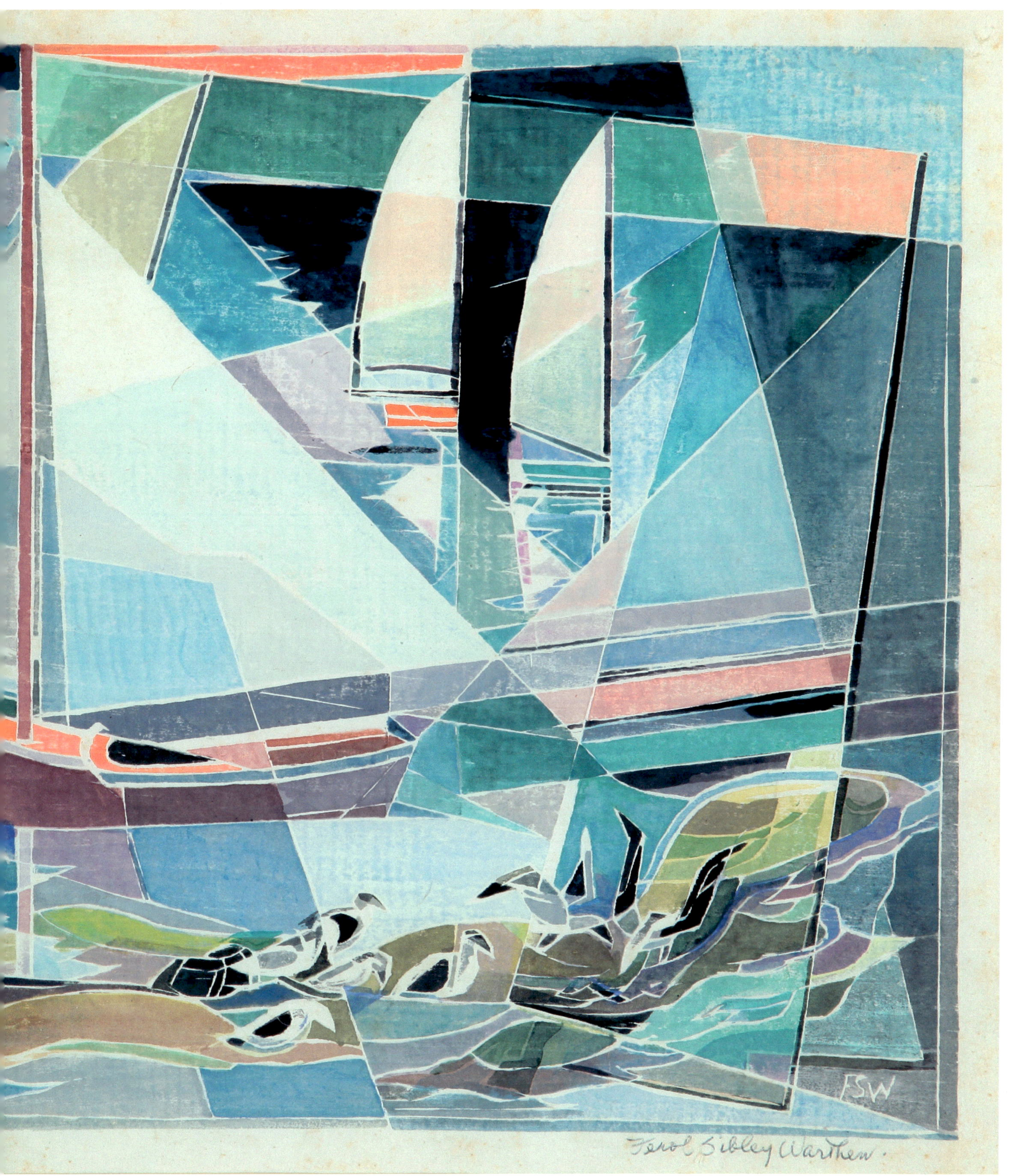

Ferol Sibley Warthen, *Provincetown Sails,* n.d. White-line woodblock on paper, 11½ × 16 inches. *Gift of Roy N. Freed, Esquire*, 1987.

EDWIN DICKINSON
(1891–1978)

After studying with William Merritt Chase at the Art Students League, Edwin Dickinson went to Provincetown in 1912 to attend Charles Hawthorne's classes. Beginning in 1937, Dickinson, who was born in Seneca Falls, New York, established a residence in Provincetown and later moved to Wellfleet.

Although his art was mostly grounded in realism, it also showed references to symbolism and surrealism as well as abstraction. An echo of El Greco's elongated figures can be seen in some of his paintings.

During Dickinson's years in Provincetown, he loved taking long walks along the beach. It was an opportunity to get in touch with nature, and he painted many landscapes. Using a limited range of colors—greens, grays, blues and browns—he could paint a landscape on the spot in a few hours. Some of these pictures verged on the abstract, as did his symbolist paintings.

In contrast to his landscapes, he often worked on his studio compositions for years as he developed complex arrangements of figures and still-life objects, sometimes finding unusual angles in his approach. *Nude Study*, in the Cape Cod Museum of Art collection, was probably done in preparation for one of those works.

Dickinson also painted portraits and many self-portraits, which are noted for their psychological insights. He straddled the nineteenth-century American romantic traditions and the more inventive European approaches, so it is hard to place him firmly in one camp. But leaning as he did toward a freer approach to his subjects and composition, he, along with Ross Moffett and Karl Knaths, were among those championing artistic innovations in Provincetown during the early years of the art colony.

Dickinson's works are in numerous public collections, including the Metropolitan Museum of Art, the Museum of Modern Art, and the Whitney Museum of American Art in New York; the Museum of Fine Arts in Boston; and the Hirshhorn Museum and Sculpture Garden in Washington, DC.

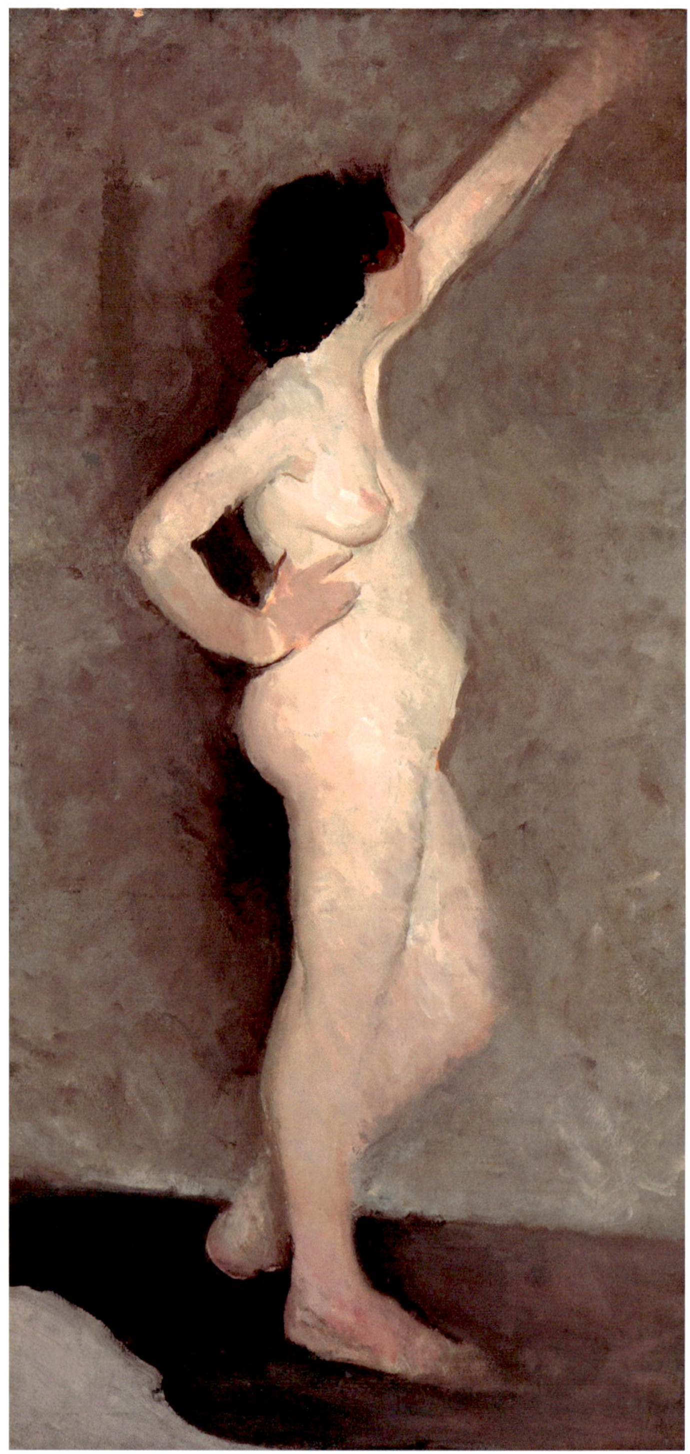

Edwin Dickinson, *Nude Study*, 1915. Oil on board, 64 × 31½ inches. *Gift of Mr. and Mrs. Frank Hogan*, 1994.

GERRIT HONDIUS
(1891–1970)

A modernist artist who divided his time between the Provincetown art colony and New York City, Gerrit Hondius was born in Holland into a family with ancestors who were artists. He studied at the Royal Academy in The Hague and the Art Students League with Max Weber and Andrew Dasburg. During the Depression, he was a Works Progress Administration artist and did murals in New York City.

His subjects included landscapes, dancers, still lifes, masked figures, the circus, and fishermen. His ink drawing *Untitled,* in the Cape Cod Museum of Art collection, is a lively image of three fishermen, which must have been inspired by Provincetown's vibrant fishing industry.

Hondius was first influenced by the Dutch paintings of The Hague School. But soon he was moved by the French and German expressionists, in particular, Georges Rouault. He worked in that tradition, often using dark outlines with fauvist colors, which show intense feelings. Despite his use of bright colors, his art has a dark and moody quality. He traveled with the circus in Holland in the 1950s and became acquainted with the performers. He depicted them in their brilliantly colored costumes and expressionistically captured their personas. He was especially interested in the clowns, whom he found often hid behind their masks.

His works are included in the collections of the San Francisco Museum of Art, the Whitney Museum of American Art in New York, the Newark Museum of Art in New Jersey, and the Provincial Museum in Kampden, Holland.

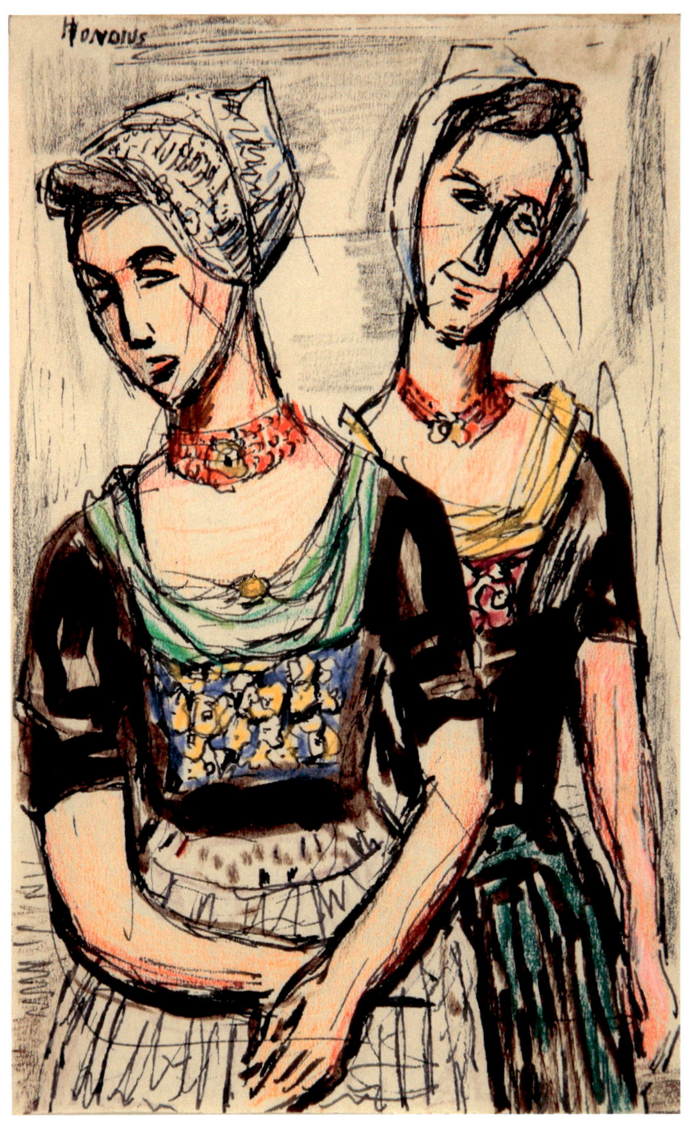

Gerrit Hondius, *Untitled,* n.d. Pen, ink, and watercolor on paper, 5 × 7½ inches. *Gift of Maria H. Sylvester in memory of Gerald Sylvester, grandson of Bart and Lilly Wirtz*, 2011.

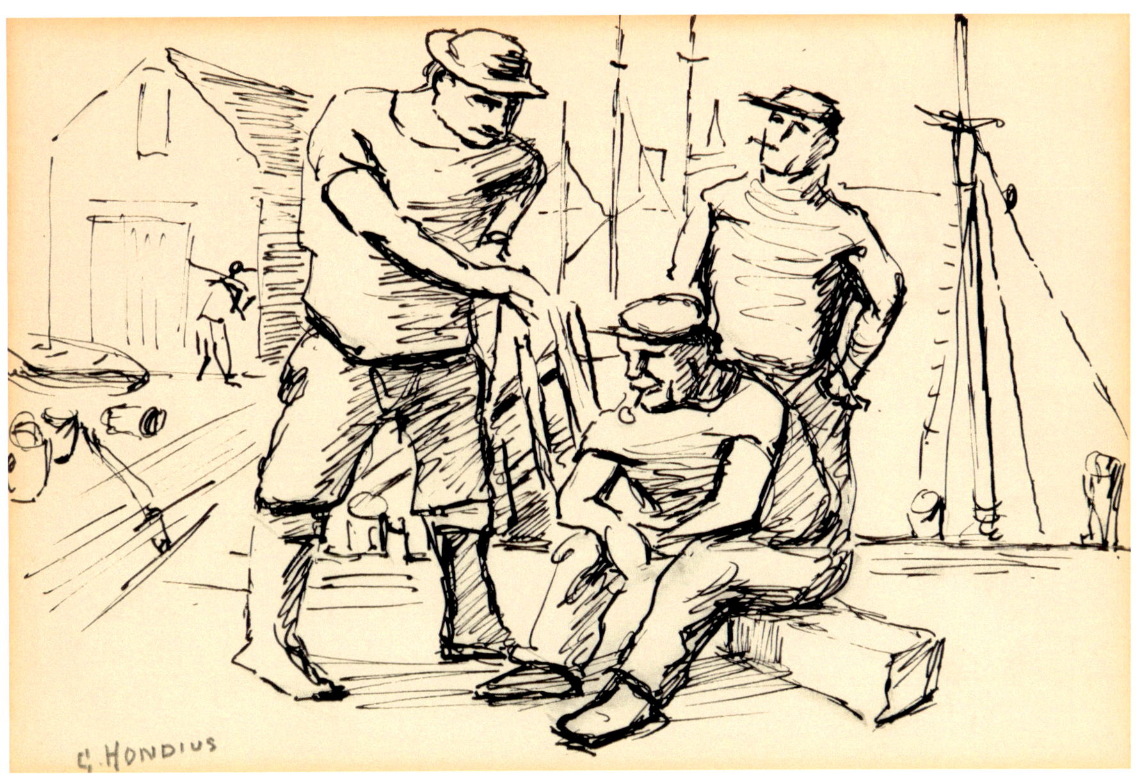

Gerrit Hondius, *Untitled*, n.d. Ink on paper, 7⅝ × 5 inches. *Gift of David Maril*, 2011.

KARL KNATHS
(1891–1971)

Although Karl Knaths spent more than a half-century painting in Provincetown and never went abroad, he was significantly influenced by the European modernists, especially Paul Cézanne and the cubists. Knaths arrived in Provincetown in 1919, five years after the establishment of the Provincetown Art Association. He lived in town until he died in 1971.

Born in Eau Claire, Wisconsin, Knaths studied at the Art Institute of Chicago, where he met Ross Moffett, who sang the praises of Provincetown. Knaths was there in Chicago working as a museum guard when the groundbreaking 1913 Armory Show arrived from New York. The rich display of European modern art had a significant impact on him.

The Armory Show, which opened in New York and caused a scandal, was one of the first opportunities most Americans had to see the revolution in art that had occurred in Paris during the previous decade. Although praise was sparse and adherents were few, Knaths was taken with the structured approach of Cézanne and the cubists. When he arrived in Provincetown, he brought with him his modernist artistic convictions, which challenged the prevailing conservatism at the Provincetown Art Association. Settling in the West End of town, not far from the Atlantic Ocean and with a view of Cape Cod Bay and close to the dunes and moors, he was stirred by the beauty of land and sea and by the fishing community, townspeople, boats and harbors, fish houses, and home interiors.

In 1922, Knaths married Helen Weinrich, a pianist and sister of Agnes Weinrich, one of the cubist-influenced Provincetown Printers. Agnes undoubtedly played a role in reinforcing in her brother-in-law the new ideas of European artists. Knaths made significant contributions to the Provincetown art colony and was a notable figure around town.

Some of his paintings have a strong figurative connection, as in the watercolor *Rooster* and woodblock print *Gathering Quahogs,* which relate to Provincetown, as does *Provincetown Landscape*, all in the Cape Cod Museum of Art collection.

Other works are abstract, boldly playing intersecting lines and forms of colors in jazzy compositions that are exhilarating. Some of his work shows the influence of Pablo Picasso, Georges Braque, and Juan Gris. Knaths beautifully represented his reality with a perceptive eye for the powerful and vibrant connections between form and color. His approach to cubism was deeply connected to the world around him. His paintings are rich in color, with rhythmic lines, robust planes, and dynamic movement. *Flight from Egypt*, *Wisconsin*, and *Untitled (Still Life)*, in the museum collection, are fine

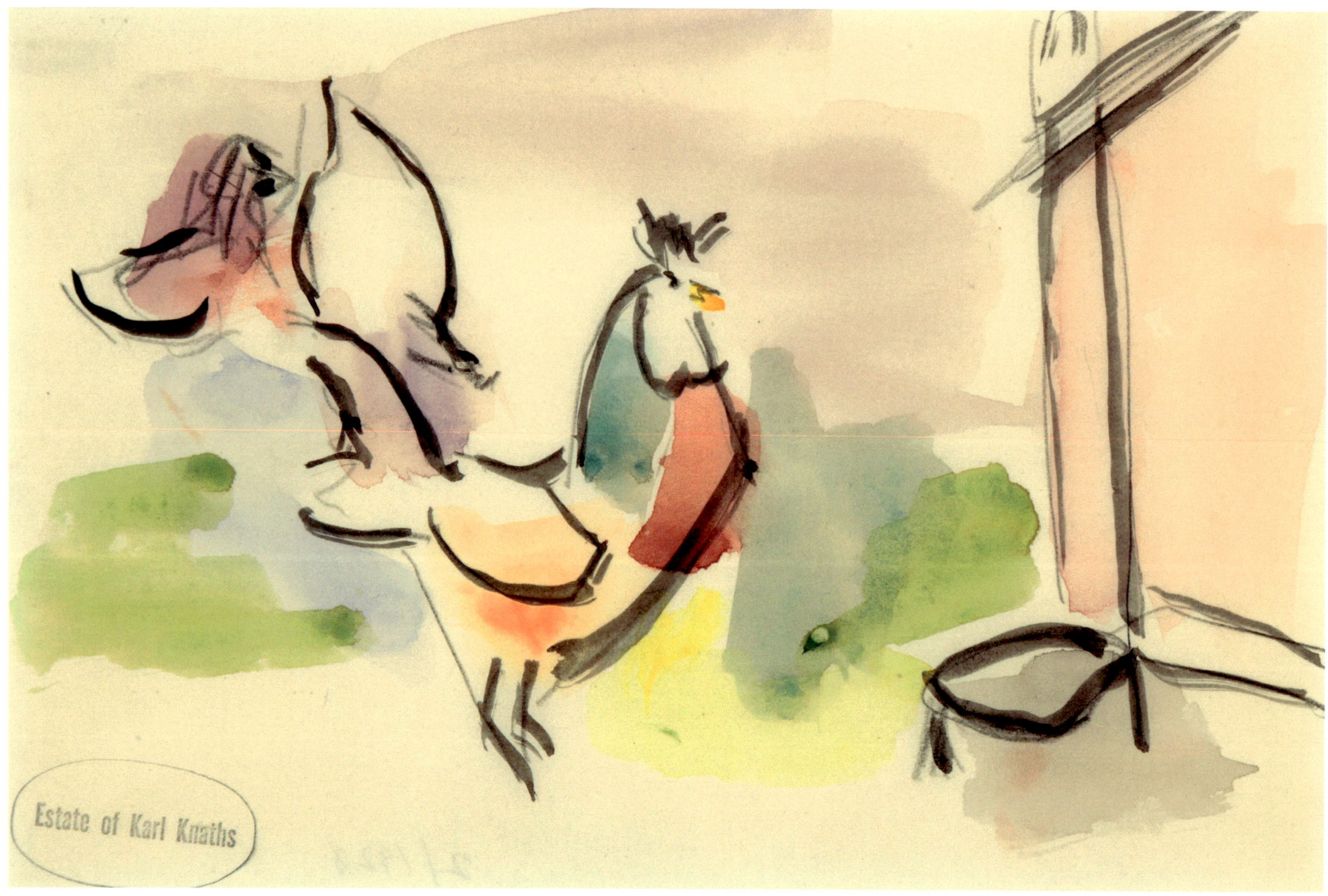

Karl Knaths, *Rooster,* n.d. Watercolor on paper, 5 × 8 inches. *Anonymous gift*, 2009.

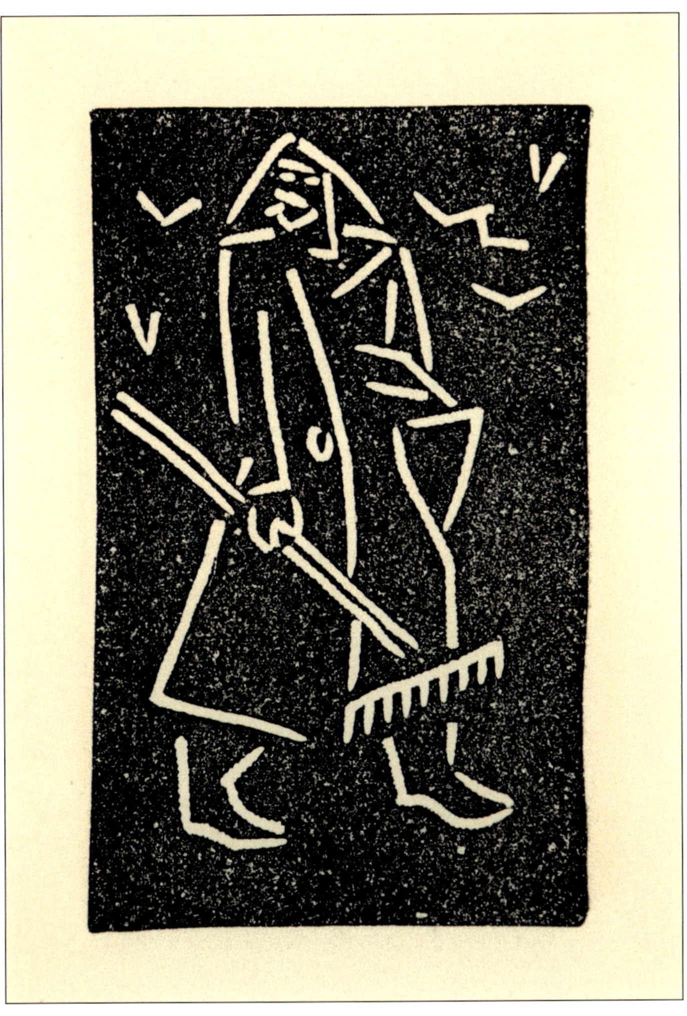

Karl Knaths, *Gathering Quahogs*, 1935. Woodblock on paper, 5½ × 3½ inches. *Anonymous gift*, 2009.

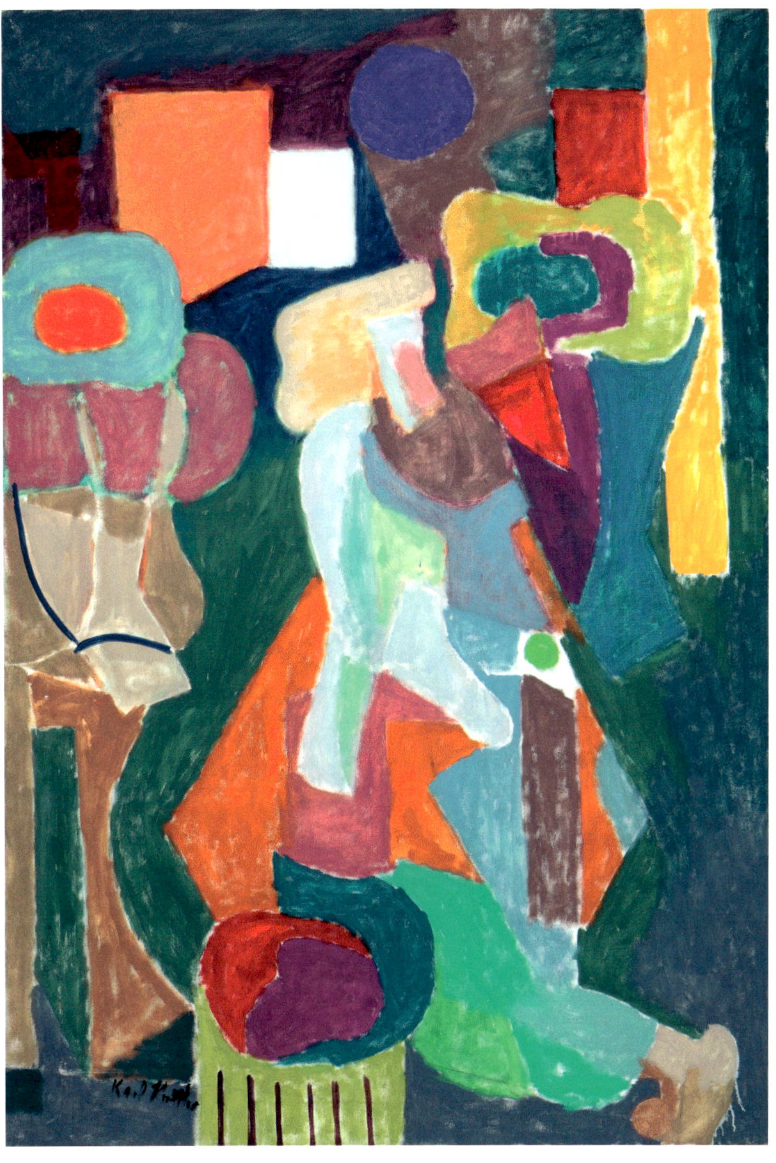

Karl Knaths, *Flight from Egypt/The Universe Maharishi*, n.d. Oil on canvas, 60 × 42 inches. *Anonymous gift*, 2009.

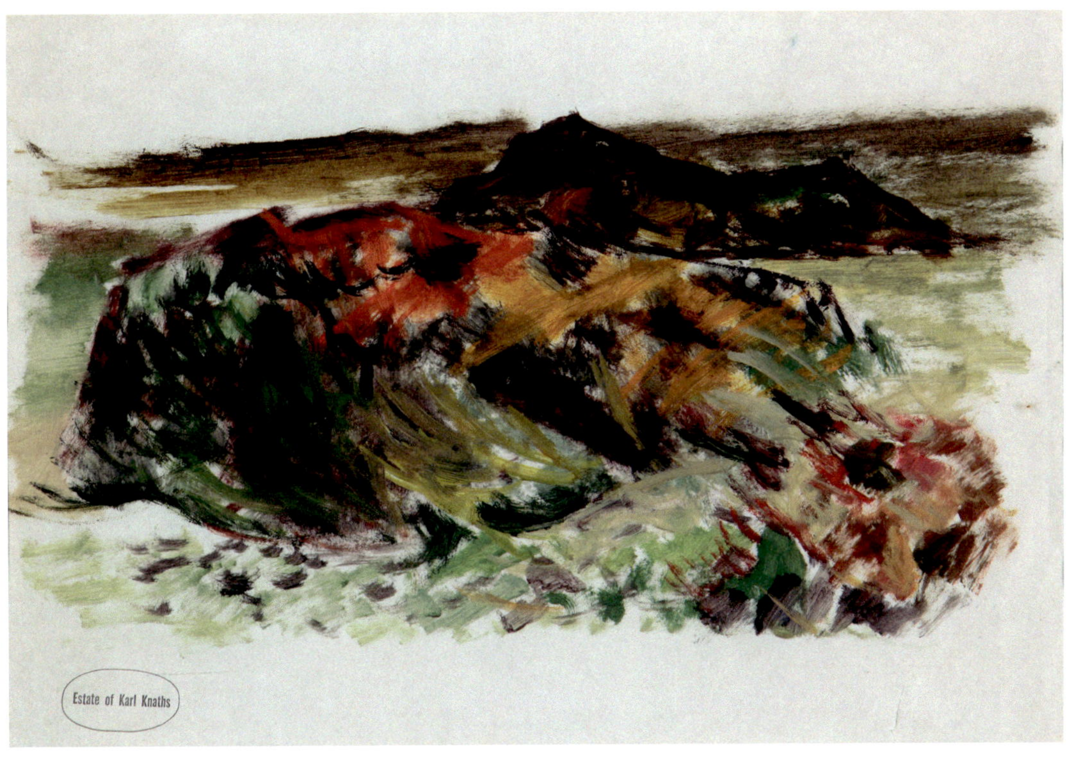

Karl Knaths, *Provincetown Landscape,* n.d. Oil on paper, 9¼ × 13¾ inches. *Gift of Roy Mennell*, 1989.

examples of his modernist works. Observing the lyricism in his work, it is not surprising to discover he saw a lively connection between music and art.

Duncan Phillips, founder of the Phillips Collection in Washington, DC, was a devoted patron and was instrumental in establishing Knaths's reputation. The Phillips Collection held his first one-person exhibition in 1929. In the 1930s, he was a prominent member of the WPA's Federal Art Project in Massachusetts, and not only produced large, lyrical oil paintings showing his debt to Matisse and Cézanne, which were highly prized by project administrators in Washington, but also produced a music-themed, symbolic mural for the Falmouth public schools.

Knaths's paintings are in major collections, including the Metropolitan Museum of Art, the Museum of Modern Art, and the Whitney Museum of American Art in New York; the Art Institute of Chicago; the Los Angeles County Museum of Art; and the Philadelphia Museum of Art.

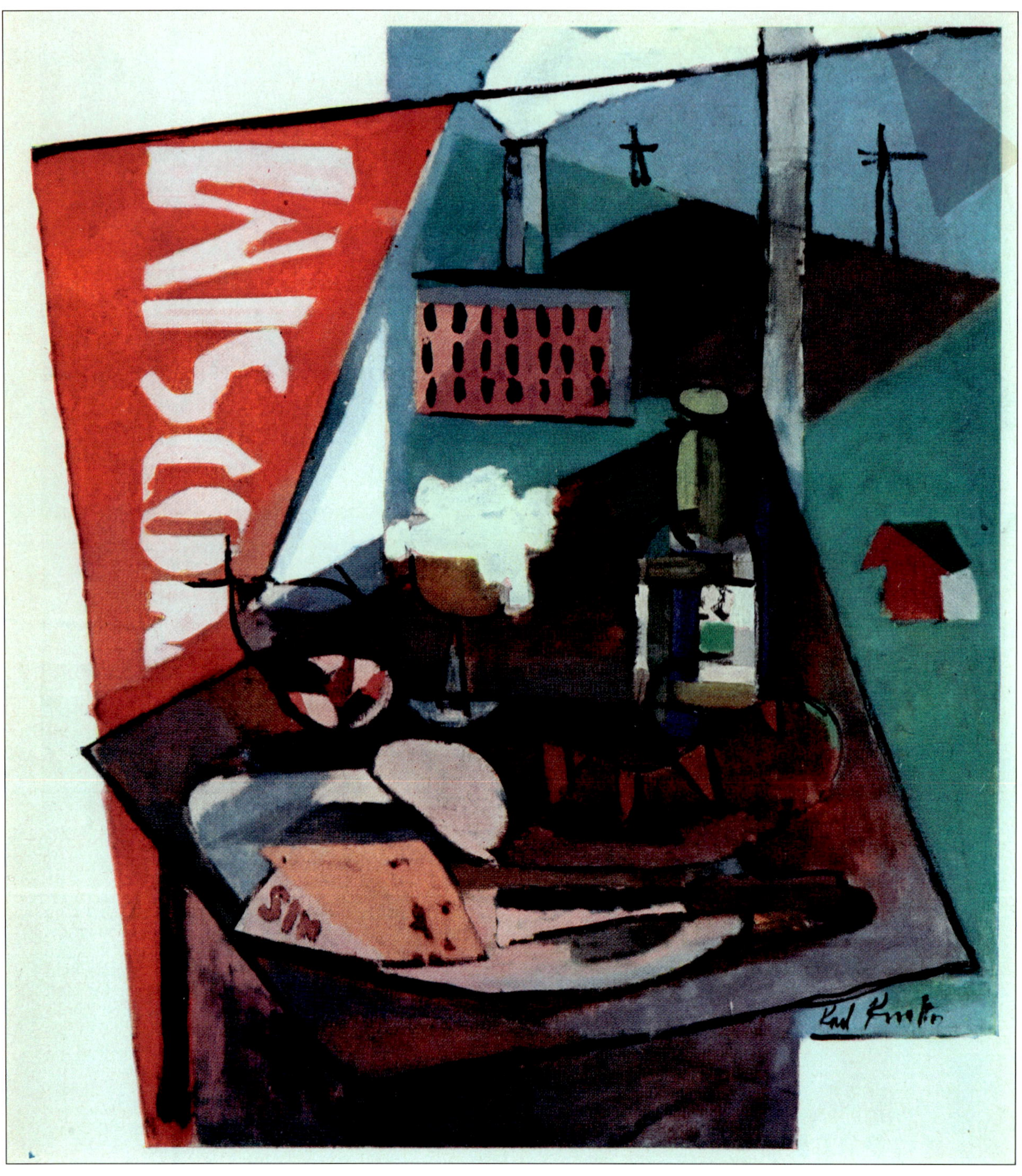

Karl Knaths, *Wisconsin,* n.d. Lithograph on paper, 8 × 7 inches. *Anonymous gift*, 2009.

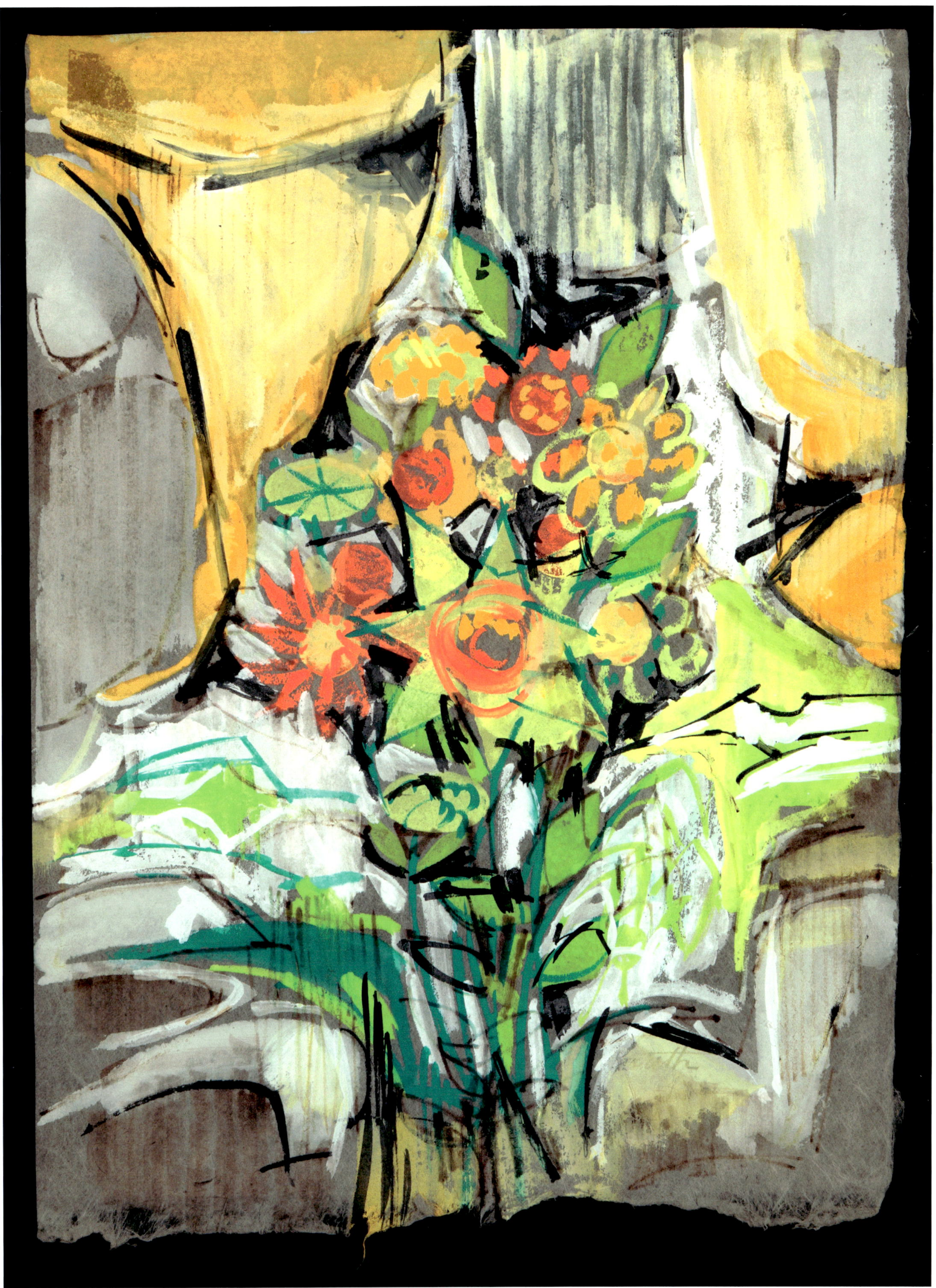

Karl Knaths, *Untitled*, n.d. Gouache on rice paper, 12¾ × 9½ inches. *Anonymous gift*, 2009.

R. H. IVES GAMMELL
(1893–1981)

Although R. H. Ives Gammell studied in Paris, he was not struck by the revolution in art that had created such a tumult in that city since the first impressionist exhibition in 1874. A committed traditionalist born in Rhode Island to a wealthy family, he attended the School of the Museum of Fine Arts in Boston. In Provincetown, he took classes with Charles Hawthorne in the summer of 1912.

Gammell had a long history in the art colony, where he spent most summers for over fifty years and taught students interested in classical training. He was part of the traditional faction of artists who were involved in the early years of the Provincetown Art Association. During the 1920s, Gammell painted in Boston; he did portraits, still lifes, interiors, and murals. He studied with William McGregor Paxton, who became a lifelong friend and mentor.

Gammell spent part of 1930 in Europe looking at the works of the great masters. Back in America he began canvases related to classical, mythological, and Biblical literature. A representational artist in the academic tradition, Gammell focused on allegories, histories, and still life. He also did etchings depicting life in Provincetown and its fishing community.

His twenty-three-panel *Hound of Heaven* series, based on Francis Thompson's poem *The Hound of Heaven*, a story of religious conversion, became Gammell's way to explore the close relationship between myths, symbols, and poetic imagery. Completed in the late 1950s, the *Hound of Heaven* series is typical of his work, reflecting great skill and technical precision. The study for *Hound of Heaven, Panel XV*, is in the Cape Cod Museum of Art collection, as is *Angel with Censer,* both dramatic paintings capturing the spirit of Gammell's fascination with the subject.

His works are included in the public collections of the Museum of Fine Arts in Boston, the Princeton University Art Museum in New Jersey, and Harvard University Art Museums in Cambridge, Massachusetts.

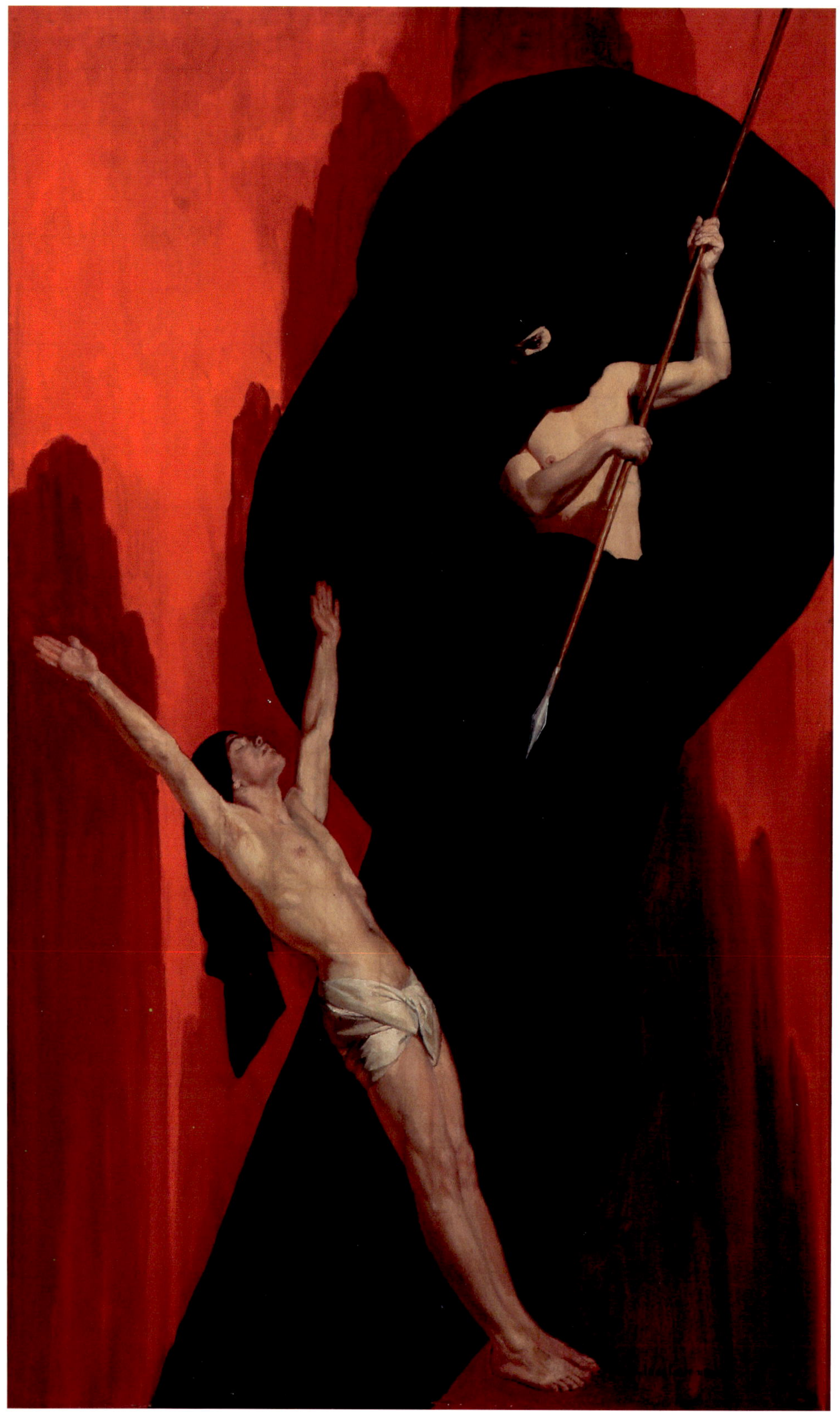

R. H. Ives Gammell, *Study, Hound of Heaven (Panel XV)*, 1949.
Oil on canvas, 60 × 23 inches.
Gift of Frank and Ruth Hogan, 1998.

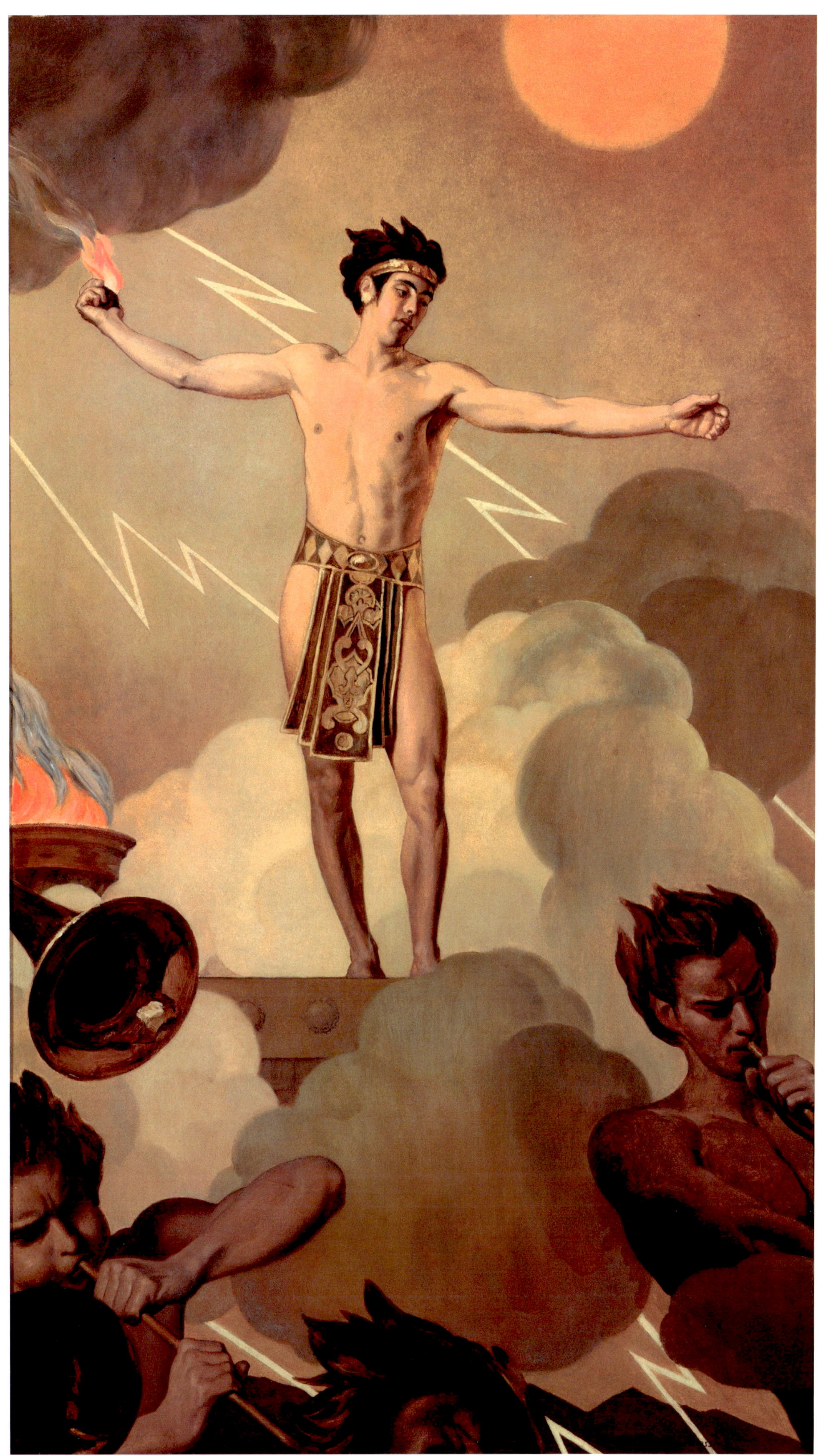

R. H. Ives Gammell, *Angel with Censer*, 1952. Oil on panel, 29½ × 17 inches. *Gift of the R. H. Ives Gammell Trust*, 1991.

GEORGE GROSZ
(1893–1959)

George Grosz was known for his grotesque, satiric drawings, collages, and paintings of life in his native Germany. From 1909 to 1911, Grosz studied at the Dresden Academy of Fine Arts and later at the Berlin College of Arts and Crafts. He became part of the Dada group, the nihilistic art movement launched in Zurich in 1916 in reaction to the horrors of World War I.

His early work was influenced by German expressionism and futurism. After observing the horrors of war as a soldier in World War I, Grosz protested with anti-war drawings, and paintings attacking a corrupt society. Perhaps best known for his drawings and watercolors of the 1920s, he took a caustically comic view of a decadent German society bitter over its defeat in 1918. Fat businessmen, wounded soldiers, and prostitutes were some of the allegorical figures he depicted to portray his critical view of Germany.

Opposed to the rise of Nazism, Grosz left Germany shortly before Hitler came to power. In 1932, he accepted an invitation to teach at the Art Students League in New York. He returned to Germany in the fall, but in January 1933, he and his family immigrated to America. He became a US citizen in 1938, and made his home in Bayside, New York. He taught at the Art Students League intermittently until 1955.

In America, although Grosz did create works critical of Nazism, he abandoned his harsh caricatures and softened his style, painting landscapes and figures. *Driftwood,* in the Cape Cod Museum of Art collection, is an example of one of those landscapes. An image that verges on the surreal, this oil painting has an ominous feeling, which you can associate with Grosz's dark earlier work when he was in Germany. Grosz returned to Germany in May 1959 and died soon after from a fall down a flight of stairs.

His works are in major museum collections, including the Metropolitan Museum of Art and Museum of Modern Art in New York, the Tate Gallery in London, the Art Institute of Chicago, Berlinische Gallery in Germany, the Los Angeles County Museum of Art, and the National Gallery of Art in Washington, DC.

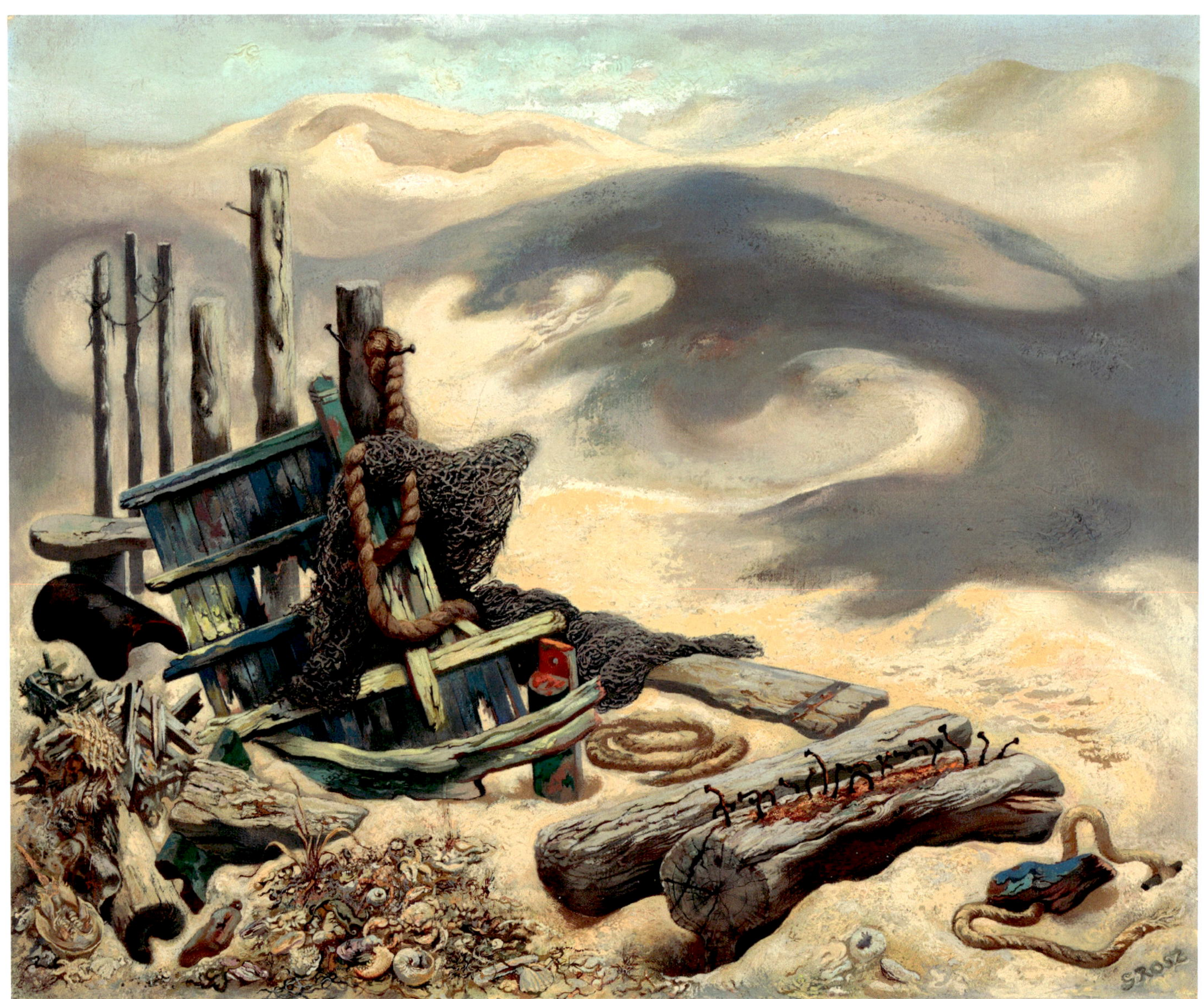

George Grosz, *Driftwood,* 1940. Oil on canvas, 21½ × 28 inches. *Gift of Timmy and Frank Wiedeman*, 2000.
© Estate of George Grosz/Licensed by VAGA, New York, New York.

VERNON SMITH
(1894–1969)

During the Depression, Vernon Smith, as regional director for the Federal Art Project of the WPA, supervising the programs on the Cape and southeastern Massachusetts, became known as one of the most progressive FAP administrators. This was because, being an open-minded, modernist-leaning painter himself, he believed in allowing artists to work undisturbed in their studios. A painter with an interest in cubist faceting and geometric forms, he later became known for his abstracted bas-relief wood carvings

Smith was born in Cortland, New York, and studied at the New York School of Fine and Applied Arts (now the Parsons School), and with Charles Hawthorne in Provincetown. In 1921, he settled in Orleans on Cape Cod, where he worked as a craftsman, repairing furniture and making sconces and pottery. He also taught in the Orleans public schools. In 1935, he became supervisor for the WPA's Federal Art Project. In 1937, he was sent to Alaska by the US Department of the Interior to paint landscapes for the Alaska Art Project.

Smith's modernist vision is apparent in *Fishing Port* and *Quiet Hour*, in the Cape Cod Museum of Art collection. These works are dynamic compositions, rich in details, which reflect the influence of cubism. In 1946, Smith began focusing on wood carvings. Two untitled works in the collection are a colorful, geometric, wood and polychrome totem-like relief and a cubistic bas-relief.

His works are in a number of museum collections, including the Museum of Modern Art in New York, the Museum of Fine Arts in Boston, and the Smithsonian American Art Museum in Washington, DC.

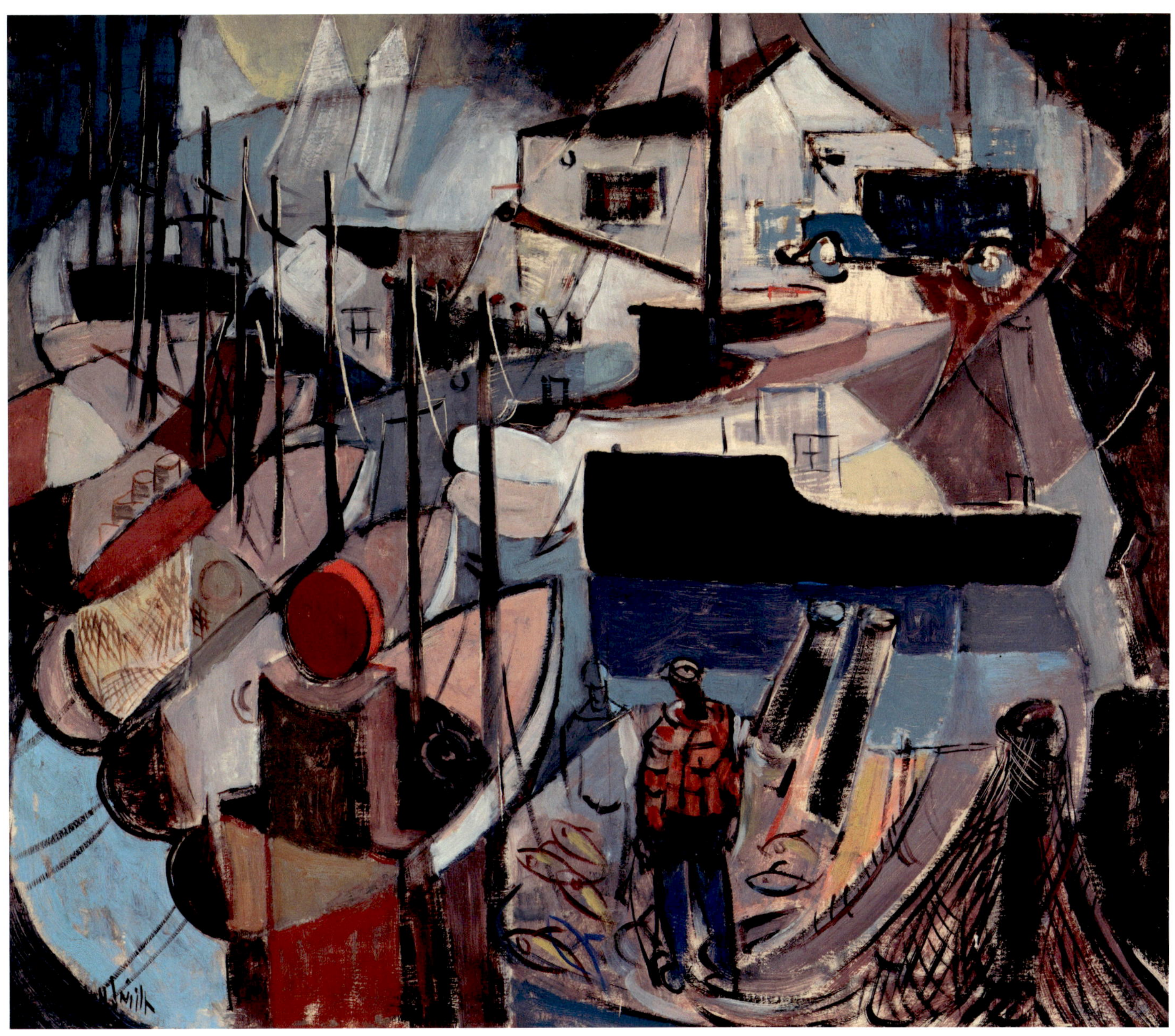

Vernon Smith, *Fishing Port*, n.d. Oil on board, 20 × 24 inches. *Gift of Harry Holl*, 1985.

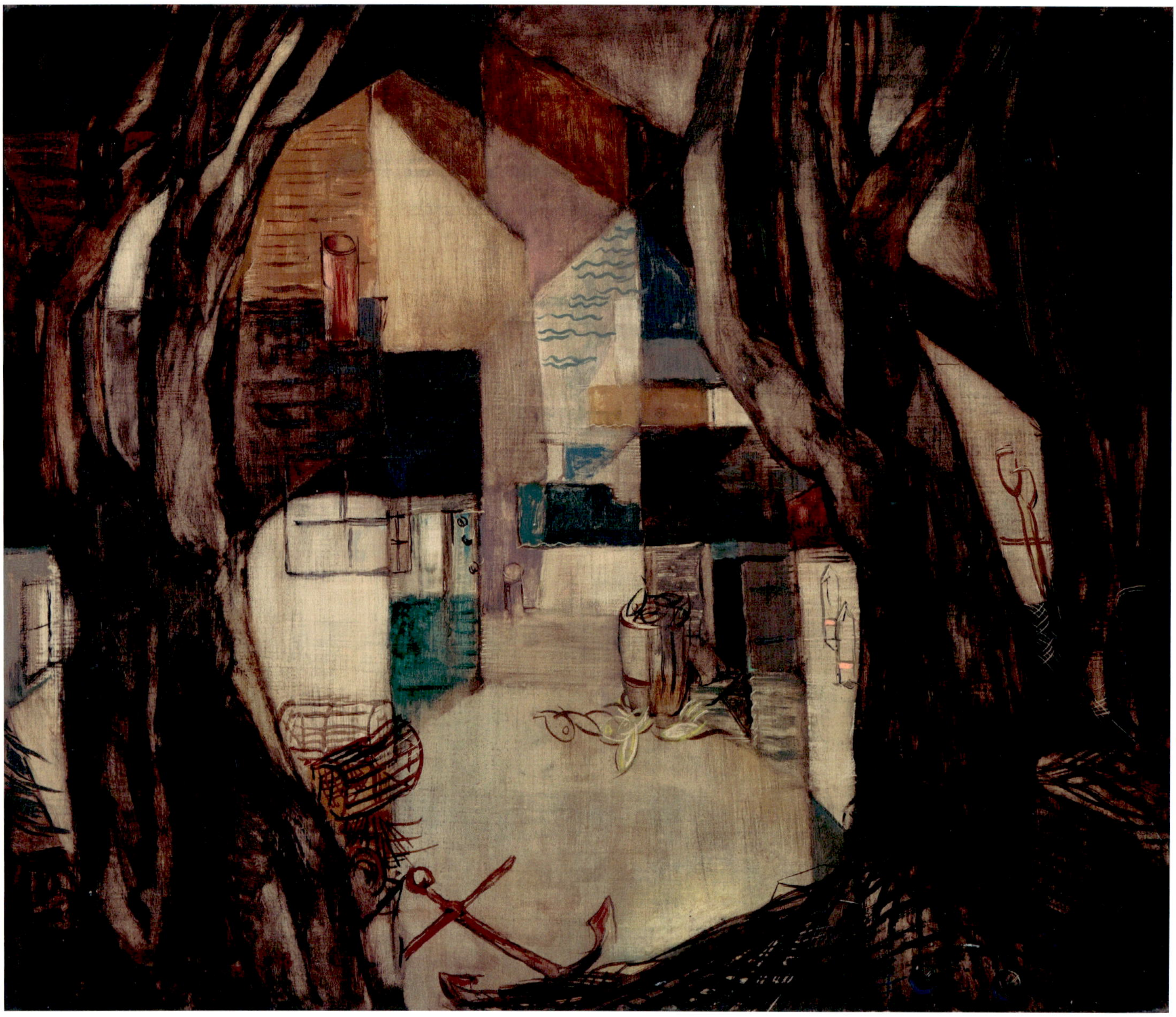

Vernon Smith, *Quiet Hour*, 1948, Oil on board, 20 × 25 inches. *Gift of Harry Holl*, 1985.

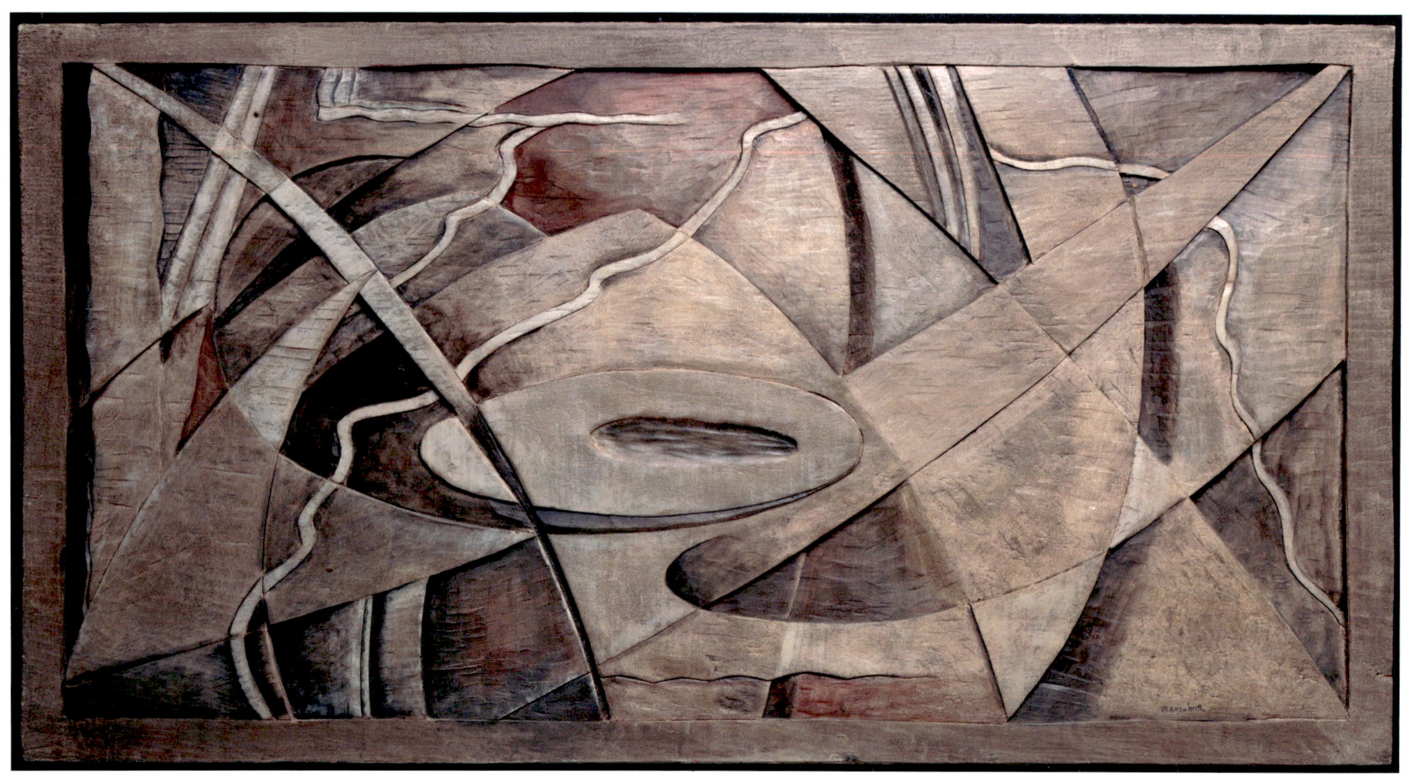

Vernon Smith, *Untitled,* n.d. Wood and polychrome relief, 51½ × 14 inches. *Gift of Anne Place in memory of Clyde Richmond Place and Mabelle Hamilton Boyd Pace,* 1987.

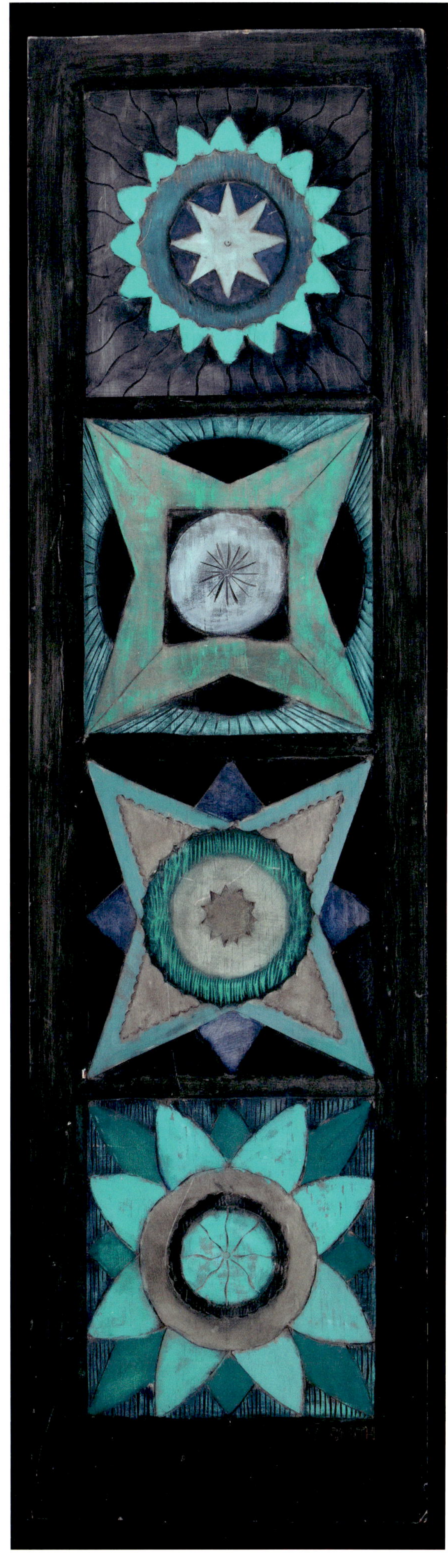

Opposite:
Vernon Smith, *Untitled,* n.d. Bas-relief on wood, 20⅜ × 38¼ inches.
Gift of the Estate of Ruth Fiske, 1996.

SOL WILSON
(1894–1974)

Sol Wilson was active in the Provincetown art colony beginning in 1947 and is known for his representational paintings of the fishing community, as well as figures and views of land and sea.

He was born in Vilno, Poland, where his father was a lithographer, and it was in his shop that the son was introduced to art. He immigrated to America in 1901, settled in New York City, and studied at Cooper Union, the National Academy of Design, and with George Bellows and Robert Henri. The latter artists were founders of the American-based group, The Eight, which later became part of the Ashcan School of painters. The Ashcan School was devoted to depicting ordinary life, which is the approach Wilson took. He felt it was important for art to be connected to its time and place. His work is influenced by Bellows, Gustave Courbet, and Albert Pinkham Ryder.

Besides Provincetown, Wilson also painted in another seaside community on Cape Ann, north of Boston. Wilson described himself as an "expressionistic realist." With his vivid colors and vibrant brushwork, he created paintings that capture the essence of a scene with the details overridden by the emotional force and mood of the work. His oil paintings *The Home* and *The Sidings of Provincetown*, in the Cape Cod Museum of Art collection, show how the energy of his brushstroke and his adventurous palette made him a true expressionist. In his work Wilson found beauty in nature's power, in a turbulent sea and a threatening sky. Although his colors are buoyant, he often captures the struggles the fisherman and laborer face.

During his nearly thirty years of summers on Cape Cod, Wilson made pen and ink and charcoal sketches of life in the area, which were the subjects for his oils and watercolors in his New York studio during the winter.

His paintings are included in the collections of the Metropolitan Museum of Art and the Whitney Museum of American Art in New York, the Tel Aviv Museum in Israel, and the Smithsonian American Art Museum and the Phillips Collection in Washington, DC.

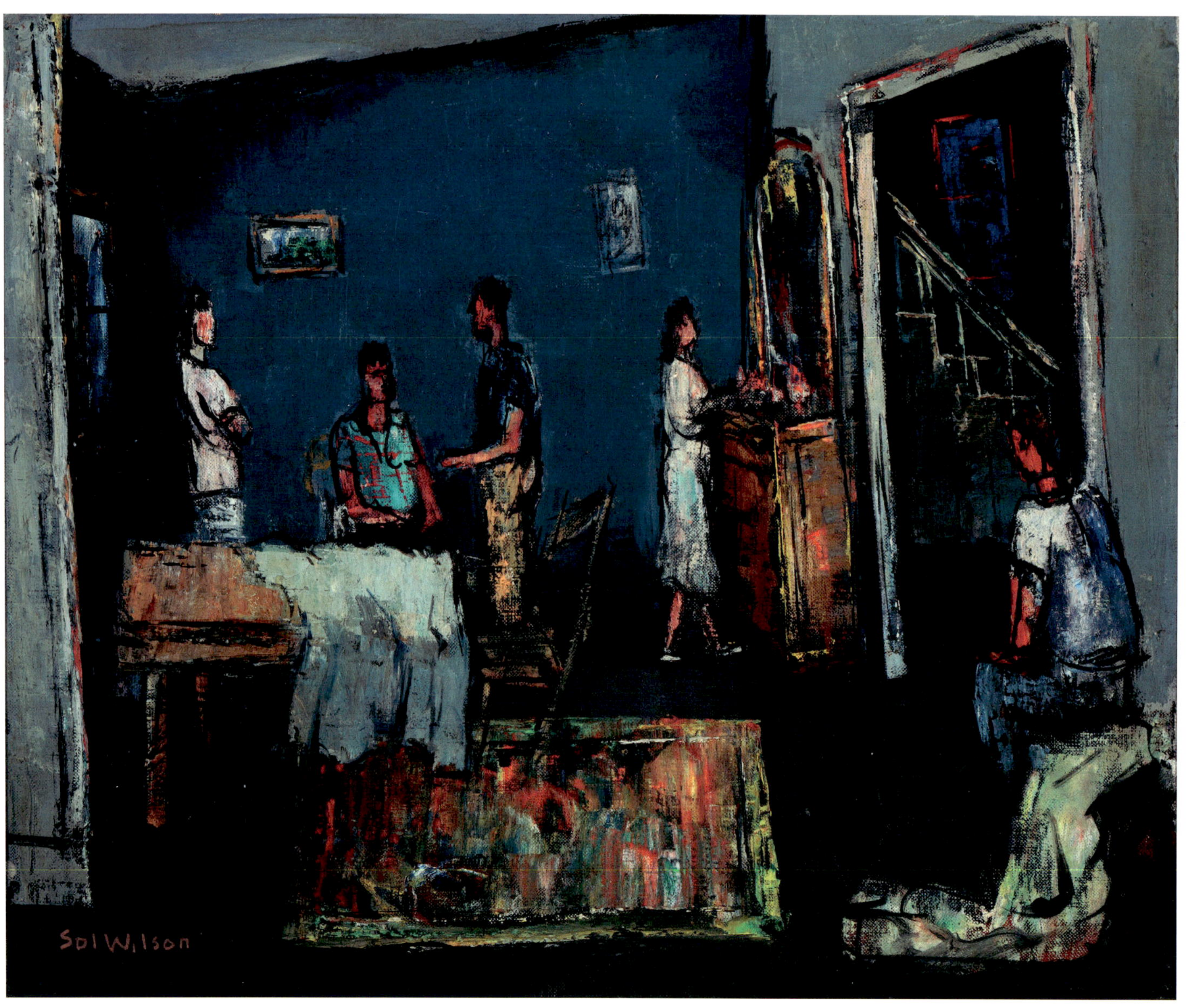

Sol Wilson, *The Home,* n.d. Oil on canvas, 21 × 28½ inches. *Anonymous gift*, 1993.

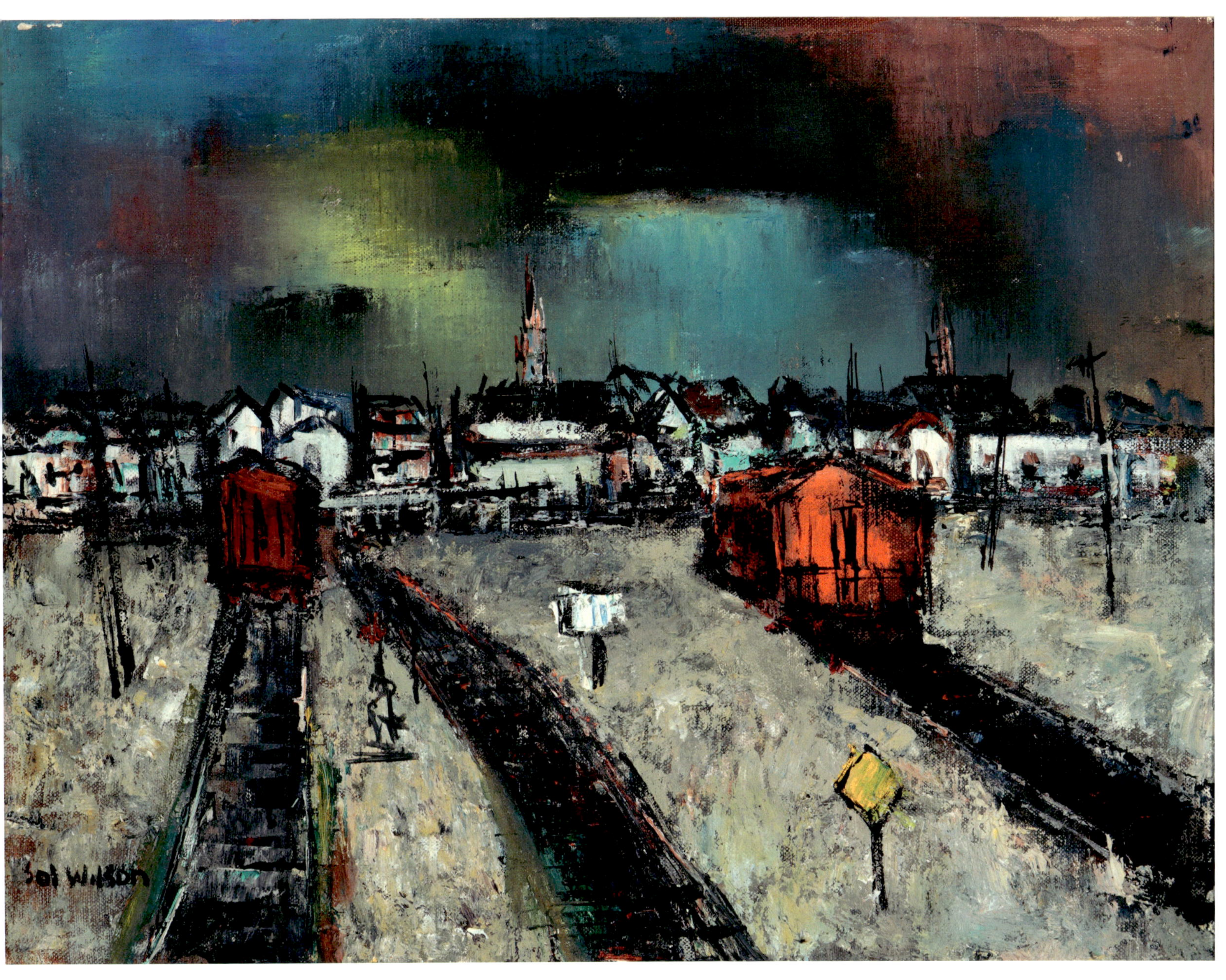

Sol Wilson, *The Sidings of Provincetown,* n.d. Oil on canvas, 11¾ × 16 inches. *Gift of Robert and Irene Wright*, 1995.

AIDEN LASSELL RIPLEY
(1896–1969)

A Massachusetts native, Aiden Lassell Ripley was rooted to his Boston training, where the traditional approach to painting, modified by impressionism, dominated even at a time when modernism was making an impact, particularly in Europe. Ripley studied at the Fenway School of Illustration, the School of the Museum of Fine Arts in Boston, and in Europe in the 1920s.

He was skilled in both oil painting and watercolor. His subjects included hunting and fishing scenes, street life, and landscapes, most often occupied by people involved in ordinary activities. His paintings of hunters and sport fishermen, inspired by his love of the outdoors and influenced by Frank Benson, who taught at the Boston Museum School, were popular with collectors. His other subjects have a strong nostalgic appeal.

The watercolors Ripley did in Europe set the scene for his later work when he returned to America in 1925. He mastered this medium, using sparkling colors, a nimble touch, and evoking a spontaneity that captures a particular moment. In both his oils and watercolors, he portrayed life at the time. He found ample subjects close to his home in Lexington, Massachusetts. He painted children sledding in Boston's Public Garden; people waiting at a train station;

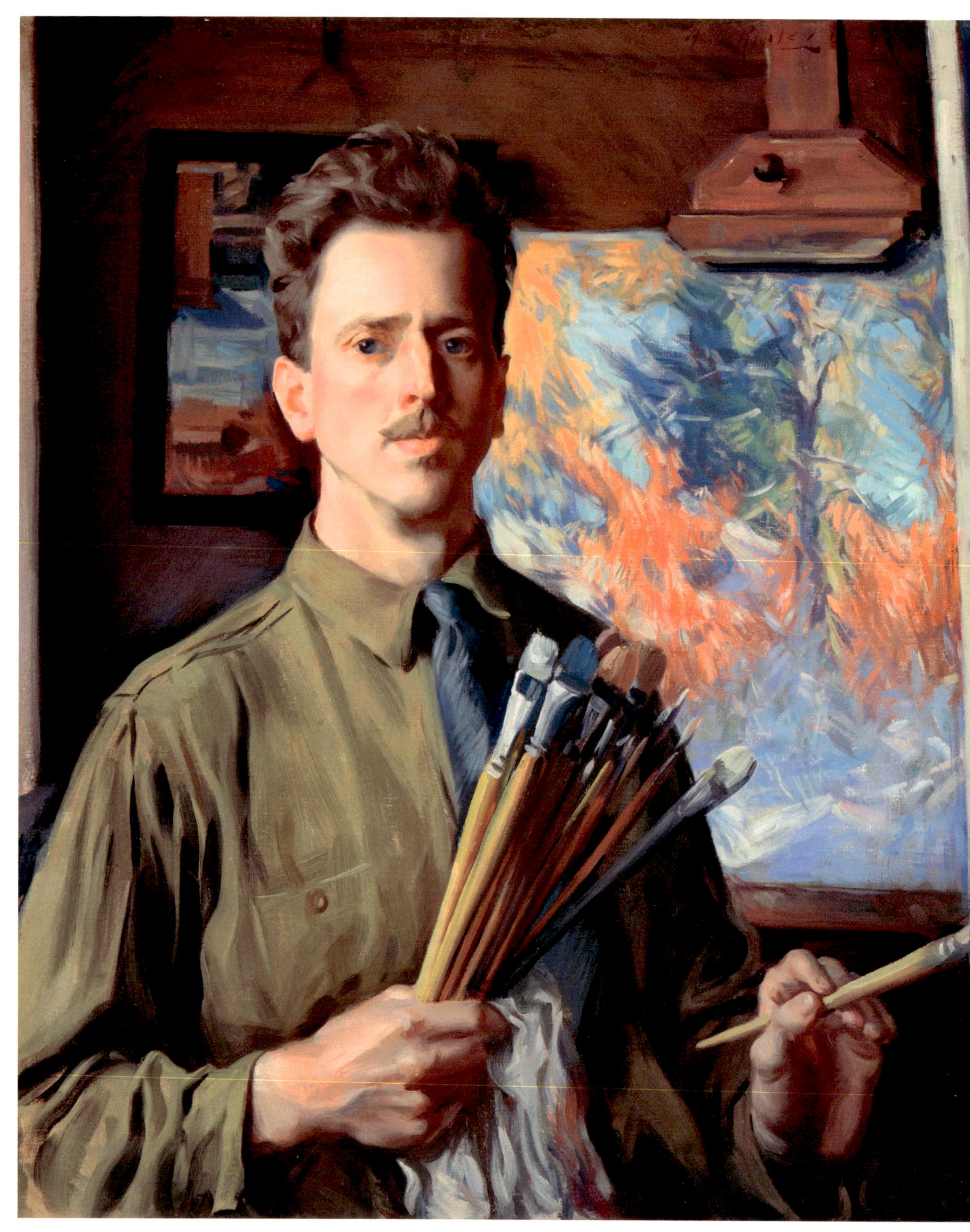

Aiden Lassell Ripley, *Self Portrait,* 1926. Oil on canvas, 36 × 30 inches. *Gift of Lawrence and Elizabeth Perera,* 2010.

snow-covered village and street scenes; and, of course, his wildlife pictures. His still lifes are artfully composed and his skill in rendering architecture is notable.

During the 1930s, Ripley received mural commissions through the Treasury Relief Art Project, depicting local historical scenes, such as *Paul Revere's Ride* for the post office in Lexington, Massachusetts. He did, however, lose one mural competition for the Holyoke, Massachusetts, post office, to Ross Moffett, who won the commission by depicting a very specific local event, while Ripley submitted a sketch of an "idealized" industrial worker.

His portraits, like the two, both named *Self-Portrait*, in the Cape Cod Museum of Art's collection, are sensitively painted and show psychological insight and awareness. The work painted in 1926 shows an eager young man, brushes in hand, in front of a brightly colored painting on an easel. The other self-portrait is subtly colored and depicts an older artist in reflection.

Ripley's works are in the collections of the Art Institute of Chicago, the Museum of Fine Arts in Boston, and the Smithsonian American Art Museum in Washington, DC.

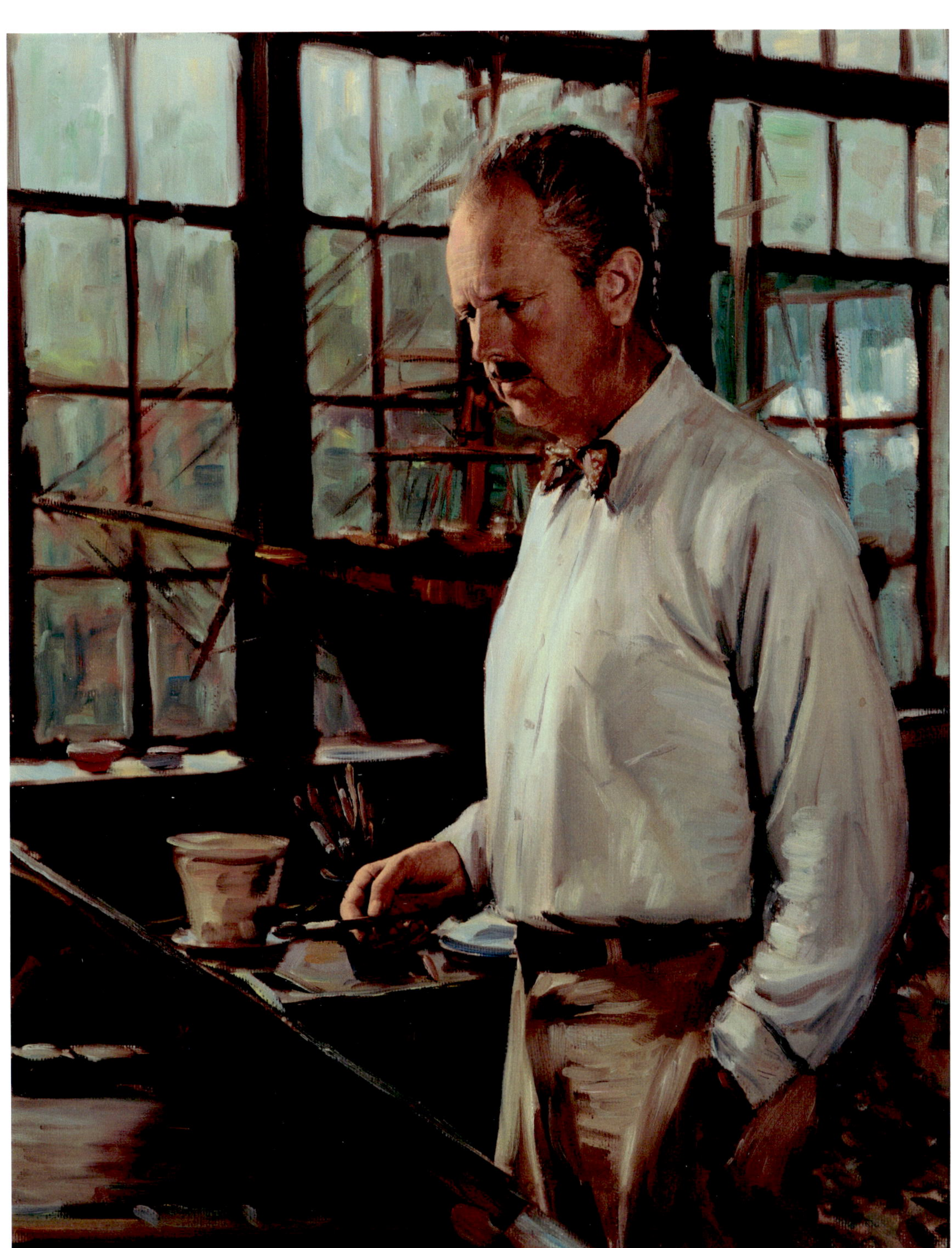

Aiden Lassell Ripley, *Self Portrait,* n.d. Oil on Board, 19¼ × 15¼ inches. *Anonymous gift*, 2011.

ARNOLD GEISSBUHLER
(1897–1993)

Arnold Geissbuhler, who was born in Switzerland, eventually settled on Cape Cod. His commitment to the Cape was sealed by the large donation he made to the new Cape Cod Museum of Art in 1985.

Geissbuhler studied sculpture in Zurich, and in Paris at the École des Beaux-Arts, the Académie Julian, and Académie de la Grande Chaumière. In Geissbuhler's representational pieces in the 1920s and 1930s, you can see the influence of Auguste Rodin and Antoine Bourdelle, with whom he studied in Paris. *Portrait of Mr. Virot,* a pewter head in the Cape Cod Museum of Art collection, is from this period in Paris. Around this time he became friends with another sculptor from Switzerland, Alberto Giacometti, who would have a later influence on his work. However, the terra cotta sculpture *Portrait of Waldo Emerson Forbes*, done in 1945, also in the museum collection, shows that Geissbuhler continued to have an interest in realism.

He first came to the United States in 1928 with his American wife, Elizabeth Chase, also a sculpture student in Paris. He came to exhibit his work at a Whitney Studio show in New York. In 1933 the Geissbuhlers returned to the United States and spent time in Boston and Cape Cod.

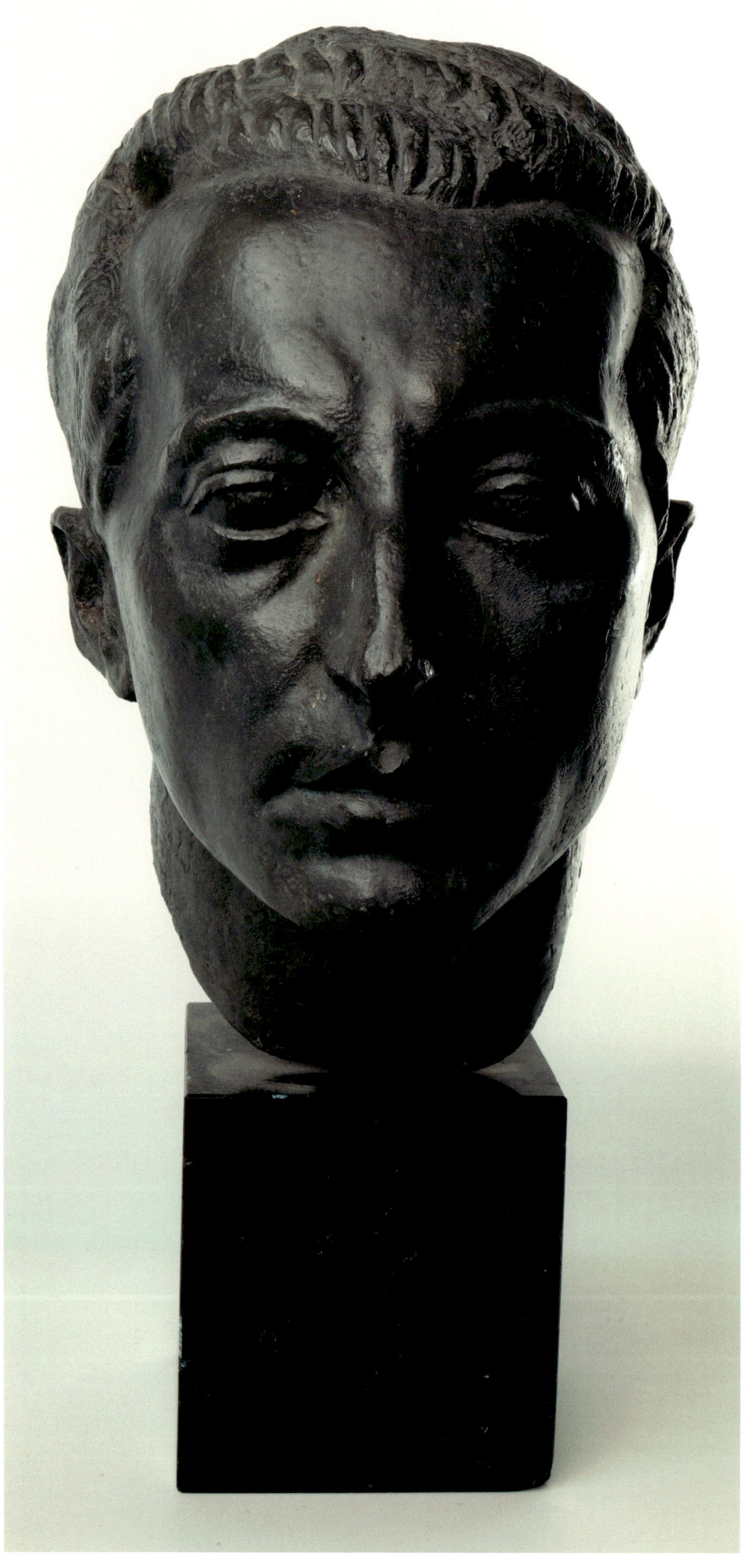

Arnold Geissbuhler, *Portrait of Mr. Virot* (Paris), 1922. Pewter on granite, 17 × 8 × 8½ inches. *Gift of Arnold Geissbuhler*, 1985.

The following year they settled in Provincetown and lived there until 1937. While Geissbuhler was there, he did a series of realistic, larger-than-life female nudes in plaster. He also did several bronzes of local people.

During the Depression, Geissbuhler worked for the Works Progress Administration, creating three bas-relief oak panels depicting the straw-weaving industry in Foxboro, Massachusetts, which were designated for the post office there. A later bas-relief in clay, *Memory of a Walk*, in the museum collection, has human figures and animals imprinted on an irregular shape.

Geissbuhler taught drawing and sculpture at Wellesley College in Massachusetts from 1937 to 1958. During World War II, he was a welder at the Quincy Shipyard. At the time, in addition to his sculpture, he did drawings in ink, charcoal, and graphite. Influenced by his experience as a welder, Geissbuhler began welding bronze castings together to create abstract works with only a slight link to his figures.

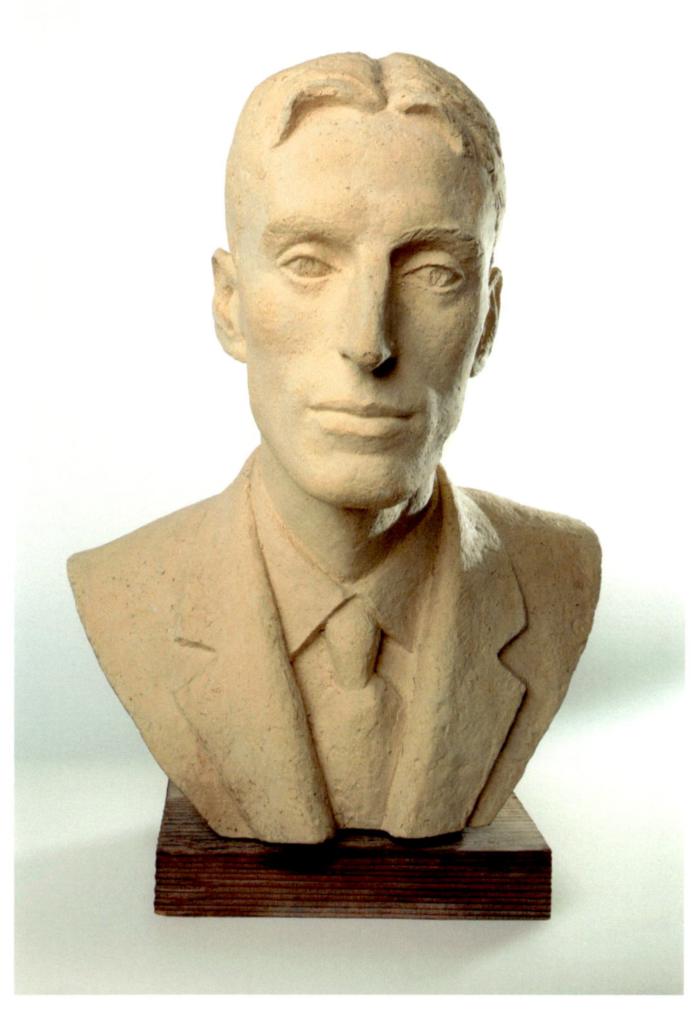

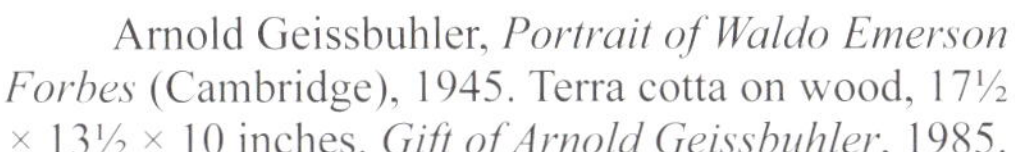

Arnold Geissbuhler, *Portrait of Waldo Emerson Forbes* (Cambridge), 1945. Terra cotta on wood, 17½ × 13½ × 10 inches. *Gift of Arnold Geissbuhler*, 1985.

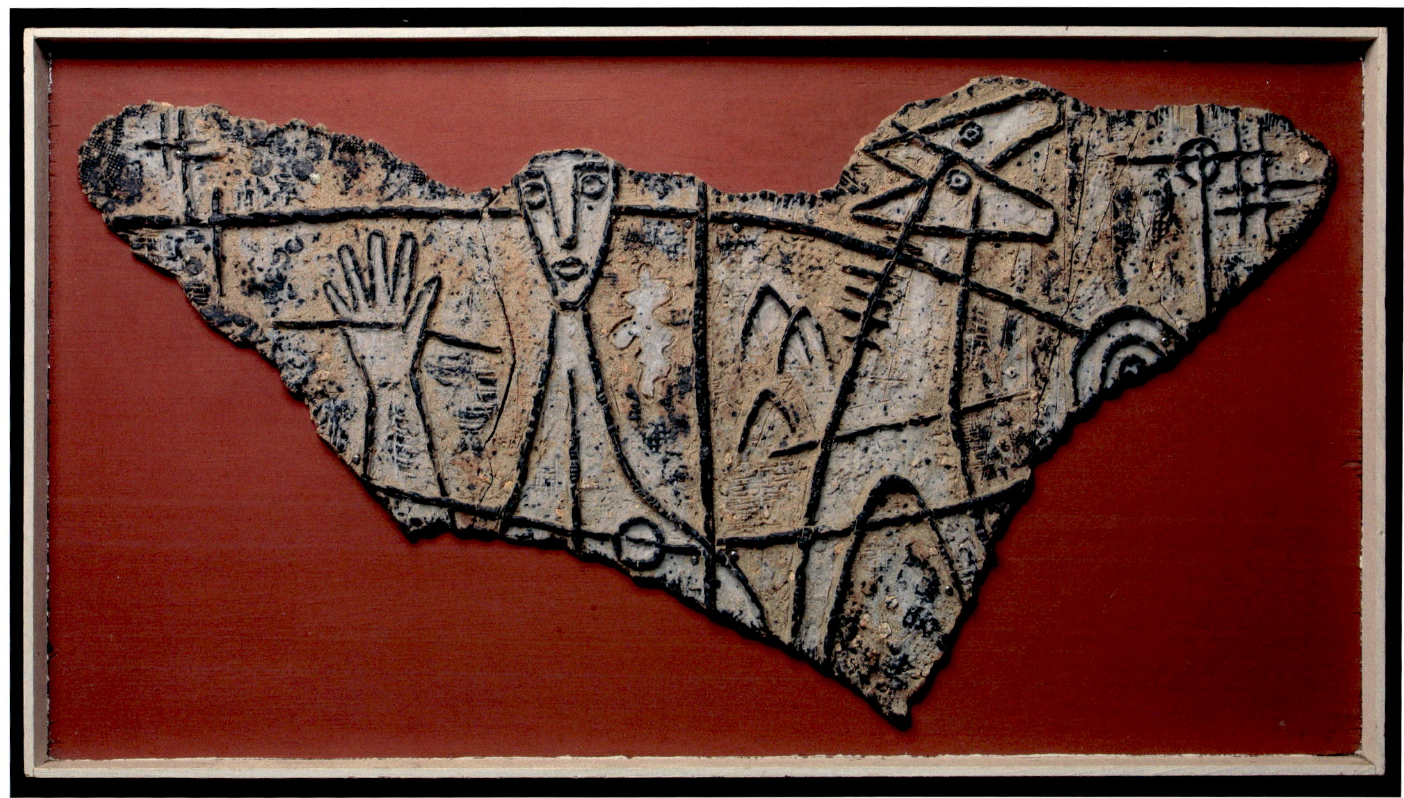

Arnold Geissbuhler, *Memory of a Walk* (Dennis), 1965. Ceramic bas-relief, 16 × 32 inches. *Gift of Arnold Geissbuhler*, 1985.

The female form occupied much of Geissbuhler's work for decades. In plaster, bronze, and ceramic, the pieces were abstracted with distortions and rounded forms. A bronze, *Female Figure*, in the museum collection, shows the influence of cubism. In the 1960s, two bronzes, *City II, Family* and *City V: Two Figures in the Garden*, in the museum collection, show the influence Giacometti eventually had on him.

During his last decades he had a home in Dennis on Cape Cod. His daughter Mirande had married Harry Holl, who not only was one of the founders of the CCMoA, but also owned Scargo Pottery in Dennis, where Geissbuhler used the kiln to create clay bas-reliefs of bird and animal forms.

In 1964, Geissbuhler was part of an exhibition in Paris that also included the work of Giacometti.

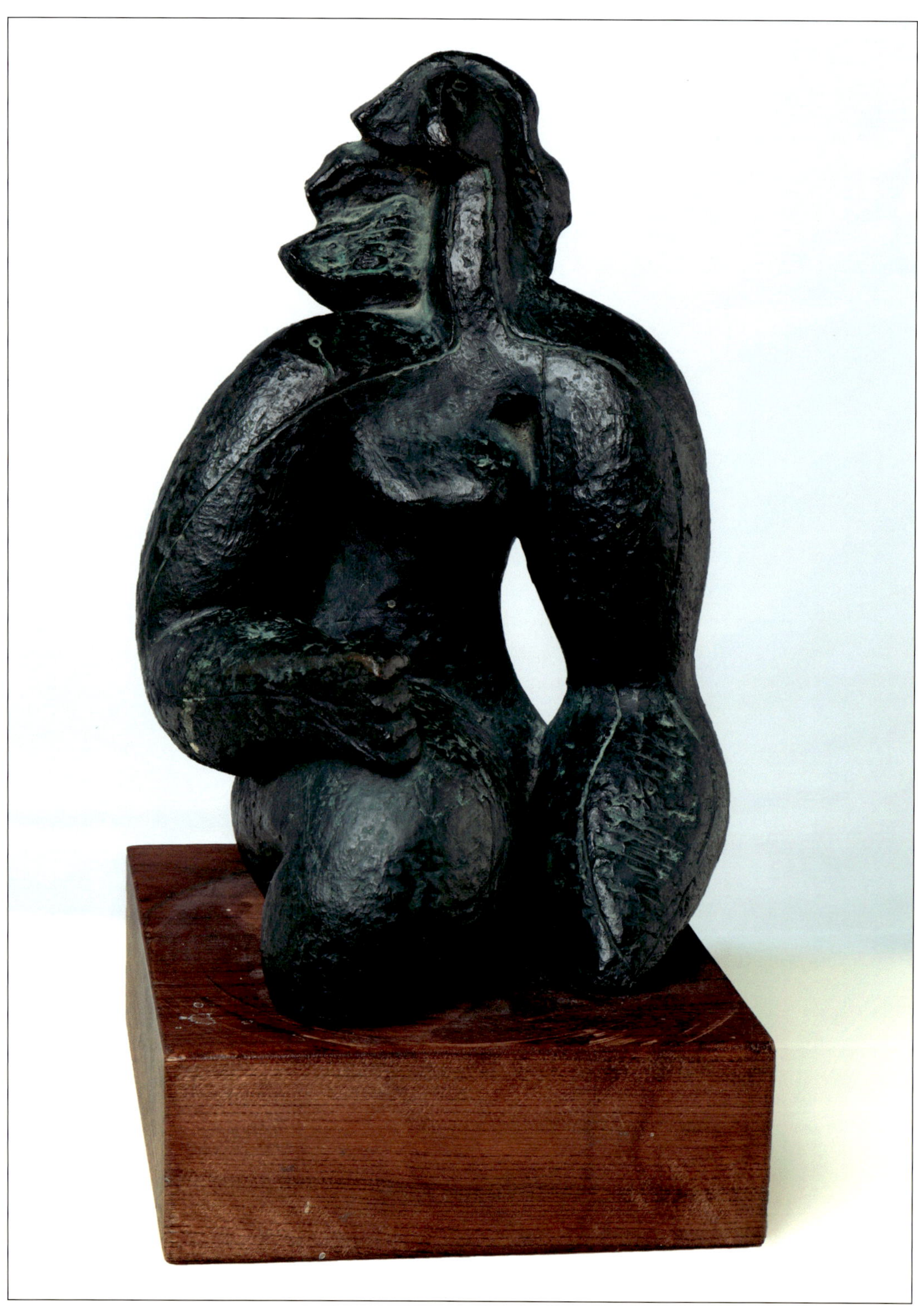

Arnold Geissbuhler, *Female Figure* 1/6, 1949. Bronze on wood, 8 × 5½ × 6 inches. *Gift of Thomas A. Gaglione*, 1990.

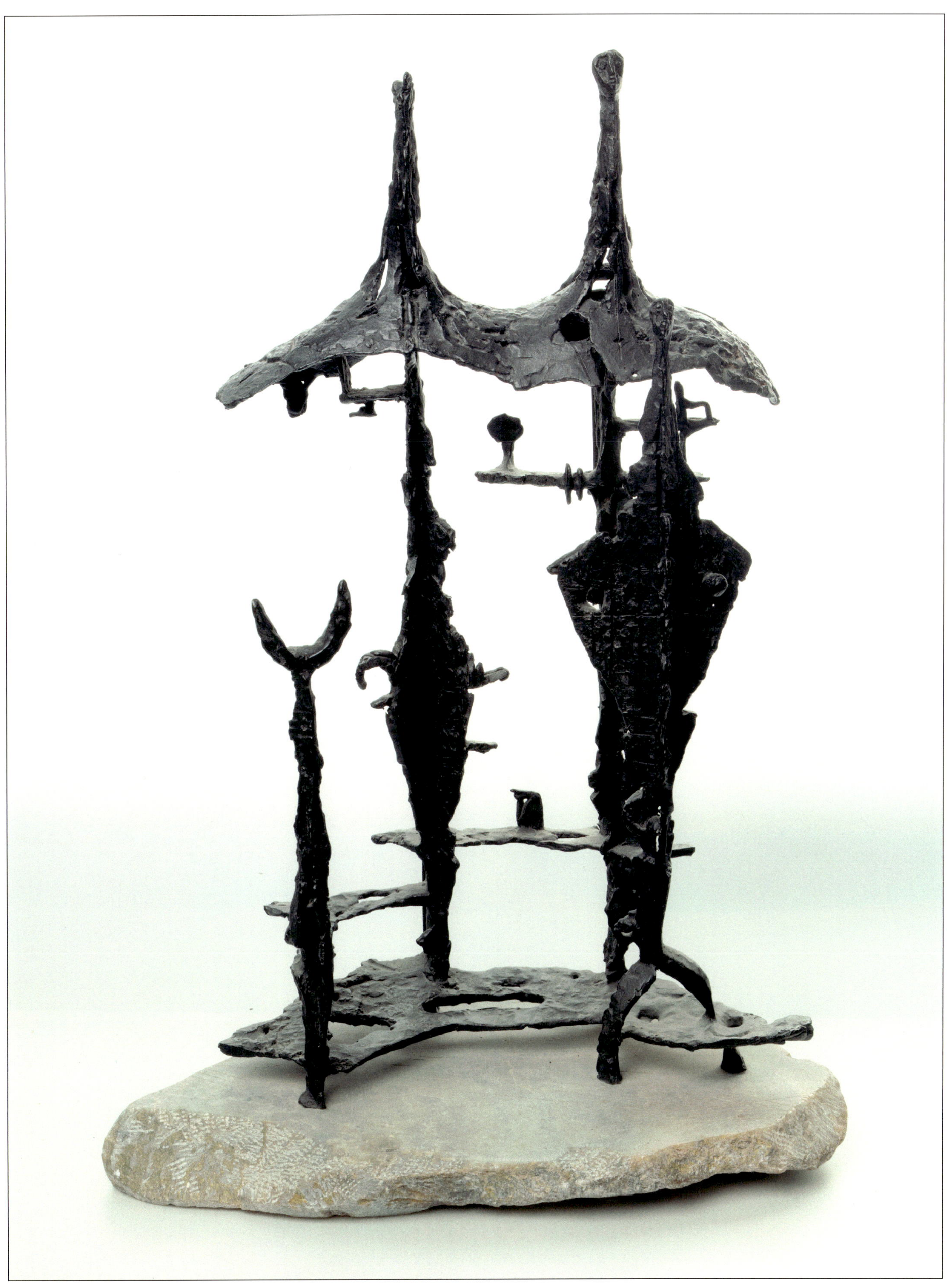

Arnold Geissbuhler, *City II, Family* (Paris), 1961–1962. Bronze on stone, 20 × 14 inches. *Gift of Arnold Geissbuhler*, 1985.

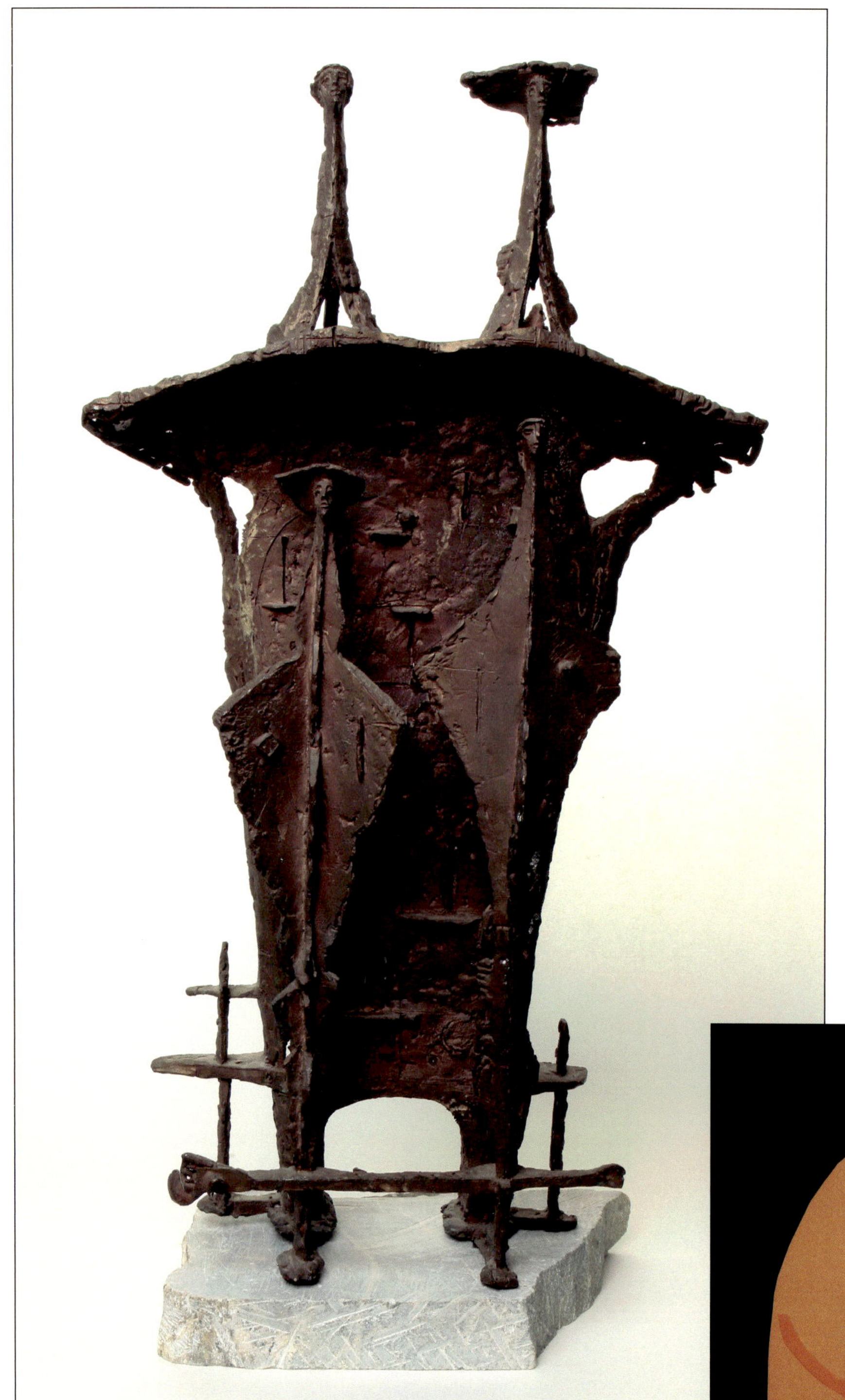

Arnold Geissbuhler, *City V, Two Figures in the Garden* (Dennis), 1966–1968. Bronze, 25 × 13½ × 5½ inches. *Gift of Arnold Geissbuhler*, 1985.

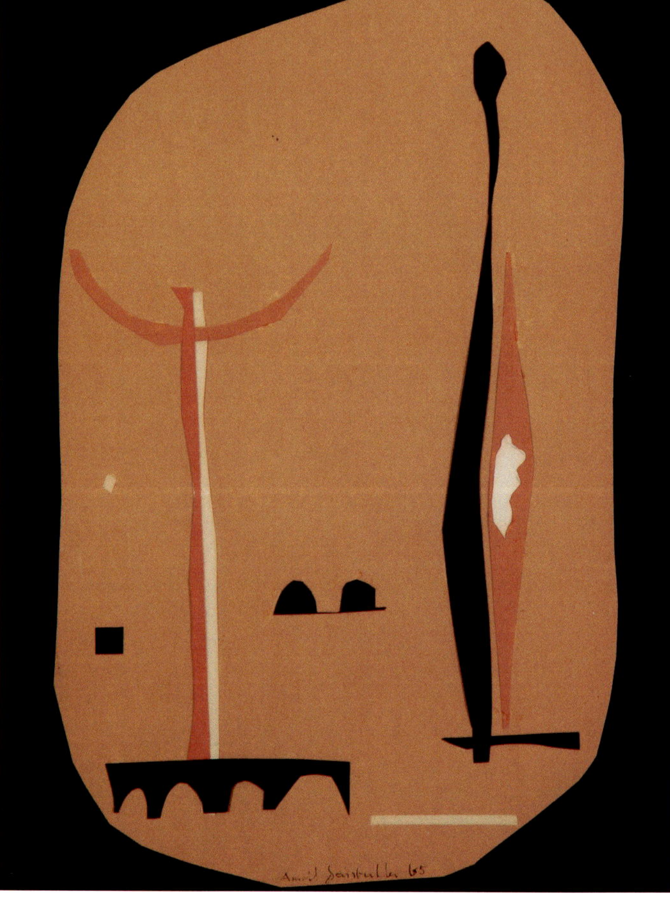

Arnold Geissbuhler, *Untitled,* 1965. Collage on paper, 12 × 9 inches. *Gift of Arnold Geissbuhler*, 1985.

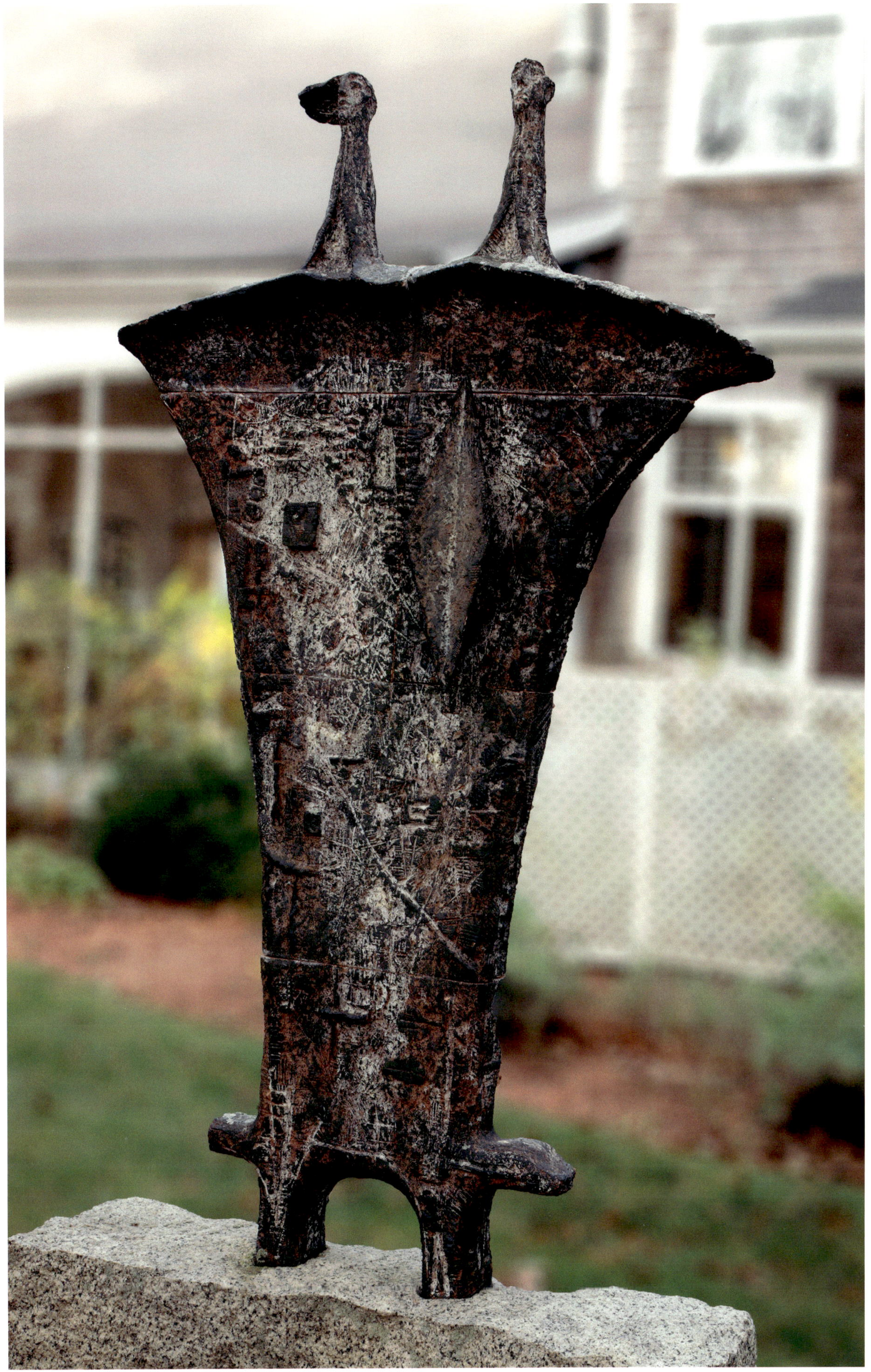

Arnold Geissbuhler, *Two Figures, Tower* (Dennis), 1963. Ceramic, 63 × 68 × 3 inches. *Gift of Arnold Geissbuhler*, 1985.

ALEXANDER CALDER
(1898–1976)

Alexander Calder is best known for his mobiles, suspended sheet metal and wire assemblages that are moved capriciously by air currents, and his monumental outdoor bolted sheet metal stabiles, which also express movement with angular shapes. He also made sculptures in wood and bronze, drew and painted in gouache, made prints, and designed jewelry.

In *La Scie et les Boules,* a lithograph in the Cape Cod Museum of Art collection, Calder used geometric forms in an uplifting composition to express a sense of movement that relates to his legendary mobiles.

Born in Lawnton, Pennsylvania, the son and grandson of artists, he made toys as a boy, which led him to study engineering at the Stevens Institute of Technology in Hoboken, New Jersey, where he received a degree in mechanical engineering in 1919. He also studied at the Art Students League with Thomas Hart Benton and John Sloan, and in Paris at the Académie de la Grande Chaumière.

As a freelance artist for the *National Police Gazette,* he sketched at the circus, which influenced his work early on when he made several constructions of animals and birds with wire and wood. His *Cirque Calder*, begun in 1926, is a miniature circus with spring-action and pull-toy performers and animals he created out of bits and pieces of cloth, yarn, cork, and wire. Some experts suggest this work allowed him to figure out the complicated physics of objects in motion and directly informed his creation of the mobile, so well balanced that it creates a moving three-dimensional form.

Inspired by Piet Mondrian, Calder began to experiment with abstract sculpture beginning in 1931 and introduced moving parts into his work a year later. His mobile forms include spheres, discs, and organic shapes adapted from plants and animals. Using simple hand tools, pliers for bending wire, and shears for cutting sheet metal, he created colorful mobiles, generally in red, blue, yellow, black, and white. His work is noted for its playfulness and sense of joy.

In 1964, Calder had a retrospective at the Guggenheim Museum and in 1976, a retrospective at the Whitney Museum of American Art. His works are included in many permanent collections, including the Whitney Museum of American Art, Solomon R. Guggenheim Museum and the Museum of Modern Art in New York; the Centre Georges Pompidou in Paris; the Museo Nacional Centro de Arte Reina Sofía in Madrid; the National Gallery of Art in Washington, DC; and the Philadelphia Museum of Art.

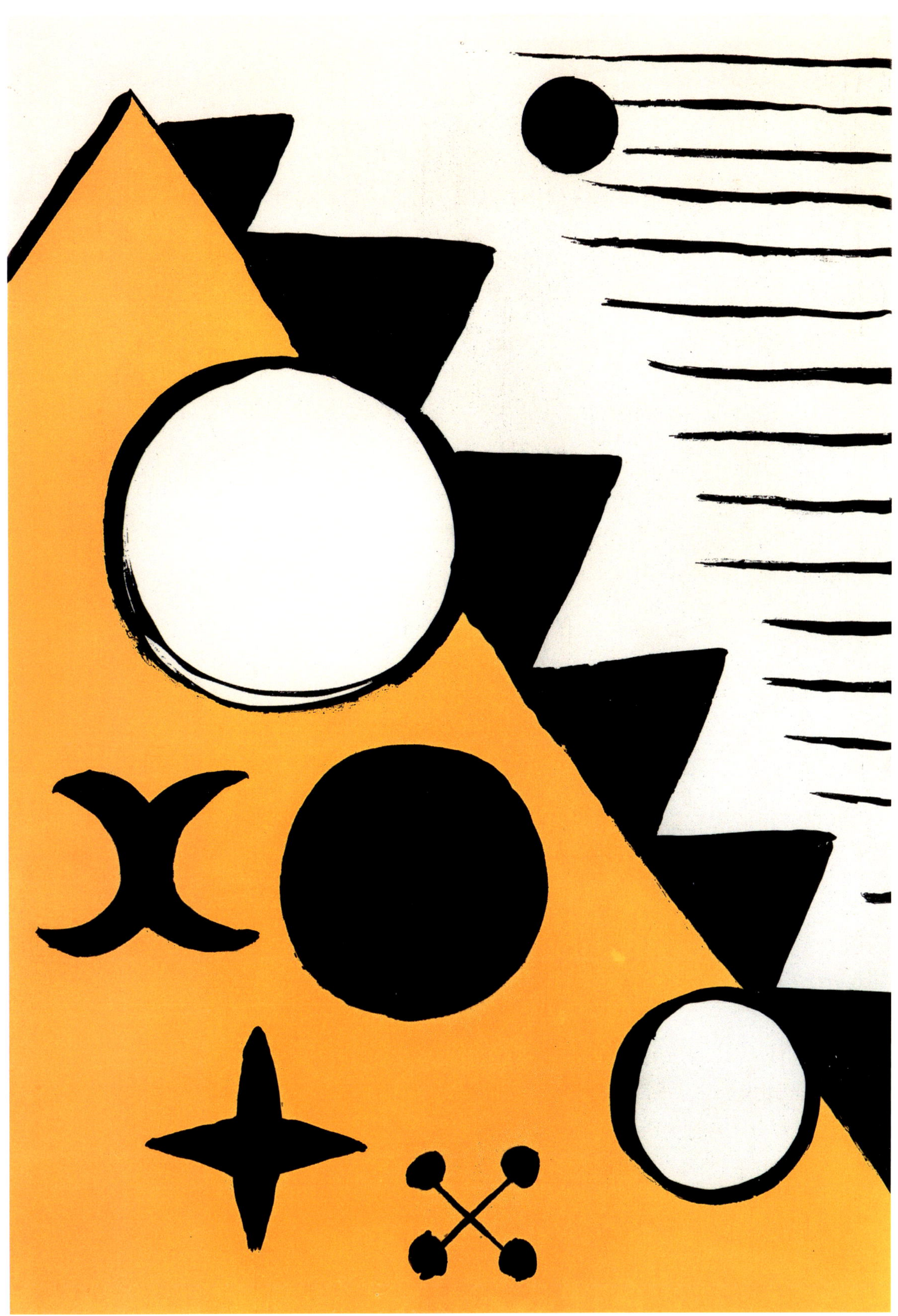

Alexander Calder, *La Scie et les Boules* 66/90, n.d. Lithograph on paper, 12 × 17¼ inches.
Gift of David and Nancy Kaplan, 2007.*© 2016 Calder Foundation/Artists Rights Society (ARS), New York.*

VERNON COLEMAN
(1898–1978)

Primarily a marine painter, Vernon Coleman had a long and varied history on Cape Cod. He was born in Norwich, Connecticut, and studied at the Corcoran Gallery School of Art in Washington, DC. Considering a practical career, he enrolled in the National Radio School to become a licensed marine radio telegrapher.

In the early 1920s when his parents decided to return to his father's boyhood home on the Cape, Coleman and his wife went along. While pursuing his art, Coleman also did other work. In 1927, he became assistant stage manager for the inaugural season of the Cape Playhouse in Dennis, Massachusetts.

During the 1930s, he was an easel artist on the Massachusetts Federal Art Project of the WPA, producing close to 100 paintings and creating murals in local schools on the Cape. Many of these oils depicted ocean themes, with strong dramatic elements of nature that evoked an intensity of mood without a specific narrative. He taught art in Barnstable for twenty-two years, and was a set designer for local theaters, including the Barnstable Comedy Club.

He is known for his seascapes and paintings of boats and clipper ships with moody skies and tossing waves. *Cape Cod '49*, in the Cape Cod Museum of Art collection, of a lighthouse with crashing waves, is typical of his work. *Cape Cod 1946*, also in the museum collection, is a darker image, of a fisherman plodding along, lowly fish shacks and boats bordering his route.

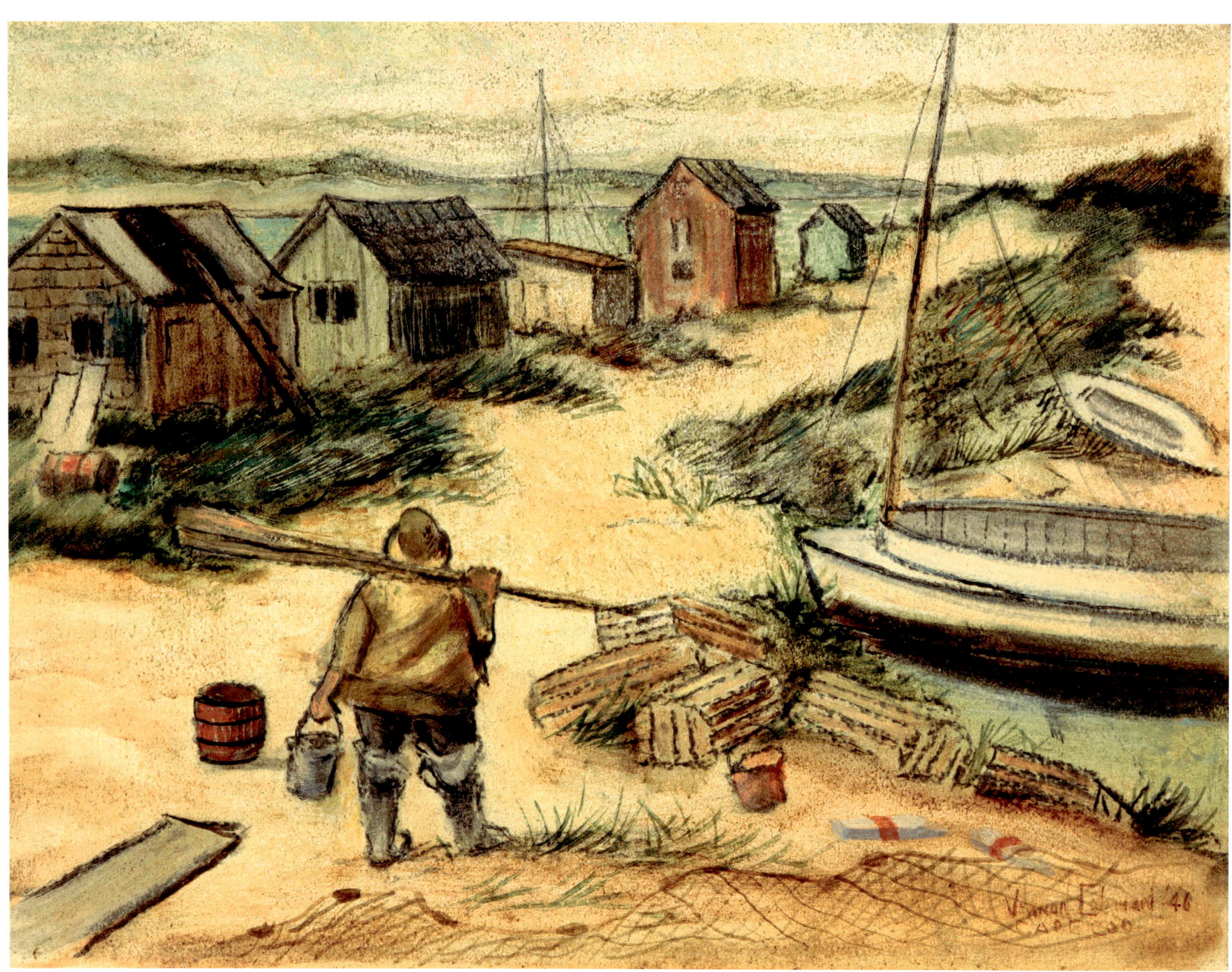

Vernon Coleman, *Cape Cod 1946*, 1946. Gouache on cardboard, 20¼ × 24 inches. *Gift of Collection of Sigmund M. and Mary B. Hyman*, 2004.

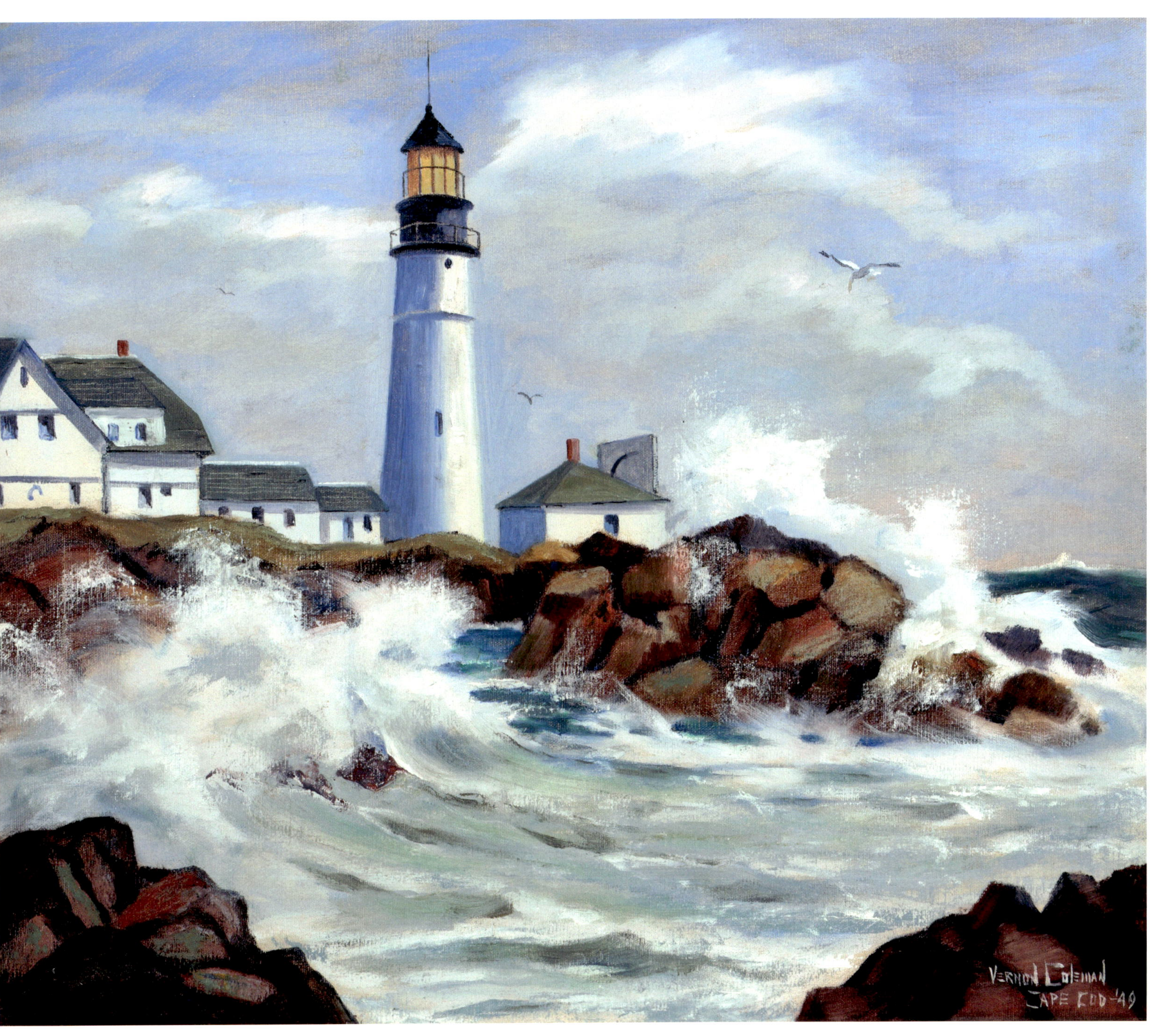

Vernon Coleman, *Cape Cod '49*, 1949. Oil on canvas, 20 × 24 inches. *Gift of Collection of Sigmund M. and Mary B. Hyman*, 2004.

XAVIER GONZALEZ
(1898–1993)

Xavier Gonzalez immigrated to America in 1925 from Spain. He studied at the Art Institute of Chicago, the San Carlos Academy in Mexico City, as well as in Paris in the 1930s, when he became acquainted with another Spanish artist, Pablo Picasso.

A versatile artist, Gonzalez painted landscapes, figures, still lifes, abstractions, and semi-abstractions, which draw from reality. He did not hesitate to improvise. In the Cape Cod Museum of Art collection are a number of pieces that show the range of his work. Dark and eerie are his expressionistic *Meditation at Patmos* and *Wellfleet III*. His brightly colored *Seascape* plays on the dynamic sails as does *Wellfleet Harbor*. The watercolor *Inland Sea* has a light-filled translucency, and *Chinese Junks, Hong Kong* shows a frenetic image of boats in a foreign land. In all of these paintings there is an emotional connection to his use of color, space, and movement.

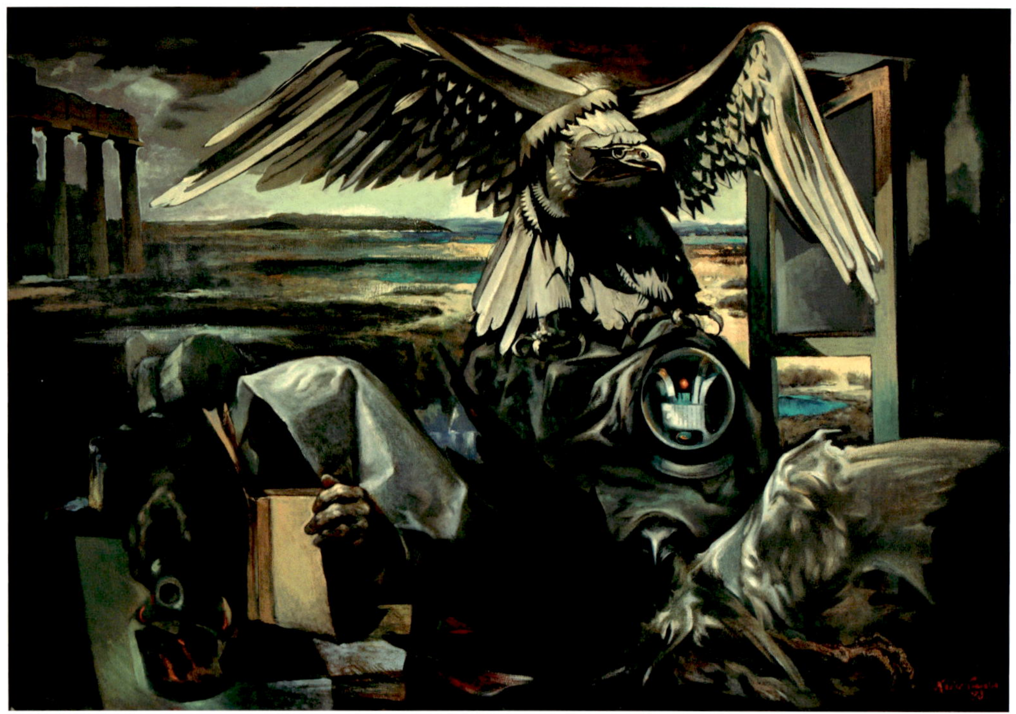

Xavier Gonzalez, *Meditation at Patmos*, n.d. Oil on canvas, 40 × 60 inches. *Gift of Roy and Sheila Mennell and Frank and Ruth Hogan*, 1997.

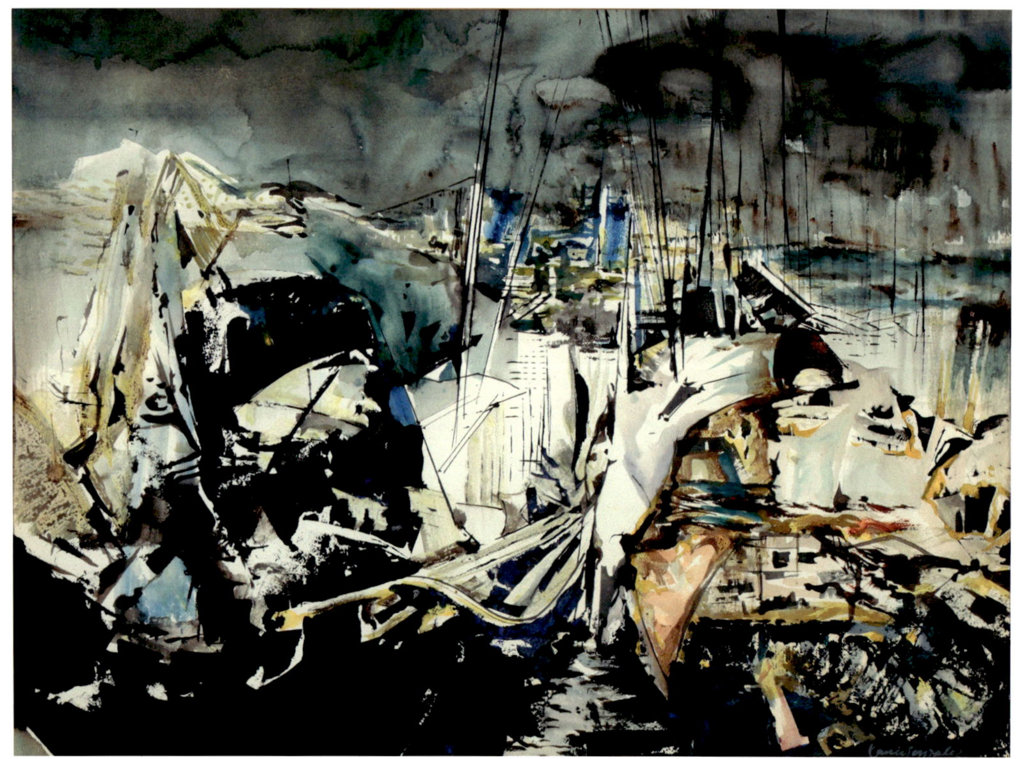

Xavier Gonzalez, *Wellfleet III*, 1960. Watercolor on paper, 22 × 30 inches. *Gift of Stuart and Kathleen Harrod*, 2006.

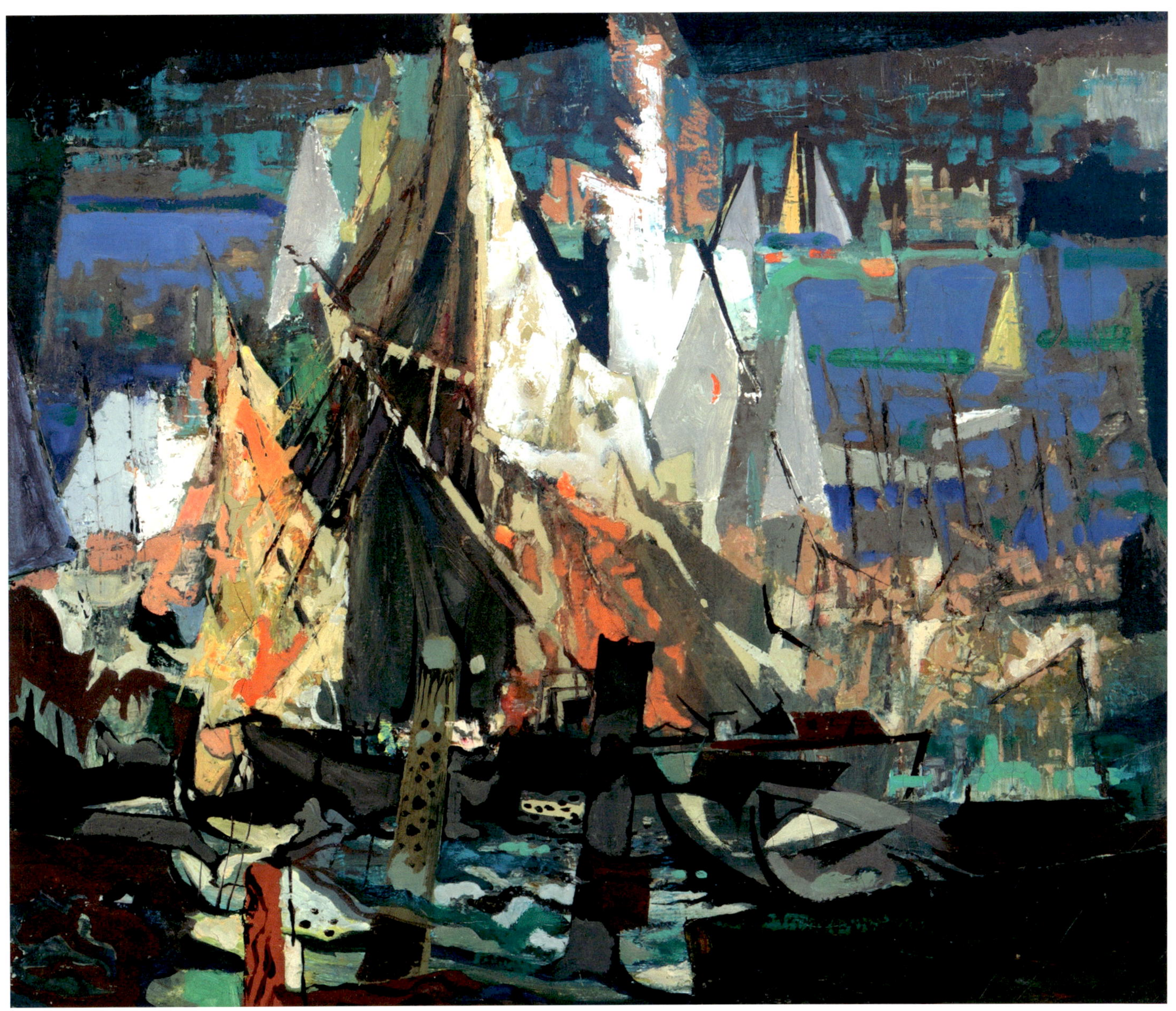

Xavier Gonzalez, *Seascape,* n.d. Oil on board, 20 × 24 inches. *Gift of Stuart and Kathleen Harrod*, 2007.

As he wrote in a catalogue for a memorial exhibition of his work in 1993 at the Art Students League Gallery: "Sometimes the basis of our work is a landscape, a figure or a gesture, and we know beforehand that the final product will be unrelated to the original idea; we shall end with another thing, another emotion."

Gonzalez worked in a number of mediums, including watercolor, plaster, and pen and ink. He was also a muralist, sculptor, and teacher. After World War II, while living in New York, he became fascinated with the beauty of Cape Cod and opened a school in Wellfleet, which he ran for a decade until the early 1970s. Wellfleet continued to be his summer home.

His works are in the collections of a number of museums, including the Metropolitan Museum of Art and the Whitney Museum of American Art in New York, the Pennsylvania Academy of Fine Arts in Philadelphia, and the Museum of Fine Arts in Boston.

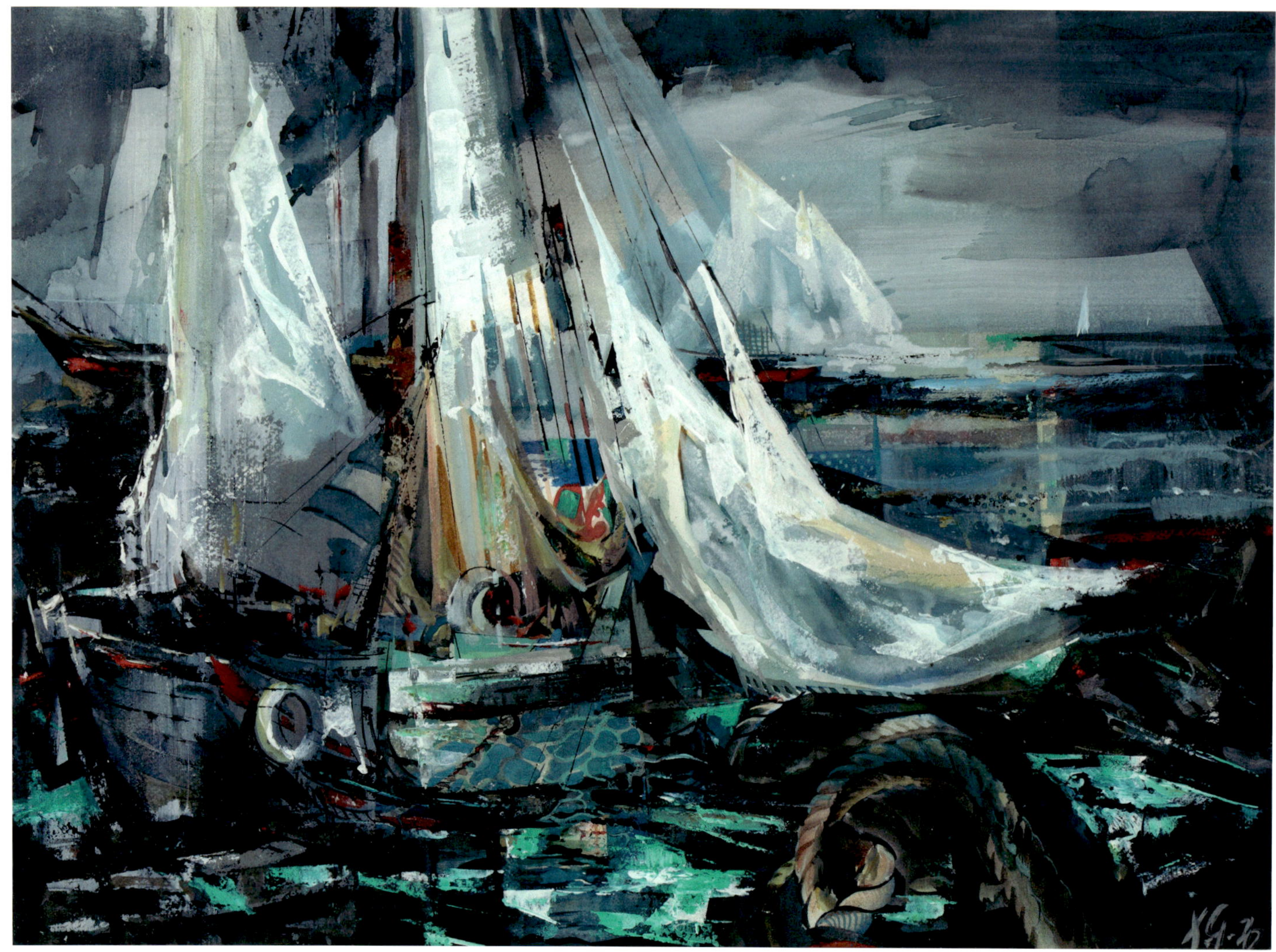

Xavier Gonzalez, *Wellfleet Harbor,* 1970. Watercolor on paper, 21½ × 29 inches. *Gift of Stuart and Kathleen Harrod*, 2008.

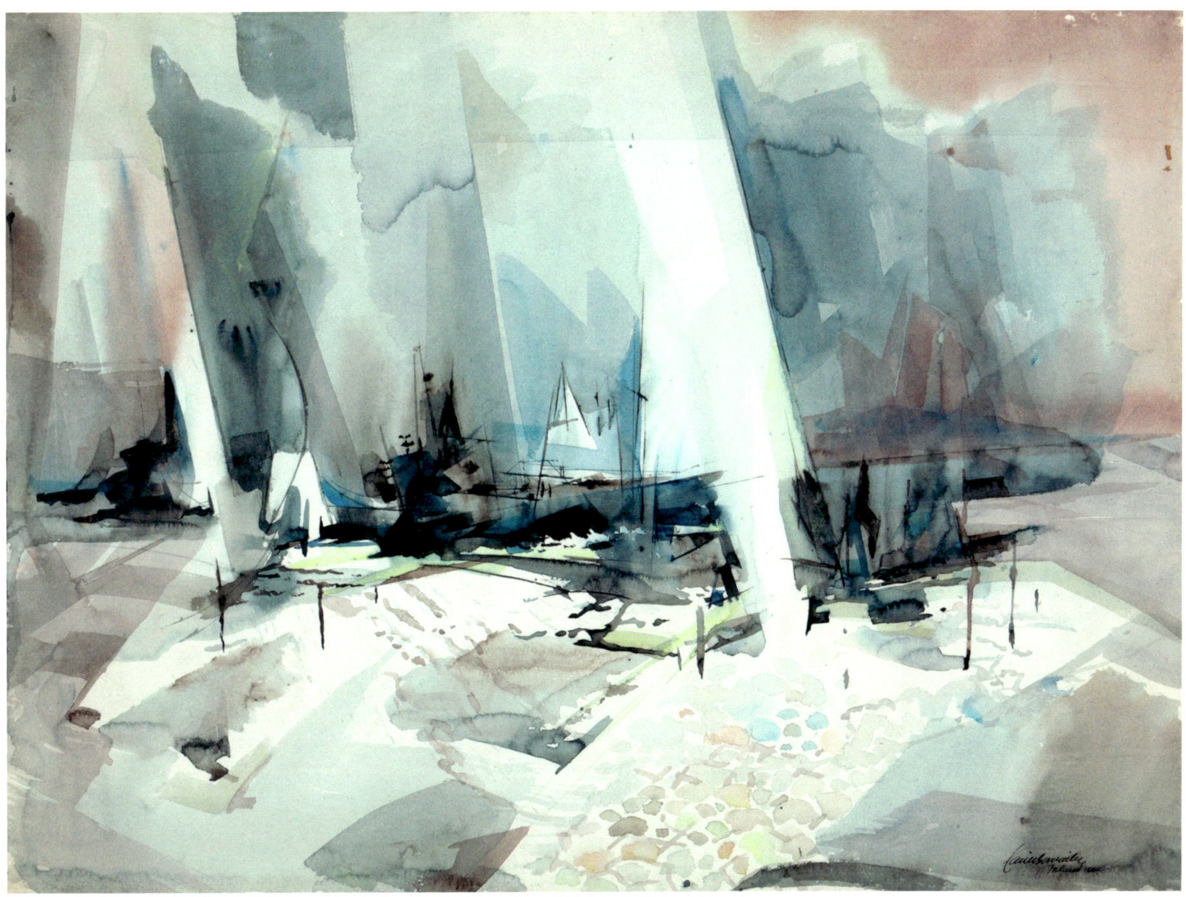

Xavier Gonzalez, *Inland Sea,* n.d. Watercolor on paper, 20¾ × 28½ inches. *Gift of Stuart and Kathleen Harrod*, 2008.

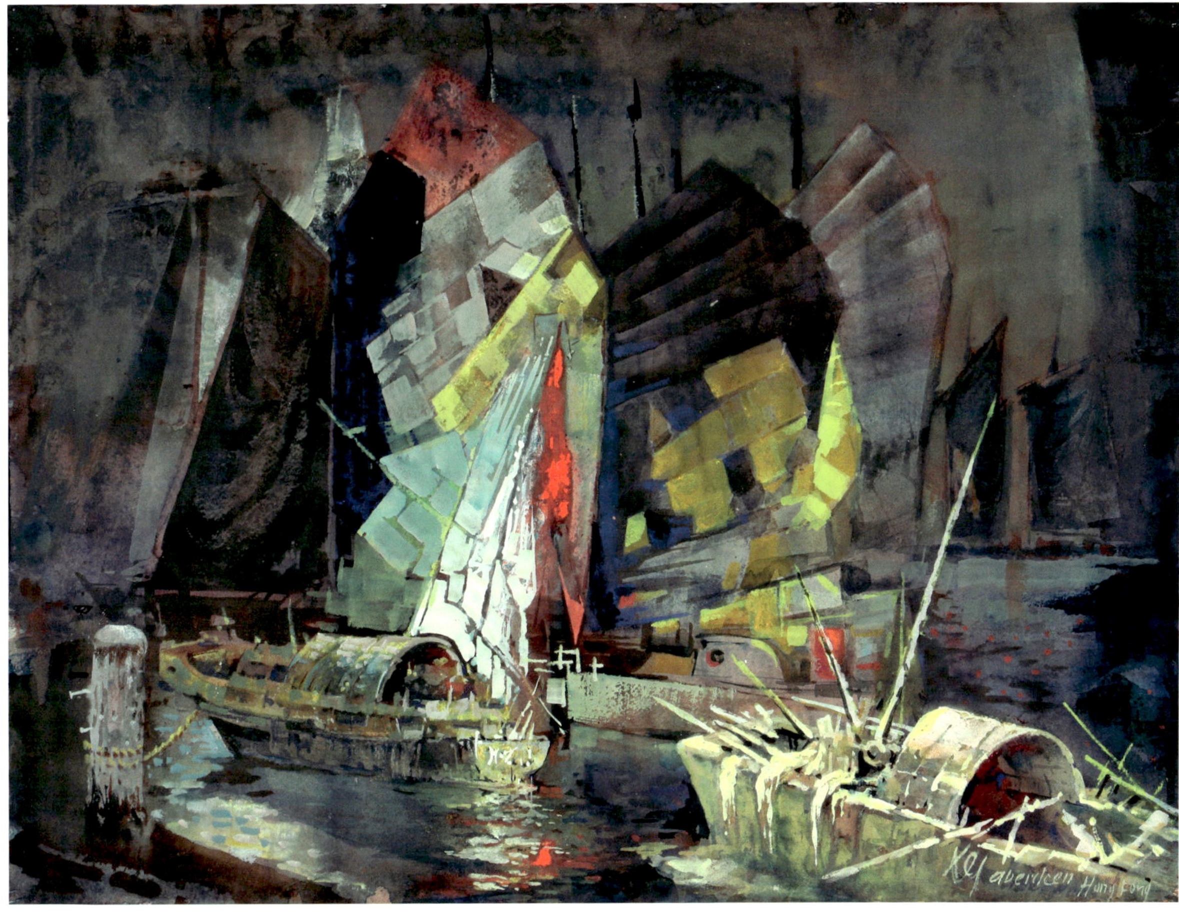

Xavier Gonzalez, *Chinese Junks, Hong Kong*, n.d. Watercolor on paper, 22½ × 31 inches. *Gift of Mary A. Eisenberg*, 2008.

CLARE LEIGHTON
(1898–1989)

Clare Leighton was born in London, the daughter of authors Robert and Marie Connor Leighton. She studied at the Brighton School of Art, the Slade School of Fine Art, and the Central School of Arts and Crafts, where she learned wood engraving, for which she is best known.

Traveling through Europe, she sketched landscapes and people and became interested in portraying rural life. These images in watercolor, pen and ink, and sepia wash became the basis for some of her wood engravings. Her strong draftsmanship and skills in composing a work produced powerful images of workers struggling with jobs on land and at sea.

The wood engraving *The Dance,* in the Cape Cod Museum of Art collection, is an excellent example of her robust, rhythmic, intense black-and-white images with swirling lines that capture a figure.

Her expressive works dramatically depict the plight and hardiness of rural laborers and fishermen as they deal with nature's whims. Devoid of figures, the wood engraving *Windblown Trees,* in the museum collection, shows the effects of a wild wind across the landscape. She also depicted images of workers in the city during the difficult years of the Depression.

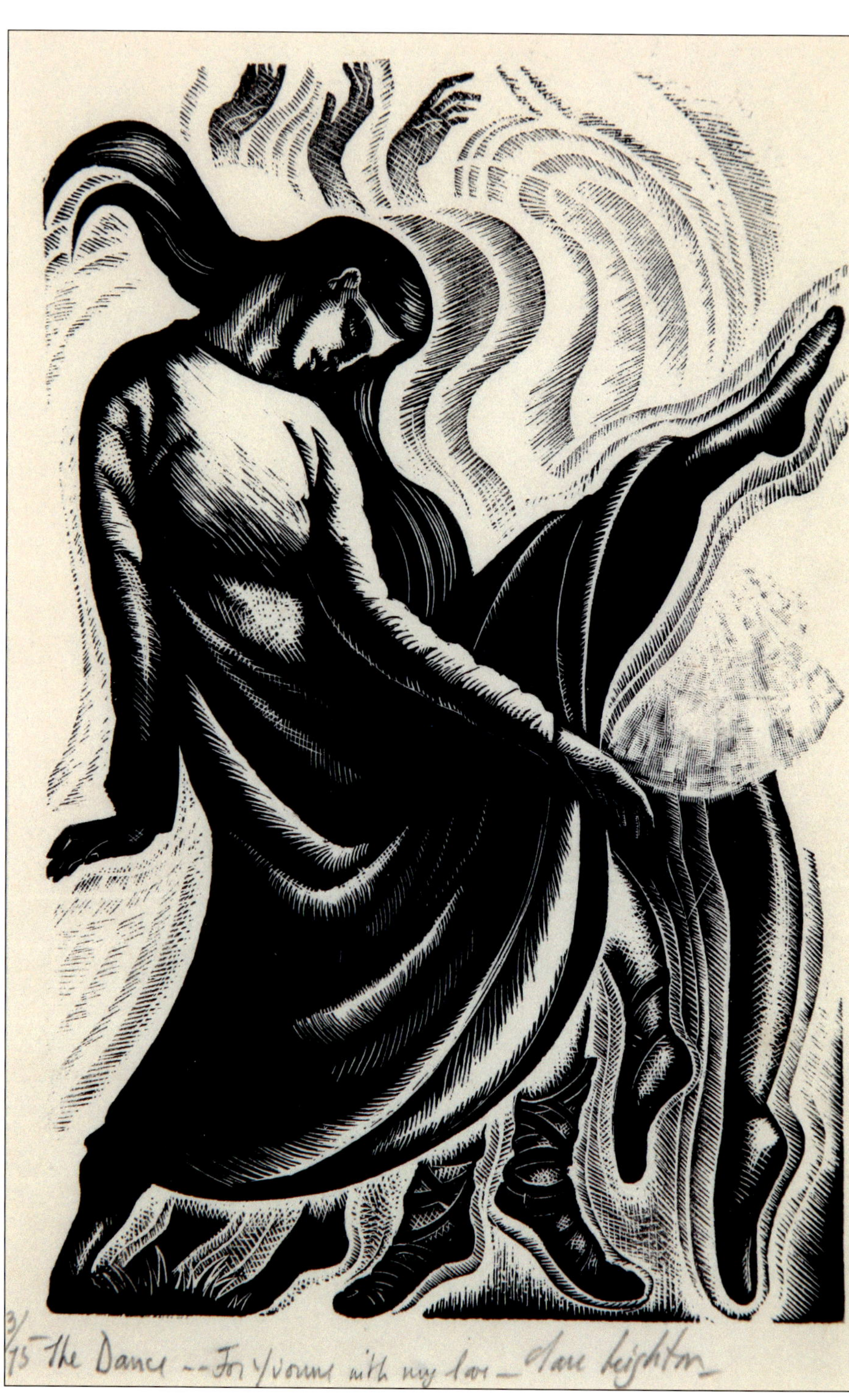

Clare Leighton, *The Dance* 3/75, n.d. Wood engraving on paper, 6½ × 4¾ inches. *Gift of Yvonne Backus*, 1988.

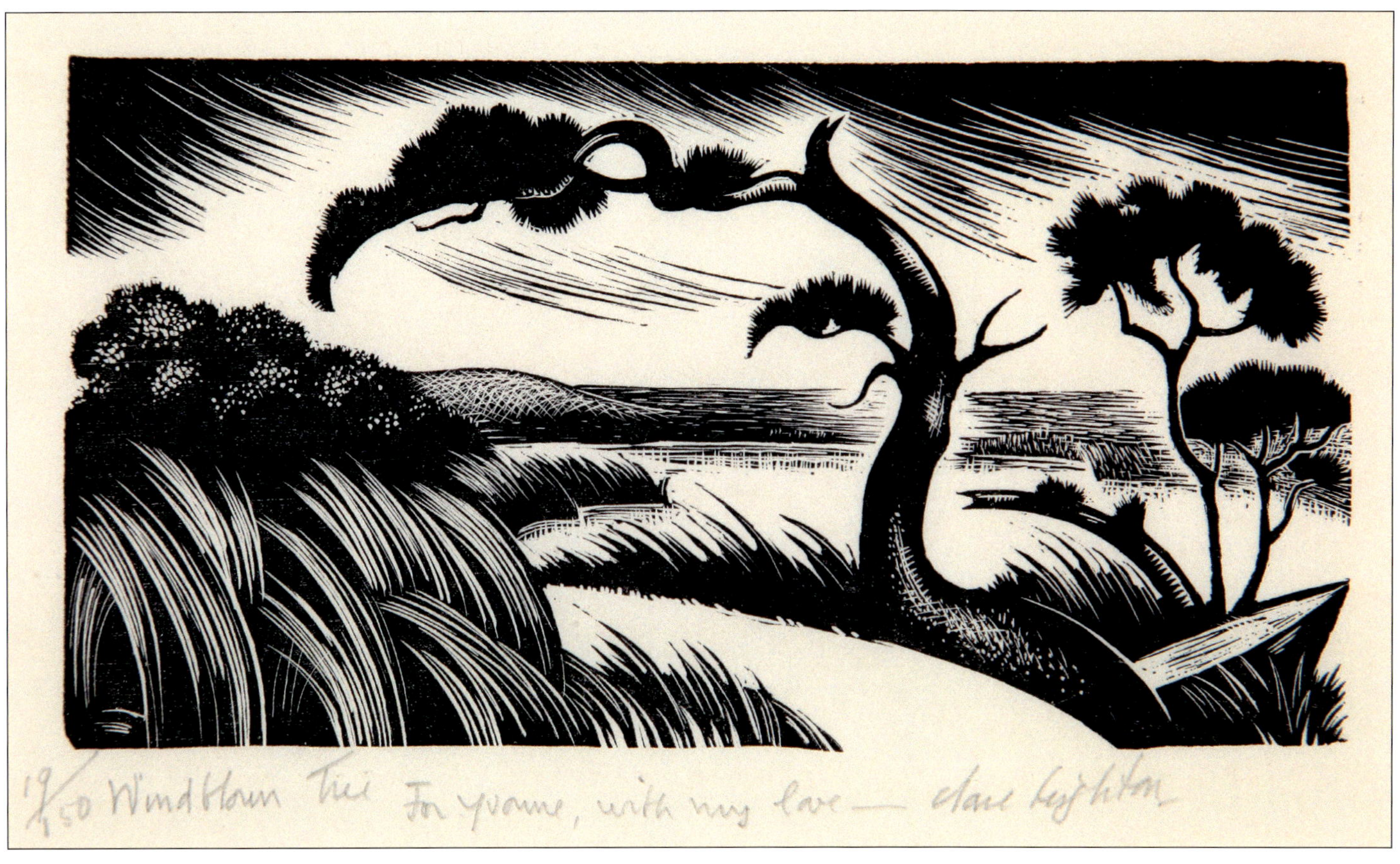

Clare Leighton, *Windblown Trees* 19/150, n.d. Wood engraving on paper, 4½ × 5½ inches. *Gift of Yvonne Backus*, 1988.

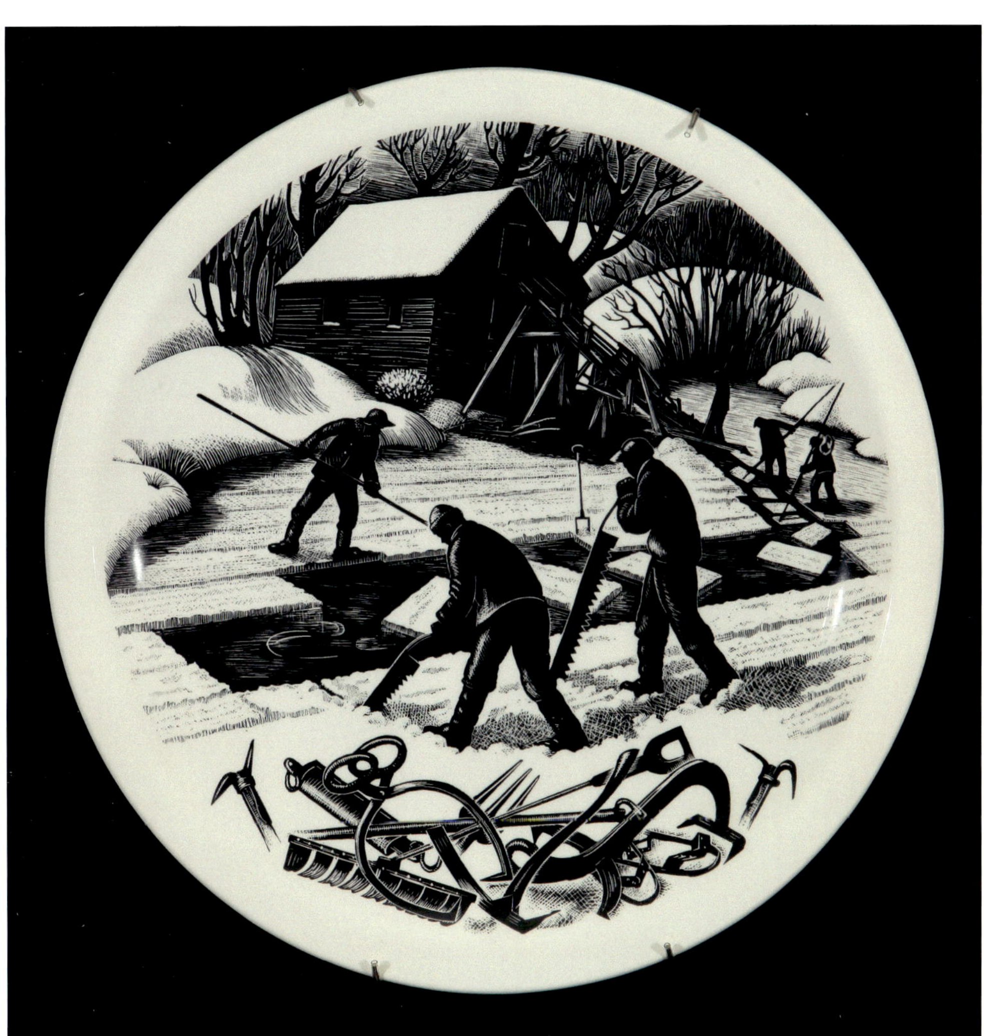

Clare Leighton, *Ice Cutting*, n.d.
Ceramic plate, 9½ diameter.
Gift of Yvonne Backus, 1988.

During the late 1920s and 1930s, Leighton visited the United States. In 1939, escaping Europe on the brink of war, she immigrated to America and in 1945 became a US citizen. She lived in Chapel Hill, North Carolina, and in the 1950s, Woodbury, Connecticut, while spending summers in Wellfleet on Cape Cod.

She wrote and illustrated books about the countryside and the people who worked on the land, among them, Thomas Hardy's *The Return of the Native*, Emily Bronte's *Wuthering Heights*, and *Where the Land Meets the Sea, The Time Line of Cape Cod*, published in 1954.

During her lifetime, she created more than 800 prints and illustrated as many as sixty-five books, among them some that she authored. In the 1950s, she created designs for Steuben Glass and Wedgwood, as well as stained-glass windows for churches in New England and for the Worcester Cathedral in England. A number of her ceramic plates are in the museum collection and include *Ice Cutting* and *Whaling,* which reference New England and the Cape.

Her prints are in museum collections, including the British Museum and Victoria and Albert Museum in London, the Metropolitan Museum of Art in New York, the Art Institute of Chicago, and the Museum of Fine Arts in Boston.

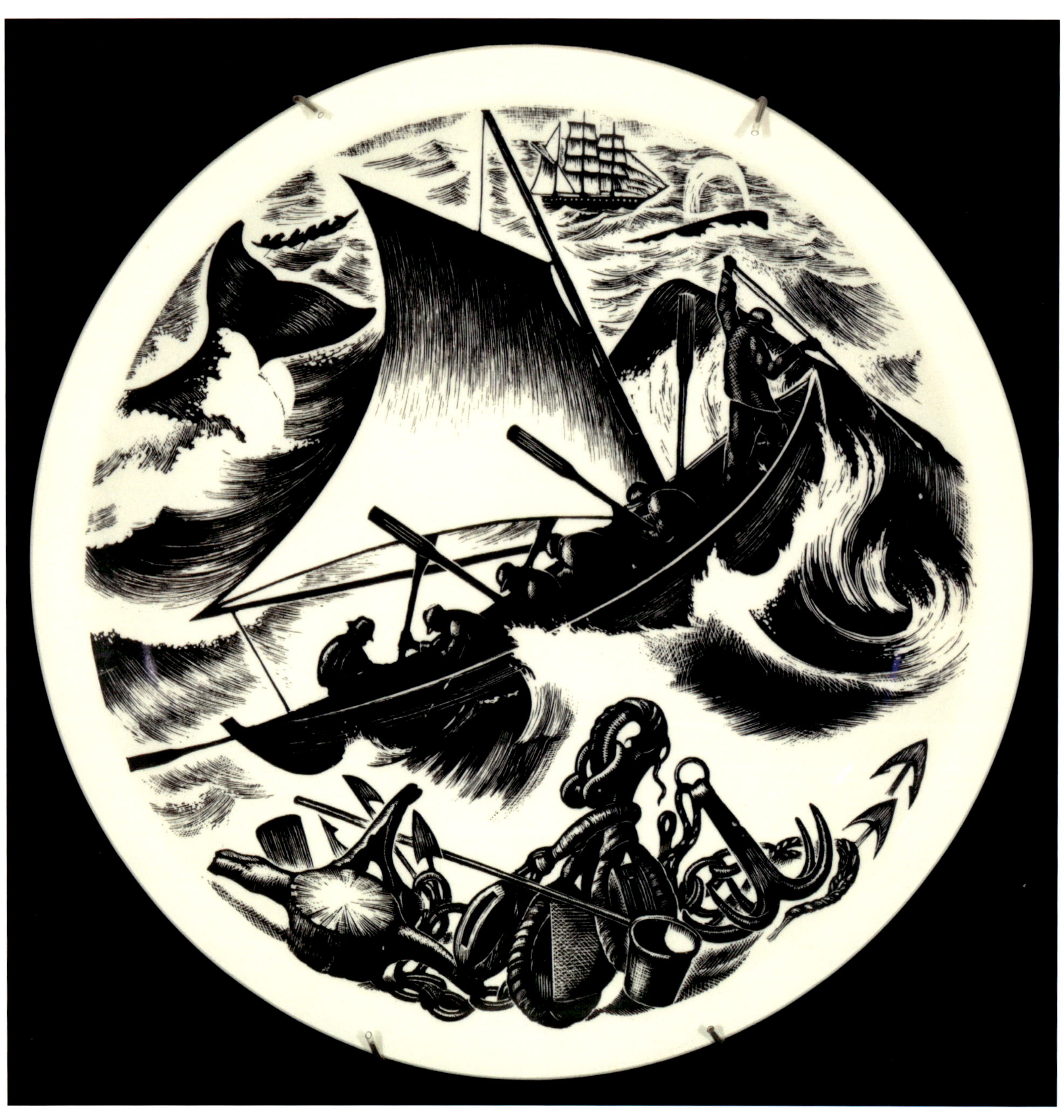

Clare Leighton, *Whaling*, n.d. Ceramic plate, 9½ diameter. *Gift of Yvonne Backus*, 1988.

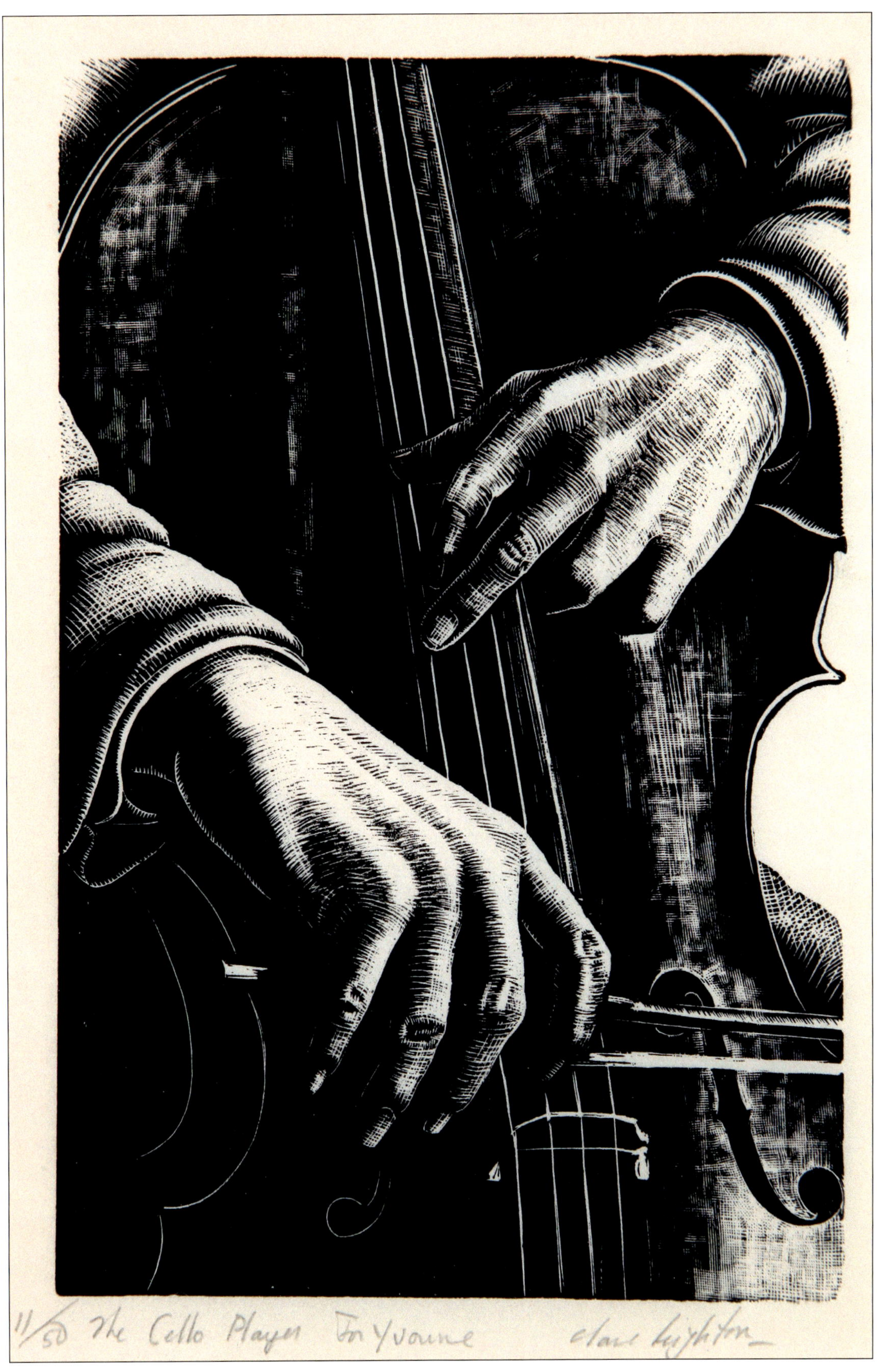

Clare Leighton, *The Cello Player* 11/50, n.d. Wood engraving on paper, 6¾ × 4½ inches. *Gift of Yvonne Backus*, 1988.

REGINALD MARSH
(1898–1954)

Reginald Marsh's paintings, drawings, and prints depict the growing metropolis of New York in the 1930s and '40s. He depicts ordinary scenes and sometimes the seedier sides of the city.

He was born in Paris to affluent American parents who were both artists. They returned to America and settled in New Jersey when Marsh was a child. Marsh graduated from Yale University's School of Art in 1920 and went to New York. He quickly succeeded as an illustrator working for the *New York Daily News* and *The New Yorker* magazine. In the 1920s Marsh studied at the Art Students League with Kenneth Hayes Miller, who focused on figures and the narrative content of a composition. Marsh also studied with Ashcan School artists John Sloan and George Luks, who influenced his approach to subject matter.

Intrigued by their view of New York, Marsh took up painting in 1923. He sketched and photographed the people on the streets, on subway trains, in nightclubs and bars, in burlesque theaters, on Coney Island beaches, and on the Bowery. Back in his studio, these sketches were the source of his paintings and prints.

Two works from the 1930s in the Cape Cod Museum of Art collection capture the mood of the Depression. *Third Avenue L*

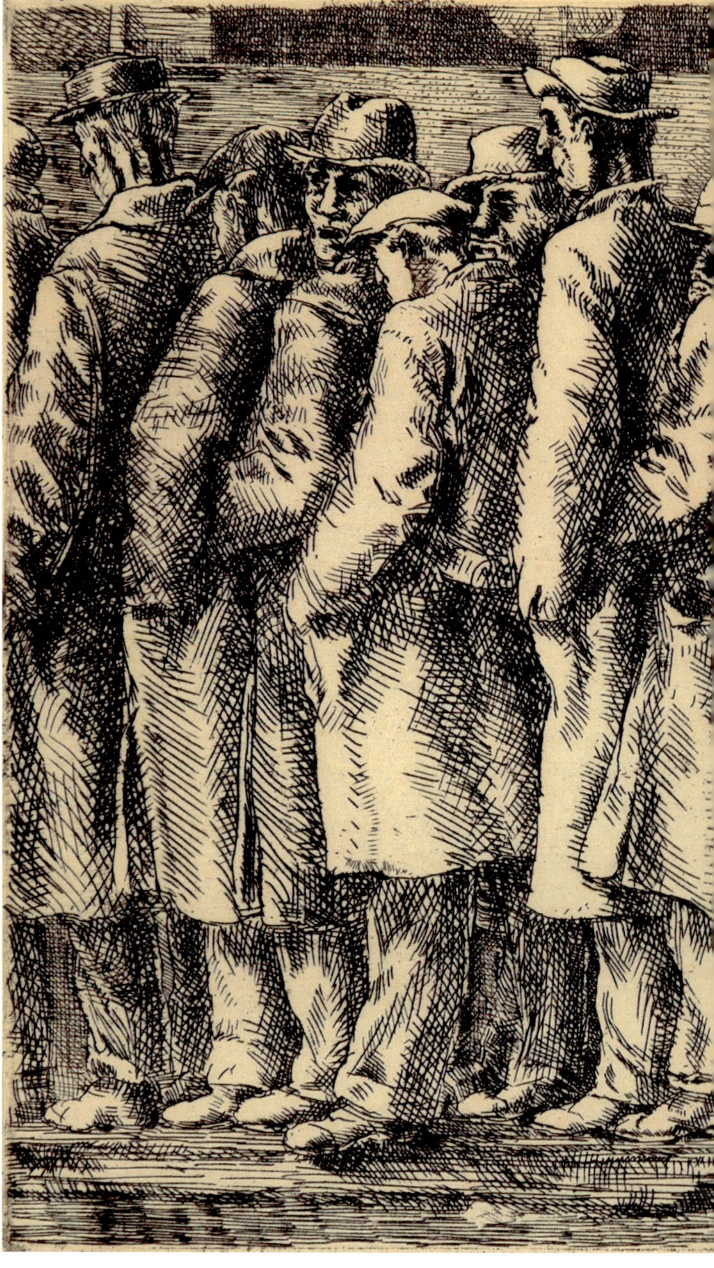

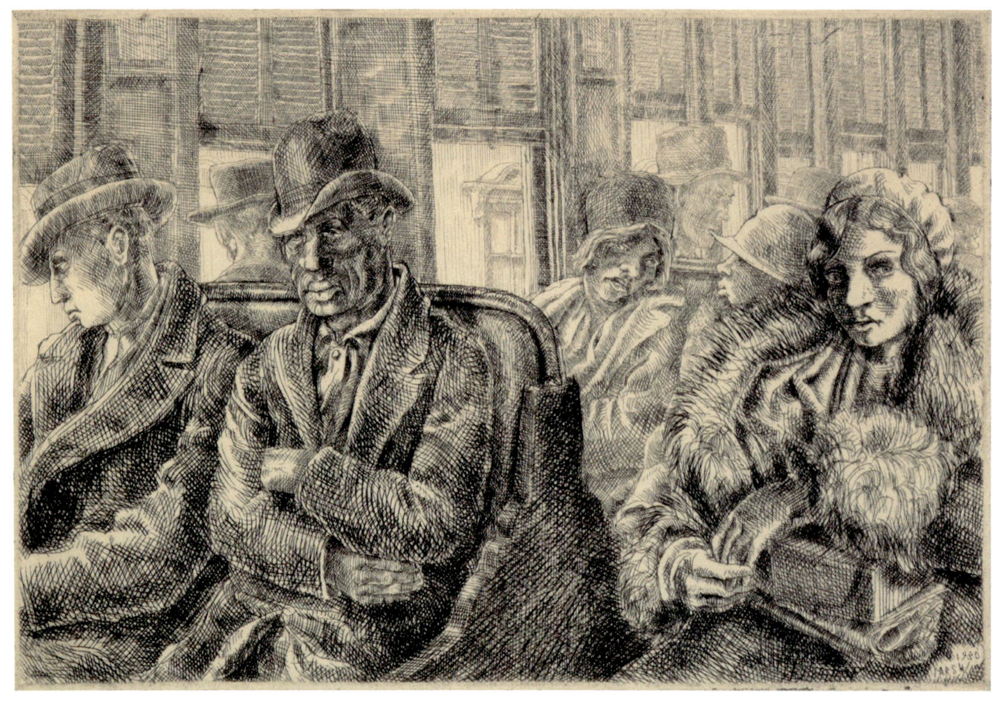

Reginald Marsh, *3rd Avenue L*, 1932. Etching on paper, 5⅞ × 8⅞ inches. *Gift of David Kaplan*, 2006.

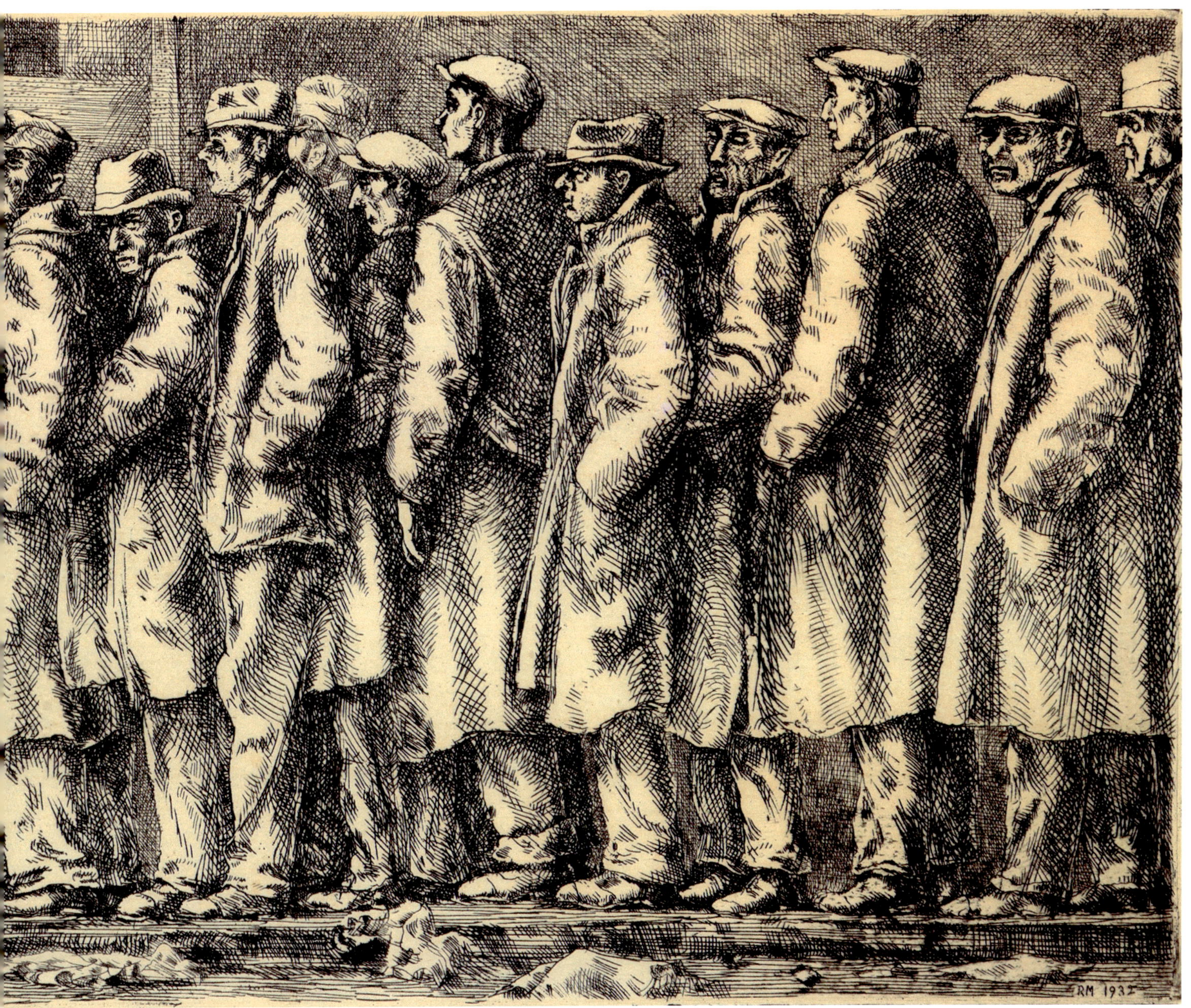

Reginald Marsh, *Bread Line, No One Has Starved*, 1930. Etching on paper, 7¼ × 12½ inches. *Gift of David Kaplan*, 2006.

depicts people on the train with somber faces, seemingly lost in the mundane. *Bread Line, No One Has Starved* shows a line of men with grim faces who are now in the position to depend on handouts.

Signs, newspaper headlines, and advertising images play a role in his art. His colors were used expressively, drab in the down-and-out scenes and boldly garish for his burlesque performers, chorus girls, and clowns. Marsh taught at the Art Students League and at the Moore Institute of Art, Science and Industry in Philadelphia.

His works are in the collections of major museums, including the Metropolitan Museum of Art and Whitney Museum of American Art in New York, the Philadelphia Museum of Art, the Art Institute of Chicago, the Museum of Fine Arts in Boston, and the National Gallery of Art and the Hirshhorn Museum and Sculpture Garden in Washington, DC.

HENRY HENSCHE
(1899–1992)

As Charles Hawthorne's assistant at the Cape Cod School of Art, Henry Hensche carried on his mentor's teaching approach at his Cape School of Art for over fifty years. An impressionist who revered nature's light and color, he was determined to teach his students the glories of his way.

Hensche was born in Germany, came to America in 1909, grew up in Chicago, and studied at the Art Institute of Chicago, where he heard about Hawthorne. He took classes at the National Academy of Fine Arts, the Art Students League, and the Beaux Arts Institute of Design before coming to Provincetown to study with Hawthorne in 1919; he became his teaching assistant in 1928.

Hensche first painted in the tonal academic tradition. His figure paintings had a narrative quality not unlike the work of the Ashcan School painters and also related to Hawthorne's depictions of Provincetown fishermen and their families. But soon color and light awakened him.

Two years after Hawthorne died in 1930, Hensche took over the school, dropping "Cod" from its name. A disciple of the Hawthorne method, Hensche taught an impressionistic approach, advocating Claude Monet's concepts of observing and painting the effects light produced on color. He was committed to *plein-air* painting. His subjects included still lifes, portraits, and landscapes. He was steadfast in his commitment to impressionism, which he considered the crowning achievement of all art.

Tea Time, in the Cape Cod Museum of Art collection, shows Hensche's light brushstroke. However, the two portraits in the museum collection truly capture his interest in impressionistic light. *Untitled* is a glittering image of a woman. *Mud Head Study of Helen and Bob* shows how, when Hensche posed his subjects with the sun behind, the facial features were blurred, causing viewers to call them "mud heads."

His works are included in the collections of the Oklahoma City Museum of Art and the Butler Institute of American Art in Youngstown, Ohio.

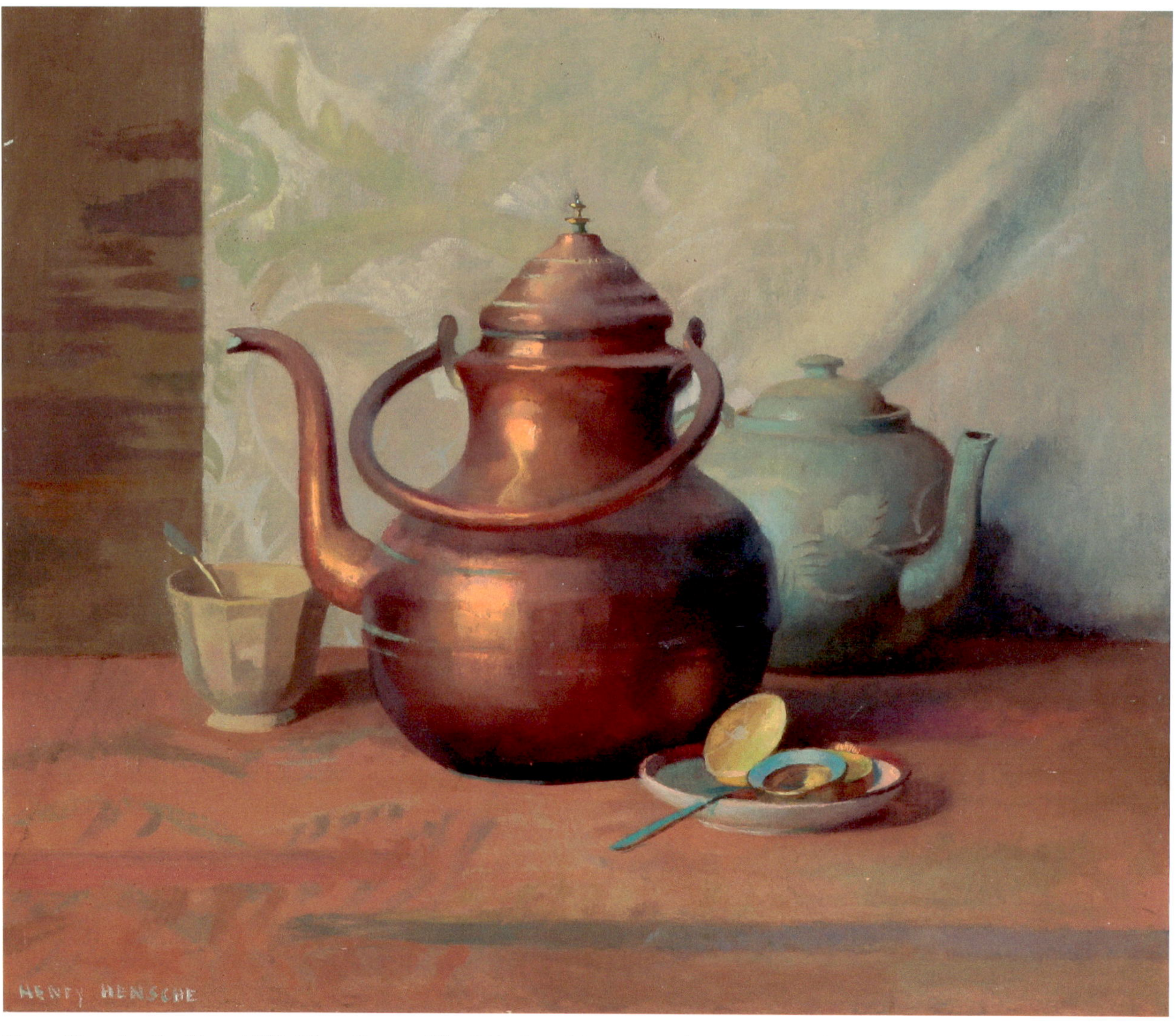

Henry Hensche, *Tea Time,* 1976. Oil on Canvas, 20 × 24 inches. *Museum purchase courtesy of Frank Hogan*, 1993.

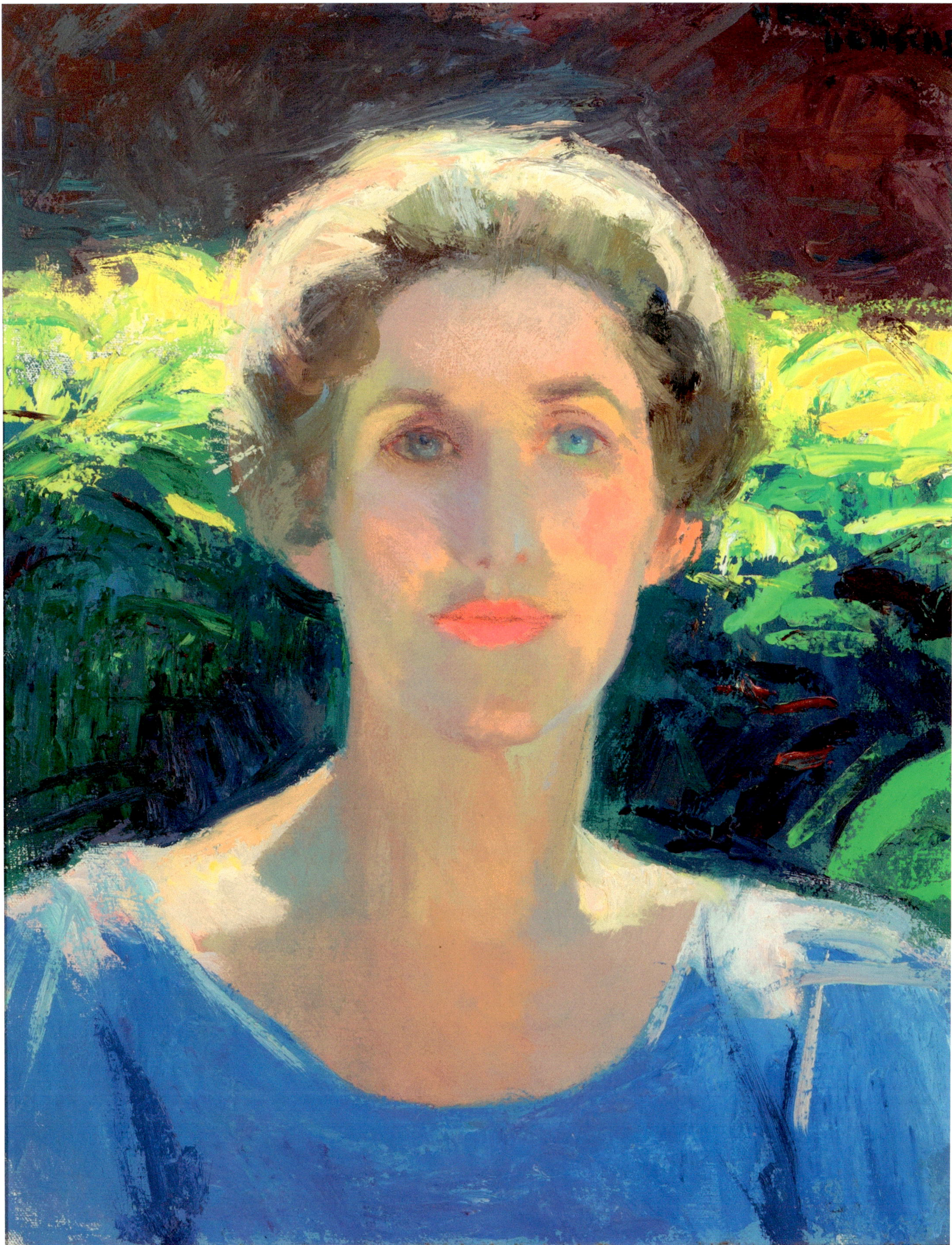

Henry Hensche, *Untitled*, n.d. Oil on canvas, 19¼ × 15½ inches. *Anonymous gift in honor of Angela Bilski*, 2009.

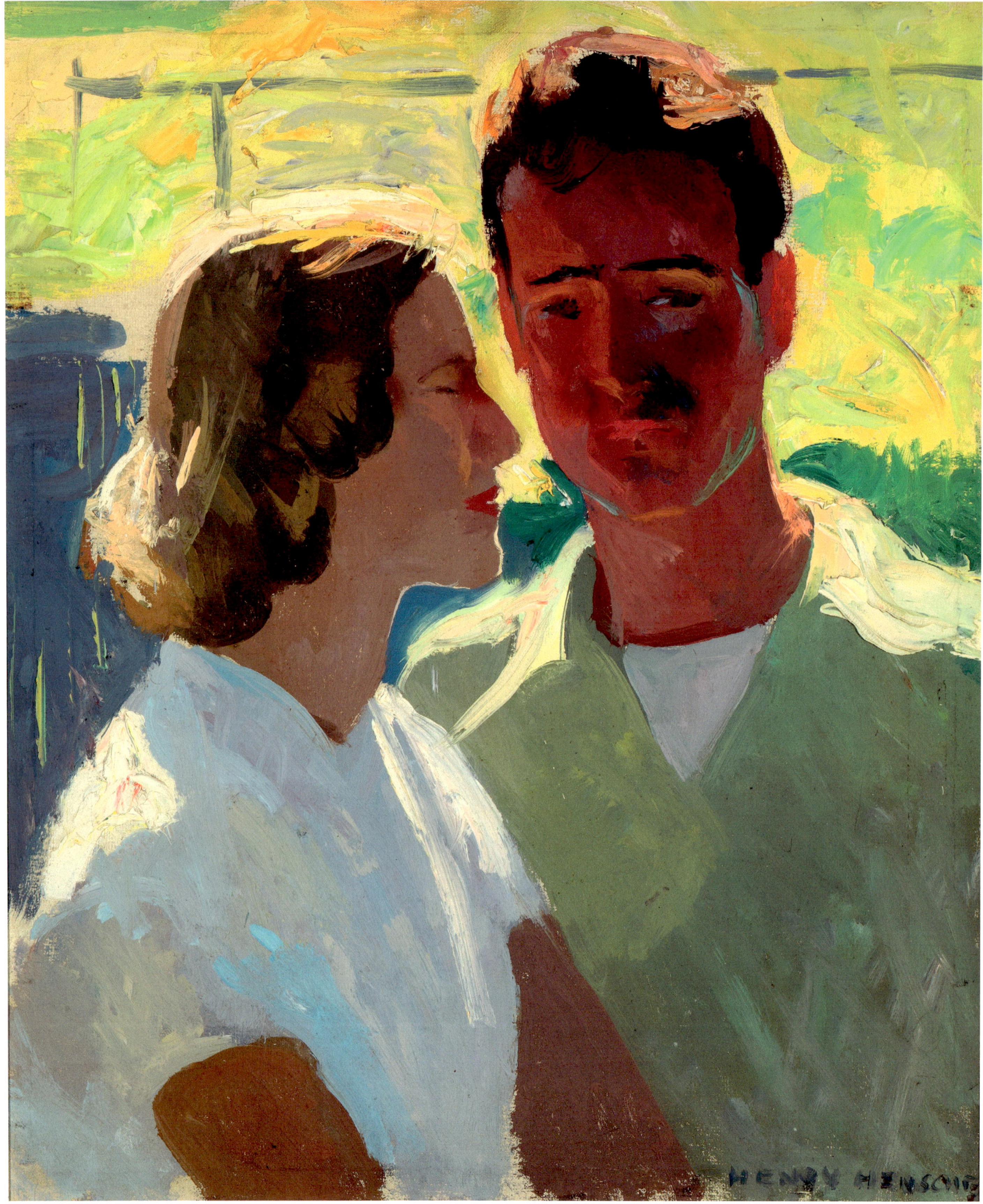

Henry Hensche, *Mudhead Study of Helen and Bob,* 1949. Oil on canvas, $21\frac{3}{8} \times 25\frac{3}{8}$ inches.
Gift of Robert Douglas and Elizabeth Hunter, 1998.

JACK TWORKOV
(1900–1982)

Jack Tworkov was always exploring new expressions in his art, from his early figurative work, through his abstract expressionist period, and finally to the late geometric paintings.

He was born in Biala, Poland, in 1900 and immigrated to the United States in 1913. He enrolled at the National Academy of Design in New York City and studied with Charles Hawthorne. In Provincetown, he took classes with Ross Moffett and met Karl Knaths. He also studied at the Art Students League.

Tworkov's early work was figurative, but by the 1940s, he came under the influence of cubism. By the late '40s he had found abstract expressionism. Works of this period have an impulsive, gestural intensity. Brash movements of line and color played across his paintings in the 1950s and '60s. His canvases are boisterous with both large and small brushstrokes and calligraphic sweeps that depict a rhythmic dance.

Tworkov had a long history in Provincetown. In 1924, he came to Provincetown to study with Hawthorne. In the 1920s and '30s, Tworkov spent summers at the Cape-tip, where he regularly exhibited at the Provincetown Art Association and lobbied for a more modern approach.

Like so many artists during the Depression, Tworkov worked for the WPA's Federal Art Project and during the Second World War was a tool designer. After the war, he became part of the abstract expressionist movement. In New York, he had a studio next to Willem de Kooning's. After a twenty-year absence from Provincetown, Tworkov returned in 1954, and he and his wife Wally purchased a house in the town's West End, where he lived and painted half the year.

De Kooning's influence is apparent in some of Tworkov's paintings, but it was Knaths who had the stronger, more lasting impact. By 1948, Tworkov was teaching at Queens College in New York and American University in Washington, DC, and he had his first one-man show at the Baltimore Museum of Art. In 1963, Tworkov became chairman of the art department at Yale University and in 1964 had a retrospective at the Whitney Museum of American Art. It was around this time that his work took a sharp 180-degree turn away from the spontaneity and personal explorations of abstract expressionism. He was searching for structure and he became interested in minimalism. His 1978 *TL #6 168/250*, in the Cape Cod Museum of Art collection, is an example of his minimalist style.

By focusing on geometry, Tworkov wanted to tap into a universality. In his need to simplify, he reduced the elements in his paintings and limited the use of color. His work took on a formality that incorporated defined grids and mathematical precision. His compositions became controlled, ordered, and meditative.

In 1982 in the spring before he died, he had an exhibition of his work at the Guggenheim Museum. His art is in major museum collections, including the Art Institute of Chicago, the Museum of Modern Art and Guggenheim Museum in New York, the Tate Modern in London, and the National Gallery of Art in Washington, DC.

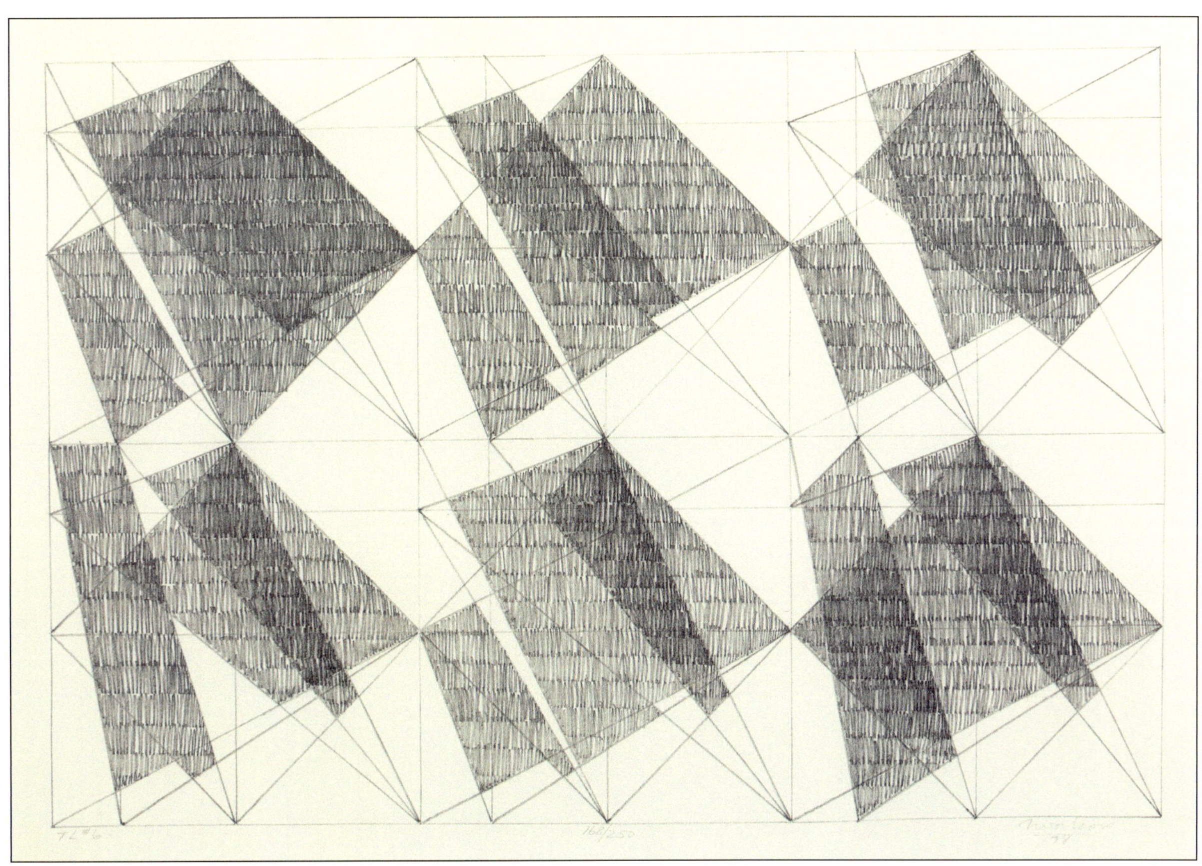

Jack Tworkov, *TL #6* 168/250, 1978. Graphite and lithograph on paper, 16½ × 22½ inches. *Anonymous gift*, 2009.

THOMAS EASTWOOD
(1902–1957)

Born in New Bedford, Massachusetts, Thomas Eastwood studied at Pratt Institute, Swain School of Design, and the Art Students League, where he worked under Thomas Hart Benton. Eastwood pursued a variety of mediums, including oil, egg tempera, gouache, pen and ink, and lithography.

Influenced by the Ashcan School, he depicted New York scenes of the subway, the East River, Washington Square, and pushcarts. His egg tempera paintings *East 19th Street* and *8th Ave. Subway*, in the Cape Cod Museum of Art collection, are modernist views, playing up the geometric elements of the scenes.

Eastwood never tired of exploring various subjects: landscapes, seascapes, figures, and still lifes. An inveterate experimenter, he also dabbled in surrealism and cubism. *Still Life* and *War Memorabilia,* also in the museum collection, show his bow to Paul Cézanne and the cubists. *War Memorabilia* goes even further than *Still Life*, rich in patterns and dallying with abstraction.

As an illustrator, Eastwood did many spot drawings referencing Manhattan for the *New Yorker* magazine, a large number of which are in the museum collection.

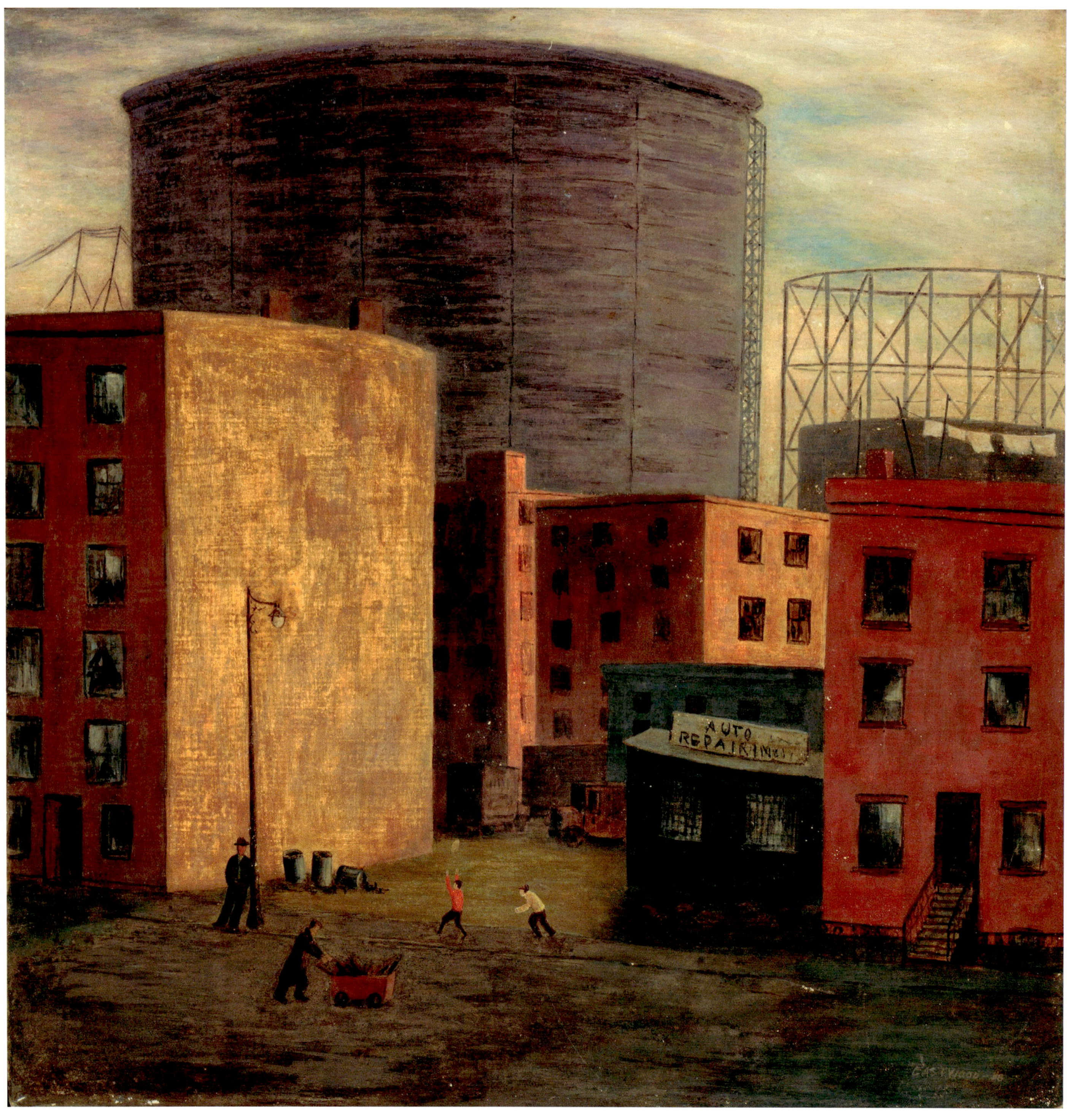

Thomas Eastwood, *East 19th Street,* 1938. Egg tempera on pressed panel, 16¾ × 16¾ inches. *Gift of Evelyn Eastwood*, 1989.

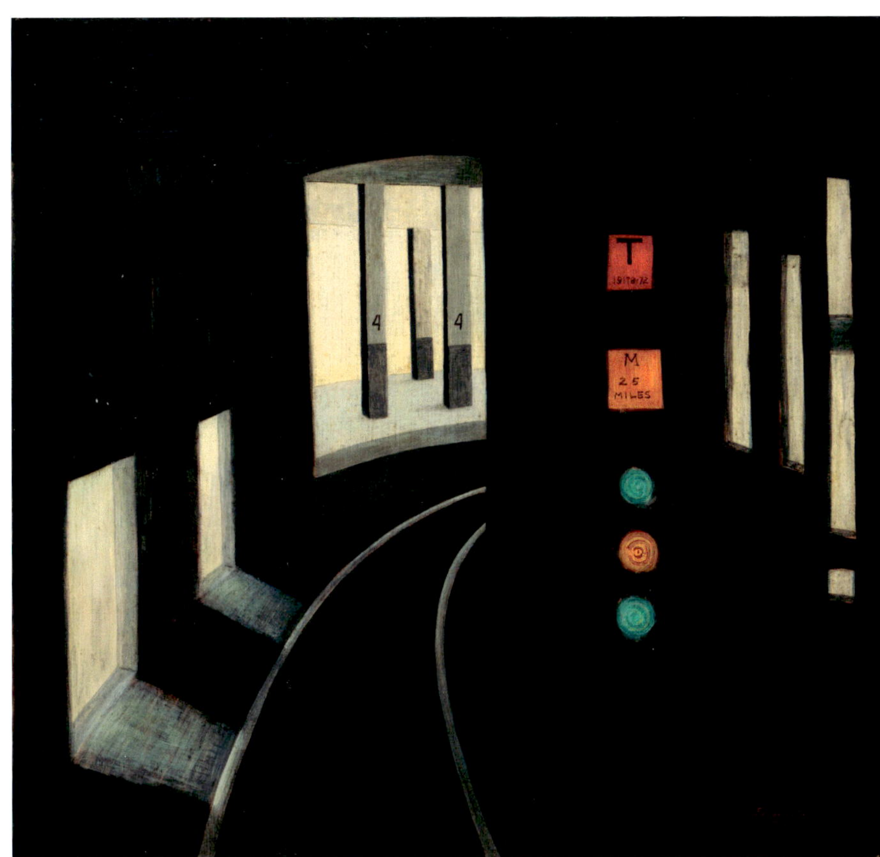

Thomas Eastwood, *8th Avenue Subway*, 1937. Egg tempera on board, 13 × 14 inches. *Gift of Evelyn Eastwood*, 1990.

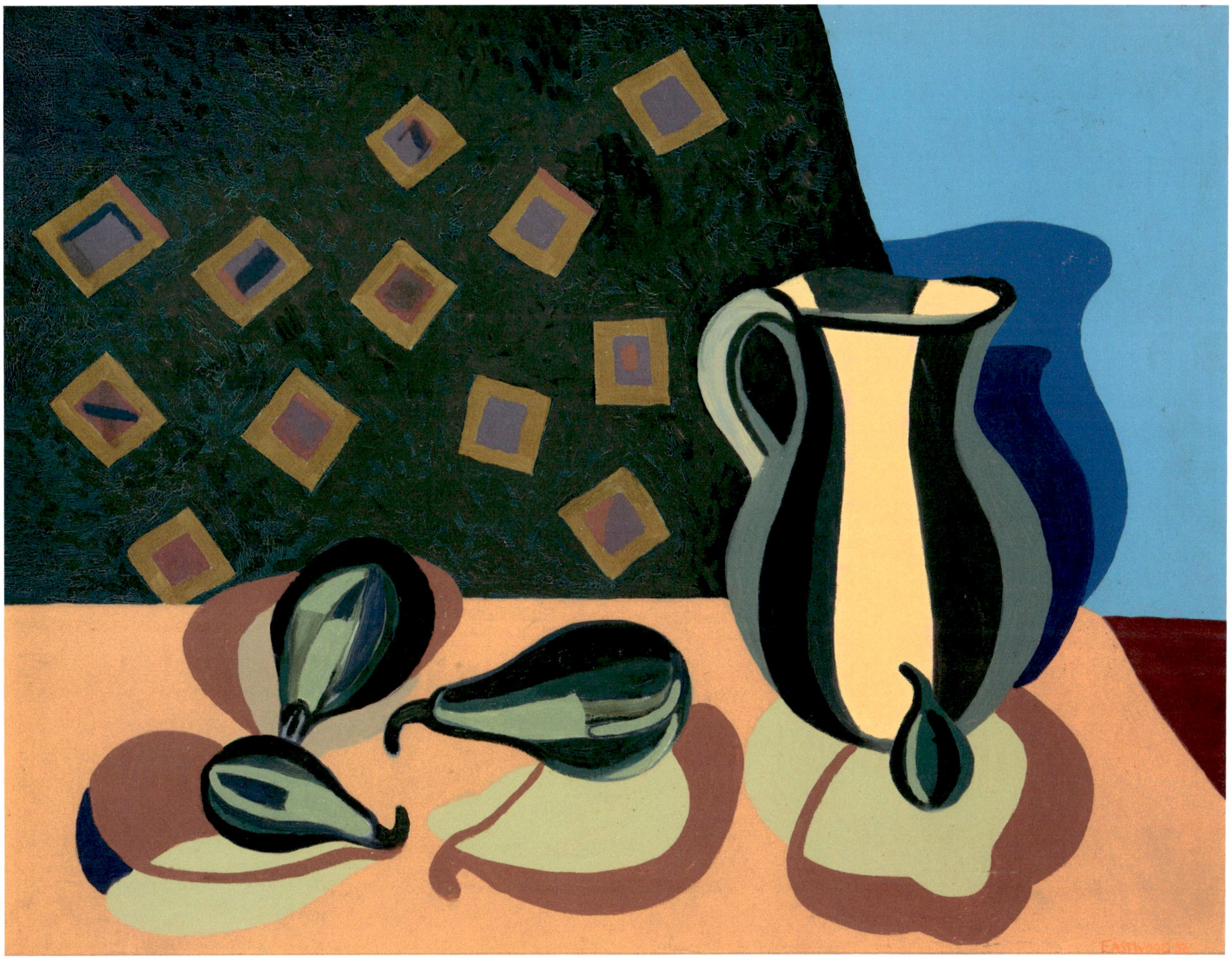

Thomas Eastwood, *Still Life,* 1956. Oil on canvas, 8½ × 11½ inches. *Gift of Evelyn Eastwood*, 1990.

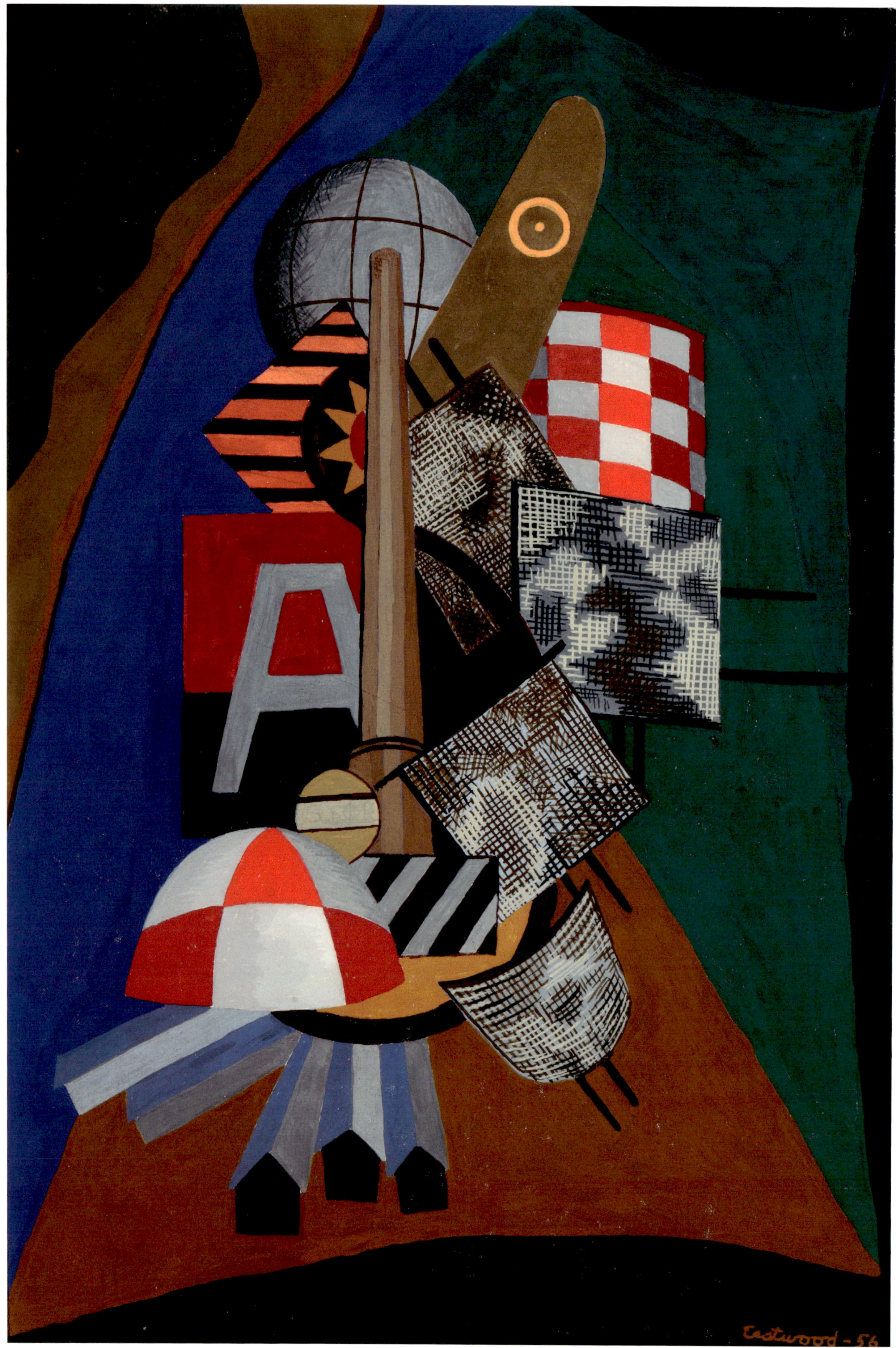

Thomas Eastwood, *War Memorabilia,* 1940s. Gouache on paper, 18 × 13 inches. *Gift of Evelyn Eastwood*, 1990.

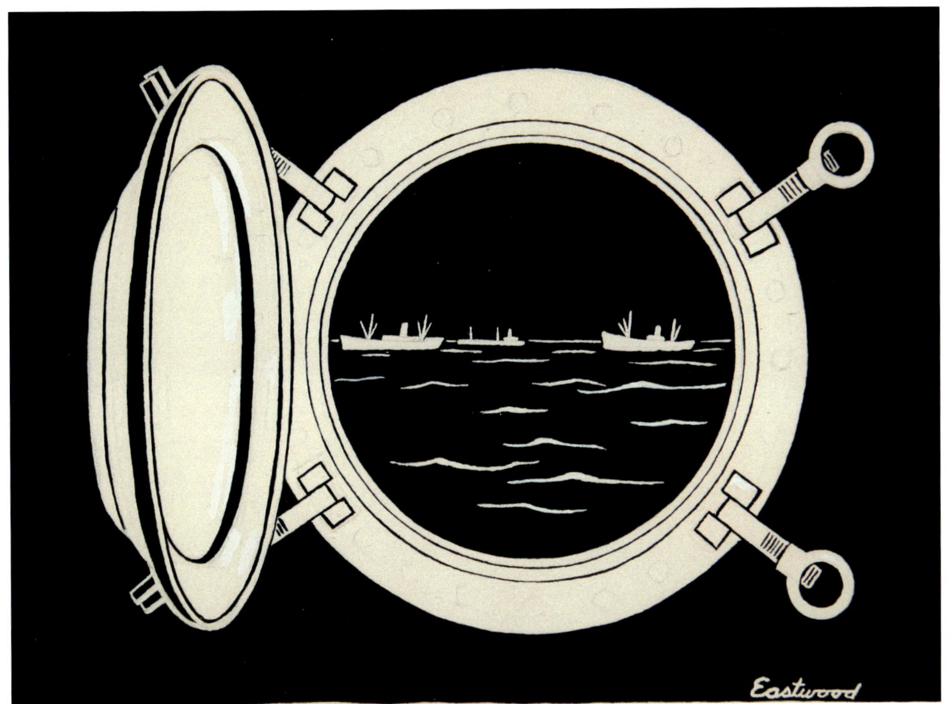

Thomas Eastwood, *Port Hole,* 1930s–1940s. Ink on paper, 5 × 7 inches. *Gift of Evelyn Eastwood,* 1990. *Courtesy of* The New Yorker *magazine*.

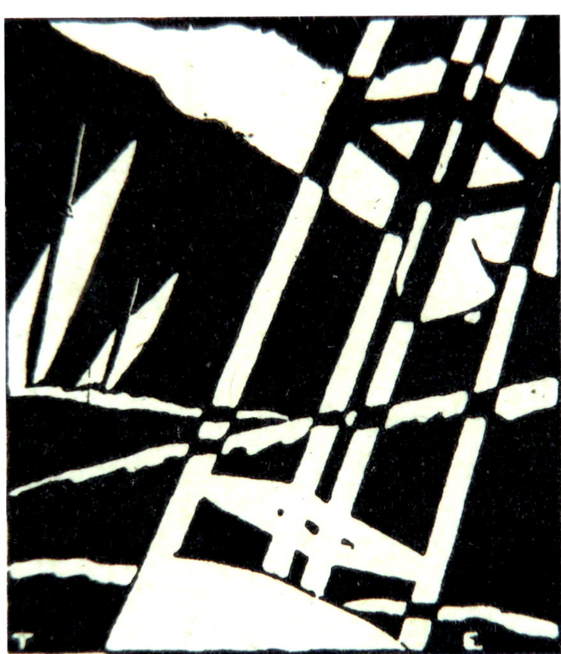

Thomas Eastwood, *Buoy*, 1930s–1940s. Ink on paper, 1 × 1 inch. *Gift of Evelyn Eastwood*, 1990. *Courtesy of* The New Yorker *magazine*.

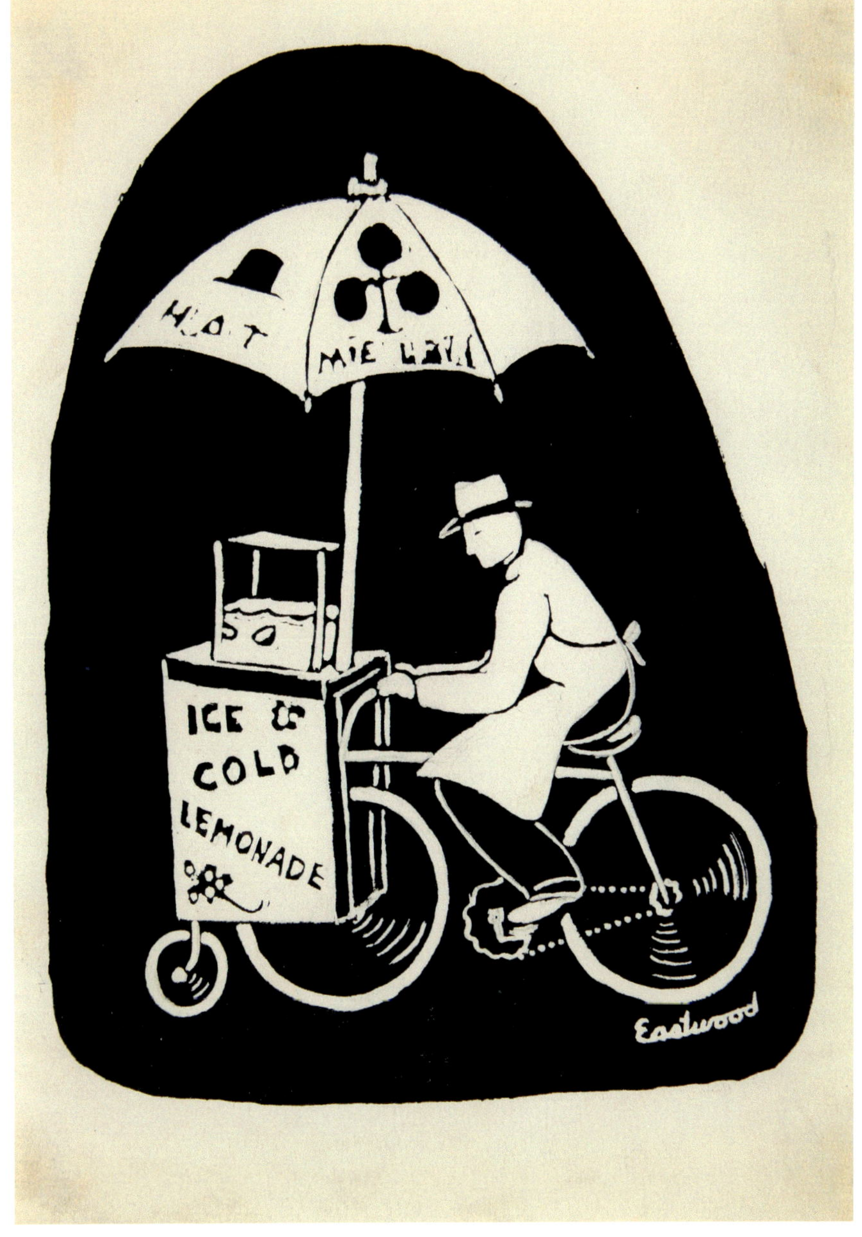

Thomas Eastwood, *Ice Cold Lemonade,* n.d. Ink on paper, 6½ × 5 inches. *Gift of Evelyn Eastwood*, 1989. *Courtesy of* The New Yorker *magazine*.

WILLIAM FREED
(1902–1984)

William Freed left Poland in 1922 for the United States. He studied at the Educational Alliance and the Art Students League. He became interested in modern European painters, who, at the time, were not in vogue in America. Paul Cézanne and Vincent van Gogh influenced his work.

Both Freed and his soon-to-be wife, artist Lillian Orlowsky, worked under the Federal Art Project of the Works Progress Administration. Freed met Hans Hofmann through Orlowsky, who already was studying with him in his New York school, and Freed began to attend his classes. Hofmann brought with him from Europe the modern trends associated with cubism and fauvism, and Freed studied with him for ten years in New York and Provincetown.

Freed and Orlowsky were married in 1942 and two years later they came to Provincetown, where they became active members of the art colony. Hofmann's influence is apparent in Freed's work as he moved on in the 1940s from representational art to still lifes with cubist distortions and riotous colors.

By the 1950s, Freed dipped into the excitement of abstract expressionism, often including geometric forms—circles, diamonds, and rectangles—that highlighted volume in the two-dimensional space and that have strong connections to Hofmann. *Resounding Echo #2*, in the Cape Cod Museum of Art collection, is an example of that approach. Freed's *Impression*, also in the museum collection, is a free-form abstraction, with dynamic rhythms and rich colors also inspired by Hofmann.

His works are in the collections of major museums, including the Metropolitan Museum of Art and Whitney Museum of American Art in New York, and the Smithsonian American Art Museum in Washington, DC.

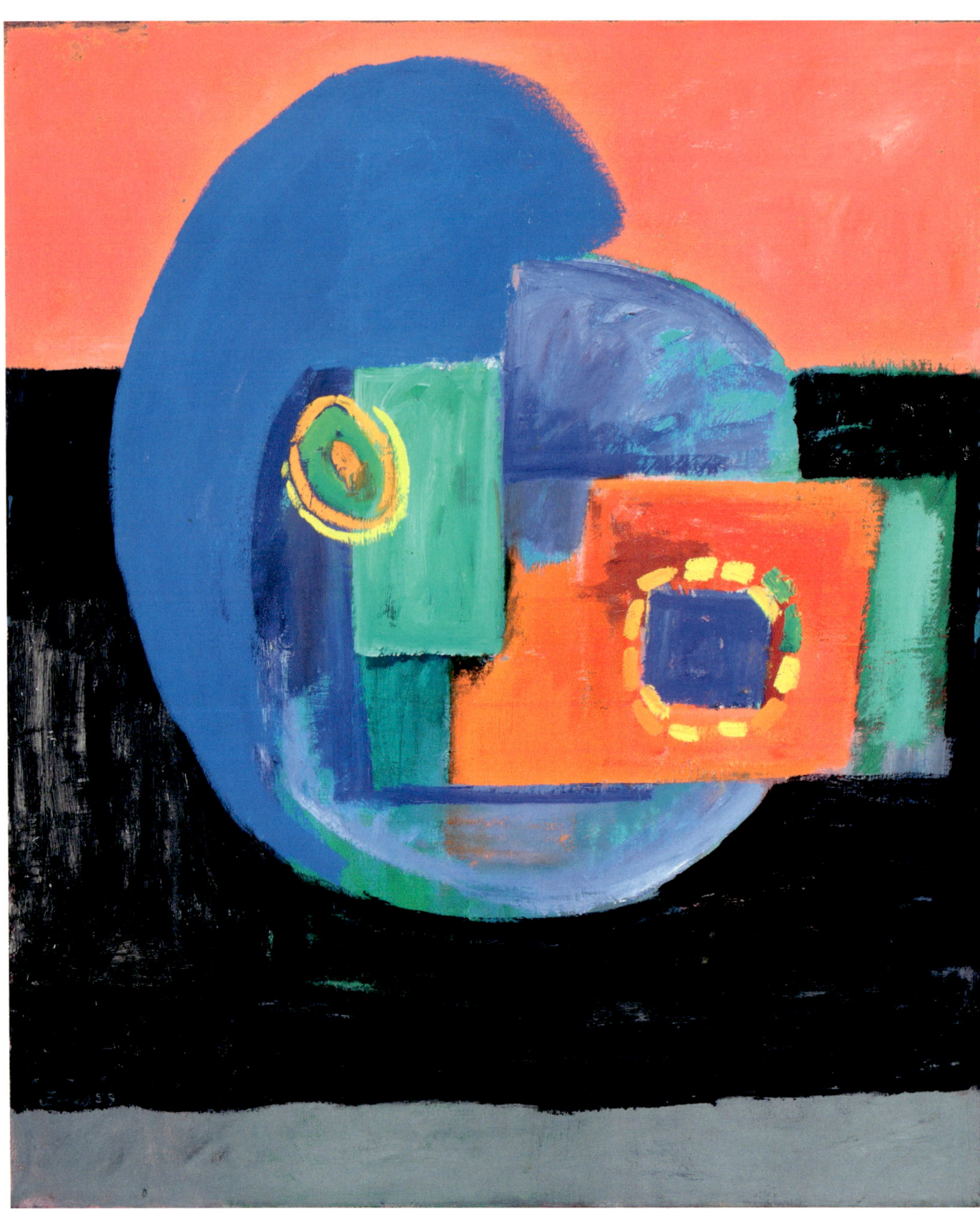

William Freed, *Resounding Echo #2,* 1959. Oil on canvas, 40 × 34 inches. *Gift of the Estate of Lillian Orlowsky Freed*, 2003.

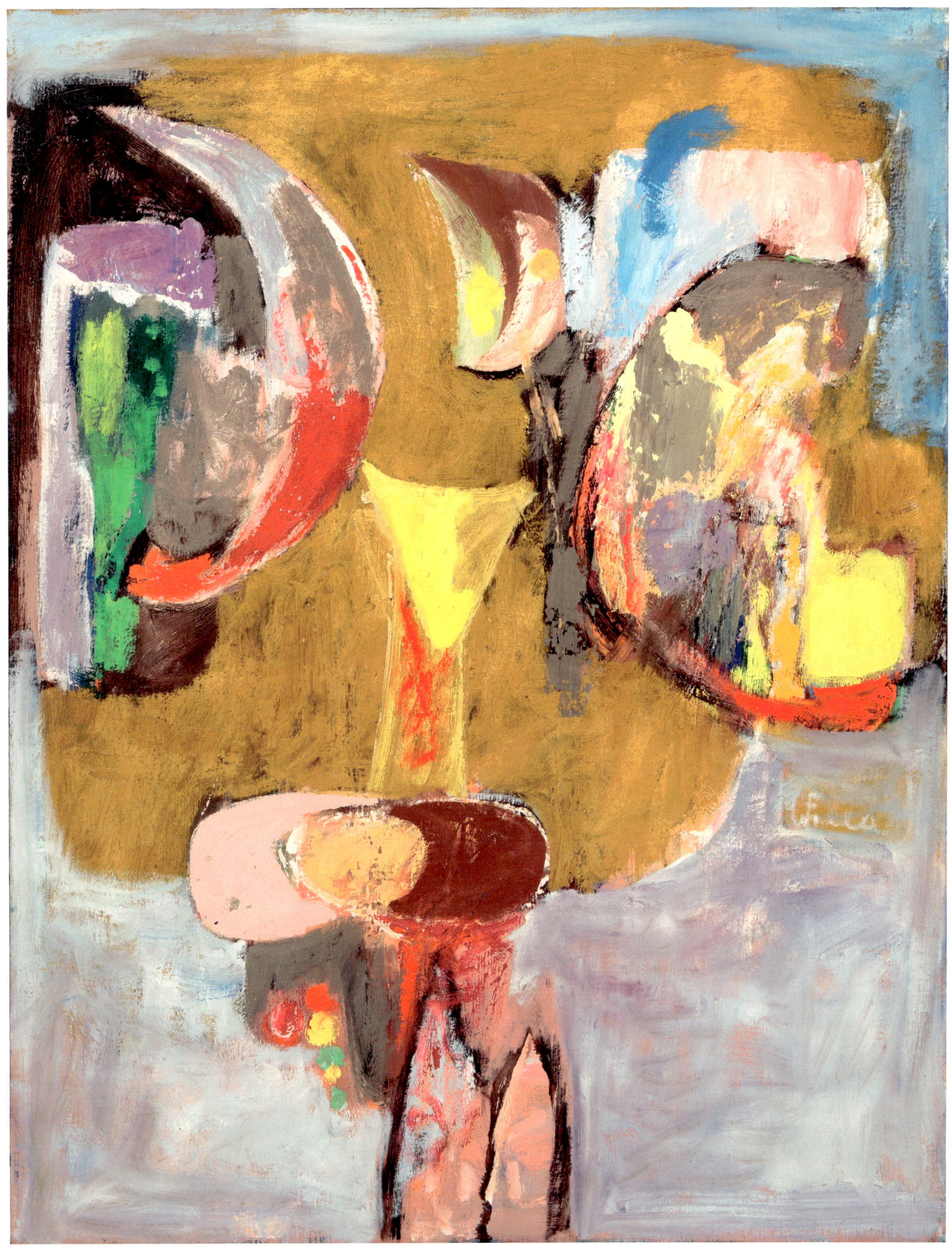

William Freed, *Impression,* 1958. Oil on canvas, 35¾ × 28 inches. *Gift of Lillian Orlowsky and William Freed*, 1995.

WILLIAM LITTLEFIELD
(1902–1969)

Like many artists of his time, William Littlefield began as a representational artist, honing his skills doing figures, portraits, and landscapes. However, by the 1950s he had turned to abstraction and became associated with abstract expressionism, which he approached in various ways.

He was born in Roxbury, Massachusetts, and went to Harvard University, where he studied at the Fogg Museum. He later studied with Adeline Wolever, an impressionist who brought to him the influences of Boston School painters Edmund Tarbell, Frank Benson, and William Paxton.

For four years, Littlefield studied in Europe, and in 1929, he had some success in France with the publication of a portfolio of six black-and-white lithographs of boxers. Later that year he returned to America, lived in Boston, and spent time at his parents' home in Falmouth on Cape Cod, where the landscape took up his interest. At the time his work was influenced by French artists Gustave Courbet and Jean-Baptiste-Camille Corot and is noted for its loose painterly style, associated with impressionism. *North Street, Woods Hole*, in the Cape Cod Museum of Art collection, is one of those images of a nearby town.

Littlefield was included in the first biennial at the Whitney Museum of American Art in New York in 1932 and in a 1936 Museum of Modern Art exhibition. His work at the time included Greek and Roman mythological themes. He also did portraits and figurative work. He worked for a time on the Massachusetts Federal Art Project, in the 1930s, producing oil paintings of local buildings and landscapes, especially around Woods Hole, and painted a mural for Falmouth High School.

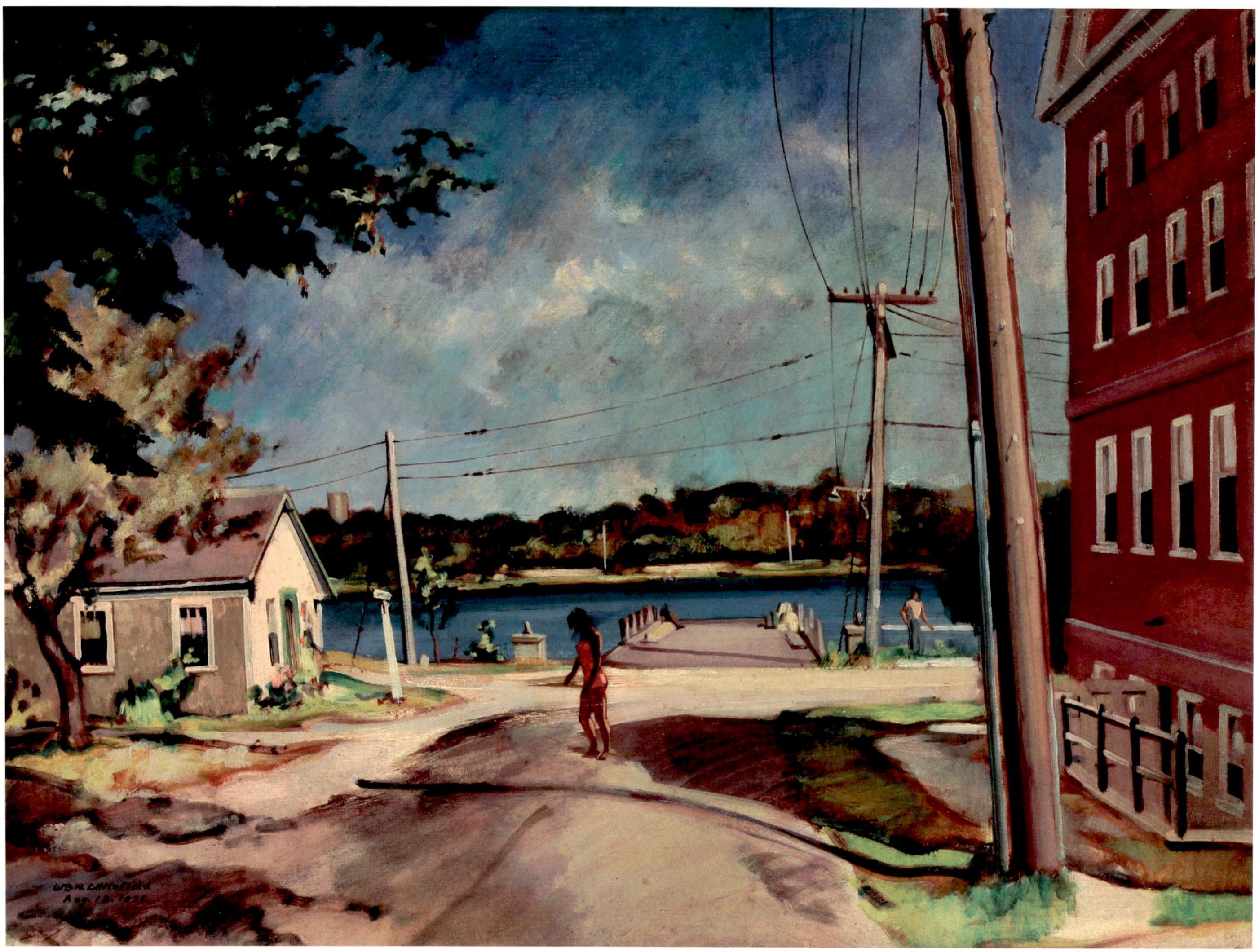

William Littlefield, *North Street, Woods Hole,* August 12, 1935. Oil on canvas, 29¾ × 32¾ inches. *Gift of Anne Bengston*, 1986.

After his military service during World War II, he moved to Falmouth. A co-founder of the Cape Cod Art Association, he exhibited at the modern juried show at the Provincetown Art Association in 1949. Littlefield studied in New York with Morris Davidson beginning in 1951 and with Hans Hofmann in Provincetown in 1952.

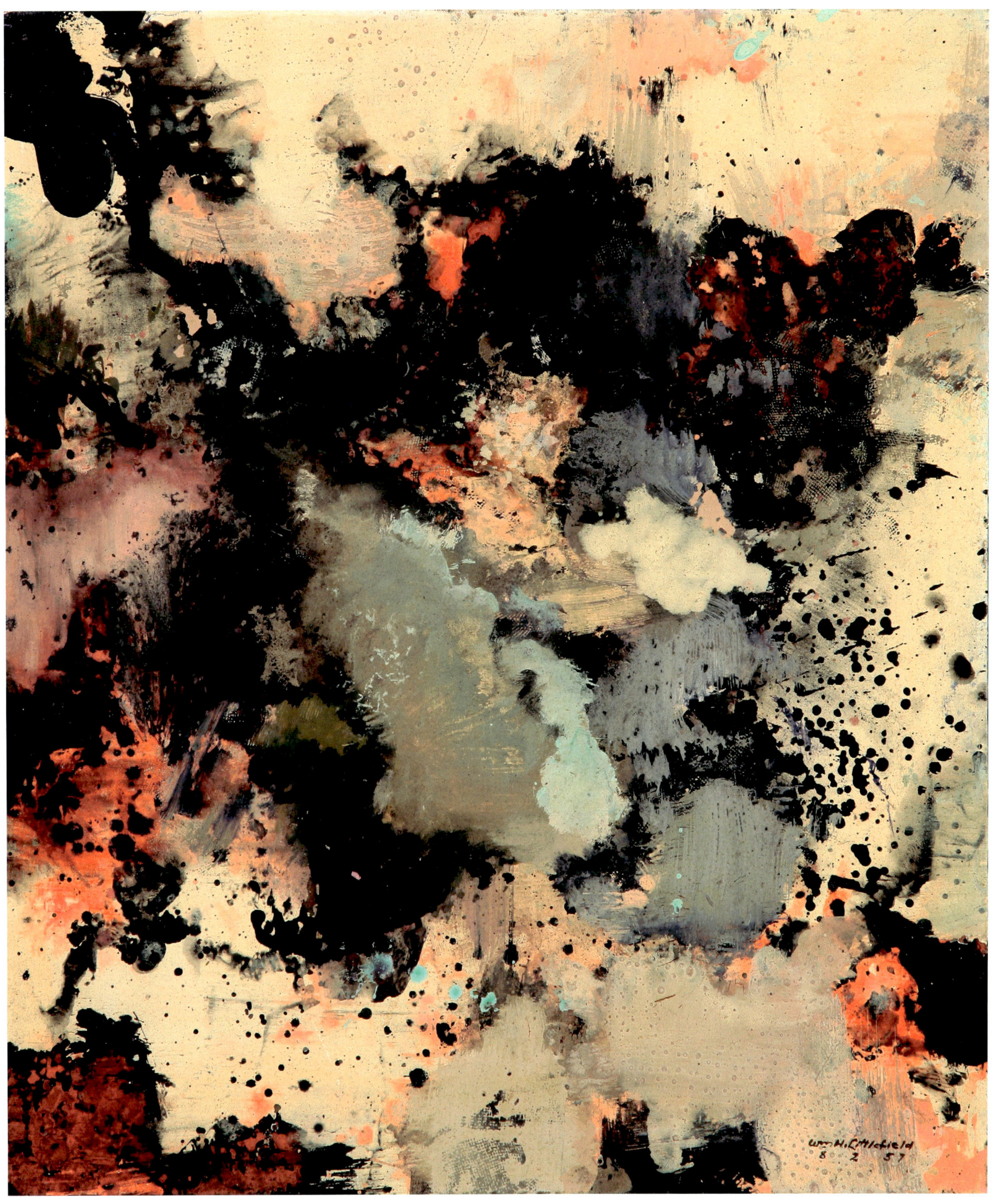

William Littlefield, *Beginning and End of Movement*, August 2, 1957. Oil on masonite, 14 × 16 inches. *Anonymous gift*, 1993.

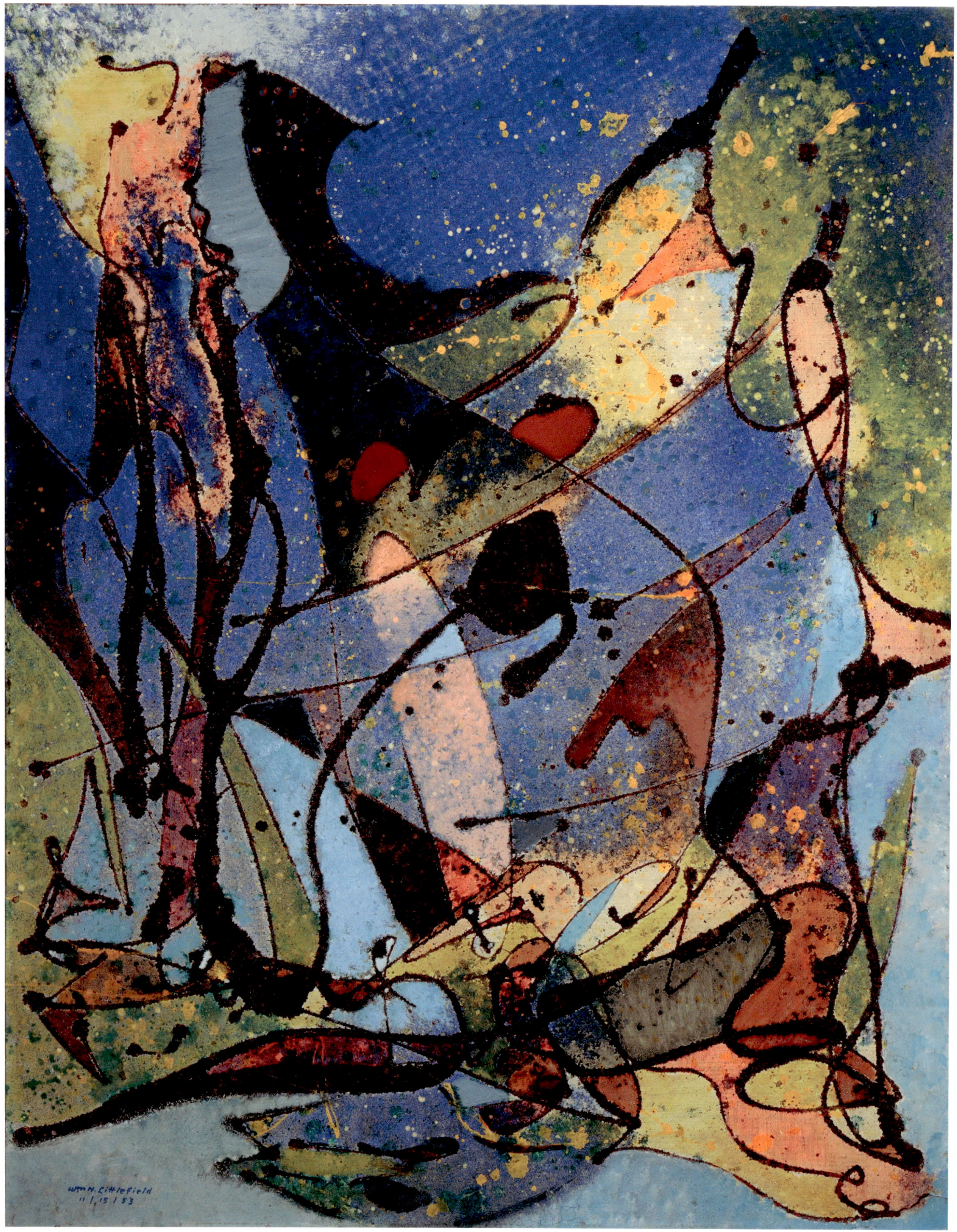

William Littlefield, *Landscape Fantasy,* November 15, 1953. Oil on canvas, 36 × 29 inches. *Gift of Anne Bengston*, 1986.

By 1950, he began working in abstraction and became associated with abstract expressionism. His art covers a spectrum of approaches. In some pieces there is the influence of cubism and hard-edged geometric abstraction. Other works are loose and gestural, as are *Landscape Fantasy*, a delightful flight of fancy abstraction, and *Beginning and End of Movement*, an intense, expressionist painting, both in the museum collection. In still others, organic forms float in a puzzle-like composition of rich colors, as with *Noesis*.

Littlefield worked in a variety of mediums including oils, collages, watercolors, drawings, and prints. His works are included in museum collections, including the Museum of Modern Art in New York, the Worcester Art Museum in Massachusetts, the Museum of Fine Arts in Boston, and the university museums of Harvard, Smith, and Vassar.

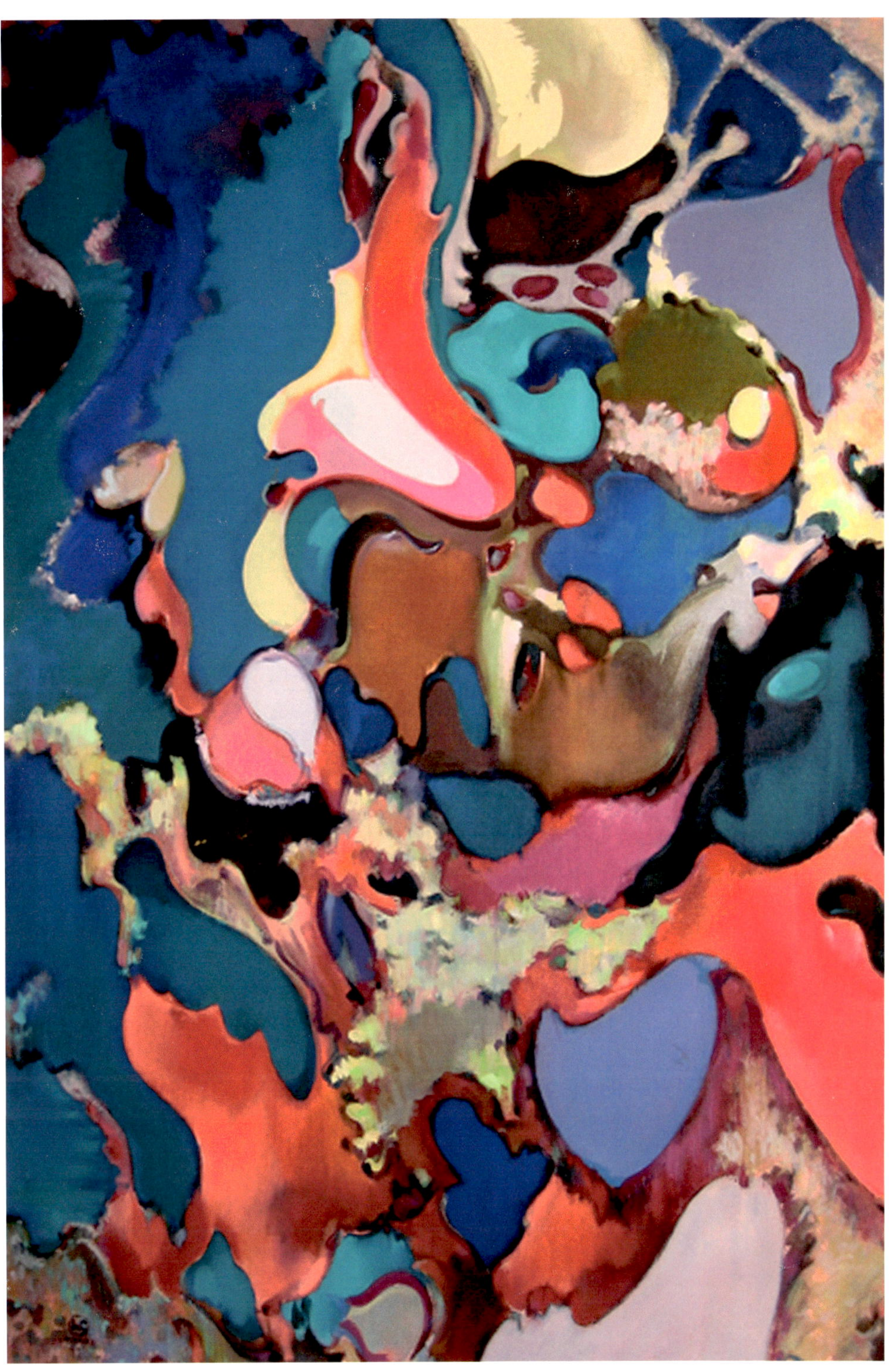

William Littlefield, *Noesis,* October 20, 1962. Acrylic on canvas, 69½ × 51¾ inches. *Anonymous gift,* 1988. *Photo courtesy of Christy King.*

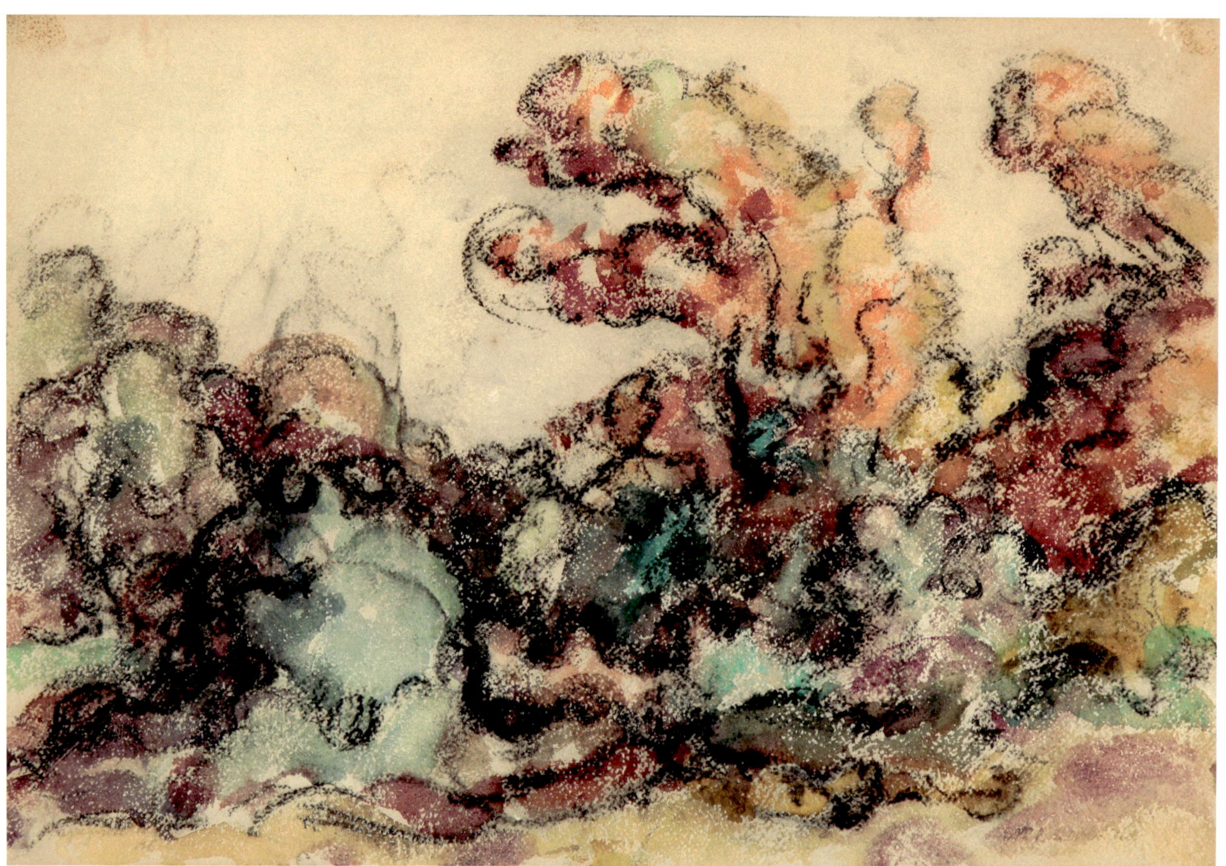

William Littlefield, *St. Tropez Trees,* December 1926. Watercolor on paper, 11⅜ × 16¾ inches.
Gift of the Estate of Fred W. McDarrah, 2013.

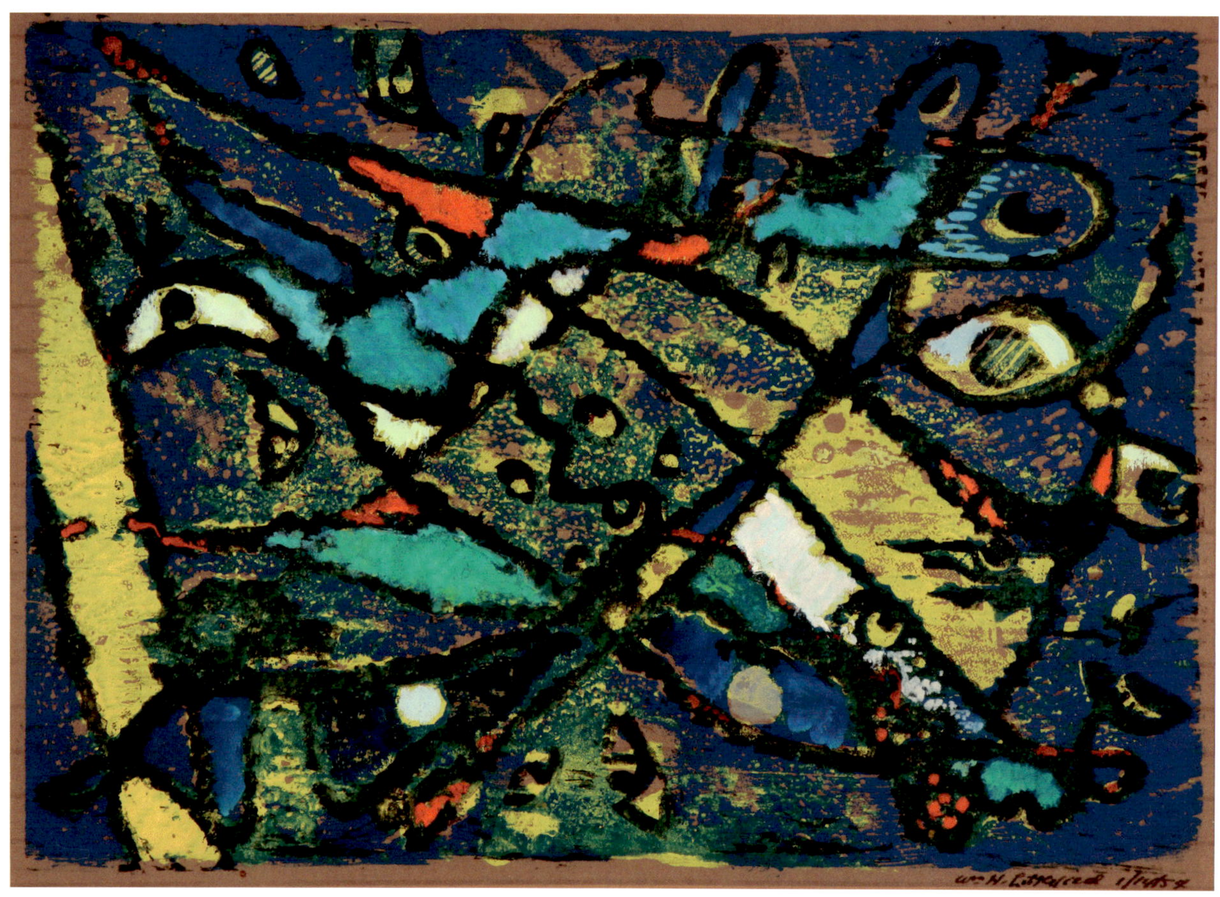

William Littlefield, *Peacock on Green Paper Bag,* January 14, 1954. Mixed media on paper, 11¼ × 16¾ inches.
Gift of the Estate of Fred W. McDarrah, 2013.

BORIS MARGO
(1902–1995)

Born in the Ukraine, Boris Margo was influenced by surrealism when he studied in Leningrad in 1927 with Pavel Filinov, a cubist-surrealist. This influence came to fruition in America, where he immigrated in 1930, not long before other surrealists, fleeing Nazism, arrived. In New York City, Margo became part of a group of rising artists, including Arshile Gorky, for whom he apprenticed, Milton Avery, and Mark Rothko.

During the Depression, Margo used materials he made or found, and developed the cellocut, a process in which plastic is melted with acetate and poured onto a surface. After the plastic hardens, etching or woodcut tools are used to create an image. The plate is then printed. Even when he could afford more materials, Margo was an inveterate experimenter with various mediums and motifs, including bas-relief and assemblage sculpture. And he continued to explore various approaches to printmaking.

In the 1930s, his work took a surrealistic approach with naturalistic forms and organic forms set in dream-like spaces, which had fantastical references. In the early 1940s he moved toward abstraction with intricate compositions, in which he floated biomorphic shapes into richly colored spaces. There is an influence of biology and astronomy on his work. Although associated with abstract expressionism, Margo maintained his individualistic style with a painterly nonobjective abstraction. In the Cape Cod Museum of Art collection are a number of his cellocuts. *Metallic Symphony* and *From Meteorites* are examples of his use of biomorphic forms. *Dancers* focuses on a meandering line spinning like a prima ballerina in a series of pirouettes.

Although New York City was his home, in 1940 he and his wife, artist Jan Gelb, began spending summers in Provincetown, where the environment—driftwood and sand and the patterns he saw in the sea and vegetation—influenced his art. *August 10, 1949*, in the museum collection, has a reference to a Cape landscape.

His works are in major museum collections, including the Art Institute of Chicago, the Metropolitan Museum of Art and the Museum of Modern Art in New York, the Philadelphia Museum of Art, the San Francisco Museum of Art, São Paulo Museum of Art in Brazil, and the National Gallery of Art in Washington, DC.

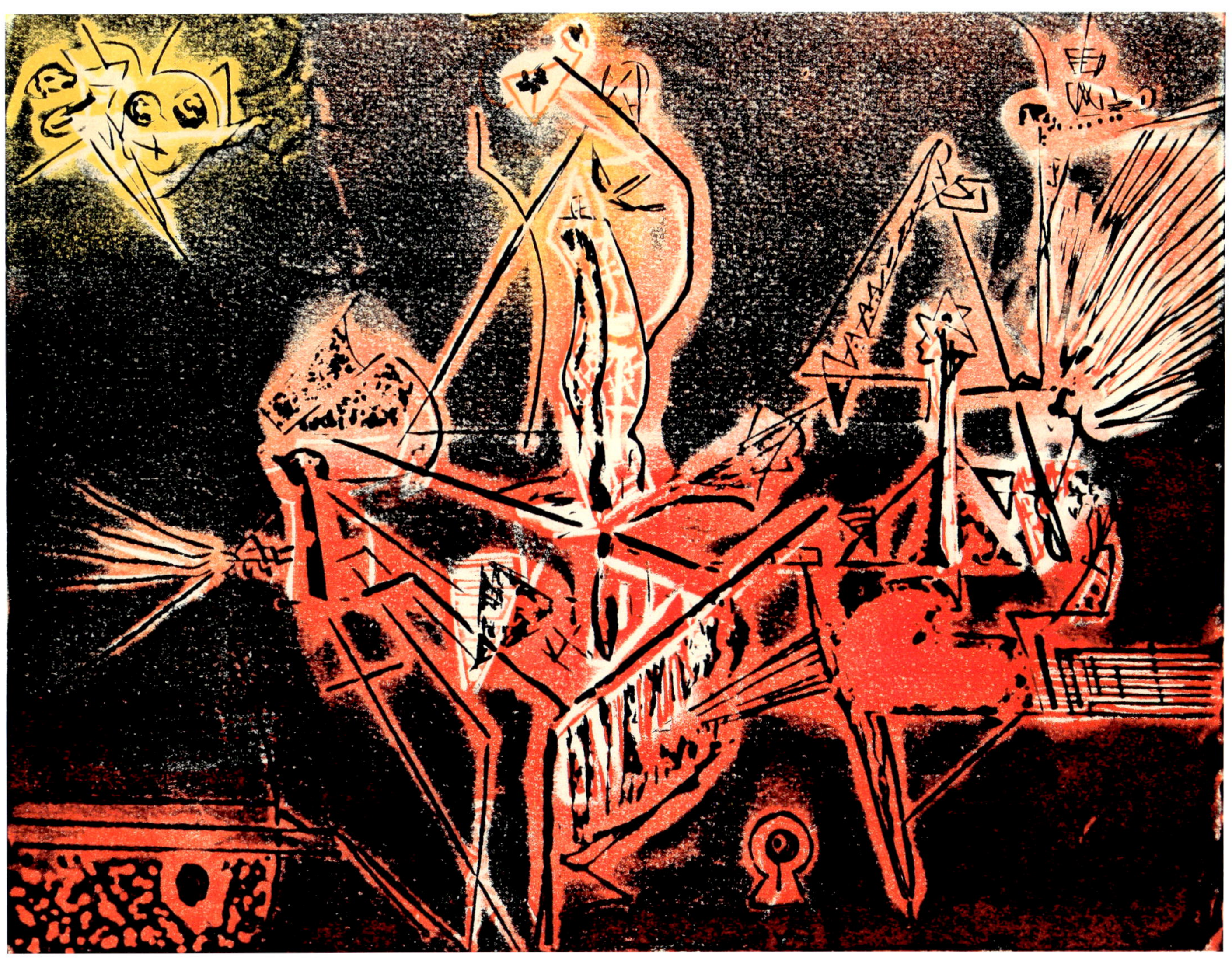

Boris Margo, *Metallic Symphony*, 1946. Cellocut on paper, 9⅛ × 11⅞ inches. *Gift of Murray and Stanley Zimiles*, 2001.

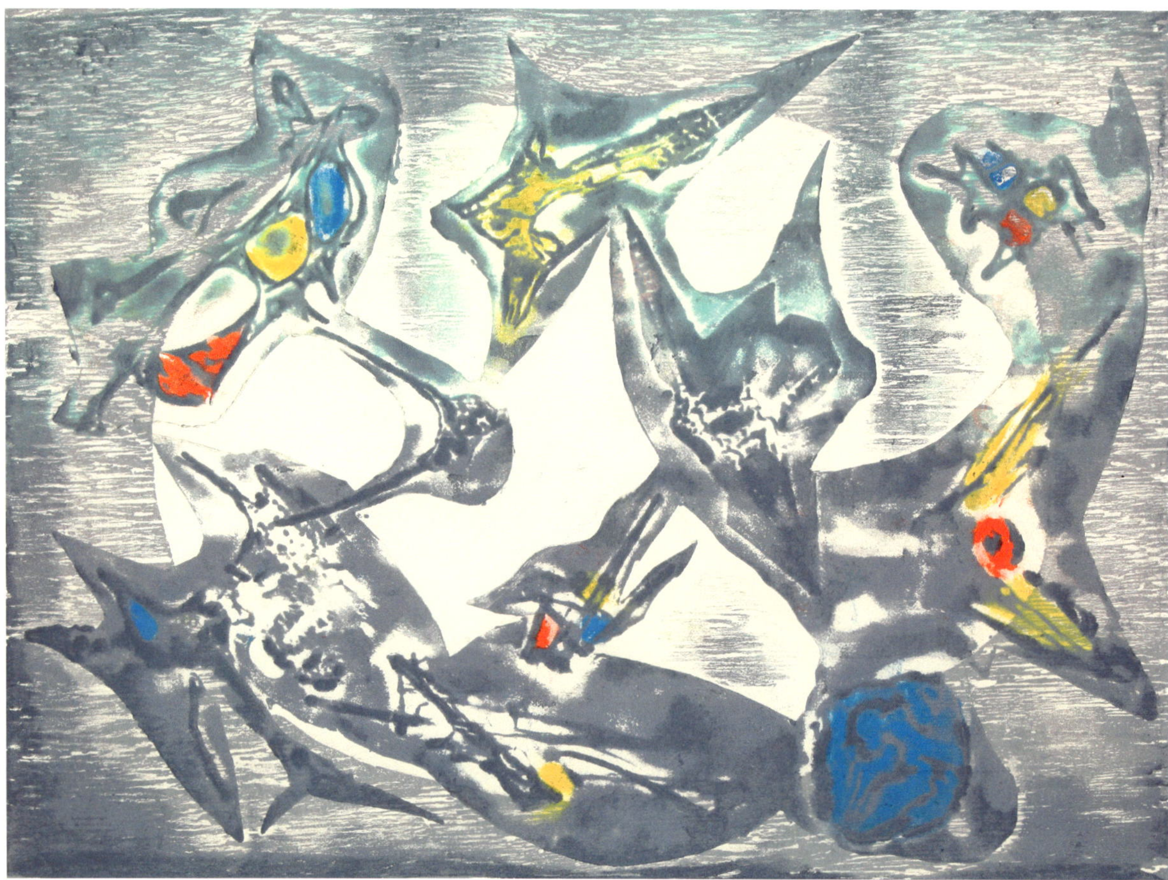

Boris Margo, *From Meteorites* AP, n.d. Cellocut on paper, 11⅝ × 15¾ inches. *Gift of Murray and Stanley Zimiles*, 2001.

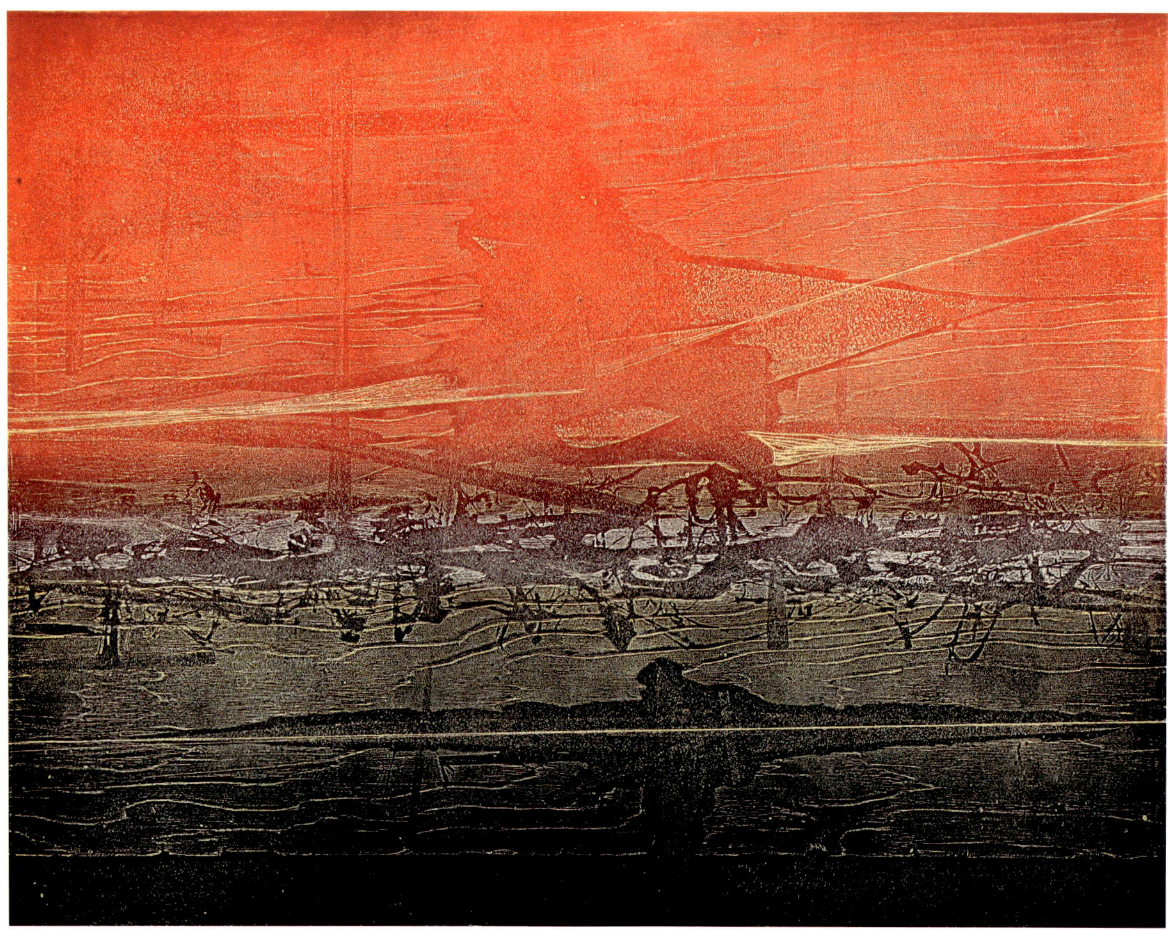

Boris Margo, *August 10, 1949* 10/10, 1949. Cellocut on paper, 12⅞ × 16⅞ inches. *Gift of Murray and Stanley Zimiles*, 2001.

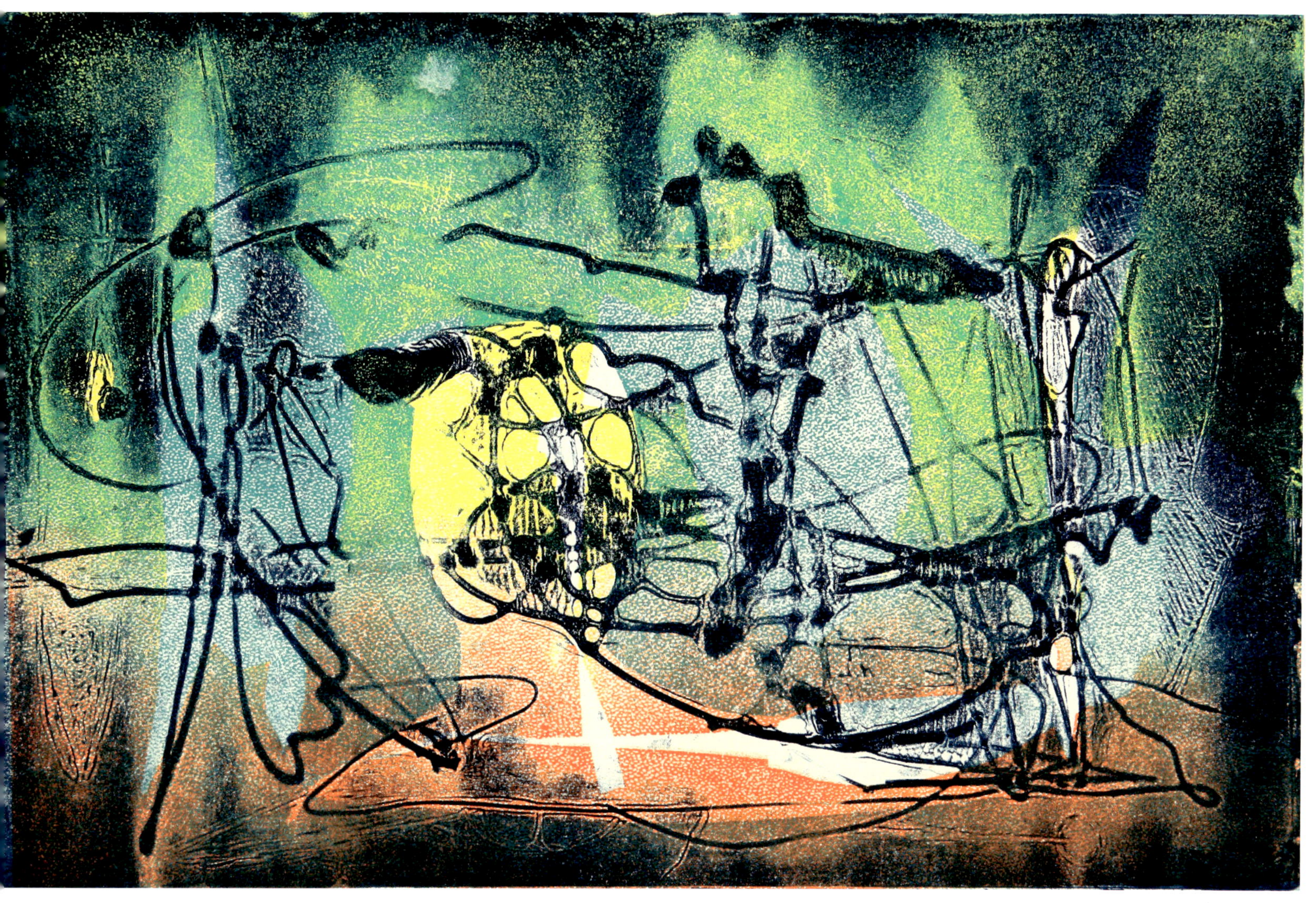

Boris Margo, *Dancers* 34/50, 1946. Cellocut on paper, 5¾ × 8¾ inches. *Gift of Murray and Stanley Zimiles*, 2001.

JOHN WHORF
(1903–1959)

John Whorf's roots were on Cape Cod, where his English ancestors settled in 1650. He was born not far from the Cape, in Winthrop, Massachussetts, and at fourteen, went to Provincetown to study with George Elmer Browne, Richard Miller, Max Bohm, and Charles Hawthorne. He then went on to the St. Botolph Studio and the School of the Museum of Fine Arts in Boston.

In 1919 he went to France and continued his education at the École des Beaux-Arts, the Académie de la Grande Chaumière, and the Académie Colarossi. While living in France he traveled to Spain, Portugal, and Morocco. He was a fine painter in oils, but after his travels, watercolor became his primary medium. His work was influenced by John Singer Sargent and Frank Benson.

Whorf's subjects include landscapes, still lifes, Boston and Manhattan street scenes, and the Provincetown fishing village with boats and seascapes. In the collection of the Cape Cod Museum of Art are several watercolors related to the sea. *The Race* is a robust image of waves dashing against rocks. The spontaneous quality of his watercolors is represented in two others from the collection: the light-filled *Brooklyn Boatyard* and *Untitled (Stormy Regatta).*

His works are represented in a number of museum collections, including the Museum of Fine Arts in Boston; the Metropolitan Museum of Art, the Whitney Museum of American Art, and the Museum of Modern Art in New York; the Los Angeles County Museum; the Art Institute of Chicago; the National Museum in Stockholm, Sweden; and Pitti Palace in Florence, Italy.

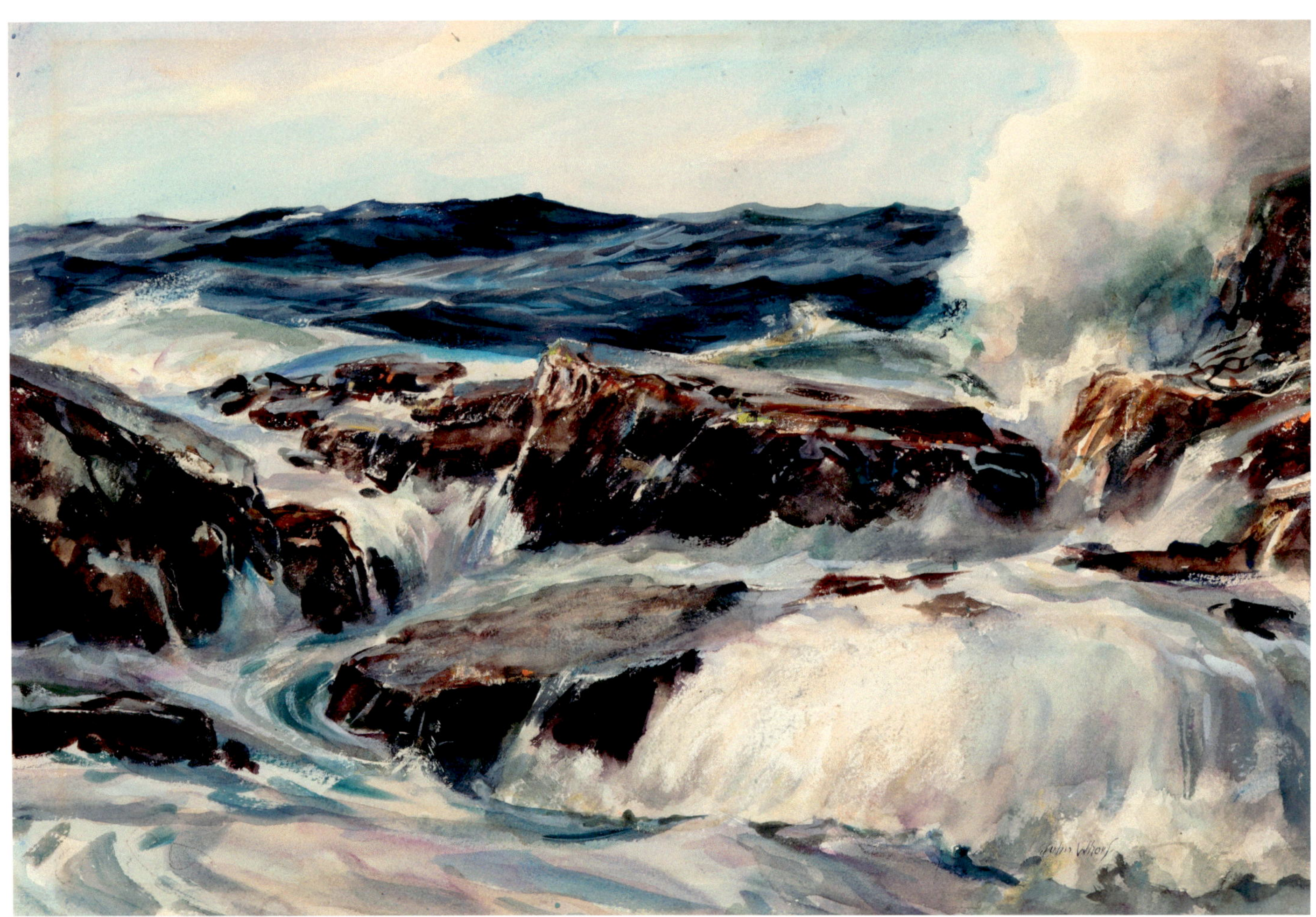

John Whorf, *The Race*, n.d. Watercolor on paper, 18¾ × 28¼ inches. *Anonymous gift*, 1990.

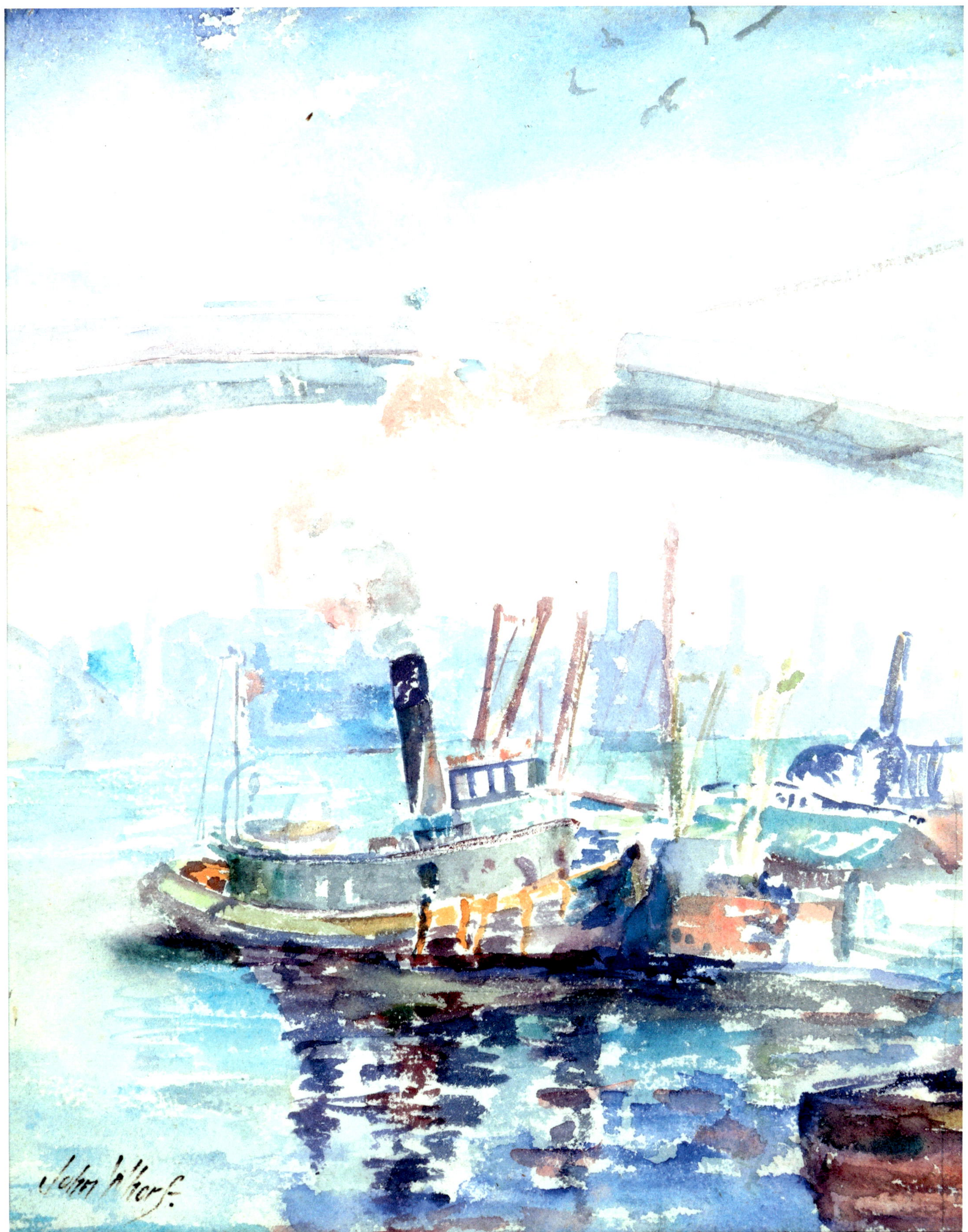

John Whorf, *Brooklyn Boatyard,* n.d. Watercolor on paper, 11½ × 9¾ inches. *Anonymous gift*, 2009.

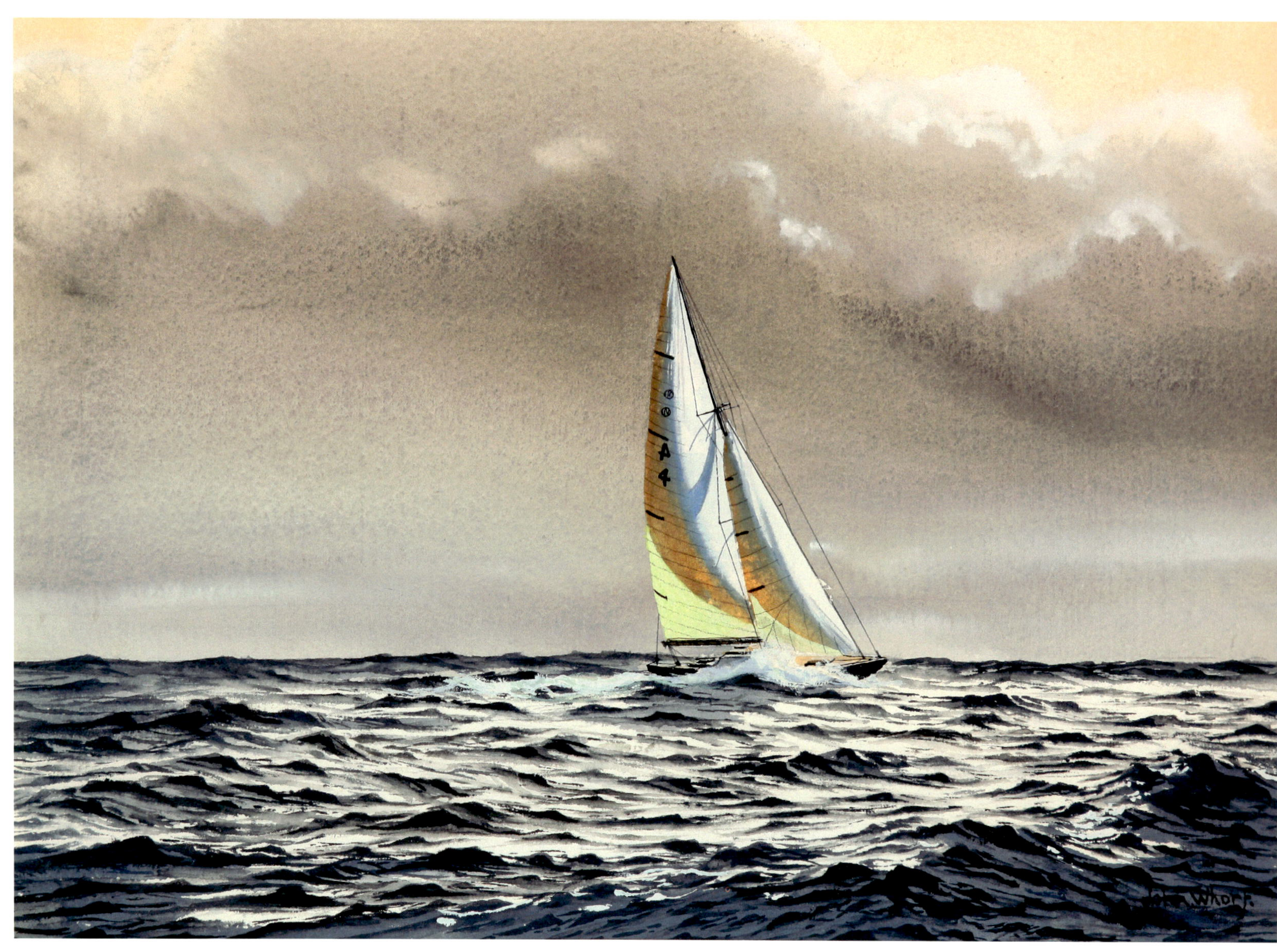

John Whorf, *Untitled (Stormy Regatta),* n.d. Watercolor on paper, 10½ × 15 inches. *Anonymous gift*, 2009.

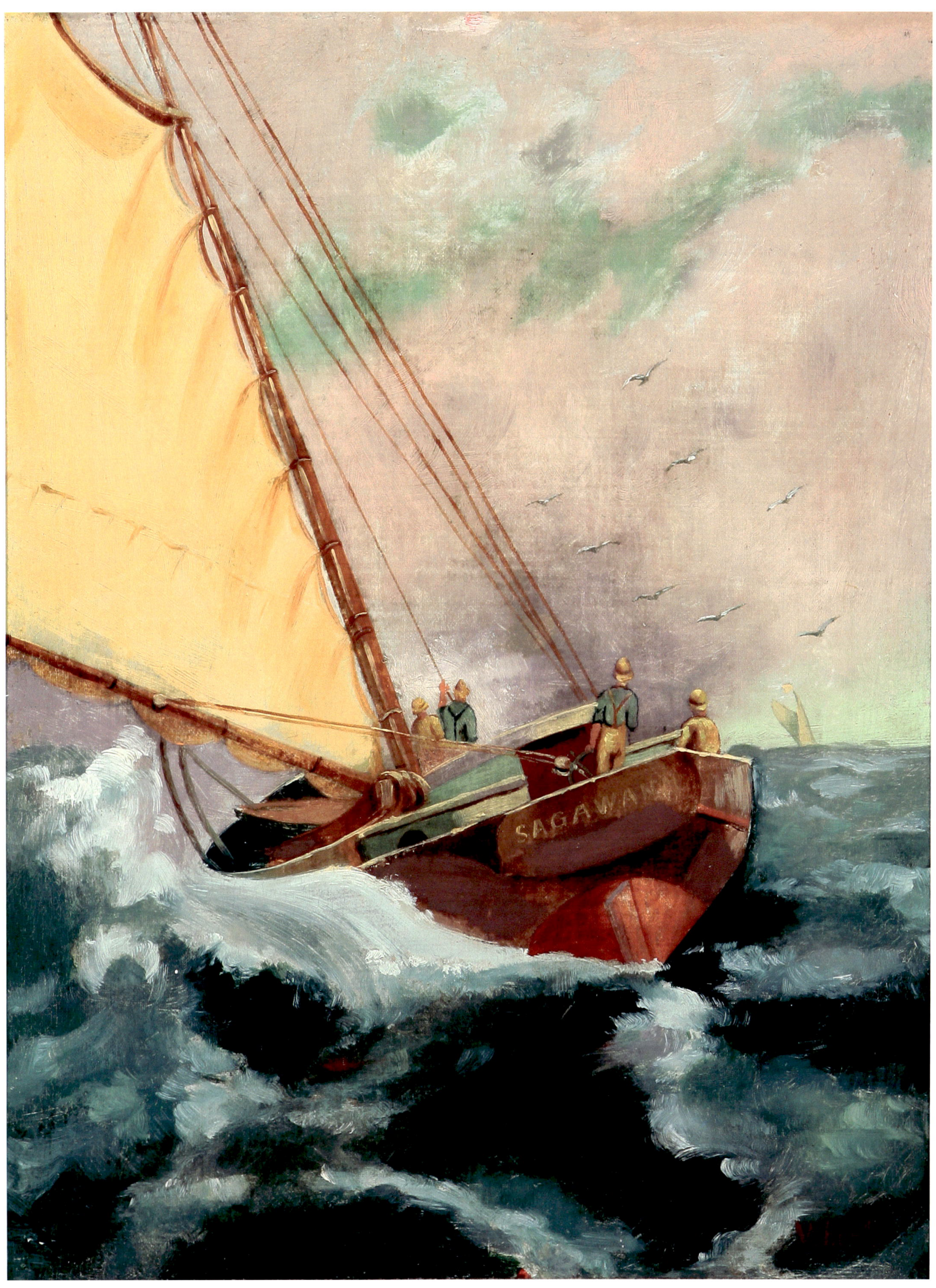

John Whorf, *Sagawann,* 1921. Oil on canvas, 18 × 14 inches. *Anonymous gift*, 2009.

HOWARD GIBBS
(1904–1970)

Howard Gibbs was influenced early on by artist Albert Pinkham Ryder, a family friend, who gave him his first paint set. He studied at the Swain School of Design in his native New Bedford before going to France in 1927 to study with Edmond-François Aman-Jean. While there, Gibbs exhibited at St. Paul du Var with Francis Picabia, Henri Matisse, and André Derain.

When Gibbs returned to Boston, his work showed the impact fauvist color had on him. His expressionistic approach was not in keeping with the conservative Boston tastes of the early 1930s, and refusing to conform, he withdrew to Harwich Port on Cape Cod. He was active at the Provincetown Art Association, exhibiting there and becoming friendly with artists in the colony, including Ross Moffett, Karl Knaths, Edwin Dickinson, and Agnes Weinrich, among others.

Gibbs was also part of the Massachusetts Federal Art Project, producing oil paintings and linocuts that ranged from portraits to landscapes. He lived for a while on a farm in North Dartmouth, and in 1945 moved to Brewster on the Cape, where he was associated with the Stony Brook circle of artists, which included painters Vernon Smith and Betty Lane, sculptors Harry Holl and Arnold Geissbuhler, and writers Conrad Aiken and John Hay.

Gibbs's work shows a range of approaches, from his expressionistic, flat, heavily outlined village scenes like *French Landscape* to the cubist-influenced still lifes, as in *Fruit and Flowers in Window*, done in the 1920s, which are in the Cape Cod Museum of Art collection. Also in the collection are the 1930 expressionistic figurative painting *The Boston Crowd*; the 1944 surreal watercolor *Continual*

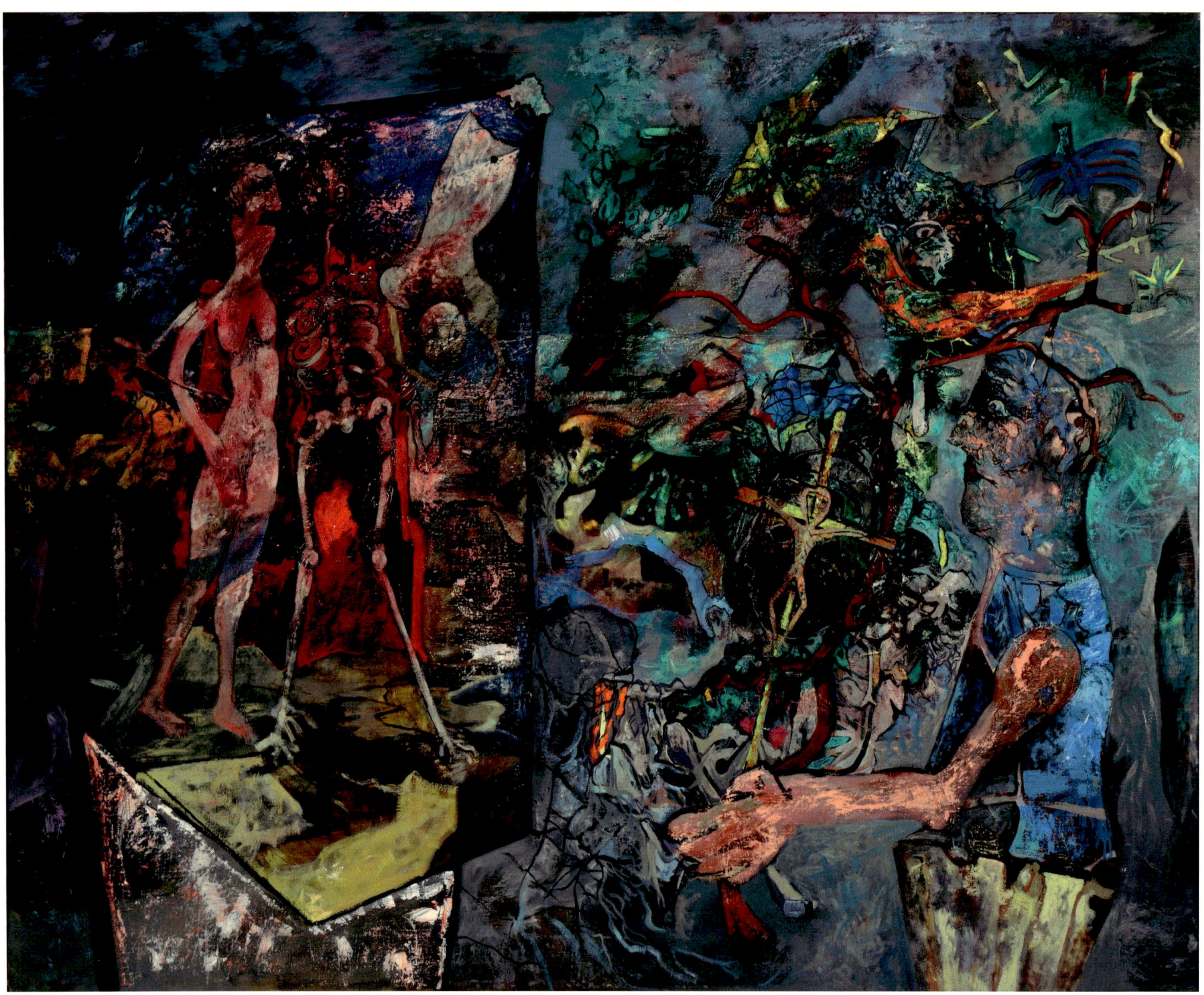

Howard Gibbs, *Oracle of the Season*, 1947–1949. Oil on canvas, 47½ × 58 inches. *Gift of Katherine Gibbs*, 1986.

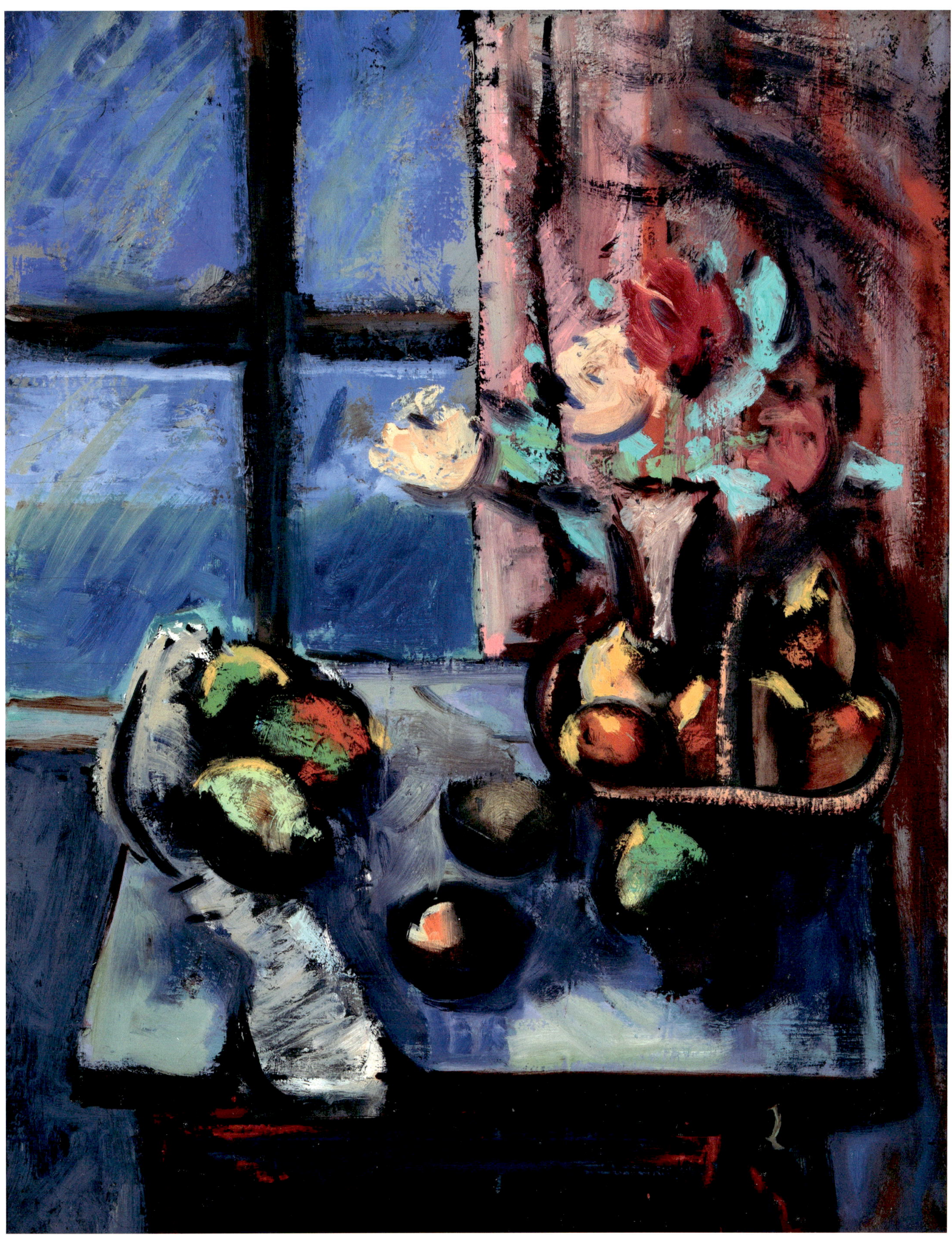

Howard Gibbs, *Fruit and Flowers in Window*, 1920s. Oil on canvas, 32 × 25½ inches. *Gift of Katherine Gibbs*, 1986.

Line with Faces; the nearly abstract 1950 landscape *Breaking the Winter Flow*; and the expressionistic abstraction *Geography of the World #1*, done in the 1960s. His work is often dark and moodily colored and evokes dream-like scenarios.

Gibbs's works were included in exhibitions at the Whitney Museum of American Art, the Museum of Modern Art, and the Metropolitan Museum of Art in New York. He had a one-man show at the Baltimore Museum of Art in 1954.

He is also represented in the collections of the Museum of Fine Arts in Boston, the Addison Gallery of American Art in Andover, and de Cordova Sculpture Park and Museum in Lincoln, all in Massachusetts.

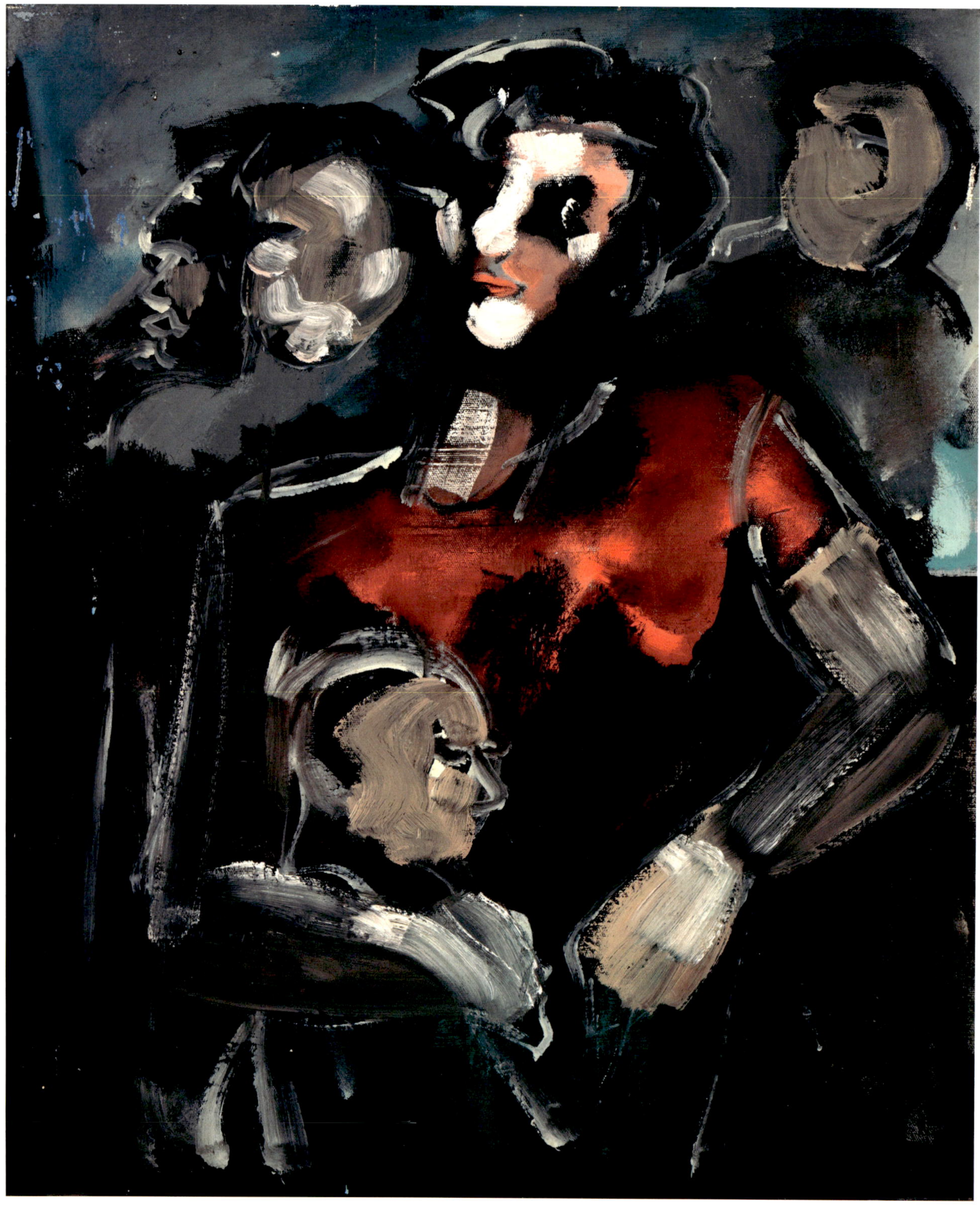

Howard Gibbs, *The Boston Crowd,* 1930. Oil on canvas, 30 × 25 inches. *Gift of Katherine Gibbs*, 1986.

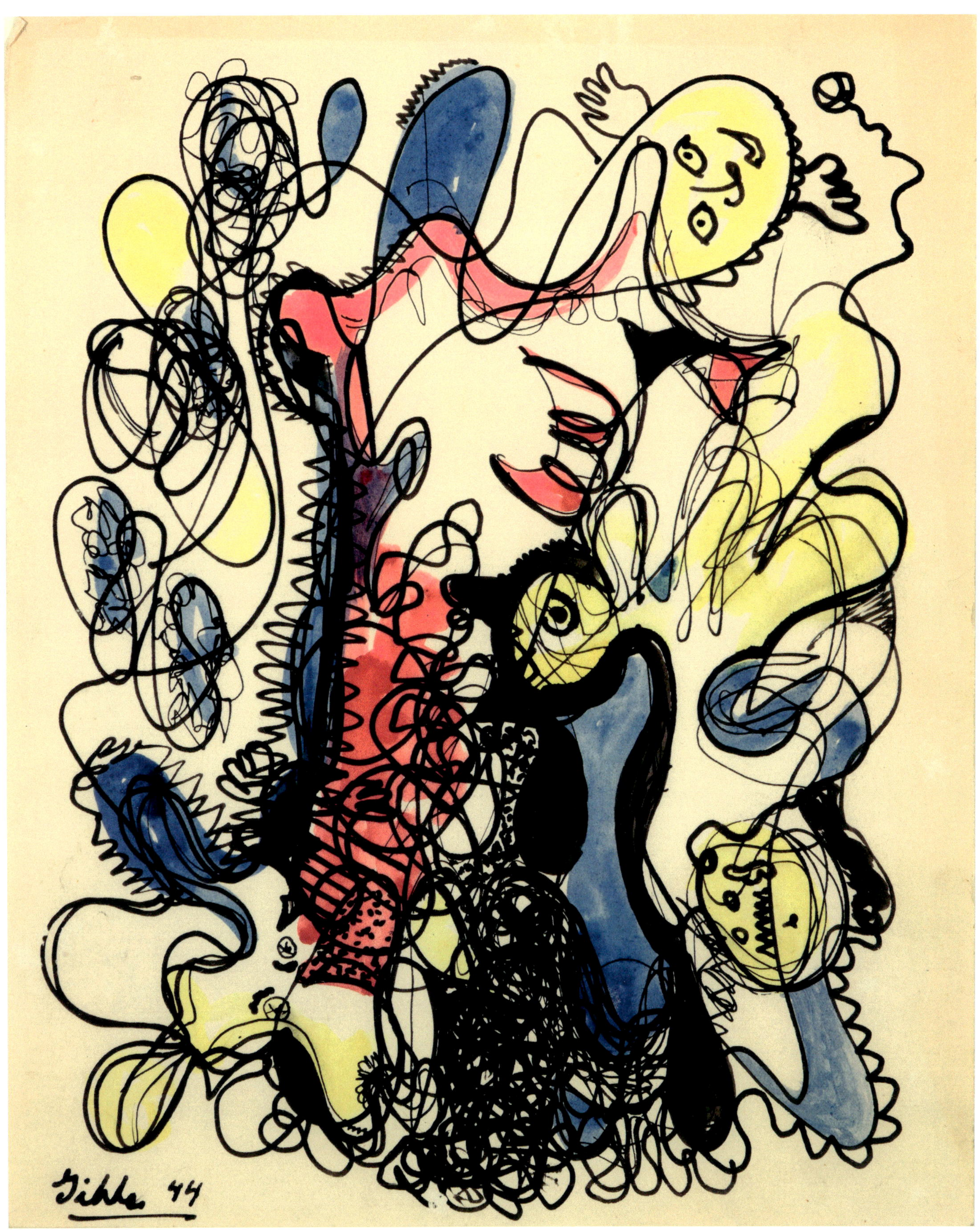

Howard Gibbs, *Continual Line with Faces,* 1944. Ink and watercolor on paper, 11⅞ × 9¾ inches. *Gift of Katherine Gibbs*, 1986.

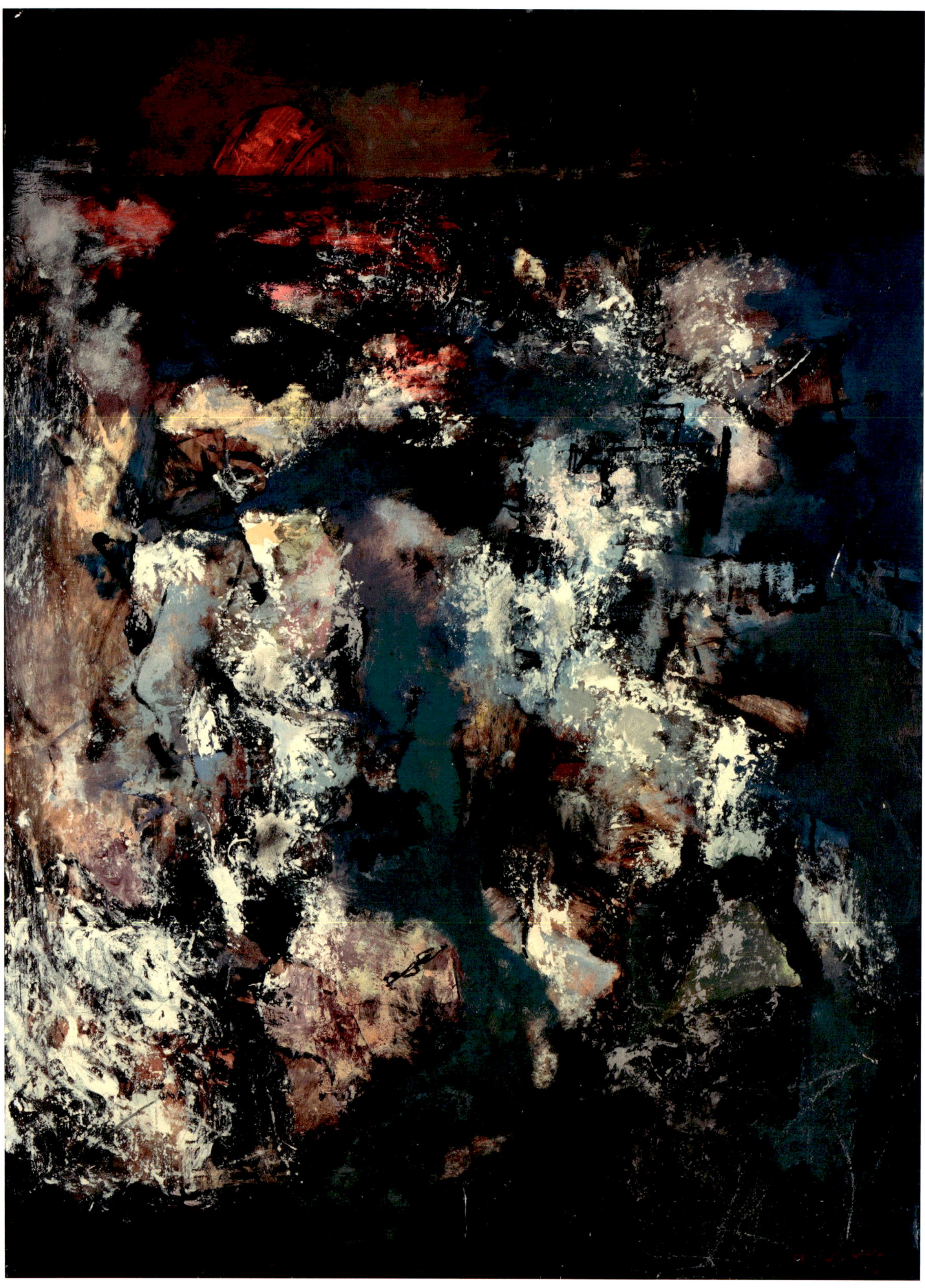

Howard Gibbs, *Breaking of the Winter Flow*, 1950. Oil on masonite, 45¼ × 35½ inches. *Gift of Katherine Gibbs*, 1986.

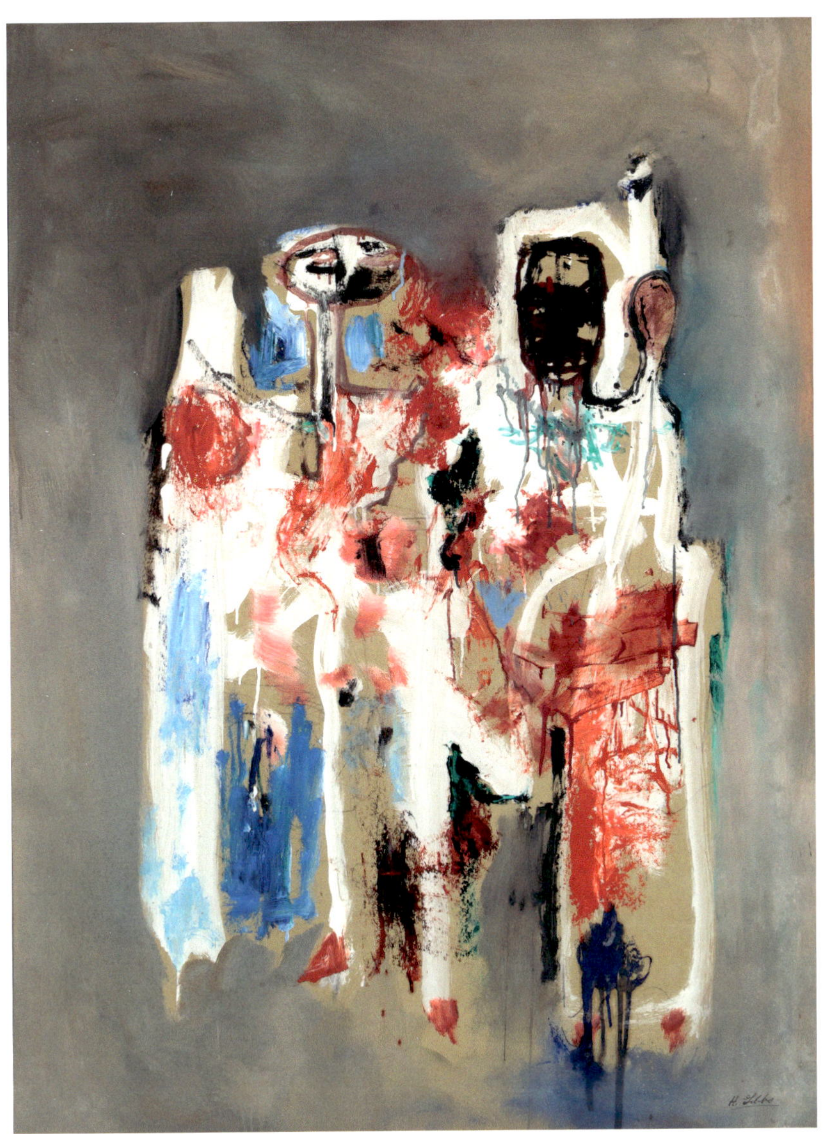

Howard Gibbs, *Geography of the World #1*, 1960s. Oil on cardboard, 40½ × 30¼ inches. *Gift of Katherine Gibbs*, 1986.

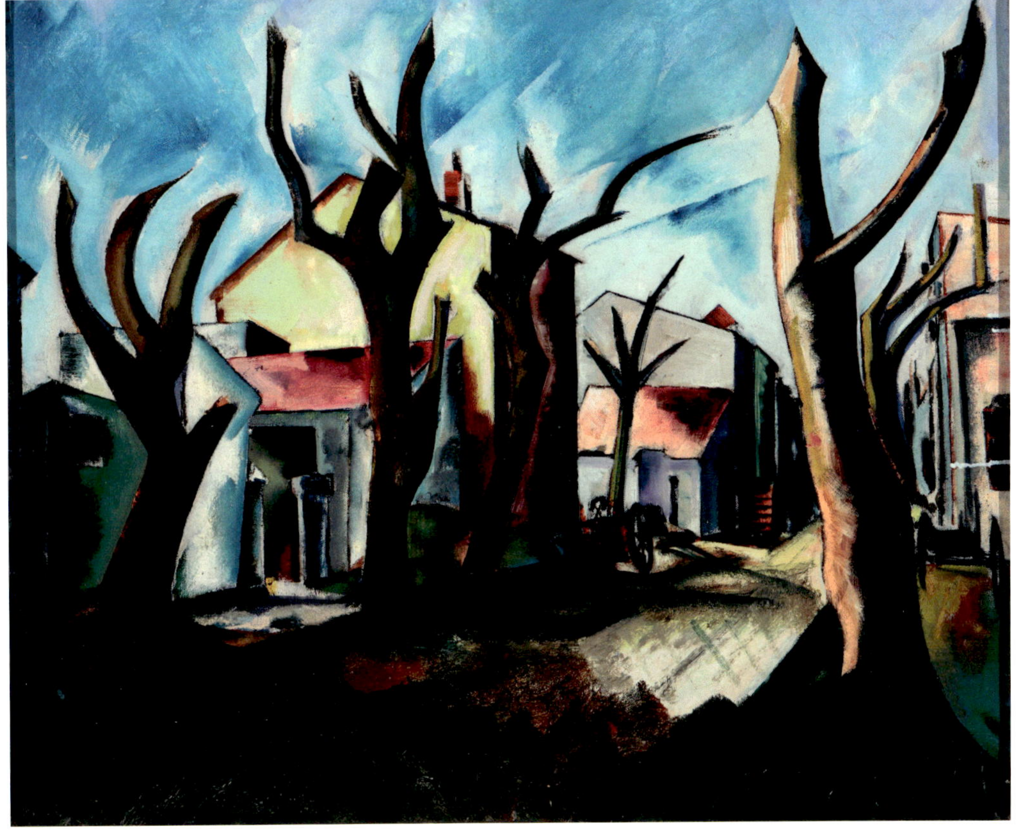

Howard Gibbs, *French Landscape*, 1920s. Oil on canvas, 24 × 30 inches. *Gift of Katherine Gibbs*, 1986.

CHAIM GROSS
(1904–1991)

Chaim Gross grew up surrounded by forests near the Galician village of Wolowa in the Carpathian Mountains of East Austria, where he was born. His father had a lumber business and Gross knew the woodcutters and carvers, so he had an early association with the wood he eventually spent his career carving.

During the First World War after his family had moved to Kolomyya, which became a pawn between the Austrians and Russians, the Gross family, along with thousands of refugees, fled from a wave of anti-Semitism. Gross was separated from his parents for a time, but later reunited. After several years in Vienna and Budapest, he immigrated to the United States in 1921 with an older brother. The rest of his family remained in Europe and died during the Holocaust.

Gross was always intent on becoming an artist, and he let nothing get in his way. While he was a student, he supported himself as a delivery boy. In the late 1920s, Gross was carving in stone and wood, which seemed a natural extension of his childhood experiences.

Works Progress Administration commissions helped him through the Depression. His fortunes improved in 1937 when the Museum of Modern Art bought one of his sculptures. A few years later, the Metropolitan Museum of Art and the Whitney Museum of American Art purchased his work for their permanent collection. By then, he was teaching at the New School for Social Research and the Educational Alliance in New York.

Gross and his wife, Renee, visited Provincetown during the war years, and in 1943 bought a home on Franklin Street, once the studio of George Elmer Browne, and divided their time between New York and Provincetown.

Primarily a sculptor, he carved in stone and his favorite, wood, and also did commissions in bronze. He didn't dwell on detail, but simplified, using a curve or line for the pure beauty of it. He also made drawings, prints, and watercolors, in which he focused on the human form, often the female, as he did in his sculpture. Two lithographs in the Cape Cod Museum of Art collection, *The Artist (IX/XV)* and *Dancers,*

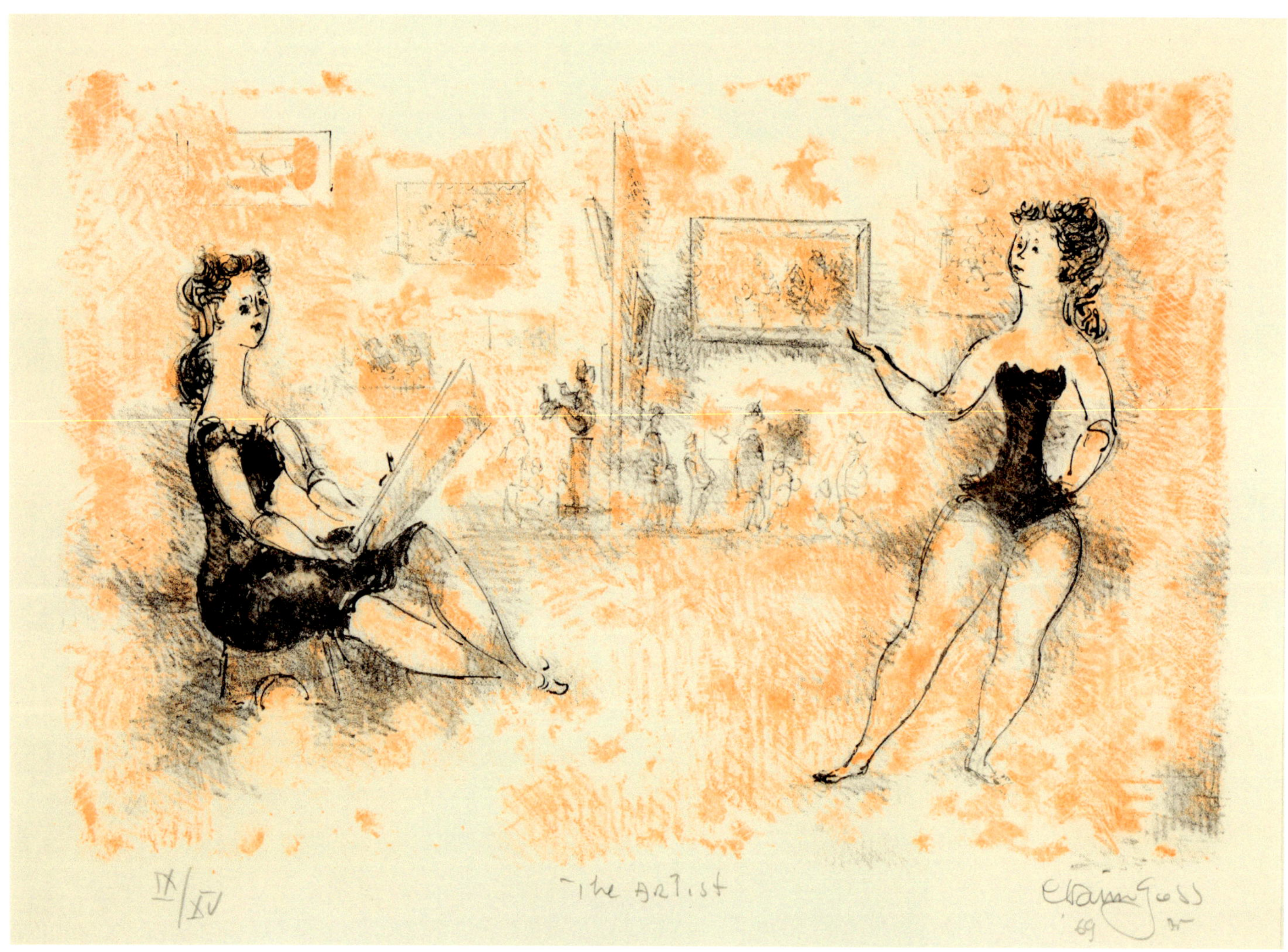

Chaim Gross, *The Artist* IX/XV, 1969. Two color lithograph on rag paper, 13⅜ × 17⅜ inches. *Gift of Chaim Gross*, 1985.

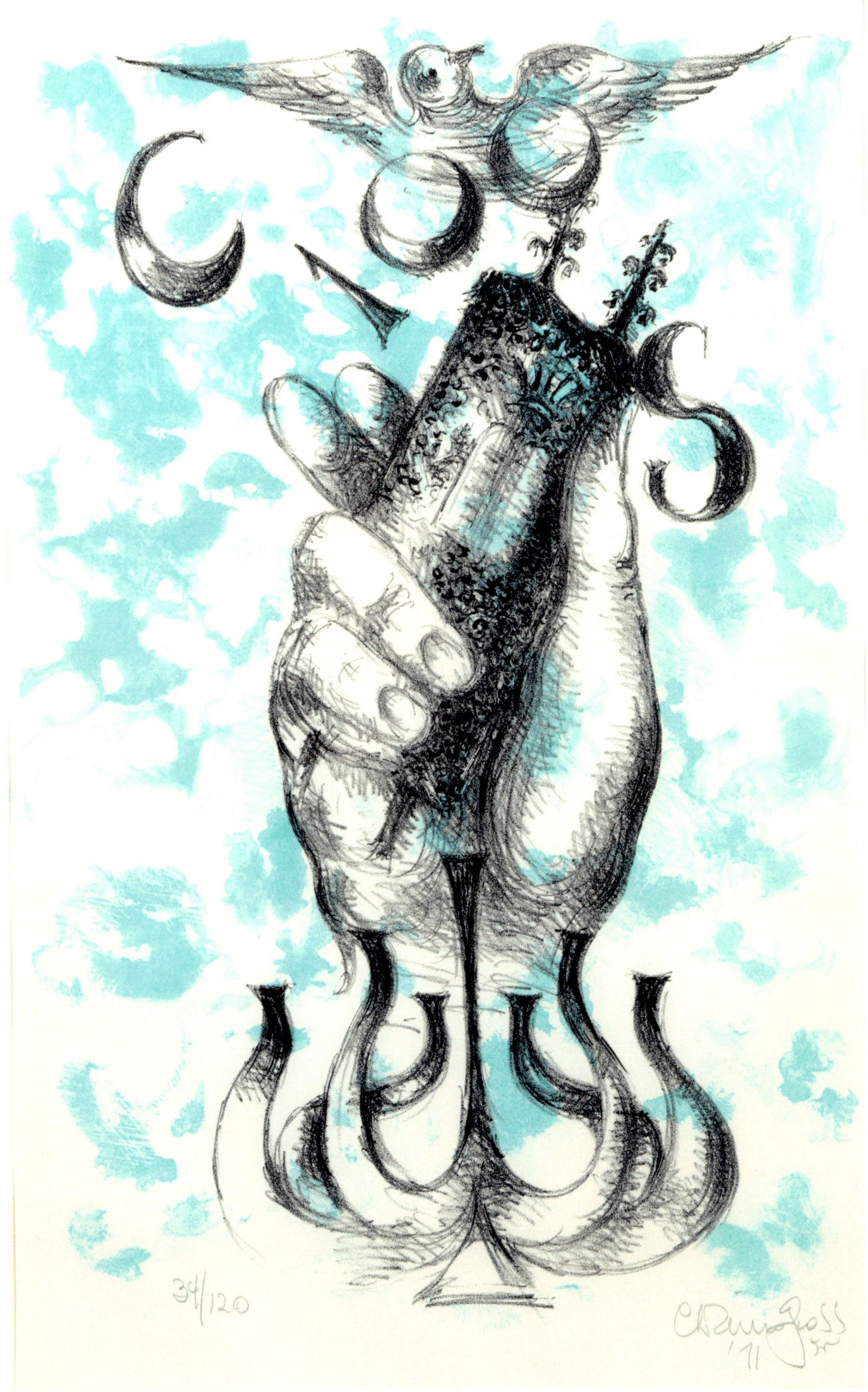

Chaim Gross, *Torah Scrolls* 34/120, 1971. Lithograph on paper, 16¾ × 10½ inches. *Anonymous gift*, 1993.

illuminate Gross's skill at draftsmanship as he nimbly captures movement and grace. His sculptures of acrobats, cubistic nudes, and playful renderings of mother and child are eloquent statements with a dramatic sense of balance, an abstracted sensuality, and a joyful sense of movement. In his lithograph *Bare Back Riders*, in the museum collection, he depicts the delight of the acrobats balancing on the horse.

In 1966, Gross created a sculpture, *Birds of Peace,* for Hebrew University in Israel, and in 1972, his large reliefs of the Ten Commandments were dedicated at the International Synagogue at John F. Kennedy Airport in New York. As these works relate to Gross's Jewish traditions, so does his lithograph *Torah Scrolls*, of those sacred writings, in the museum collection.

His works are in the collections of major museums, including the Art Institute of Chicago, Metropolitan Museum of Art in New York, the Philadelphia Museum of Art, and the Smithsonian American Art Museum and the Hirshhorn Museum and Sculpture Garden in Washington, DC.

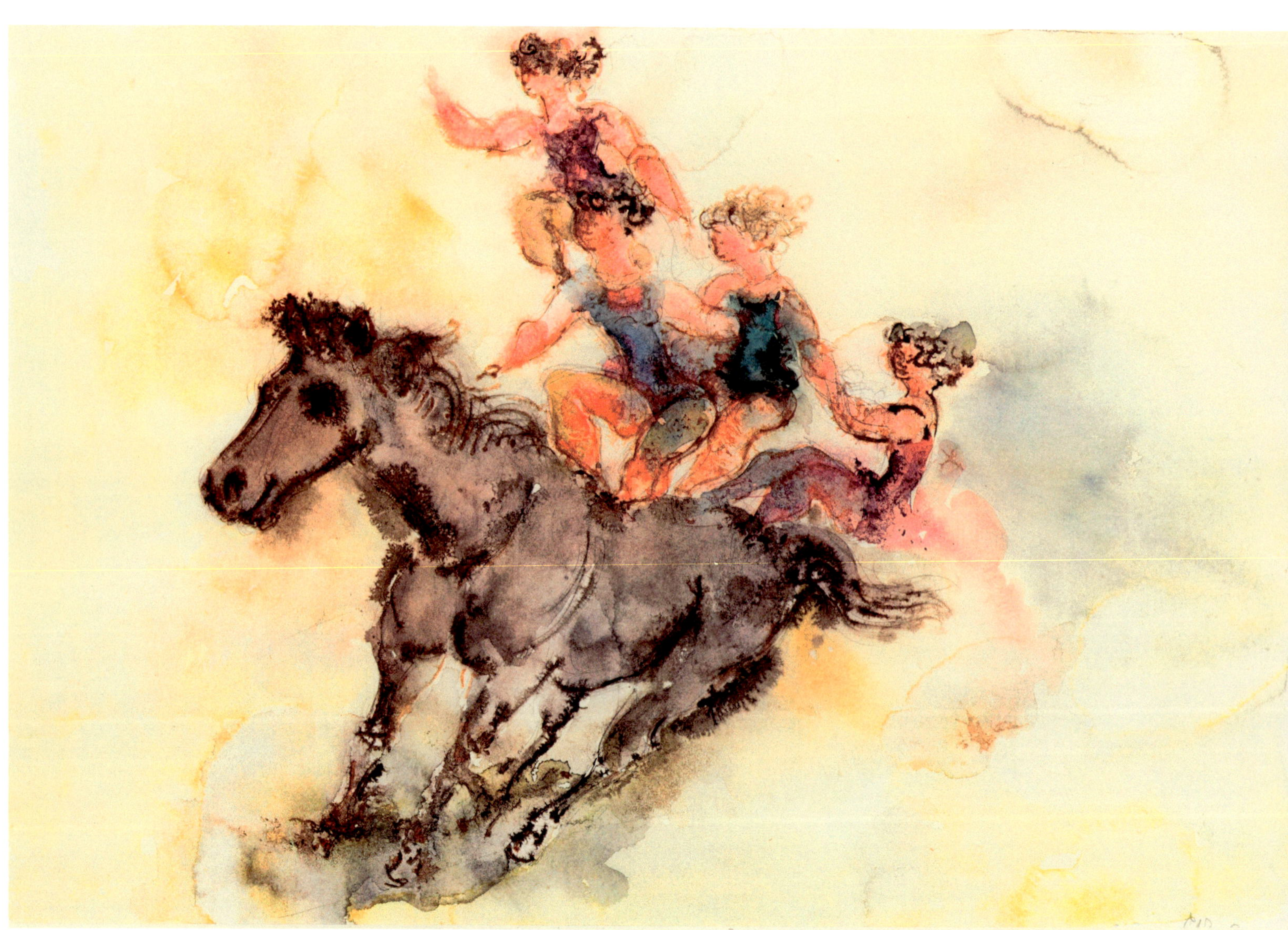

Chaim Gross, *Bare Back Riders*, n.d. Lithograph on paper, 19 × 27¾ inches. *Gift of Philip and Lisa Weiss*, 2007.

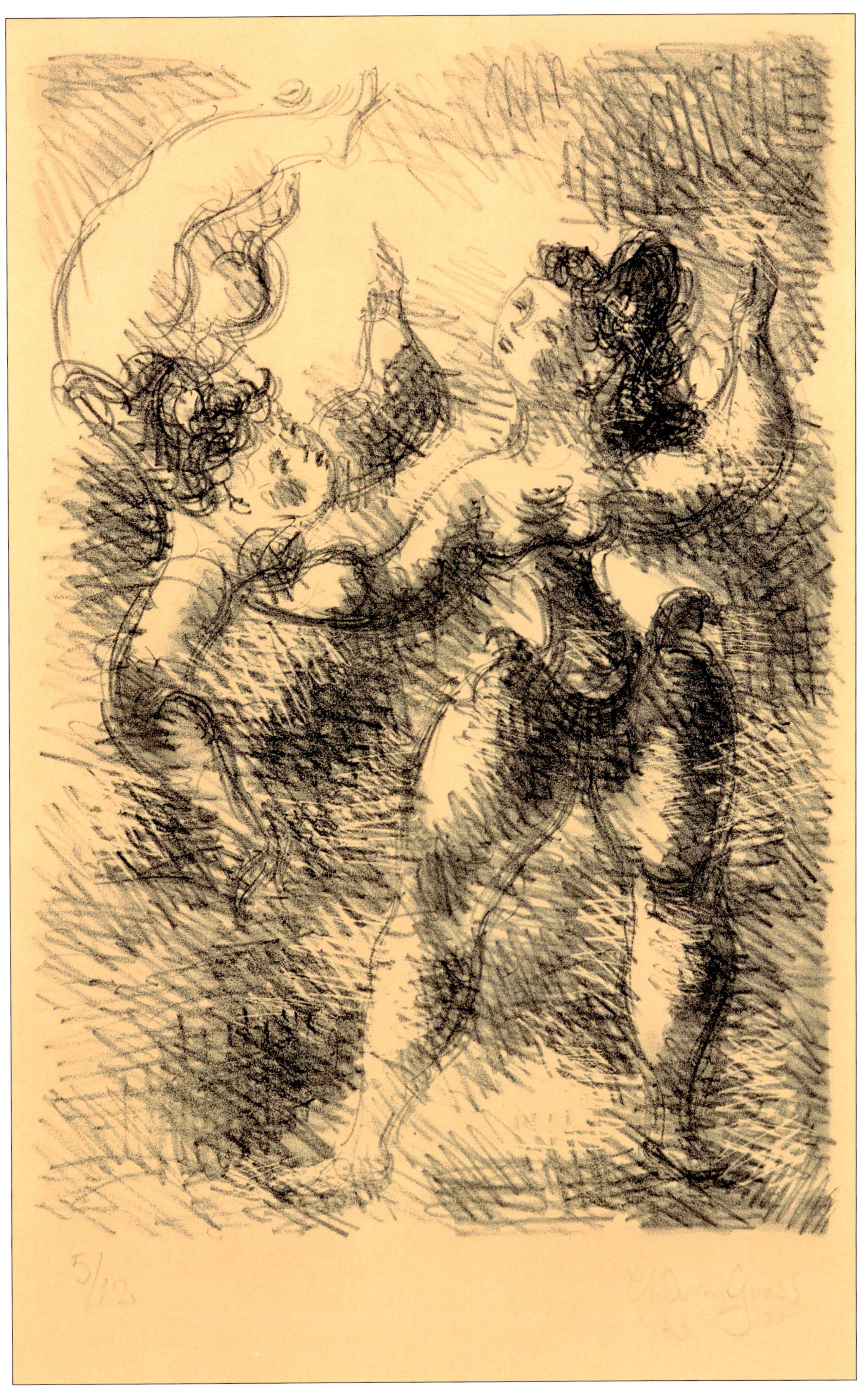

Chaim Gross, *Dancers*, 1963. Lithograph on paper, 15 × 9½ inches. *Gift of Pearl and Joel M. Wolfson*, 1987.

ELLIOT ORR
(1904–1997)

Elliot Orr's representational portraits and landscapes are in the tradition of nineteenth-century romantics, including the French Camille Corot, the British John Constable, and the American Albert Pinkham Ryder. It was a tradition that imposed imagination and emotion on the subject. Orr was included in the exhibition *Romantic Painting in America* at the Museum of Modern Art in 1943.

He was born in Flushing, New York, and studied at Grand Central Art School with George Luks, and with Charles Hawthorne in Provincetown in the 1920s. Later he settled in Chatham on Cape Cod.

Nature inspired Orr's art. His Cape Cod landscapes are noted for: low horizons with land stretching into the distance; restless, cloud-filled skies; stormy seas; and shipwrecks. When he added figures, they were struggling against nature's forces, sailing boats, or at leisure on the beach. His subjects include Tenth Avenue in New York, a path through the woods, and clam diggers. His paintings from the Massachusetts Federal Art Project continue in his realist mode, always tempered by romanticism and mystery.

His work can be serene and sometimes dark and moody, as in *Mother and Child* and *Into the Night*, in the Cape Cod Museum of Art collection. In the watercolor *Mother and Child*, despite the shadowy colors, a warmth exudes in the way he depicts the mother holding the child. *Into the Night*, saturated in blue, is a distant view of a house across the water, and is like others he has done of lonely houses. His other subjects include weathered barns and fishermen's shacks, which have a rugged quality.

Orr was interested in capturing a pristine and nostalgic view of Cape Cod as well as of southwest Florida. Even when he settled in Naples, he continued to paint the subjects he had grown to love on the Cape. In the 1930s and '40s, his work tended toward subtly colored, somber images, but his colors brightened after traveling to Mexico.

His works are in the collections of museums, including the Whitney Museum of American Art in New York, the Brooklyn Museum of Art, the Detroit Institute of Arts, and the Phillips Collection in Washington, DC.

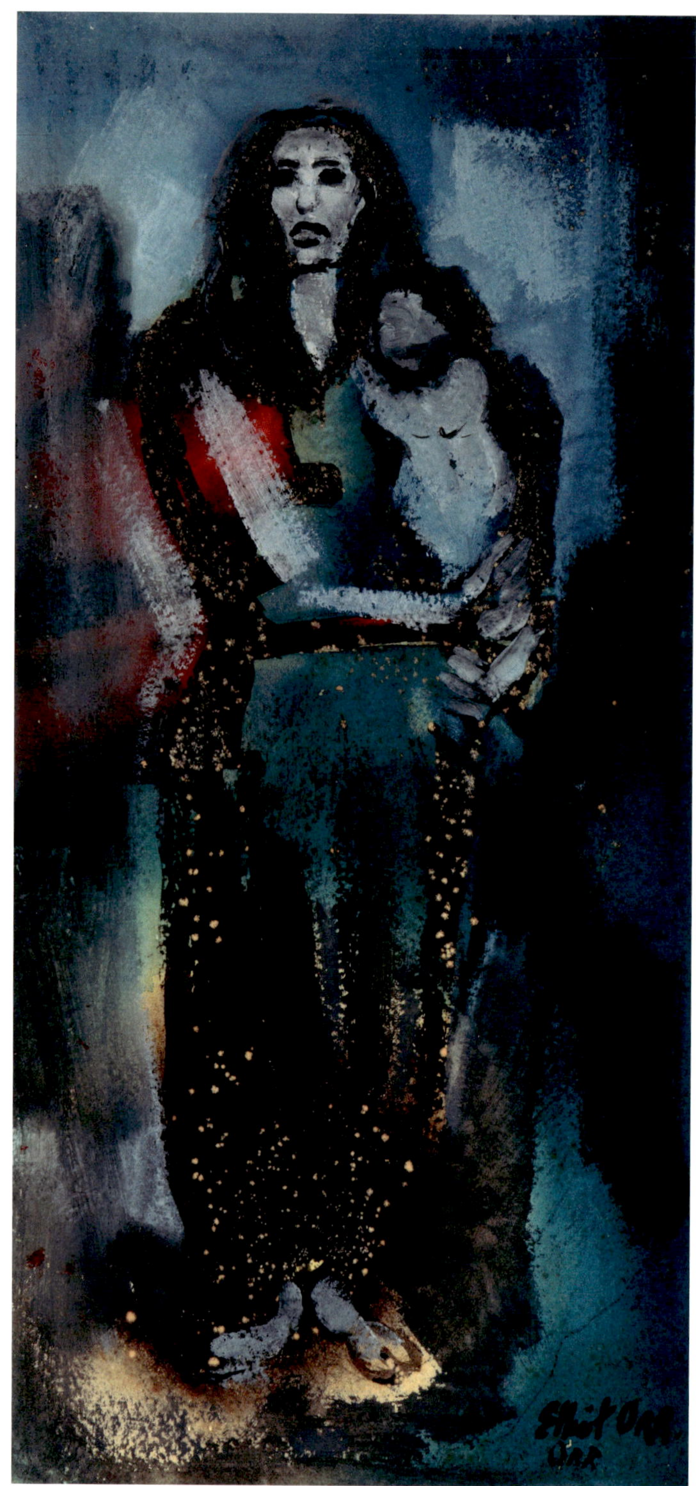

Elliot Orr, *Mother and Child*, 1932. Watercolor on paper, 15 1/8 × 7½ inches. *Anonymous gift*, 2011.

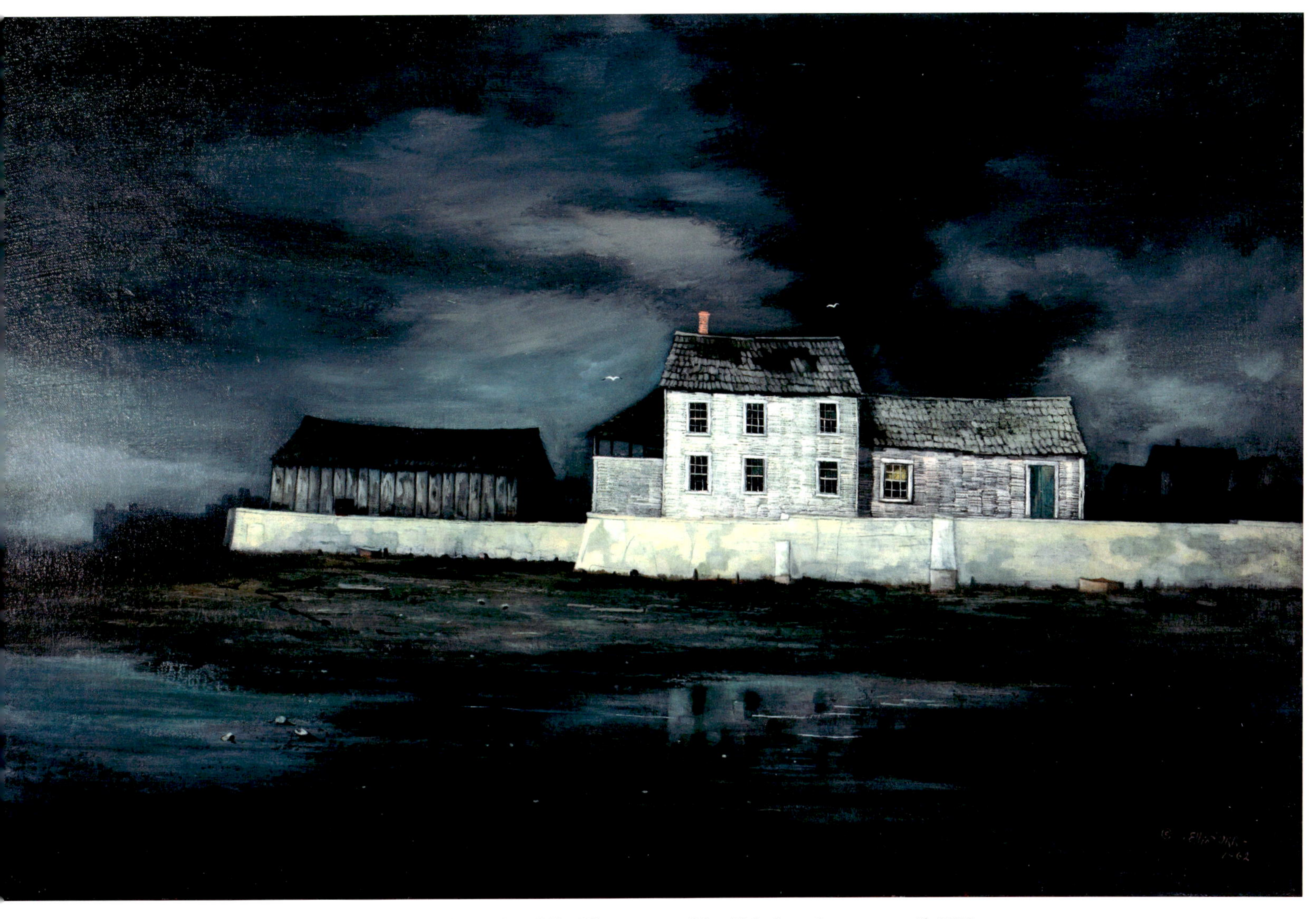

Elliot Orr, *Into the Night,* 1962. Oil on canvas, 26 × 30 inches. *Anonymous gift*, 2011.

MARTHA CAHOON
(1905–1999)

Martha Farham, better known as Martha Cahoon, was living with her family in Harwich on Cape Cod when she met Ralph Cahoon, whom she married in 1932.

Martha's father, Axel Farham, decorated furniture and she worked with him. After she and Ralph married, she taught him the craft. They settled in the neighboring town of Osterville and began decorating tables, chairs, dressers, chests, and other items including tin trays and wooden bowls. Their work followed in the Swedish, Pennsylvania Dutch, and American folk traditions. During World War I, Ralph painted battleships at the shipyard in Quincy.

After the war, Ralph and Martha bought the 1775 Crocker house in Cotuit. The building is now the Cahoon Museum of American Art. The couple began creating their own folk designs and soon took up painting. Ralph's whimsical folk art is best known for depicting sailors and mermaids in New England seaside settings adorned with lighthouses, clipper ships, and hot-air balloons. Martha's nostalgic views of country scenes and flower and fruit still lifes are in the same folk tradition. However, Martha's *Mermaid and Sea Serpent* and *Balloons,* in the Cape Cod Museum of Art collection, relate to her husband's work by incorporating a mermaid in a sea view and hot-air balloons floating among the clouds.

In 1953, Joan Whitney Payson began showing the couple's work at the Country Art Gallery on Long Island. By 1960, the Cahoons were exhibiting their work on Nantucket and in Boston and Florida. Their work was collected by members of the Kennedy, Mellon, and duPont families. Josiah K. Lilly III founded Heritage Plantation of Sandwich (now Heritage Museums and Gardens) in Sandwich, Massachusetts, which has many Cahoon works in its collection, as does the Cahoon Museum of American Art in Cotuit, Massachusetts.

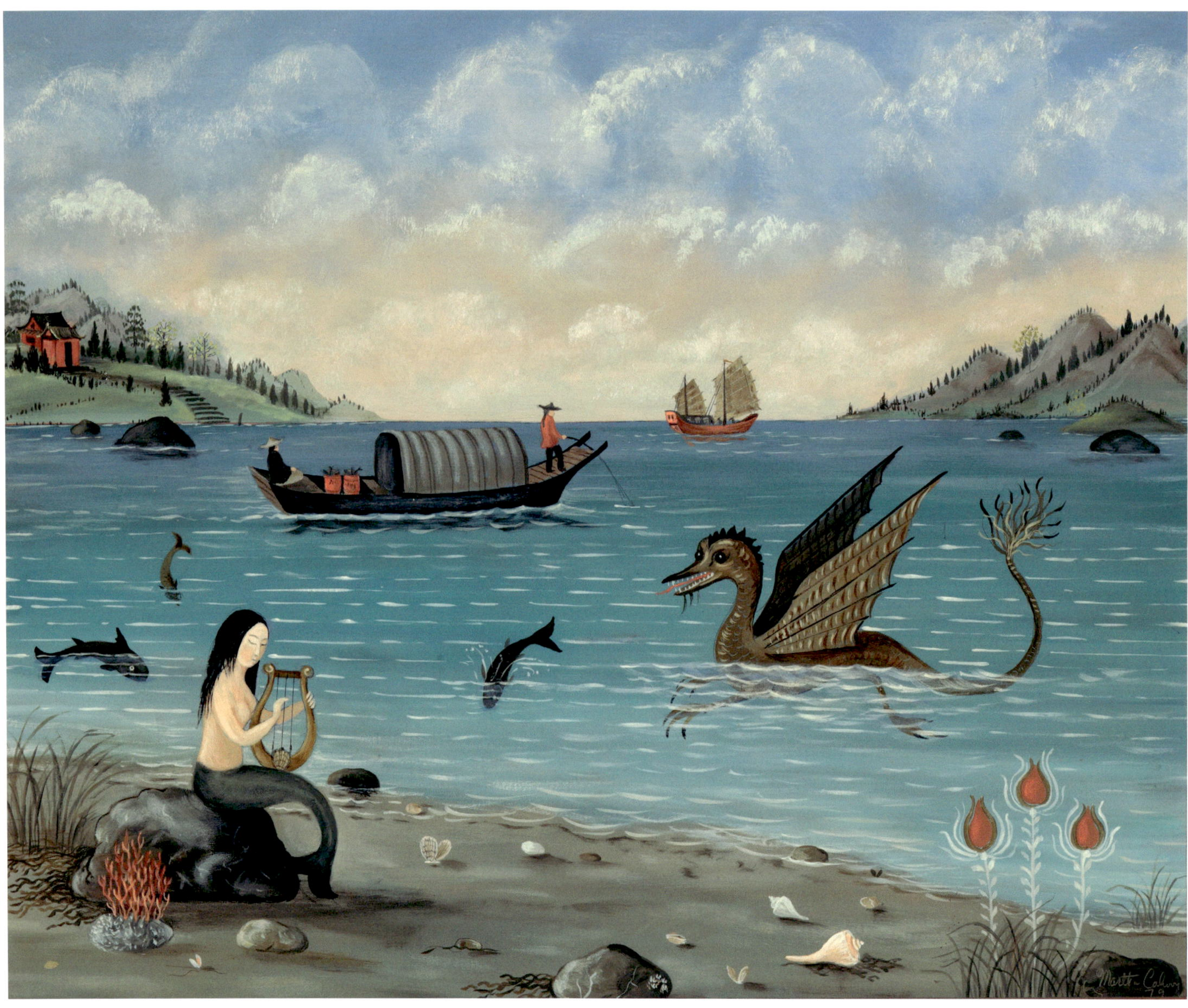

Martha Cahoon, *Mermaid and Sea Serpent*, n.d. Oil on masonite, 15½ × 20 inches. *Anonymous gift*, 1990.

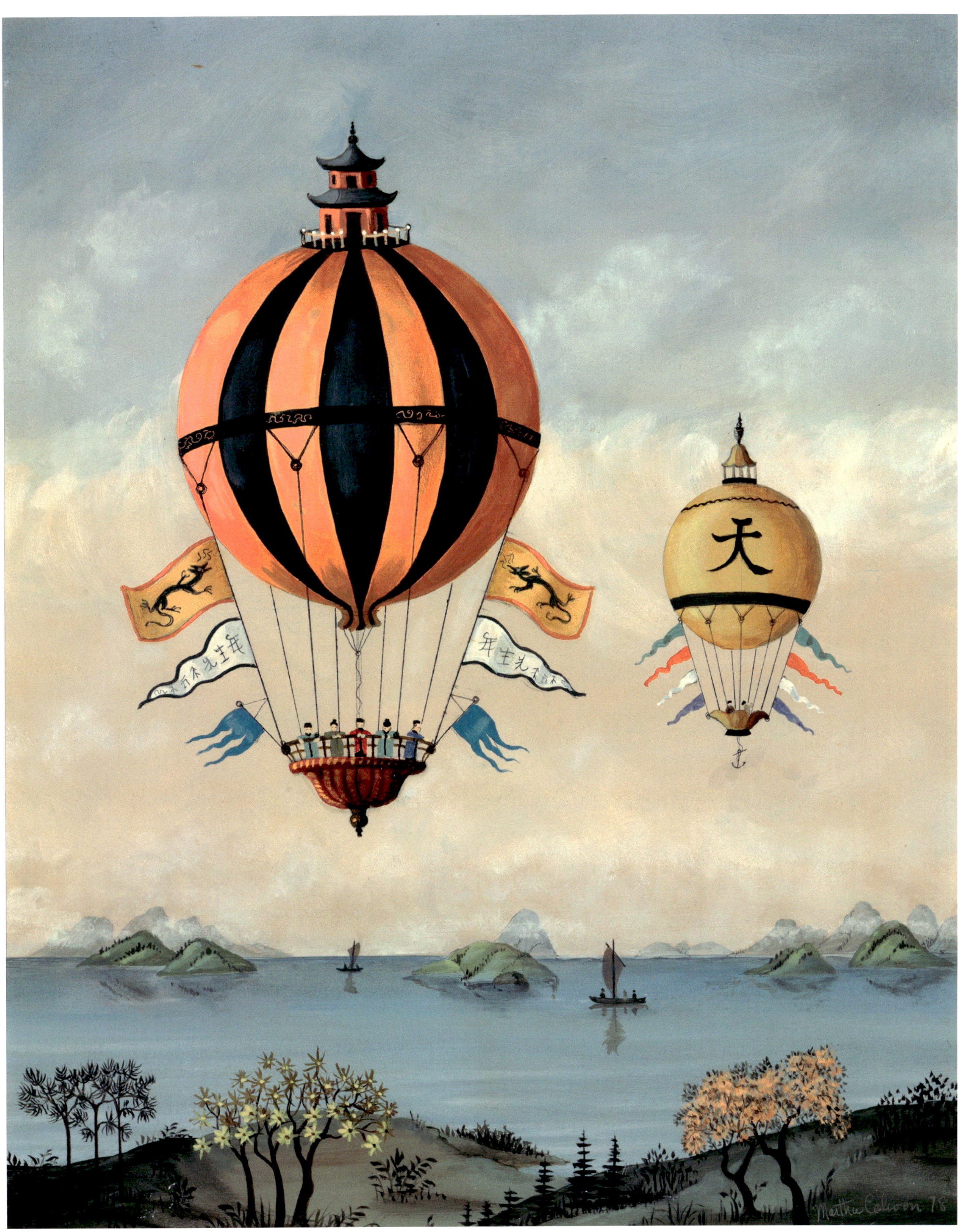

Martha Cahoon, *Balloons,* 1978. Oil on masonite, 15½ × 12½ inches. *Anonymous gift*, 1990.

BETTY LANE
(1907–1996)

Betty Lane's art runs across a spectrum of styles and subjects, which is largely representational, but sometimes flirts with abstraction.

Born in Washington, DC, she studied at the Corcoran School of Art, in Washington, DC, and then transferred to Massachusetts Normal Art School (now Massachusetts College of Art). In 1928, she went to Paris to study with cubist André L'Hote. Two years later she returned to Washington, and Duncan Phillips of the Phillips Memorial Gallery (now the Phillips Collection) gave her an exhibition.

She returned to Europe, and in England met and married Gerald Noxon, a Canadian writer and filmmaker. In 1939 with the start of World War II, Lane, Noxon, and their son went to Canada, and Lane returned to her art.

Lane's early work was influenced by surrealism, but by the 1940s, she began painting portraits of family and friends, which are straightforward, simple compositions yet reveal an intimate connection and an insightfulness into the personality of the subject. *Self-Portrait (Retired, Liberation, MPS)* in the Cape Cod Museum of Art collection, shows a somber Lane, apparently pondering her future after retiring from a fourteen-year stint teaching at Miss Porter's School in Farmington, Connecticut. *Portrait of Geissbuhler,* in the collection, is an expressionistic rendering of artist Arnold Geissbuhler.

Lane's paintings have strong and lively colors and evoke a buoyancy and spontaneity. Although she rarely departed from representational subjects, her modernism is revealed in the flatness of her landscapes, as in *Gay Head*, in the museum collection, and the harmonic patterns that spread across her compositions.

After retiring from teaching, Lane settled in Brewster on Cape Cod, and became part of the Stony Brook circle of artists, which included painters Howard Gibbs and Vernon Smith, sculptors Harry Holl and Geissbuhler, and writers Conrad Aiken and John Hay.

Her works are in the collections of several museums, including the Metropolitan Museum of Art in New York and the Phillips Collection in Washington, DC.

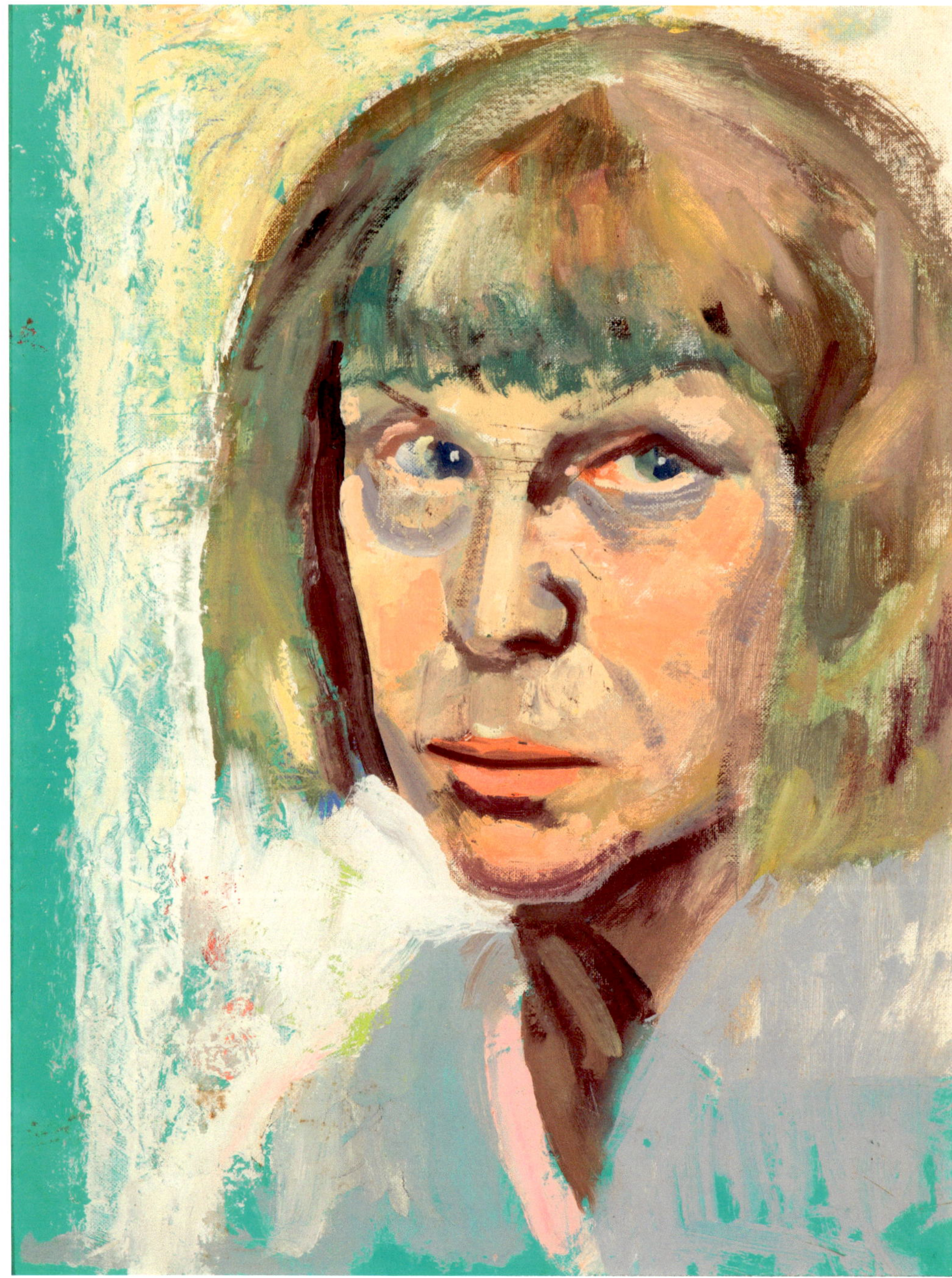

Betty Lane, *Self Portrait* (Retired, Liberation, MPS), 1966. Oil on board, 18 × 14 inches. *Gift of Nicholas and Nicky Noxon*, 2006.

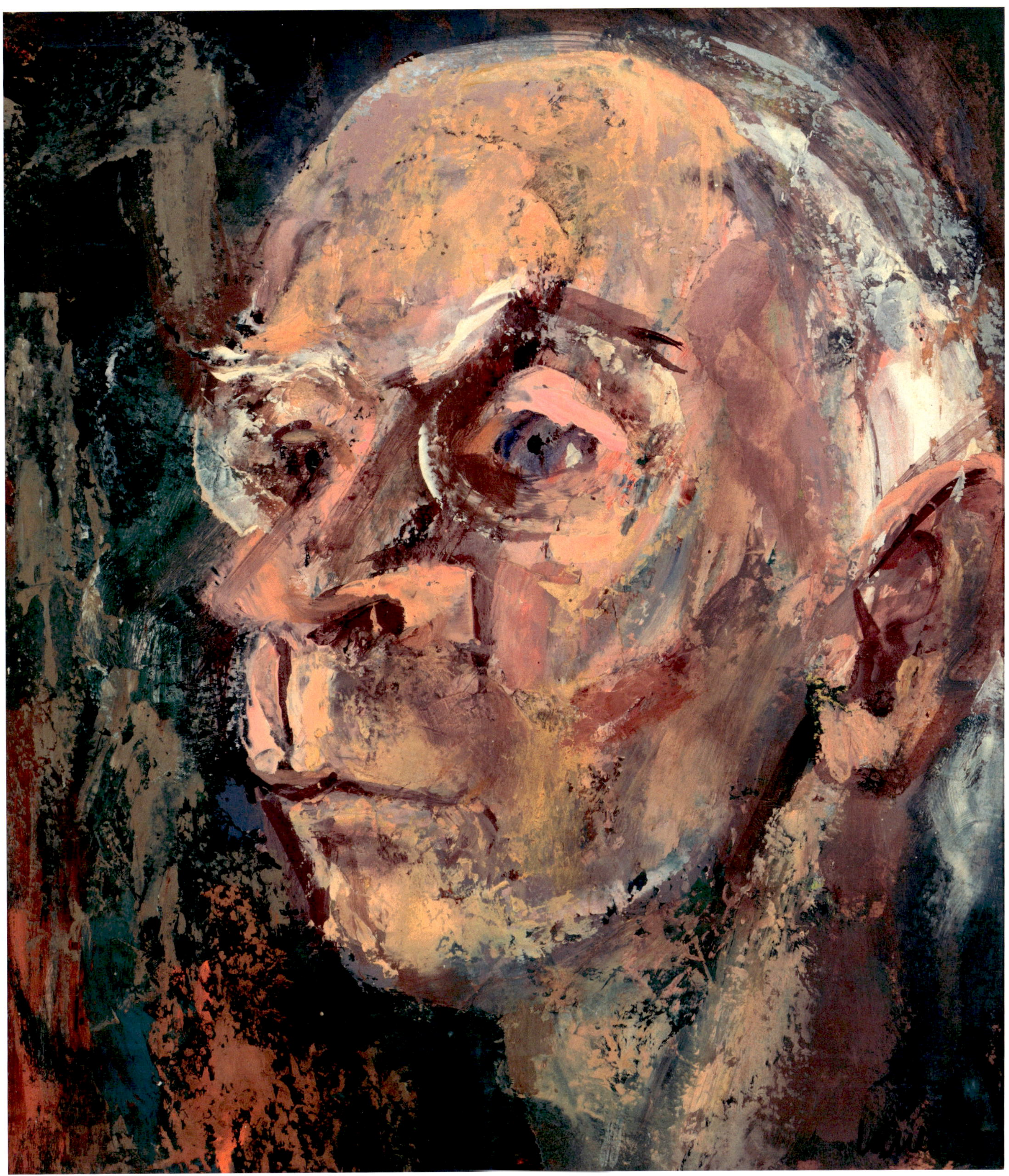

Betty Lane, *Portrait of Geissbuhler,* 1962. Oil on board, 15 × 13 inches. *Gift of Nicholas and Nicky Noxon*, 2006.

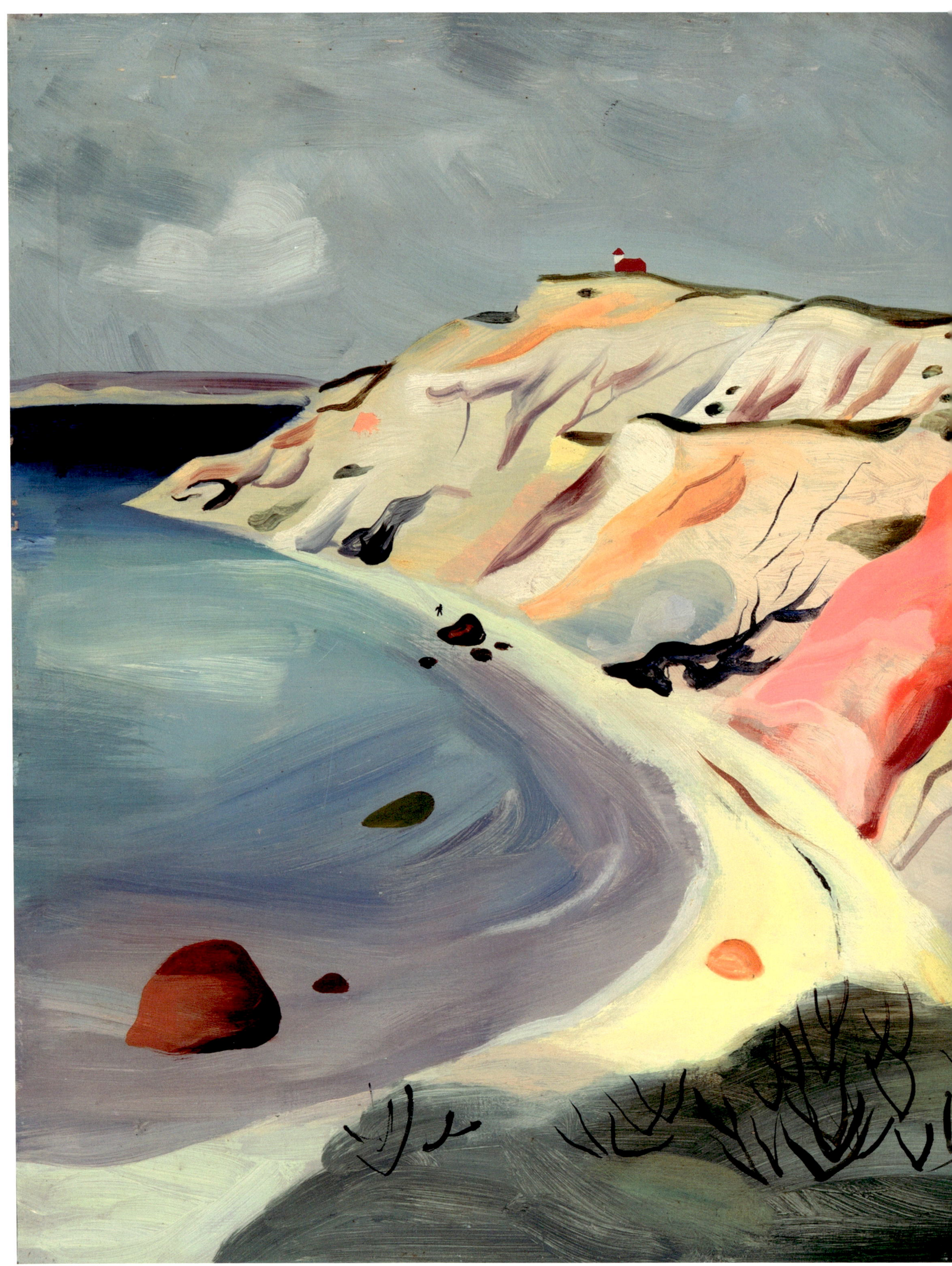

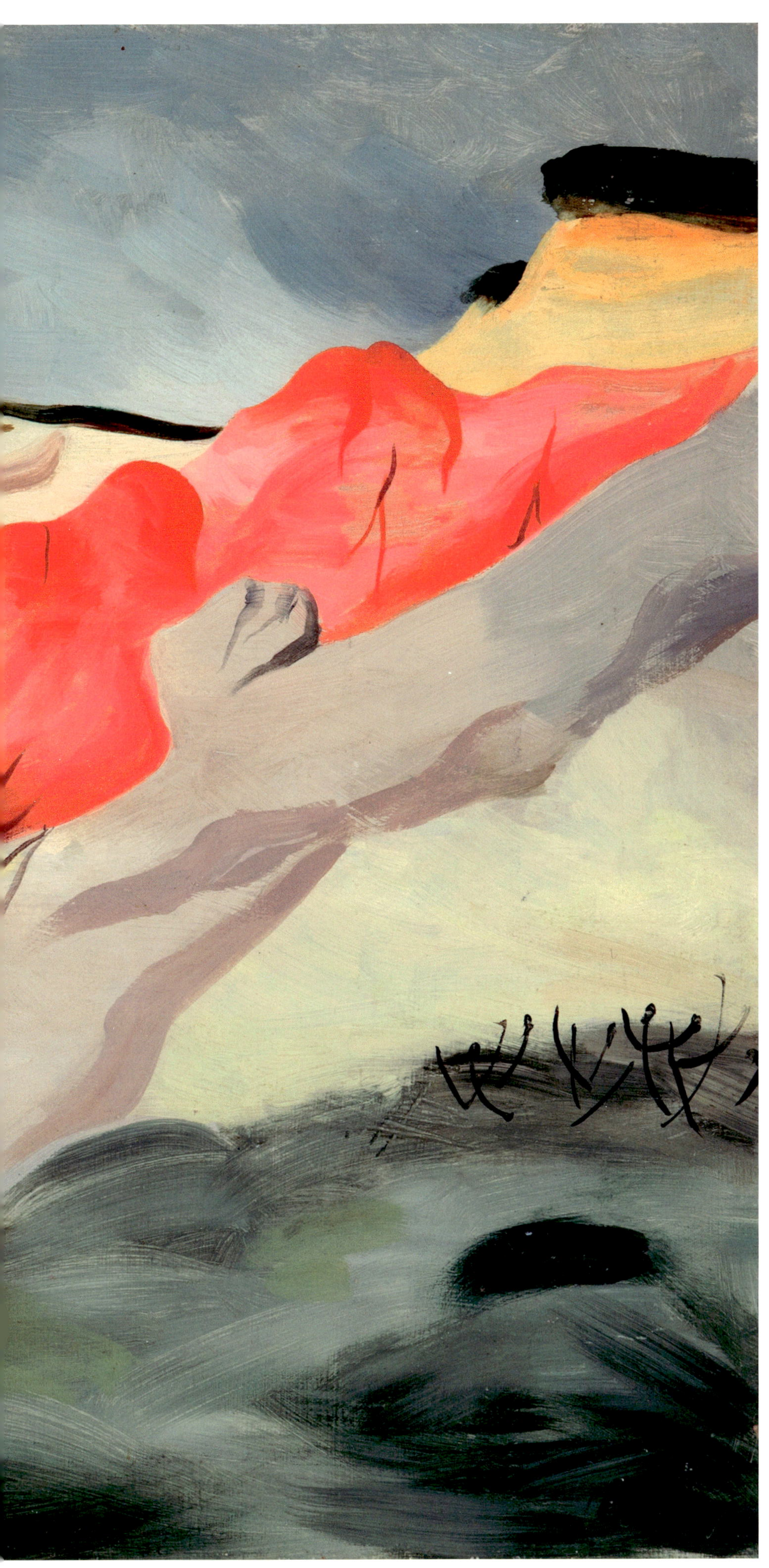

Betty Lane, *Gayhead*, 1947. Oil on board, 17¾ × 23½ inches. *Gift of Nicholas and Nicky Noxon*, 2006.

KENNETH STUBBS
(1907–1967)

Kenneth Stubbs molded figures from the clay of his native Georgia in his childhood, and went on to study at Corcoran School of Art in Washington, DC, from 1926 to 1930. In the 1930s, he took classes with E. Ambrose Webster in Provincetown. He also traveled to Italy to study at Accademia di Belle Arti in Florence.

Stubbs was influenced by cubists Juan Gris and Georges Braque. He was interested in conveying a sense of motion largely with straight lines and color. The cubist influences resulted in paintings composed of flat or semi-flat patterns in bright, fresh colors and angular, faceted forms that provide a dynamic energy to the works. His work also included lyrical watercolors and Japanese brush drawings.

He was an active member of the Provincetown art colony for years, and many of his paintings capture the seaside and the town's streets and cottages in simple cubistic shapes and vibrant colors. In the Cape Cod Museum of Art collection is *Shore Scape,* depicting a topsy-turvy assemblage of pared-down cottages. Stubbs's still lifes are bold and complex arrangements that recall the work of Gris, but with a bright American sense of joy added through his faceting of planes marked by lively colors. *Still Life with Melon*, also in the museum collection, goes even further and is essentially abstract.

Stubbs taught painting and drawing at the Corcoran School of Art in Washington, DC, for seventeen years both before and after World War II. His work is in the collections of the National Portrait Gallery in Washington, DC, and the University of Maryland.

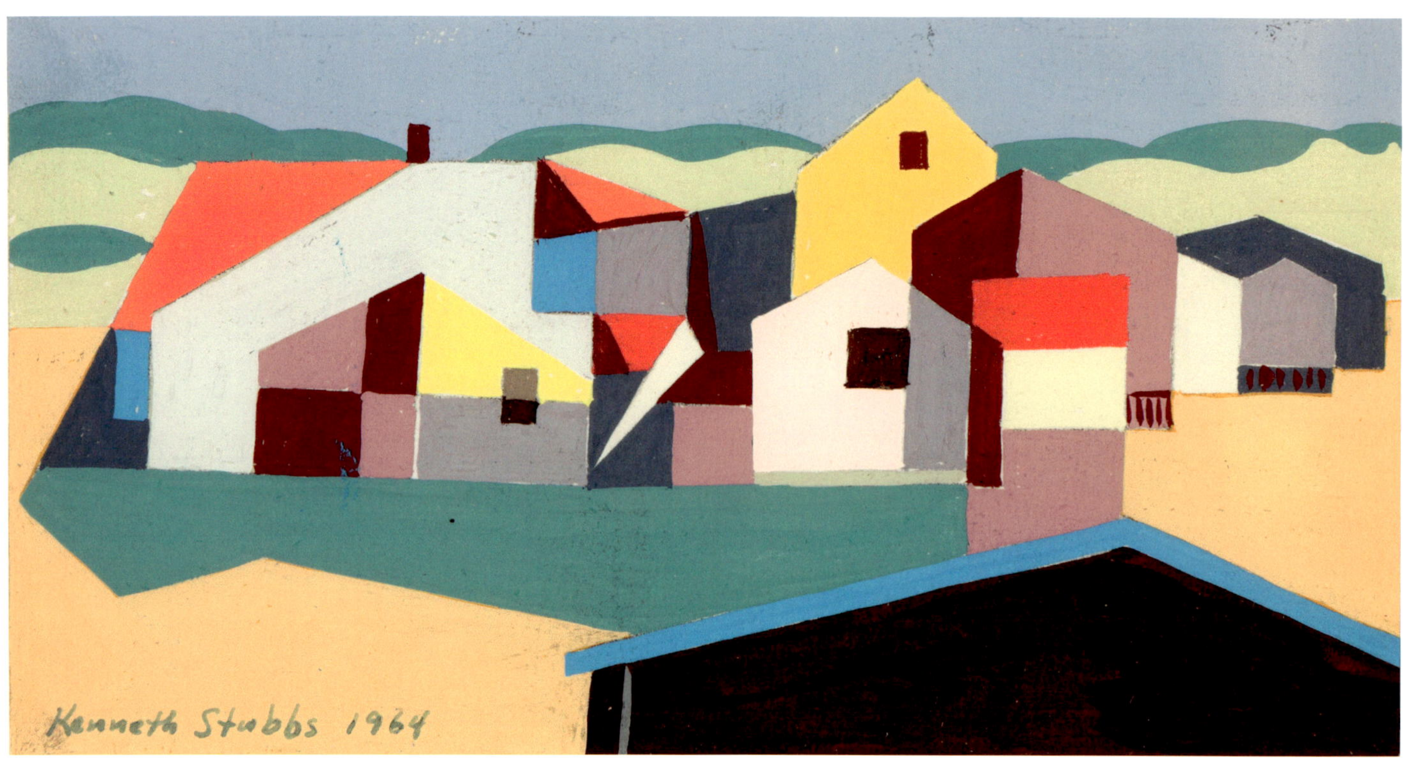

Kenneth Stubbs, *Shore Scape*, 1964. Casein on paper, 9¼ × 11¾ inches. *Gift of Miriam Stubbs*, 1989.

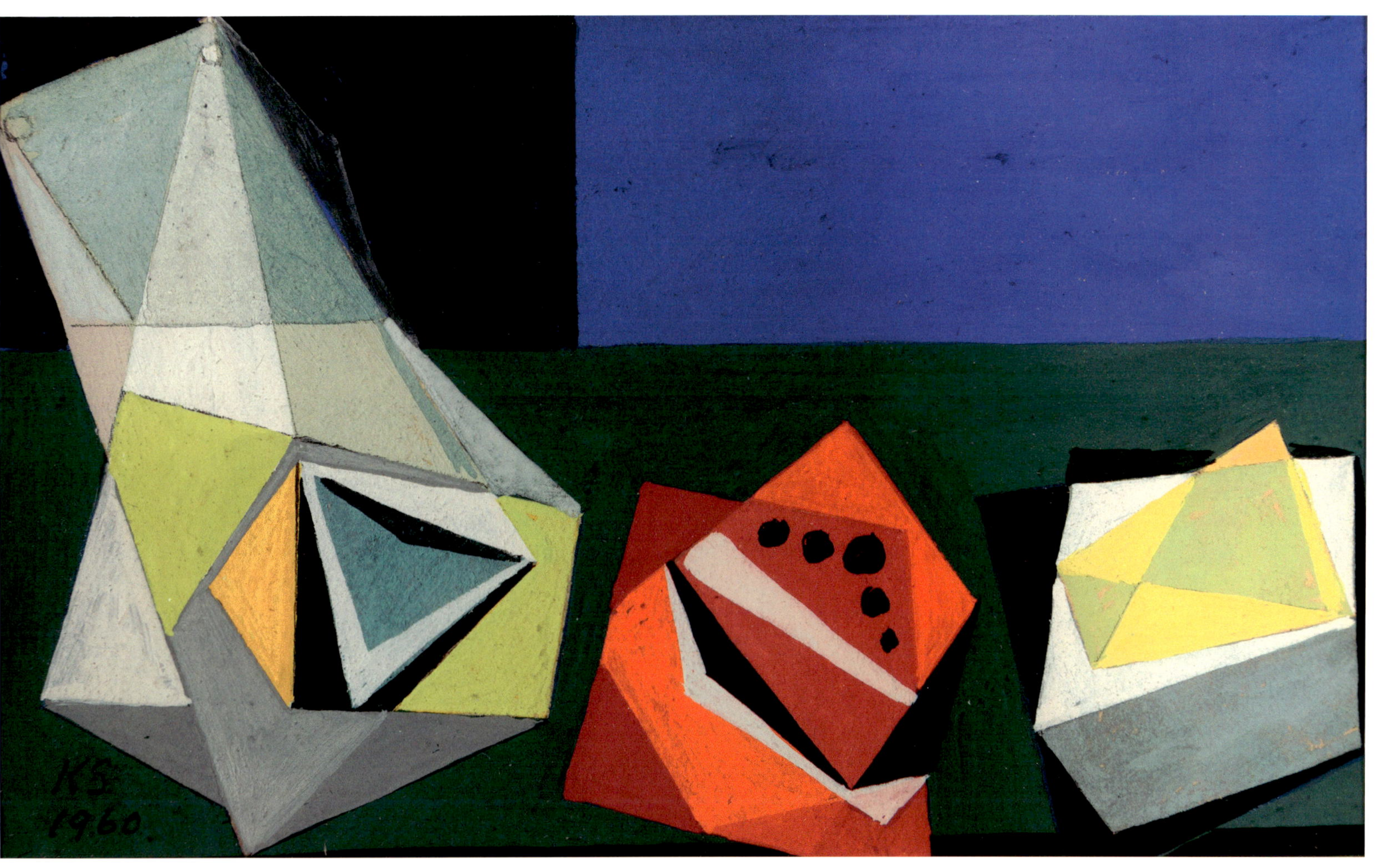

Kenneth Stubbs, *Still Life with Melon*, 1960. Casein on paper, 3⅓ × 5⅓ inches. *Gift of Miriam Stubbs*, 1989.

PHILIP C. MALICOAT
(1908–1981)

Philip Malicoat studied at the John Herron Art Institute in his native Indiana in the late 1920s. From there he went to Provincetown to take classes with Charles Hawthorne during the summers of 1929 and 1930. After seeing the ocean for the first time this Midwesterner became enamored with the area and in 1931, he made Provincetown his home. He went on to study drawing with Edwin Dickinson during the winter of 1931–32.

Provincetown and the surrounding area became the subject of his atmospheric paintings. They capture various views of the sea from quiet to turbulent. He is known for his loose brushwork, sedate colors, and diffused contours. During the late 1930s, Malicoat was employed by the Massachusetts Federal Art Project, and submitted oils that depict local Provincetown scenes with subtle coloring and almost dream-like images. In the Cape Cod Museum of Art collection, the drawing *Thumbprint*, which shows the fragment of a nude torso, is a fine example of his diffused style.

Malicoat was a fixture in the art colony, as an active member of the Provincetown Art Association and later one of the founders of the Fine Arts Work Center. He was a member of the Beachcombers, a social group that included artists Gerrit Beneker, Edwin Dickinson, William Paxton, Karl Knaths, Ross Moffett, and Frederick Waugh.

He was also active in Woodstock, New York, and exhibited at various museums including the National Academy of Design, the Art Institute of Chicago, and the Pennsylvania Academy of Fine Arts. His works are included in the museum collections of the Hirshhorn Museum and Sculpture Garden in Washington, DC, and the Chrysler Museum of Art in Norfolk, Virginia.

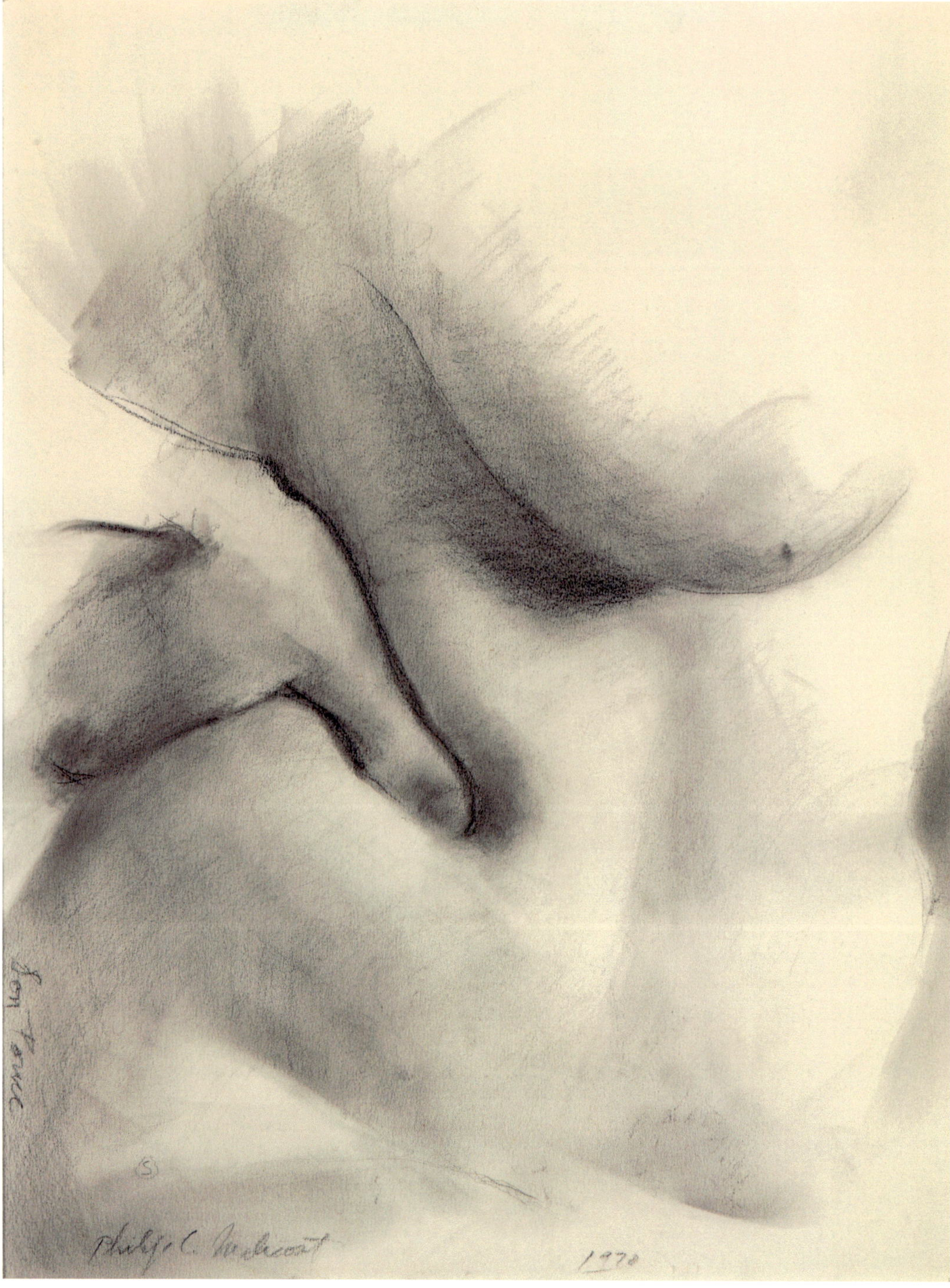

Philip C. Malicoat, *Thumbprint*, 1970. Pencil and charcoal on paper, 13 ⅜ × 10⅜ inches. *Gift of Maria Sylvester in memory of Gerald D. Sylvester*, 1987.

HERMAN MARIL
(1908–1986)

Herman Maril's art was inspired by nature and the world around him. His seascapes, landscapes, and interiors were simplified, and like so many representational artists of the twentieth century, abstraction played a role in his compositions.

Born in Baltimore, he studied at what is now the Maryland Institute College of Art. In 1934, he first visited Provincetown, and in subsequent years spent many summers at the tip of Cape Cod, where he was struck by the light that has attracted artists there for more than a century. In Provincetown he painted the seaside, as in *Angry Waters* and *Fish House*, in the Cape Cod Museum of Art collection. In Baltimore, his theme was the city. In the 1930s, Duncan Phillips, founder of the Phillips Collection in Washington, DC, discovered Maril and began collecting his works.

Maril was influenced by the art of Mark Rothko, Milton Avery, and Karl Knaths. You can especially see the influence of Avery in Maril's flat areas of color and his emphasis on the harmony of his spatial planes, as in *The Flats* and *Dark Waters* in the museum collection. Maril also was influenced by what he observed in his travels to a variety of places, including Mexico, Spain, Portugal, California, New Mexico, and Maine.

In the late 1930s, working with the Works Progress Administration, he was commissioned to paint murals in the post offices of Scranton, Pennsylvania, and Alta Vista, Virginia. He also had a painting selected by Eleanor Roosevelt to hang in the White House, which is now in the Smithsonian American Art Museum collection. After his World War II military service, he had a long career as professor in the art department of the University of Maryland.

In 1967, the Baltimore Museum of Art published a monograph on Maril, in conjunction with a solo exhibition of his works. The National Institute of Arts and Letters honored him in 1978. His works are also included in the collections of the Whitney Museum of American Art and the Museum of Modern Art in New York, and the Baltimore Museum of Art.

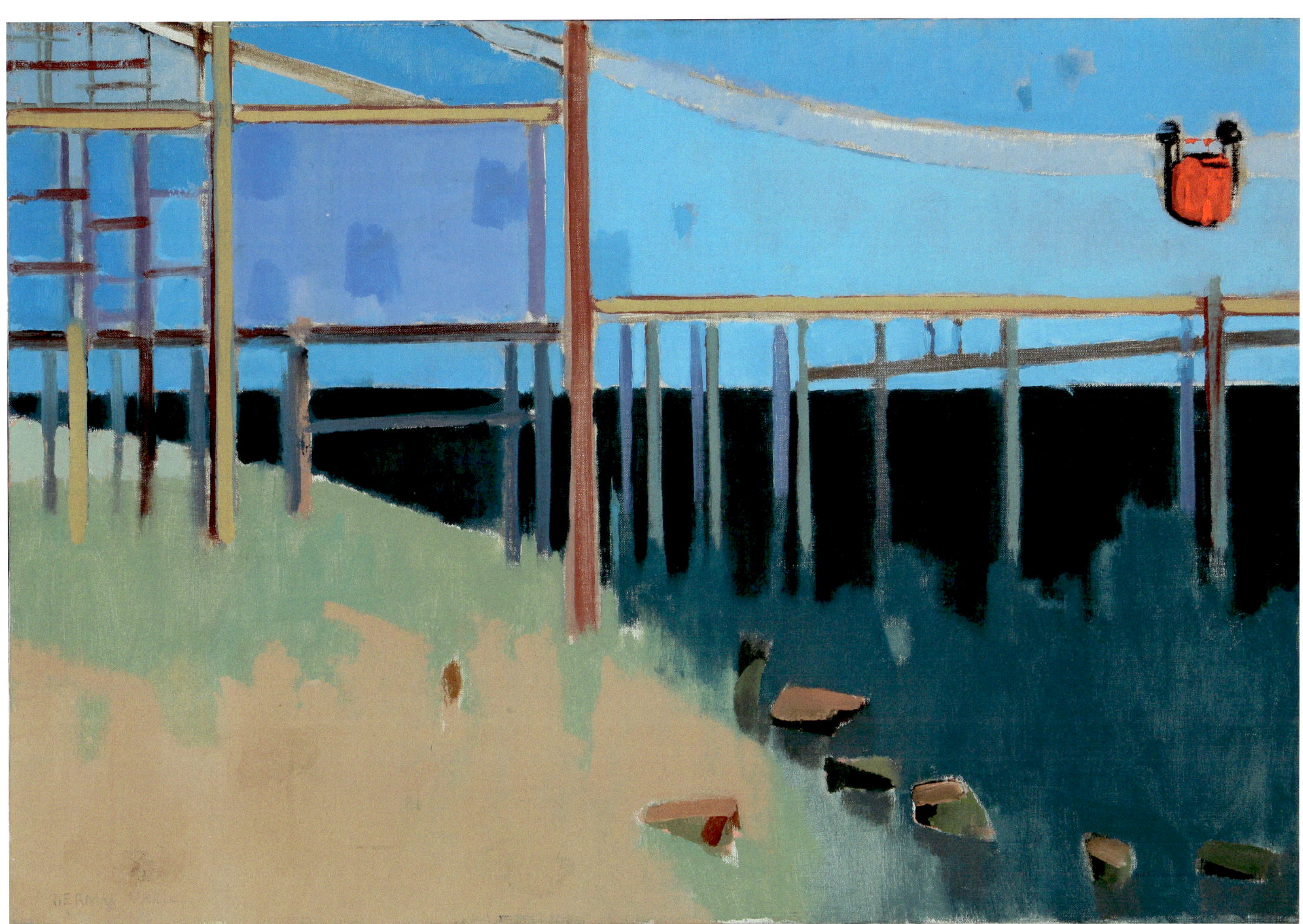

Herman Maril, *Fish House*, 1971. Oil on canvas, 18 × 26 inches. *Gift of Esta C. Maril*, 1991.

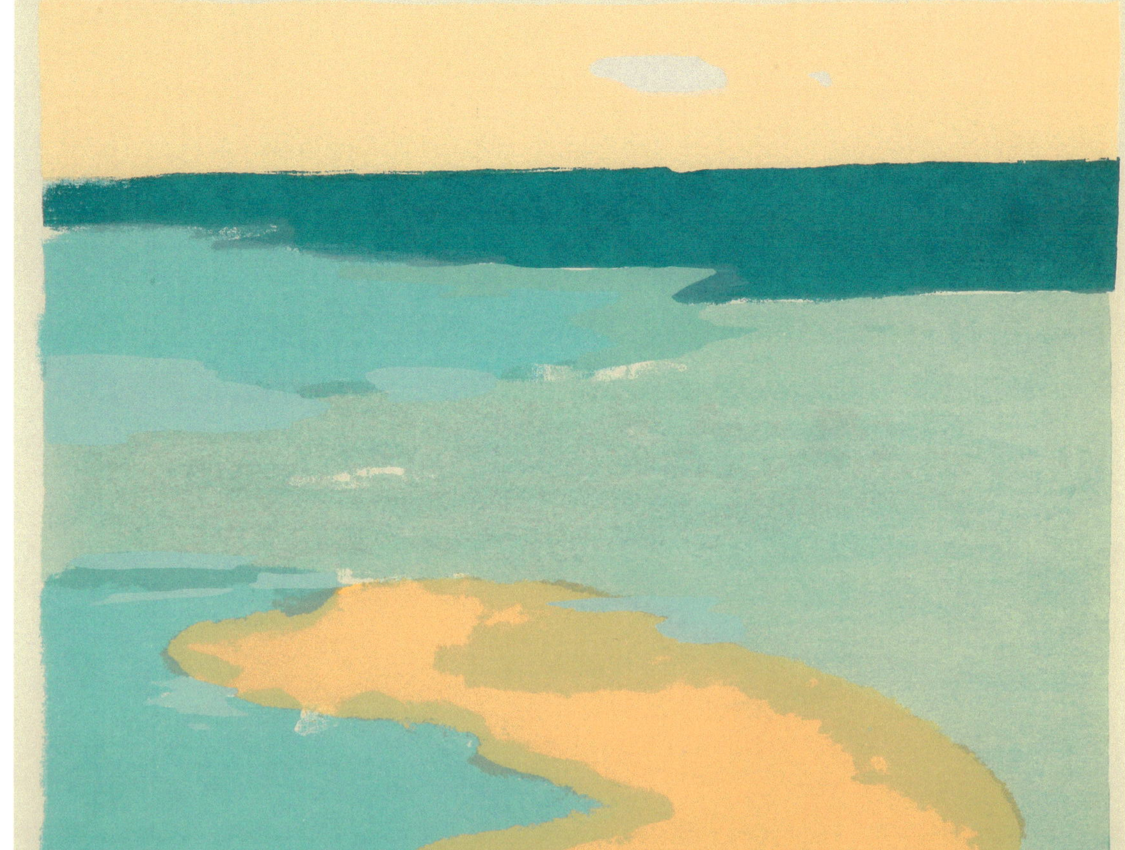

Herman Maril, *The Flats* 56/100, 1975–1980. Serigraph on paper, 16½ × 19¾ inches. *Gift of Esta C. Maril*, 1988.

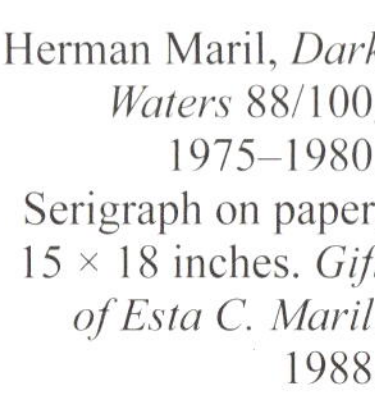

Herman Maril, *Dark Waters* 88/100, 1975–1980. Serigraph on paper, 15 × 18 inches. *Gift of Esta C. Maril*, 1988.

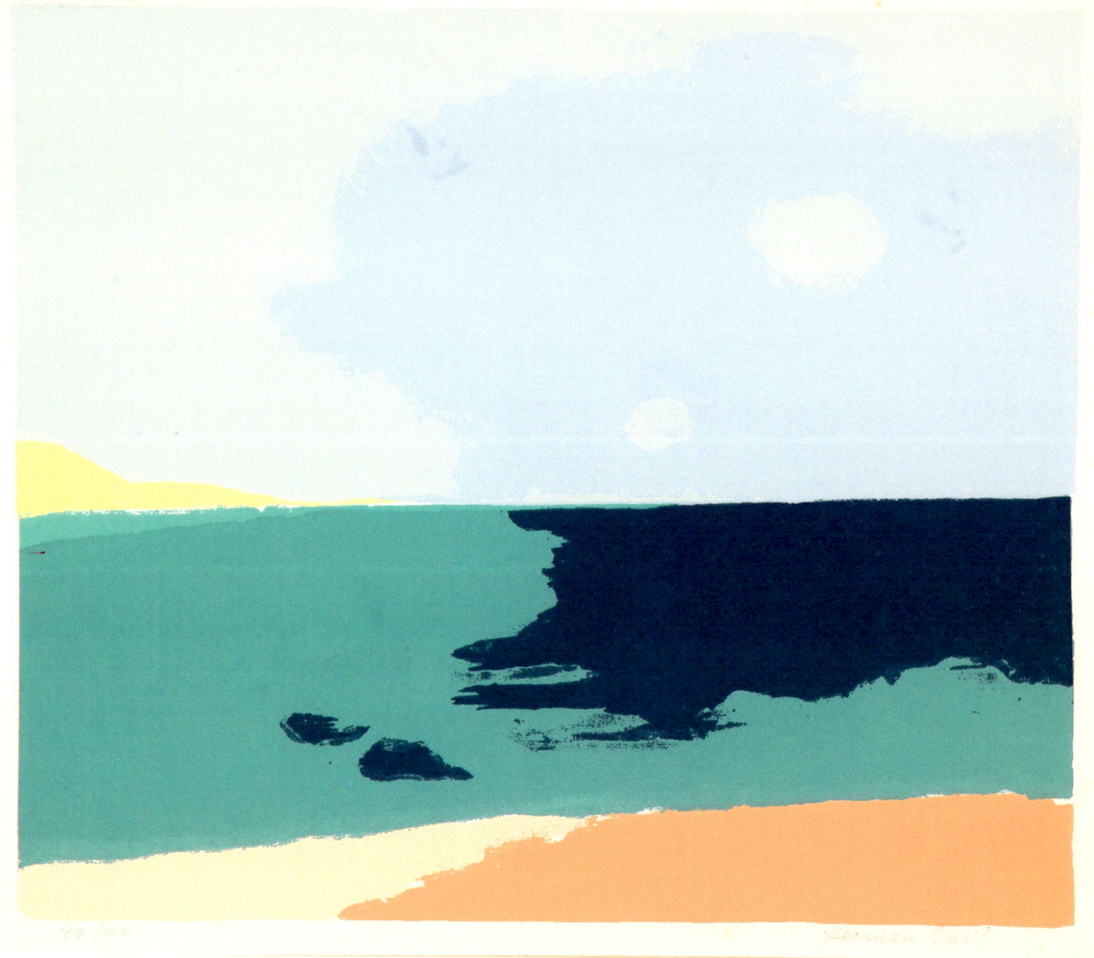

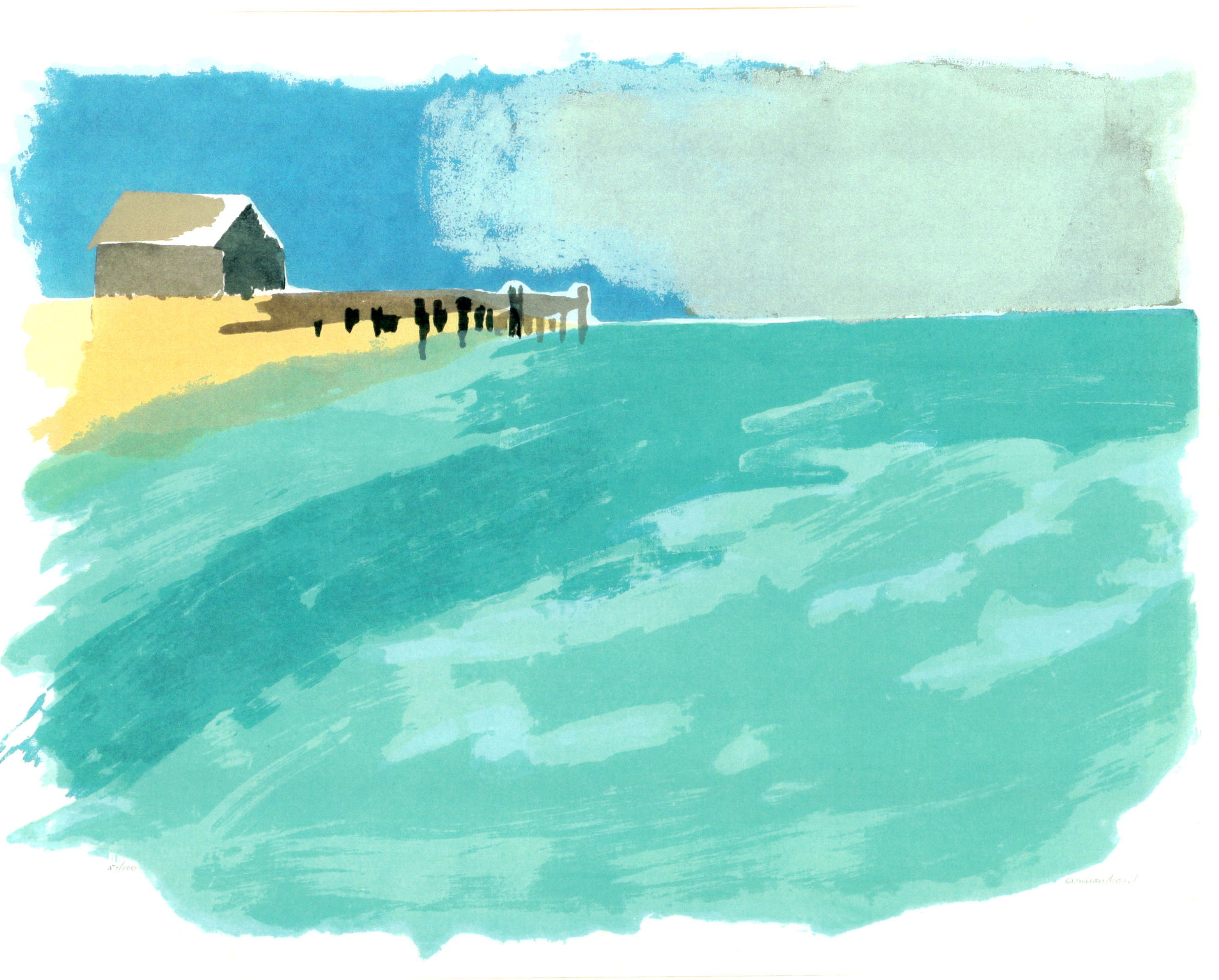

Herman Maril, *Angry Waters* 51/100, 1975–1980. Serigraph on paper, 26¼ × 30½ inches. *Gift of Esta C. Maril*, 1988.

GEORGE MCNEIL
(1908–1995)

Although George McNeil was included in the second wave of abstract expressionist artists, in the 1960s he moved on to figurative expressionism with paintings that vibrate in rambunctious colors and highly charged images relating to contemporary life. Faces and objects erupt in perpetual motion in these works.

McNeil was born in Brooklyn and studied at the Pratt Institute, the Art Students League, and with Hans Hofmann from 1932 to 1936, and the Hofmann influence is present in his bold colors and pulsating rhythms. During the Depression, he worked with the Federal Art Project of the Works Progress Administration. McNeil spent summers in Provincetown from the mid-1930s until the early '60s. In 1936, he was a founding member of the American Abstract Artists, an organization committed to promoting abstract and nonobjective art. He taught at the University of Wyoming, University of California at Berkeley, and New York Studio School and Pratt Institute in New York City.

From the abstract expressionist *Post Position*, in the Cape Cod Museum of Art collection, he moved onto the figurative expressionist *No Uncertain Terms*, also in the museum collection. Big eyes emboldened by the riotous colors stare out while an outstretched hand seems to be reaching out to stop the viewer.

His *Disco* paintings, in which dancers gyrate in blazing colors, erupted from the time he spent watching MTV. Works from the 1980s evoke a picture of the razzle-dazzle and throbbing of urban life, of a wild, turbulent world, exciting and disorienting; these works are a big, brash circus of great emotions. His bold colors and emotionally drawn figures, which have a childlike reference, exude a playful quality, and at the same time a sensation of angst.

His works are in numerous museum collections, including the Museum of Modern Art, the Metropolitan Museum of Art, and the Whitney Museum of America Art in New York; the San Francisco Museum of Modern Art; the Los Angeles Museum of Contemporary Art; and the Walker Art Center in Minneapolis.

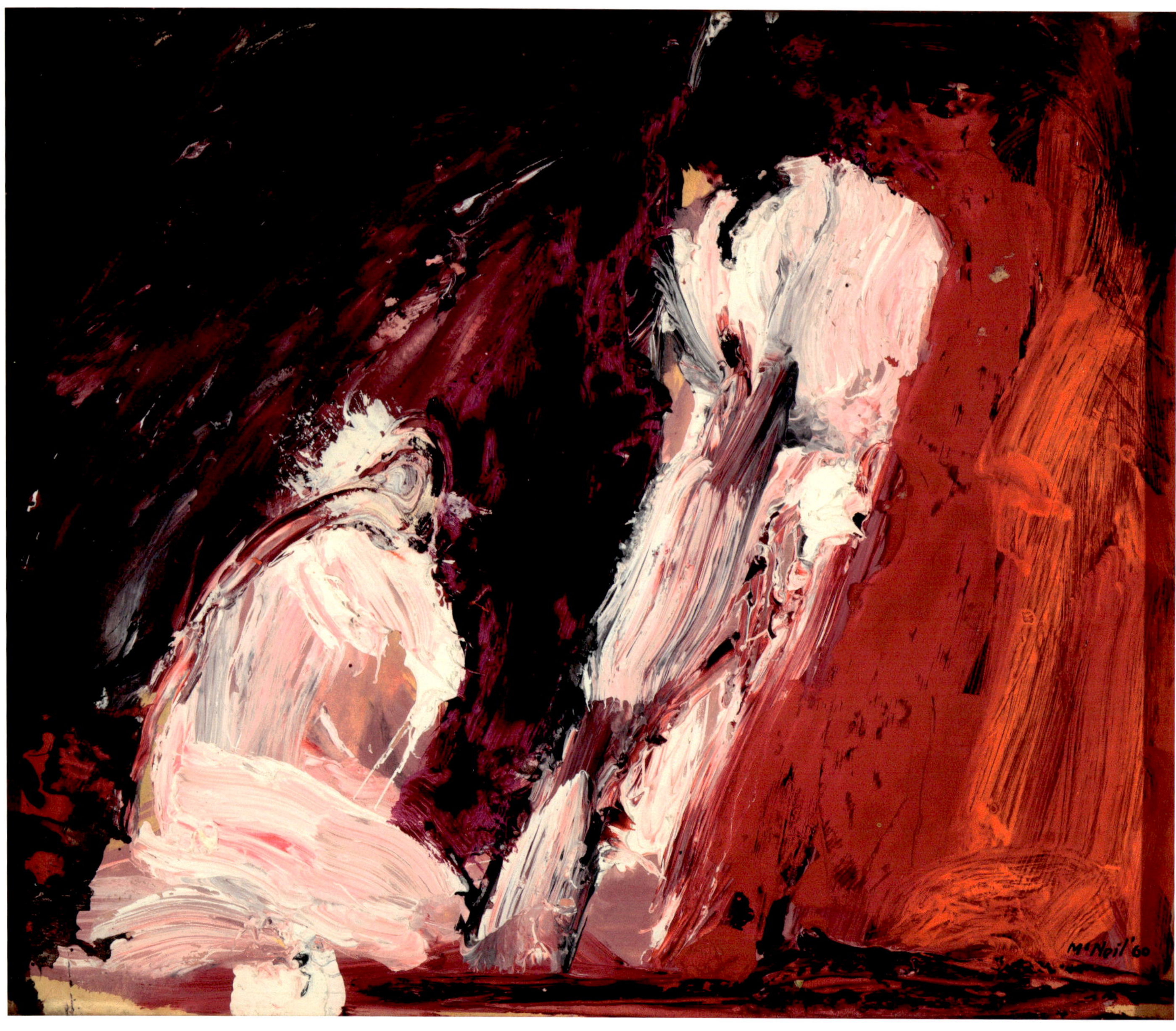

George McNeil, *Post Position,* 1960. Oil on paper, 13 × 16 inches. *Anonymous gift*, 1999.

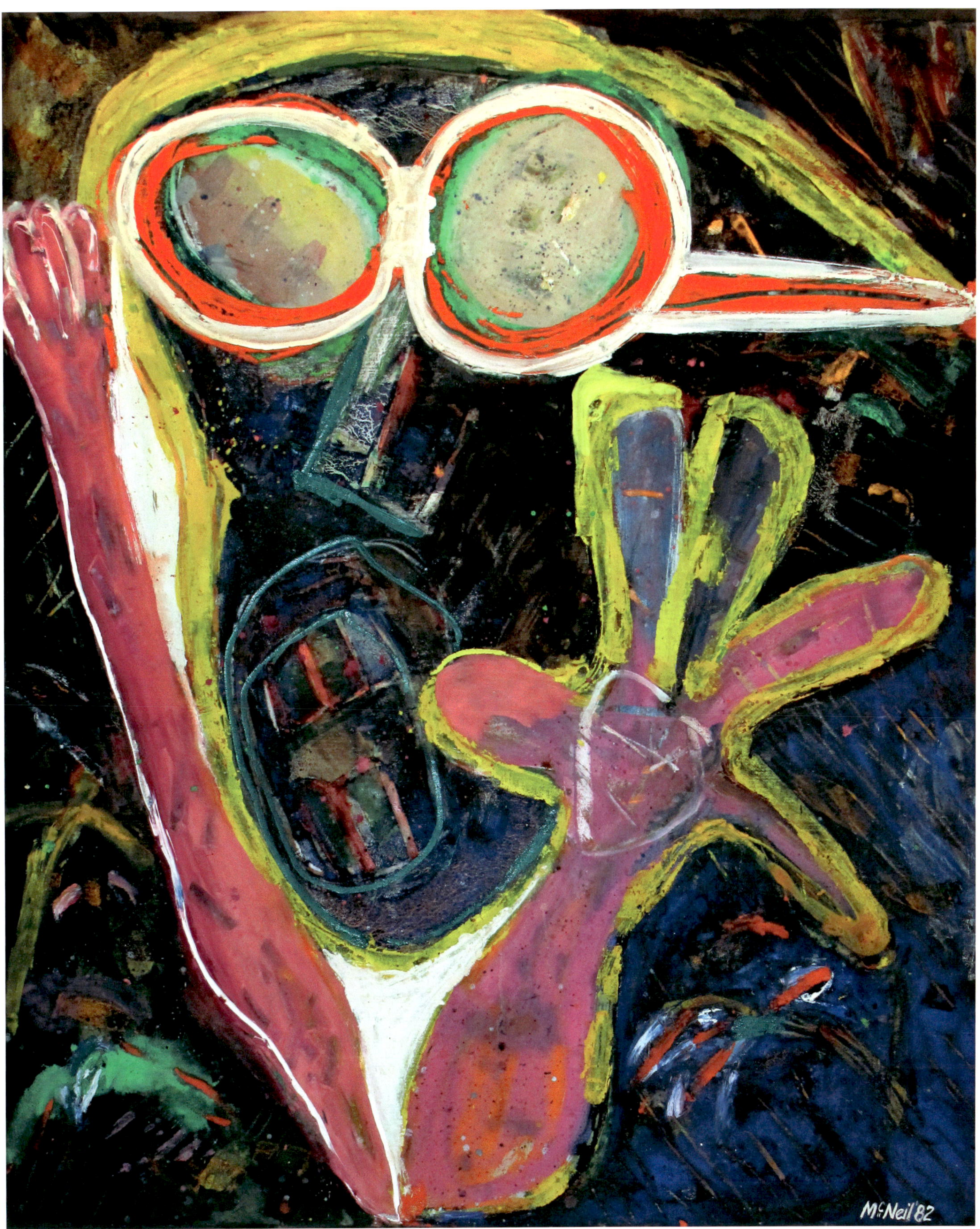

George McNeil, *No Uncertain Terms,* 1984. Oil on canvas, 67¼ × 56 inches. *Gift of the George McNeil Charitable Trust,* 2004.

LAWRENCE KUPFERMAN
(1909–1982)

Although Lawrence Kupferman was born and educated in Boston, known for its conservative approach to art, he became an abstract artist as early as the 1940s. In the late 1920s, Kupferman attended Boston's School of the Museum of Fine Arts and found the teaching of Philip L. Hale too rigid. Later, in 1932, he studied at the Massachusetts College of Art.

In the 1930s, working under the Federal Art Project of the WPA, his art was a realistic series of etchings and dry points, mostly of the facades of buildings, often Victorian architecture. His art changed to a more expressionistic style in the early 1940s, and soon after, abstract imagery took hold. Credited with bringing abstract expressionism to Boston, he was a link to New York painters through Provincetown, where he began spending summers in the 1940s.

Kupferman found Boston's artistic conservatism stifling, and Provincetown's freedom was a breath of fresh air. There he became friendly with New York progressives Mark Rothko, Hans Hofmann, Adolph Gottlieb, William Baziotes, Robert Motherwell, and Karl Knaths.

He was pouring paint on his canvases as early as 1941, allowing it to make its own way. His connection to the surrounding waters was realized in fluid brushwork and tiny, organic marine-like forms that float in a sea of color. His watercolor *Driftwood and Beach*, in the Cape Cod Museum of Art collection, is an example of his loose brushwork in a work that has a surreal quality. *Nauset Light*, also in the museum collection, is an abstract rendering, perhaps of the light that emanates from the Cape Cod lighthouse.

As a Jew growing up in an Irish-Catholic neighborhood, he felt the sting of anti-Semitism, so the Holocaust during World War II had a powerful influence on him. His work at the time exploded into images of figures lost and dissolving into veils of paint.

Kupferman taught painting at the Massachusetts College of Art. His works are in a number of other museum collections, including the Art Institute of Chicago, the Philadelphia Museum of Art, and the Harvard University Art Museums.

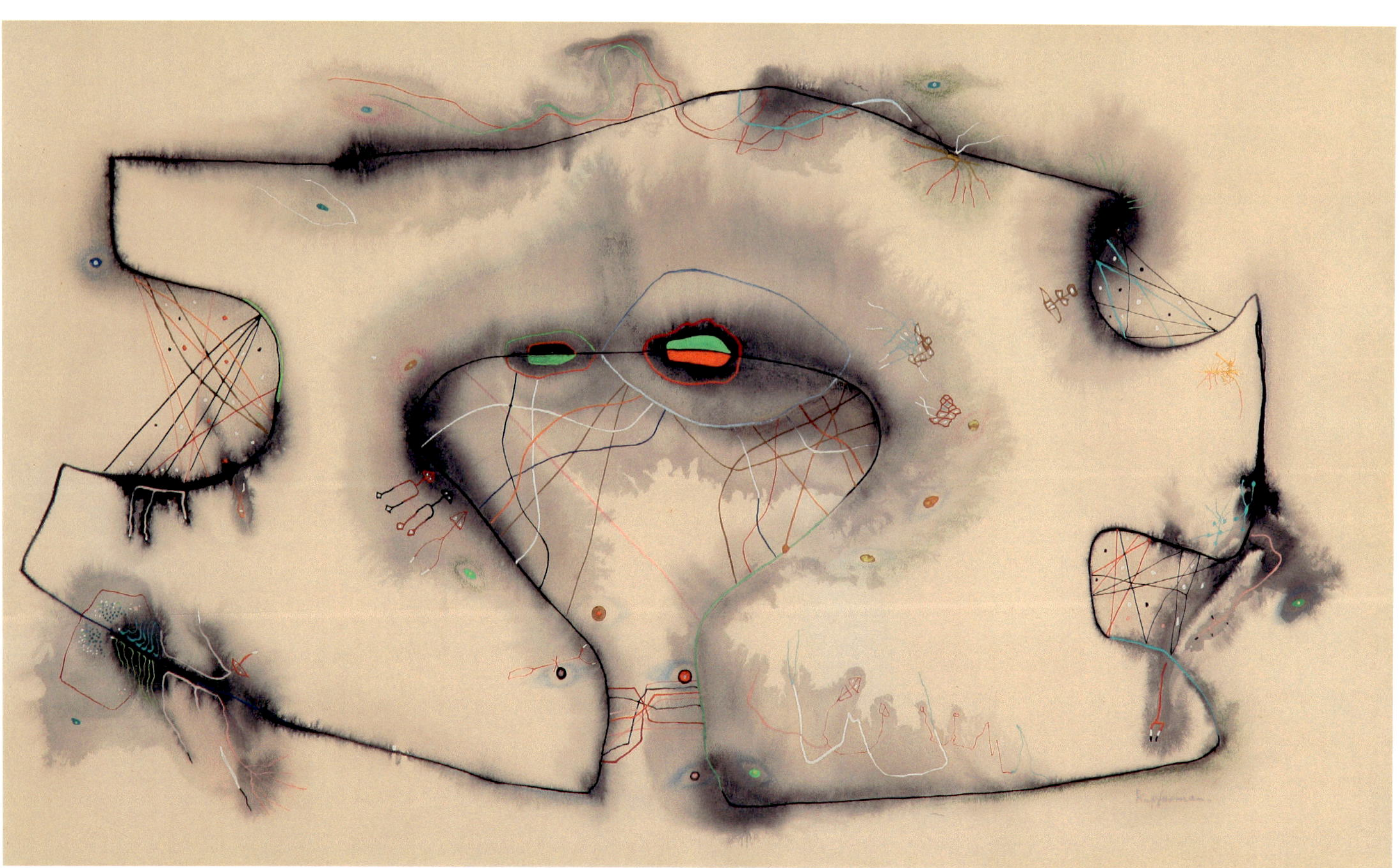

Lawrence Kupferman, *Nauset Light*, 1949. India ink on casein on paper, 21½ × 12¾ inches. *Gift of Sara Gorfinkle*, 1995.

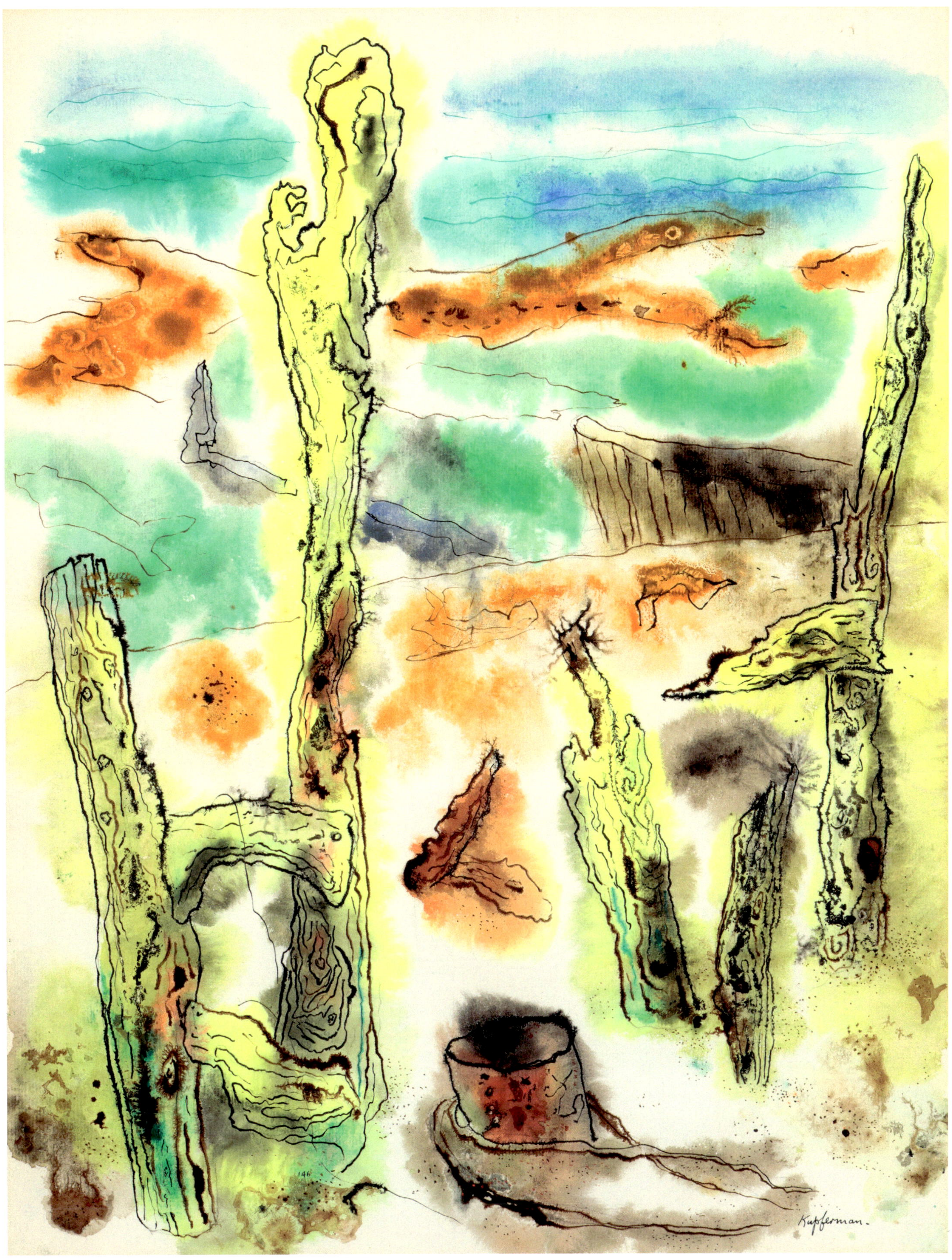

Lawrence Kupferman, *Driftwood and Beach*, 1946. Watercolor and ink on paper, 18½ × 14¾ inches. *Gift of Sara Gorfinkle*, 1995.

GEORGE DAVID YATER
(1910–1993)

George Yater's love of Cape Cod is engagingly depicted in his nostalgic paintings of the area. He is also known for his photographs of artists and friends in Provincetown, which are a historic document of the art colony.

He was born in Madison, Indiana, and by the time he was in fourth grade, his artistic talent was recognized. He studied at the Herron School of Art in Indianapolis and then went to Provincetown to take classes with Henry Hensche. Hensche was continuing in the tradition of Charles Hawthorne, using colors to create form, placing one spot of color next to another to build a picture. Yater spent many years in Provincetown and later had a home in Truro. He was a vital member of the art colony, although he spent time in Florida and the Virgin Islands. He was director of the Provincetown Art Association for fifteen years beginning in 1947.

His early work with a palette knife is looser than his later works, which tend to be more defined and have more structure. His watercolors also show a sense of freedom with the brush and have an atmospheric quality, as in *Shirley on the Beach*, in the Cape Cod Museum of Art collection, which is full of light and shows Yater's quick brushstroke.

His use of light and color is reminiscent of the Hawthorne-Hensche style. His brushwork is animated, yet the compositions show a vivid determination. His subjects include landscapes, the fishing community, Provincetown's harbors and village life, portraits, and still lifes. He masterfully captured historic buildings and Cape landmarks, like Eastham's nineteenth-century *The Penniman House*, which is in the museum's collection. In this work, you can see his command of technique and understanding of architectural structure.

A number of photographs Yater took of artists and others in the Provincetown art colony are in the museum collection and include: the legendary Hans Hofmann; early modernist Ross Moffet; a strong image of John Whorf; impressionist Henry Hensche; and Budd Hopkins, an abstract expressionist who later committed himself to hard-edge geometric works.

Yater's works are in the collections of the Chrysler Art Museum in Norfolk, Virginia; DePauw University in Greencastle, Indiana; and Indiana University in Bloomington.

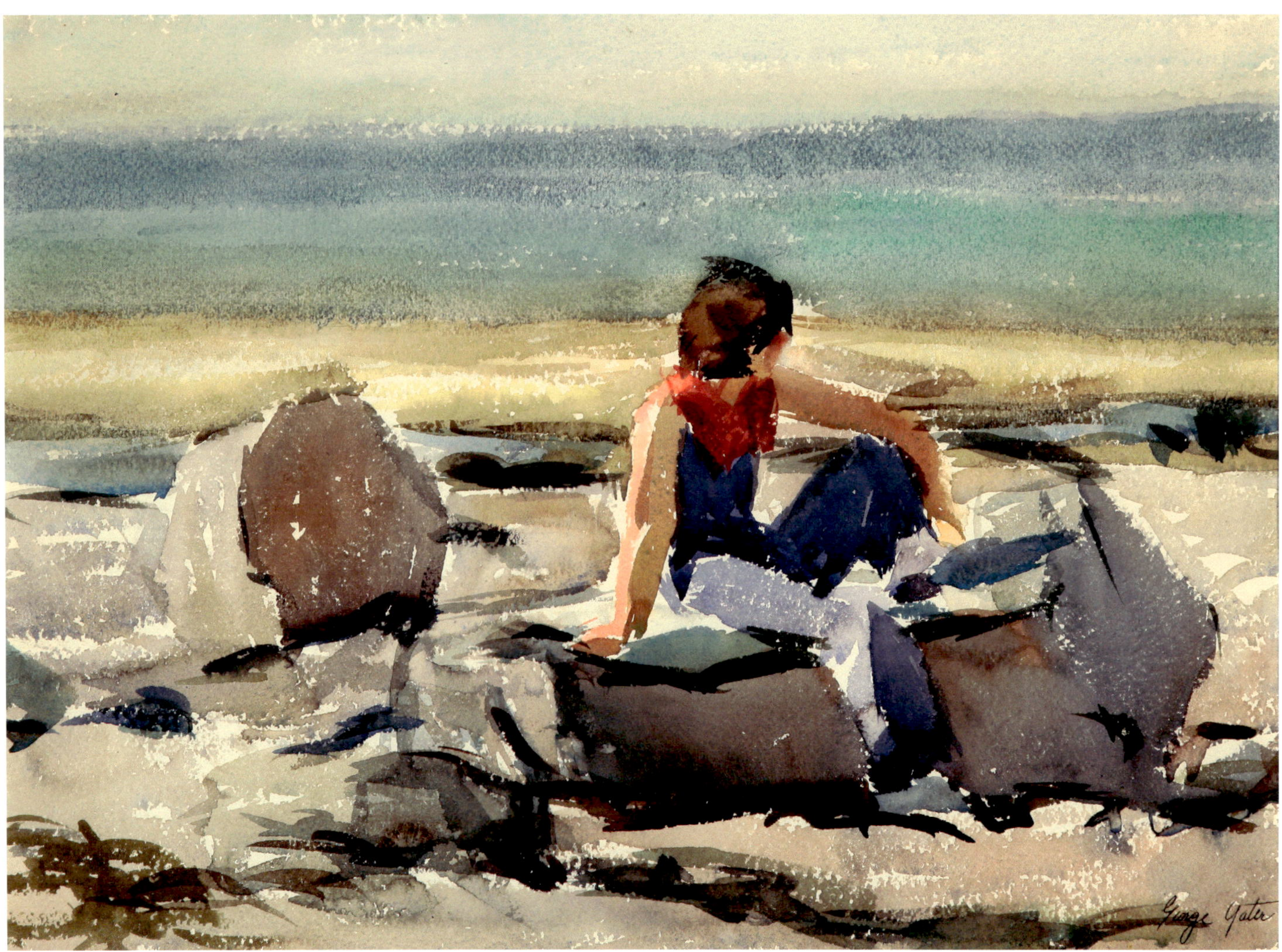

George Yater, *Shirley on the Beach*, 1932. Watercolor on paper, 12½ × 17½ inches. *Gift of George and Shirley Yater*, 1989.

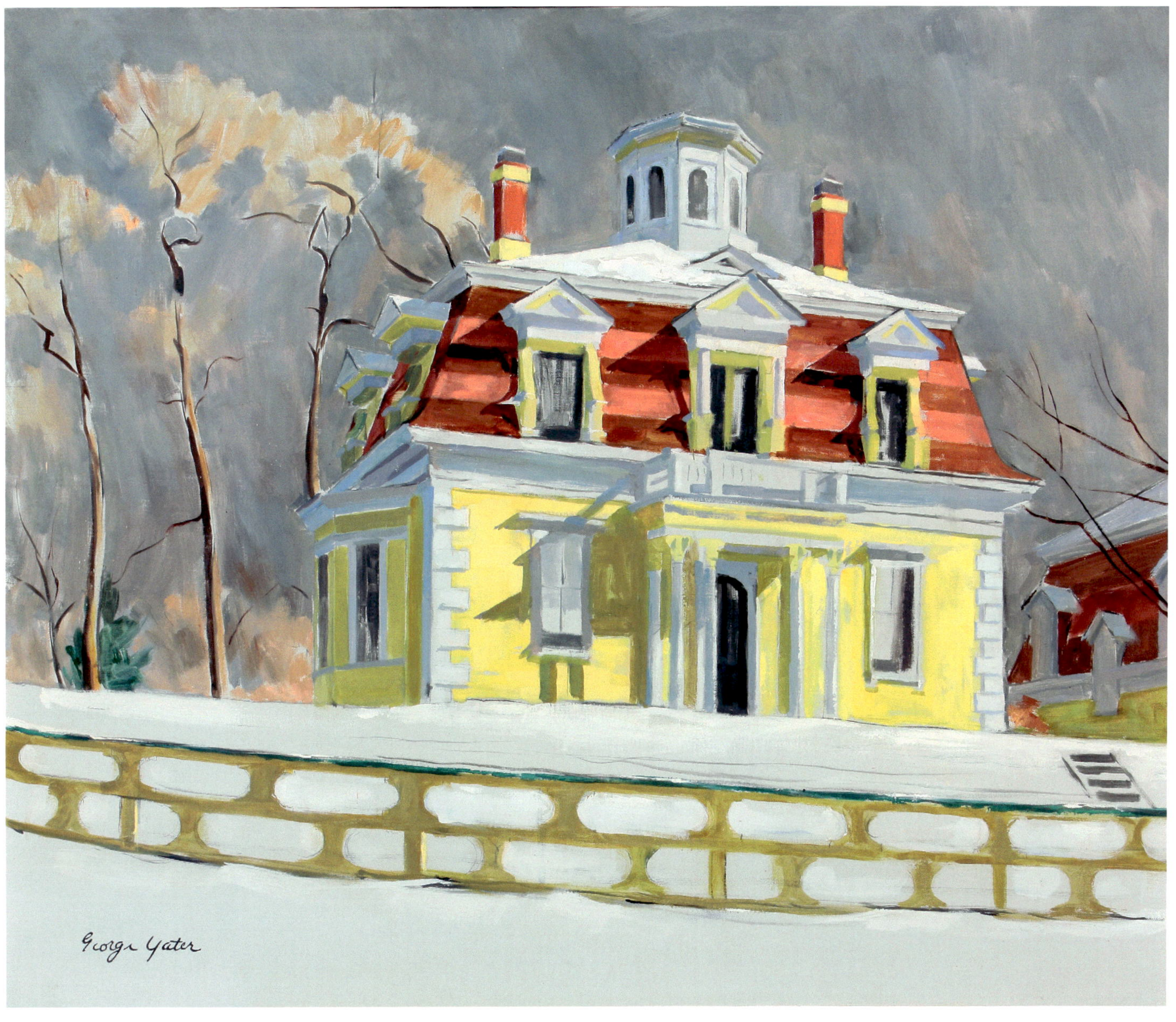

George Yater, *The Penniman House,* n.d. Oil on canvas, 30 × 36 inches. *Gift of Marjorie Yater*, 2005.

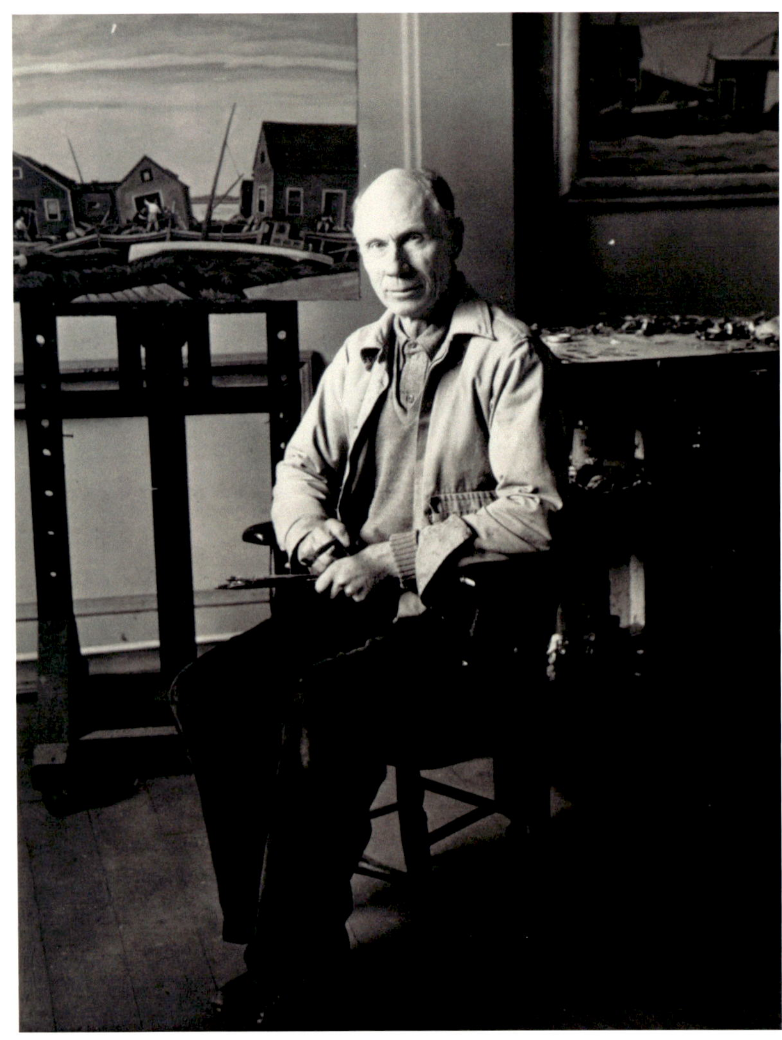

George Yater, *Ross Moffett,* n.d.
Silver gelatin print, 7 × 5 inches.
Gift of Shirley Yater, 1993.

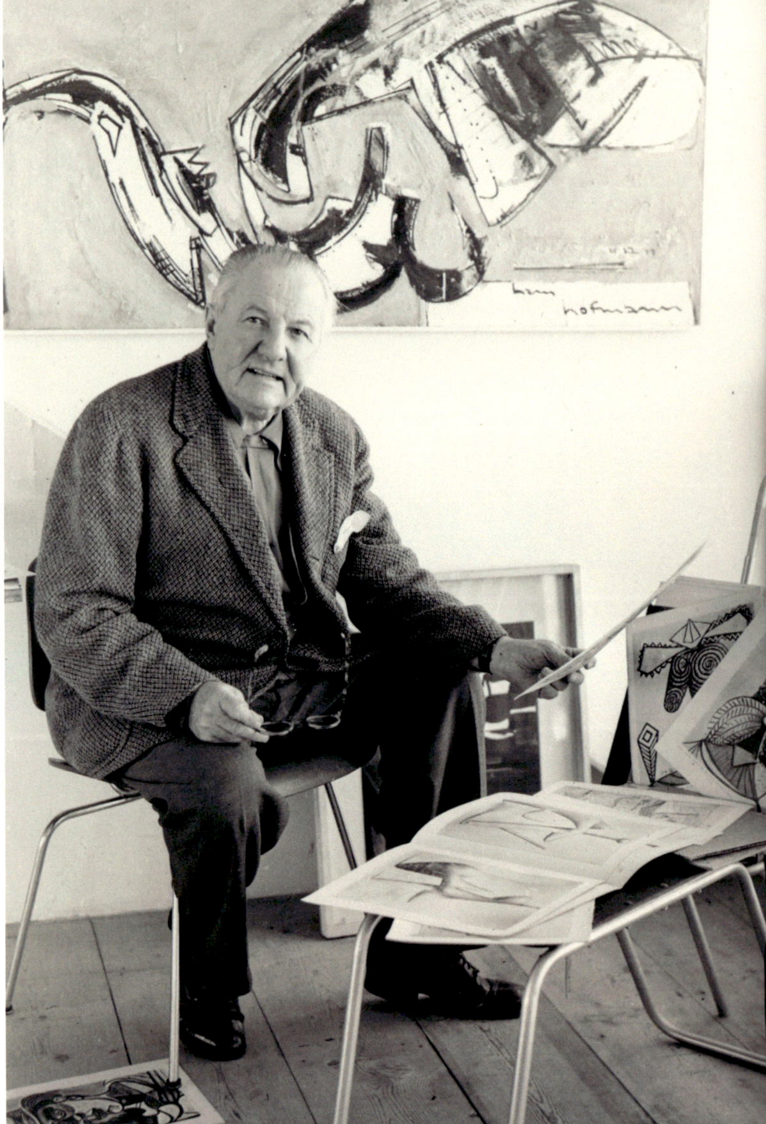

George Yater, *Hans Hofmann,* n.d.
Silver gelatin print, 10 × 8 inches.
Gift of Shirley Yater, 1993.

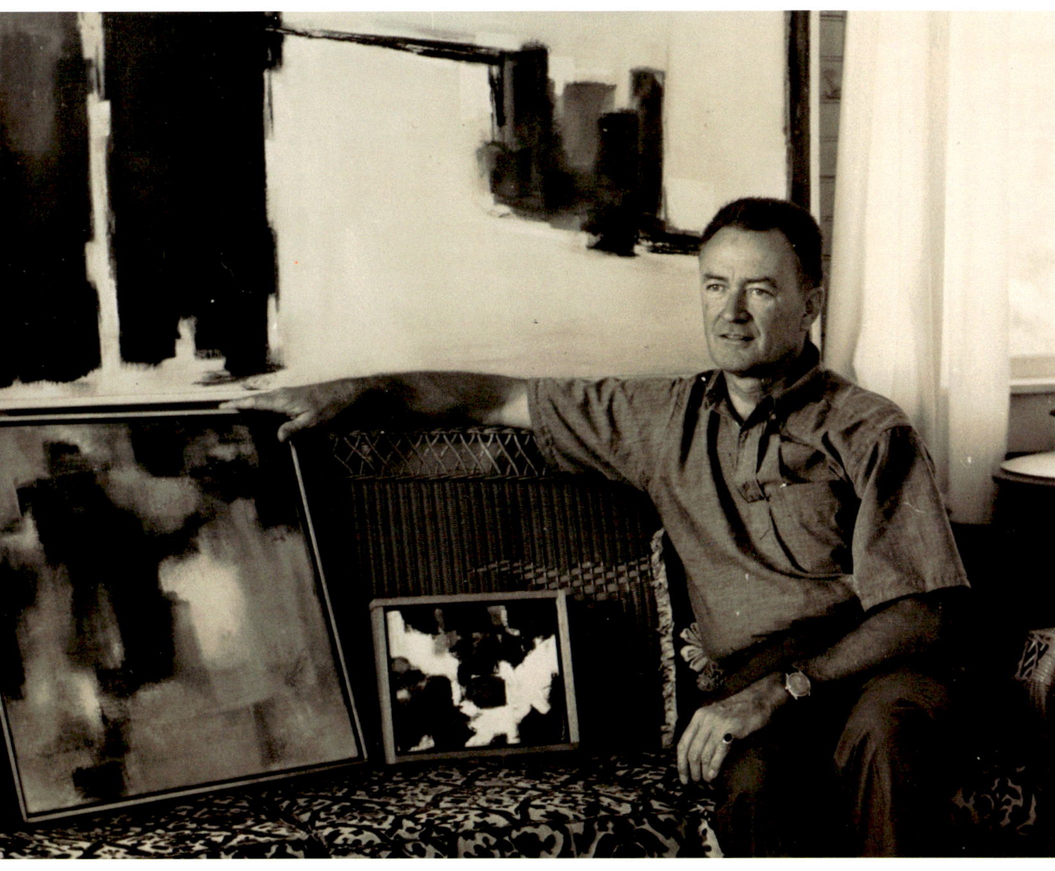

George Yater, *Budd Hopkins,* n.d.
Silver gelatin print, 8 × 10 inches.
Gift of Shirley Yater, 1993.

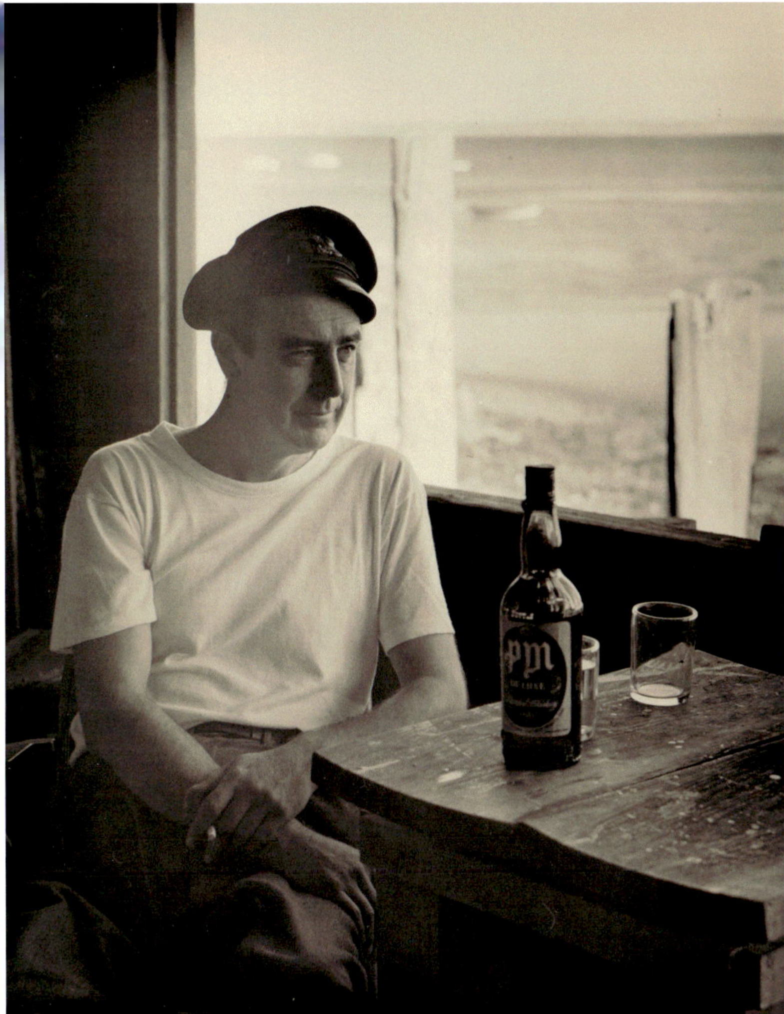

George Yater, *John Whorf*, n.d. Silver gelatin print, 10 × 8 inches.
Gift of Shirley Yater, 1993.

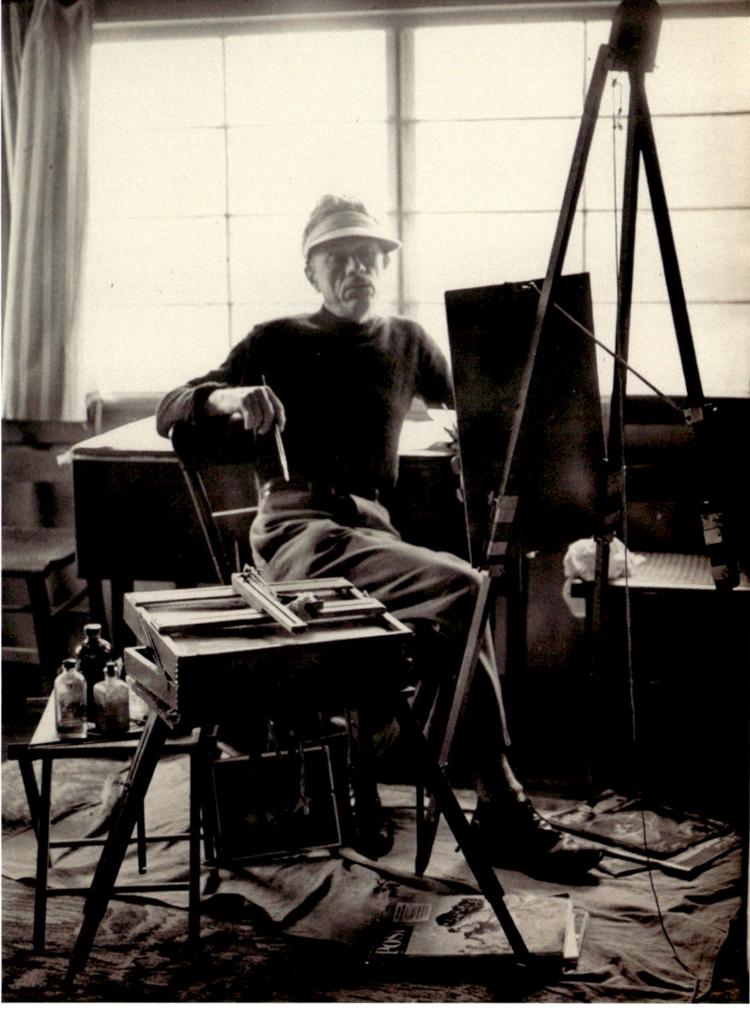

George Yater, *Henry Hensche,* n.d. Silver gelatin print, 10 × 8 inches.
Gift of Shirley Yater, 1993.

WILL BARNET
(1911–2012)

Although Will Barnet may be best known for his figurative art, he did spend a good part of his career working abstractly. And, for him, there was a definite link between the two. It actually worked both ways in his work, because of the crossover between the two approaches. Like many representational artists, he found that an abstract structure was a vital part of his composition, and in his abstract work, the shapes he composed are linked to forms in real life.

Barnet, who lived in New York and died there at the age of 101, spent many summers in Provincetown in the 1950s and 1960s. Because he was born on the North Shore in Beverly, Massachusetts, and Provincetown was a convenient place to visit, it became an inspiration for his abstractions.

Studying at the School of the Museum of Fine Arts in Boston in the 1920s and early '30s, Barnet became committed to the tradition of classical French painters. Despite that interest, he never considered himself an academic painter; he always thought of himself as a modernist. Barnet moved to New York in the 1930s, studied at the Art Students League, and became interested in printmaking; he was designated the League printer in 1935. In this medium, he worked in a variety of techniques, including lithography, woodcut, and serigraphy. He went on to work in graphic arts for the WPA's Federal Art Project.

In the 1940s and 1950s when abstract expressionism was flying high, Barnet developed his own form of abstraction. In the 1950s, he became associated with the Indian Space painters who created geometrical abstract paintings with forms found in Native American art. Barnet volleyed between abstract and figurative work throughout his career. His stylized figurative work was precisely linear, and often focused on his family, his wife, children, and his cats. He said he never drew a figure realistically. There is a formal quality, which defined the structure. When looking at his representational works, it is important to pay attention to the shapes and the two-dimensionality of his forms.

By reducing a figure or object and the background to flat planes of color, a composition develops, which can be translated into the basic shapes of an abstraction. Barnet saw the value of background spaces becoming positive elements, just as the figures and objects were. There is no negative space. It is all positive. And by simplifying his figures, he made them more generalized, less individualistic, broadening their relevancy and connecting them with the universalities of the human condition.

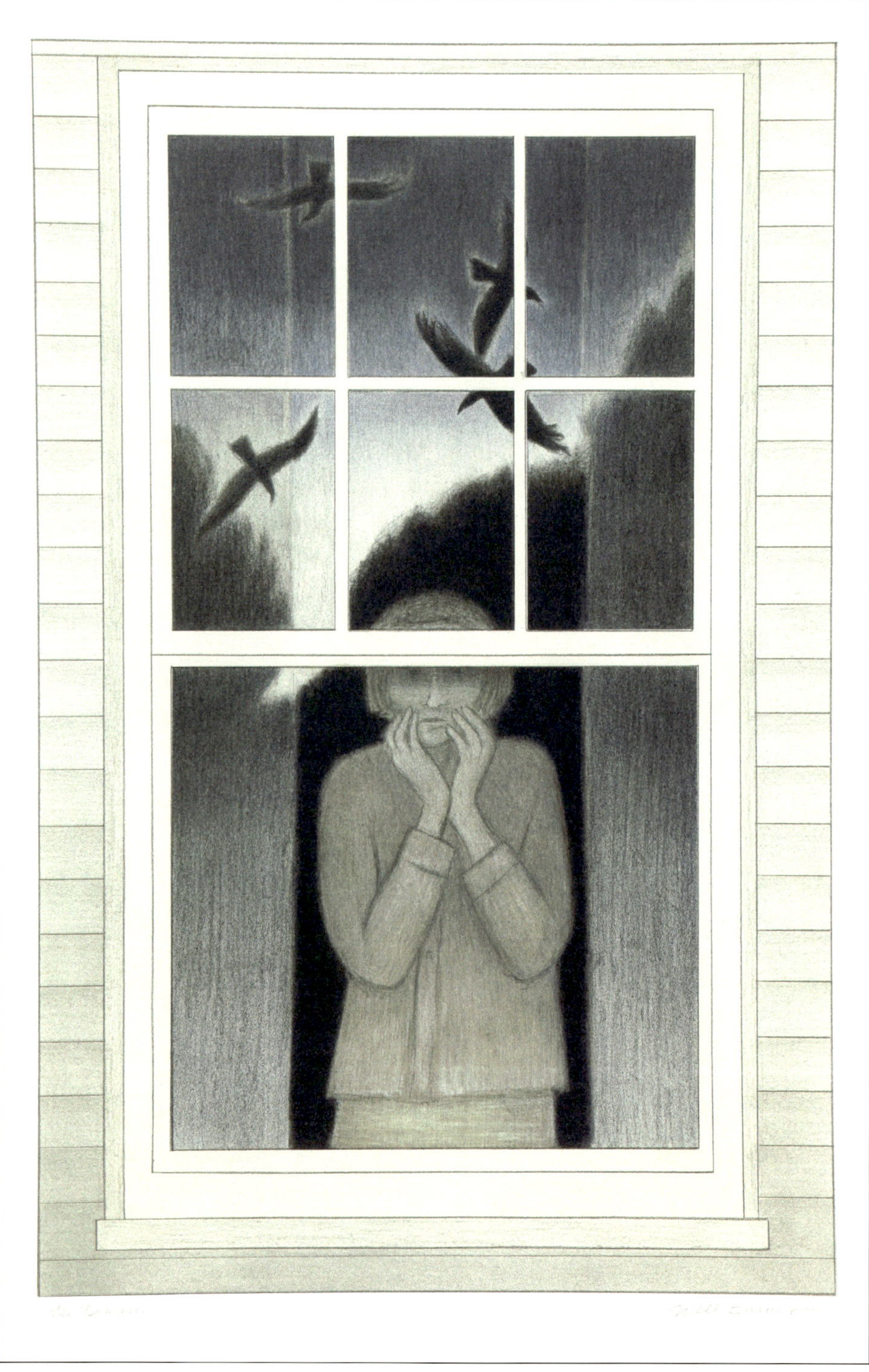

Will Barnet, *The Dream*, circa 1990. Lithograph on paper, 28 × 19 inches. *Gift of Will Barnet*, 2003. *© Will Barnet Trust/Licensed by VAGA, New York, New York.*

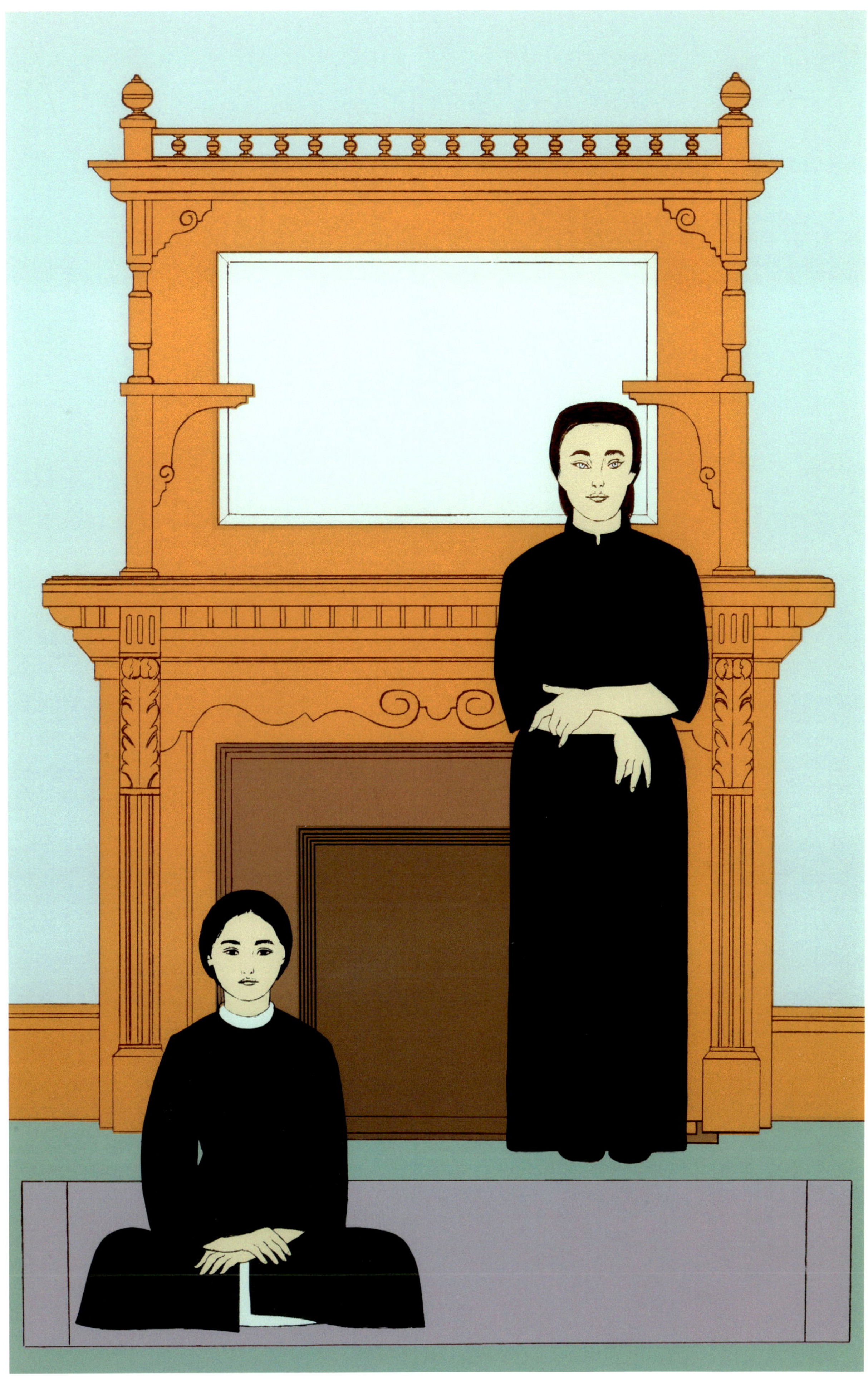

Will Barnet, *Reflection* 115/225, n.d. Silkscreen on paper, 24½ × 17 inches. *Gift of David Kaplan*, 2005.

His women reading, holding a cat, climbing stairs, smelling a flower, or simply musing are mostly quietly composed, as they are in *Reflection*, in the Cape Cod Museum of Art collection. These images are not specific personalities, but rather timeless representations. He has carefully placed his forms and chosen his colors so that there is a sense of balance and composure.

Cats were a favorite subject for Barnet. The museum collection houses both *The Sled*, of a child with a cat sitting on his sled, and the beautifully patterned *Cat and Canary*. These works are fine examples of how Barnet flattened familiar images. Windows also play a role in his work, and *The Dream*, in the museum collection, is one of his more straightforward portrayals.

In 2003, Barnet returned to producing abstract paintings, which contain bold images of geometric and biomorphic forms, and in which the influence of Native American art is apparent. These compositions are more complex than his figurative works and they are more animated and dynamic.

Barnet's works are included in the collections of major museums, including the Metropolitan Museum of Art, the Museum of Modern Art, the Whitney Museum of American Art, and the Guggenheim Museum in New York; the National Gallery of Art in Washington, DC; the Museum of Fine Arts in Boston; the Philadelphia Museum of Art; the British Museum; and the Vatican Museums.

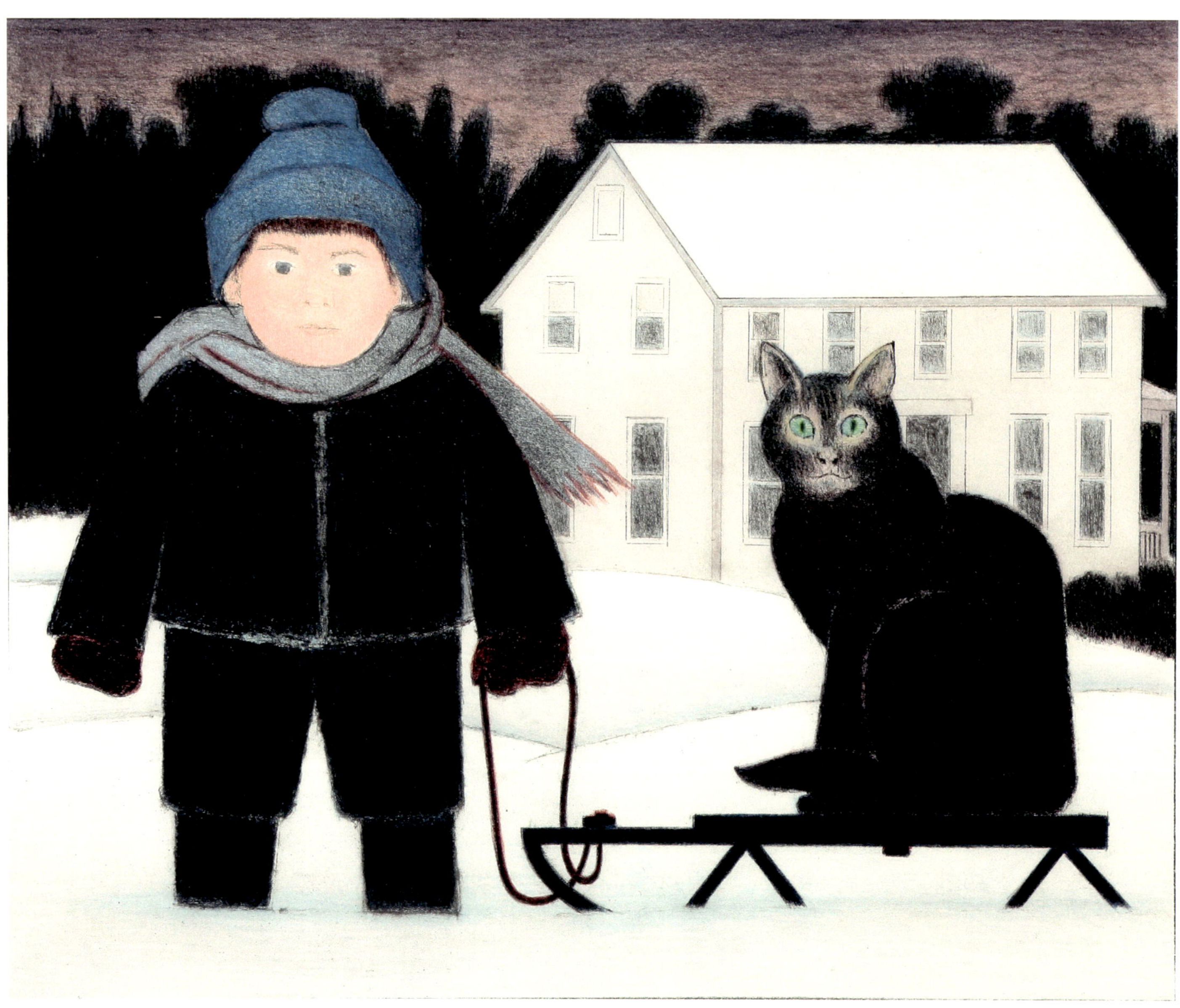

Will Barnet, *The Sled* AP, circa 1984. Lithograph on paper, 21¼ × 25 inches. *Gift of Will Barnet*, 2003.
© Will Barnet Trust/Licensed by VAGA, New York, New York.

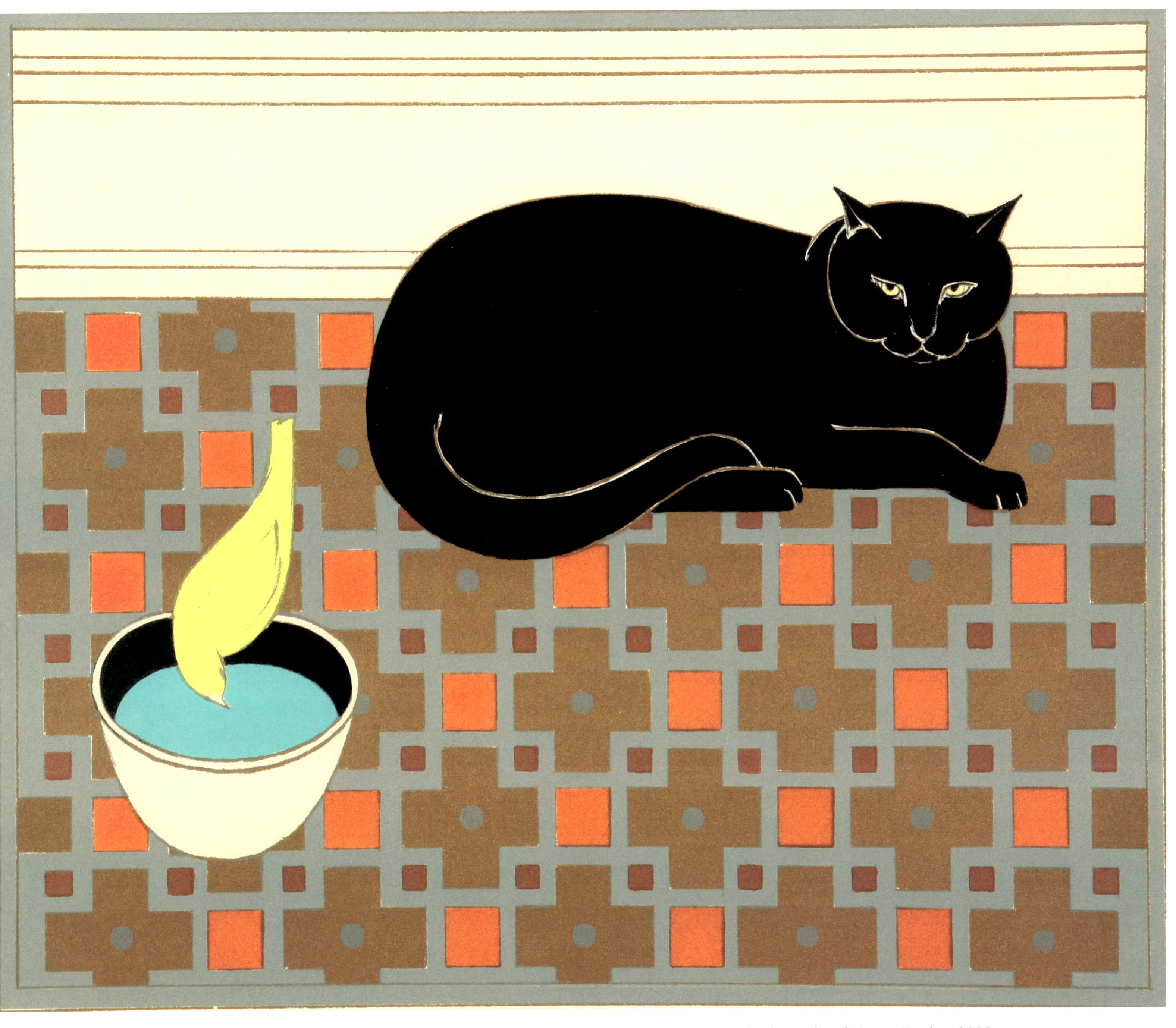

Will Barnet, *Cat and Canary* 194/255, n.d. Silkscreen on paper, 23½ × 30 inches. *Gift of David and Nancy Kaplan*, 2007.

NANNO DE GROOT
(1913–1963)

Nanno de Groot, part of the New York School of abstract expressionists in the 1950s, was born in the Netherlands, and went to nautical school in Amsterdam. During World War II, he was in the Dutch navy stationed in Java until he was sent to San Francisco to serve as liaison officer to the US Army and Navy. He was lieutenant commander in charge of the Dutch Port Authority in San Francisco. After the war, at age thirty-three, he received American citizenship, and soon after moved to New York and took up painting full time. In 1961, de Groot moved to Provincetown and became a part of the abstract expressionist activity there.

His early work is noted for spontaneous black lines suggesting figures, as in *Two Figures* in the Cape Cod Museum of Art collection. Later he added color and representations of animals and birds. In the 1950s, he moved into figurative expressionism and painted female nudes in bold colors. *Ladies by the River*, in the museum collection, is a robust example of this approach. In the late '50s, his subjects included peonies and poppies. In 1959 on a visit to Provincetown, he painted landscapes and more flowers: zinnias, daisies, sunflowers, and cornflowers. That winter, in Stamford, Connecticut, he painted snow scenes. With its black outlined trees and its stark snowy whites, *Winter Pastoral*, also in the museum collection, is a contrast to his brilliantly colored works and exudes a hushed feeling. In the 1960s, he moved on to paintings of fields, sunlit waters, and fruits and vegetables, and made ink drawings of the harbor and boats in Provincetown.

His works are included in major museums, including the Hirshhorn Museum and Sculpture Garden in Washington DC, and Hebrew University in Israel.

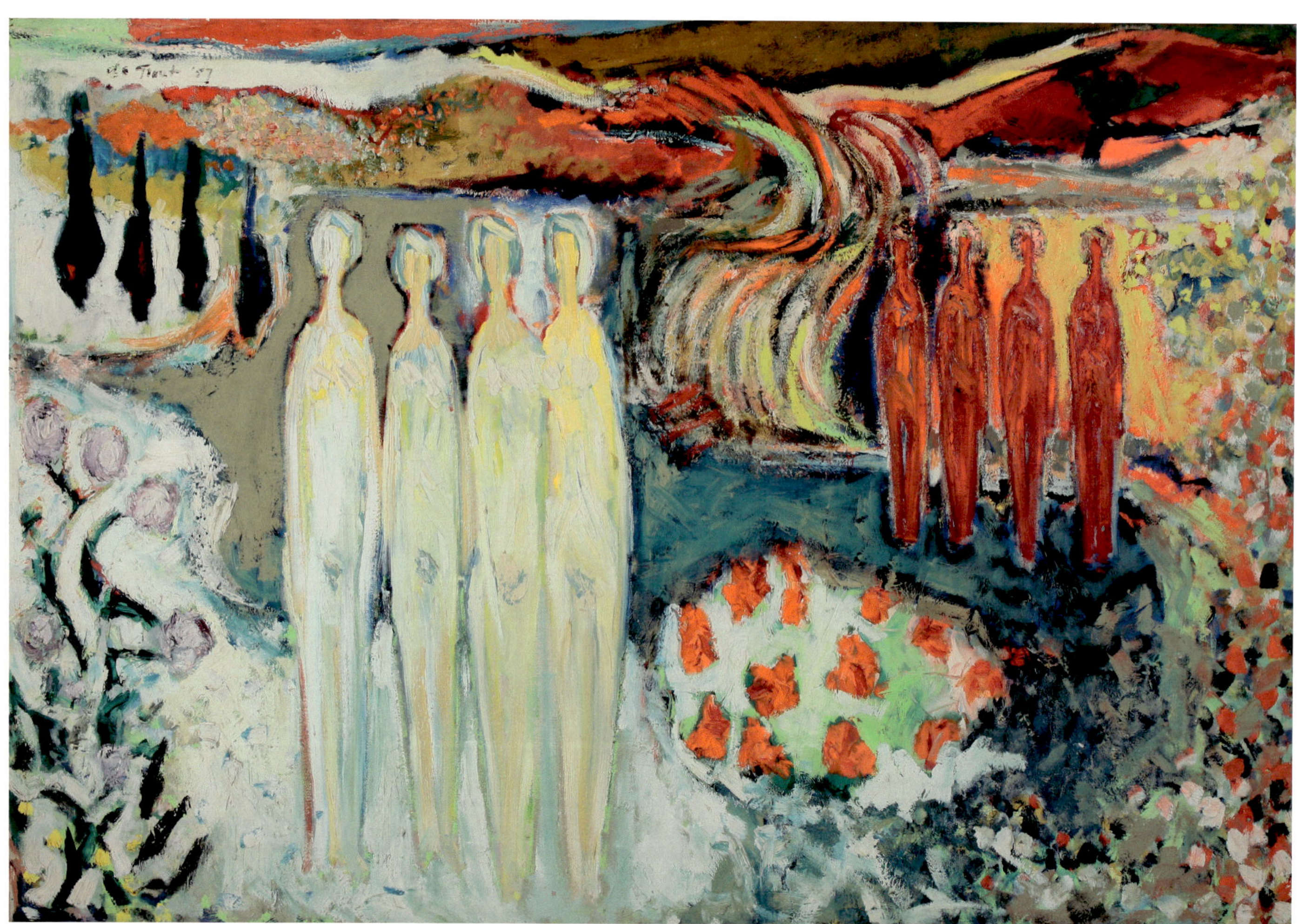

Nanno de Groot, *Ladies by the River*, 1957. Oil on canvas, 50 × 74 inches. *Gift of Pat de Groot*, 2000.

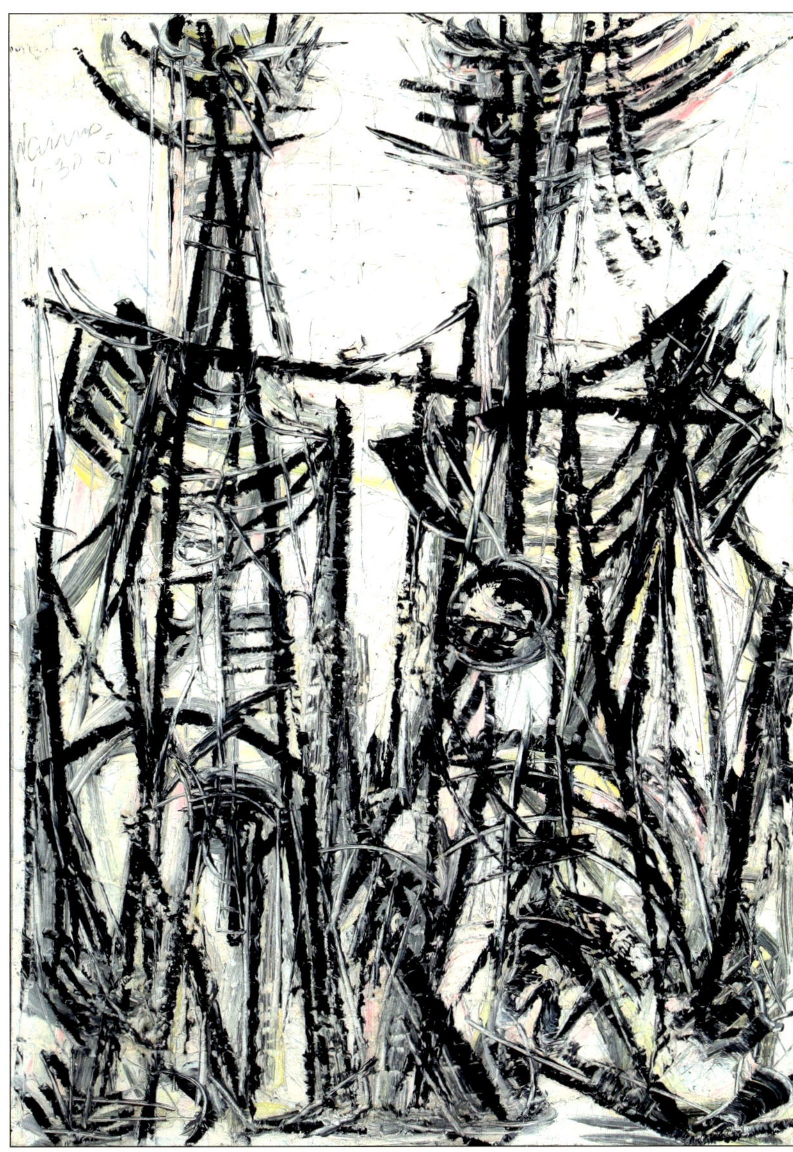

Nanno de Groot, *Two Figures,* 1951.
Oil on canvas, 37 × 24½ inches.
Gift of Pat de Groot, 2000.

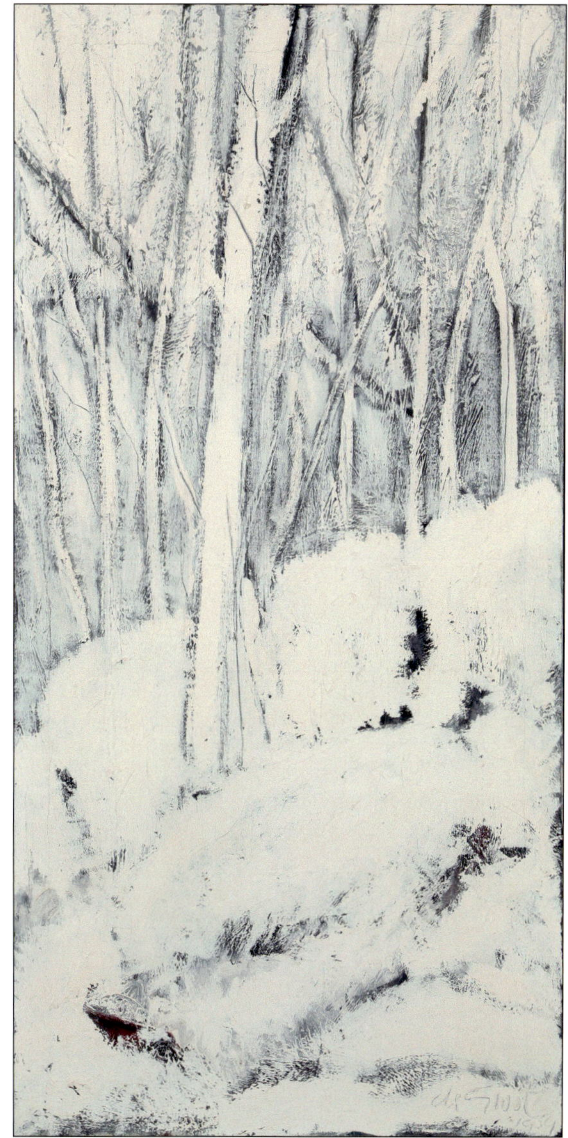

Nanno de Groot, *Winter Pastoral*,
1959. Oil on canvas, 45 × 22¾ inches.
Anonymous gift in honor of Mr. Hudson Duffy, 2009.

PETER BUSA
(1914–1985)

Peter Busa studied at the Carnegie Institute of Technology in his native Pittsburgh, and at the Art Students League with Thomas Hart Benton at the same time as Jackson Pollock. From 1935 to 1938, he took classes with Hans Hofmann in New York and Provincetown. During the 1930s, he also worked on the Federal Art Project of the Works Progress Administration. He later taught at a number of schools, including Cooper Union, New York University, and University of Michigan.

New York's Fourteenth Street School was home for Busa in the 1940s and early 1950s when he had a close friendship with modernist Stuart Davis. At the time, he was part of the budding abstract expressionist movement. His approach to form, movement, and dramatic use of color can be associated with Hofmann, who merged cubist influences on structure and fauvist emphasis on color. But Busa also took cues from a variety of sources, including Davis, Arshile Gorky, and the surrealists Roberto Matta and William Baziotes.

He also worked figuratively, and moved back and forth in various genres throughout his career. He could work on a hard-edge, geometric painting, like *Kiss #1* in the Cape Cod Museum of Art collection, a free abstract expressionist canvas, and a surrealist automatic drawing experiment all in the same day. His various styles included works made up of biomorphic shapes and geometric patterns, which came together in colorful, rhythmic compositions. Busa had become interested in the economy of forms and simplicity of Native American art in the 1930s, and its motifs became part of his Indian Space series. He abandoned this direction in his painting in the heady atmosphere of the 1950s abstract expressionism, only to return to a new exploration of its visual ideas in the 1980s. *Untitled (Petrograph)*, in the museum collection, represents this approach in his work.

Busa's works are in the collections of the Metropolitan Museum of Art and Whitney Museum of American Art in New York, the Walker Art Center in Minneapolis, and the Smithsonian American Art Museum, Washington, DC.

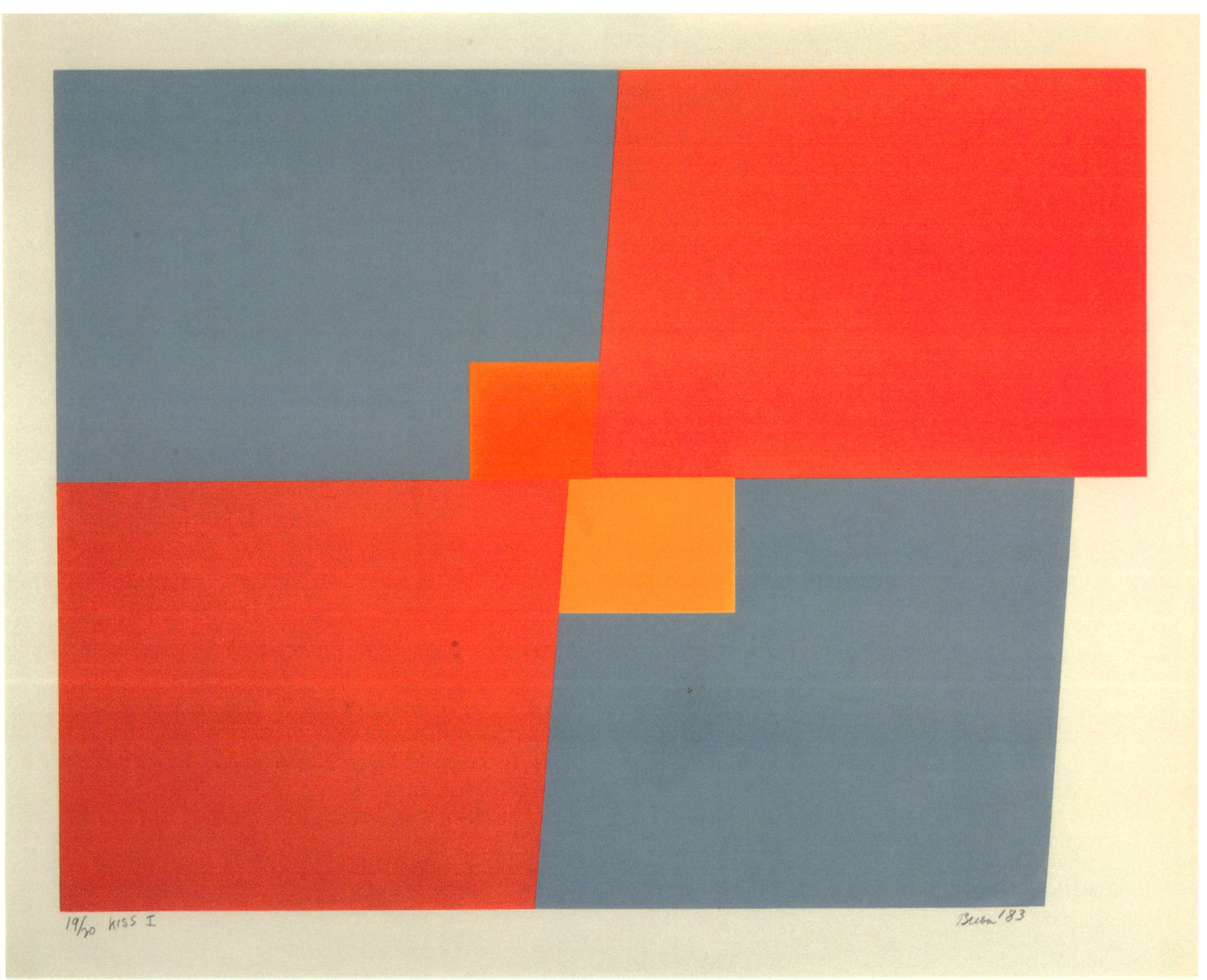

Peter Busa, *Kiss #1* 19/20, 1983. Silkscreen on paper, 22¼ × 30⅛ inches. *Gift of Stephen Borkowski in honor of Chris Busa*, 2011. *Courtesy of Chris Busa for the Estate of Peter Busa.*

Peter Busa, *Untitled* (Petrograph), n.d. Ink on paper, 25½ × 19⅝ inches. *Gift of Christopher Busa*, 2000.
Courtesy of Chris Busa for the Estate of Peter Busa.

LEO MANSO
(1914–1993)

Leo Manso was a vital member of the Provincetown art colony beginning in the 1940s. Born in New York City, he was educated at the National Academy of Design and the New School of Social Research.

Early in his career, his work was linked to nature and influenced by light and impressionism, as in his 1949 abstracted *Biomorphic Experiment—Meditation on Seaside Objects*, in the collection of the Cape Cod Museum of Art, which is a forerunner of the spiritual aspects of Manso's later work.

Looking for something more permanent than the fleeting sensation of nature, he pursued more lasting images in the myths of past civilizations. In the 1960s, Manso's work developed a strong foundation in geometric shapes—the circle, triangle, and square. He used these objective forms as personal expressions with mythological references. In the mid-1970s, his art became freer, influenced by his travels to Nepal, Tunisia, and Italy.

Manso began summering in Provincetown in the 1940s, and in 1958 opened a school there, which ran for eighteen

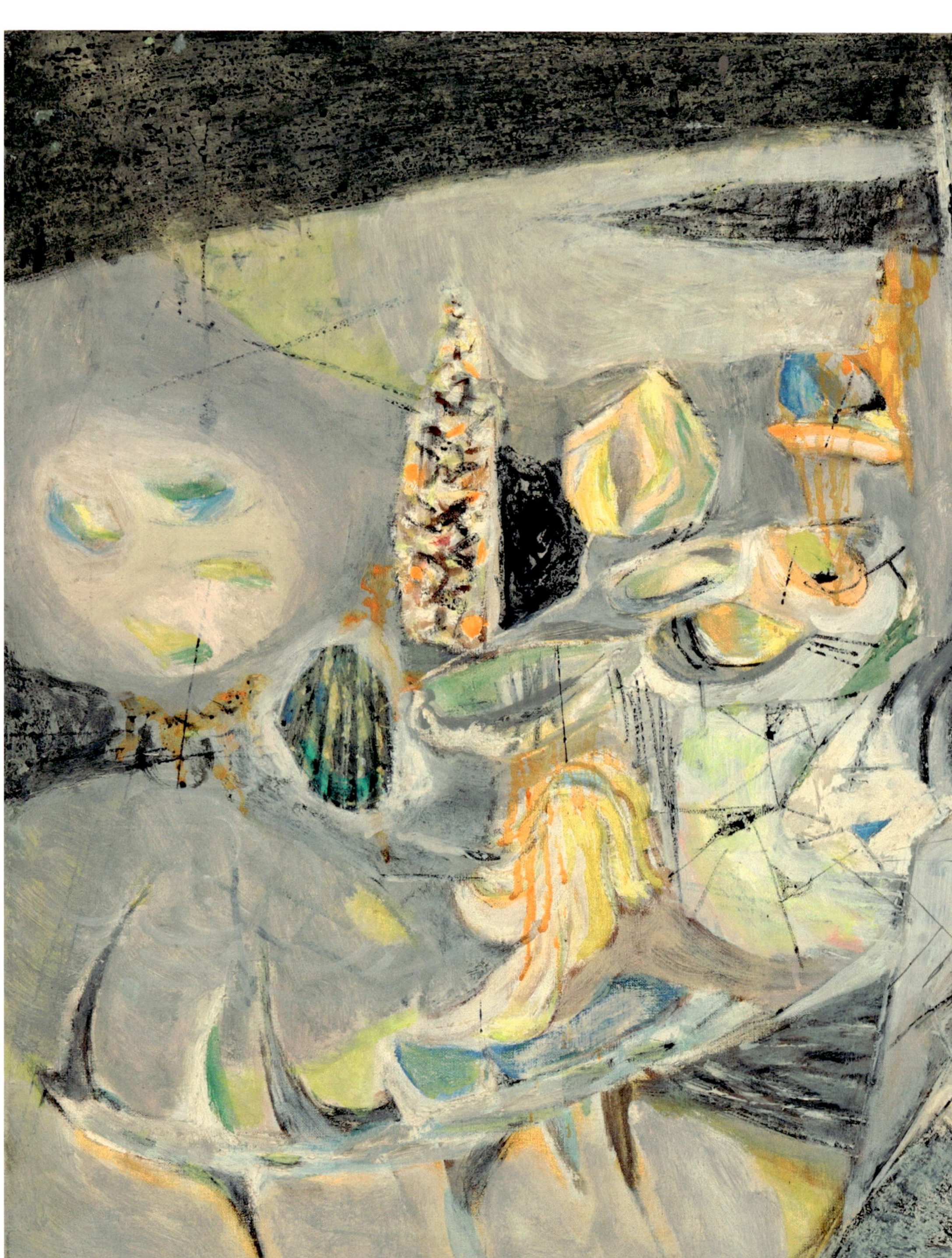

Leo Manso, *Bimorphic Experiment Meditation of Seaside Objects*, 1949. Oil and casein on canvas, 22 × 42 inches. *Gift of the Estate of Lawrence Kupferman*, 1994.

years. He was a founding member of the cooperative Gallery 256 and was a member of Long Point Gallery. Working in a narrow shed behind his East End home in Provincetown, Manso accumulated a collection of ancient books and documents, fragments of slate, old photographs, antique quilts, and piles of painted cloth and paper. He scavenged flea markets from Rome to Cape Cod for the materials he brought together for bold and striking, sometimes dark and mysterious, collages.

Manso experienced his abstract art as a meditative process. His acrylic paintings are subtle and thoughtful, rather than bold and theatrical like his collages. Yet all his work has a mystery that seduces the viewer to linger and contemplate.

His works are in major museum collections, including the Museum of Modern Art and Whitney Museum of American Art in New York, the Museum of Fine Arts in Boston, the Pennsylvania Academy of Fine Arts in Philadelphia, and the Brooklyn Museum of Art.

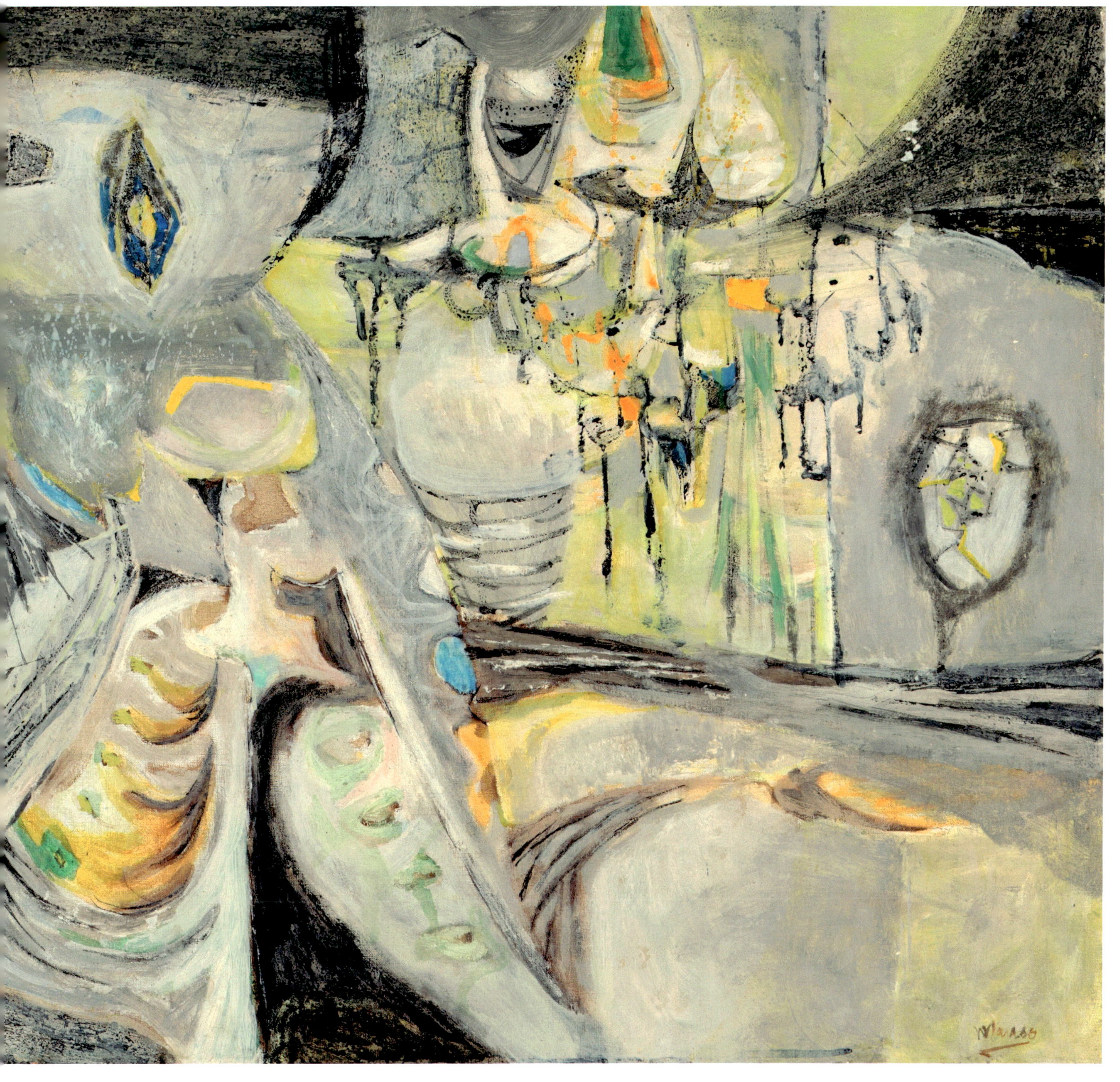

LILLIAN ORLOWSKY
(1914–2007)

As a New Yorker, Lillian Orlowsky had a diverse art education. She learned a traditional approach at the Educational Alliance in New York in the 1930s. Her early figures showed a cubist angularity, but after studying with Hans Hofmann, she developed a new appreciation and understanding of the picture plane. Her paintings and collages evolved from formally structured work in the 1940s to a free-form abstract expressionism in the 1950s.

There is a clear relationship between Orlowsky's work and Hofmann's. In the late '50s and early '60s, her collages are rich in allusions, and have an extemporaneous feel, as seen in *The Doll*, part of the Cape Cod Museum of Art collection. In most of her paintings, her colors are daring, and there is a dynamic exchange between them. *Untitled* and *Floating Form*, also in the museum collection, are lively abstractions, which have a spontaneity that is commanding.

Orlowsky was an important member of the Provincetown art colony. She and her husband, William Freed, moved to Provincetown in 1942, and they worked at Days Lumberyard in the 1940s and '50s. She was part of the artistic camaraderie of that era, when studios were $50 for the season, when Hofmann, Fritz Bultman, and Myron Stout shared bathrooms, and when there were only ice boxes and two-burner kerosene stoves. In the late '50s, Orlowsky and her husband bought a lot on Brewster Street in Provincetown and built a home and studio, where they lived for six months of the year. She painted into her eighties, and continued to experiment and search for new forms of expression.

Her works are in major museum collections, including the Museum of Modern Art and Metropolitan Museum of Art in New York, the Museum of Fine Arts in Boston, and the Baltimore Museum of Art.

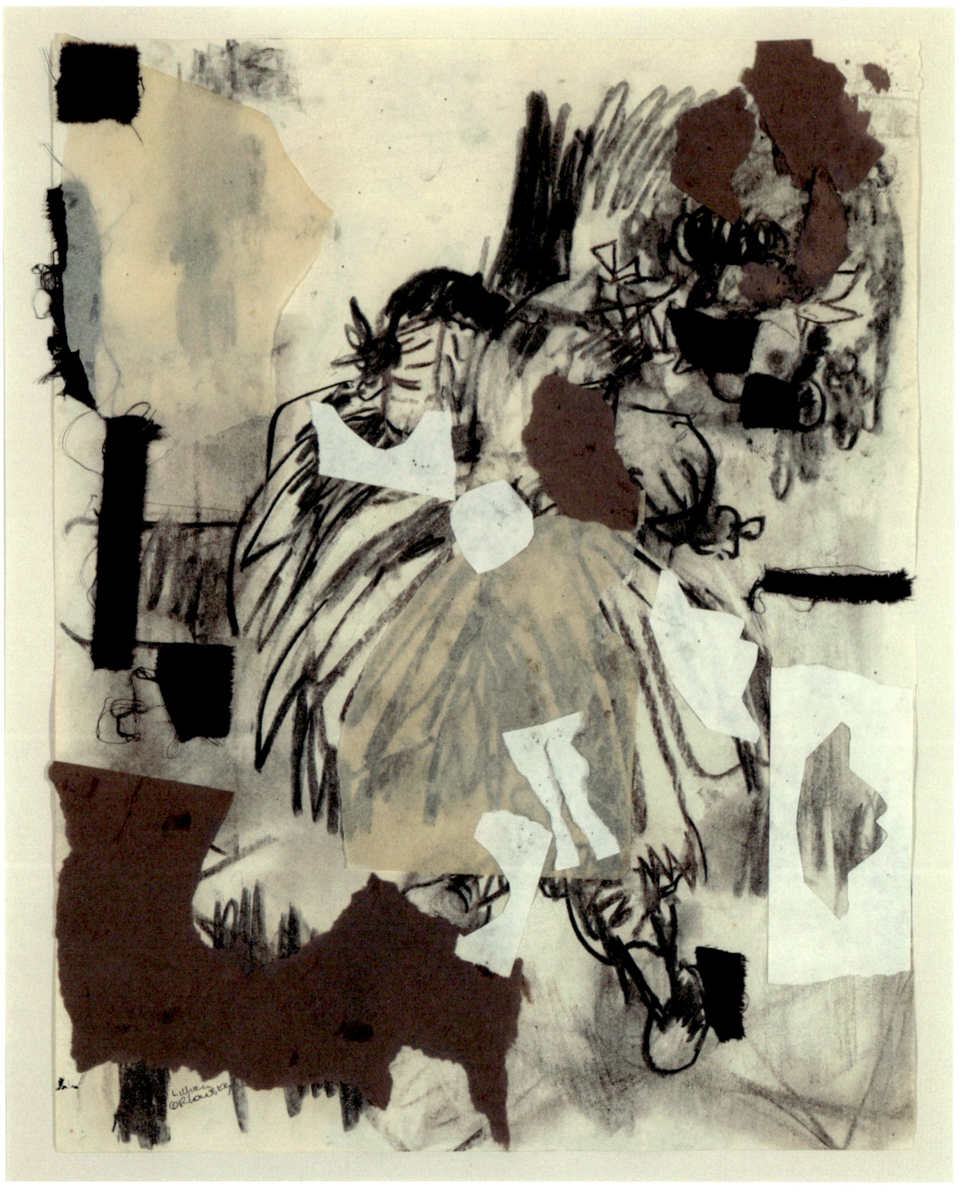

Lillian Orlowsky, *The Doll*, n.d. Collage on paper, 17 × 14 inches. *Gift of Lillian Orlowsky*, 1993.

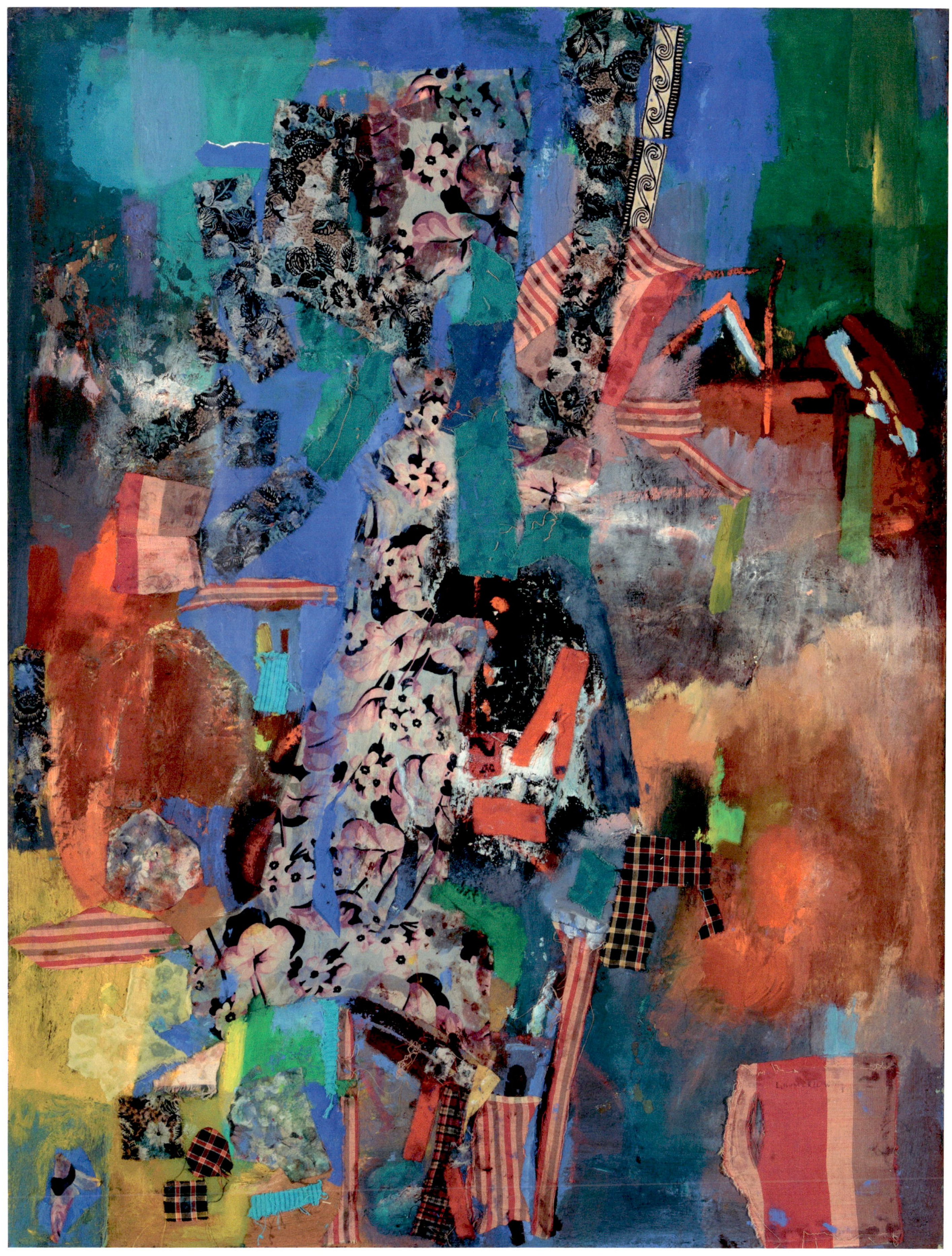

Lillian Orlowsky, *Untitled*, late 1950s/early 1960s. Oil and fabric collage on canvas, 36 × 28 inches. *Gift of Lillian Orlowsky*, 1993.

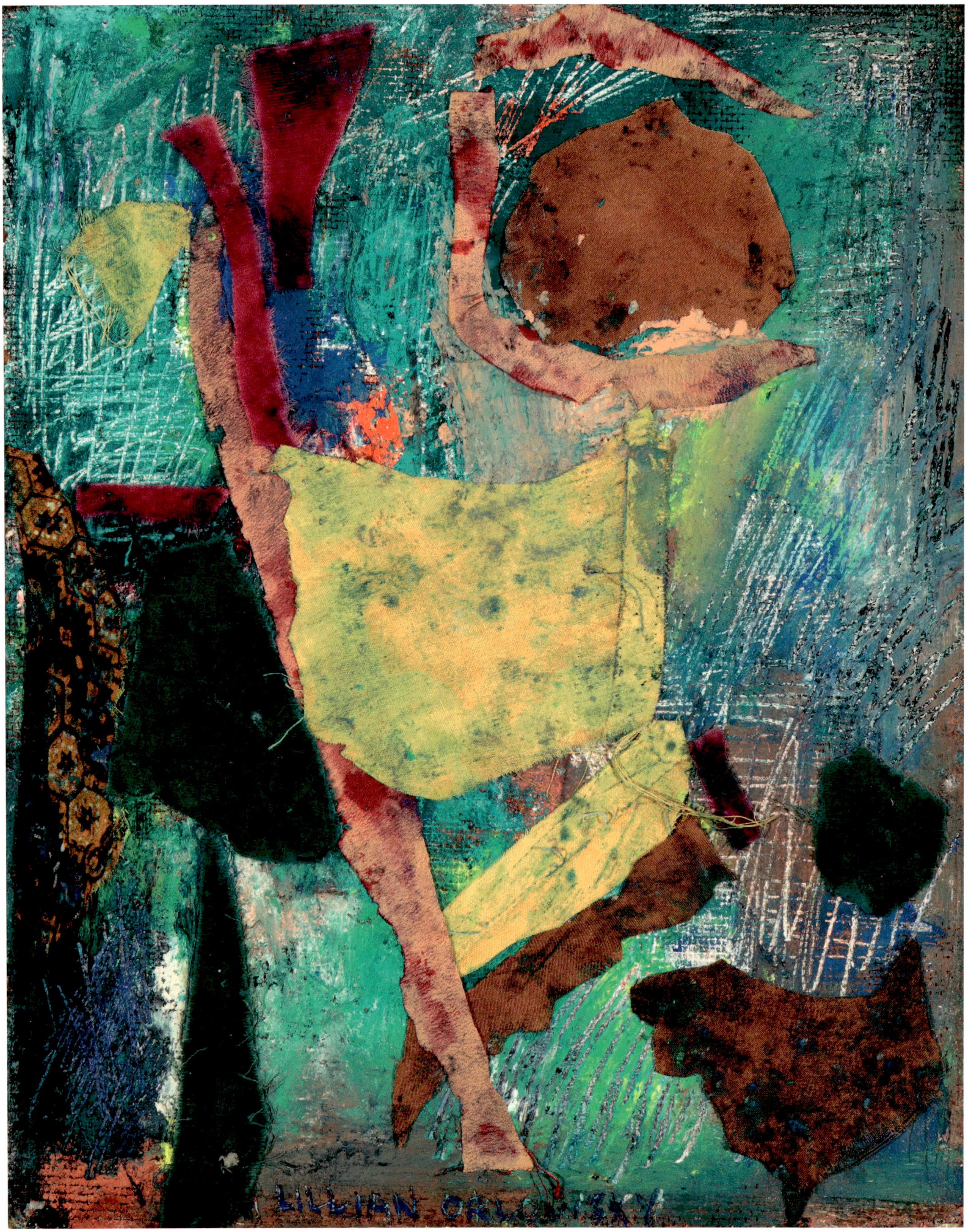

Lillian Orlowsky, *Floating Form*, n.d. Oil and mixed media on masonite, 12 × 10 inches. *Gift of Lillian Orlowsky*, 1993.

SAM FEINSTEIN
(1915–2003)

Born Samuel Lawrence Feinstein in Russia, Feinstein came to the United States when he was five years old and grew up in Philadelphia. He graduated in 1936 from Philadelphia College of Art, where he later taught. During World War II, Feinstein served as an artist for the army. After the war, he taught at Pratt Institute. Feinstein first came to Cape Cod in 1949 to study with Hans Hofmann in Provincetown, and his teacher became an enormous influence on his life and art.

For fifty years, Feinstein taught painting in workshops in New York, Philadelphia, Princeton, Toronto, and Cape Cod, carrying on Hofmann's principles of composition and the dynamics of color. He focused on the relationships between shapes and colors and the flow between them. A friend of Hofmann, Feinstein co-wrote, filmed, and edited a documentary film, *Hans Hofmann*, which previewed at the Metropolitan Museum of Art in New York City.

Feinstein's early work was realistic, but in the late 1930s and 1940s, his painting became expressionistic with swift, commanding strokes of color and elements of cubism as he depicted the boats and docks in his paintings of Gloucester, Massachusetts. *Harbor* and *Wharf*, in the Cape Cod Museum of Art collection, are bold images from this period.

By the early 1950s, he had escaped any suggestion of real objects as he moved into pure abstraction with a powerful

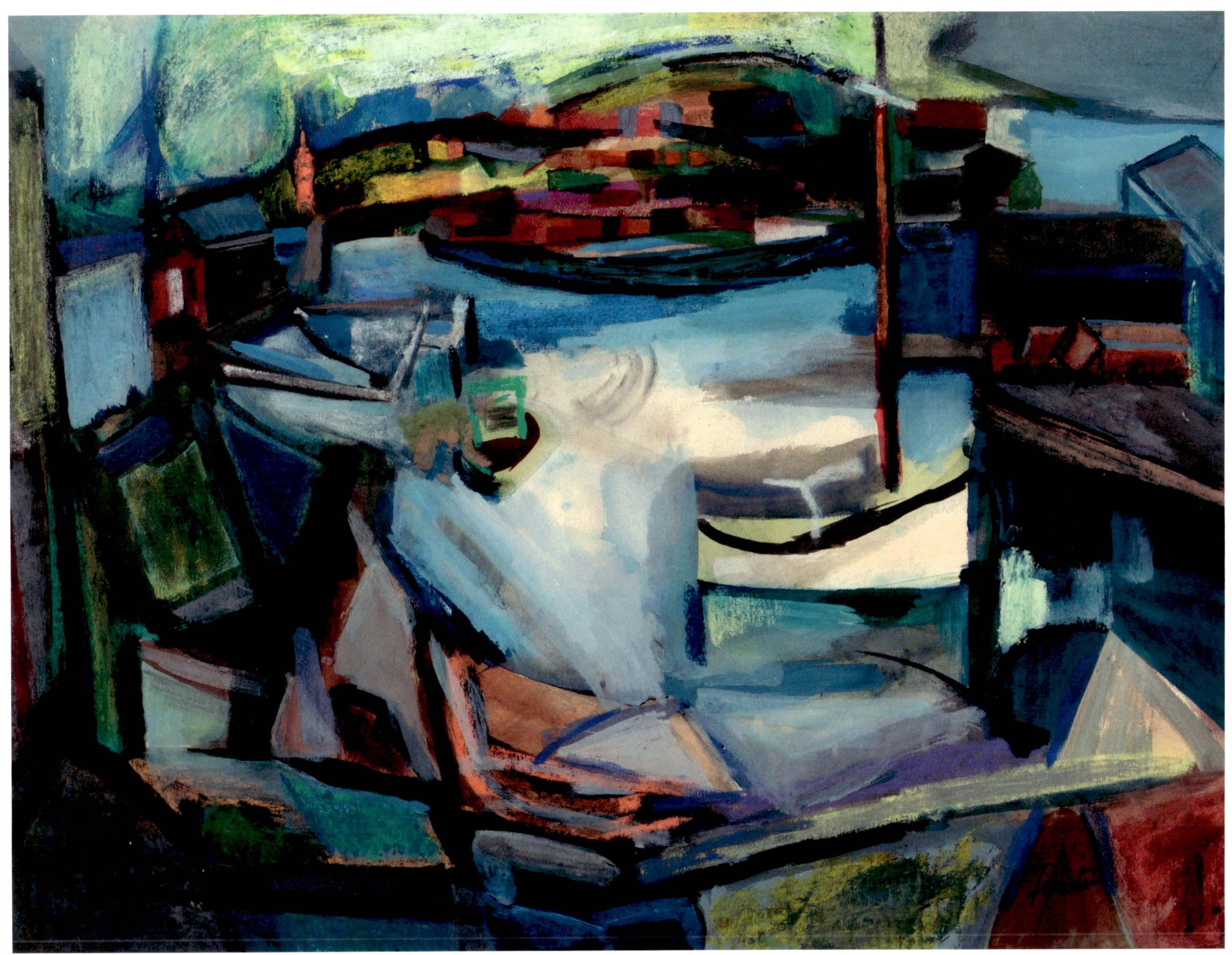

Sam Feinstein, *Harbor,* 1948. Casein, ink, and pastel on paper, 19 × 25 inches. *Gift of the Samuel L. Feinstein Trust, Patricia Stark Feinstein, Trustee*, 2015.

use of color and shapes, which explode like fireballs into bursts of energy. Forms that had some structure earlier began to dissolve in heavily textured seas of hot colors and ravishing flows of paint: almost Monet-like, except for the richness of the palette. *Summertime*, in the museum collection, is an exhilarating example from this master colorist, who saw color forms as the building blocks of a painting.

After exhibiting in New York, Provincetown, and Philadelphia from the 1930s through the 1950s, Feinstein made the decision to stop showing and selling his art, a decision that he continued through the end of his life. His work has become part of many museum collections, including the Metropolitan Museum of Art in New York, the Philadelphia Museum of Art, and the Pennsylvania Academy of Fine Arts.

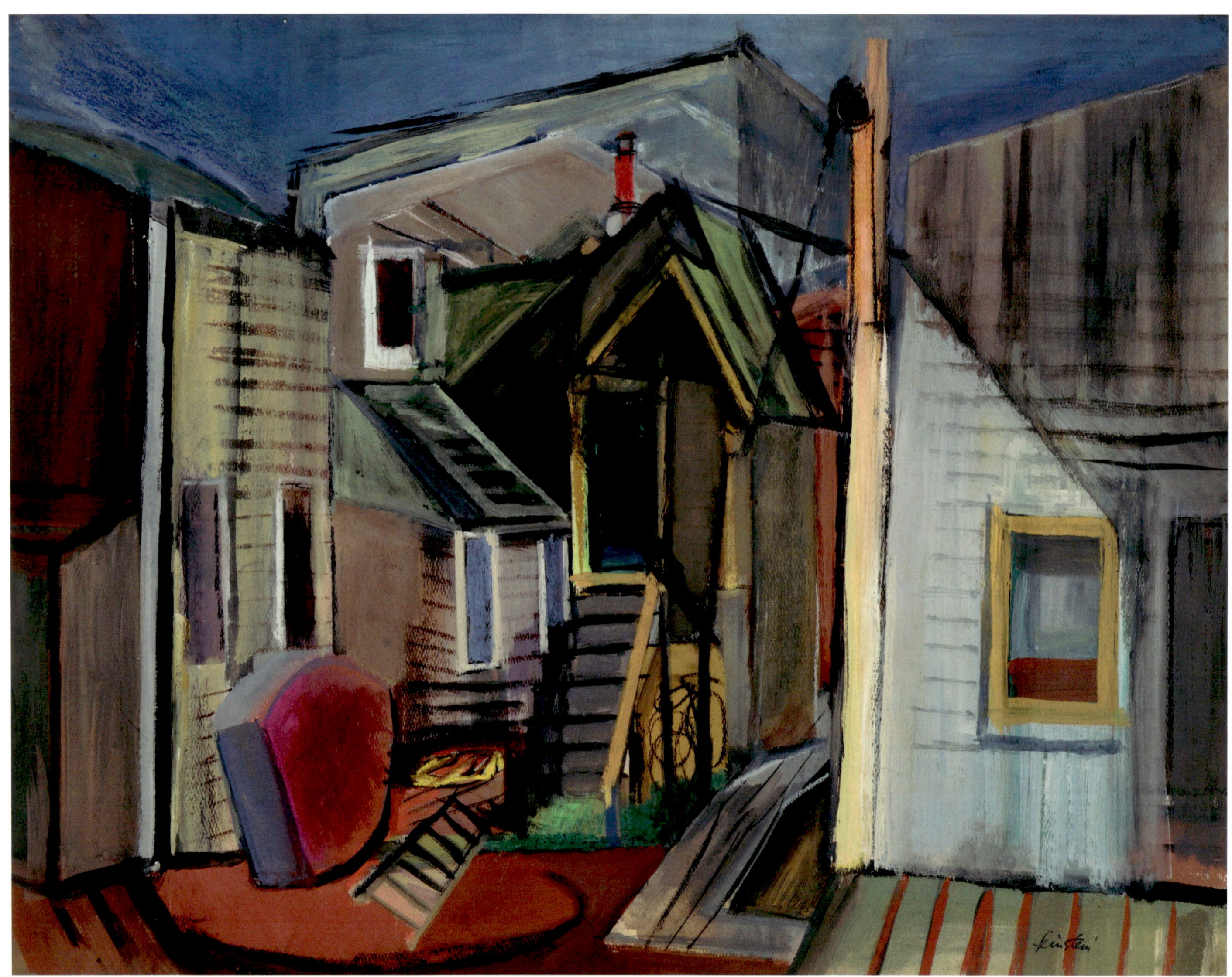

Sam Feinstein, *Wharf,* 1948. Casein, ink and pastel on paper, 19½ × 24½ inches. *Gift of the Samuel L. Feinstein Trust, Patricia Stark Feinstein, Trustee*, 2015.

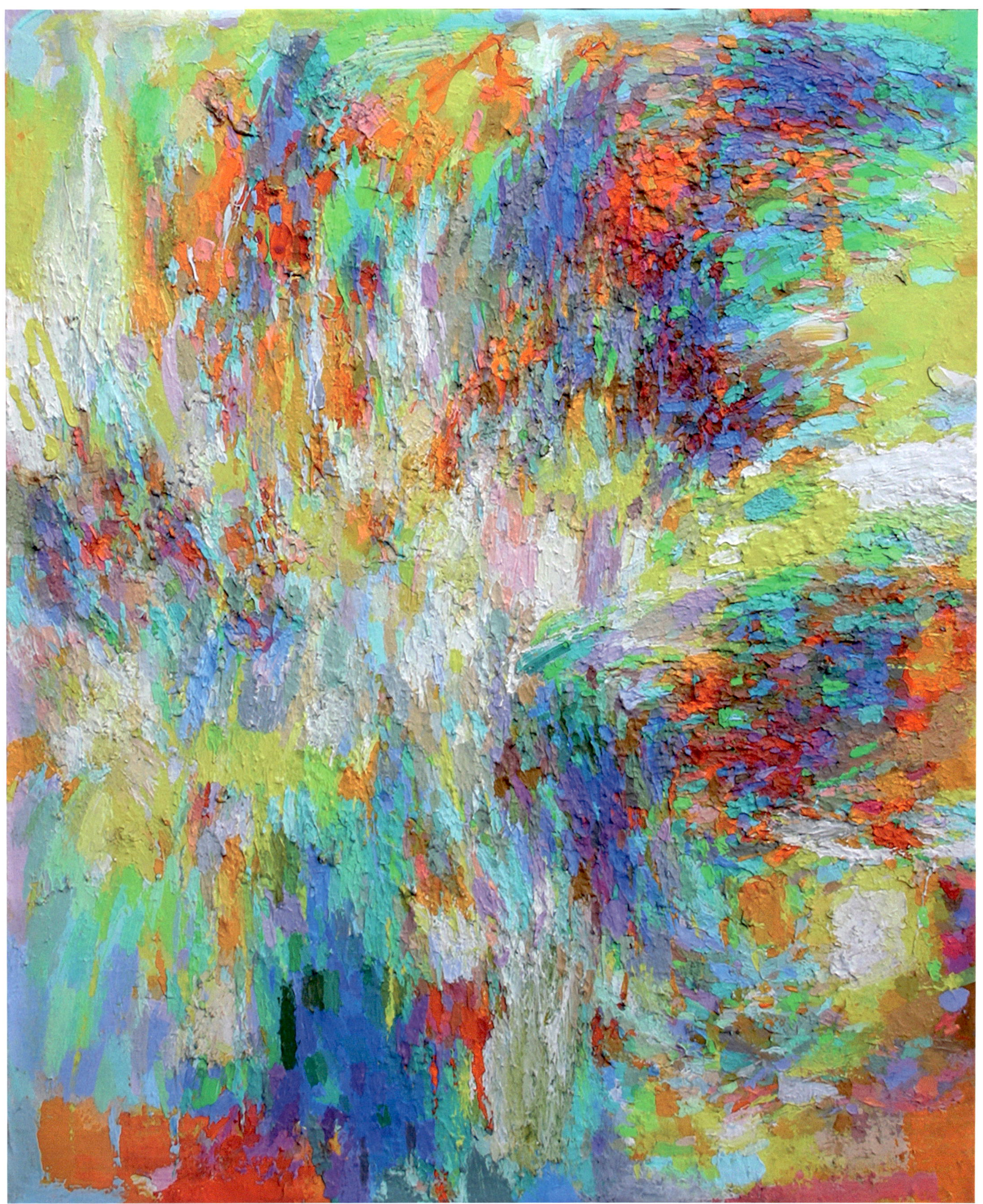

Sam Feinstein, *Summertime,* 1970s. Acrylic on canvas, 53 × 44 inches. *Gift of the Samuel L. Feinstein Trust, Patricia Stark Feinstein, Trustee*, 2004. *Photo courtesy of Patricia Stark Feinstein.*

ROBERT MOTHERWELL
(1915–1991)

When Robert Motherwell sat on the deck of his bayside Provincetown home and looked out at the water, he mused about being obsessed with the light and the color blue. A leading abstract expressionist, he found inspiration in this tiny fishing village at land's end as so many artists have. He spent summers there from the mid-1950s until he died there in 1991. He was one of the many abstract expressionists who were drawn to Provincetown. With Mark Rothko, Adolph Gottlieb, Franz Kline, Willem de Kooning, and Jackson Pollock in town during the 1940s and '50s, the burst of artistic energy that was captivating New York spread into this already well-established art colony. Of that group, Motherwell stayed the longest.

Although Motherwell spent most of the 1940s and early '50s summering in East Hampton, Long Island, it was in 1953 that Provincetown beckoned. He left the Hamptons and the hub of artistic activity swirling around Jackson Pollock and Willem de Kooning because he admired the egalitarian aspects and informal lifestyle of Provincetown, enjoyed the company of the many artists who were there, and wanted to leave the high pressure of New York behind.

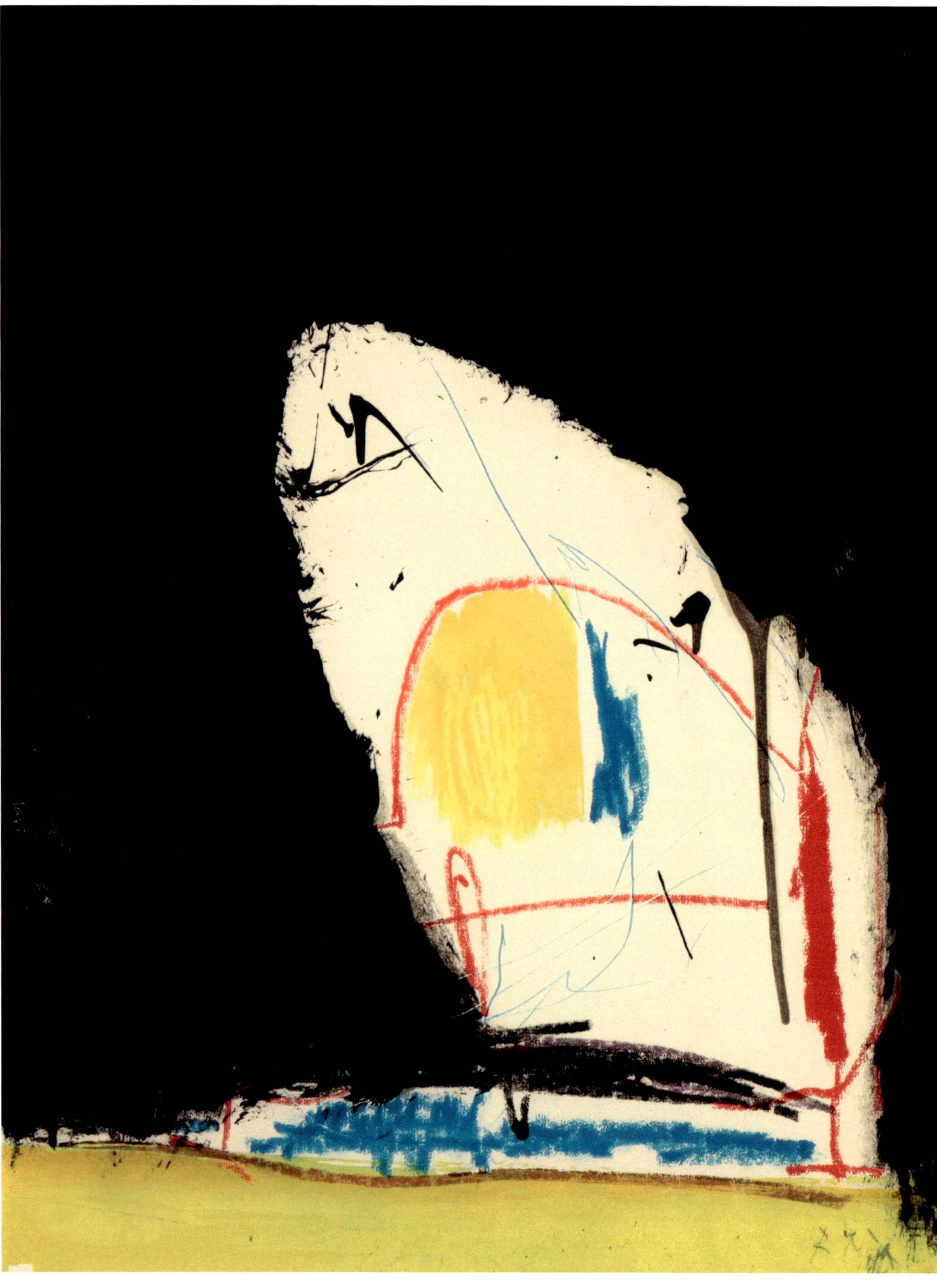

Robert Motherwell, *Capriccio,* 1961. Collotype and photo silkscreen on paper, 20⅜ × 15⅝ inches. *Gift of Jack T. Ahlin,* 2003. *© Dedalus Foundation, Inc. / Licensed by VAGA, New York, New York.*

Born in Aberdeen, Washington, he spent his summer seaside vacations on Washington's Olympic Peninsula, so Provincetown felt familiar.

Motherwell had very little formal art training. He studied briefly at the California School of Fine Arts in 1932, but switched his major from art to philosophy at Stanford University. While there he had the opportunity to view a private collection of works by Henri Matisse and was so profoundly impressed that Matisse became a continuous influence on his painting and collages. After earning a philosophy degree at Stanford, he went east, studied at Harvard University and then enrolled in the graduate program in art history at Columbia University. There he met art scholar Meyer Schapiro, who introduced him to European artists Marcel Duchamp, Max Ernst, Roberto Matta, and André Masson, who had come to New York to escape the war in Europe. Many of the surrealist artists, as well as Marc Chagall, Piet Mondrian, and Fernand Léger, were in Manhattan at the time.

Although in the early 1940s Motherwell's work had a figurative element, he soon moved into abstraction. He is celebrated for his rugged gestural paintings, his inscrutable series *Elegy to a Spanish Republic*, his painterly *Open* series, and his lyrical collages. When he used black, as in his *Elegy* paintings, he saw it as a raw, spontaneous form with an exotic power. His dynamic use of black and the gestural approach of abstract expressionism is shown in *Capriccio*, a collotype and photo silkscreen print, in the collection of the Cape Cod Museum of Art.

Some consider his collages his most beautiful work, with their broad areas of luscious colors, punctuated with items from everyday life: a fragment of sheet music, a Gauloises cigarette package, a cheese label, an invitation, a theater ticket, or postage stamp. *Gemini,* a lithograph in the museum collection, shows how Motherwell used a collage element to activate flat areas of color.

Besides exhibitions in the United States, Motherwell had major museum shows in Mexico, Dusseldorf, Stockholm, Vienna, Paris, London, and Edinburgh. His works are in the collections of major museums, including the Metropolitan Museum of Art, the Museum of Modern Art, the Whitney Museum of American Art, and the Guggenheim Museum in New York; the Los Angeles County Museum of Art; the National Gallery of Art in Washington, DC; the Philadelphia Museum of Art; the San Francisco Museum of Modern Art; the Tate Modern in London, England; Centre Georges Pompidou in Paris; and Museo Nacional Centro de Arte Reina Sofia in Madrid.

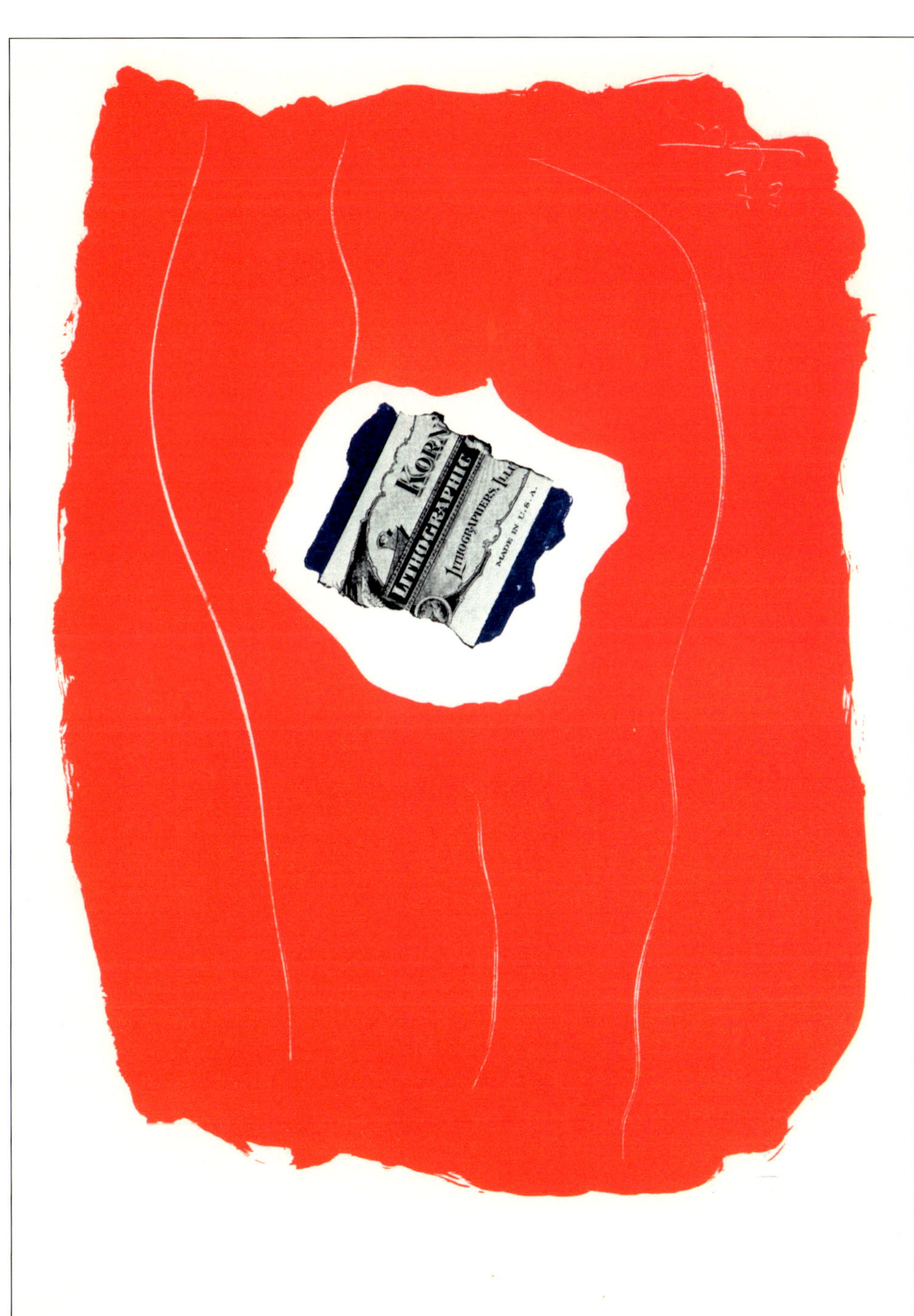

Robert Motherwell, *Gemini*, 1973. Lithograph on paper, 14 × 10¼ inches. *Anonymous gift*, 2009. © *Dedalus Foundation, Inc. /Licensed by VAGA, New York, New York.*

RICHARD FLORSHEIM (1916–1979)

Richard Florsheim, a printmaker, painter, and sculptor, is known for his abstracted treatment of cityscapes. In his views of the city and harbor scenes, he placed an emphasis on man-made lights and their effect on the viewer's experience of the built environment.

Born in Chicago, Florsheim studied at the University of Chicago, at the Museum of Modern Art and the Metropolitan Museum of Art in New York, and at the Musée Nationale d'Art Moderne in Paris, where he exhibited at the Salon des Réfusés. In 1939, he returned to Chicago and began working in lithography. In 1942, Florsheim enlisted in the US Navy, served in the Pacific theater as a cartographer, and obtained patents for his radar plane-spotting technique. After the war, he resumed his artistic career.

His lithographs are well represented at the Cape Cod Museum of Art. His work, whether of city or seaside, explores structure, form, line, and light, and how they can be manipulated in an abstracted composition. For example, in his *Untitled* harbor view, wide horizontal bands are set against the sharp vertical lines of masts and their watery reflections.

Florsheim's skylines, often night-lit, as in the black-and-white lithograph *Untitled*, in the museum collection, show facets of light projecting from the buildings. His *City Morning* depicts a low-lying skyline against a red sky. His skyscrapers are often reflected in the water, as in another *Untitled* work, bathed in green with lights shooting up into the sky.

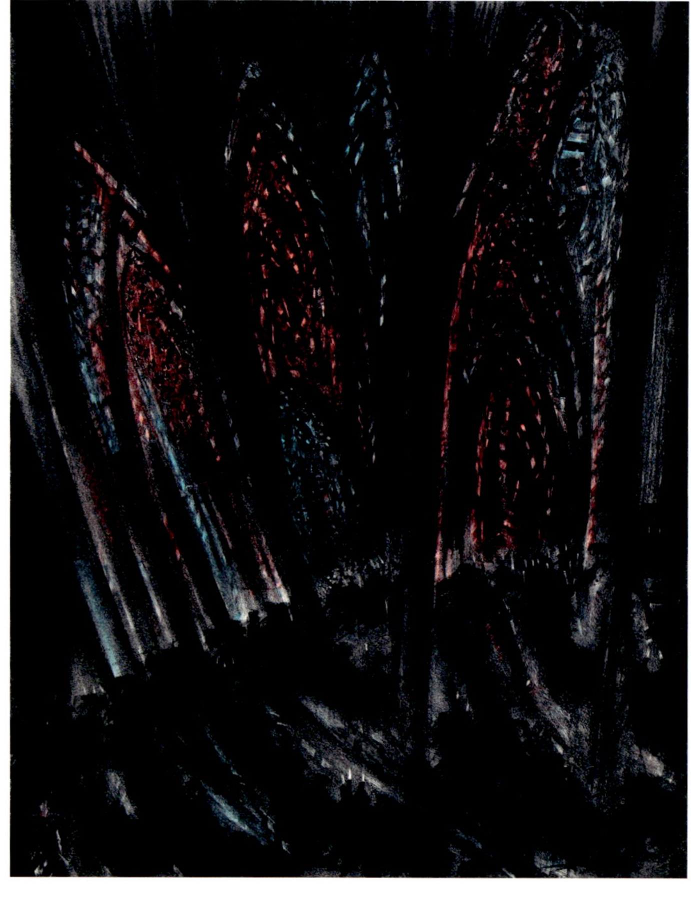

Richard Florsheim, *Untitled* 37/50, n.d. Lithograph on paper, 26 × 20 inches. *Gift of the Richard Florsheim Art Fund*, 2004.

Florsheim's fascination with light and how it can distort and dramatize night scenes is demonstrated in one of the museum's lithographs showing streams of light from speeding cars blurred in a line across a highway. The depiction of stained-glass church windows in another untitled lithograph in the museum's collection shows how he could capture the drama of light streaming through an interior space.

Florsheim had a summer home in Provincetown, and was a trustee and honorary vice president of Provincetown Art Association and Museum.

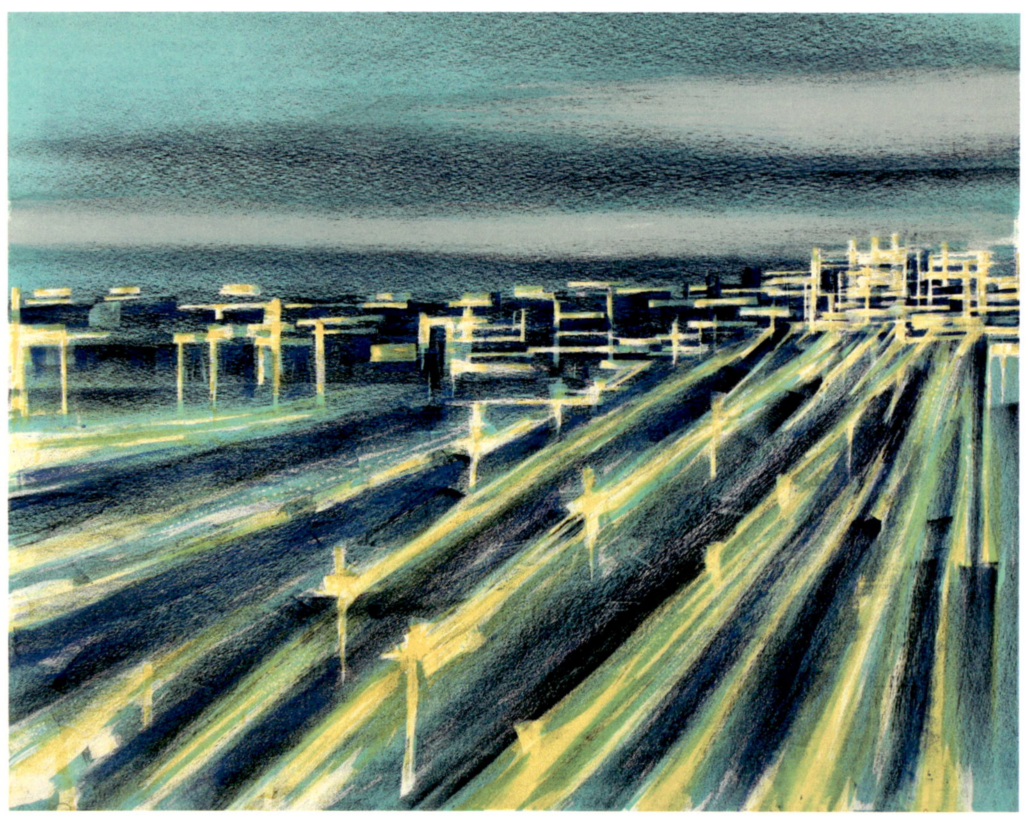

Richard Florsheim, *Untitled* AP, n.d. Lithograph on paper, 19¼ × 26 inches. *Gift of the Richard Florsheim Art Fund*, 2004.

His lithographs and paintings are in the collections of a number of museums, including the Art Institute of Chicago; the National Gallery of Art in Washington, DC; the Philadelphia Museum of Art; the Metropolitan Museum of Art in New York; the Victoria and Albert Museum in London, England; Kunsthalle in Hamburg, Germany; La Bibliothèque nationale de France in Paris; and Galleria d'Arte Moderna in Milan, Italy.

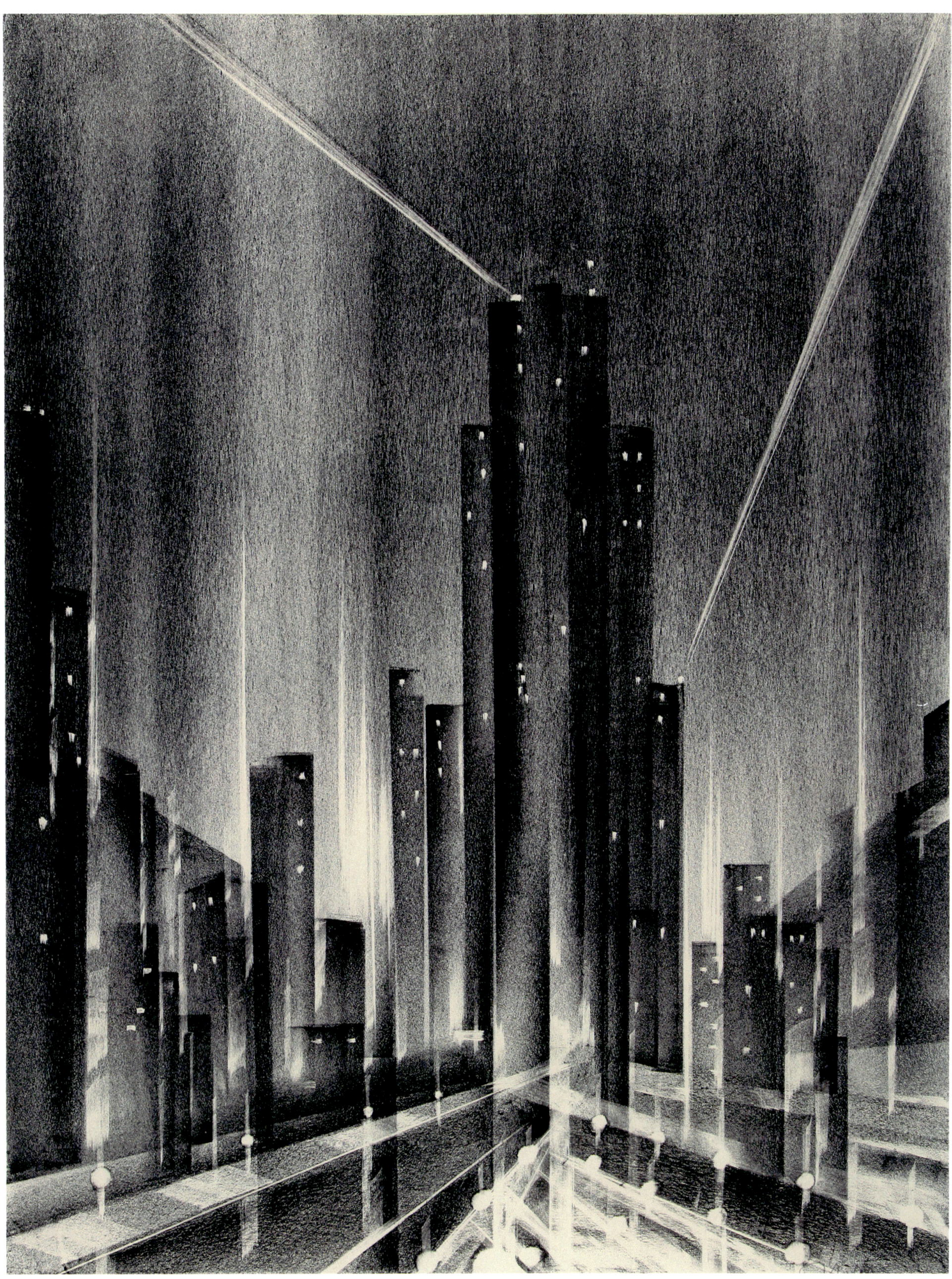

Richard Florsheim, *Untitled* 34/35, n.d. Lithograph on paper, 21¾ × 17¼ inches. *Gift of the Richard Florsheim Art Fund*, 2004.

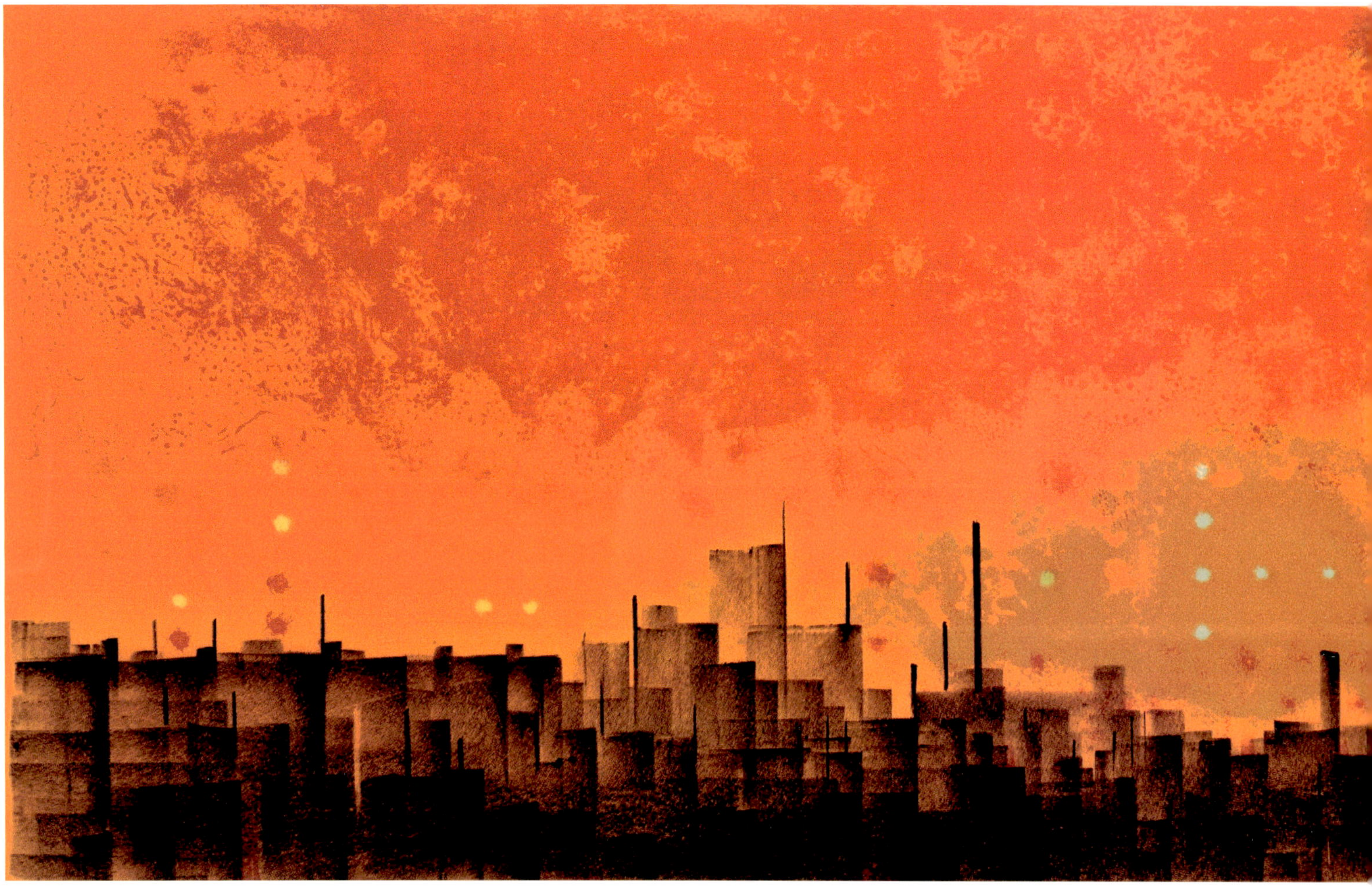

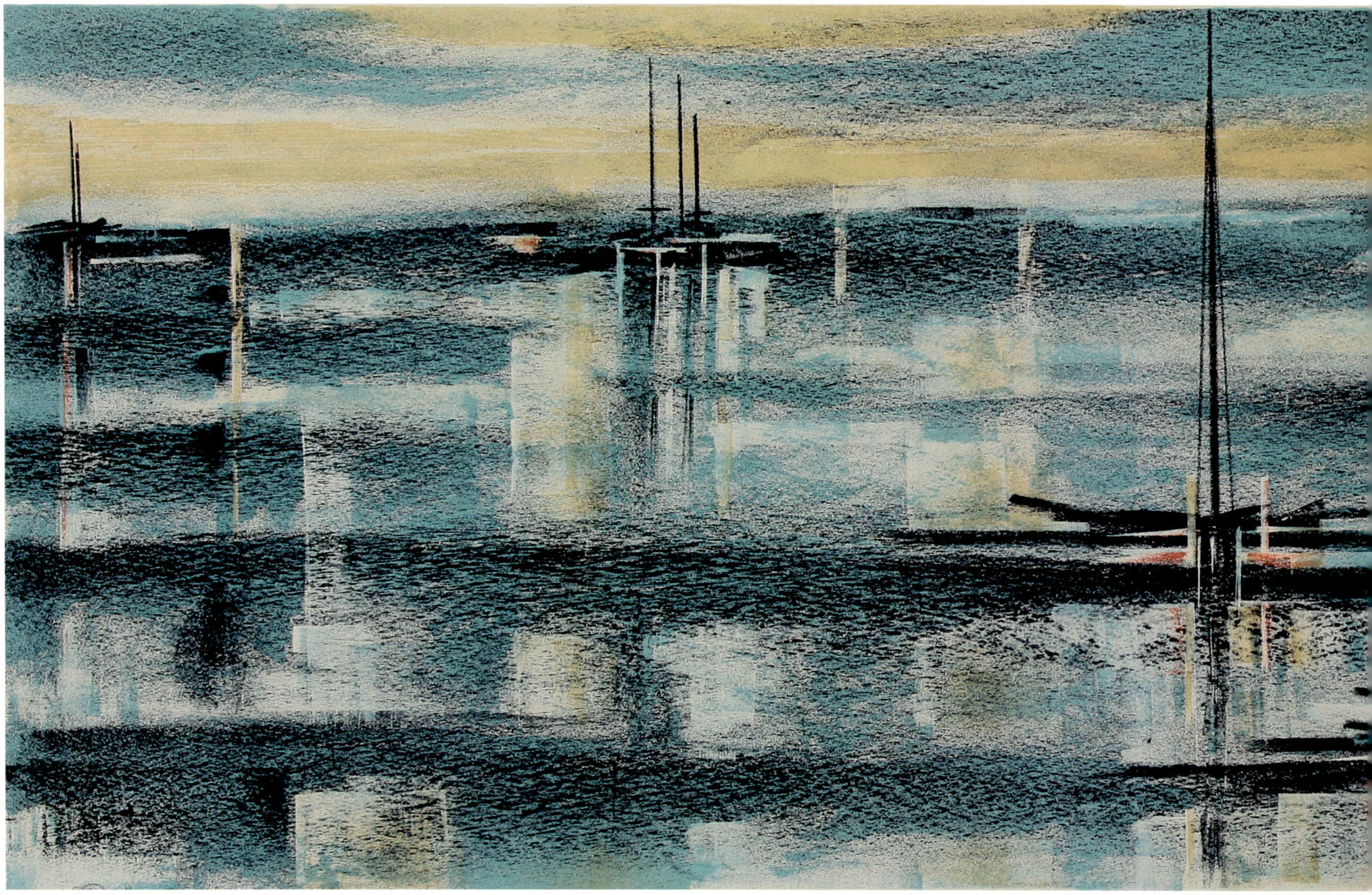

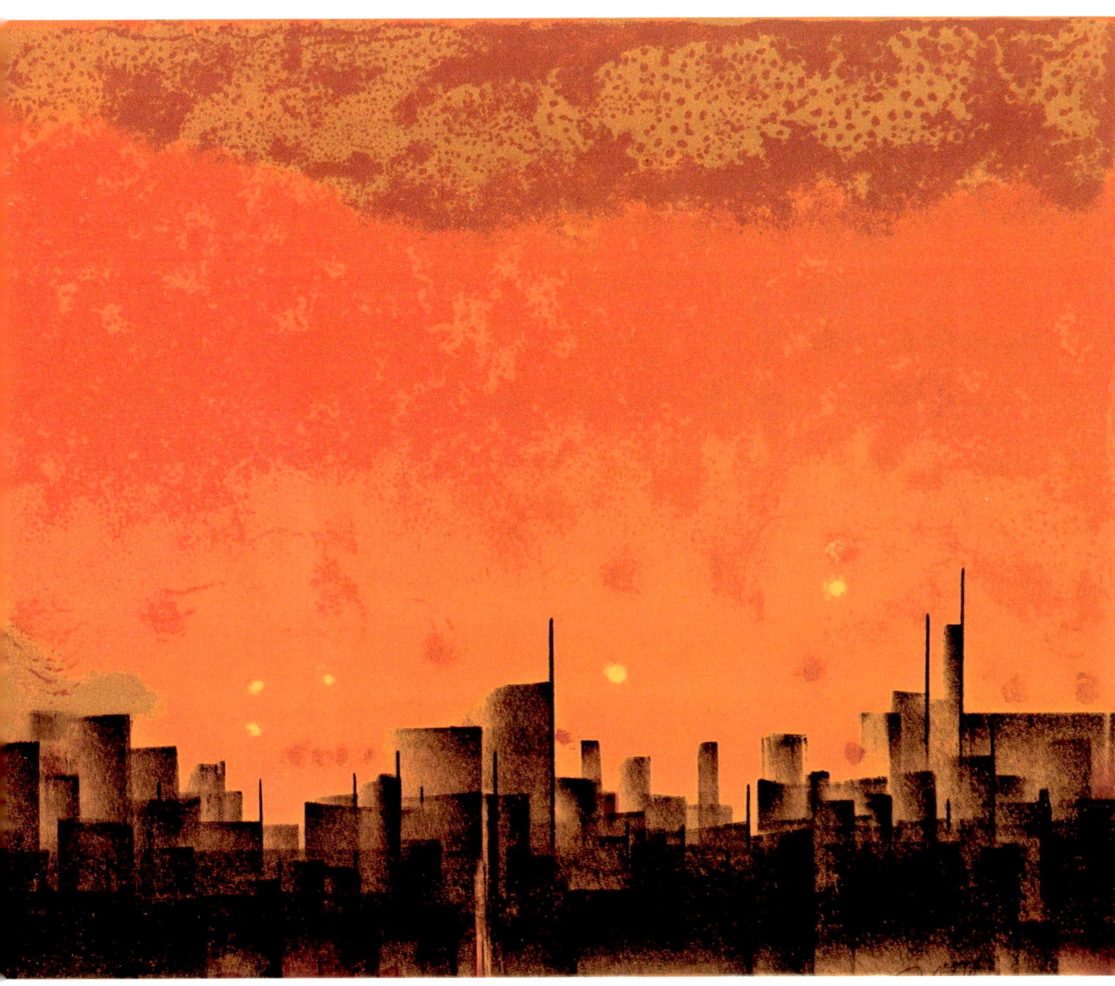

Richard Florsheim, *City Morning* 15/250, n.d. Lithograph on paper, 18½ × 37½ inches. *Gift of Reverend and Mrs. Albert C. Ronander*, 1986.

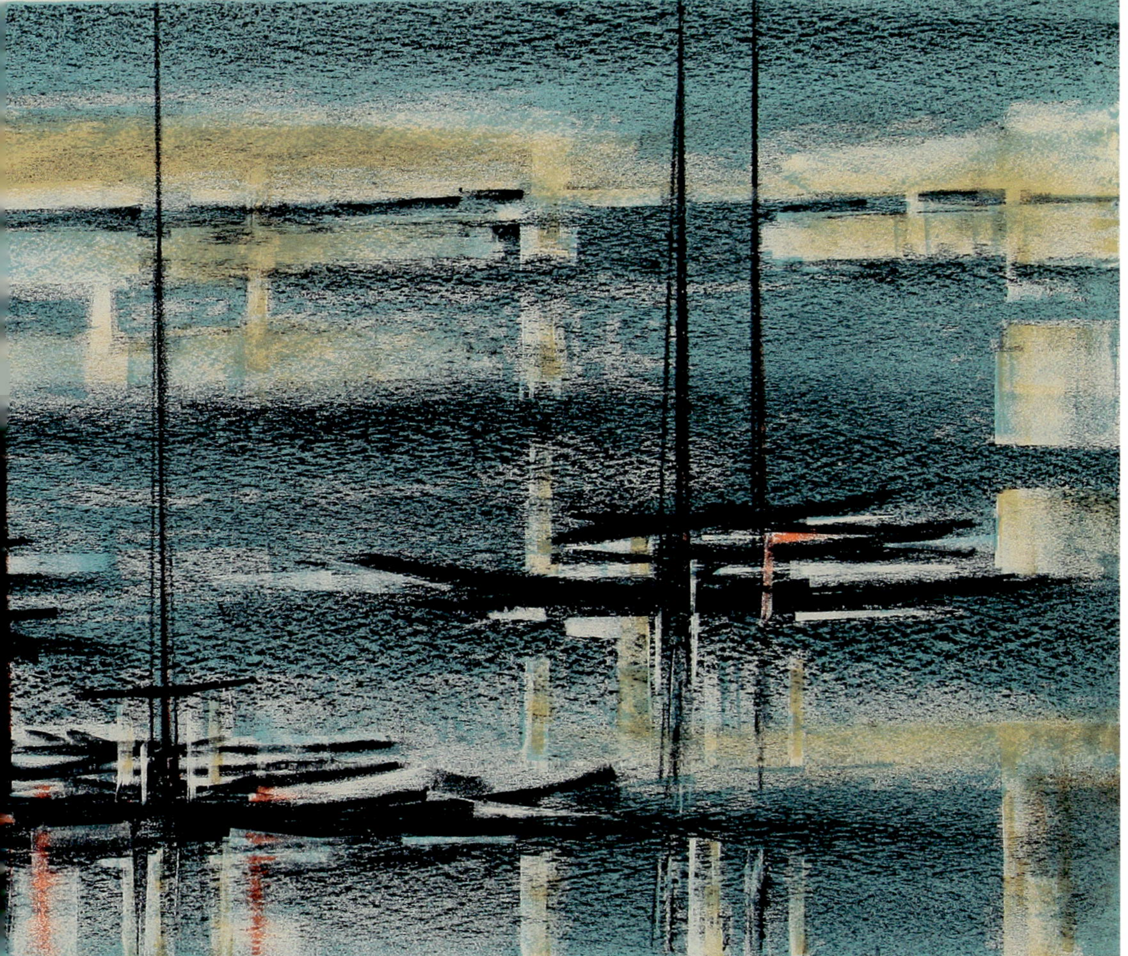

Richard Florsheim, *Untitled* AP-B, n.d. Lithograph on paper, 14½ × 34½ inches. *Gift of the Richard Florsheim Art Fund*, 2004.

ROY FREED
(1917–2014)

Roy Freed, who had a summer home on Cape Cod, was a co-founder of the Cape Museum of Fine Arts in 1981, which was later renamed the Cape Cod Museum of Art. He was an attorney who also made sculpture with steel, found objects, and artifacts.

He was born in New Haven, Connecticut, attended Yale University and Yale School of Law. He graduated in 1940 and began working for the US government. Freed served in the Army Ordnance Corps and in the Petroleum Administration during World War II, and worked with the Department of Justice's Antitrust Division until 1951, when he went to work in a private law firm. Studying new computer technology, he helped develop the field of computer law.

Freed's sculpture, which he began creating in 1975, is abstract, yet often has specific references, such as *Rising Pheasant* and *Flight*, in the Cape Cod Museum of Art collection, both of which have sweeping shapes and a strong sense of movement. And despite its descriptive title, the abstracting trends of cubism are quite obvious in *Woman with Flower*, a steel sculpture on a wood base.

Some of Freed's work references dada, which spawned assemblage, collage, and use of found objects. His sense of humor is apparent in some of his sculptures, which use elements not originally meant for art, in the process of creating abstract forms. Often these objects—a pottery mold, a clamp, even a fire extinguisher—are identifiable, which adds to the piece's expression. Texture and color are often used to enhance the dimension of the sculpture. Freed's titles play a role in the appreciation of the work, which combines unrelated, often ordinary, objects in imaginative ways.

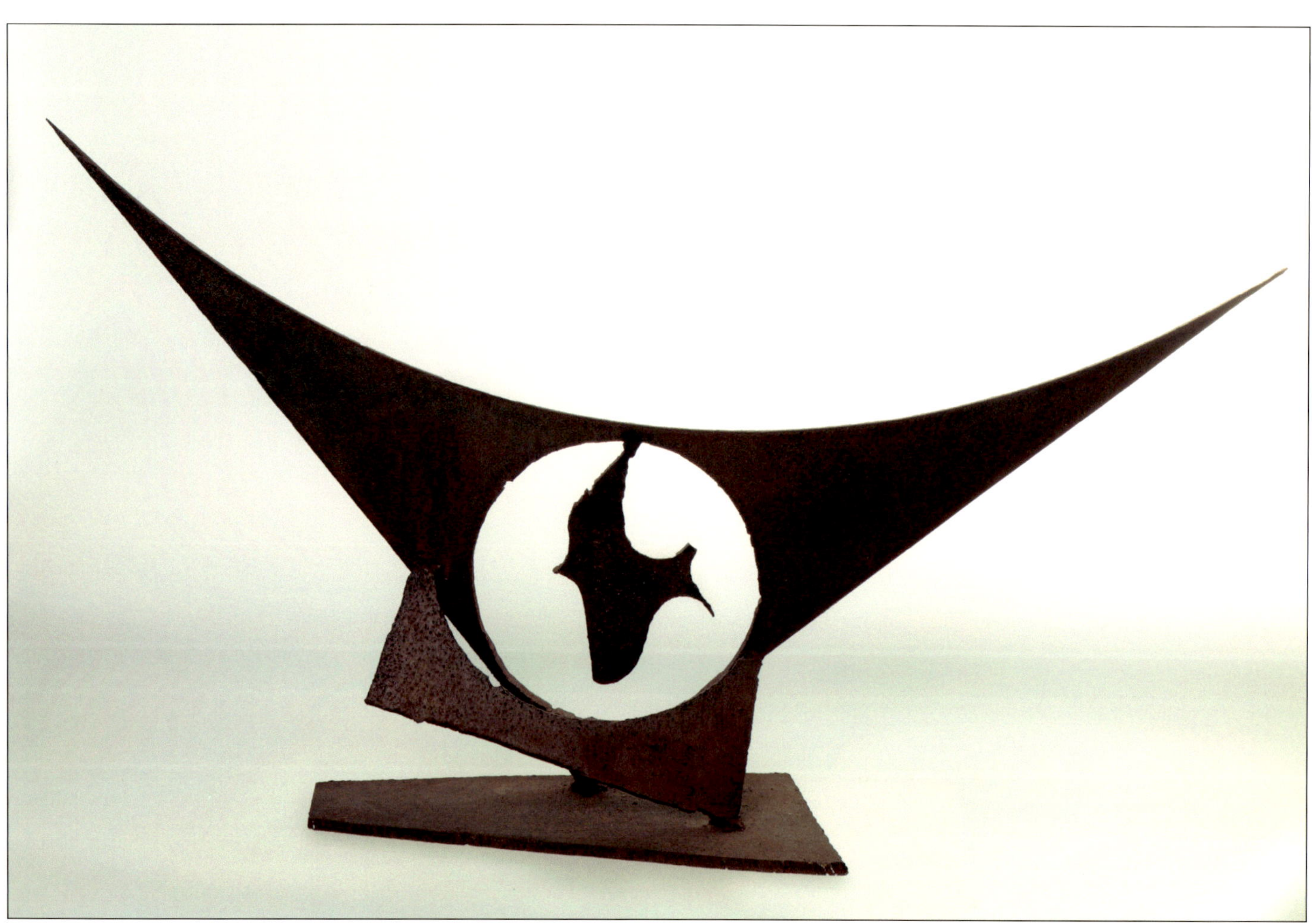

Roy Freed, *Flight*, n.d. Steel, 18 × 39 × 7½ inches. *Gift of Roy and Anne Freed*, 2006.

Roy Freed, *Woman with Flower*, n.d. Steel with wood base, 44½ × 21½ inches. *Gift of Roy and Anne Freed*, 2006.

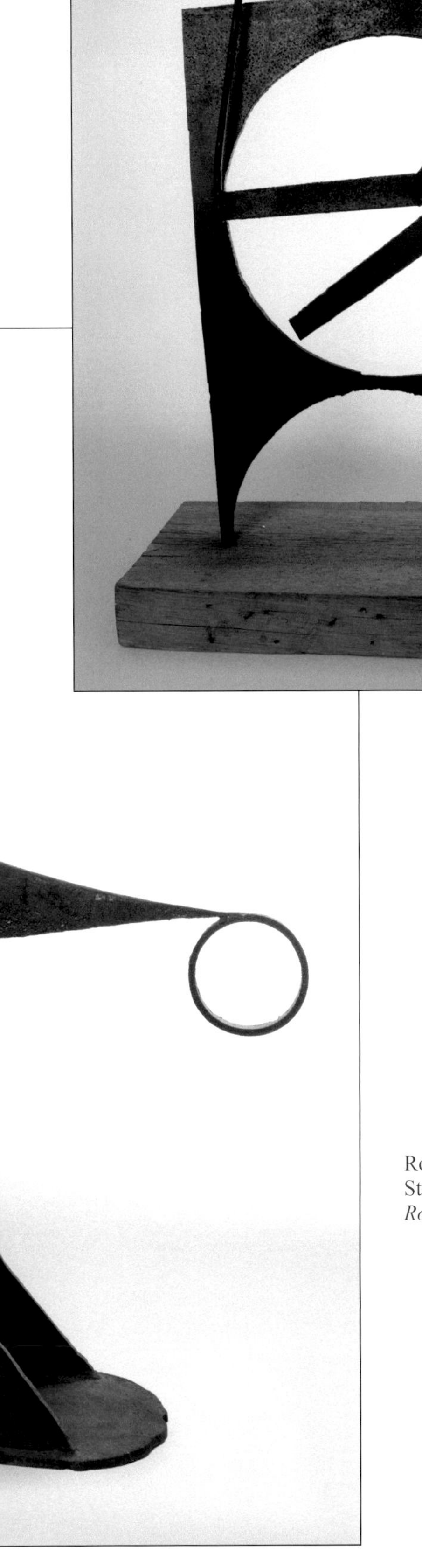

Roy Freed, *Rising Pheasant,* n.d. Steel, 30 × 30 × 7 inches. *Gift of Roy and Anne Freed*, 2006.

JOHN GRILLO
(1917–2014)

John Grillo grew up in Connecticut, and in the 1930s, while a student at the Hartford School of Fine Arts, he became interested in the work of the Ashcan School and George Luks, Robert Henri, Thomas Hart Benton, and Reginald Marsh. But when he later saw a collage by Robert Motherwell, he was inspired to jump into abstraction.

After the Second World War, during which he served in the US Navy in the South Pacific, he studied at the San Francisco School of Fine Arts under the GI Bill. Mark Rothko was one of his teachers and Grillo was influenced by other abstract expressionists, as well as Pablo Picasso, Piet Mondrian, and Joan Miró. While in California, he became the leader of the West Coast branch of abstract expressionism.

In 1948, Grillo went east, joined the New York circle of abstractionists, began studying with Hans Hofmann, and confirmed his adulation of intense color. Much later, in 1967, he moved into figurative work when he began teaching at the University of Massachusetts in Amherst, where he taught for twenty-five years. He retired in 1991 and moved to Wellfleet, Massachusetts.

Major themes in Grillo's figurative work are found in his *Tango* and *Circus* series, both begun in the 1980s. Exotic and seductive, his dancers capture the heat of the tango. In the Cape Cod Museum of Art's collection is a six-foot acrylic on wood triptych, *Tango Dancers*, which captures a scene in which a sinister-looking man peeks out from behind a curtain at three voluptuous women, while a lively couple comes together to dance. The exotic image exults in brilliant patterns and the robust rhythms of the tango.

His circus pictures are lively and flatly painted in ebullient colors. *At the Zoo*, also in the museum collection, is a view of five people in front of a cage with an elephant. Mother, father, and son appear involved with the elephant, but the other two, a man and woman, are clutching at one another, hardly aware of where they are.

Grillo was infatuated with curvaceous women. His female figures are voluptuous superstars, as seen in his *Marilyn* series, based on the shapely form of Marilyn Monroe. His nudes and self-portraits recall Henri Matisse's fauve paintings with their use of expressive color.

Grillo ventured back and forth between abstract and figurative works his entire career. Like many artists, he was an intuitive painter, driven by instincts and feelings. And all of his work—whether they are his free-wheeling abstractions; tight mosaics; or figurative paintings on the themes of the circus, the tango, Marilyn Monroe, or provocative nudes—are filled with vibrant colors, robust lines, exotic interpretations, and a zestful mood.

Grillo's works are in the collections of major museums, including the Metropolitan Museum of Art, the Whitney Museum of American Art, and the Guggenheim Museum, all in New York.

John Grillo, *Tango Dancers* (Triptych), n.d. Acrylic on wood, 76 × 125⅛ × 1 inches. *Gift of John Grillo*, 2009.

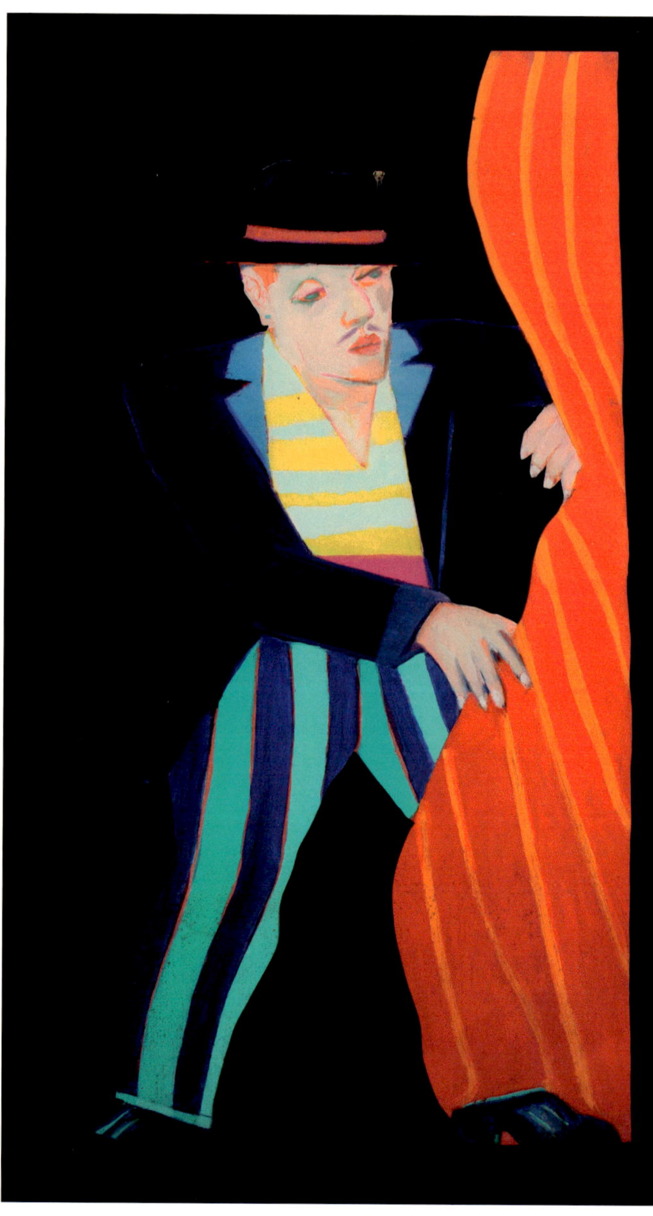

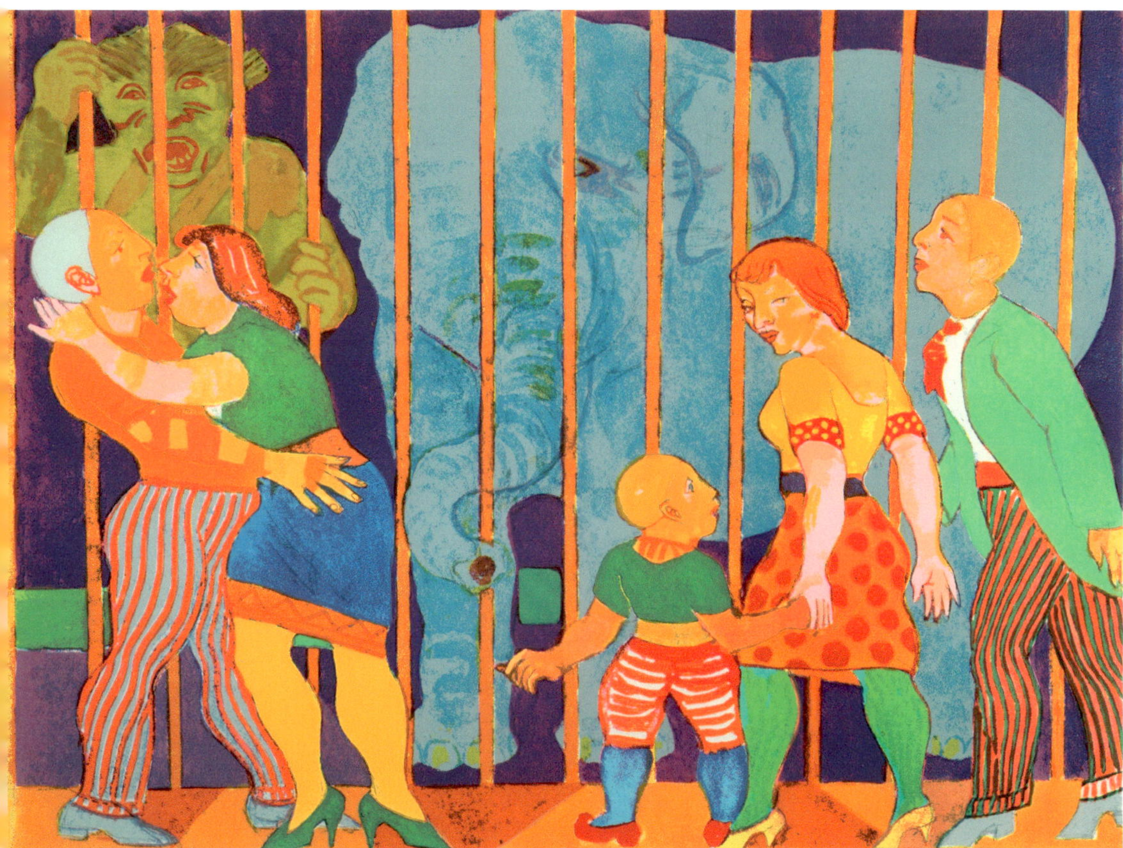

John Grillo, *At the Zoo* 34/50, 1991. Color lithograph on paper, 19½ × 26 inches. *Anonymous gift*, 2000.

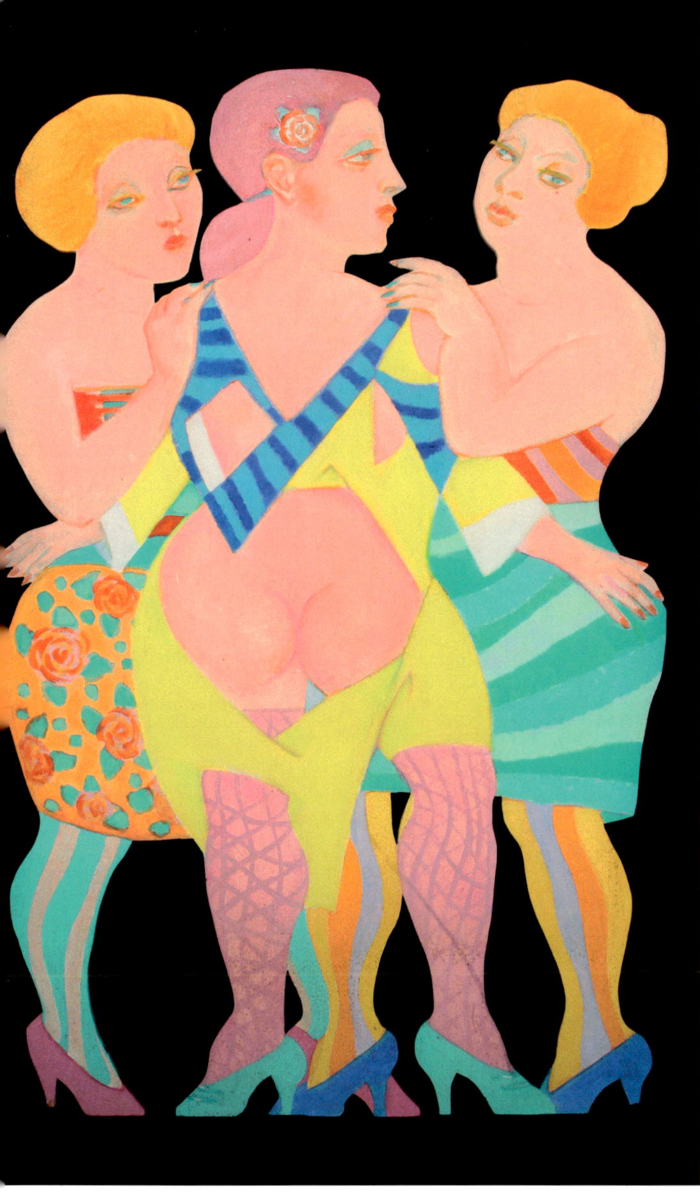

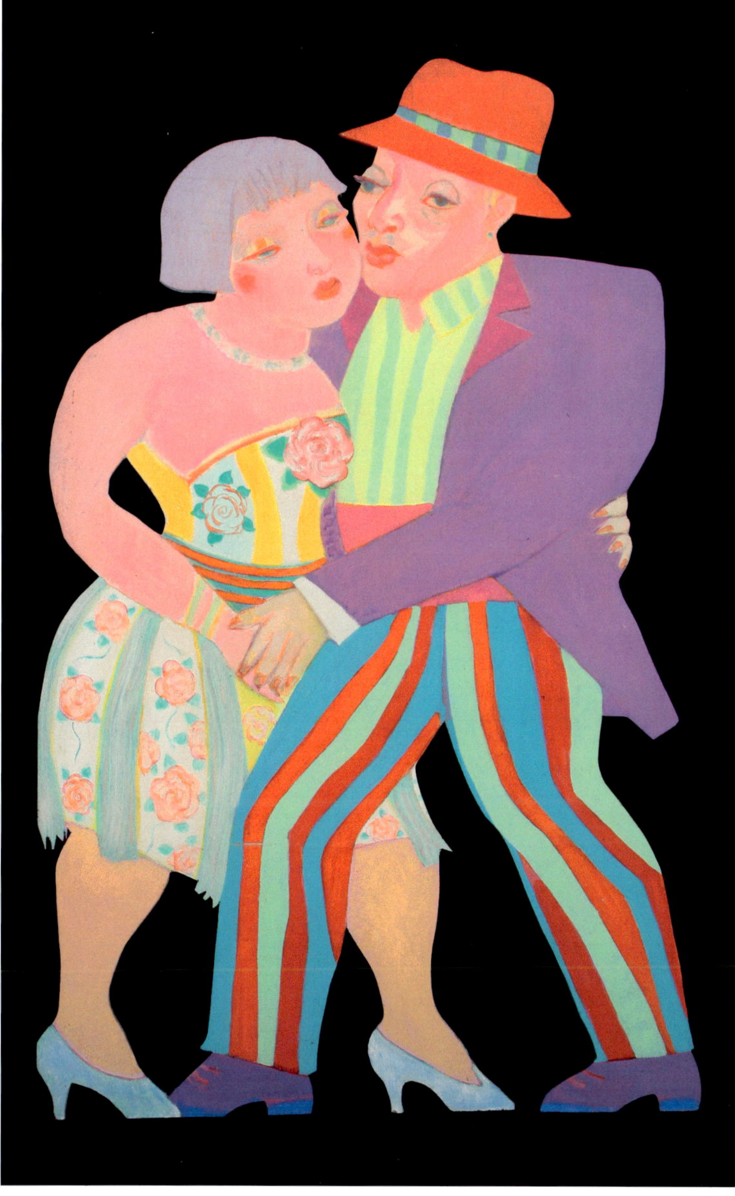

SIDNEY SIMON
(1917–1997)

Sculptor Sidney Simon carved wood, cast bronzes, shaped terra cotta and clay, built mixed-media constructions, and did large commission works for public places. His art encompassed abstract and figurative pieces, and he always seemed to incorporate some kind of story. Simon had a home in Truro and was active in the Provincetown art colony for many years.

Born in Pittsburgh, he studied art at Carnegie Institute of Technology, the Pennsylvania Academy of Fine Arts, the University of Pennsylvania and the Académie de la Grande Chaumière in Paris. During World War II, he was a captain in the Army Corps of Engineers, in charge of organizing war artists. When he returned from military service, abstract expressionism was in full swing. But he found abstractions impossible after his war years, and focused on representing the figure. The conté crayon drawing *Reclining Nude*, done in 1975, in the collection of the Cape Cod Museum of Art, is typical of his focus on the female form, and his work from the live model.

After the war, Simon spent time in France. Despite an association with Georges Braque, he maintained his commitment to representational painting. He turned to sculpture in the mid-1950s and did create some abstract pieces. However, in the 1960s, he revisited figurative works, structured by abstract principles. Simon's wry sense of humor and his penchant for puns often found their way into his sculpture. Like the man himself, his work was full of humor and whimsy, parody and irony. In *Headstand*, in the museum collection, you can see his amusing play on words, which refers not only to the inverted position of the black walnut carved figure but also to the base where the head seems to be stuck inside.

His public commissions include the 1989 Four Seasons fountain sculpture in Worldwide Plaza in Manhattan and the 1987 fountain sculpture in City Hall Plaza in Philadelphia. A founder of the Skowhegan School of Painting and Sculpture in Maine, Simon also taught at Parsons School of Design, the Art Students League, Brooklyn Museum School, Columbia University, and Cooper Union. His works are in museum collections, including the Whitney Museum of American Art in New York and the Williams College Museum of Art in Williamstown, Massachusetts.

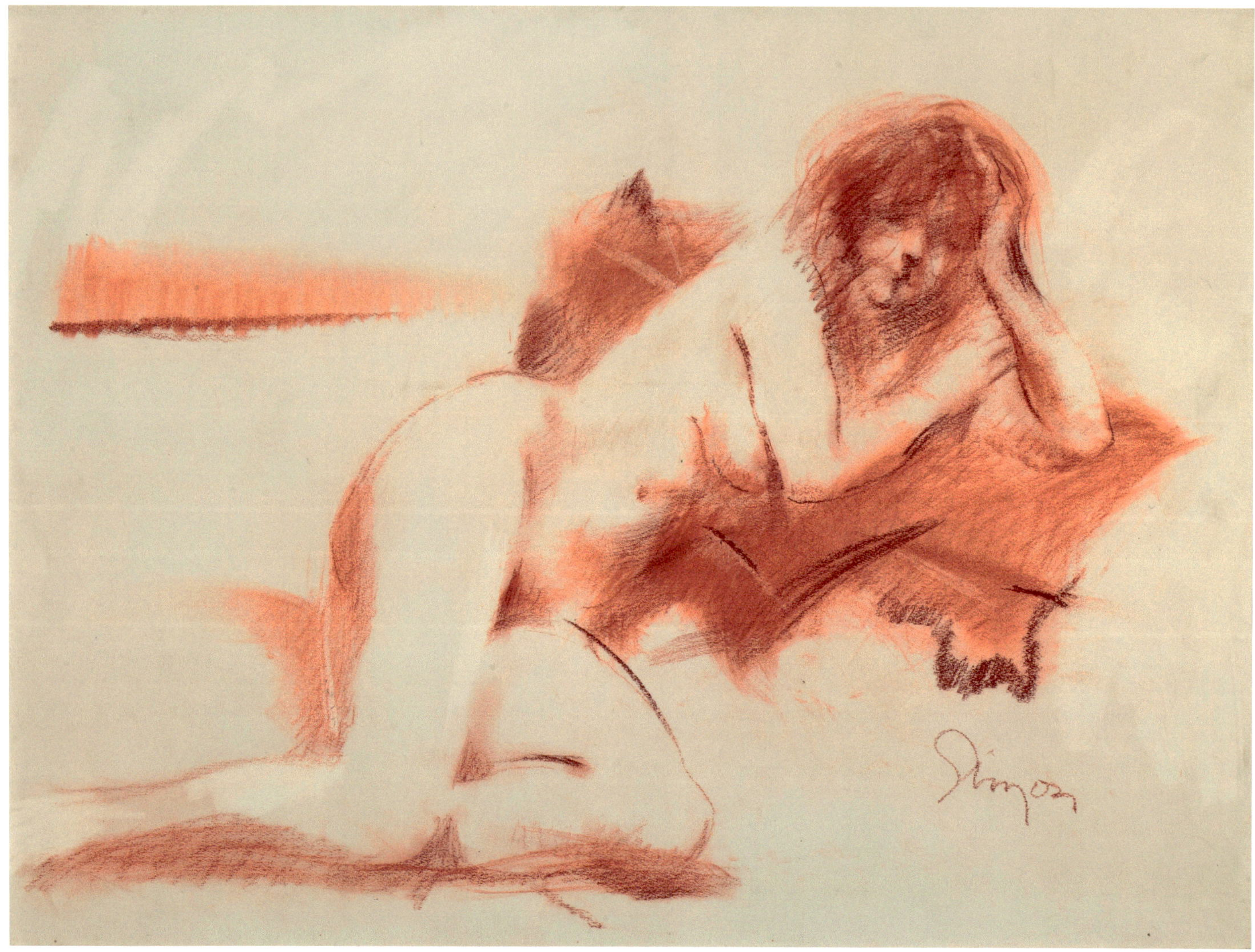

Sidney Simon, *Reclining Nude*, 1975. Conte crayon on paper, 21⅝ × 29⅝ inches. *Gift of Sidney Simon*, 1989.

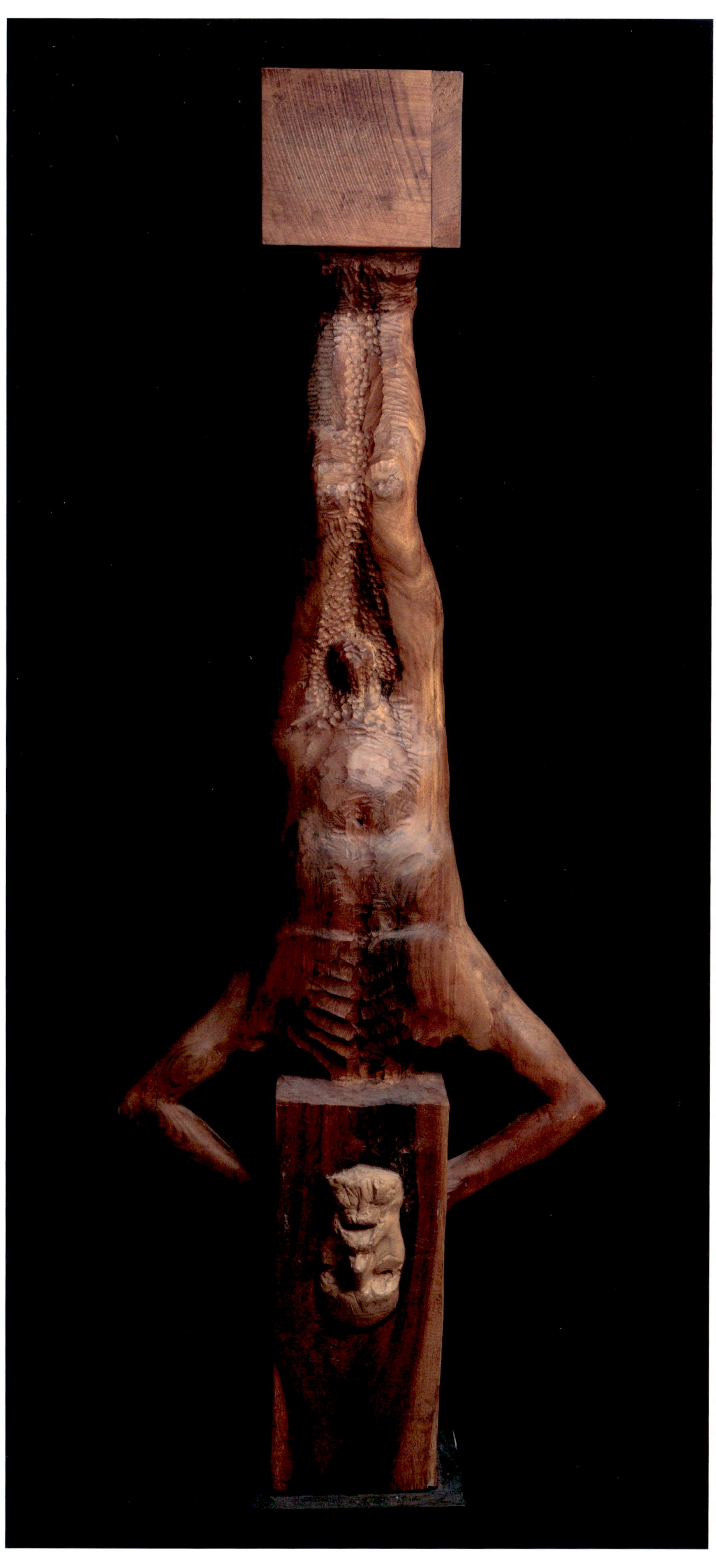

Sidney Simon, *Headstand*, 1994. Black walnut with metal base, 72 × 14 × 27 inches. *Gift of the Estate of Sidney Simon*, 2007.

SISTER MARY CORITA KENT
(1918–1986)

When you drive into Boston on the Southeast Expressway, it is hard to miss the rainbow arc design by Corita Kent painted in primary colors on Boston Gas Co.'s 150-foot-high natural gas storage tank in Dorchester, two miles south of the city. But Kent's tank design is just a small part of her contributions to American art in the twentieth century. Her primary medium was silkscreen, a printmaking technique also known as serigraphy.

Before Andy Warhol made serigraph prints a media sensation, Kent was working to establish the technique as a fine-art medium, and experimenting with collage, photography, and bold, flat colors. Warhol's work did later influence her, and like him, she used elements from popular commercial graphics to create her pop art images. However, because of her spiritual background, she often combined typical advertisements, newspaper clippings, and song lyrics with biblical and morally uplifting images and the language of peace and love. This spiritual focus is evident in her silkscreen, *Sacrifice of Abraham*, in the Cape Cod Museum of Art collection, which references a story from the Bible. *Benedictio*, also in the museum collection, is sparked by graphic elements, which add additional energy to her striking colors.

Kent created hundreds of serigraph designs for posters, book covers, and murals. And she designed the 1985 US Postal Service "Love" stamp. Her art ranged from representational to abstract, and her work almost always expressed hope and optimism.

She was born Frances Elizabeth Kent in Fort Dodge, Iowa, and became a nun in 1936 when she joined the Roman Catholic order of Sisters of the Immaculate Heart of Mary in Los Angeles, and took the name Sister Mary Corita. She studied at Otis College of Art and Design and Chouinard Art Institute, and later earned her bachelor's degree from Immaculate Heart College, and a master's in art history at the University of Southern California. She taught at Immaculate Heart College for many years, became chair of the art department, and drew around her a circle of forward-thinking artists and designers, such as Saul Bass, John Cage, Buckminster Fuller, and Charles and Ray Eames. In 1968, she left the order because of her progressive social and political views, and moved to Boston, where she devoted herself to art.

Kent's papers are held at the Schlesinger Library in Radcliffe Institute at Harvard University. Her works are in numerous museum collections, including the Museum of Fine Arts in Boston, and the Metropolitan Museum of Art and Whitney Museum of American Art in New York.

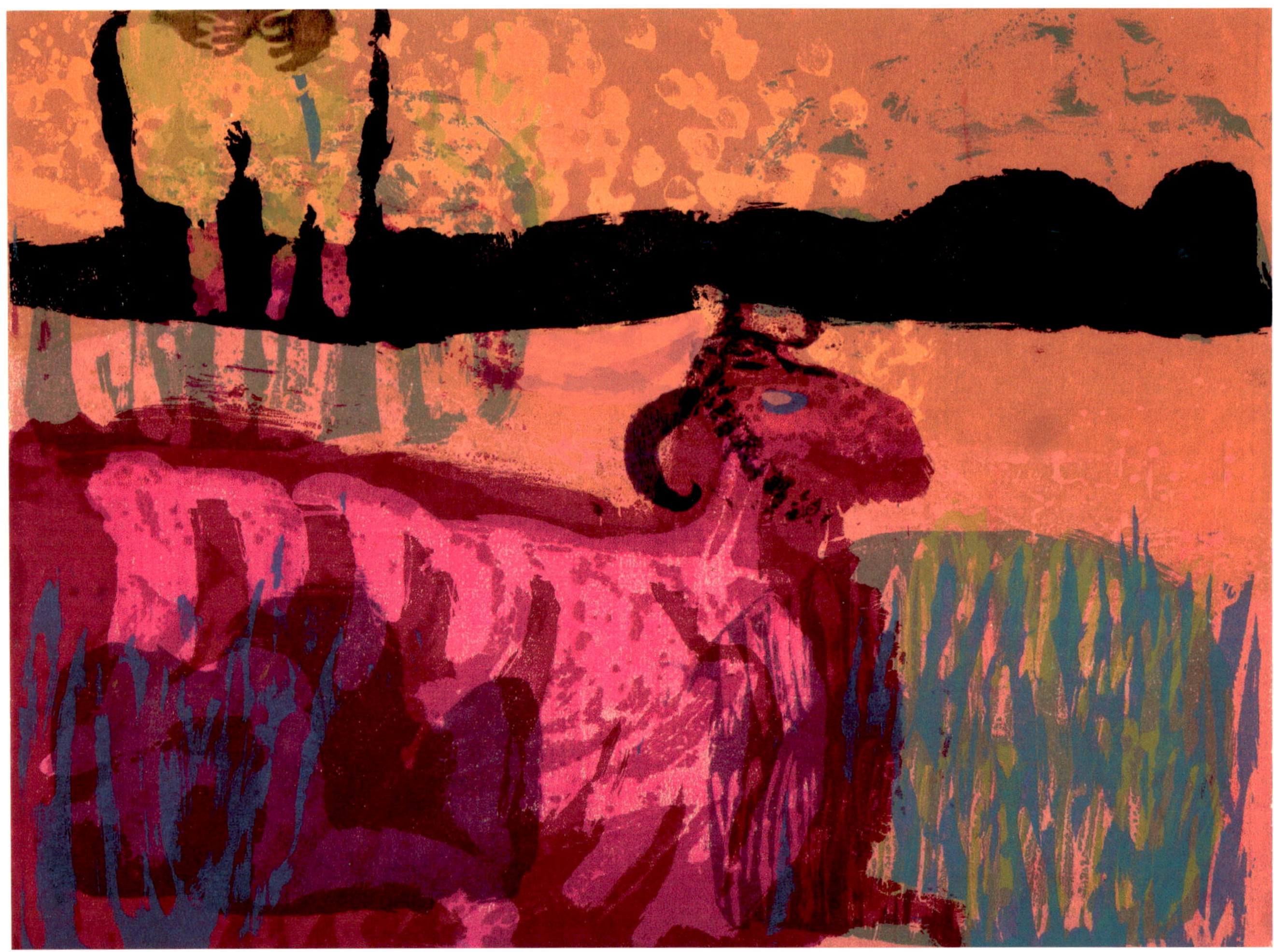

Sister Mary Corita Kent, *Sacrifice of Abraham*, 1959. Silkscreen on paper, 22½ × 31½ inches. *Gift of Reverend William G. O'Brien*, 1987. *Courtesy of Corita Art Center, Los Angeles.*

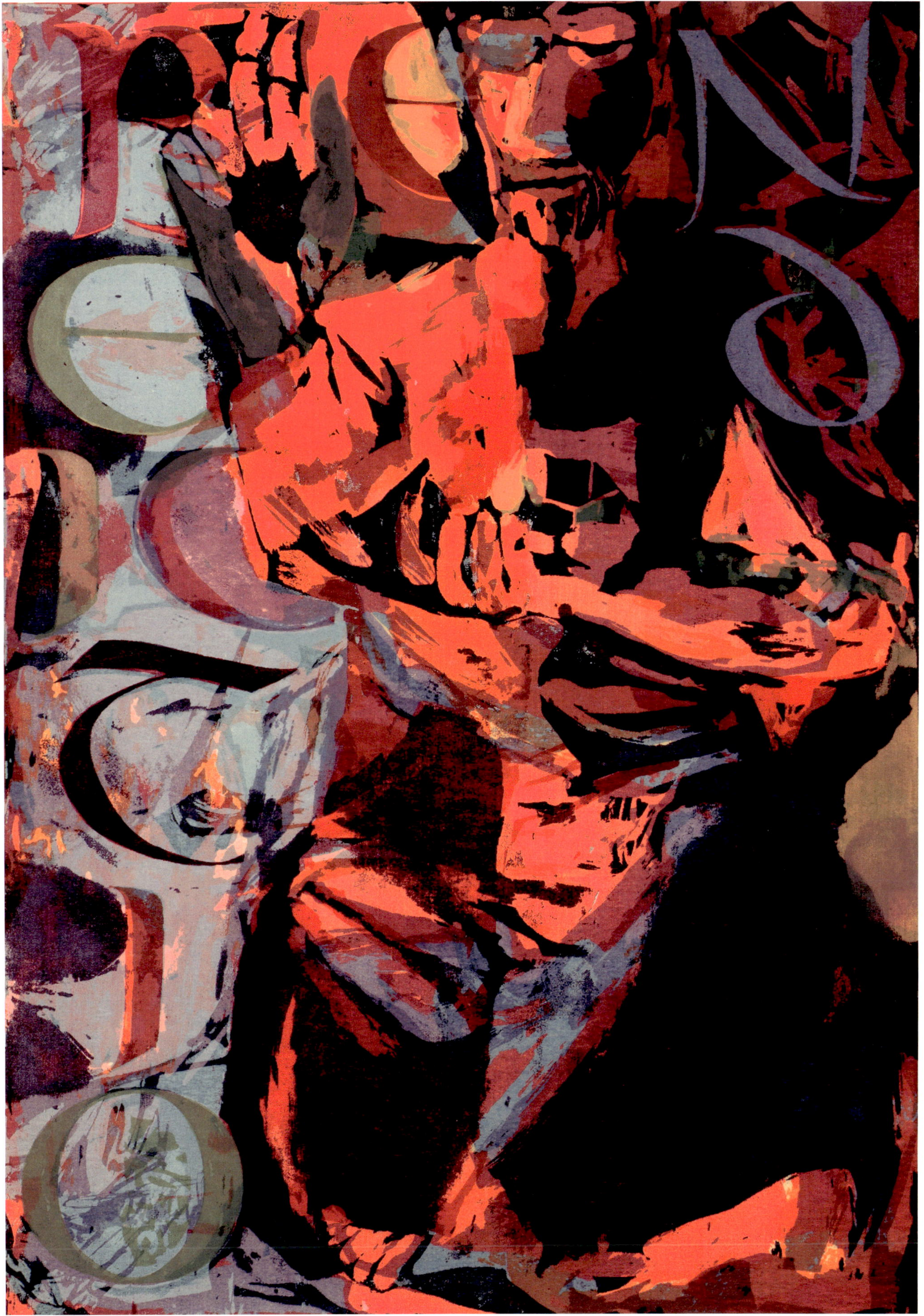

Sister Mary Corita Kent, *Benedicto,* 1954. Serigraph on paper, 21⅜ × 15½ inches. *Gift of Reverend William G. O'Brien*, 2006. *Courtesy of Corita Art Center, Los Angeles.*

FRITZ BULTMAN
(1919–1985)

A member of the New York School of abstract expressionists, Fritz Bultman was significantly influenced by Hans Hofmann, with whom he studied in New York and Provincetown from 1938 until 1941.

Bultman was born in New Orleans and after studying there and at the New Bauhaus in Chicago, he went to Germany to study at Munich's Bauhaus in 1935. However, by the time he arrived, the school had been closed by Hitler. While he was in Munich, he rented a room from Hofmann's wife, who had remained there when her husband left Germany to teach at the University of California at Berkeley.

There is no denying the connection between Hofmann and Fritz Bultman, who had a deep personal relationship with his teacher. Bultman's abstract collages are cascades of rhythmic movement in vivid colors, strongly influenced by Hofmann's style and teaching.

His collages are composed of large pieces of paper that he painted with gouache. Primary colors dominate, but there are also creams, browns, and blacks. The pieces of painted paper rendezvous in large, strong, well-defined patterns. Seductive curves and clean, straight edges manage a delicate balancing act and evoke a lyrical tempo. The jazz so deeply rooted in Bultman's native New Orleans made its way into the artist's consciousness and became a fluent part of his work.

Several of his collages suggest the undulating shape of a female torso, which he loved to capture in his representational drawings. Other pieces capture his impressions of the ocean, as in *Blue Yoke I*, in the Cape Cod Museum of Art collection, which is dominated by a mighty U-shape turned upside-down that feels like the rise of a giant wave. The robust and simplified forms representative of Bultman's late work evolved from a rich and variegated abstract expressionism to clear-sighted collages that evoke Henri Matisse's *papiers collés*.

Although his paintings and collages are essentially abstract, he regularly drew nude studies from live models. In these drawings, his curvilinear lines move with lively curiosity around the figure. It is the same line that is defined with alacrity in his cut-paper collages.

His works are included in major museum collections, including the Metropolitan Museum of Art, the Museum of Modern Art, the Whitney Museum of American Art, and the Guggenheim Museum, in New York; the Smithsonian American Art Museum in Washington, DC; the Museum of Fine Arts in Boston; and New Orleans Museum of Art.

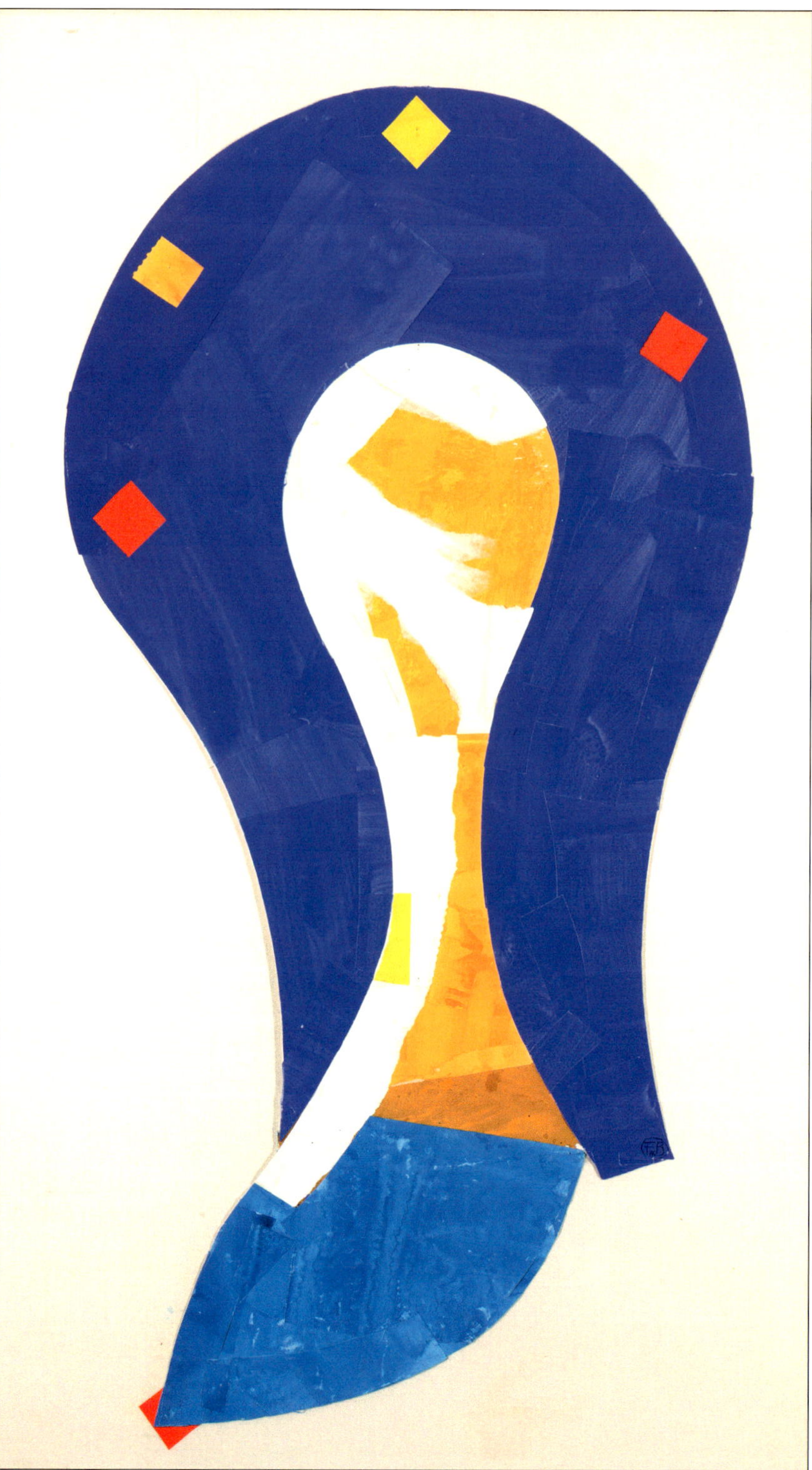

Fritz Bultman, *Blue Yoke I*, 1976.
Collage with painted paper on fabric, 44½ × 25 inches.
Gift of Mrs. Jeanne Bultman, 1998.

GILBERT FRANKLIN
(1919–2004)

Born in England, Gilbert Franklin grew up in Attleboro, Massachusetts. He learned about metals from his father, who was a jeweler. He studied sculpture at the Rhode Island School of Design, at the Museo Nacional de Arte in Mexico City, and the American Academy in Rome. In 1938, he came to Provincetown to take classes with John Frazier, and continued spending summers on the Cape for the rest of his life.

The human figure was a major part of his work. Influenced by Greek and Roman classical sculpture, his pieces nevertheless took a contemporary turn with their simplifications, fluid lines, and sharp contours. *New England Woman*, a nearly life-size bronze in the Cape Cod Museum of Art collection, is a beautifully curved form without a head or arms, which evokes a sense of New England austerity. *Torso*, a polished travertine marble figure in the museum collection, is a voluptuous shape seductively accentuating breasts and hips.

Some of Franklin's sculpture is abstract, yet still relates to the human figure and objects in the real world. Many are inspired by the natural world's organic shapes and come from the shells and rocks he saw on the Cape. In addition to bronze and marble, Franklin worked in wood.

He taught at the Rhode Island School of Design, Harvard, Yale, and the University of Pennsylvania. Franklin also completed numerous public commissions, including the US Navy Memorial in Washington, DC; the Harry S. Truman Memorial in Independence, Missouri; and the Orpheus Ascending Fountain at the Frazier Memorial in Providence, Rhode Island.

His works are in a number of public collections, including the Museum of Fine Arts in Boston, the Rhode Island School of Design Museum in Providence, the National Academy Museum in New York, and the National Portrait Gallery in Washington, DC.

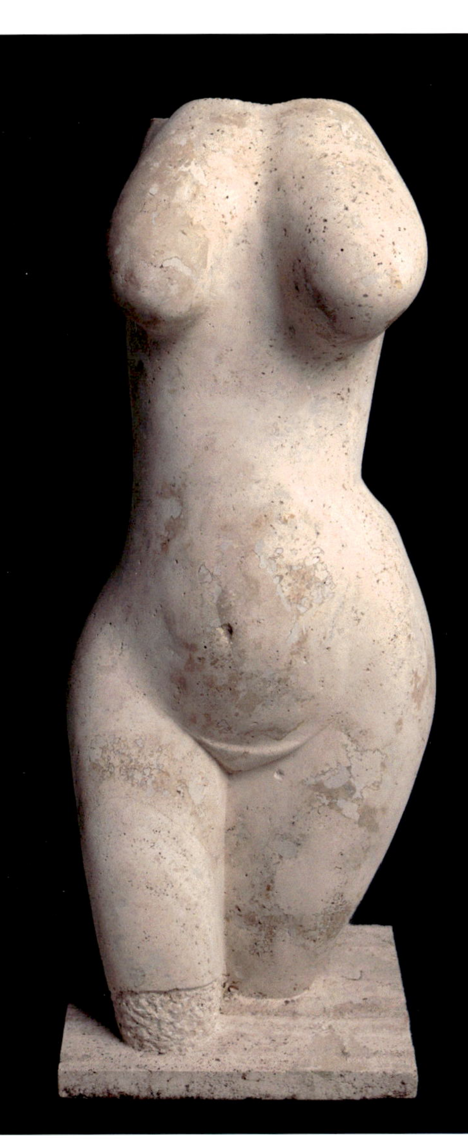

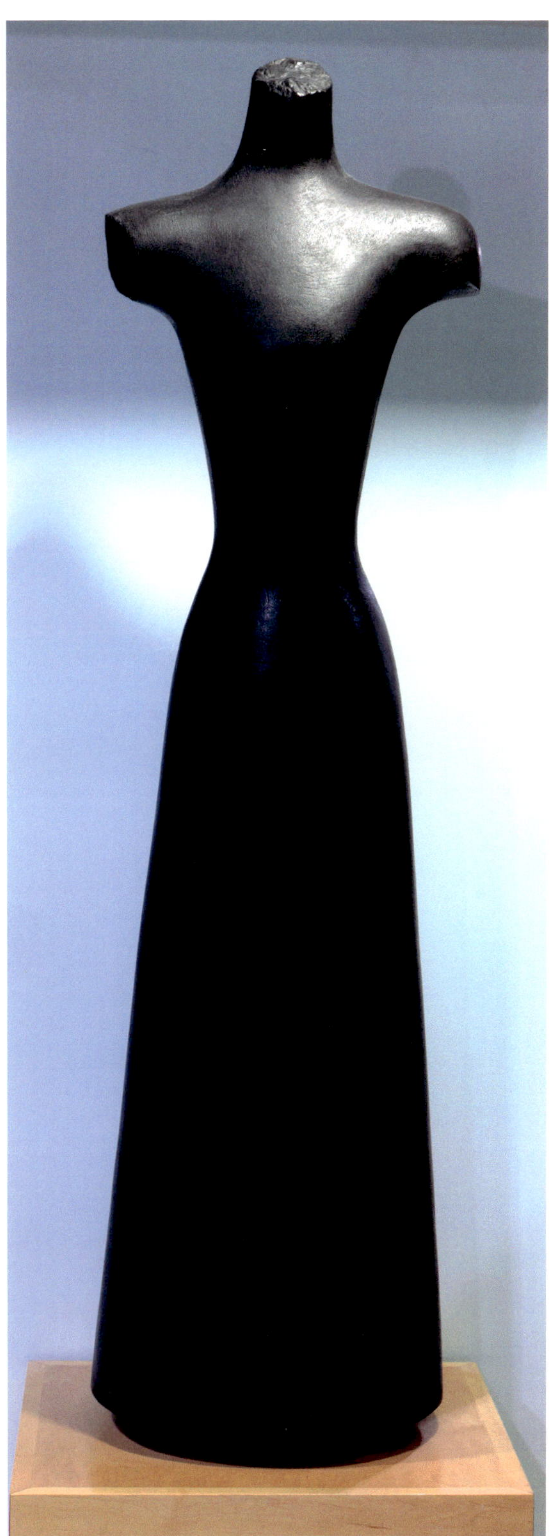

Right: Gilbert Franklin, *Torso*, 1965. Polished travertine marble, 35 × 14 × 12 inches. *Gift of Gilbert and Joyce Franklin*, 1991.

Far right: Gilbert Franklin, *New England Woman*, 1998. Bronze on wood base, 46 × 12 × 11 inches. *Gift of Gilbert Franklin, Dr. Linda B. Miller, and the Florsheim Art Fund*, 1998.

TARO YAMAMOTO
(1919–1994)

Although Taro Yamamoto was born in Hollywood, California, his childhood education was in Japan. He returned to California to study art. After military service during World War II, he went east to study in New York. It was 1950 when he enrolled at the Art Students League, and abstract expressionism was on the rise. He went on to Hans Hofmann's School in New York in the early 1950s. In 1953 he went to Europe to study with abstract artist Willi Baumeister in Germany. At a residency at MacDowell Colony in Peterborough, New Hampshire, he worked with Stuart Davis, Milton Avery, and abstract expressionists Willem de Kooning, Jackson Pollock, and Mark Rothko.

Hofmann's influence brought Yamamoto to Provincetown, where he lived for many years. Hofmann was a continual inspiration for him, which can be seen in his abstract expressionist work. The vibrant color, the free-wheeling gestures, the splatters and drips of paint, even the rectangles can all be seen as Hofmannesque. With its randomly spaced rectangles, *Dawn*, in the Cape Cod Museum of Art collection, has a distinct relationship to Hofmann's later work. And Yamamoto's 1972 *Untitled*, in the museum collection, has the drips and speckles that define his approach to abstract expressionism.

Yamamoto's brushwork was fluid and spontaneous, sometimes swirling, other times building into irregular shapes. His colors, always vibrant, evoke various moods, whether boisterous in spills of red, or pondering in blues encrusted over a sea of other colors. His work has dynamism and energy. His large-scale paintings fill the space around them, and almost engulf the viewer.

In the 1980s, Yamamoto took on a hard-edge style, referencing an earlier period when he was interested in Piet Mondrian's geometric abstractions.

His works are included in various public collections, including the Museum of Fine Arts in Boston, the Miami Museum of Modern Art in Florida, La Jolla Museum of Art in California, and the Hirshhorn Museum and Sculpture Garden in Washington, DC.

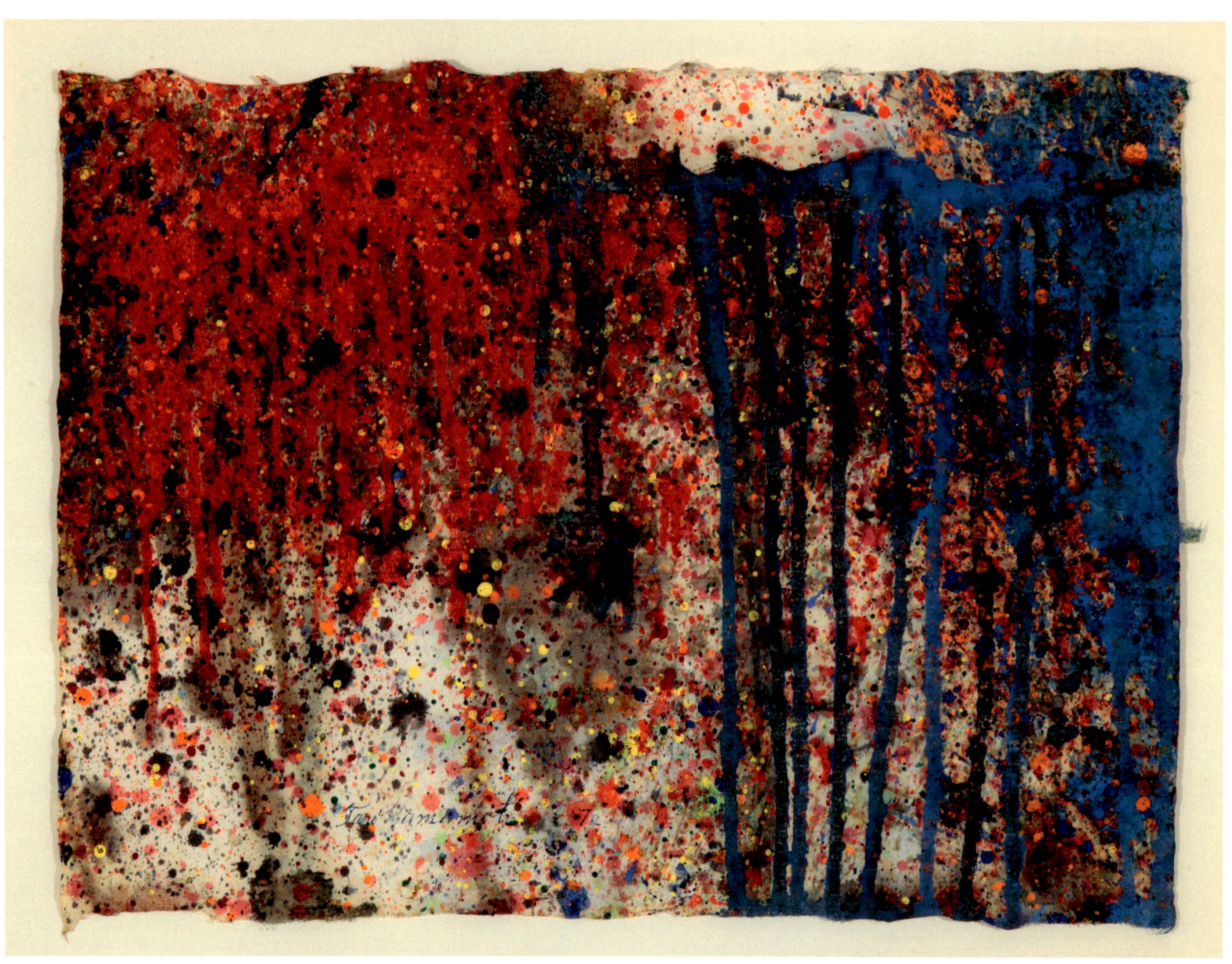

Taro Yamamoto, *Untitled,* 1972. Ink and watercolor on rice paper, 12 × 16½ inches. *Gift of Greta Waldas,* 1993.

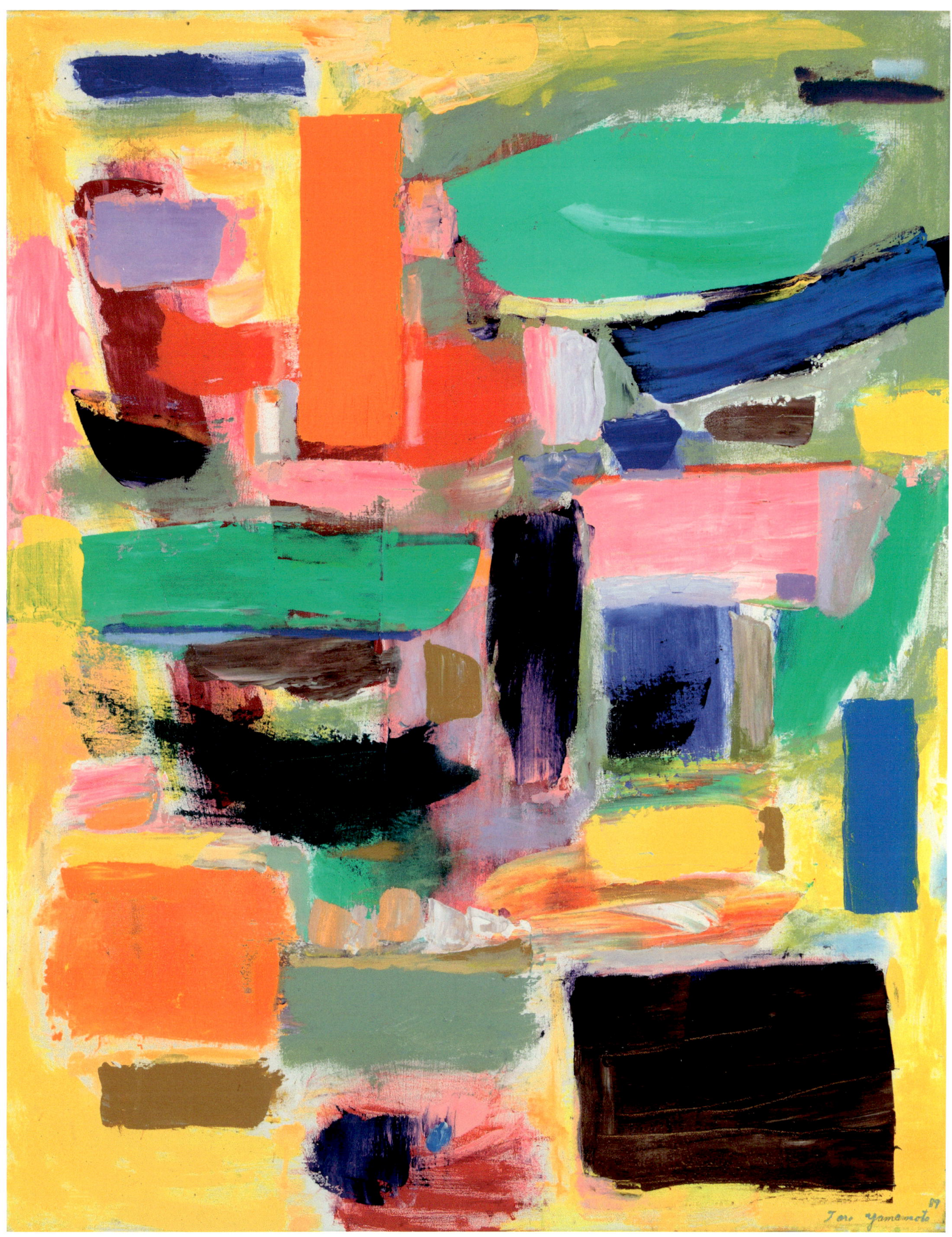

Taro Yamamoto, *Fried Egg Sandwich,* 1989. Oil on canvas, 49½ × 39½ inches. *Gift of George Zhouf*, 1995.

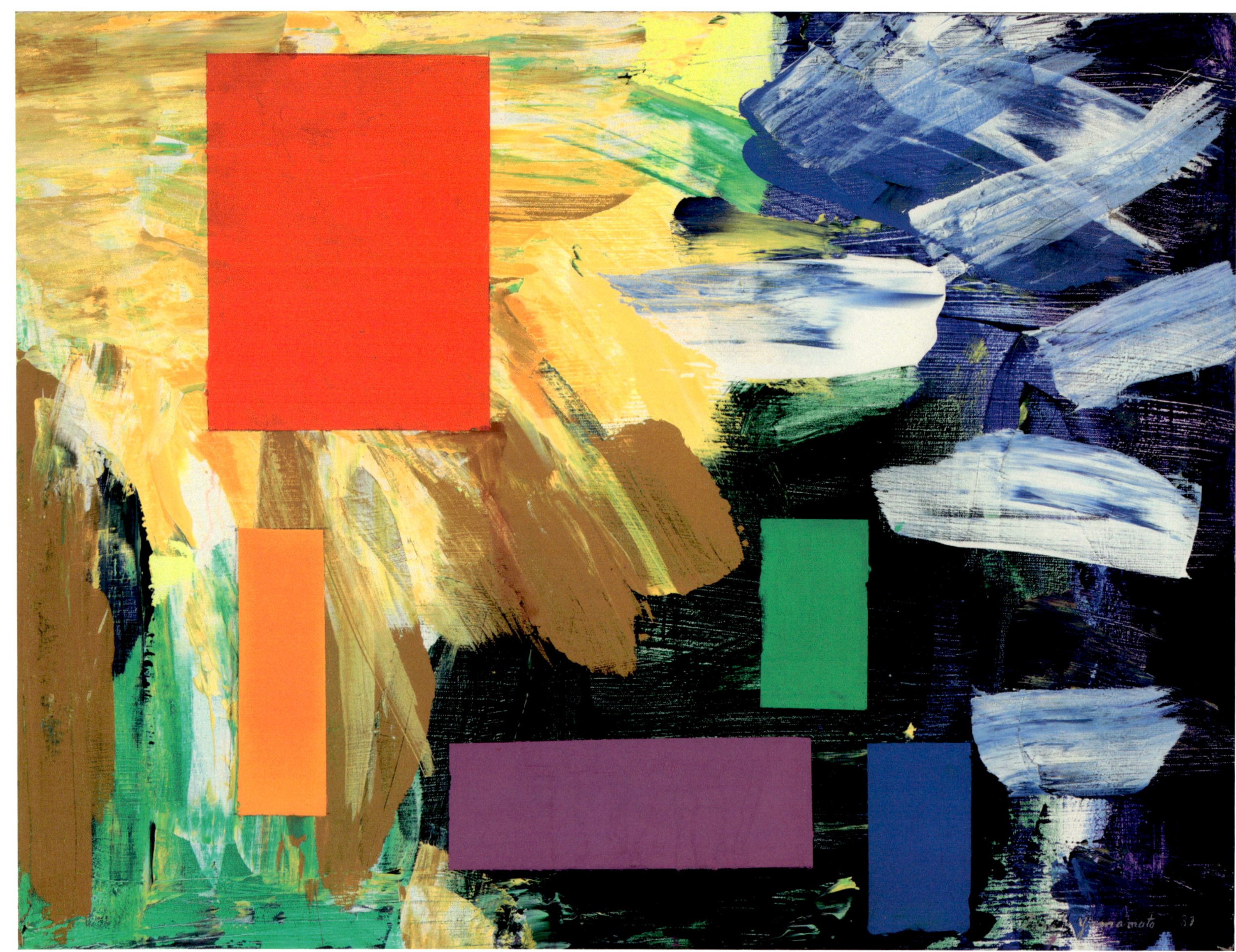

Taro Yamamoto, *Dawn,* 1987. Oil on canvas, 30 × 40 inches. *Gift of George Zhouf*, 1995.

SIDEO FROMBOLUTI
(1920–2014)

Sideo Fromboluti grew up in South Philadelphia and never saw the ocean as a child, but as an artist who spent part of the year in Wellfleet, he became enamored with the water.

Fromboluti's father, who was from Tuscany in Italy, was a stonemason and had a passion for art, which influenced his son. He studied at Temple University's Tyler School of Art in Philadelphia, where he met fellow artist Nora Speyer. They married while he was in the army, stationed at Fort Riley in Kansas. In 1948, the couple went to New York where abstract expressionism was hot, but not of interest to them. Nonobjective art seemed like a dead end.

The Wellfleet home where Fromboluti and Speyer spent summers since the 1950s looked out on the serene Higgins Pond. Pickerelweed blooms grew in the pond; it was an idyllic setting, full of shimmering lights in the water and intense shadows where the woods thicken. Fromboluti painted this scene over and over again in rich impasto oils full of mood and dripping with sensuality. One acre with two ponds, a meandering brook, and a forest of trees were the subjects of hundreds of his paintings. Fromboluti could paint the images he saw every day when he was in his studio because he painted as much by what he knew and experienced as by what he saw.

His work is rich with radiant light that emerges from his expressionistic application of paint, so thick that he creates the textures of the bark of a tree and blades of grass on the canvas. Even when he stepped away from the ponds and trees, as with *Pig on a Paint Table*, in the Cape Cod Museum of Art collection, his impasto and expressionistic approach created a vibrant, textured canvas.

Although he never abandoned the image that inspired him, whether landscape or figure, there is a legacy from modernist abstraction that is reflected in the close-up textures of his paintings. He created a nonobjective world of drips, squiggles, and swirls of luscious, loaded colors—blues and greens, purples and pinks, yellows and mauves. Some of his work almost crosses the line into abstraction, like one of Monet's late water lilies. Others are seen through an incandescent veil, as if a luminous mist has descended on the pond. Still others feel wet as if they were drenched by a quiet summer rain. And most, despite the turbulence of the paint, are meditative and peaceful.

His works are in several museum collections, including the Museum of Modern Art in New York and the Provincetown Art Association and Museum.

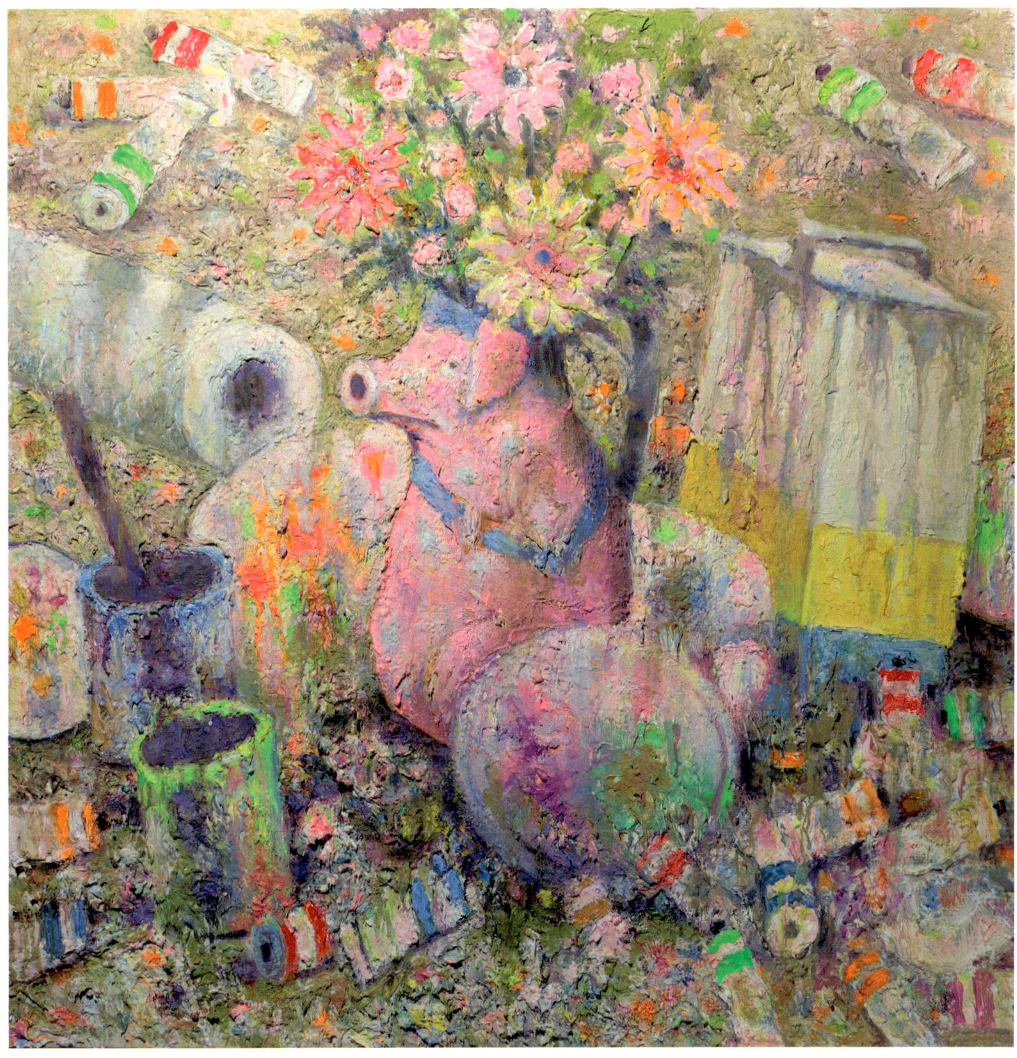

Sideo Fromboluti, *Pig on Paint Table*, 2006. Oil on canvas, 40 × 40 inches. *Gift of Sideo Fromboluti*, 2006.

LEONARD BASKIN
(1922–2000)

Leonard Baskin, a figurative artist who worked in a range of mediums, was born in New Brunswick, New Jersey, and by the time he was a teenager, wanted to be a sculptor. He studied with sculptor Maurice Glickman, and later studied art at New York University's School of Architecture and Applied Arts, and Yale University. He became interested in printmaking and founded The Gehenna Press, which during his lifetime issued more than a hundred finely printed books.

After military service during World War II, he earned a degree at the New School for Social Research and went on to study at the Académie de la Grande Chaumière in Paris and Accademia di Belle Arti in Florence.

As a graphic artist, he is well known for his large woodblock prints, which brought him recognition in the 1950s. His wood, limestone, and bronze sculptures are also numbered among his significant achievements. His portraits are psychologically astute images. A number of etchings he did of artists and

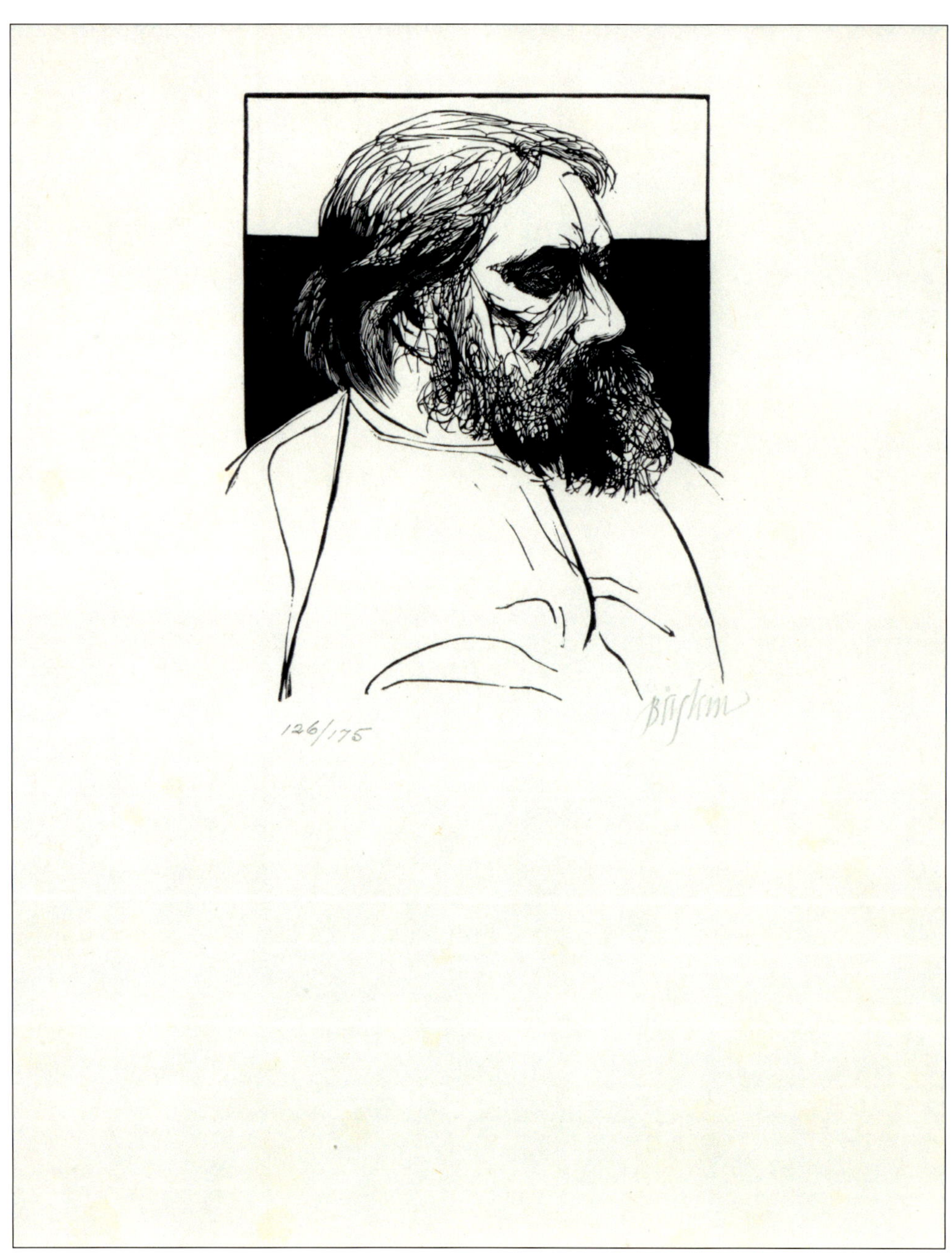

Leonard Baskin, *Gustave Courbet* 126/175, n.d. Wood engraving on paper, 9¾ × 7¾ inches.
Gift of Mrs. James L. Tedrick, 2007.

writers that comprise the book *Laus Pictorum* are in the Cape Cod Museum of Art collection. They include J. F. Millet, Théodore Rousseau, Gustave Courbet, Thomas Eakins, William Morris, and Camille Corot.

Other subjects Baskin pursued were themes from the Old Testament and Greek mythology. He also depicted birds, Native Americans, and figures of death. His commissions include the bas-relief of a funeral cortege created for the Franklin Delano Roosevelt Memorial in Washington, DC, and a grief-stricken, seven-foot, cast-bronze figure for the Ann Arbor Holocaust Memorial in Michigan.

Baskin illustrated books of works by Dante, Homer, Joseph Conrad, and Jonathan Swift, as well as children's books. He taught sculpture and printmaking in Massachusetts at Smith College in Northampton and Hampshire College in Amherst.

His works are in major museums, including the Metropolitan Museum of Art and the Museum of Modern Art in New York, the Art Institute of Chicago, the Museum of Fine Arts in Boston, the British Museum in London, and the Vatican Museums in Rome.

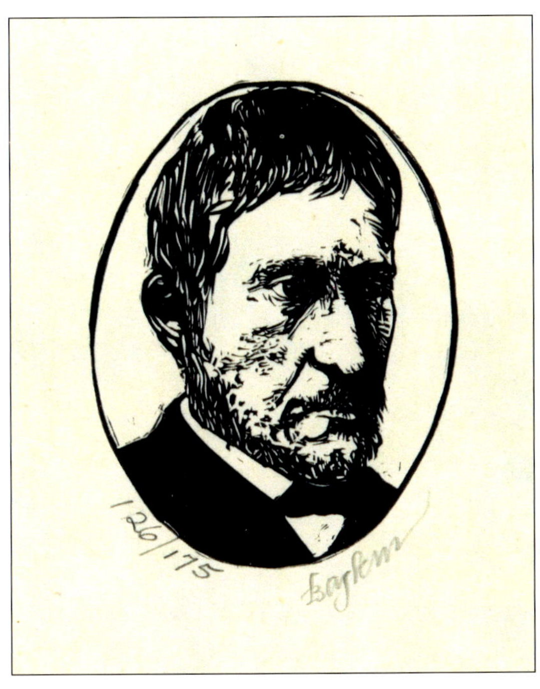

Leonard Baskin, *Thomas Eakins* 126/175, n.d. Wood engraving on paper, 2 × 1¾ inches. *Gift of Mrs. James L. Tederick*, 2007.

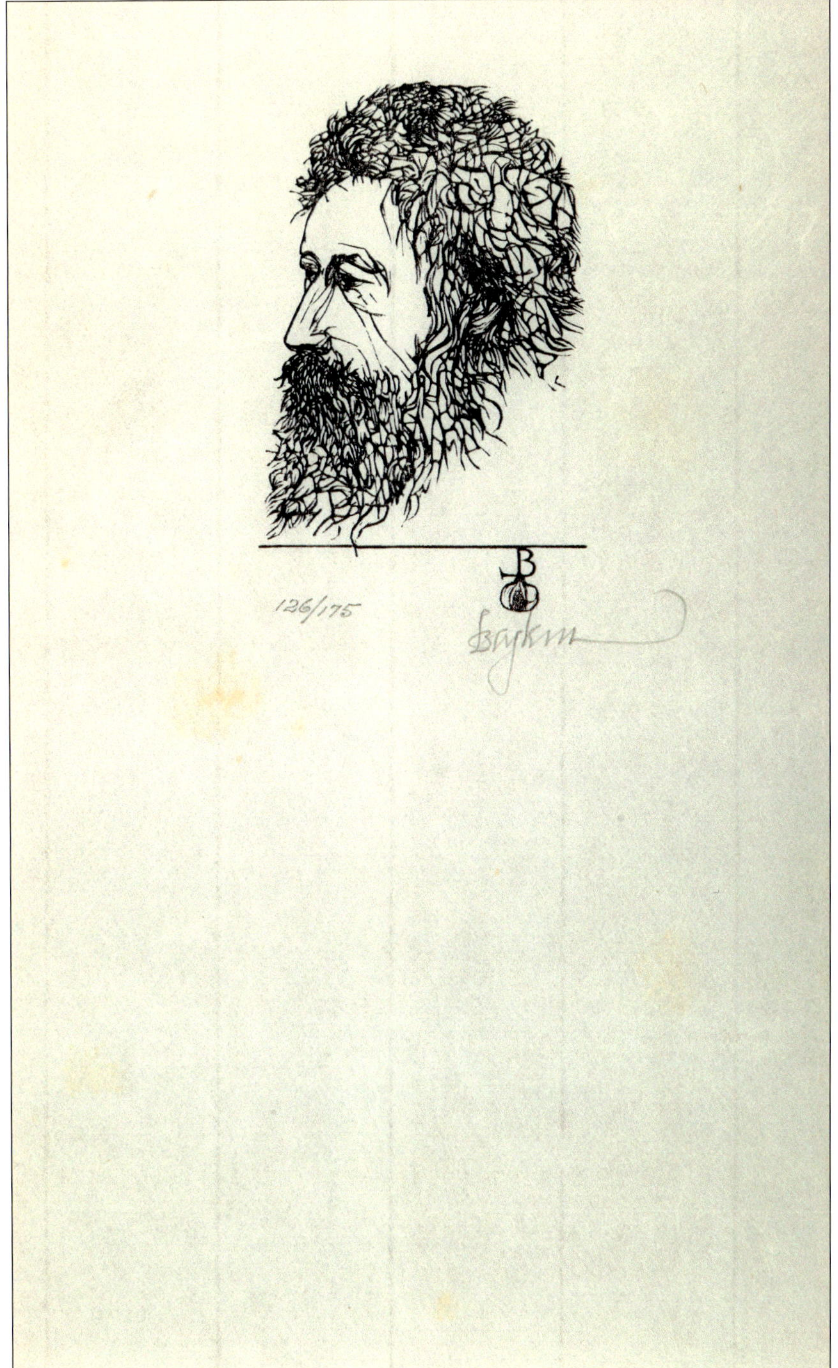

Leonard Baskin, *William Morris* 126/175, n.d. Wood engraving on paper, 9¾ × 5¾ inches. *Gift of Mrs. James L. Tederick*, 2007.

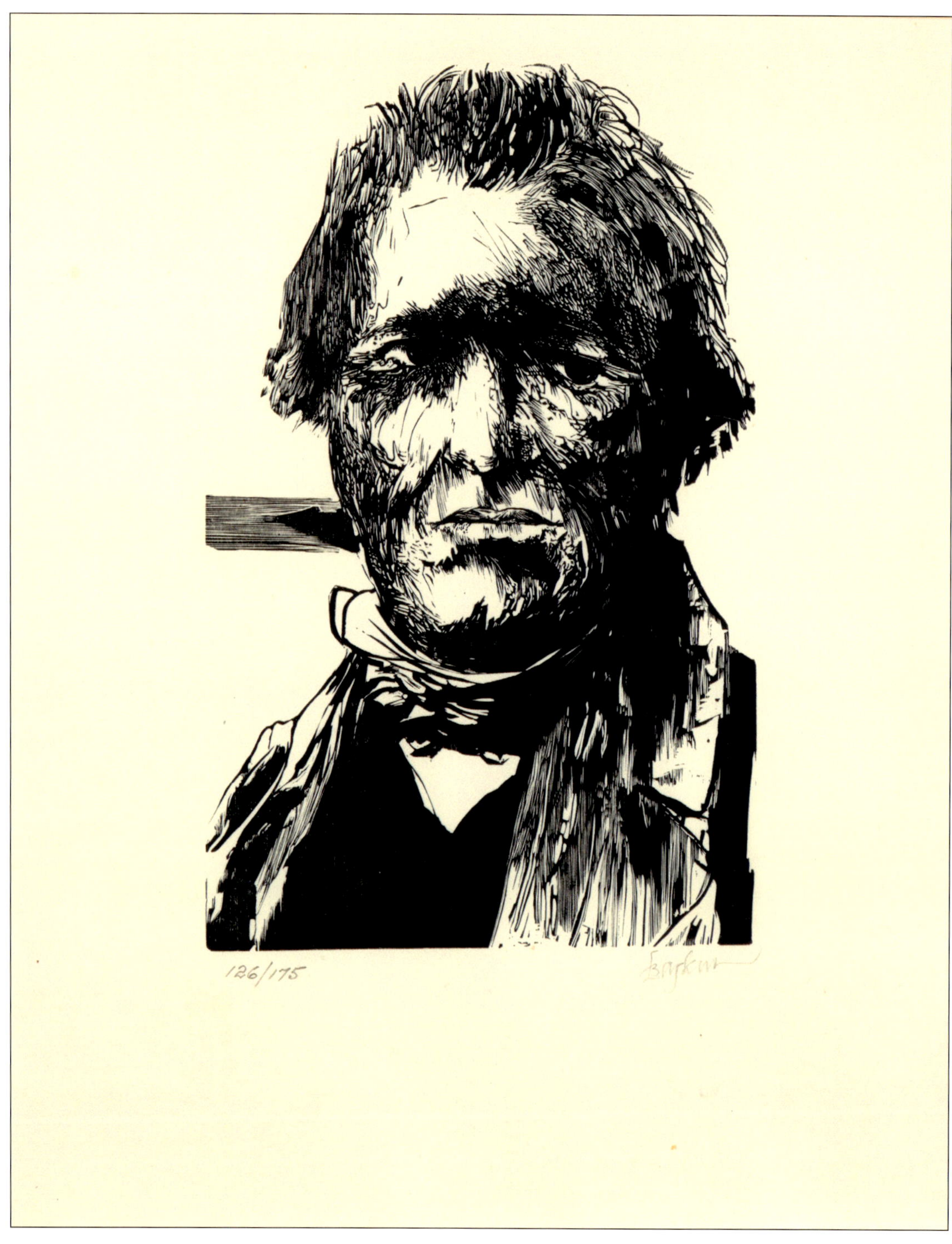

Leonard Baskin, *Camille Corot* 126/175, n.d. Wood engraving on paper, 7¼ × 4⅝ inches.
Gift of Mrs. James L. Tederick, 2007.

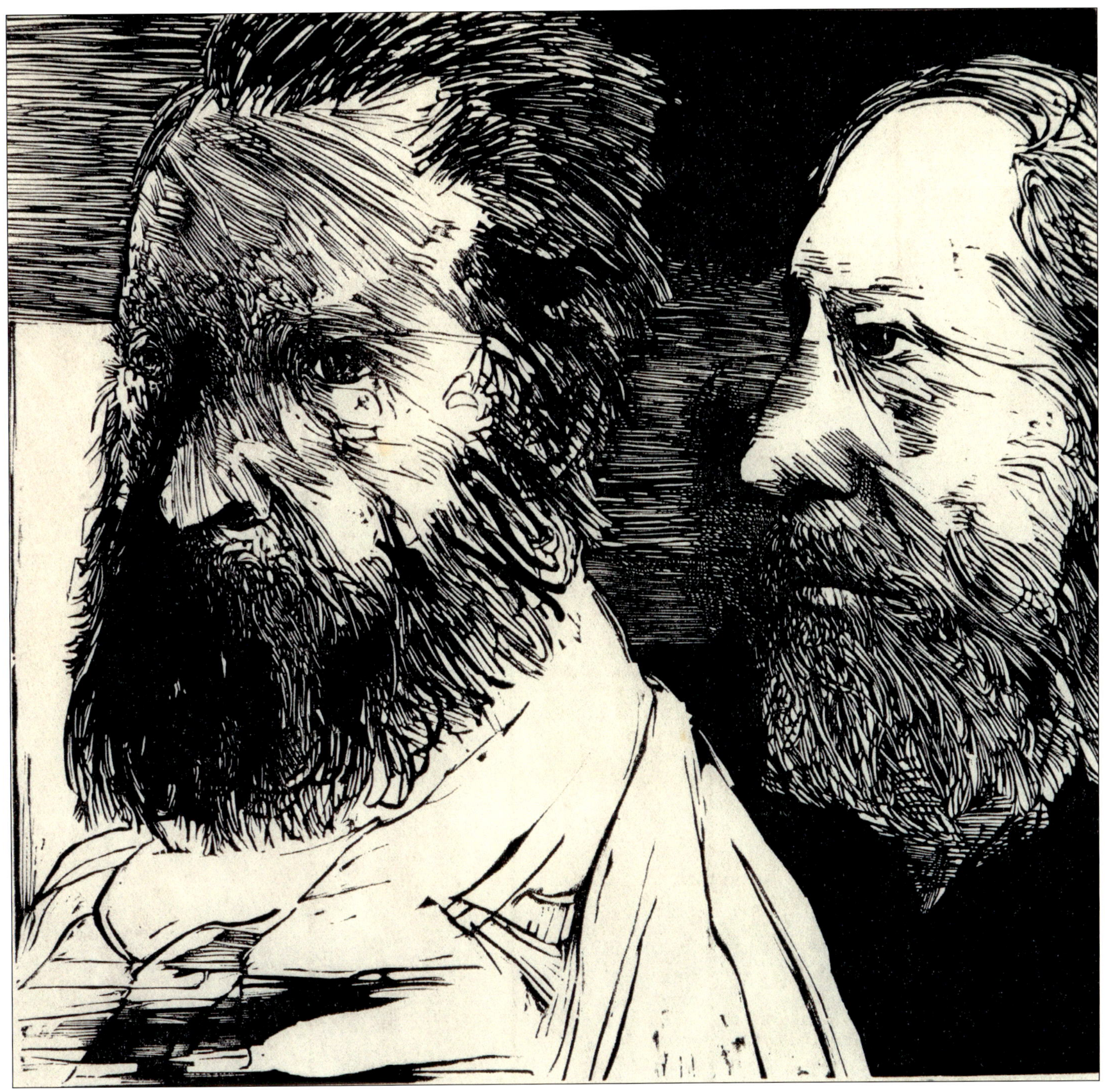

Leonard Baskin, *J. F. Millet & Th. Rousseau* 126/175, n.d. Wood engraving on paper, 6¼ × 6½ inches. *Gift of Mrs. James L. Tederick*, 2007.

HARRY HOLL
(1922–2014)

Harry Holl was something of a legend on Cape Cod. Holl was the co-founder, with Roy Freed, of the Cape Cod Museum of Art, and helped to found the Society of Cape Cod Craftsmen and the Cape Cod Museum of Natural History. His Scargo Pottery in Dennis, which he established in 1952, is an oasis of artistry in a wooded area adjacent to Scargo Lake. During his lifetime, it was a place to visit to see his work and the work of his students and to watch them on the wheel turning clay into pots, bowls, vases, and the various shaped components that would emerge as bird-feeder castles.

Although Holl, who grew up in the Bronx, New York, is best known for his pottery, he was also a sculptor and painter. He painted in high school and later studied at the Beaux-Arts Institute of Design in Manhattan. During World War II, he was a bombardier in the Army Air Corps. After the war, he studied at the Art Students League in New York and then Black Mountain College in North Carolina, where he met Mirande Geissbuhler, his future wife, whose father, Arnold, was a sculptor and had property in Dennis.

Holl was teaching at the Portland Art Museum in Oregon when he met Japanese potter Shoji Hamada, a Zen Buddhist whose life and philosophy strongly influenced Holl. He discussed this influence in the 2002 documentary *A Centered Universe: The Life and Art of Harry Holl*, and upon settling on Cape Cod, he seemed to embrace Hamada's philosophy of focusing on his work—his art and pottery, his dedication to preserving the culture, and his responsibility as a teacher—as the center of his world.

In addition to his ceramic bowls, vases, fantastical castles, and bas-reliefs, his work includes sculpted portraits and figures, granite sculptures, charcoal drawings, and abstract paintings. When visitors arrive at the Cape Cod Museum of Art, they are greeted by Holl's ceramic mask *Untitled (Large Female Head)*, which focuses wide-eyed on them. Other works in the collection include expressionistic figurative images on ceramics, including a bowl, *Untitled (Mother & Child)*, and a bas-relief, *Four Sisters*, referencing Holl's four daughters. *The Potter*, an energetic, faceted cubist figurative painting, is also in the collection.

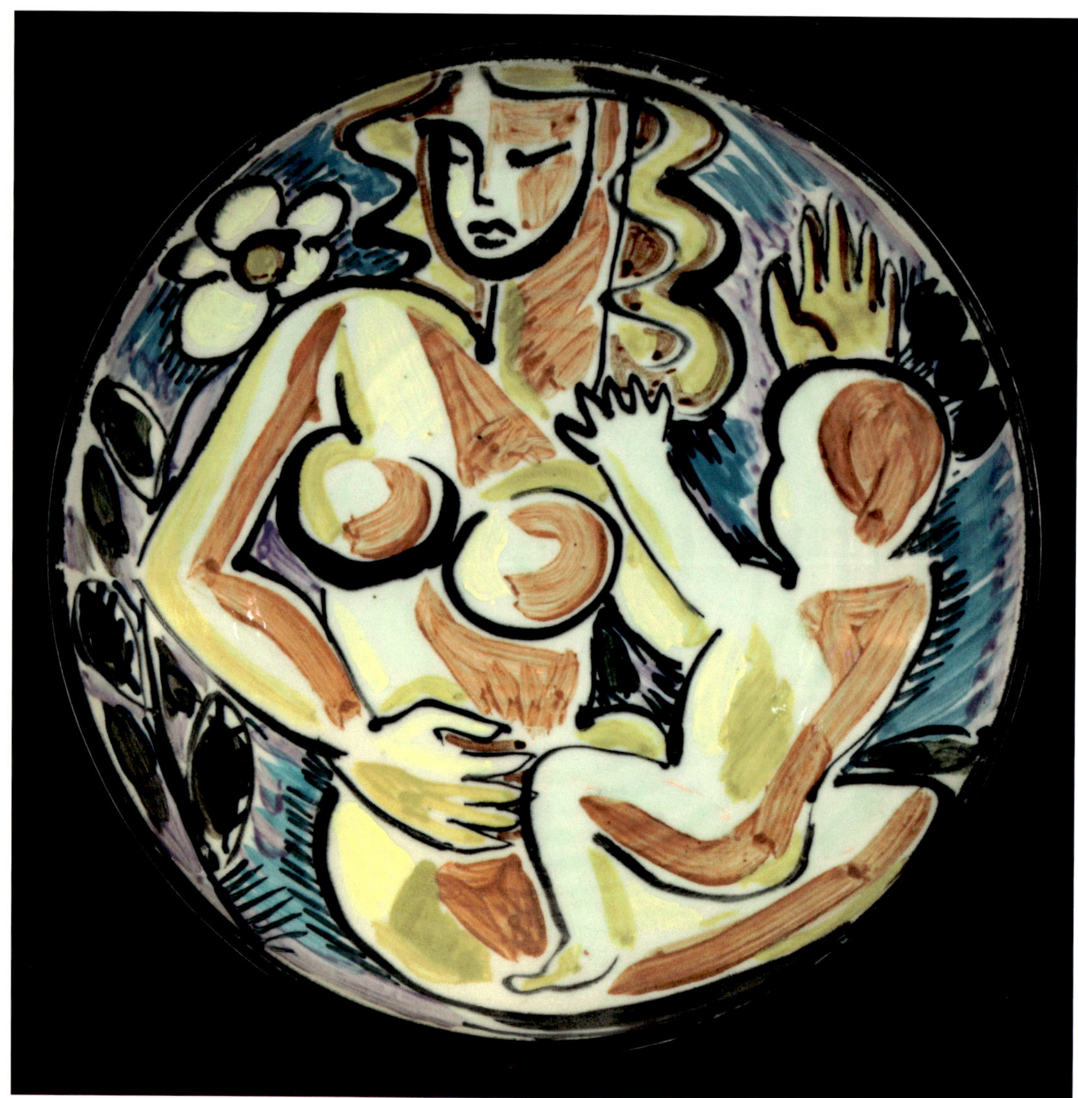

Harry Holl, *Untitled (Mother & Child)*, n.d. Ceramic bowl, 11½ diameter. *Gift of Roy N. & Anne O. Freed*, 2007.

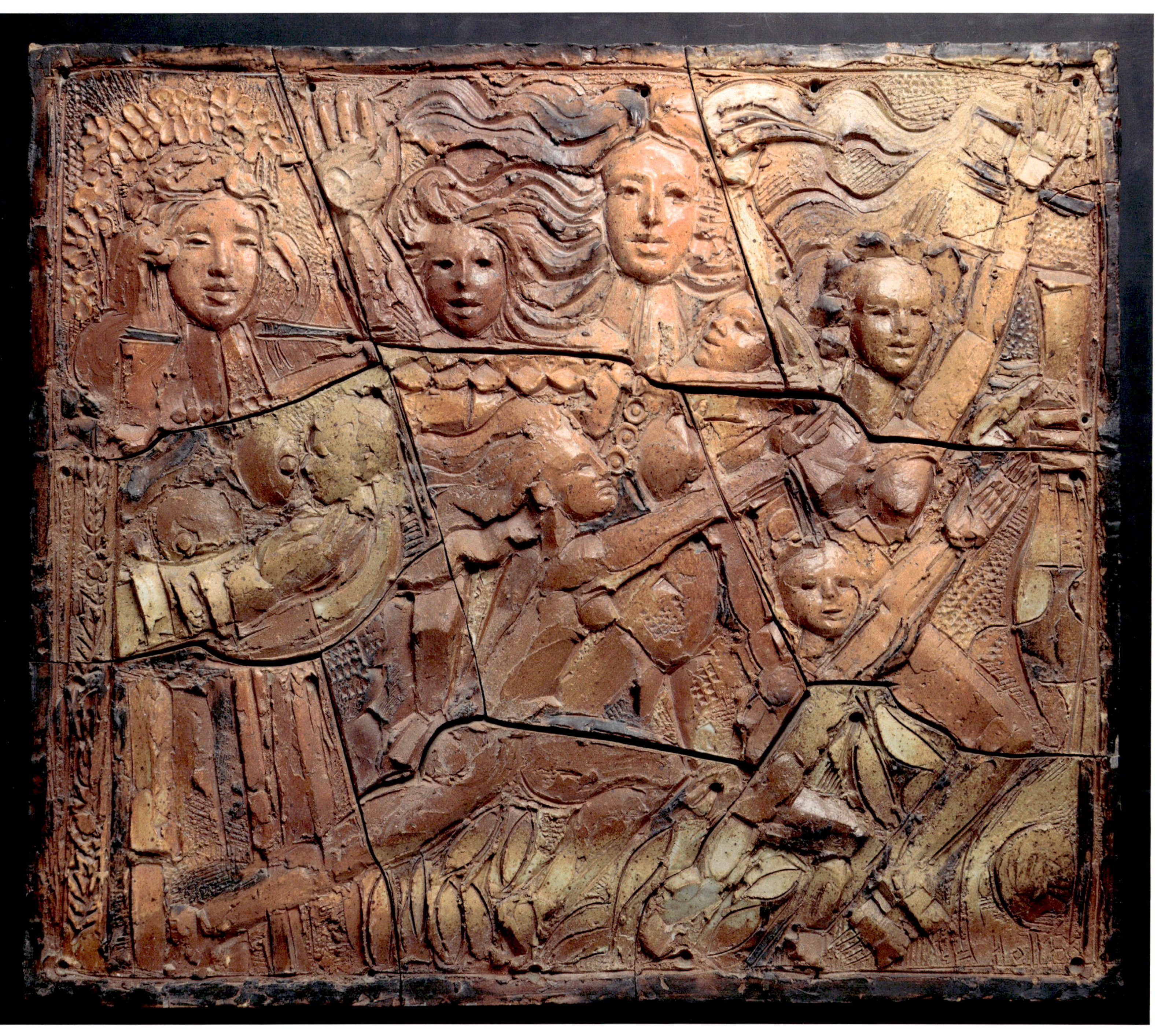

Harry Holl, *Four Sisters,* 1987. Ceramic bas-relief, 29 × 35 inches. *Gift of Ann Bengston*, 1987.

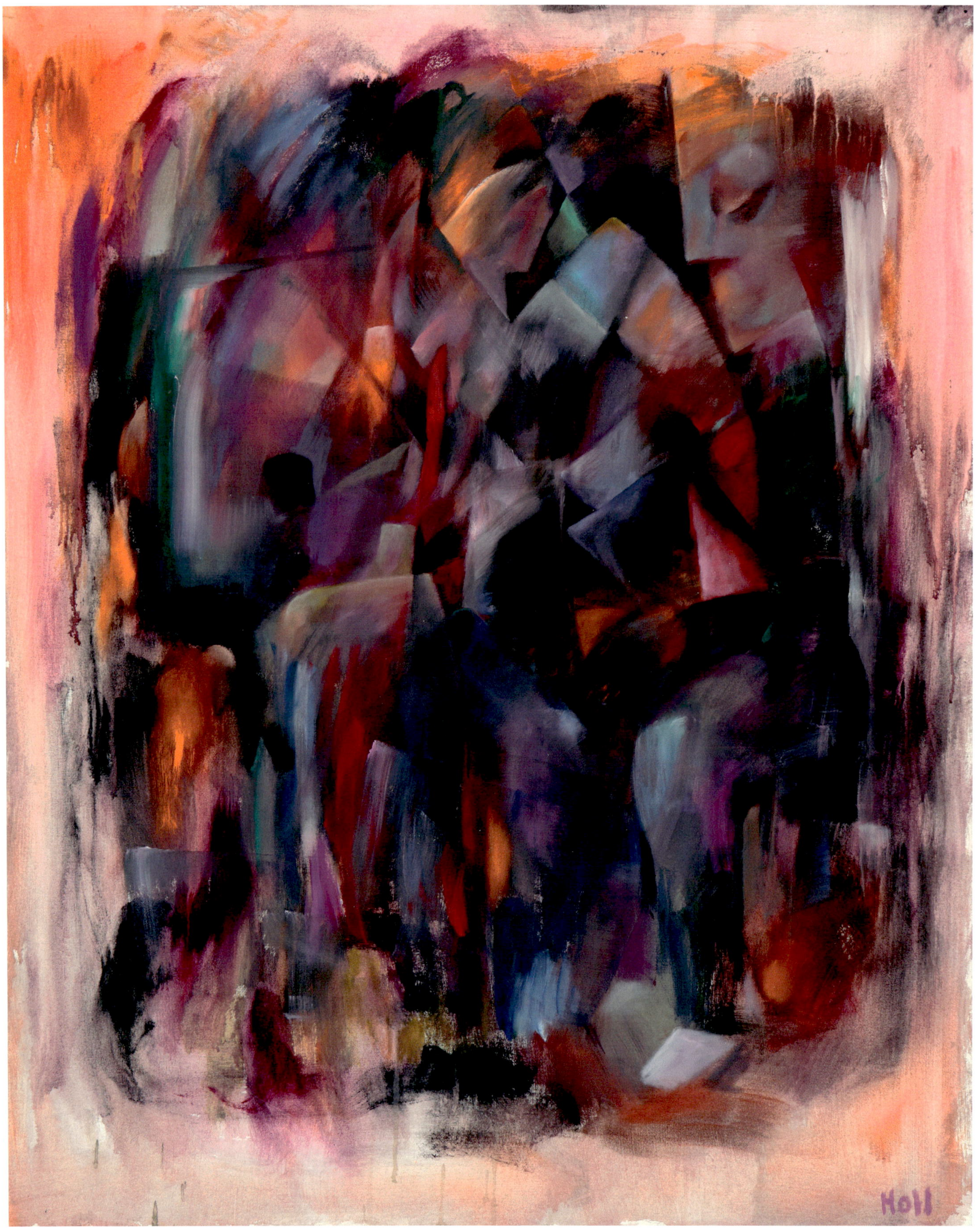

Harry Holl, *The Potter,* 2008. Oil on canvas, 54 × 44⅛ inches. *Gift of Jo Ann Hughes and Charles Weiner*, 2008.

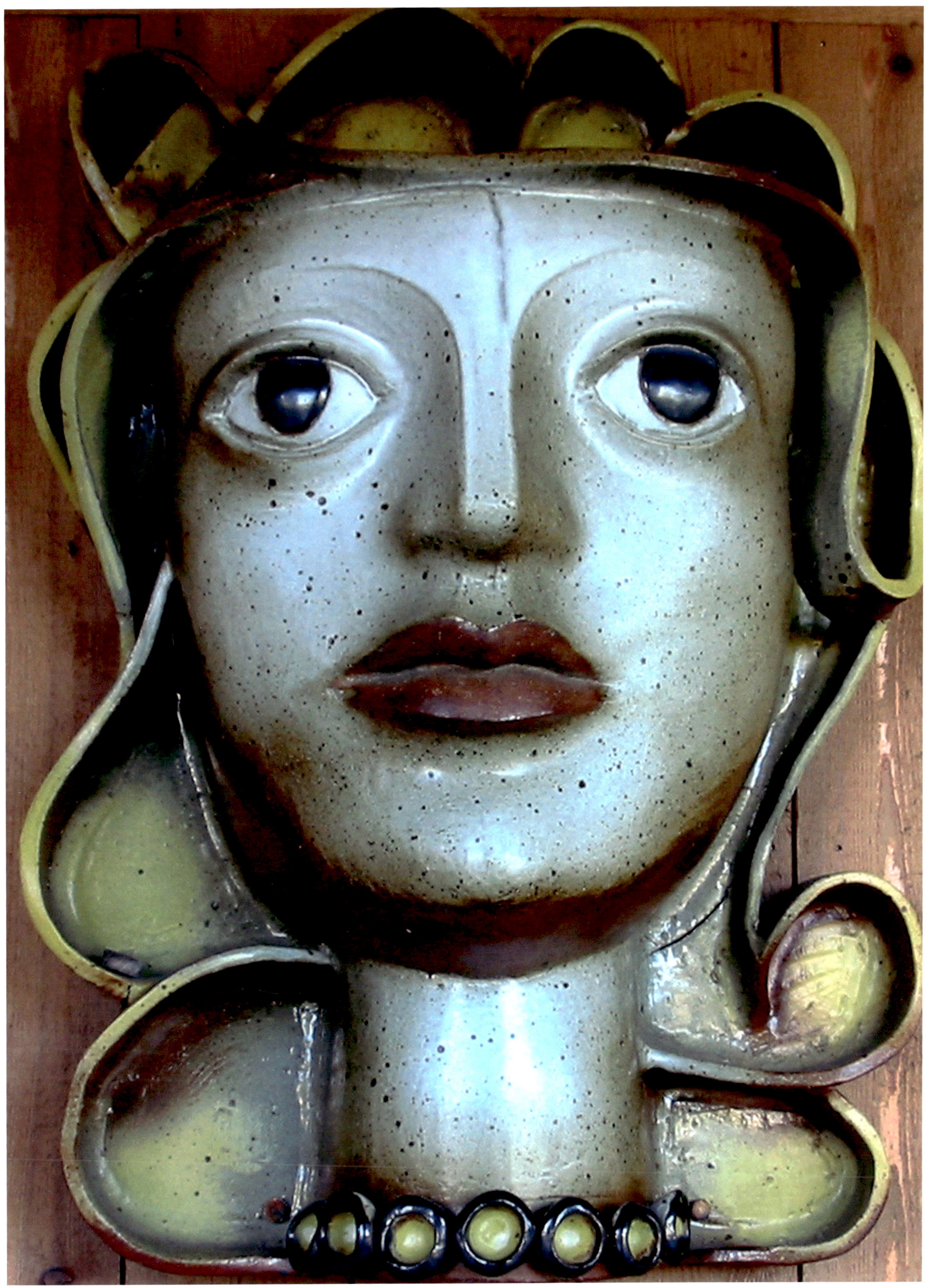

Harry Holl, *Untitled* (Large Female Head), n.d. Ceramic, 28 × 20 × 9 inches. *Anonymous gift*, 2004. *Photo courtesy of Christy King.*

ROBERT BEAUCHAMP
(1923–1995)

Robert Beauchamp's work is wild in color and form with female nudes, comical and frightening faces, and robust gestures that relate him to abstract expressionism, although, for most of his career, he fit more comfortably into the category of figurative expressionism.

Born in Denver, Colorado, he studied at Colorado Springs Fine Arts Center and Cranbrook Academy of Art in Michigan. He moved to New York City in the early 1950s and spent time with the abstract expressionists at their hangout in Cedar Tavern and studied with Hans Hofmann in New York and Provincetown for three years. In 1959 he traveled to Italy on a Fulbright Award. When he returned to America he lived in Provincetown and exhibited at the Sun Gallery, known for the pioneering figurative expressionists who were challenging the reigning abstract expressionists.

Beauchamp's paintings have an explosive spontaneity. Some of his female figures relate to those of Willem de Kooning, whom he knew from New York. He painted grotesque faces in riotous colors, as in *Self-Portrait*, *The Family*, and *Untitled (Male Portrait)* in the Cape Cod Museum of Art collection. His work is a dashing array of objects: flowers, feathers, fish, roosters, baboons, dogs, snakes, and so much more. *Allegorical Scene*, also in the museum collection, is an array of fish-like forms floating in a sea of reds.

Beauchamp's heavily encrusted paintings resulted from spattering, layering, and pouring paint from a can in a hit-or-miss application. Forms whirl and swirl and sometimes melt into another. There is no gravity in his paintings. Figures fly into space or float on air. Objects spin and tumble, appearing to go nowhere and everywhere at the same time. Color never cools to less than a boil. The world in his paintings is phantasmagoric and psychedelic. It never stops spinning in a free-wheeling exuberance that stirs the imagination into new territories.

Beauchamp's works are in major museum collections, including the Metropolitan Museum of Art, the Museum of Modern Art, and the Whitney Museum of American Art in New York; the Hirshhorn Museum and Sculpture Garden and National Gallery in Washington, DC; and the Denver Museum of Art.

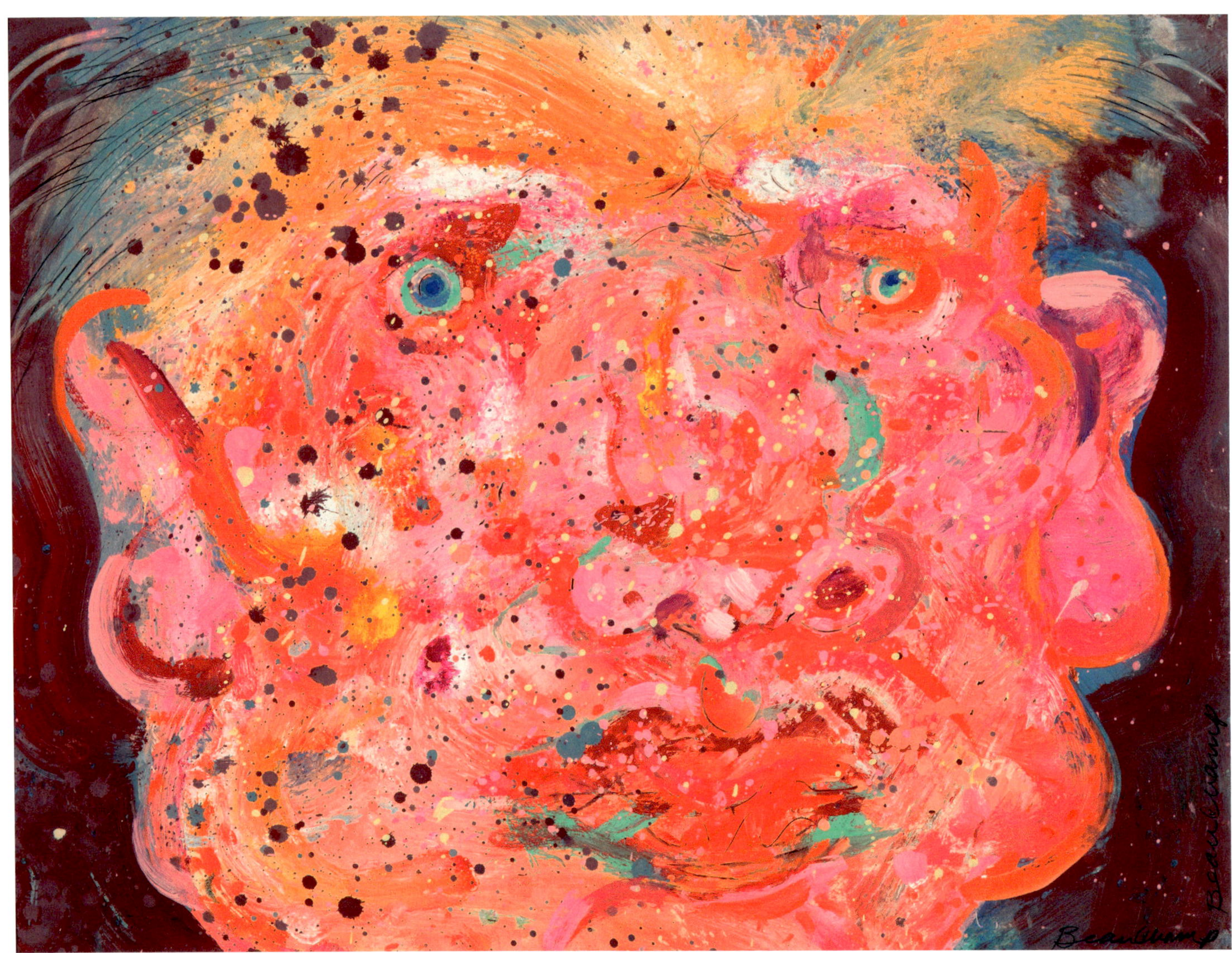

Robert Beauchamp, *Untitled* (Male Portrait), n.d. Oil on board, 12 × 16 inches. *Anonymous gift*, 2009.

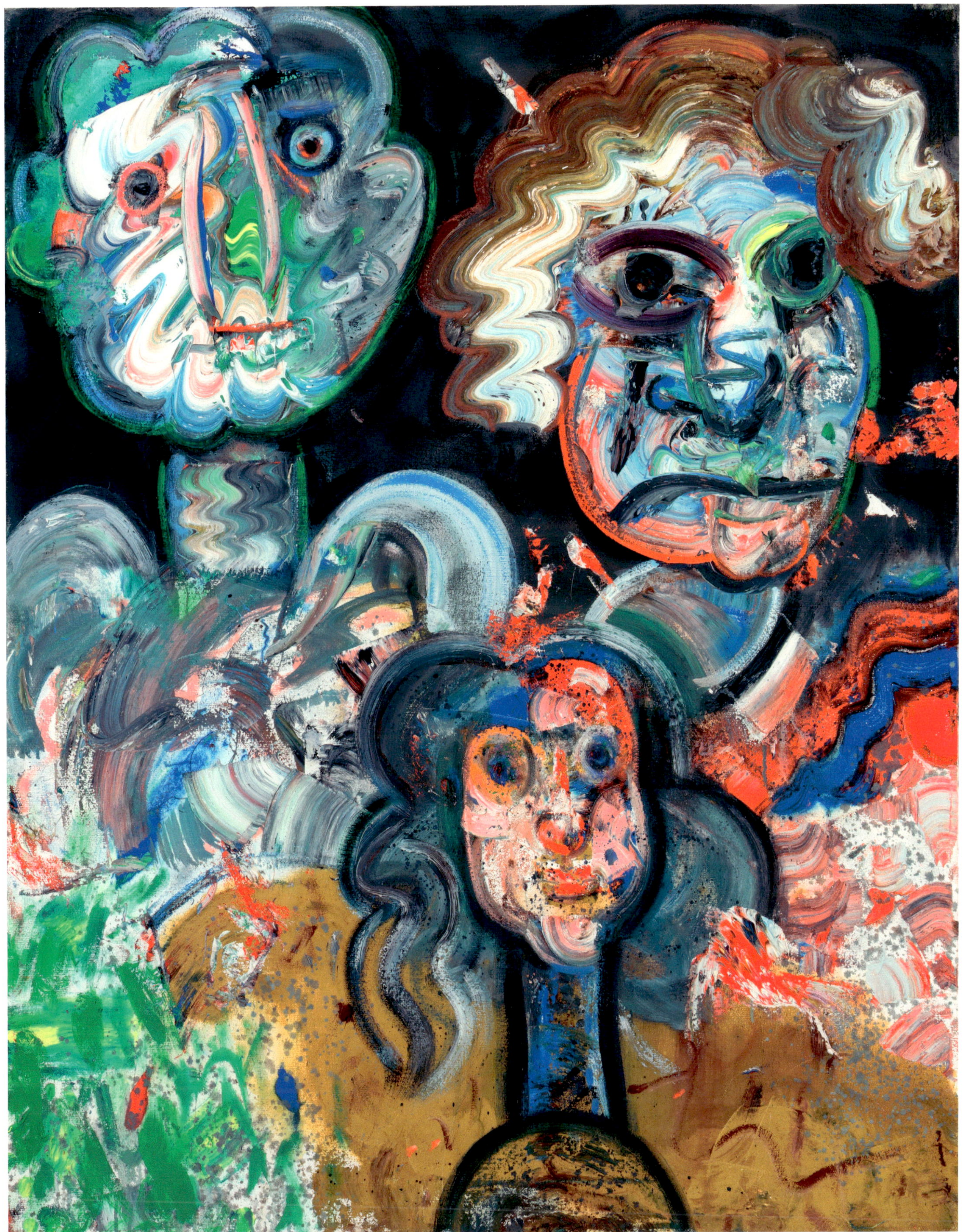

Robert Beauchamp, *The Family,* 1990. Oil on canvas, 50 × 40 inches. *Gift of the Robert Beauchamp Estate*, 2000.

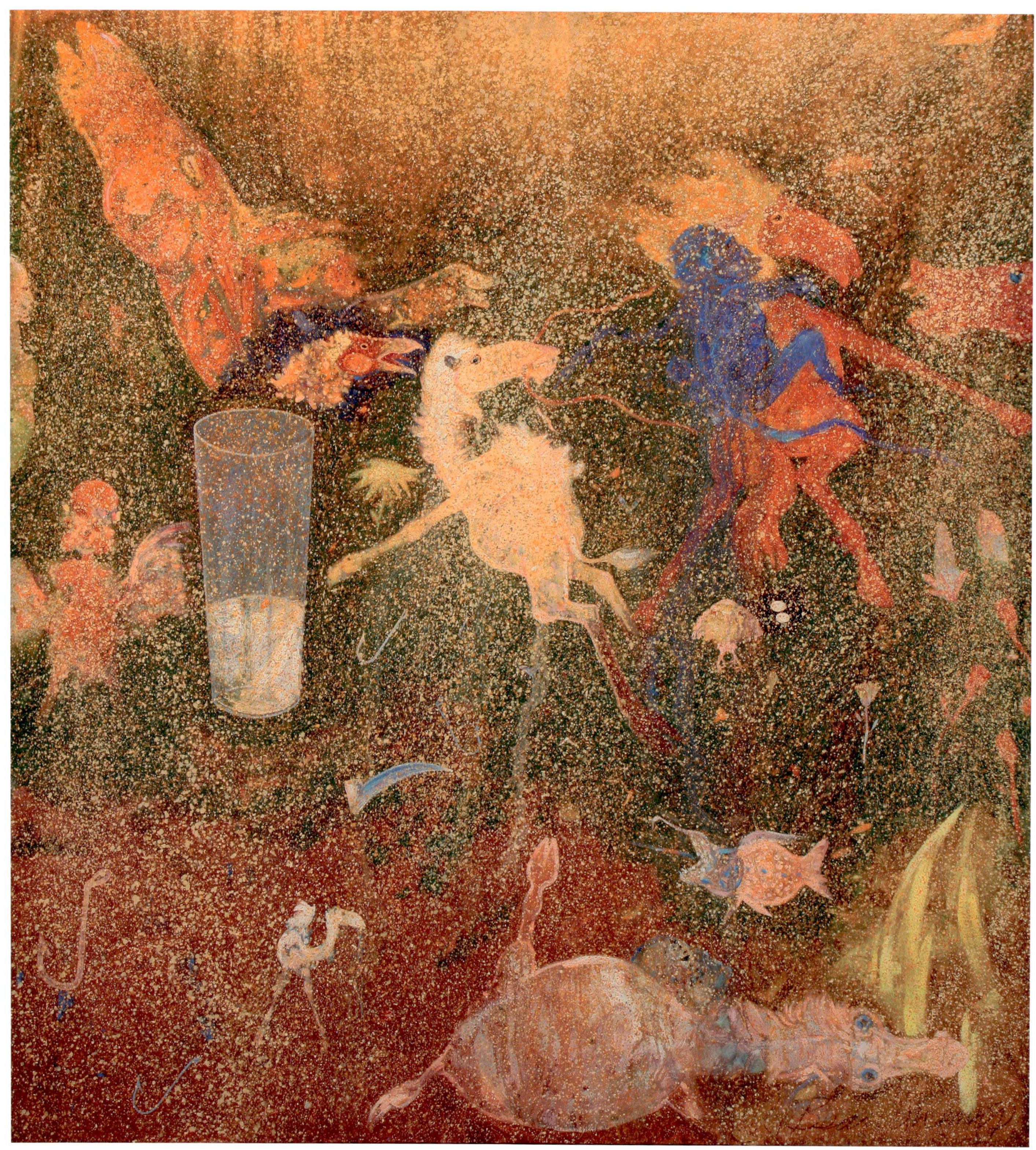

Robert Beauchamp, *Allegorical Scene*, 1969. Oil on canvas, 64 × 60 inches. *Gift of the Robert Beauchamp Estate*, 2000.

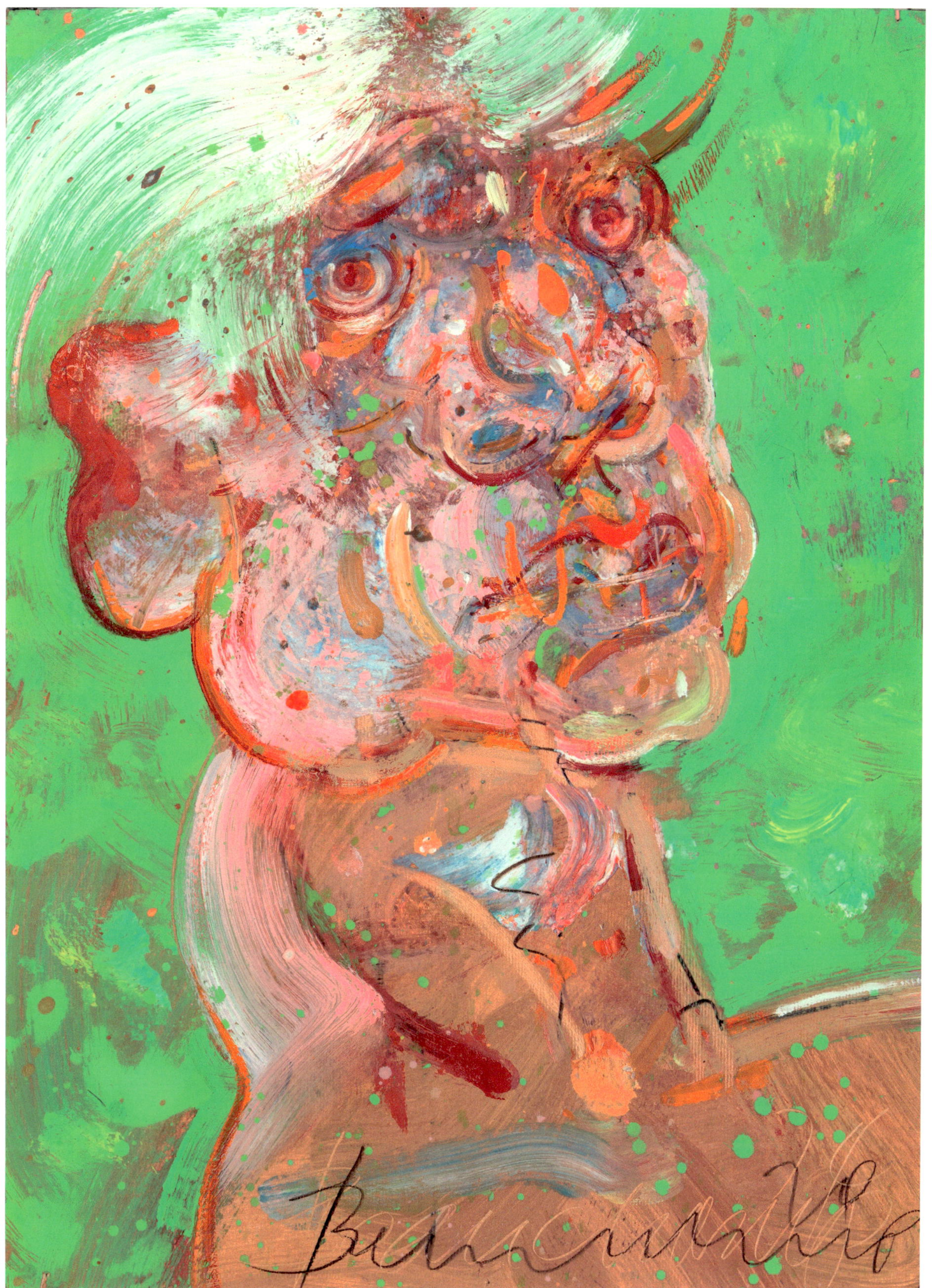

Robert Beauchamp, *Self Portrait*, 1974. Oil on canvas, 15 × 11½ inches. *Gift of the Robert Beauchamp Estate*, 1999.

VARUJAN BOGHOSIAN
(1926–)

Varujan Boghosian's collages, assemblages, and constructions are made to surprise, delight, and, sometimes, confound. He has a deadpan sense of humor, which he often incorporates into his mixed-media constructions.

He was born in New Britain, Connecticut, served in the navy during World War II, and studied at the Vesper George School of Art in Boston, where he met the artist and teacher Henry Hensche. Although he first came to Provincetown in 1948 with friends who wanted to study with Hensche, Boghosian never did study with him. He worked in restaurants and started beachcombing, which initiated his art of assemblage.

Although he had a home in Provincetown from the late 1940s on, his most important connection there came in the late 1970s when he joined Long Point Gallery. He taught for many years at Cooper Union in New York, then Brown University in Rhode Island, and finally Dartmouth College in Hanover, New Hampshire, and was often away from the camaraderie of the art colony. For him, Provincetown has always remained a collecting place for objects and material, which have made their way into his art.

He has created unusual juxtapositions of ordinary, old, and weathered objects to express new ideas, forms, or meanings. By bringing together the commonplace, he creates uncommon images, which sometimes have a narrative quality. Boghosian's collages and constructions are made with objects he finds in antique shops, yard sales, and flea markets. He combines antique toys, blocks, hat forms, wooden shoe trees, miniature mannequins, wheels, bells, diagrams and pictures from books, old photographs, tools, and even tenpins in unpredictable, ambiguous, and paradoxical ways, which reach back to memory or myth. So time, past and present, is a constant theme in his work.

Poetry (by William Butler Yeats and T. S. Eliot, for example) and art history influence his work, as do dada and surrealist art. *Something for Magritte*, in the Cape Cod Museum of Art collection, is an example of his tribute to the surrealist artist René Magritte. *Rose C'est La Vie (Blimp)* and *Rose C'est La Vie (Simple Borders)*, also in the museum collection, reference Man Ray's portraits of dada artist Marcel Duchamp portraying his female alter-ego, "Rrose Sélavy," a pun on "Eros, c'est la vie" (thus the addition of the extra "r"). Boghosian often

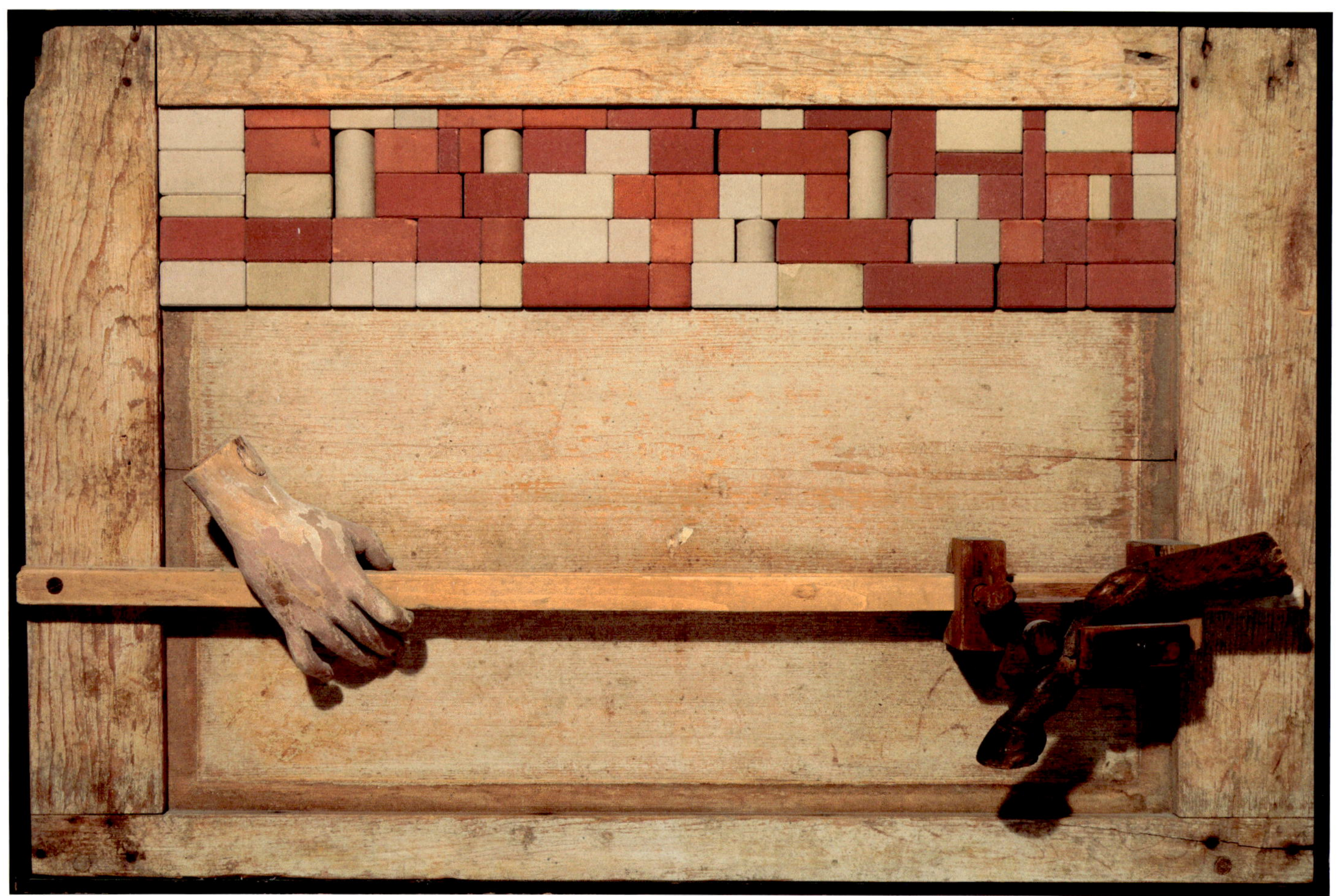

Varujan Boghosian, *Something for Magritte*, 1975. Mixed media sculpture, 19½ × 30 × 2⅛ inches. *Gift of Gilbert and Joyce Franklin*, 1991.

relates the original identity of the object to the meaning of his assemblage, as in *Why Knot?*, which combines a knot of wood with the wooden letter "Y."

His pieces are not always a quick take. Some require pondering, such as other pieces in the museum collection, *Red House* and *Bird & Butterfly*, which entail a certain mystery and surprise. His later work has become simpler, three-dimensional still-life constructions with children's blocks, spheres from tabletop croquet sets, ivory cue balls, and hockey pucks. The objects are arranged on a shelf with no backdrop, and like the paintings of the Italian painter Giorgio Morandi, they are simple arrangements of objects of geometric shapes.

Boghosian's works are in the collections of a number of major museums, including the Metropolitan Museum of Art, the Museum of Modern Art, and the Whitney Museum of American Art, all in New York.

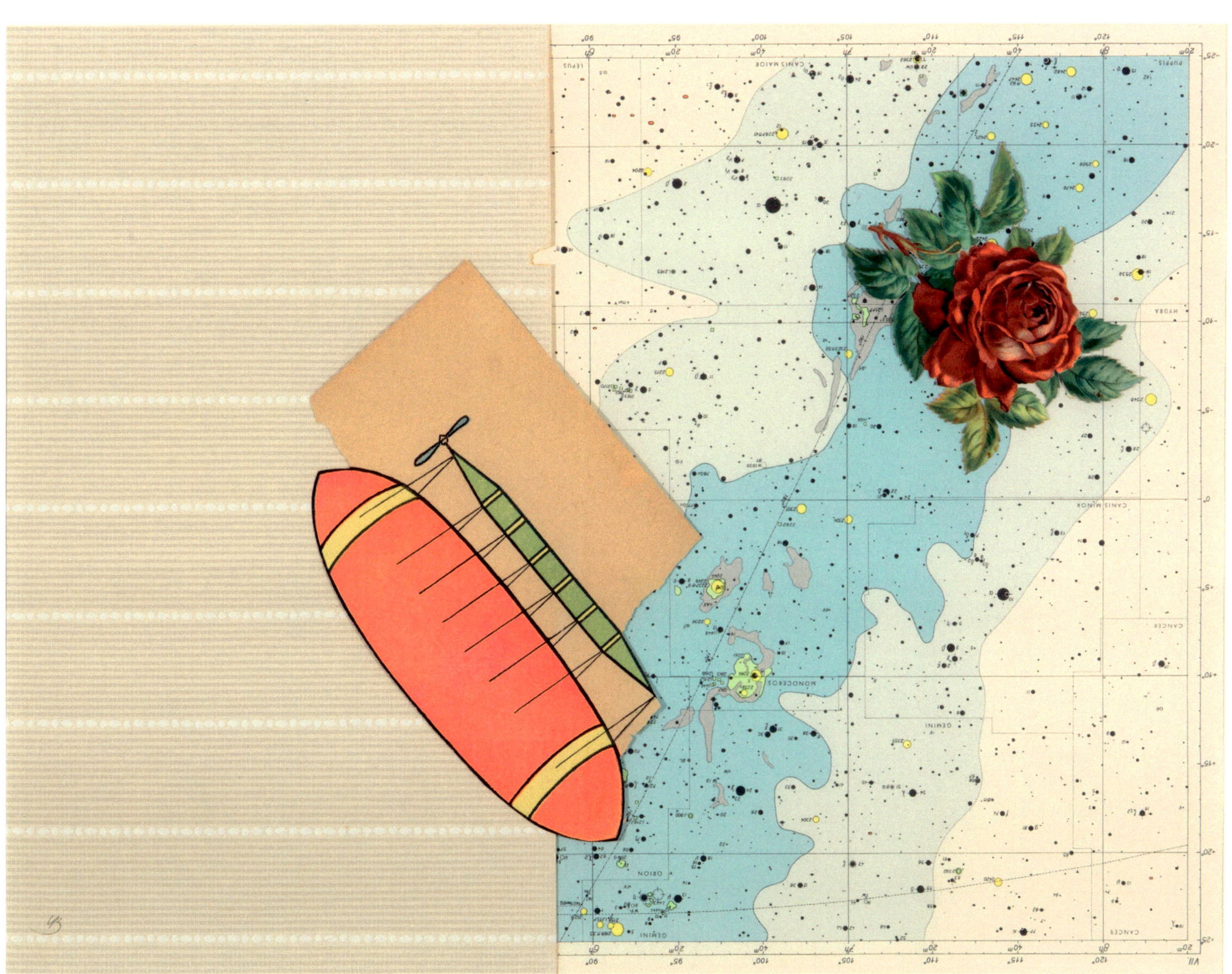

Varujan Boghosian, *Rose C'est La Vie* (Blimp), 1999. Collage on paper, 15¾ × 20¾ inches. *Gift of Lester Heller*, 2000.

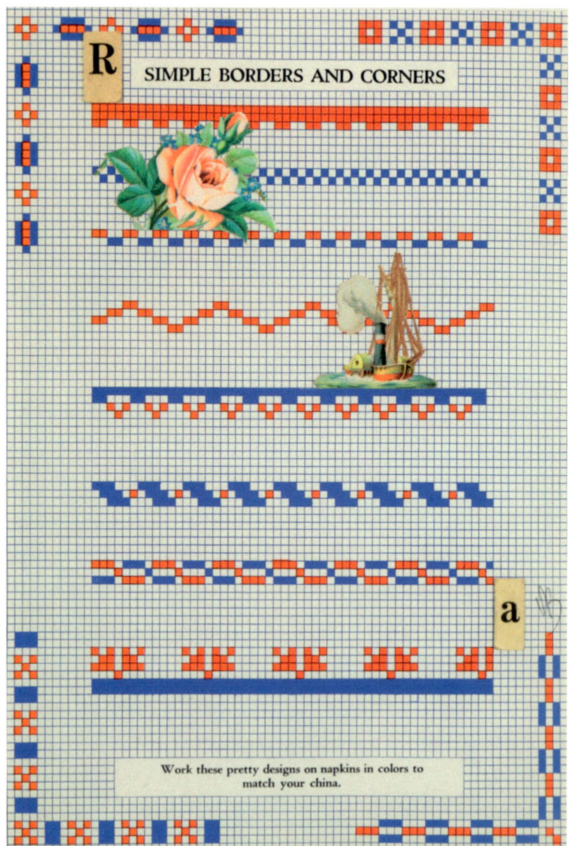

Varujan Boghosian, *Rose C'est La Vie* (Simple Borders), 1999. Collage on paper, 10½ × 7¼ inches, *Gift of Lester Heller,* 2000.

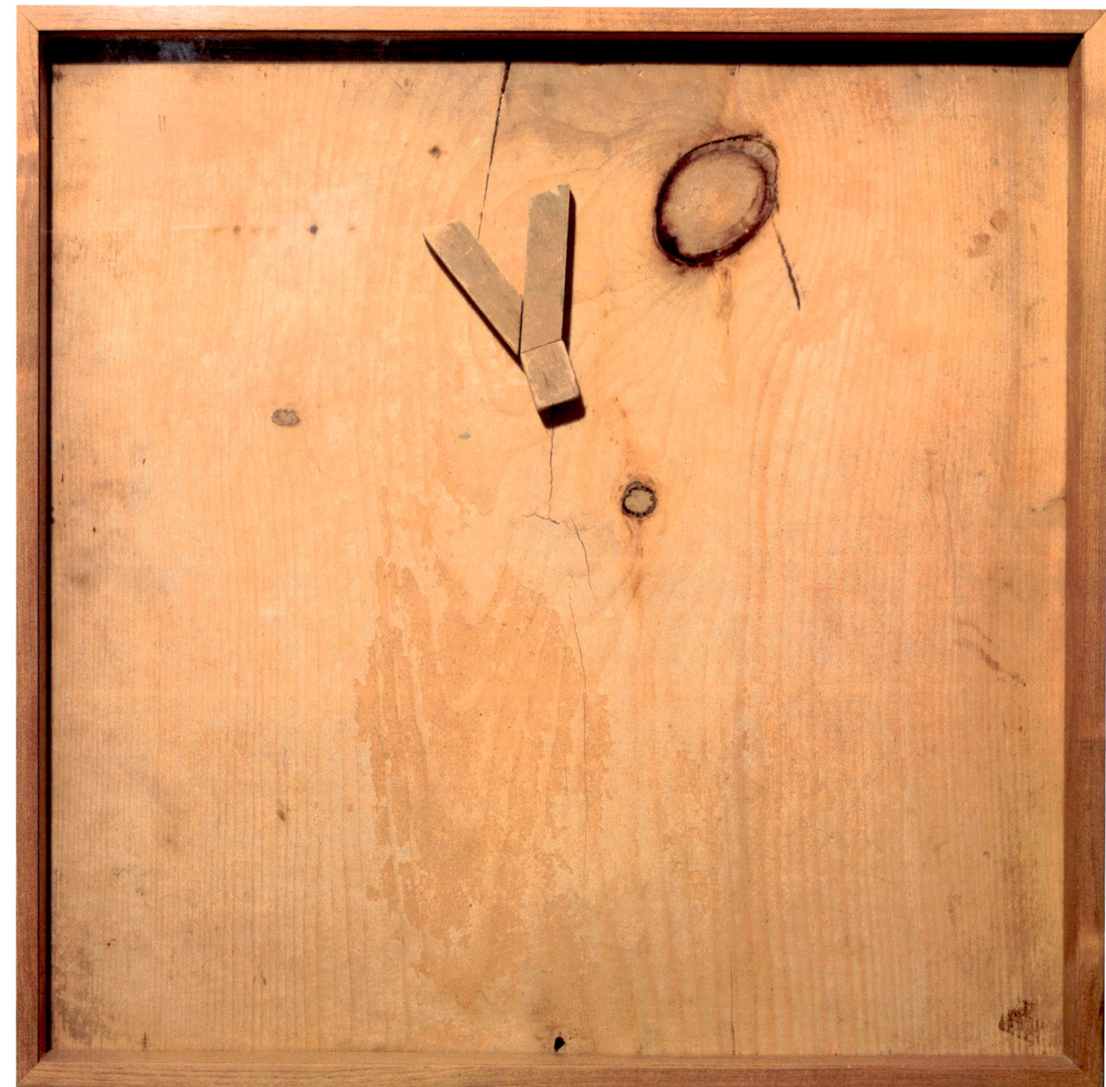

Varujan Boghosian, *Why Knot* ?, 1995. Mixed media on paper, 21 × 22 inches. *Gift of Adele and Lester Heller*, 1998.

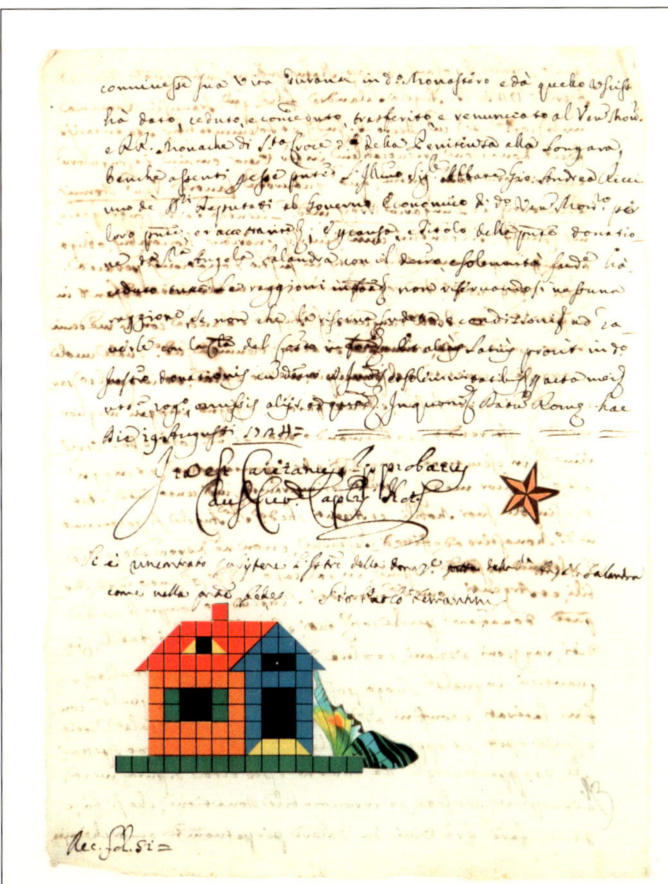

Varujan Boghosian, *Red House*, 1999. Collage on paper, 10½ × 7¾ inches. *Gift of Lester Heller,* 2000.

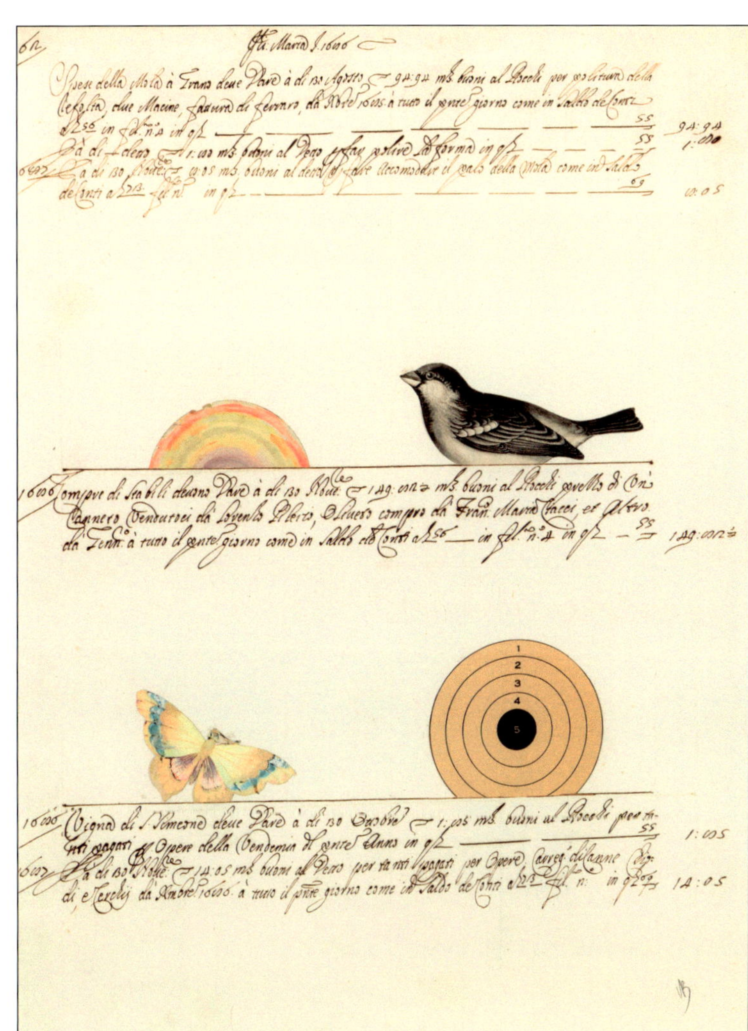

Varujan Boghosian, *Bird & Butterfly*, 1999. Collage on paper, 20½ × 15 inches. *Gift of Lester Heller*, 2000.

CARMEN CICERO
(1926–)

Long before Carmen Cicero stepped into his current world of enigmatic scenes, he was working in abstraction. Like so many artists of his era, he was an abstract expressionist when he began painting, but he soon moved on to a fierce figurative expressionism and then into what he calls a "visionary" style of dream-like, mysterious, and enigmatic images.

Born in Newark, New Jersey, he has been part of the Provincetown art scene since the 1960s. Cicero divides his time between his New York loft and his home in Truro, once the South Truro railroad station. On the property is a large studio built with a $90,000 Lifetime Achievement Award from the Pollock-Krasner Foundation.

In graduate school at Hunter College, he had studied with Robert Motherwell, whom many years later, he joined as a member of Long Point Gallery in Provincetown. In the late 1940s, he became part of the abstract expressionist scene and was in six Whitney Museum shows with the major pioneers of the movement.

By the 1960s, a realistic structure was emerging from his abstract work, and in the '70s, his figures took on a decidedly nervous tension and angst. These boldly colored paintings often depict conflict. His figures are engaged in heated, animated interaction. The paintings are intense, edgy, and sometimes violent, as in *The Rage*, in the Cape Cod Museum of Art collection, which depicts a fierce man wielding a knife chasing a woman. *The Story of Life*, also in the museum collection, is allegorical with a serpent, devil, and animals seemingly threatening a female figure. These images are painted with bold outlines and free-wheeling strokes of inventive colors.

Beginning in the '90s, his painting took on a calmer, more reflective, quality. Although his newer work is still somewhat disconcerting and certainly provocative, there is a meditative tone. His precise application of paint meticulously delineates blades of grass along a road, foliage in a forest, or a stone wall in a deserted neighborhood. Yet the realism contains a surreal, haunting aura, and a suggestion of a mysterious narrative.

This later work is a significant change from the previous angst-filled images, and often depicts solitary figures in lonely settings. One of these characters, introduced in 1995 in *Tracer of Lost Persons*, is a man in a trench coat and a 1940s-style fedora taking long strides across a bridge, his shadow stretched out in the moonlight. Another figure he used on occasion is a man in a car on a lonely road, which could be one of those isolated ones in Truro. In *Collins Road, Truro*, in the museum collection, there is an owl-like creature with a ferocious stare, planted in the middle of a secluded road, shadowed by silhouetted trees, a full moon overhead. Like many of his other late works, the content is dark and mystifying.

Cicero's works are in the collections of major museums, including the Metropolitan Museum of Art, the Whitney Museum of American Art, and the Guggenheim Museum in New York; and the Hirshhorn Museum and Sculpture Garden in Washington, DC.

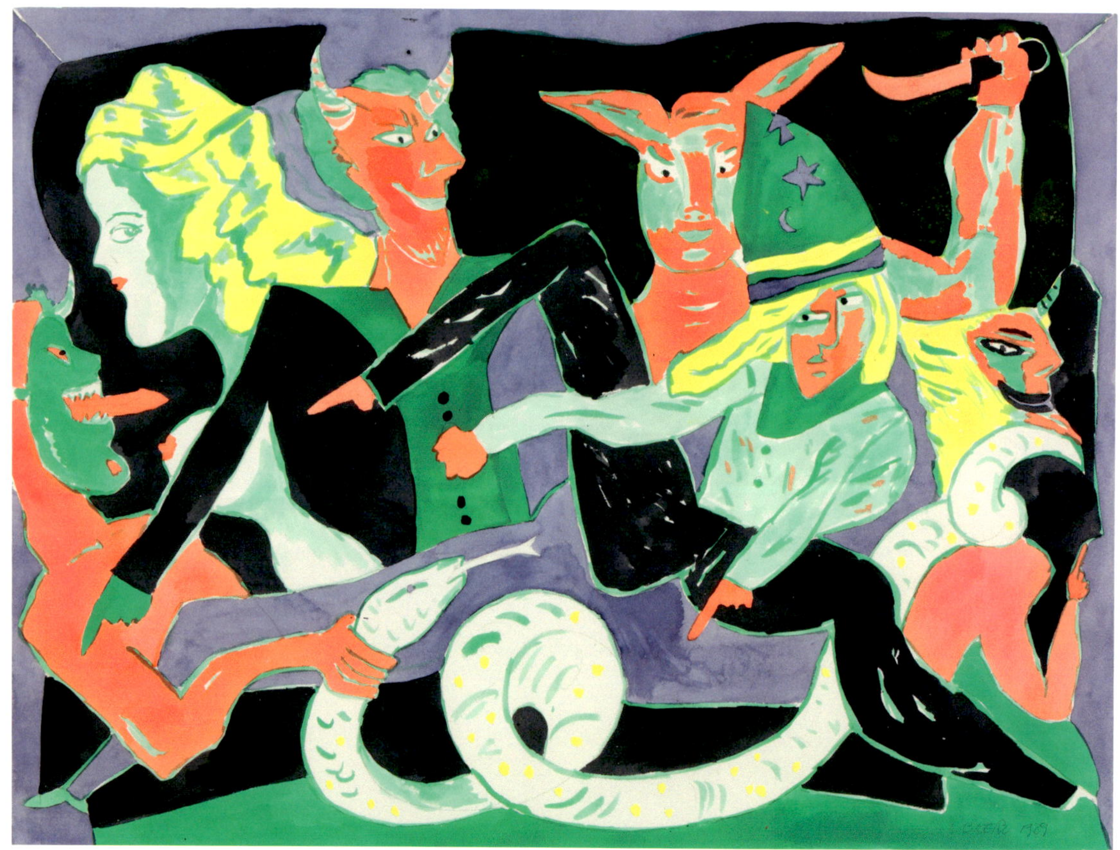

Carmen Cicero, *The Story of Life*, n.d. Watercolor on paper, 20 × 30 inches. *Gift of Carmen L. Cicero*, 2001.

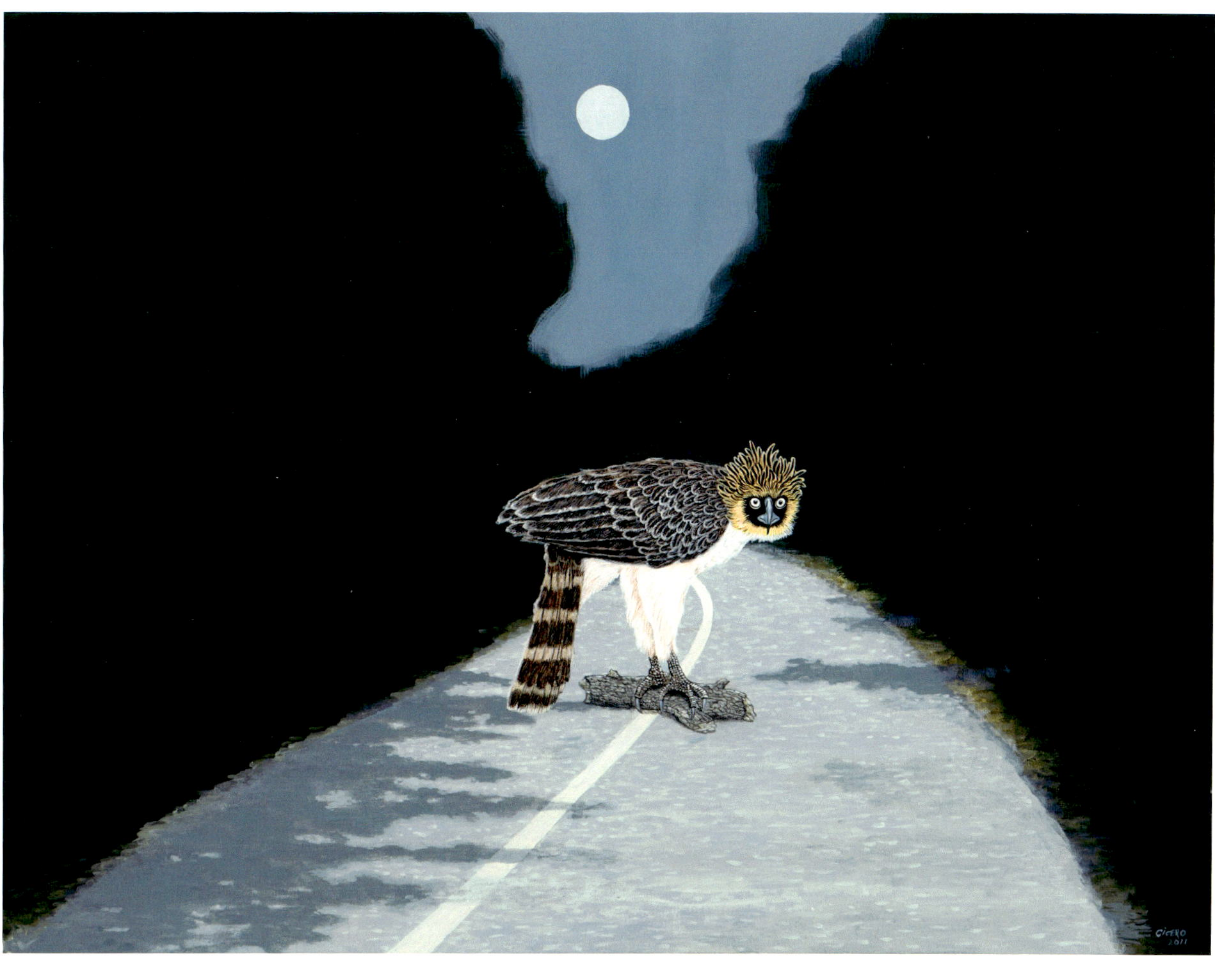

Carmen Cicero, *Collins Road, Truro,* 2011. Acrylic on canvas, 30 × 40 inches. *Gift of Carmen L. Cicero*, 2015.

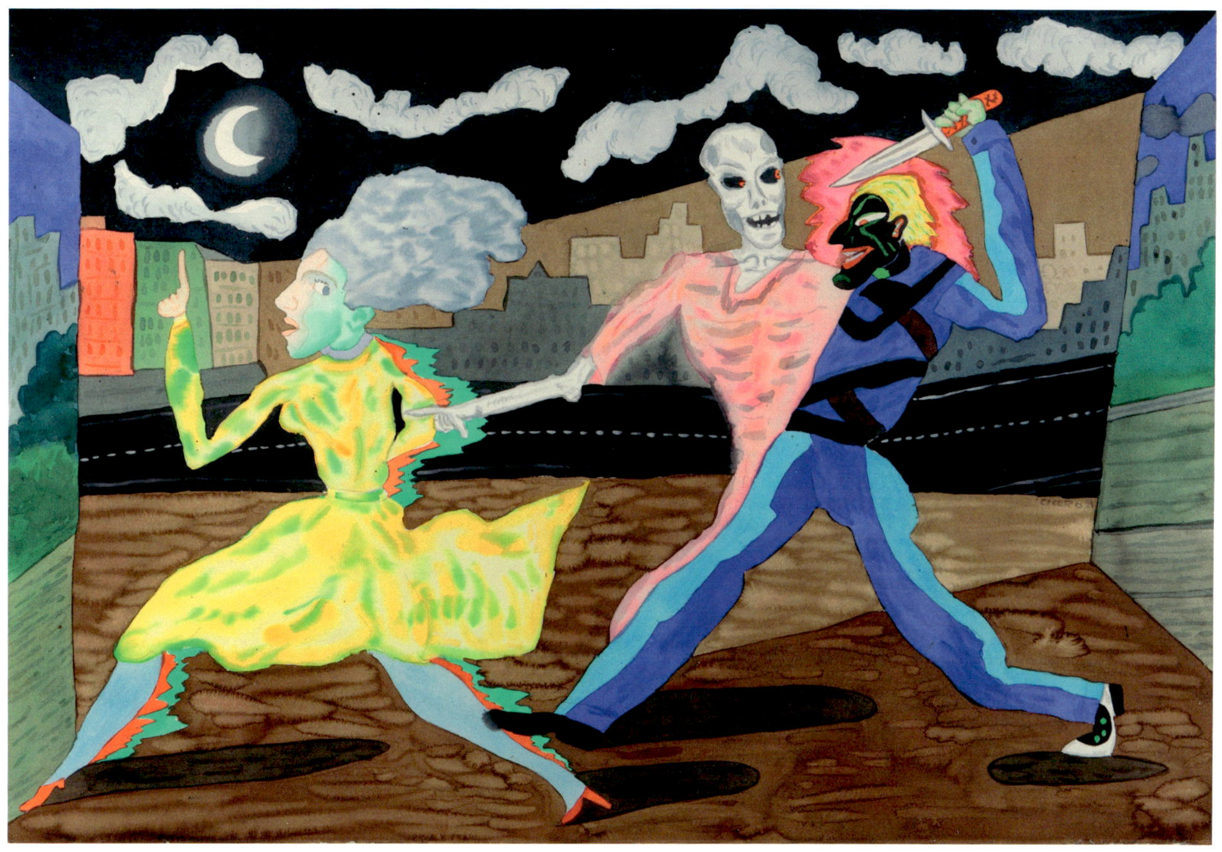

Carmen Cicero, *The Rage*, 1995. Watercolor on paper, 40 × 60 inches. *Gift of Carmen L. Cicero*, 2001.

EDWARD GIOBBI
(1926–)

Edward Giobbi met Henry Hensche when he was studying at the Vesper George School of Arts in Boston. Hensche encouraged him to come to Provincetown to attend his Cape School of Art, and in 1949 he arrived. Giobbi learned valuable lessons from Hensche about color and its relationship to nature, which he has continued to use. A founding member of the prestigious Long Point Gallery in Provincetown, Giobbi spent many summers there.

Born in Katonah, New York, Giobbi grew up in Waterbury, Connecticut. He studied at the Whitney School of Art and the Art Students League in New York, and Accademia di Belle Arti in Florence, Italy.

His art includes collages, constructions, and gouaches. His work is noted for its skillful draftsmanship, dry humor, and fascinating juxtapositions. His collages are made up of found elements with unusual textures. Employing symmetry and hard-edge forms, he often makes pictures on unusually shaped canvases, combining figurative images like flowers from his garden and abstract elements. He is influenced by literature, history, and mythology, and a diversity of periods, including the ancient art of the Etruscans and Romans, Renaissance and baroque art, as well as Italian futurism. His 1962 *Untitled* drawing in the Cape Cod Museum of Art collection is an example of his abstract work, evoking a mystery that is evident in a number of his works.

His works are included in the collections of major museums, including the Museum of Fine Arts in Boston and the Whitney Museum of American Art in New York.

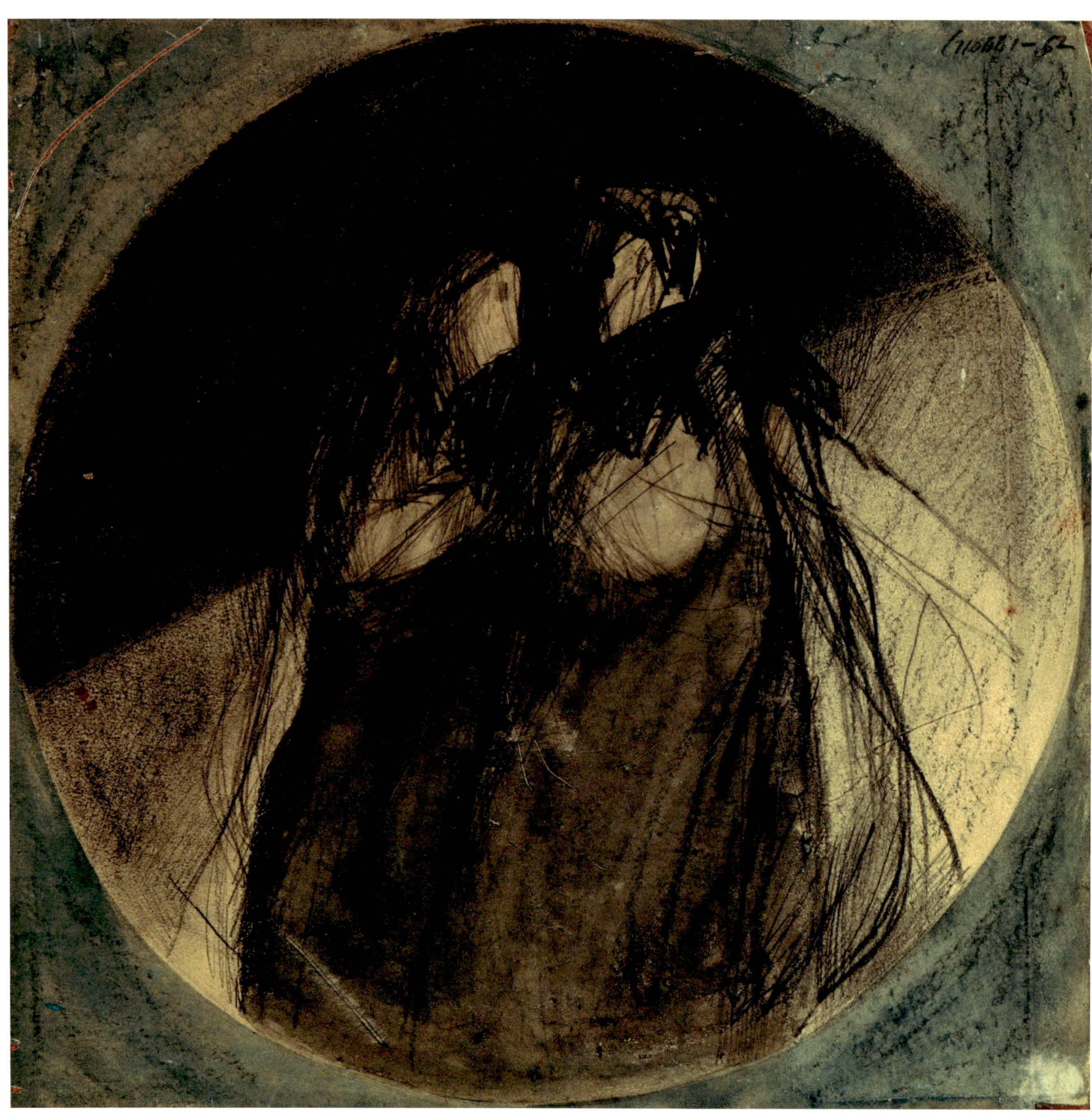

Edward Giobbi, *Untitled*, 1962. Pencil on paper, 12 × 12 inches. *Anonymous gift*, 1998.

TONY VEVERS
(1926–2008)

To escape the Blitz during World War II, Vevers left his native England for America in 1940, when he was a teenager. He served in the US Army during the Second World War and then went on to earn an art degree from Yale University. He studied in Italy and with Hans Hofmann.

When abstract expressionism was the primary art movement in New York, Vevers joined the crowd at the Cedar Bar in Greenwich Village, the tavern where Jackson Pollock, Franz Kline, Mark Rothko, Willem de Kooning, and Robert Motherwell hung out and doused their art discussions with a good portion of alcohol. Vevers tried his hand at gestural abstraction, but by the 1950s he turned to figurative works.

He made his initial mark on the Provincetown art colony in the 1950s when he was one of the rebellious Sun Gallery artists who were challenging the reigning abstract expressionists with a new approach to figurative art. That gallery gave Vevers his first major one-man show in 1958. Provincetown soon became his summer home, and when he retired from teaching at Purdue University in 1988, it became his year-round residence.

During his figurative period, Vevers's loosely painted figures set in a landscape are dreamy images in muted colors, and they often have a story to tell. His paintings of Provincetown are sweeps of color forming flat patterns, as in the 1956 *Winter Landscape* in the Cape Cod Museum of Art collection. Although some of these works are similar to the paintings of Milton Avery, a friend of his, the images are softer, as if seen through a veil of memory.

Ironically, in the late 1970s, Vevers became associated with Robert Motherwell, one of the leaders of abstract expressionism, at the Long Point Gallery in Provincetown. By that time, Vevers had found his way back to abstraction through the use of sand and found objects. These pieces are made up of fragments of sand-coated canvas, salvaged from previous works, and rope or buoys found on Provincetown beaches. Although these assemblages are essentially abstract, they broach reality by using real found objects, and paradoxically, have an actual physical connection to the real world—to Provincetown—that painted representational works can never have.

Vevers's works are in permanent public collections, including the Hirshhorn Museum and Sculpture Garden in Washington, DC; the Walter Chrysler Museum in Norfolk, Virginia; the deCordova Sculpture Park and Museum in Lincoln, Massachusetts; and the University of Massachusetts.

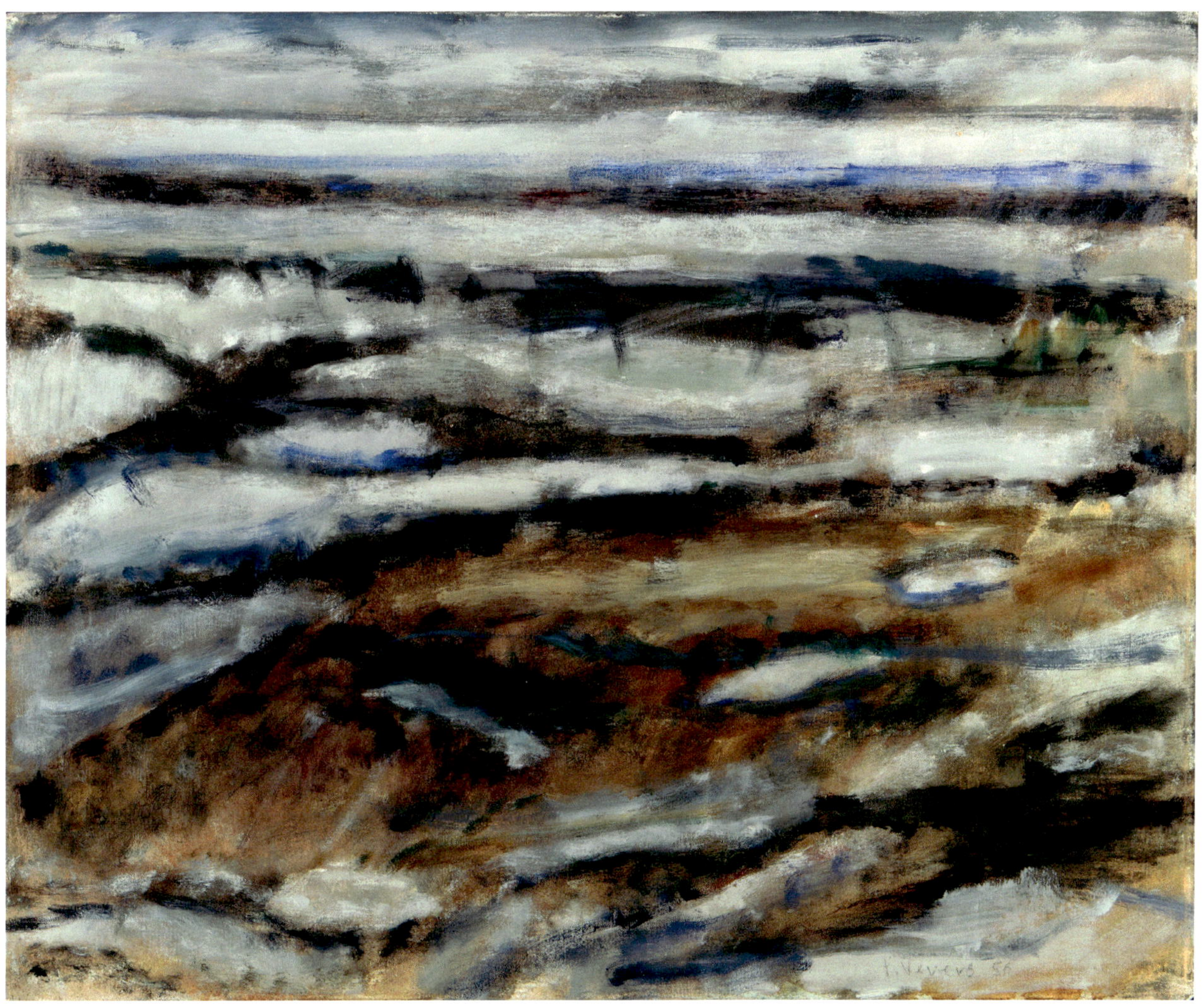

Tony Vevers, *Winter Landscape*, 1956. Oil on canvas, 24 × 30 inches. *Gift of Tony Vevers*, 1997.

ROBERT VICKREY
(1926–2011)

Robert Vickrey was a representational artist associated with magic realism, a movement noted for its precisely detailed paintings, which also add a note of fantasy, mystery, and ambiguity. He is known for his technical skills in egg tempera and meticulous compositions, populated by children and nuns with picturesque headgear, in which shadows play a masterful role. The narrative aspect of his paintings explores dream-like settings that seem to hover between reality and imagination. Although provocative, his paintings often have a hushed feeling as if time has been frozen.

Born in Manhattan, Vickrey studied at the Art Students League with Reginald Marsh and Kenneth Hayes Miller and in 1950 received a bachelor of fine arts degree from Yale University. It was at Yale that he mastered the medium of egg tempera, which he used to create his highly refined, moody realism.

In the 1950s and '60s, Vickrey was included in nine Whitney Museum exhibitions. He also created seventy-eight cover paintings for *Time* magazine. Forty-eight of these covers are in the permanent collection in the Smithsonian Institution's National Portrait Gallery. Although Vickrey's reputation diminished somewhat in the era of the abstract, nonobjective, and formalist movements, by the 1980s, when the art world was becoming more diverse and magic realism was being reevaluated, Vickrey's work was reconsidered for its individuality.

Despite his hyper-realism and the narrative aspects of his work, there is an abstract element in his compositions,

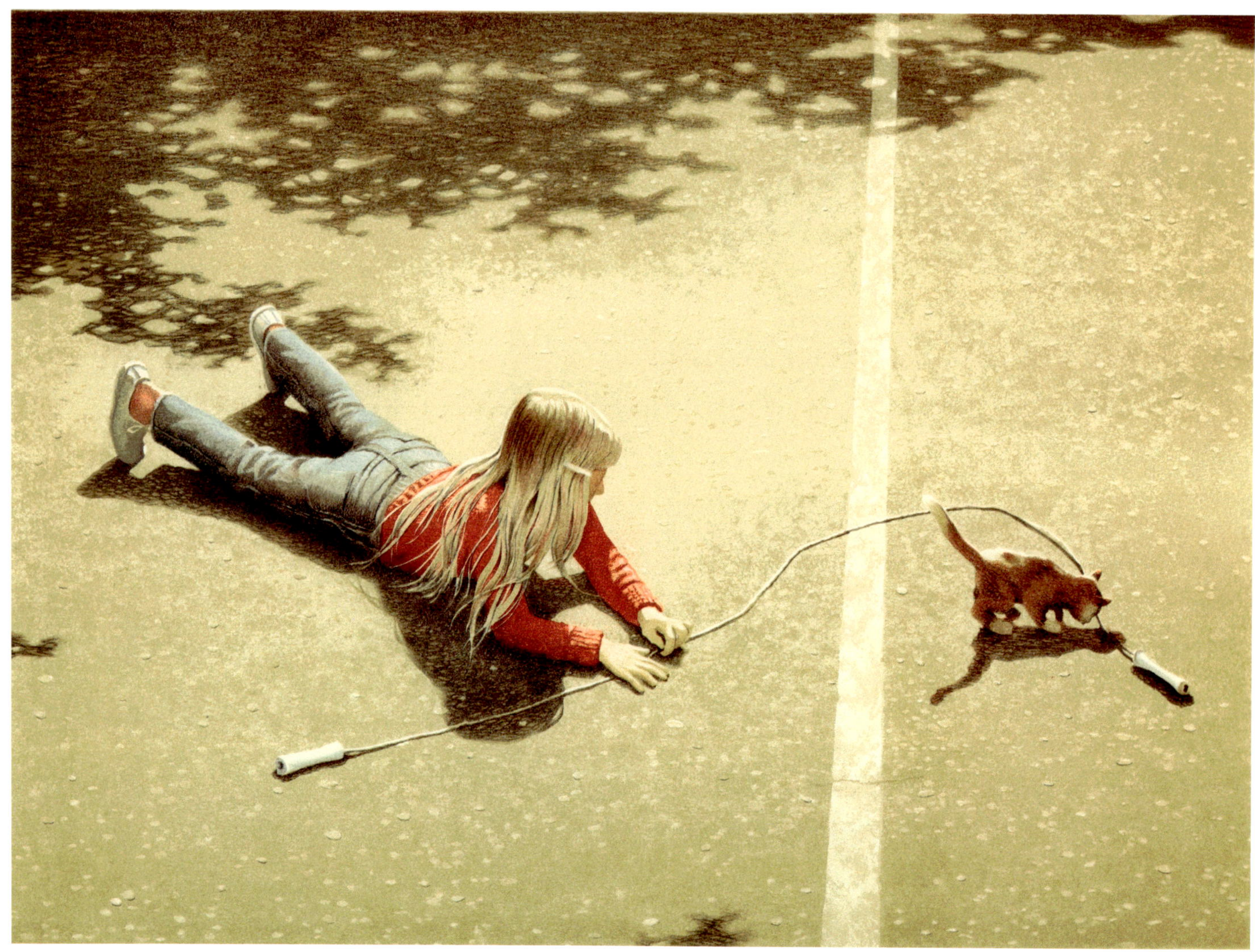

Robert Vickrey, *Skip Rope* 249/250, n.d. Serigraph on paper, 18 × 24½ inches. *Gift of Robert Vickrey*, 1990.
© The Estate of Robert Vickery/Licensed by VAGA, New York, New York.

particularly in his use of shadows as material forms, which can be scattered across a pavement reflecting an intricate arrangement of bicycle wheels, or become patterns of snowflakes, foliage, or angular grids on a street or brick wall. His serigraph *Skip Rope*, in the Cape Cod Museum of Art collection, is a fine example of how he worked his shadows to play a distinct role in his compositions.

His work has a surreal quality at times. Sometimes he created ambiguity with a double exposure of images on a wall or reflections in a glass window. Or he erected ominous shadowy figures on a wall mysteriously hovering over a child. He chose the nuns of the St. Vincent de Paul order because of the abstract shape of their historic, winged headgear, which allowed him to show it in a diversity of ways as light and shadow play over its angles. His egg tempera *The Nun*, in the museum collection, represents his perennial interest in this figure and the design of her hat, and also his deftness in using shadows to elevate a composition's abstract elements. Like his children, his nuns are often shown against a wall of light reflections or of shadowy figures from another time.

Vickrey spent many years on Cape Cod in his Orleans home. His works are in the collections of numerous museums, including the Metropolitan Museum of Art and the Whitney Museum of American Art in New York, and the Smithsonian American Art Museum in Washington, DC.

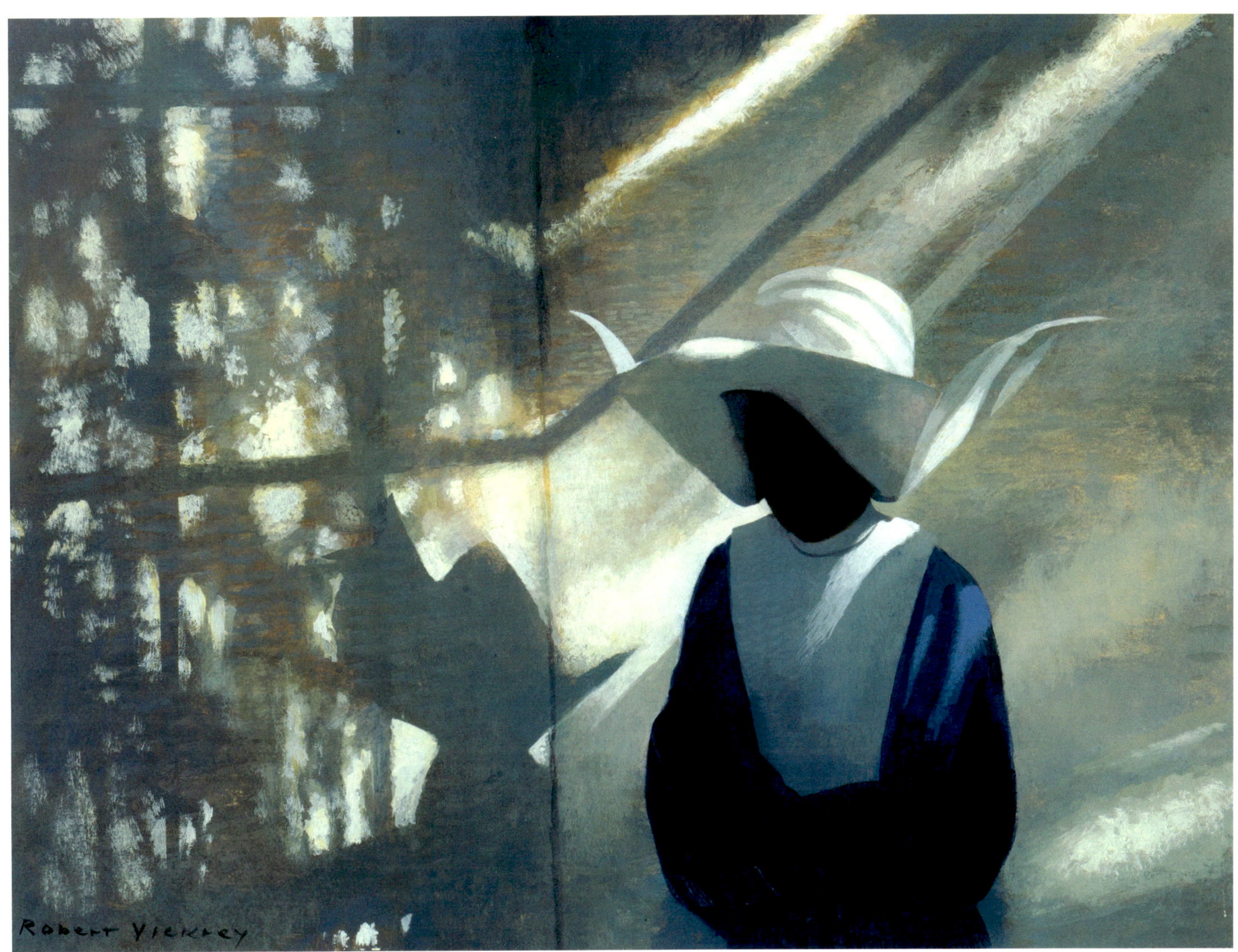

Robert Vickrey, *The Nun*, n.d. Egg tempera on board, 11 × 14¾ inches. *Gift of Frank H. Hogan*, 1991.

ROMANOS RIZK
(1927–2009)

Romanos Rizk had a long history in the Provincetown art colony. He was born in Providence, Rhode Island, and studied a traditional approach at the Vesper George School of Art in Boston. When fellow student Salvatore Del Deo encouraged him to come to Provincetown to study with Henry Hensche in 1948, he was enthusiastic to see a different approach.

While studying with Hensche, Rizk adopted his teacher's style with portraits and paintings of the town and harbor. He became fascinated with impressionism and its emphasis on color. But after two years with Hensche, Rizk felt that he needed to integrate more formal structure into his work, which he found in Asian art, in particular, in calligraphic ink brush paintings. This approach—which integrates the philosophical approach of Zen, and involves the ideas of asymmetry, the free movement of the brush, and spontaneity—is demonstrated in the abstract collage *Seeking the Tao*, in the Cape Cod Museum of Art collection.

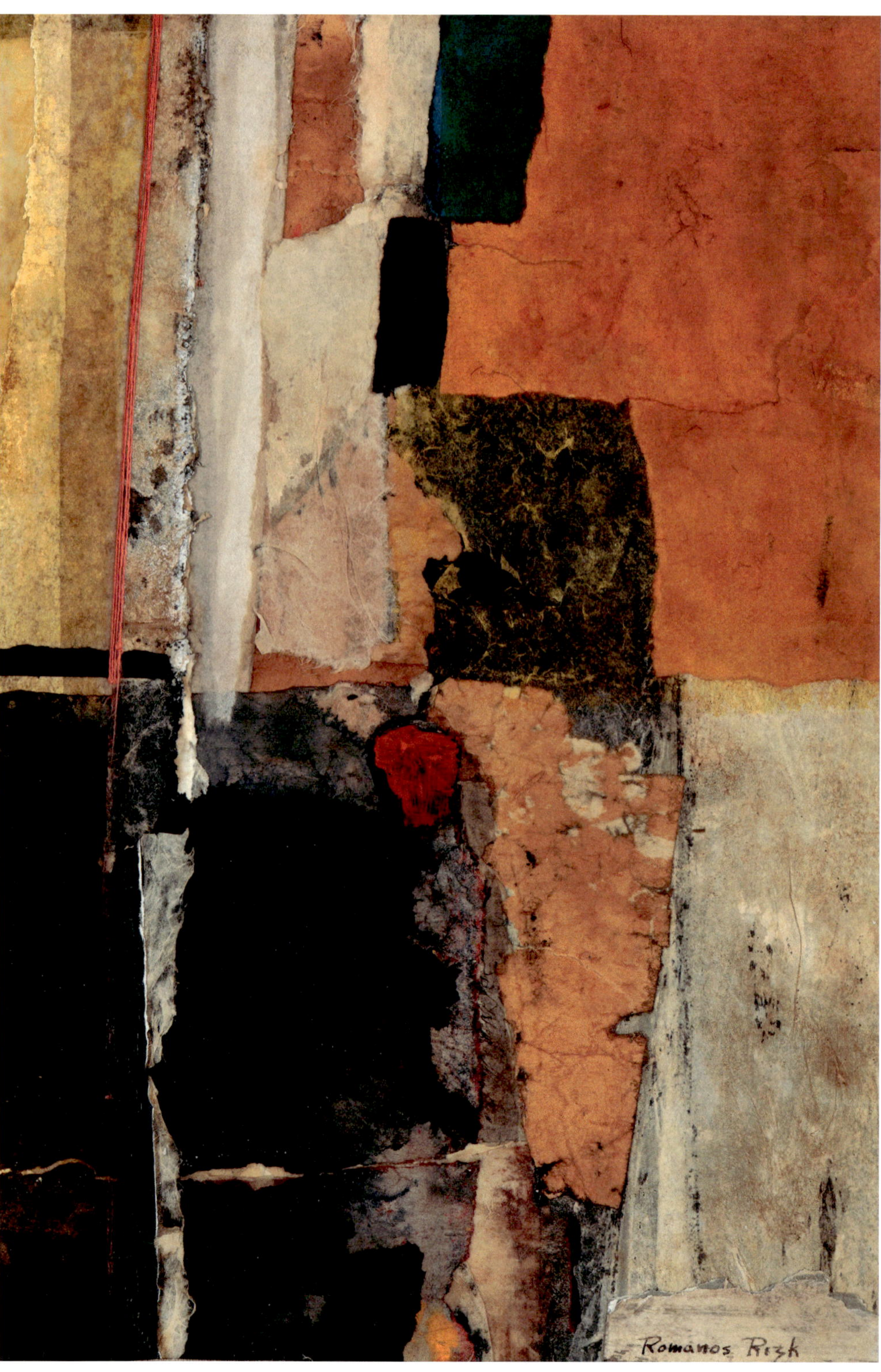

Romanos Rizk, *Seeking the Tao*, n.d. Collage on paper, 13¼ × 9¼ inches. *Gift of Elizabeth and Robert Douglas Hunter*, 1991.

Abstract art pointed the way for Rizk. A painting for him was not only about color, but also about relating shape, color, line, and texture in a harmonious way. For many years, he painted in this manner, but during the last decade of his life he revisited Hensche's impressionism, with Monet-inspired, luminous, and atmospheric lily ponds, figures, and still lifes.

The softly painted acrylic and collage *Still Life #15*; the boldly colored, atmospheric lily pond *Landscape Impression #6*; and the fiery *Pond #5 Beechwood Forest*, in the museum collection, are fine examples of Rizk's various styles. He never stayed still. His body of work formed a circle in the way he transformed his art and then returned to what must have felt like home. But also, it was a path with twists and turns, experiments, and constant exploring.

Rizk's work is represented in numerous private and corporate collections, including the Ford Motor Company, John Hancock Insurance, Nissan Motors, Weyerhaeuser, and JP Morgan Chase Bank, as well as in the collections of the Fine Arts Museum, Mobile, Alabama; Fitchburg Art Museum in Fitchburg, Massachusetts; and Slater Memorial Museum in Norwich, Connecticut.

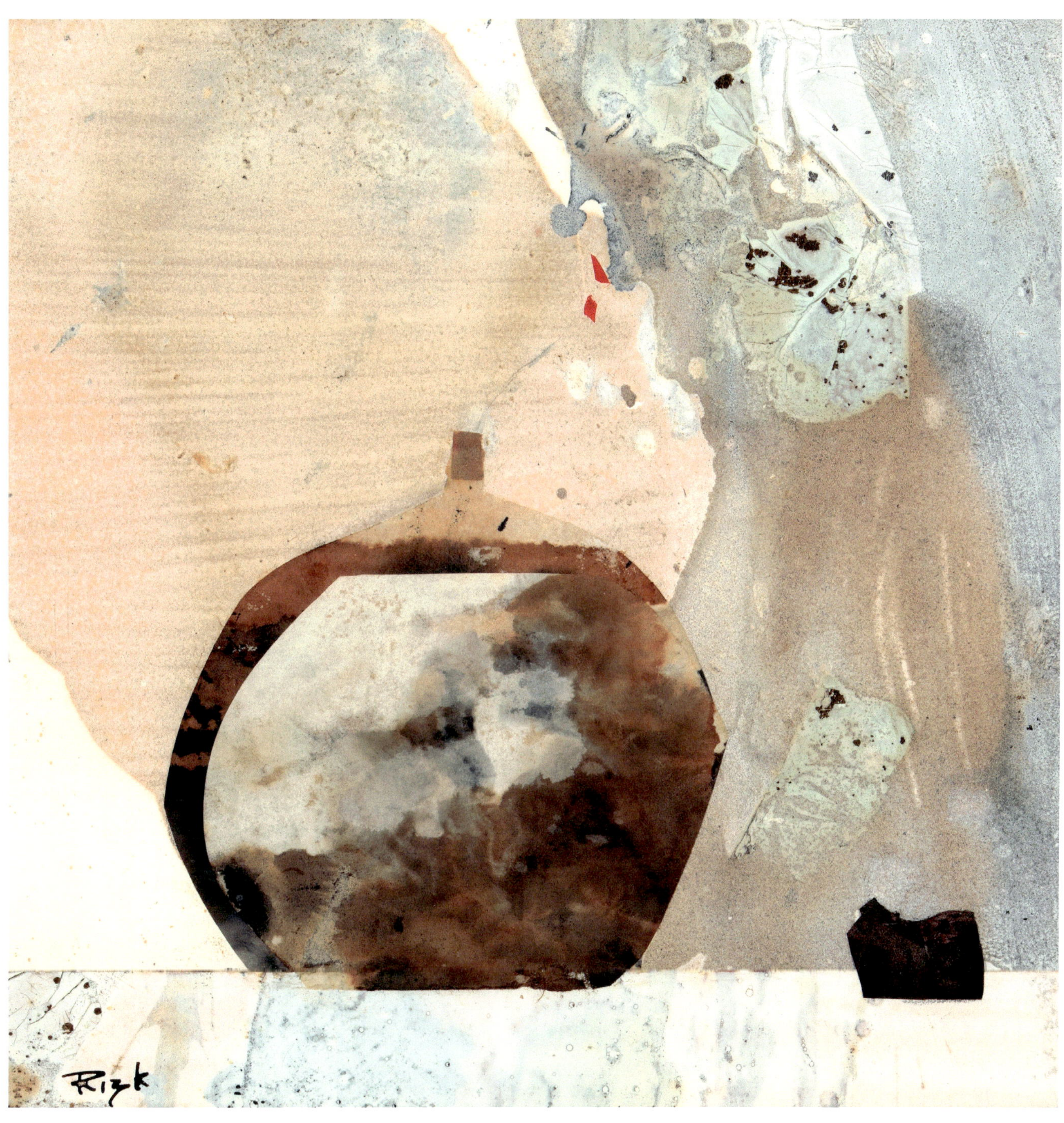

Romanos Rizk, *Still Life #15*, n.d. Acrylic polymer and collage on paper, 10 × 10 inches. *Gift of Richard Polak*, 2004.

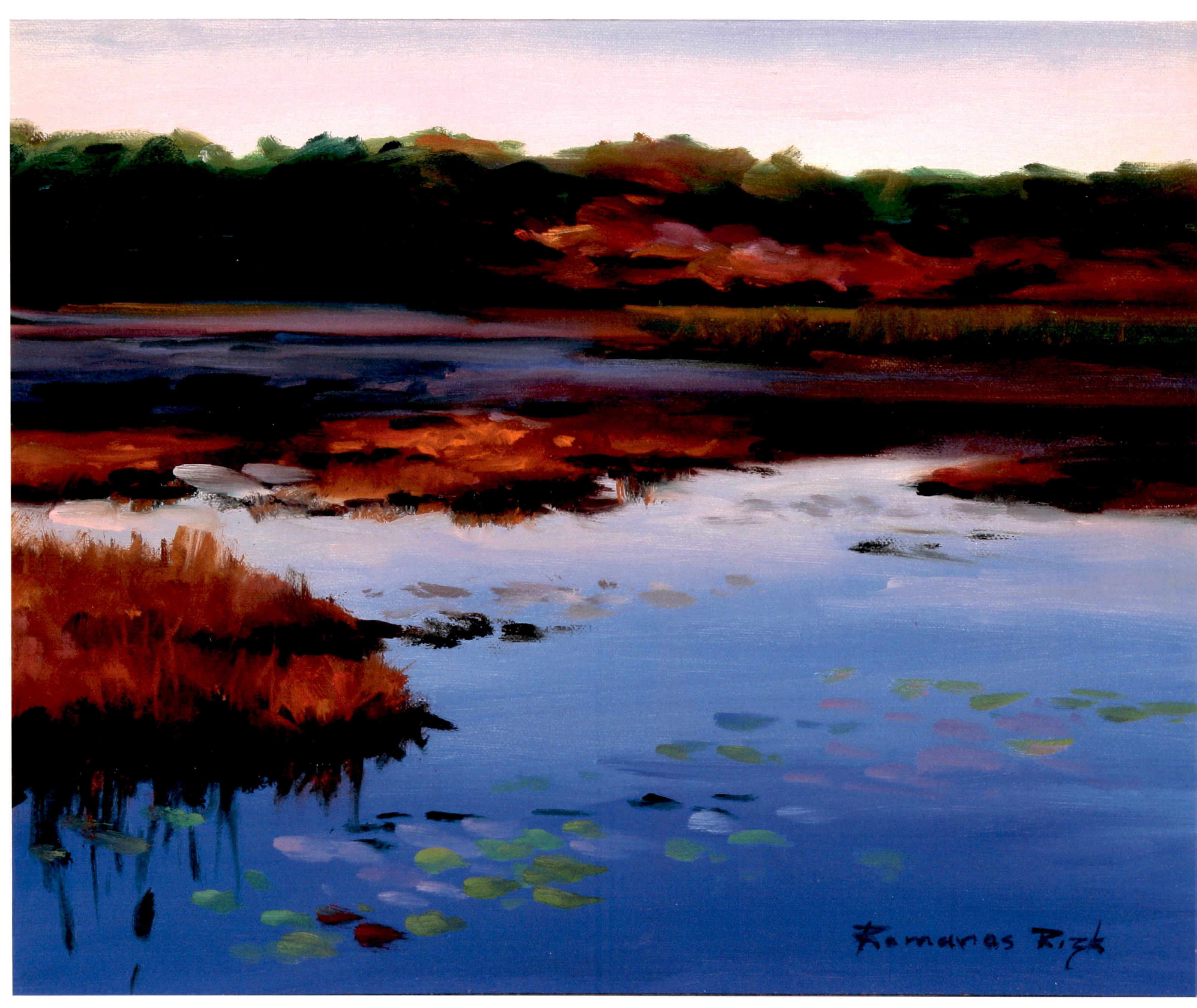

Romanos Rizk, *Pond #5 Beechwood Forest*, n.d. Oil on canvas, 11 × 14 inches. *Anonymous gift*, 2009.

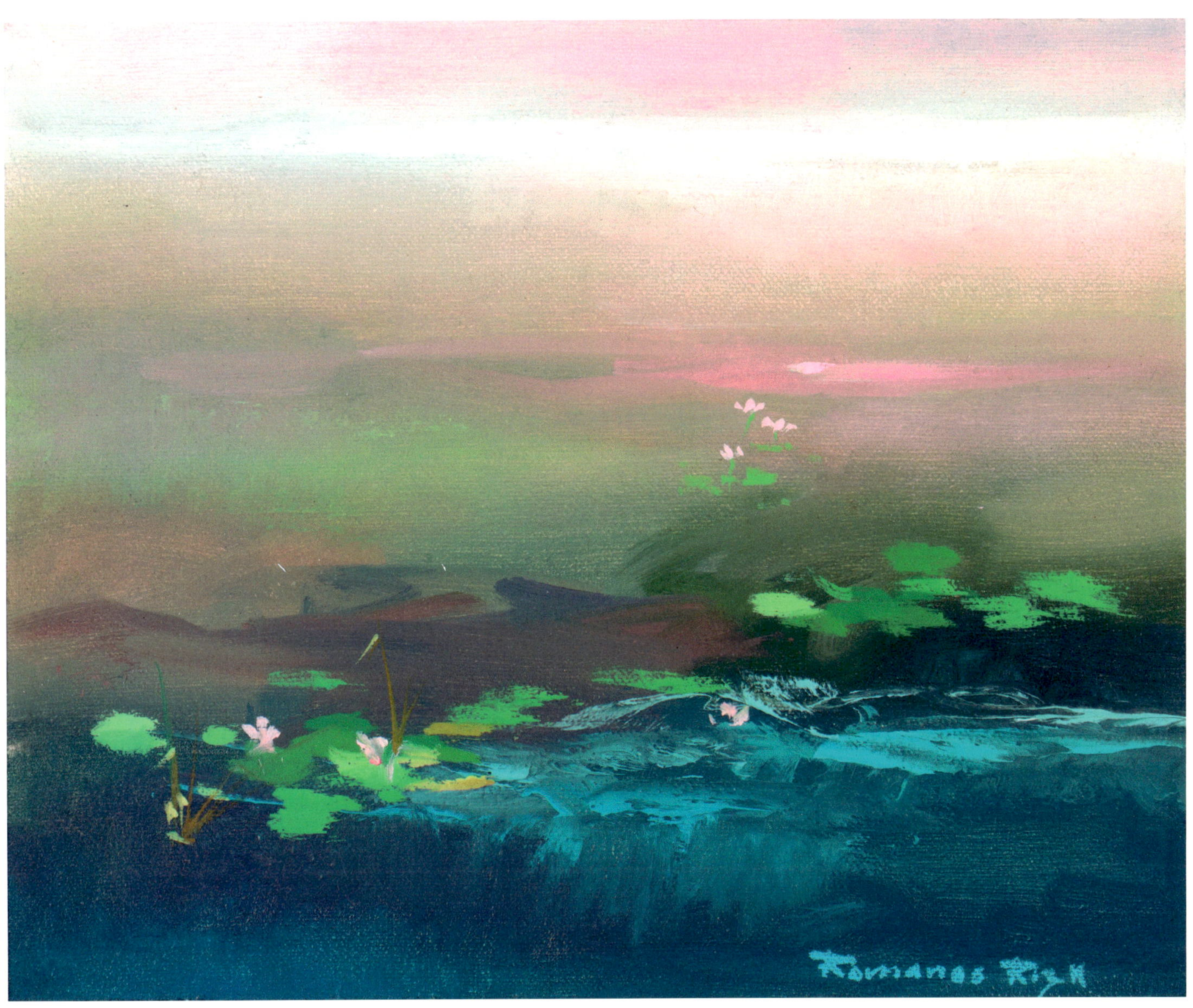

Romanos Rizk, *Landscape Impression #6,* n.d. Oil on canvas, 7½ × 9½ inches. *Anonymous gift*, 2009.

DONALD STOLTENBERG
(1927–2016)

Donald Stoltenberg's world is not the natural one of land and sea, but the one of manmade structures that occupy so much of the space on our planet. His interest in architecture and engineering informed the boats, bridges, trains, and airplanes he painted. His work is about shapes and space, about breaking down the space into shapes. Those subjects—bridges, the grid work under an elevated train station, the diagonal lines of a Cape Cod house, the dramatic angles of a cruise ship—occupy his paintings.

Born in Milwaukee, Stoltenberg moved to Chicago when he was five. In the late 1940s, he studied at Chicago's Institute of Design, which was founded in 1937 as the New Bauhaus. Bauhaus design and architecture informed his imagery, and his style was influenced by Cézanne and cubism, with its splintered forms and diverse viewpoints. Other influences were the work of the precisionist Charles Sheeler, who turned fractured forms into polished images of urban and industrial subjects, and the art of Charles Demuth and Lyonel Feininger.

Those who delight in nature's scenic splendors may view the engineering feat of a bridge as just so much steel and girders, a necessity, but hardly a thing of beauty. But Stoltenberg's paintings of bridges are just that. His compositions build from the angle and particular segment of the structure he chose. He wove together the various shapes and lines into an intricate pattern that heralds not only the genius of the construction but also the sheer beauty of its form.

In his work, like the oil *Railway* and the watercolor *Cleveland Arcade*, in the Cape Cod Museum of Art collection, he faceted the light that streams through the architectural forms, creating sharp angles and prismatic transparencies, which produce dazzling effects and dynamic movement and enhance the abstract elements of the painting.

Focusing on architecture, Stoltenberg painted buildings, such as *House in Harwich*, again with prismatic effects. He also captured buildings under construction. Most of his paintings take up unorthodox perspectives, like the underside of a bridge or of an elevated train. Although color is integral to his painting, his focus was more about defining the shapes,

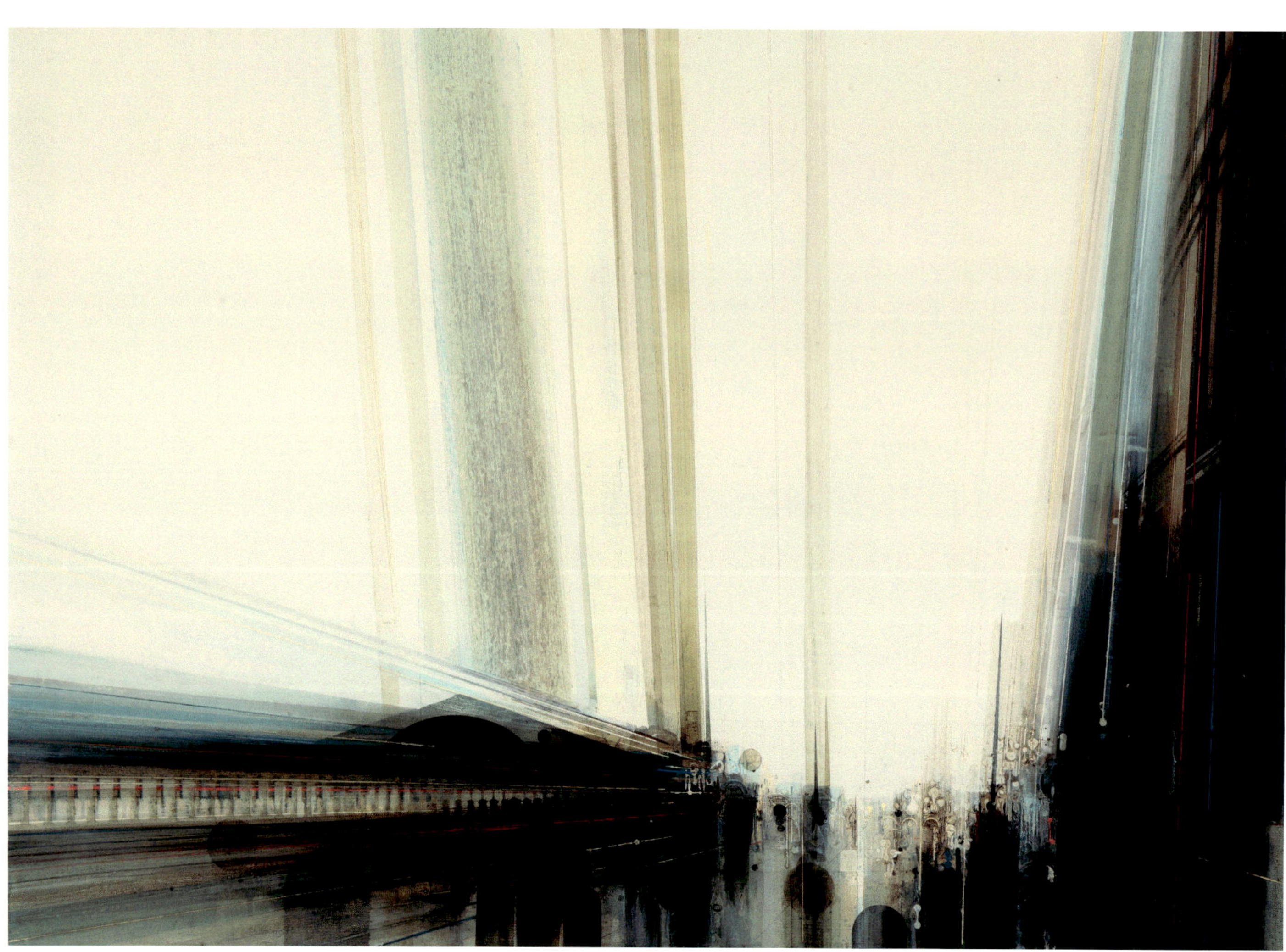

Donald Stoltenberg, *Railway,* 1965. Oil on canvas, 35 × 50 inches. *Gift of Mr. & Mrs. John McKee*, 2005.

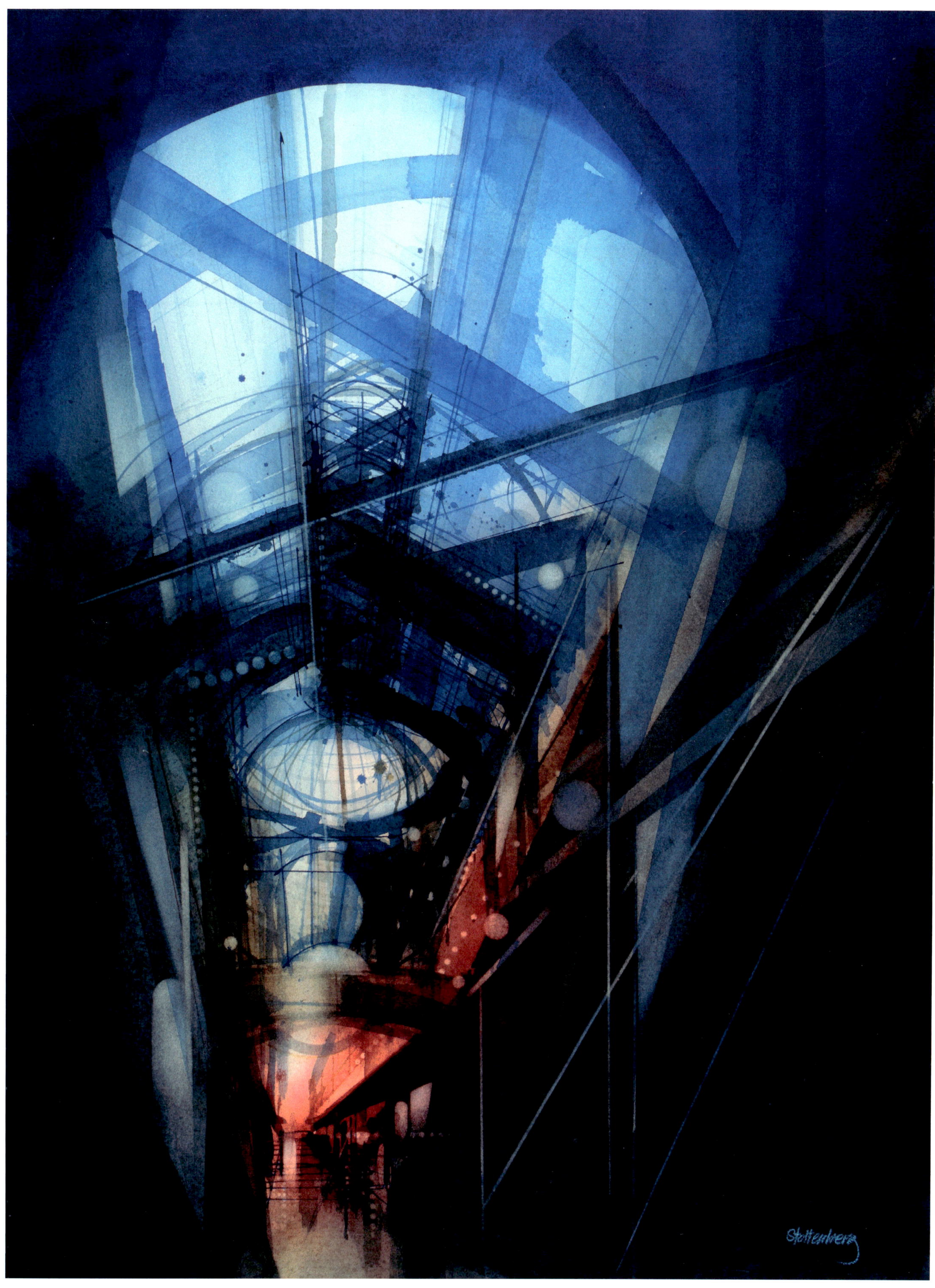

Donald Stoltenberg, *Cleveland Arcade*, 1970. Watercolor on paper, 22½ × 11 inches. *Gift in memory of Kenneth Swallow*, 2015.

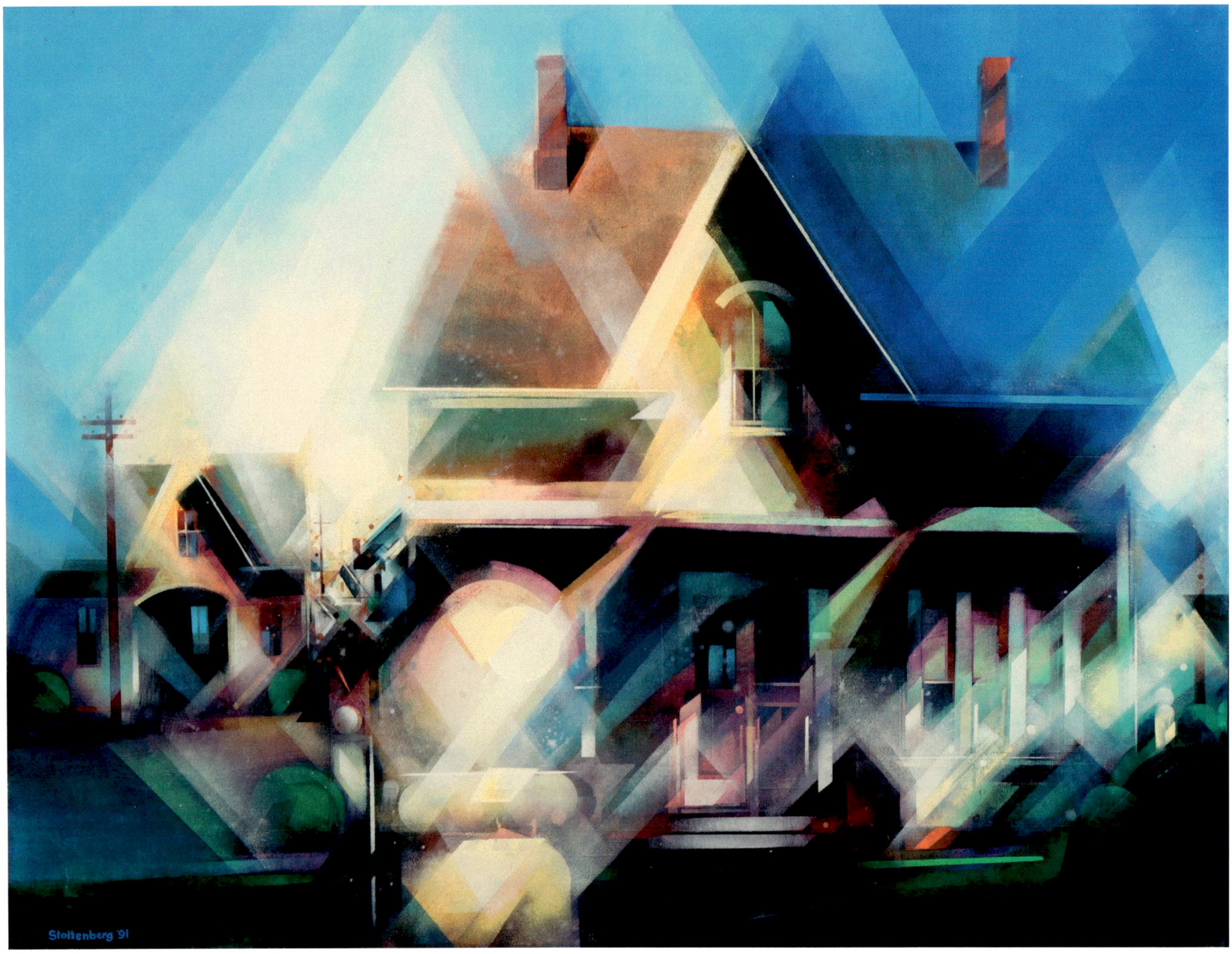

Donald Stoltenberg, *House in Harwich,* 1991. Oil on canvas, 30 × 40 inches. *Gift in memory of Kenneth Swallow*, 2015.

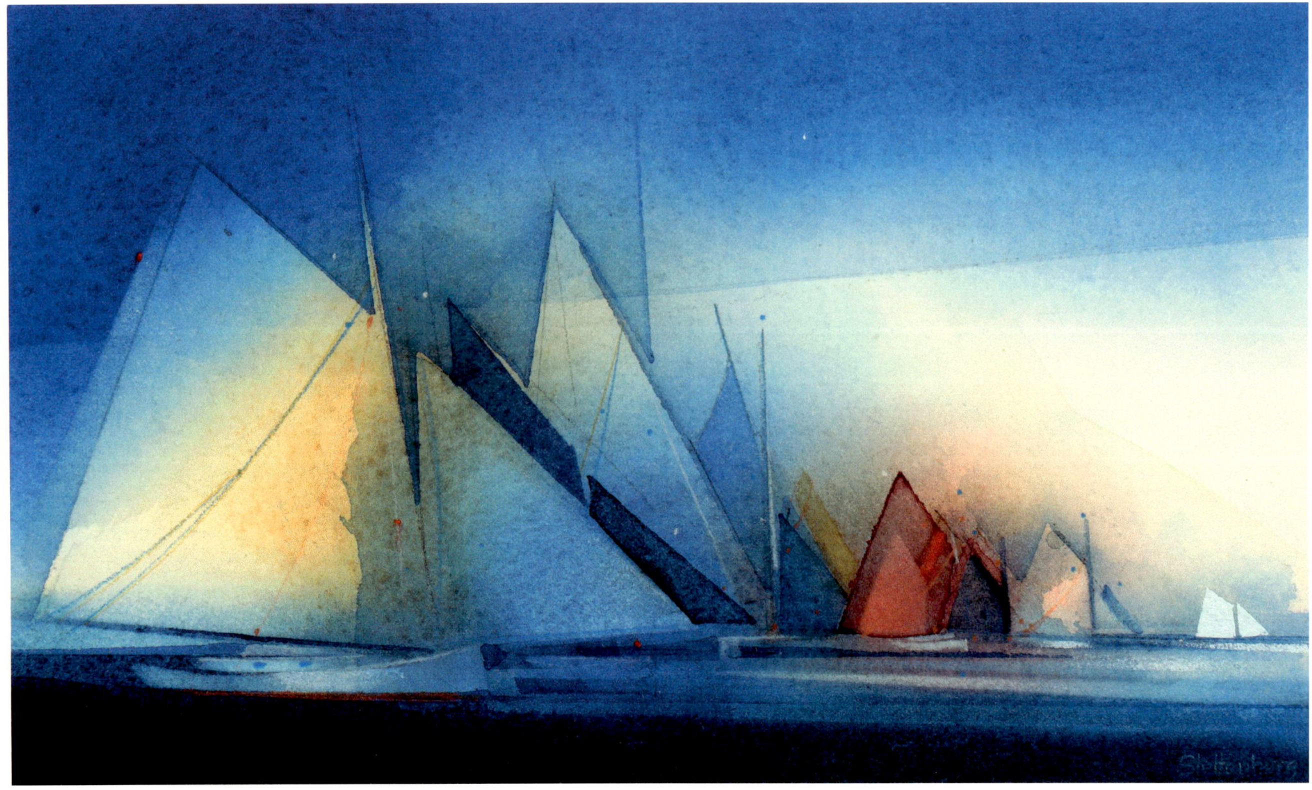

Donald Stoltenberg, *Gaft Sail Study*, 1989. Watercolor on paper, 4¾ × 8 inches. *Gift of Yvonne Backus*, 1989.

stretching the lines, and emphasizing the diagonal, which gives so much life to his work.

Stoltenberg lived in Brewster for more than fifty years. He moved there from Boston where he was living on Commercial Wharf, and devoted himself full time to painting after a career as a graphic designer. From his location on the Boston waterfront, he had a view of ships, which only expanded his interest in boats that began when he was a boy. He is known for his faceted paintings of sailing yachts, as in *Gaft Sail Study*, and the very abstracted images that use color and light building to a crescendo, including *Battleship in Drydock*, both in the museum collection. He also made detailed collographic prints by building up delicate, precise surfaces on a flat plate and printing them on a press, such as the oval image of sailing ships, *Spinnakers*, in the museum collection.

Stoltenberg exhibited his work in major museums, including the Metropolitan Museum of Art in New York City, the Art Institute of Chicago, and the Museum of Fine Arts in Boston.

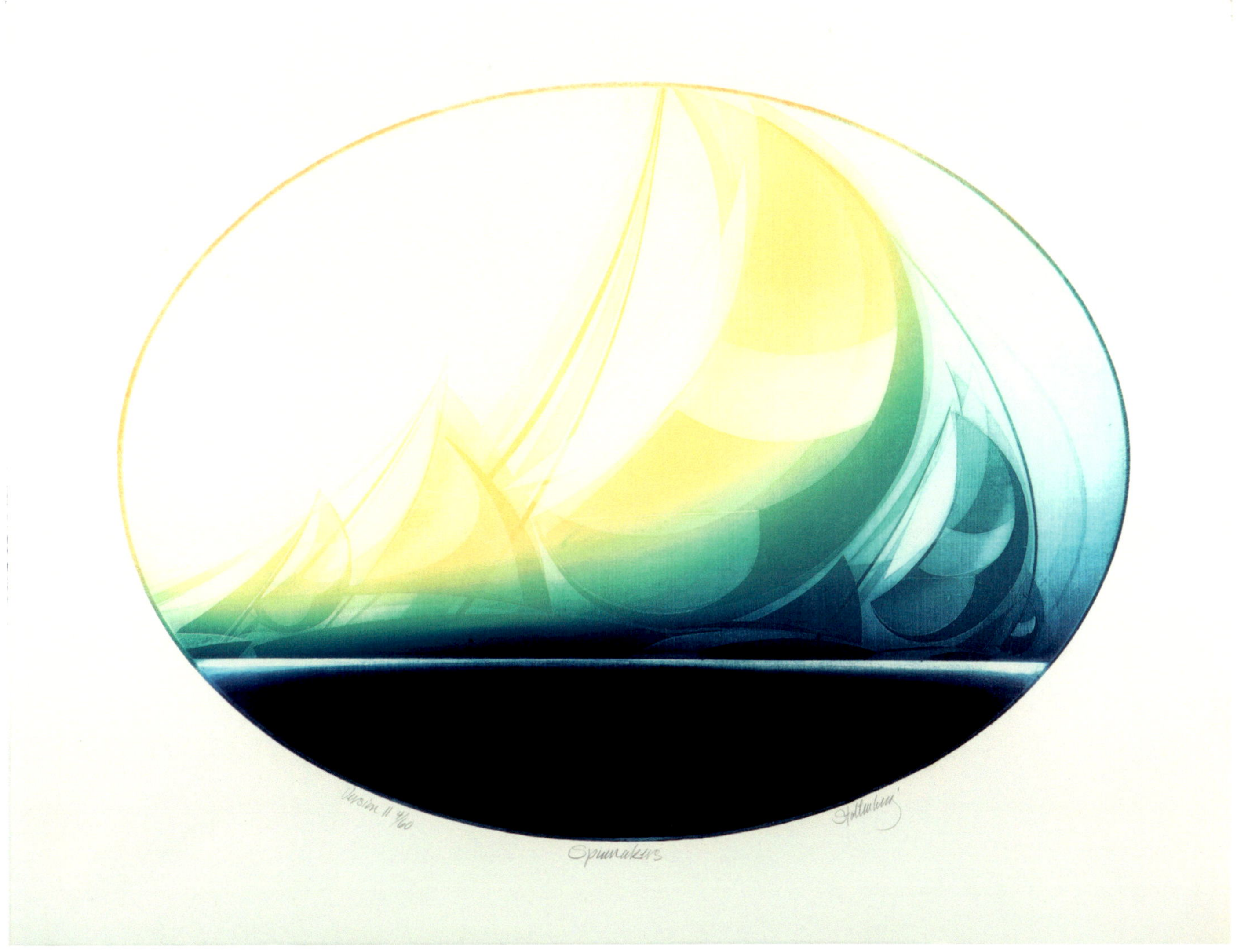

Donald Stoltenberg, *Spinnakers* Version II 4/60, 1972. Collagraph on paper, 18 × $23\frac{7}{8}$ inches. *Gift in memory of Kenneth Swallow*, 2015.

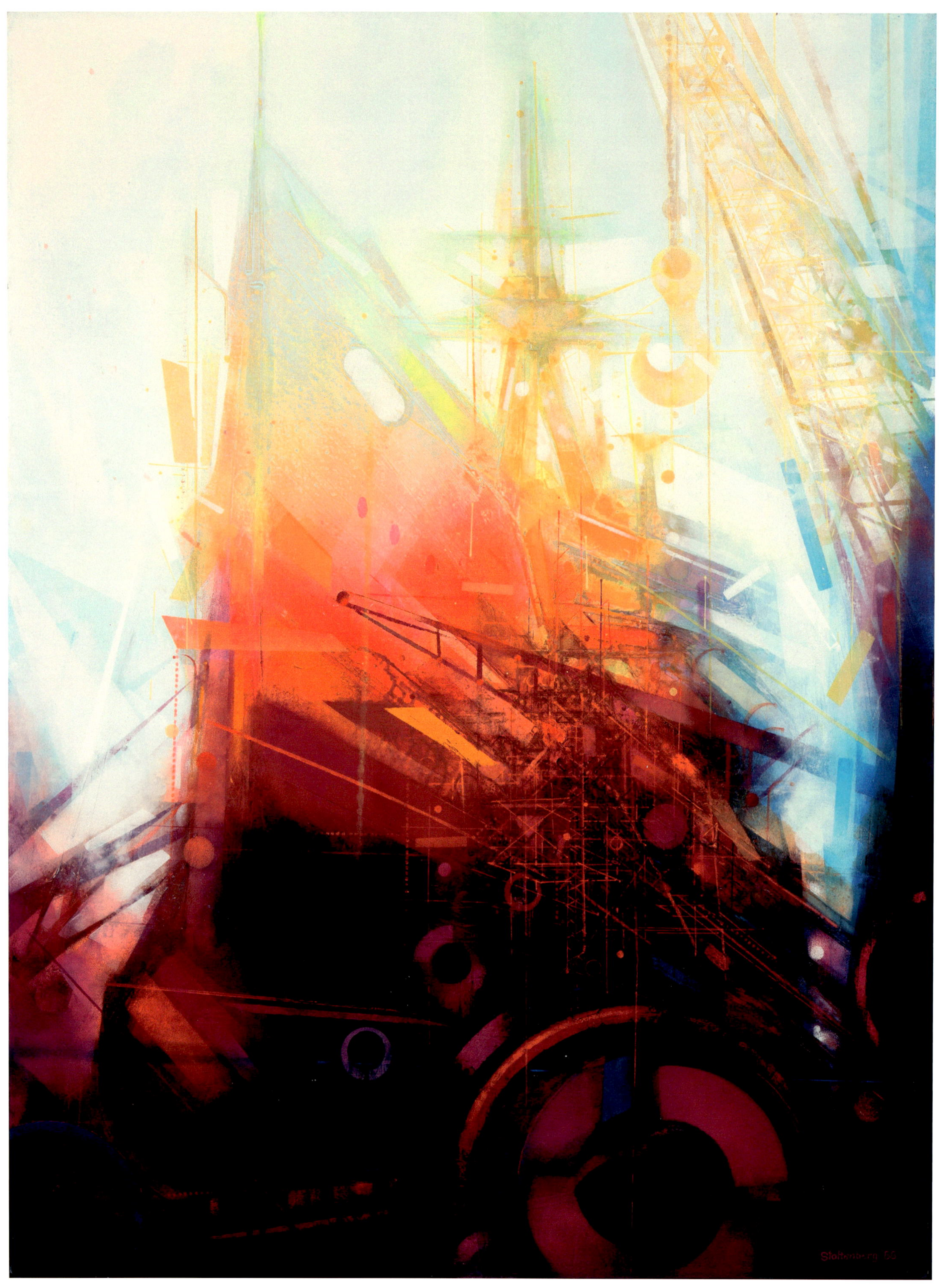

Donald Stoltenberg, *Battleship in Drydock*, 1988. Oil and acrylic on linen canvas, 41 × 30½ inches. *Gift of the Artist*, 1991.

ARTHUR COHEN
(1928–2012)

Arthur Cohen painted the places he lived in and loved—New York and Provincetown. He was born in New York and studied with Edwin Dickinson at both Cooper Union and the Art Students League, as well as with Robert Gwathmey and Reginald Marsh.

For fifty years he divided his time between city and seaside life. Although there are contrasts of the views of the two places, whether the serene images of Provincetown's shoreline, harbor, boats, and marshes, and the skyscrapers of New York, his work has a calm and gentle quality that is created with mostly muted colors, soft brushstrokes, and a veil of time. Although not precisely a *plein-air* painter, because he often painted under the cover of his car, which was fitted with the palette, brushes, and paint, he nevertheless painted on site.

His work is noted for its simple planes of color and a reflective quality. In his oil paintings, photographs, and etchings, he often depicted specific locations—MacMillan Pier in Provincetown or the Brooklyn Bridge. In the Cape Cod Museum of Art's collection are works of both places. The oil painting *Provincetown* shows the curve of the shoreline with sky and water lit by soft colors. The etching *Provincetown* is a long view that emphasizes the open space that is so inviting. *MacMillan Pier*, bathed in blue, is also a long view over water to the buildings on the pier.

His New York images in the museum collection include *Flat Iron Building*, an etching of the iconic 1902, wedge-shaped, twenty-two-story skyscraper at the triangular block formed by Fifth Avenue, Broadway, and East 22nd and 23rd Streets. The aquatint *Brooklyn Bridge* softly captures the grandeur of the giant span, a monumental engineering structure completed in 1883.

His works are included in the collections of the Metropolitan Museum of Art, the Museum of the City of New York, the Brooklyn Museum of Art, the New York Historical Society, the Museum of Fine Arts in Boston, and the Hirshhorn Museum and Sculpture Garden in Washington, DC.

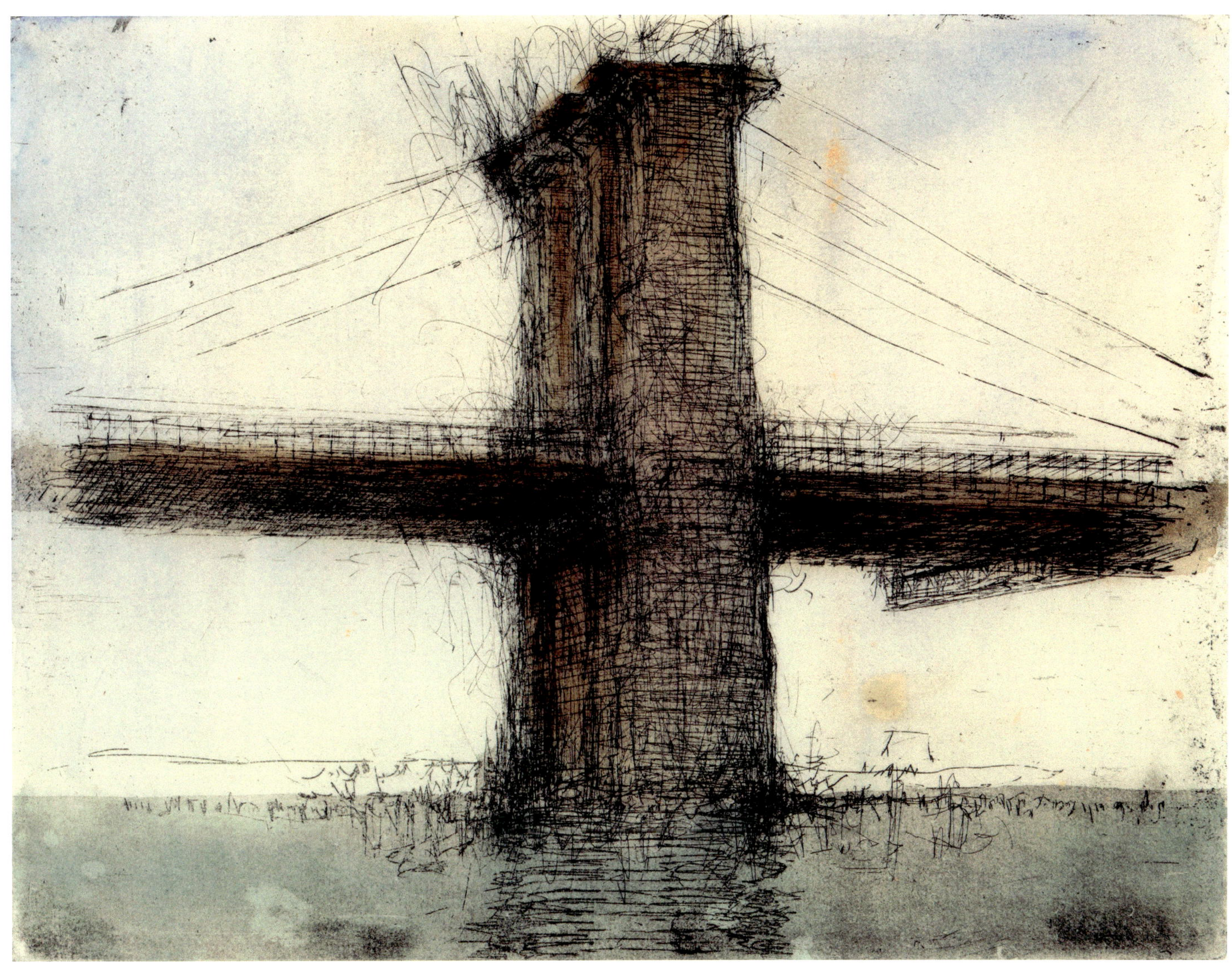

Arthur Cohen, *Brooklyn Bridge*, 1983. Aquatint on paper, 9½ × 12¼ inches. *Anonymous gift*, 2009.

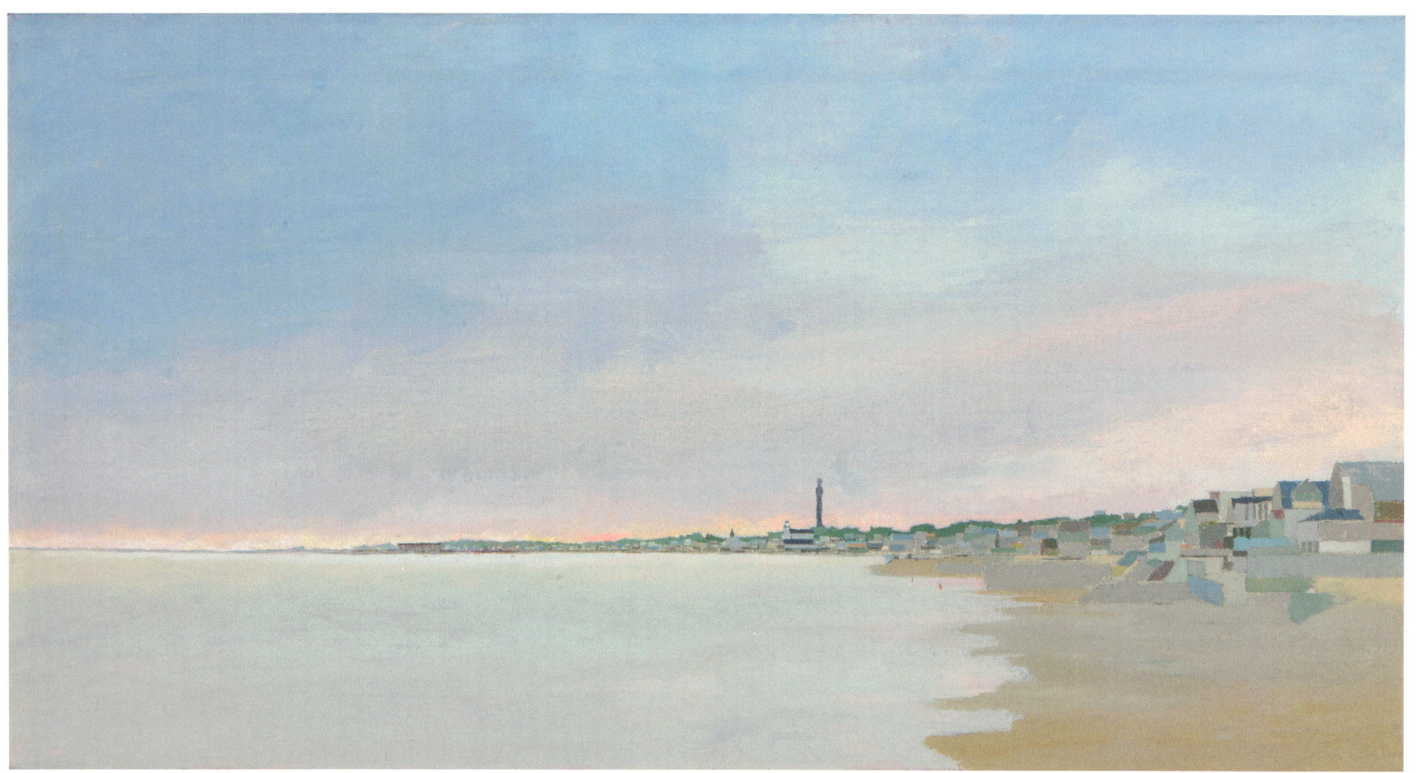

Arthur Cohen, *Provincetown,* n.d. Oil on canvas, 18 × 34 inches. *Gift of Arthur Cohen*, 1991.

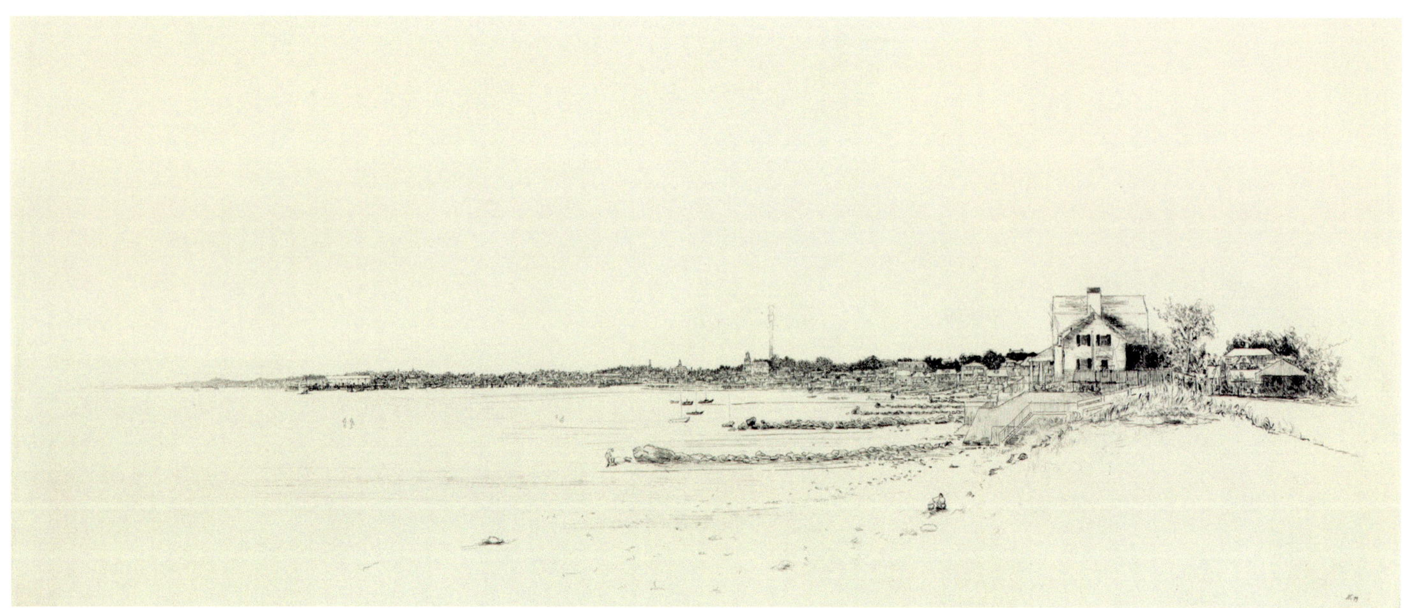

Arthur Cohen, *Provincetown* 10/25, 1979. Etching on paper, 9 × 23¾ inches. *Gift of Dr. Linda B. Miller*, 1999.

Arthur Cohen, *MacMillian Pier,* n.d. Oil on canvas, 15¾ × 19¾ inches. *Gift of Arthur Cohen*, 2004.

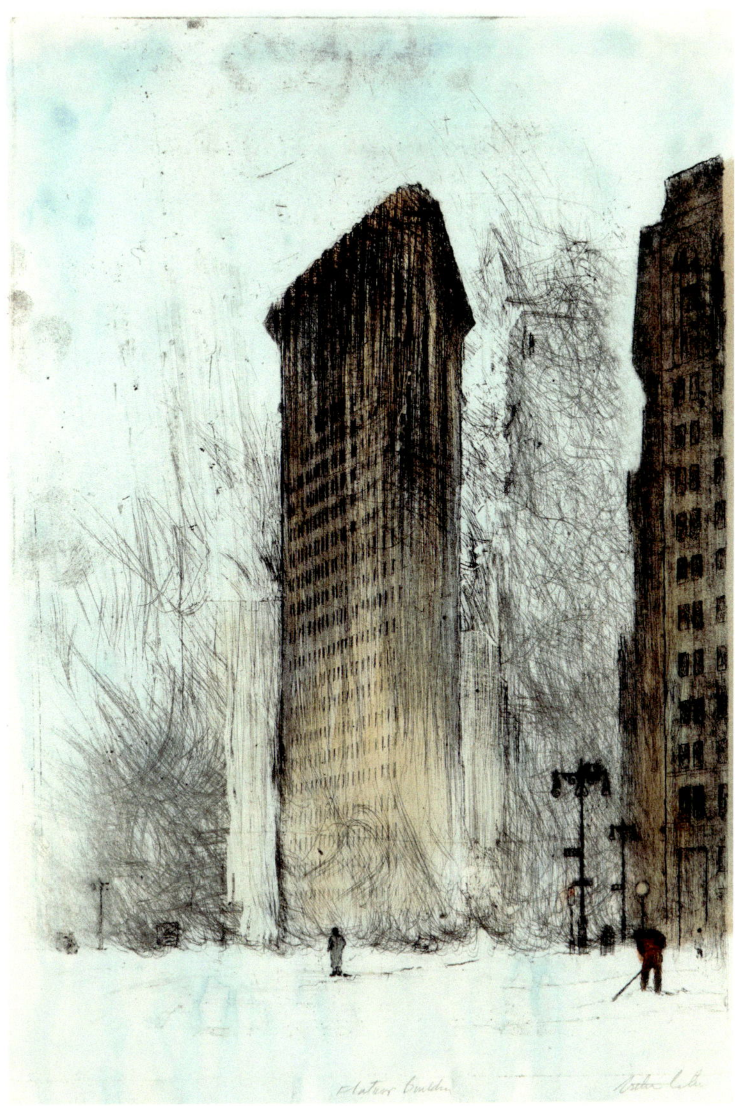

Arthur Cohen, *Flat Iron Building*, n.d. Etching on paper, 20 × 14 inches. *Anonymous gift*, 2009.

SALVATORE DEL DEO
(1928–)

Salvatore Del Deo's commitment to Provincetown is long and deep. He first arrived in Provincetown from Providence, Rhode Island, in 1946 to study with Henry Hensche. He also took classes with Edwin Dickinson, whom he considered an important teacher. He had studied with Dickinson at the Art Students League in New York and knew him in Provincetown as well.

When in 1953, Del Deo and his wife, Josephine, an art historian, married, they decided to settle in Provincetown. He has remained there ever since, running restaurants, fishing, even working as a carpenter, and all the time painting. Several of the artists who have influenced him—Ross Moffett, Dickinson, and Karl Knaths—were painters who had a long connection to the Provincetown art colony.

Del Deo has painted a wide range of subjects. In the Cape Cod Museum of Art collection is *Eidolon*, a charcoal figure sketch, and the painting *Studio Concept II*, a still life, intricately and colorfully composed of figures—a plaster model of a nude and a mannequin—ready as inspiration for the artist. He also has produced many scenes of Provincetown: the dunes; figures on the beach; and the life of a small town, the fishermen, their boats, and the activity at the wharf.

Although his pictures of fishermen have a sober aspect, showing the difficulty of the job, similar to Ross Moffett's paintings, Del Deo's colors are bright, so the works end up being uplifting, depicting the struggle and a quiet drama. Some of his landscapes are quiet, even somber; others are light-filled, expressing his love of Provincetown.

His paintings are in several public collections, including the National Portrait Gallery of the Smithsonian Institution in Washington, DC; Harvard University in Cambridge, Massachusetts; the Provincetown Art Association and Museum; and Williams College Museum of Art in Williamstown, Massachusetts.

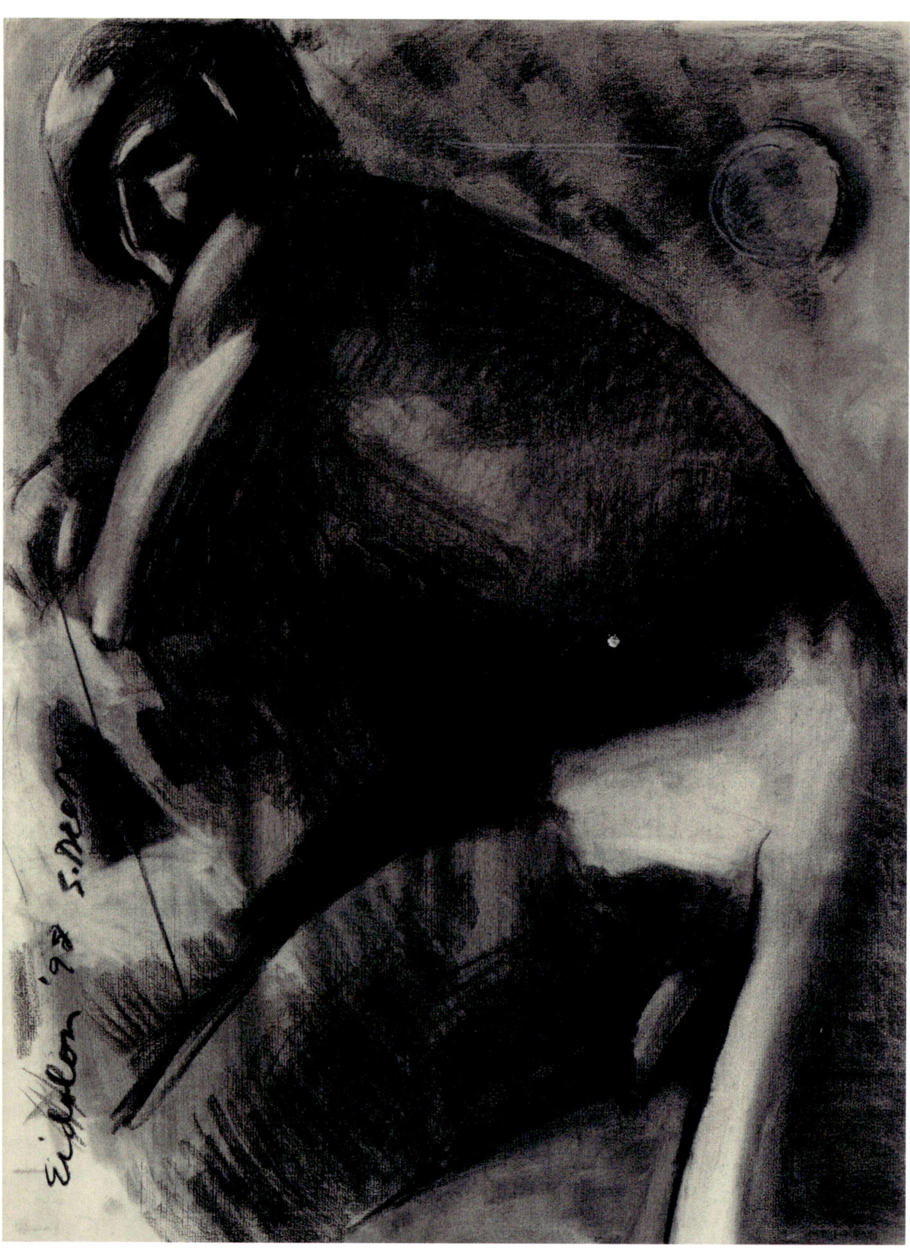

Salvatore Del Deo, *Eidolon,* 1998.
Charcoal on paper, 25 × 19 inches,
Gift of Salvatore Del Deo, 2003.

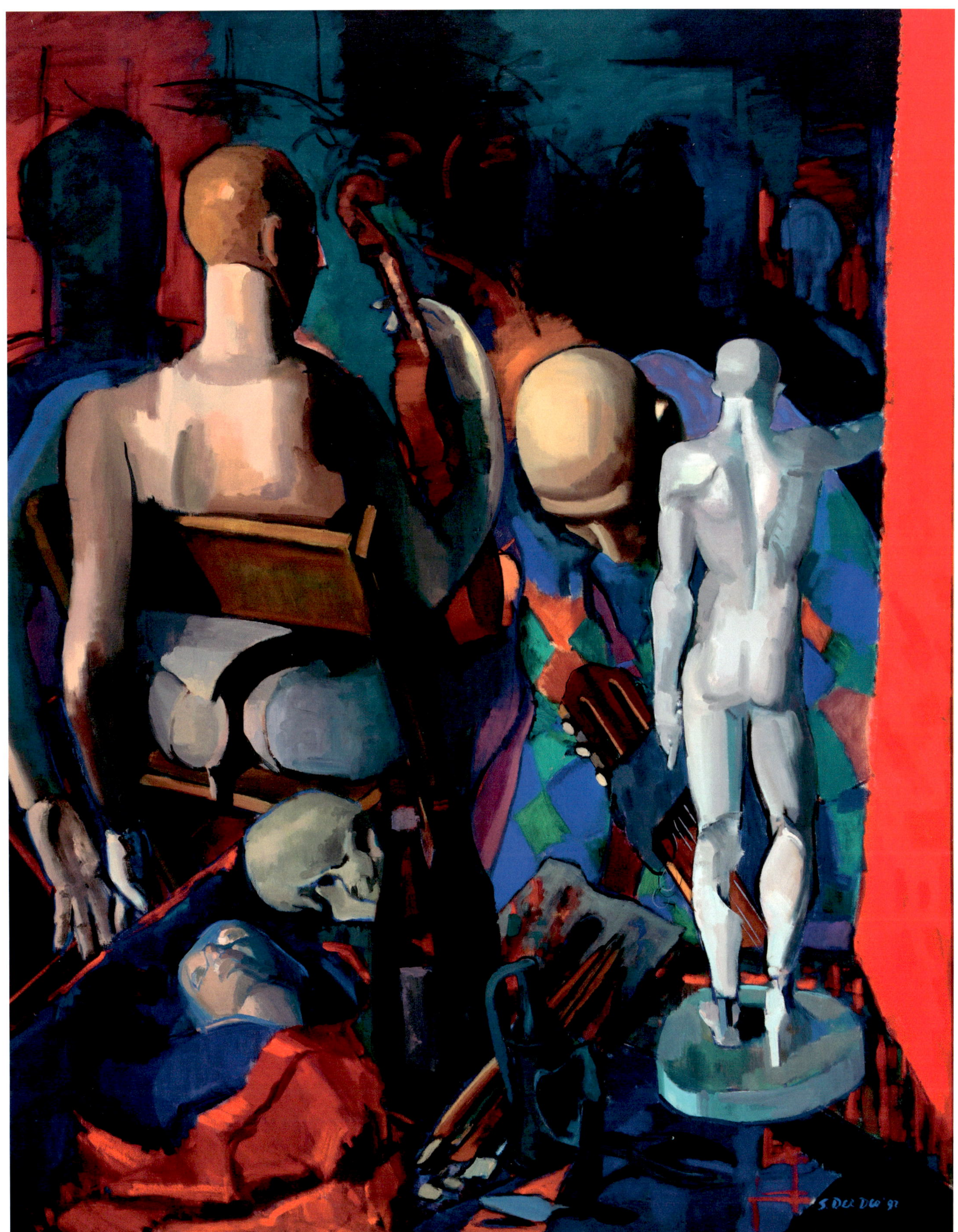

Salvatore Del Deo, *Studio Concept II*, 1992. Oil on canvas, 50 × 40 inches. *Gift of Salvatore Del Deo*, 2003.

ROBERT DOUGLAS HUNTER
(1928–2014)

Robert Douglas Hunter's world, similar to the studio where he worked in his Walpole, Massachusetts, home, was a tranquil place filled with old crockery, glass bottles, earthenware jugs, pewter and brass bowls, Chinese porcelain, dried hydrangeas, branches of red berries, and seashells, all of which eventually found a place in his beautifully composed paintings.

A Boston native, Hunter graduated from the Vesper George School of Art and studied in Provincetown with Henry Hensche and R. H. Ives Gammell. He spent thirty-one summers in Provincetown, where he fell in love with the dunes. Like his teachers, Hunter remained a realist, although early on he experimented with abstraction. He admired the realism of artists like William Morris Hunt, William Paxton, and other Boston School painters.

Yet Hunter's meticulously crafted and luminous still lifes are structured with a modern eye and an insightful understanding of the abstract elements of a composition—color, form, and balance. They are elegantly painted, balancing forms and unifying the color relationships. Although these paintings each have their own distinctive qualities, what is consistent is the way Hunter arranged the objects he chose to build a composition of shapes and colors. Bowls and bottles, vases, and fruit are unified into a harmonious whole

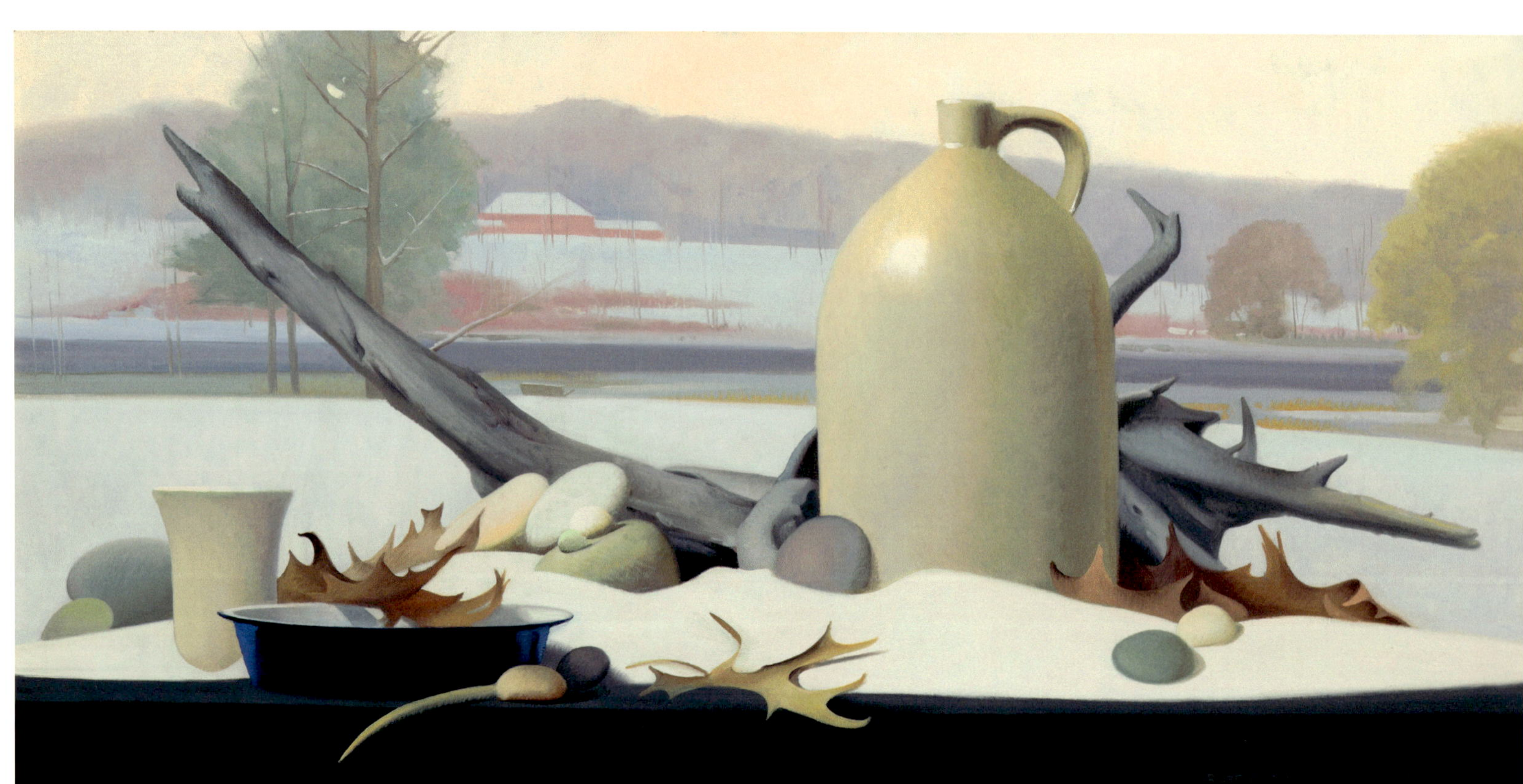

Robert Douglas Hunter, *Crockery, Driftwood and Snow*, 1990. Oil on canvas, 20 × 40 inches. *Gift of Elizabeth Hunter*, 1991.

and evoke a sense of calm that transports you to a place of serenity.

Three still lifes in the collection of the Cape Cod Museum of Art are beautiful examples of his work: *Crockery, Driftwood, and Snow* evokes a wintery sensation; *Arrangement with a Small Blue Bowl* captures the warmth of a country kitchen; and *In Honor of Frederick Waugh* is actually a still life with a framed painting by the marine painter as a background for a collection of shells and stones.

Hunter never tired of painting still lifes, which took days to complete. But when he painted landscapes outdoors, he worked quickly because of the ever-changing light. These works are softly painted in an impressionistic style, as in *Morning Haze*, in the museum collection. Several of Hunter's portraits are also in the museum collection, including *Fourteen, Jerry Irmer*, which is impeccably painted, similar to his still lifes.

Hunter's paintings are in the permanent collections of the Ackland Art Museum in Chapel Hill, North Carolina; the Chrysler Art Museum in Norfolk, Virginia; the Maryhill Museum in Goldendale, Washington; and the Michelson Museum of Art in Marshall, Texas. He has a gallery wing named in his honor at the Cape Cod Museum of Art, where his wife, Elizabeth Ives Hunter, was director for several years.

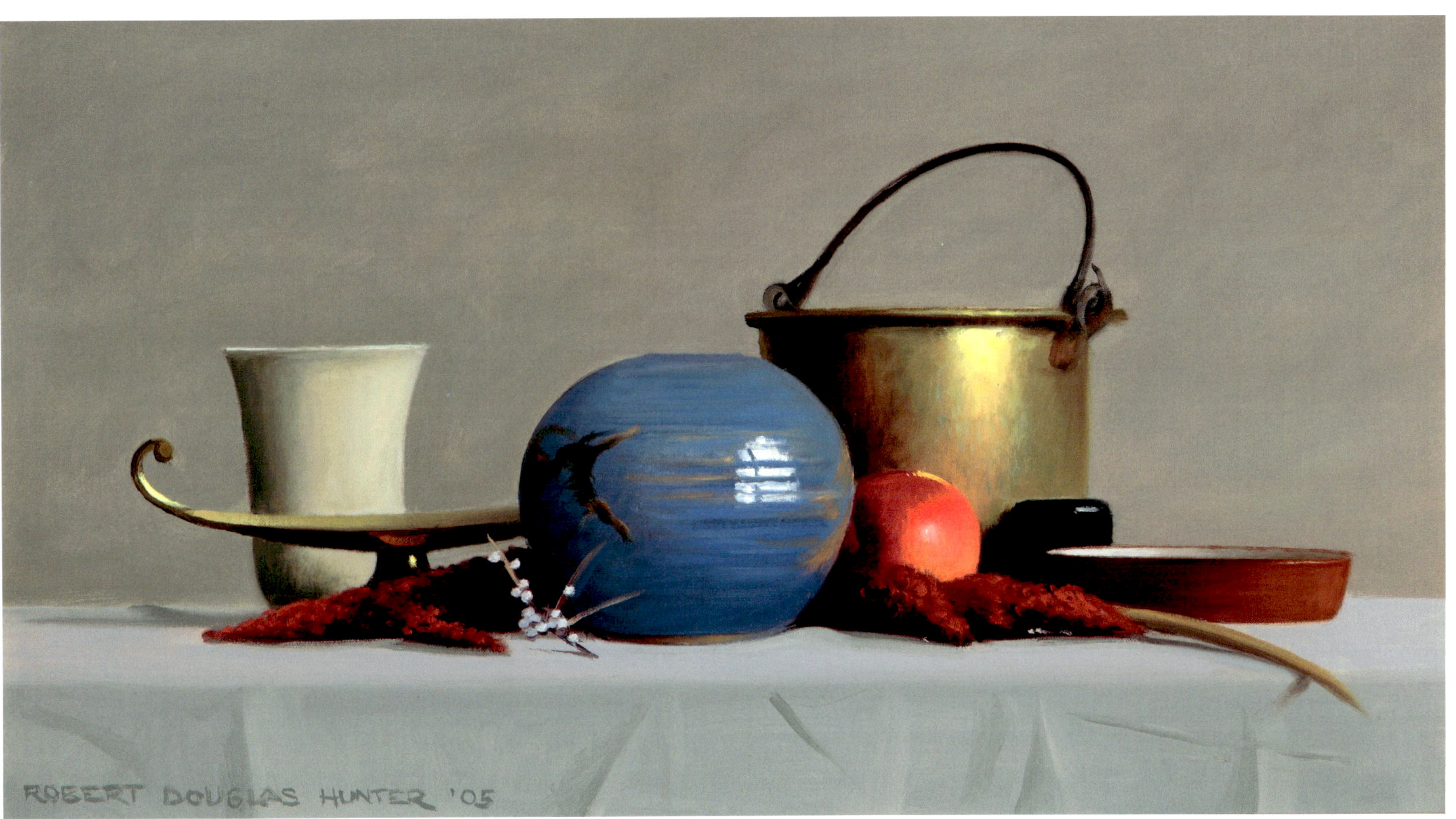

Robert Douglas Hunter, *Arrangement with a Small Blue Bowl*, 2005. Oil on canvas, 14 × 26 inches. *Gift of Sam and Hannah Vokey*, 2006.

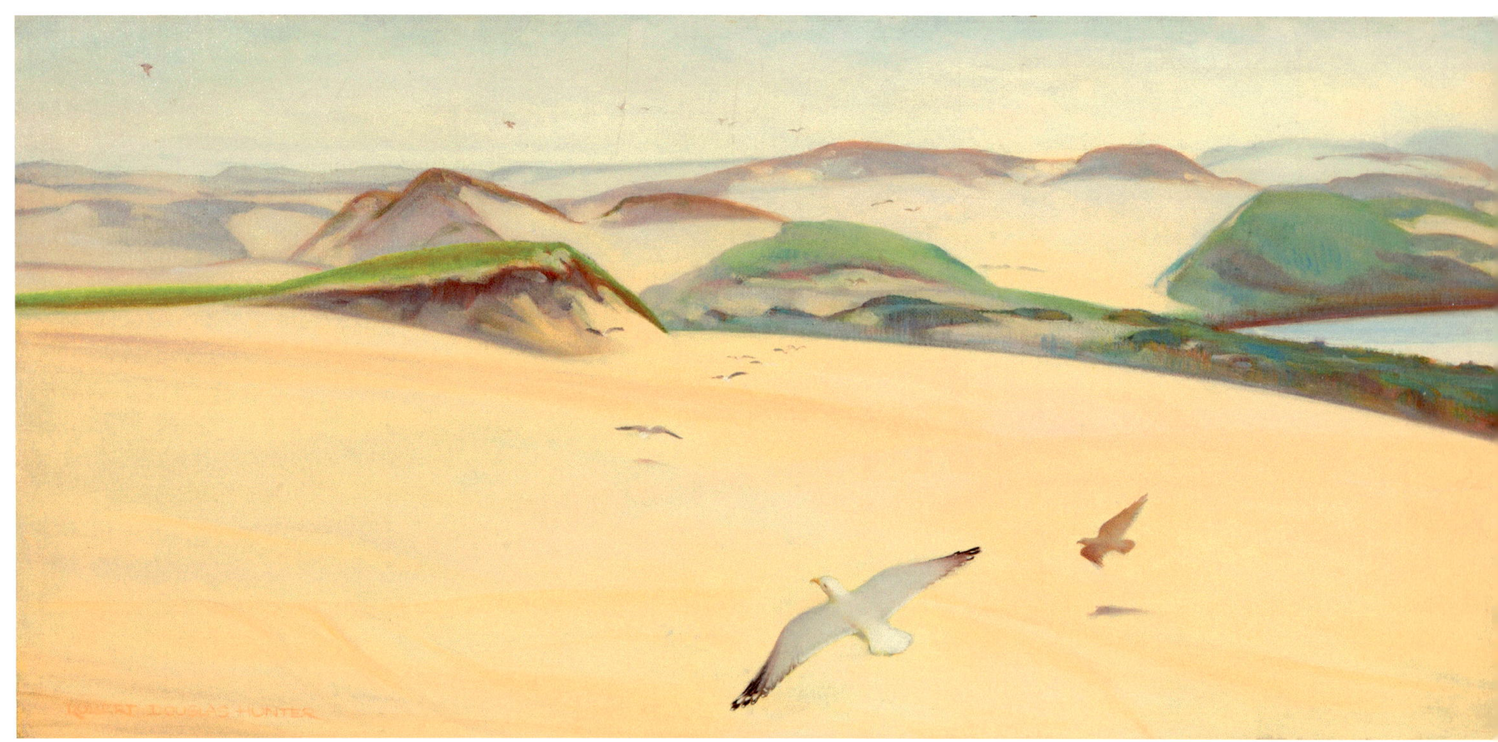

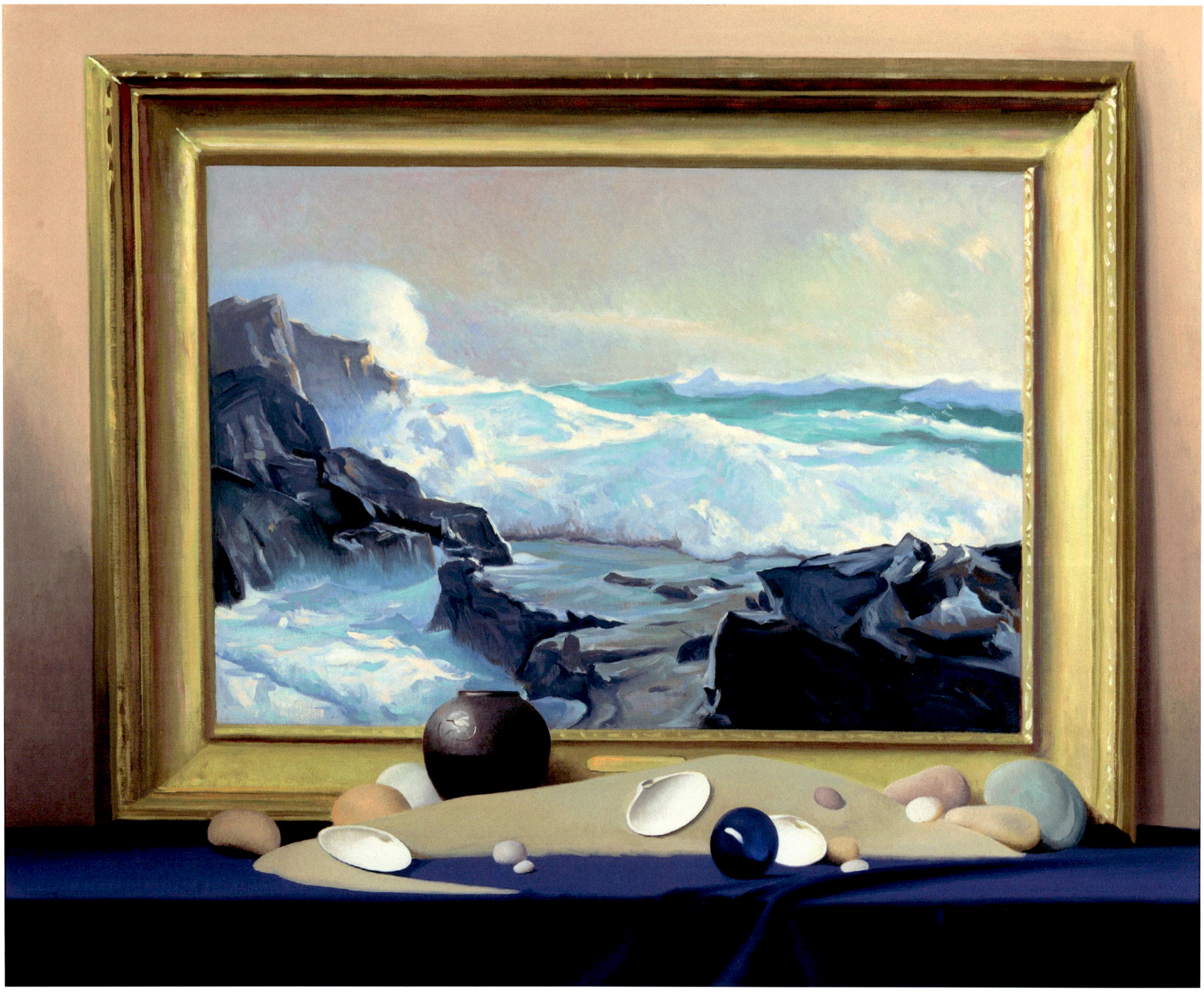

Robert Douglas Hunter, *In Honor of Frederick Waugh*, 1992. Oil on canvas, 36 × 46 inches. *Gift of Robert Douglas Hunter*, 1993.

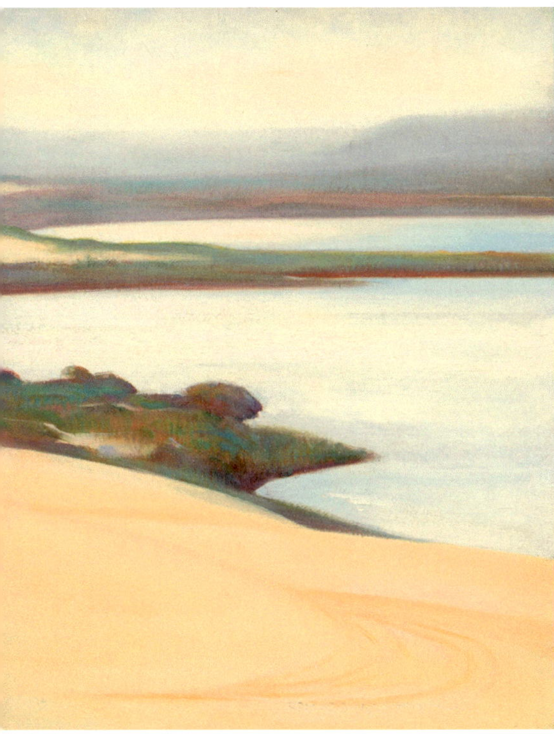

Robert Douglas Hunter, *Morning Haze*, circa 1952. Oil on canvas, 12 × 36 inches. *Anonymous gift*, 2003.

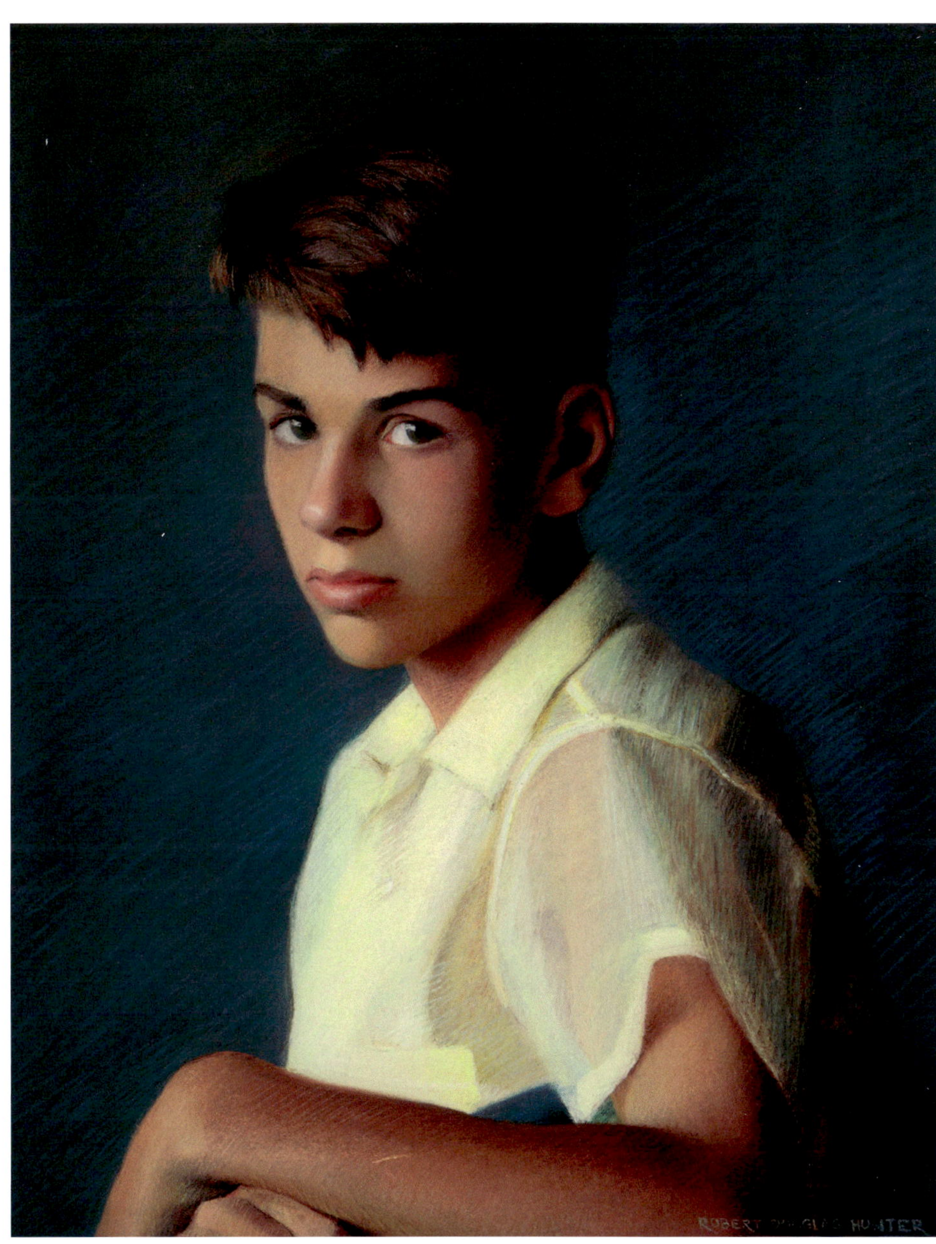

Robert Douglas Hunter, *Fourteen, Jerry Irmer*, mid 1950s. Pastel on paper, 22 × 17 inches. *Gift of Robert Douglas Hunter*, 2010.

PAUL RESIKA
(1928–)

Paul Resika began studying art as a child in New York. Important inspiration came from his early teacher Sol Wilson, and his studies in the mid-to-late 1940s with Hans Hofmann in New York and Provincetown. He abandoned his early abstract works in 1950 when he went to Europe—Paris, Rome, and Venice. He became enamored with traditional European painting. He found even impressionism was too modern for him at the time. In Paris he studied at the Académie de la Grande Chaumière, and then moved to Italy. He spent two years in Venice, where he studied the work of the eighteenth-century master painter Giovanni Canaletto, as well as the art of the Renaissance masters Titian, Tintoretto, and Paolo Veronese, and followed those traditions.

When he returned to America in 1953, abstract expressionism was in full swing and pop would soon take over, but Resika persisted in doing his more representational paintings. In this period, he was producing mostly subtly shaded and fluid landscapes, which show the influences of nineteenth-century painters, such as Camille Corot, and the twentieth-century Provincetown painter Edwin Dickinson.

In the 1970s, his colors brightened and in the 1980s, he began to simplify his objects to archetypal emblems set in flattened space. His paintings of Provincetown's piers depict simple structures of the buildings on MacMillan Wharf and the accompanying boats. *Provincetown Harbor,* a charcoal drawing with the towering Pilgrim Monument, and *Long Point and Black Roof*, an oil on paper of simple cottages lining the shore, both in the collection of the Cape Cod Museum of Art, are examples of his spare iconic images of the area. *Red Roof*, also in the museum collection, shows the brilliance of his colors, clearly indicating Hofmann's influence, which has remained with him throughout his career.

Although recognized for the buoyancy of his palette, Resika also claims the importance of the basic shapes of his subjects, which he pares down to the simplest geometric forms—those neat little houses in profile and those swishes of color that define his boats and piers. His paintings are often just a suggestion of a scene, but it is enough to spark a memory, evoke a mood, or illuminate a dream.

Resika has continued to be a part of the Provincetown art colony, where he has spent summers since the 1980s when not in Manhattan. The Cape is where he is inspired to paint his familiar iconic images of the area: piers, boats, cottages, flowers, figures on the beach, and lighthouses, which float in a sea of sparkling color. His buildings are constructed of flat planes and angled roofs. His brushwork is adventurous and expressionistic, gently picking up some of the gestures of the abstract expressionists. The forms are made up of a shorthand of strokes. If he eliminates the horizon, the objects glide in a sea of color, which catches fire and blazes across the painting. His loosely painted flowers, like his images of pickerels, sometimes verge on the abstract.

Resika's works are in collections of major museums, including the Metropolitan Museum of Art, the Museum of Modern Art and the Whitney Museum of American Art in New York; and the National Museum of American Art in Washington, DC.

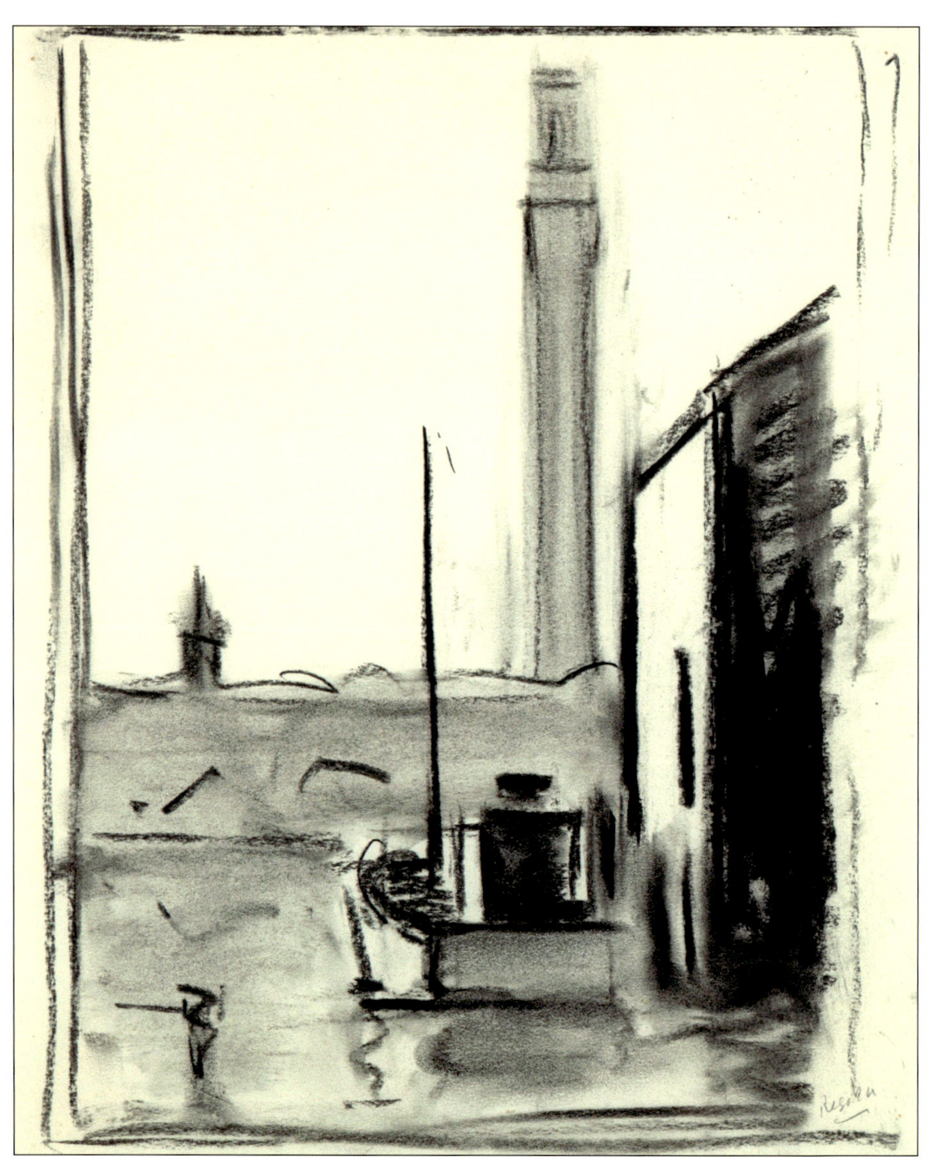

Paul Resika, *Provincetown Harbor*, 1986. Charcoal on paper, 17 × 14 inches. *Anonymous gift*, 2009.

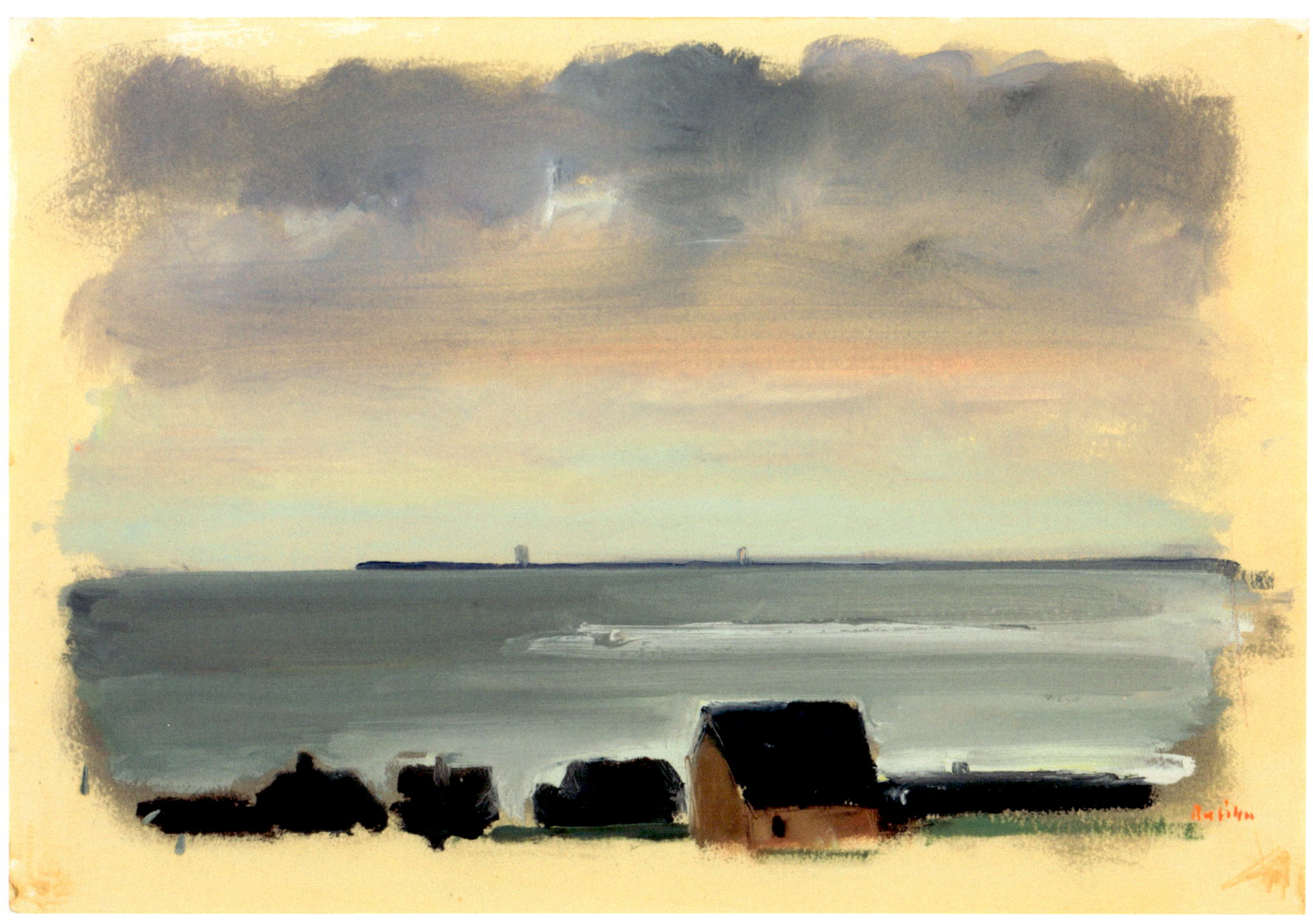

Paul Resika, *Long Point and Black Roof*, 1988. Oil on paper, 15 × 22¾ inches. *Gift of Gilbert and Joyce Franklin*, 1991.

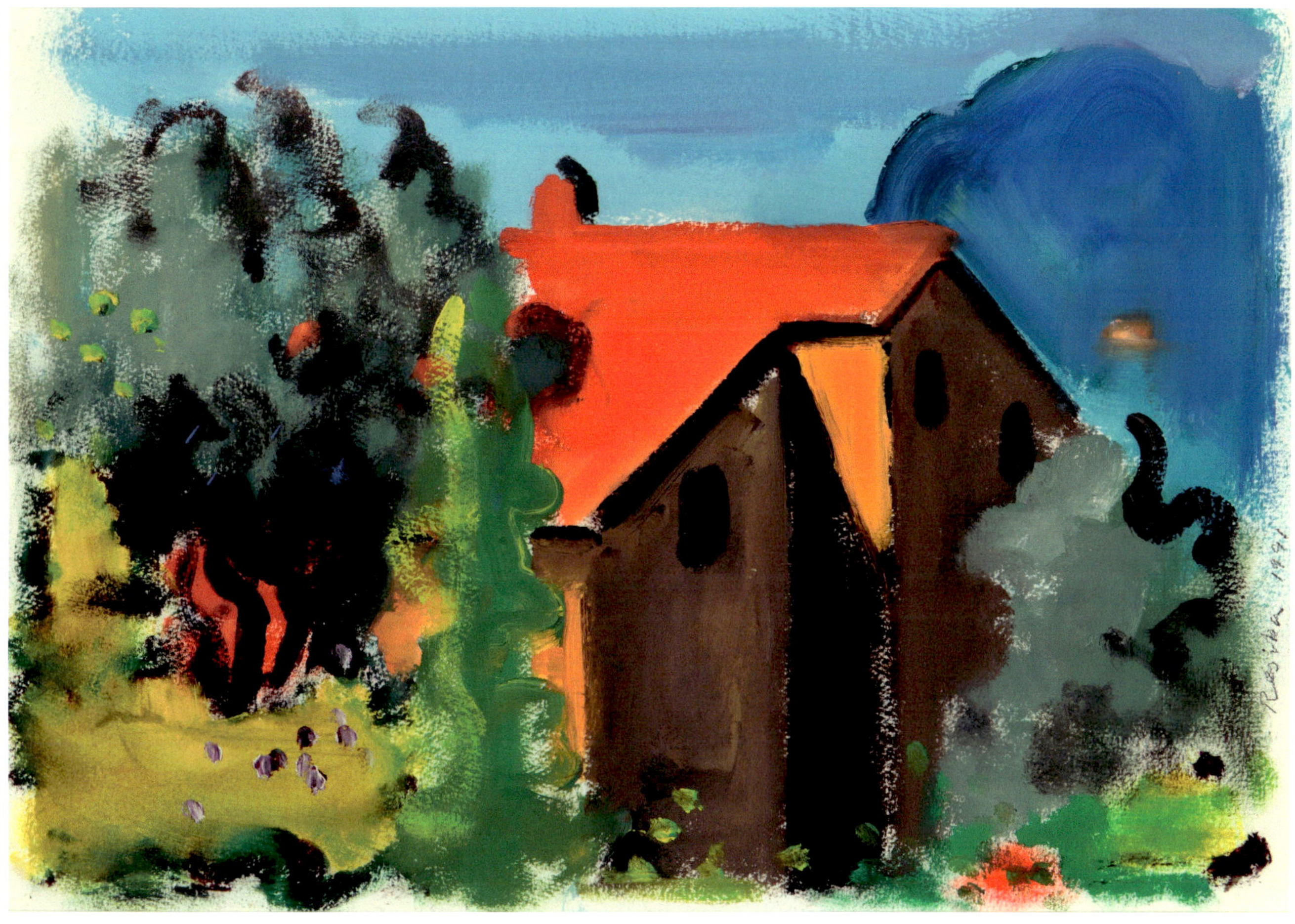

Paul Resika, *Red Roof*, 1991. Oil on paper, 14 × 21 inches. *Anonymous gift*, 2009.

DEL FILARDI
(1929–)

With degrees in physical education and dance, Del Filardi has translated her interest in movement and choreography into corten steel and bronze sculptures of birds. From her home on Cape Cod, overlooking the Pamet River in Truro, she spends a great deal of time birdwatching, with a special interest in the birds' musculature and powerful movement. Her sculptures of feathered creatures, although often constructed in hard metal, seem to take flight with wings spread, or appear ready to move forward as they hesitate on their perch. Her *Northern Bald Eagle* and *Heron*, in the Cape Cod Museum of Art collection, are more than just realistically represented; they have a power and energy that command respect.

Filardi's sculptures present formidable creatures; her work evokes their strength and endurance. Her series on endangered birds captures the beauty of the various species, which makes us long for their preservation. Filardi also has created mixed-media sculptures from objects found in her scavenging adventures, hiking the marshes and trails around her home.

Before her career as an artist, Filardi earned degrees in health and physical education from the State Teachers College in Cortland, New York, and her master's degree in dance and education from Columbia University. She taught dance and physical education for twenty years, at first taking up sculpture as a hobby, and later devoting herself full time to her art.

She has exhibited her work at the Smithsonian National Academy of Science in Washington, DC, and the Boston Museum of Science.

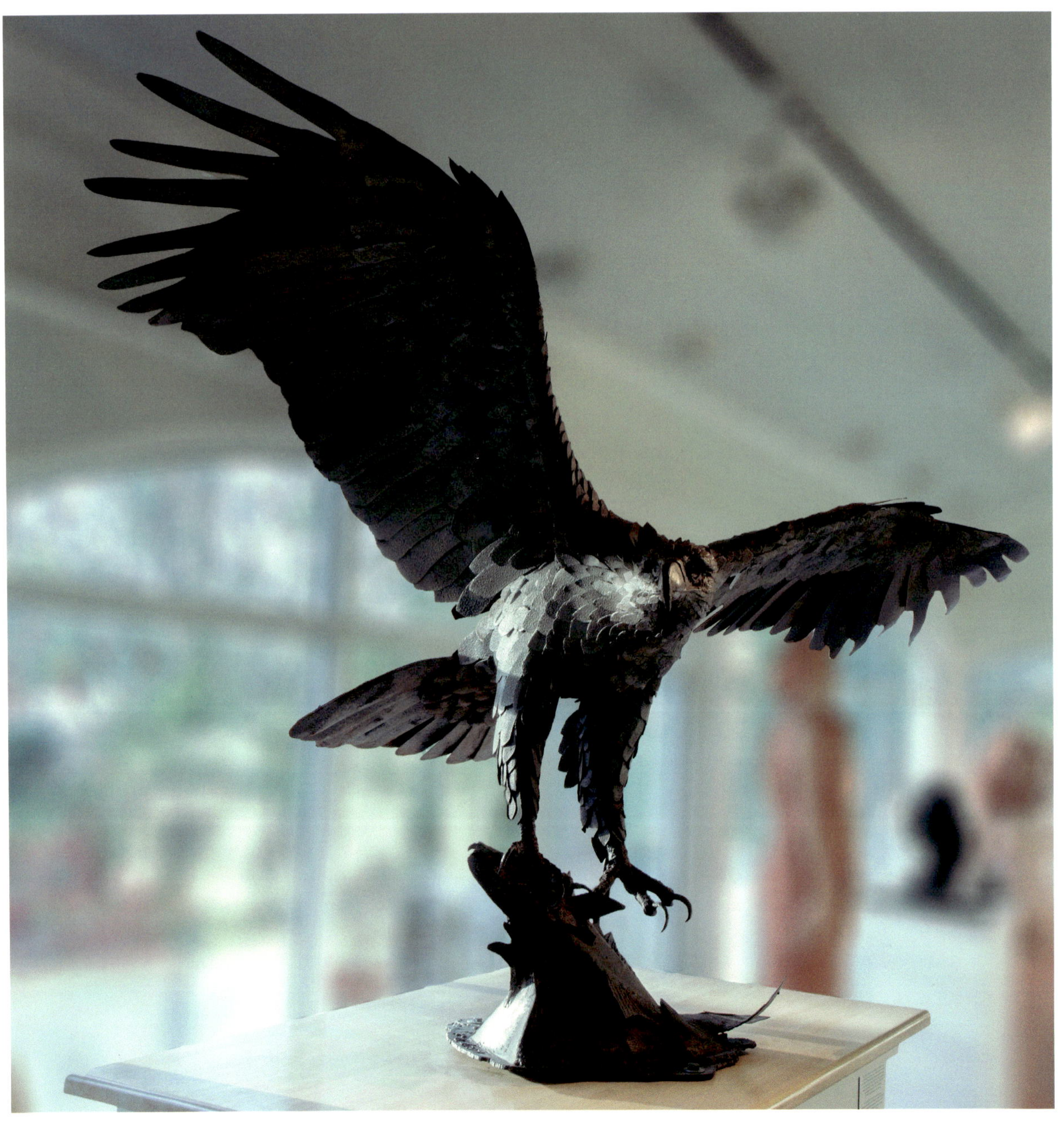

Del Filardi, *Northern Bald Eagle (Female)*, 1983. Corten steel, 56 × 84 inches.
Gift of Henry and Helen Keller, Dr. Linda B. Miller, Harriet F. Rubin, and Other Friends, 1993.

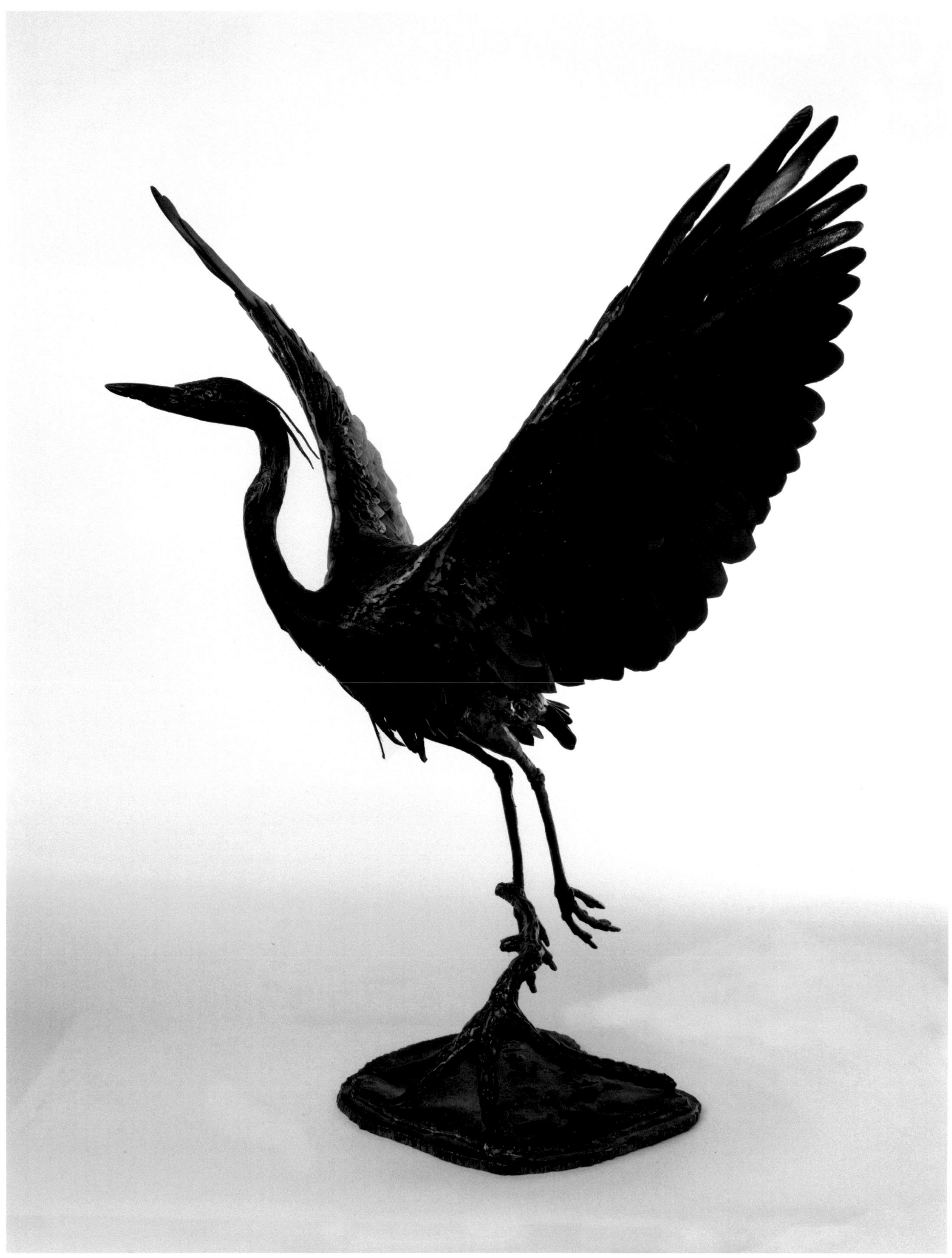

Del Filardi, *Heron,* 1996. Corten steel, 23½ × 20½ × 23½ inches. *Gift of Constantine Filardi*, 2009.

ELSPETH HALVORSEN
(1929–)

Provincetown has bred several generations of artists, as the sons and daughters who are imbued with talent and inspiration follow in their parents' or grandparents' paths. The Vevers-Halvorsen family is one example. For Elspeth Halvorsen, the matriarch of this family, Provincetown holds a primary place as the inspiration for her box constructions. The town, where she has been a summer resident since the 1950s, is often represented by found objects from the area or ones she constructs.

Halvorsen, who was born in Purdy, New York, met painter Tony Vevers when they were painting on Monhegan Island in Maine. They married, and in 1964, Halvorsen and Vevers bought the Provincetown house that she lives in today from abstract expressionist Mark Rothko. In 1988, when her husband retired from teaching art at Purdue University, Provincetown became their year-round home. Vevers, Halvorsen, and their daughter, artist Tabitha Vevers, have been active in the Provincetown art colony for many years and their work is represented in the Cape Cod Museum of Art collection.

Halvorsen's boxes are inhabited by elements from the real world, and are either directly connected to the object itself or have a symbolic meaning. Her works can be viewed as miniature stage sets and often represent what she sees around her in Provincetown, but are not limited to that. Her concerns are universal. Miniature ladders, swings, balance scales, female torsos, tiny Pilgrim Monument models, mirrors, iron scrolls, aluminum, and scavenged wood occur again and again in her work. There are a multitude of reference points and many interpretations. An idea for an artwork may be sparked by an object she finds. She has used remnants of piers, horseshoe crab shells, a bird skull, or a piece of driftwood she finds on the beach in her box constructions.

The circular shape, as sun and moon, is often a central image in her work, as with *Sun Eclipse*, in the Cape Cod Museum of Art collection. In this construction, the suggestion of a seascape is framed by a circle. An elliptically shaped sun rises above a horizon, and is reflected below, seemingly setting into a scalloped sea. The various layers of materials and the play of light on them encourage a variety of interpretations.

Halvorsen's rich imagination is sparked not only by Provincetown, but also by social and political concerns, which are played out in her works. Philosophical and psychological explorations are embodied in assemblages that are often haunting and almost always mysterious; they hold deep feelings and her constant search for meaning.

Halvorsen has received a Massachusetts Cultural Council Award and the Emily Lowe Award, and her work may be found in many private and public collections, including the Greater Lafayette Art Association and Museum in Lafayette, Indiana, the Provincetown Art Association and Museum, and the Ward Eggleston collection in New York, New York.

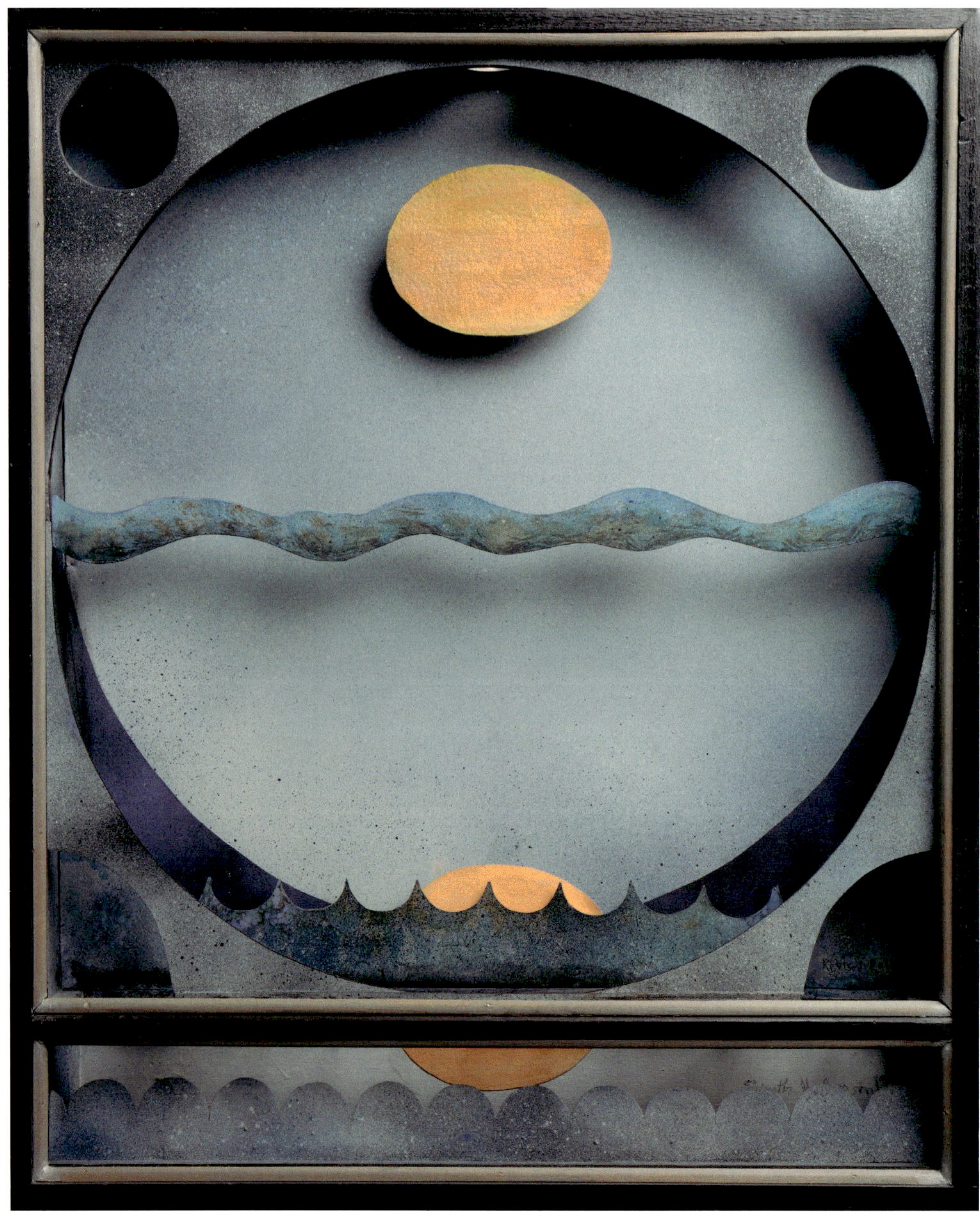

Elspeth Halvorsen, *Sun Eclipse*, 1993. Mixed media sculpture, 23½ × 19½ × 4 inches. *Gift of Elspeth Halvorsen*, 2015.

JOYCE JOHNSON
(1929–2014)

Joyce Johnson had a long history on Cape Cod. She first arrived with her parents in 1929, the year she was born. Her parents bought a summer place in North Eastham, and each summer they would travel to the Cape from their home in Concord, Massachusetts.

She studied sculpture for two years in Spain in the 1950s, and earned a degree in sculpture at the School of the Museum of Fine Arts in Boston. Since the mid-1960s, she lived on the Cape full time and was devoted to the natural world, which was a constant inspiration for her art. As founder of the Truro Center for the Arts at Castle Hill, Johnson's position in the art community became part of the Cape's cultural history.

Sculpture had fascinated Johnson since childhood. Before she was ten, she was whittling. And up until her death, she continued to carve wood and stone, model clay, and paint. Her favorite woods were poplar, linden, mahogany, and walnut. Inspiration could be a Provincetown dune, a weed, a flower, or a figure, yet most of her pieces were honed down to simplified forms. Her wood and bronze works are both figurative and abstract. In the Cape Cod Museum of Art collection are two bronzes: the representational, yet smoothed and simplified, *Woman with Hat,* and *Reclining Figure,* which is abstracted into cubist planes.

The many years Johnson spent time in the Provincetown dunes enhanced her connection to nature. She had the opportunity to live in one of the dune shacks, where artists go to experience an ascetic life and seclusion among the mountains of sand in the Cape Cod National Seashore. Because of these interests and experiences, the natural world was a continual influence on her work, which covered an impressive range of materials, themes, images, forms, and subjects. Her raku *Birds in Flight*, also in the museum collection, is an expression of Johnson's love of nature.

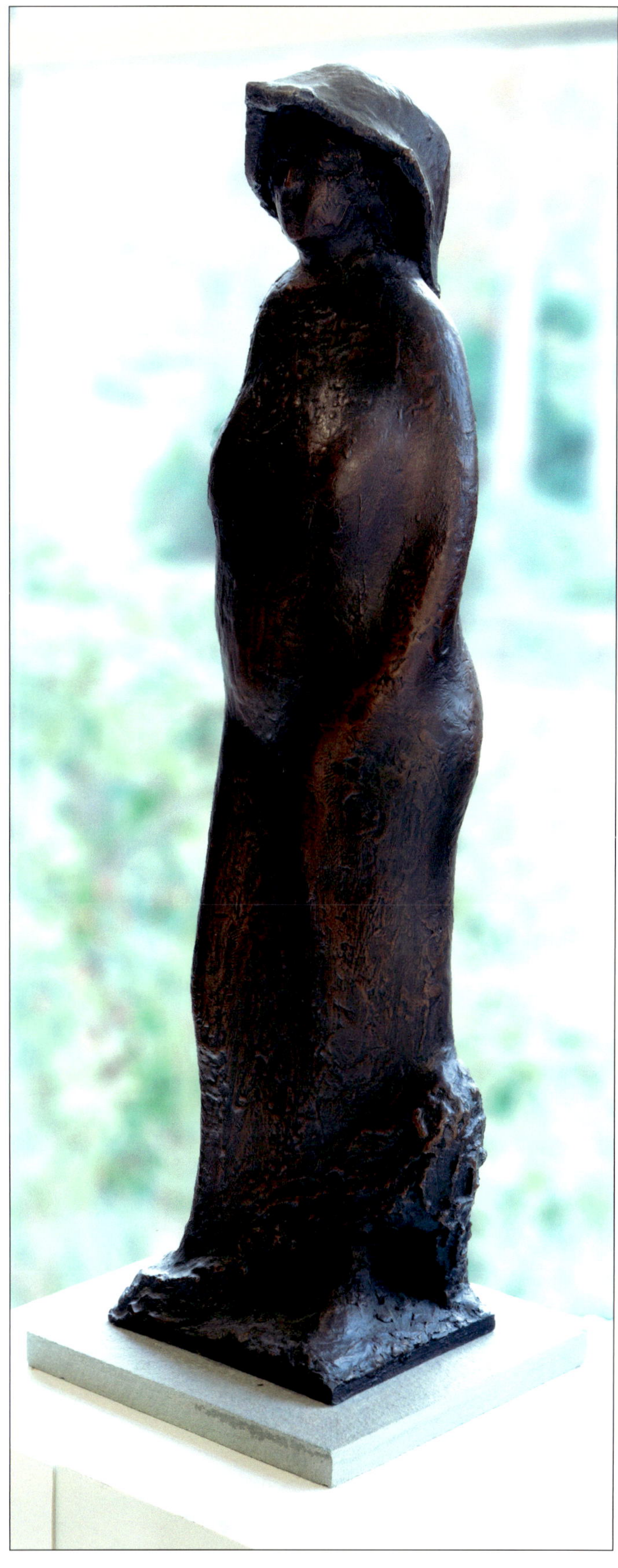

Joyce Johnson, *Woman with Hat*, 2009. Bronze, 34 × 8 × 9 inches. *Museum purchase from proceeds from the Joyce Johnson Sculpture Fund*, 2009.

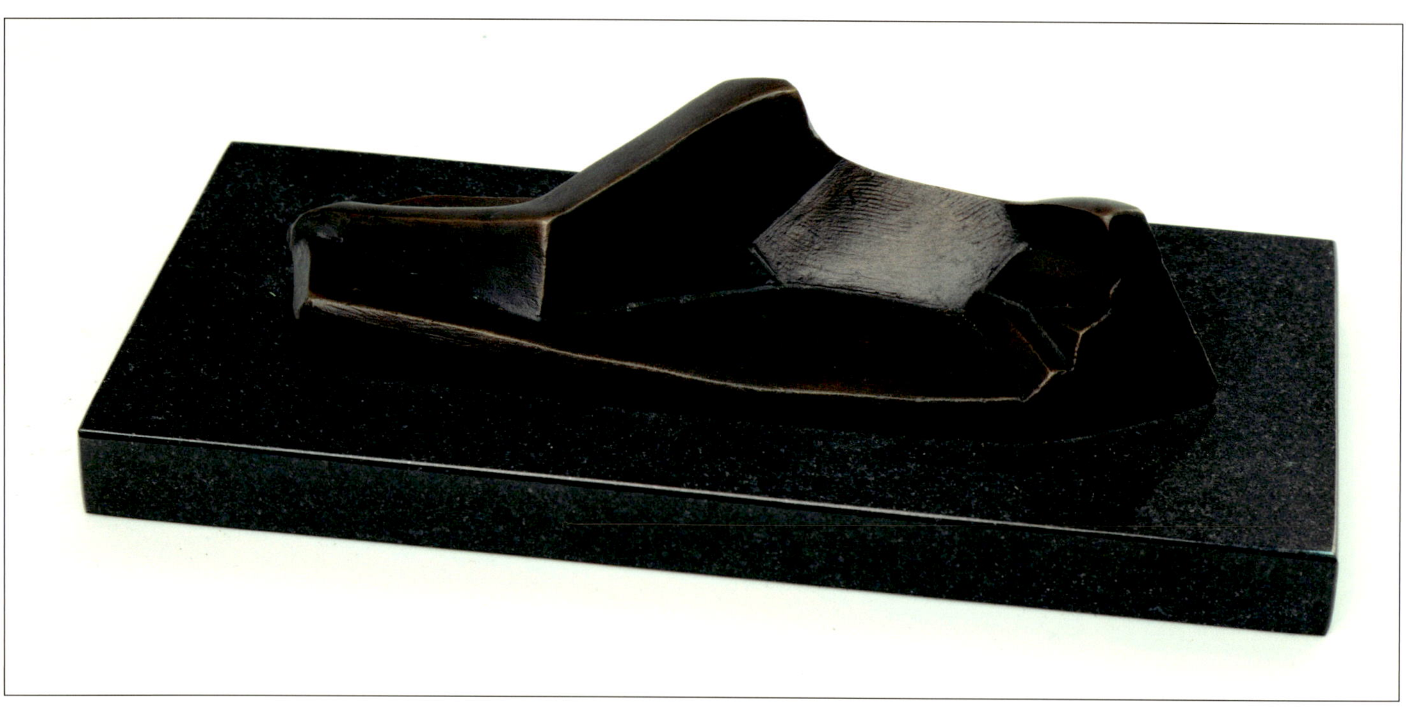

Joyce Johnson, *Reclining Figure* (edition of 10), n.d. Bronze on granite, 9½ × 4½ × 3 inches. *Gift of Ann Harrison*, 2009.

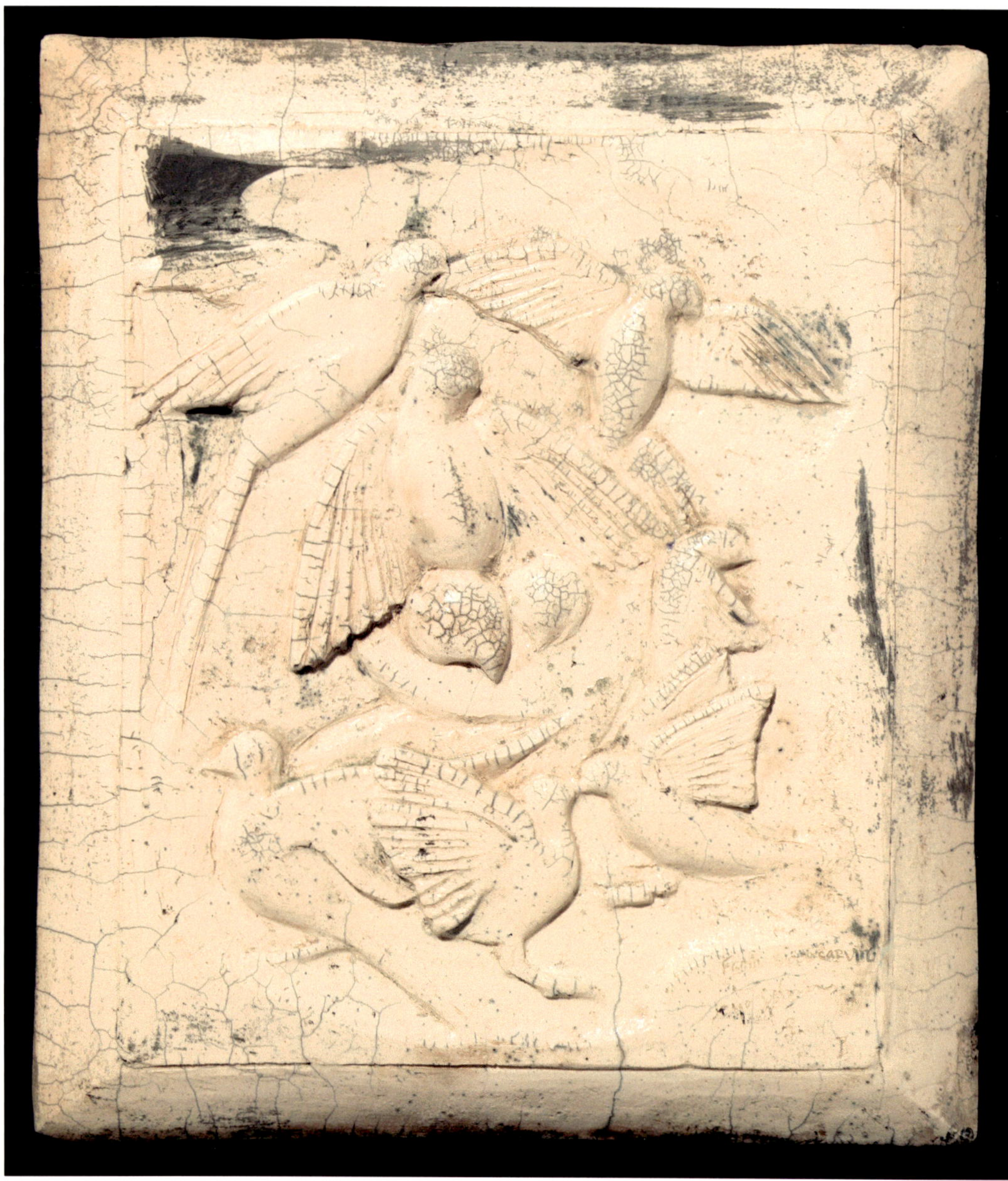

Joyce Johnson, *Birds in Flight*, n.d. Raku, 15½ × 14 inches. *Gift of Dr. Linda B. Miller in memory of Joyce Johnson & Robert Douglas Hunter*, 2014.

HAYNES OWNBY
(1929–2001)

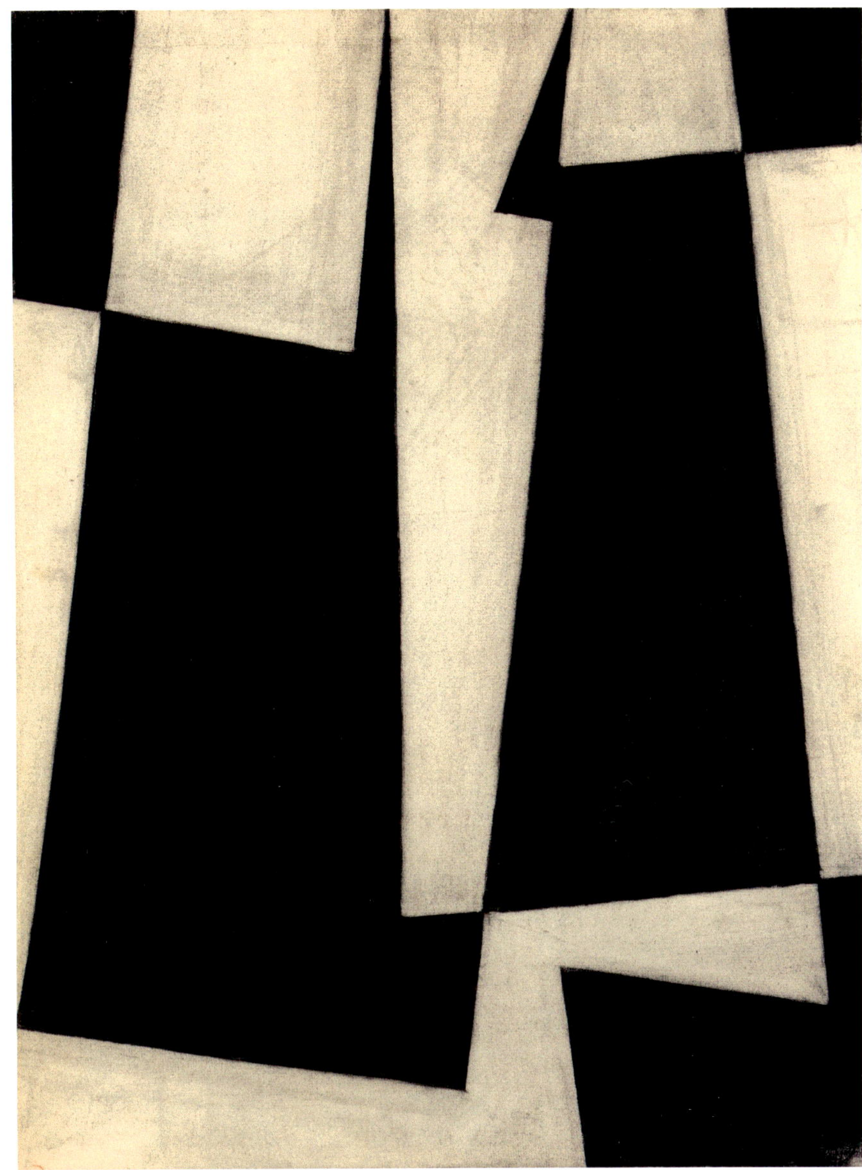

Haynes Ownby, *Untitled*, 1952. Charcoal on paper, 24¾ × 19 inches. *Gift of Joann Heiser, Estate of Haynes Ownby*, 2004.

Even before Haynes Ownby studied with Hans Hofmann, he was interested in abstract art. Born in Dallas, Texas, he studied art at Southern Methodist University in Dallas, and early on was attracted to the works of Piet Mondrian and Pablo Picasso.

Ownby first met Hofmann in 1951 in Provincetown and studied with him in New York and Provincetown from 1952 through 1955. Although influenced by Hofmann's approach to the use of space, light, rhythm, movement, and his legendary concept of "push and pull," Ownby, like all of his teacher's students, took his own approach to abstract art. He found another of Hofmann's students, Myron Stout, particularly inspirational, and like him, Ownby explored a hard-edge geometric approach in his work. *Untitled, 1952 (Geometric Drawing)*, in the Cape Cod Museum of Art collection, shows the strong influence that Stout had on him.

Although, similar to Stout, Ownby did considerable work in black and white, as in *Quintet (Black and White)*, in the collection, many of his paintings are animated with brilliant color, such as *Homage to a Crop Circle*. Ownby's precise forms—rectangles, squares, triangles, jagged shapes, arcs, and wide and narrow bars—are used for the tension they create and to express movement. These shapes, which on their own have an emotive quality, vibrate in complex patterns and jangling effects, and are dramatically depicted in *Fugue in World War II*. His work is a lot about rhythm, which he related to music—jazz in particular—and to dance, as in rock and roll.

Ownby spent many years in Provincetown off and on between travels in Europe, a time in Taos, New Mexico, and time in Austin, where he earned his MFA at the University of Texas and wrote his thesis, "Movement, Rhythm and Epiphanies." Finally, he spent the last twenty years of his life in the art colony where Hofmann had played such an important role in inspiring him.

Ownby was awarded grants from the Richard Florsheim Art Fund and the Gottlieb Foundation. His work is in the collections of the Dallas Museum of Art and the El Paso Museum of Art in Texas, the Provincetown Art Association and Museum, and the AT&T collection.

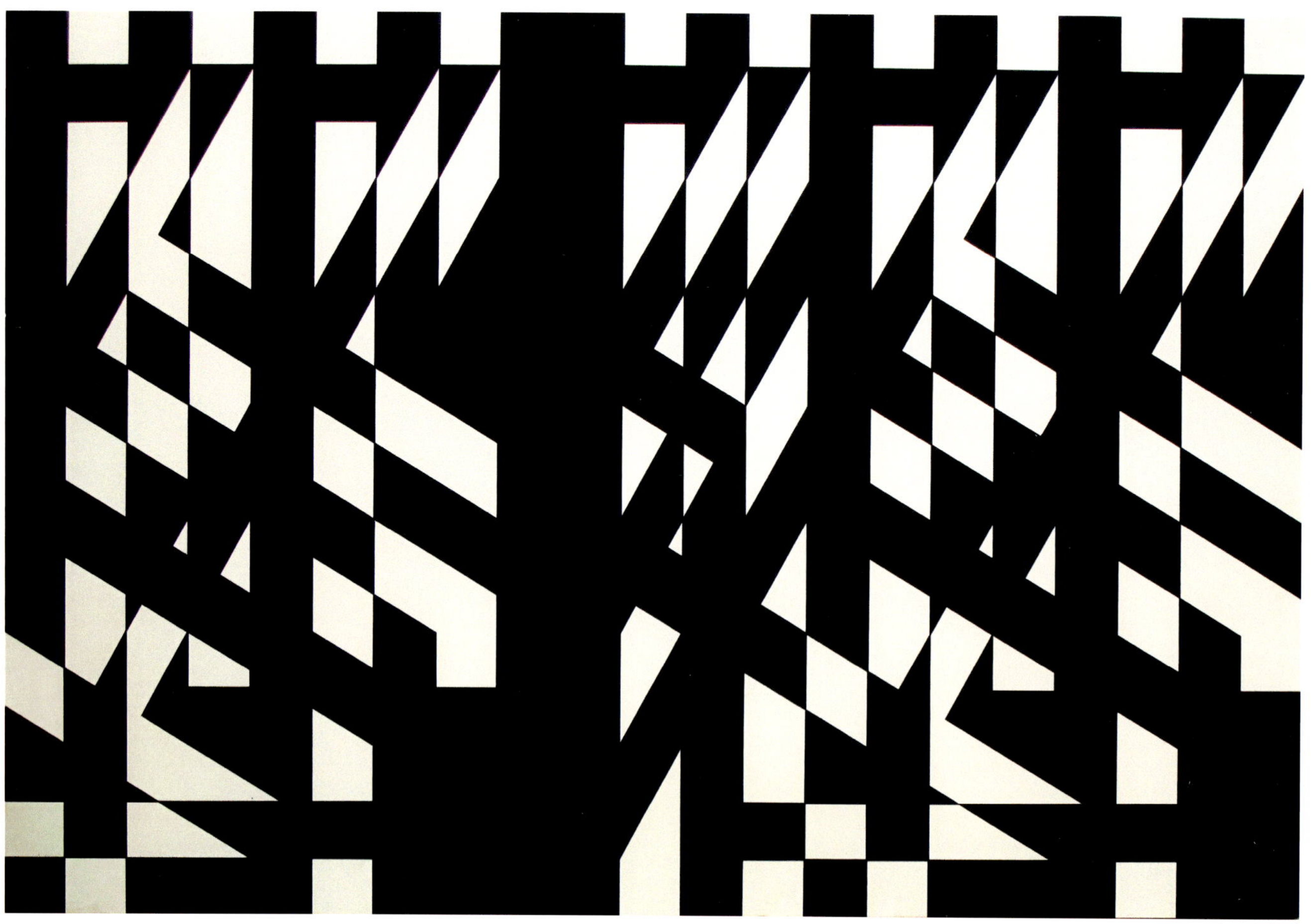

Haynes Ownby, *Quintet,* 1984. Acrylic on masonite, 48 × 96 inches. *Gift of Joann Heiser, Estate of Haynes Ownby*, 2004. *Photo courtesy of Christy King.*

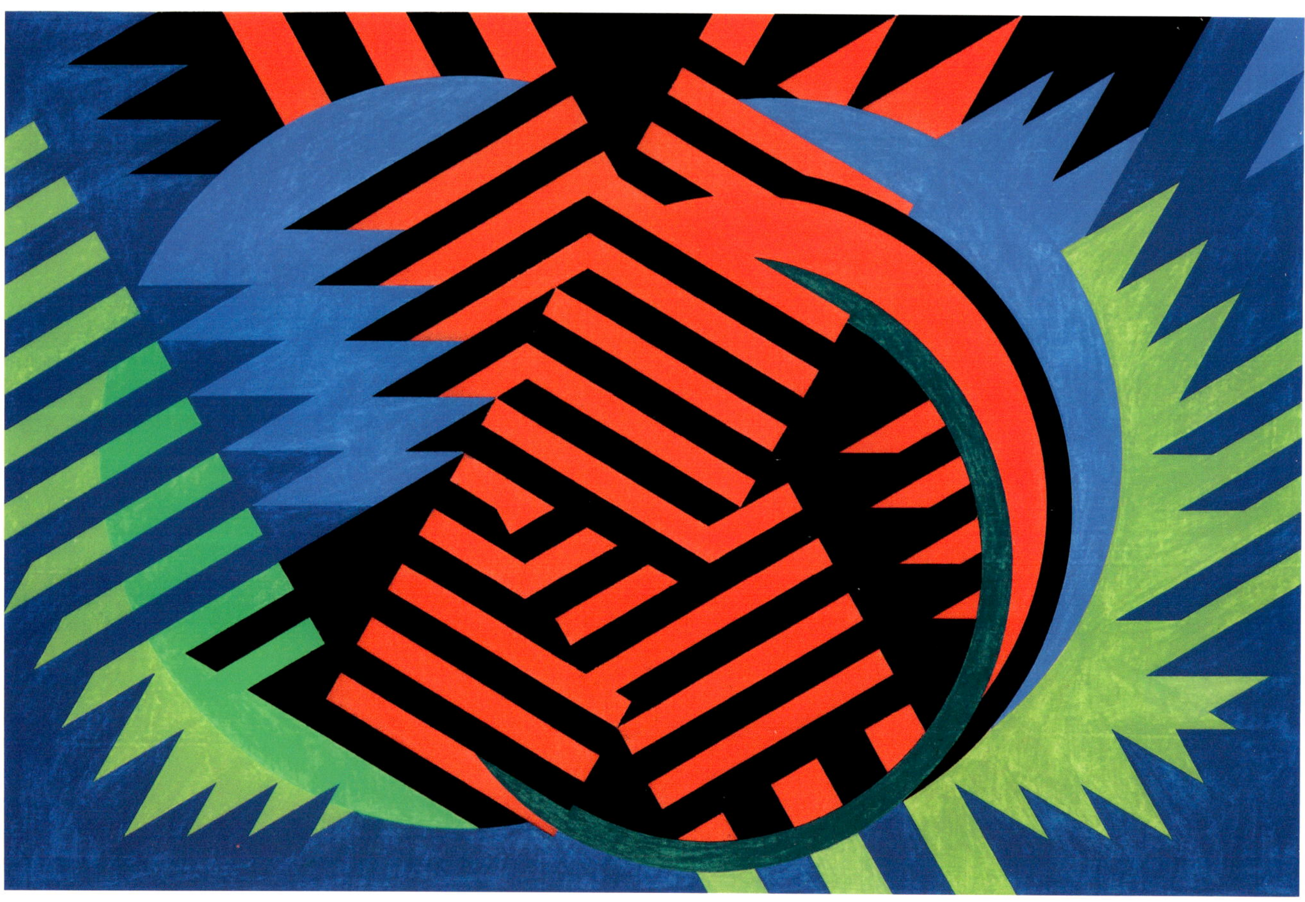

Haynes Ownby, *Rock and Roll*, 1990. Gouache and pencil on paper, 16 × 24 inches. *Gift of Myrna Harrison*, 1995.

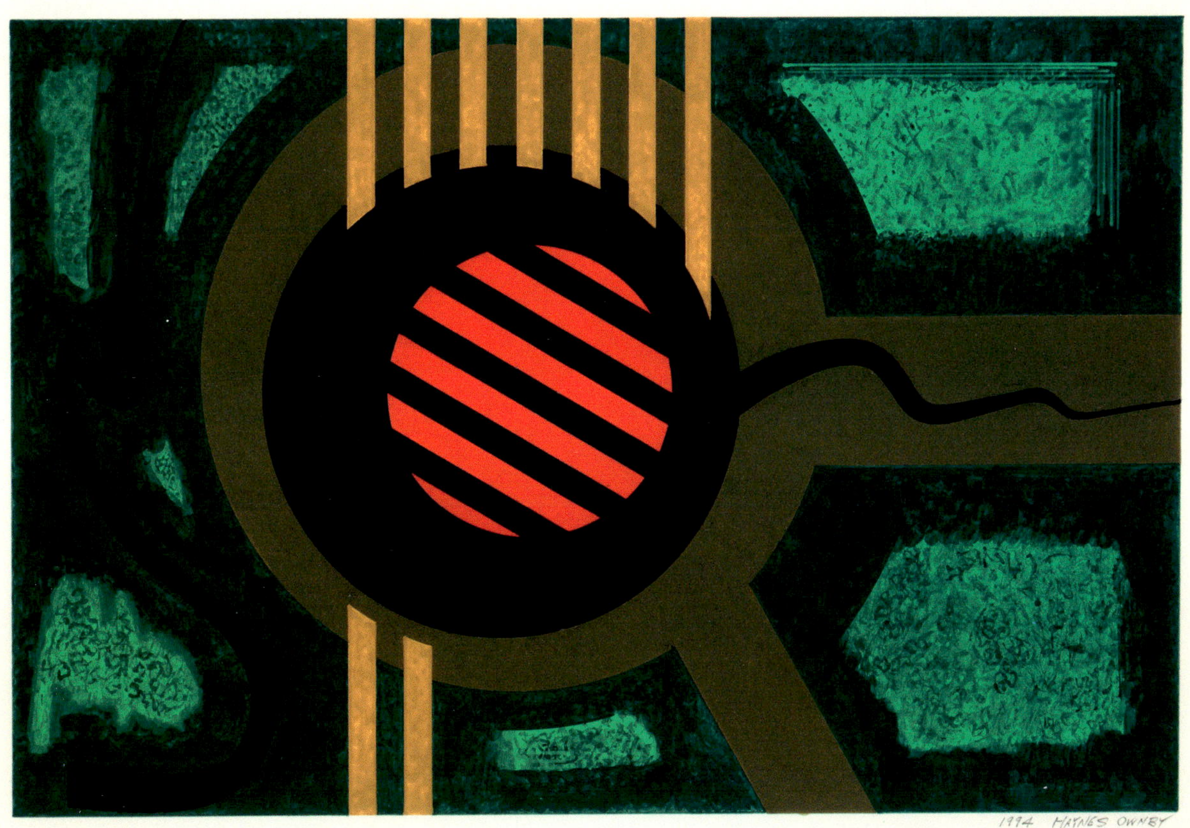

Haynes Ownby, *Homage to a Crop Circle*, 1994. Gouache on paper, 8 × 12 inches. *Gift of Myrna Harrison*, 1995.

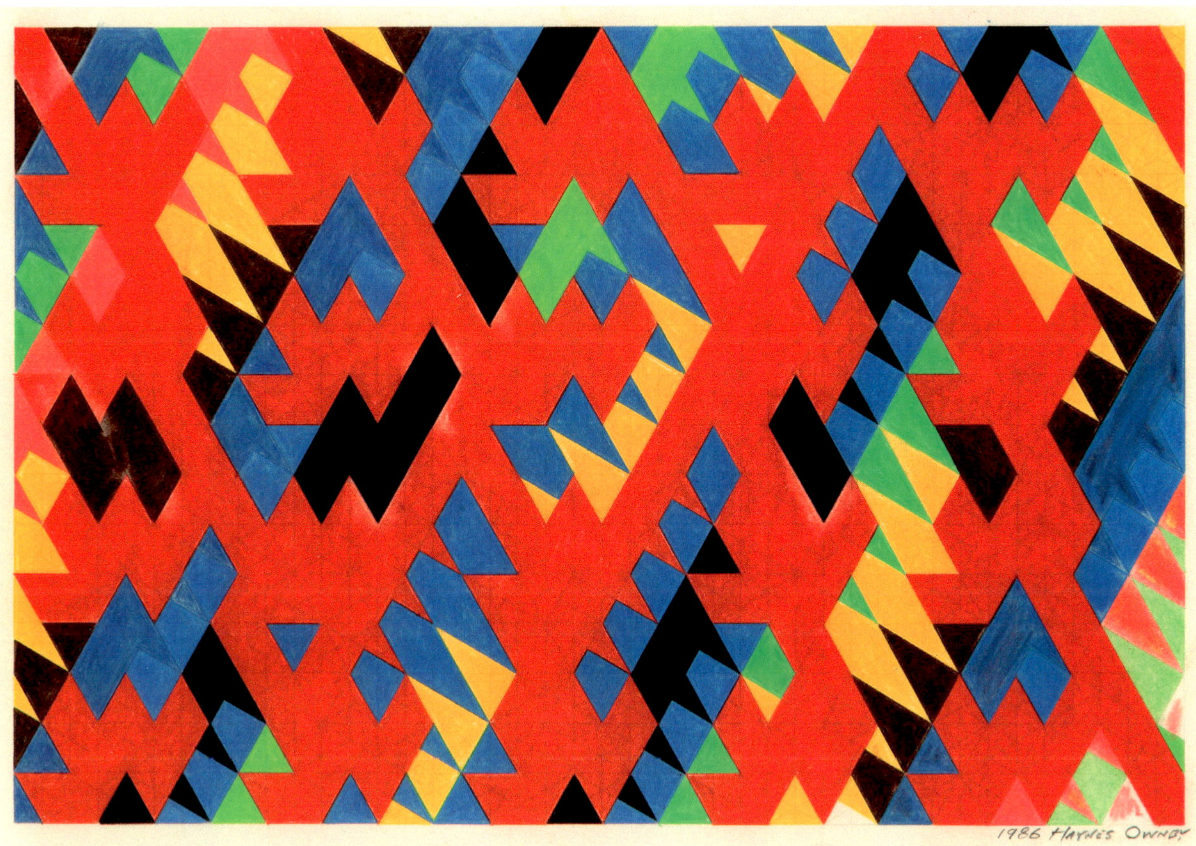

Haynes Ownby, *Fugue in WWII*, 1986. Colored pencil on paper, 12½ × 9¾ inches. *Gift of Joann Heiser, Estate of Haynes Ownby*, 2004.

JUDITH SHAHN
(1929–2009)

Like her father, Ben Shahn, Judith was a representational artist, working in several mediums: painting, drawing, and printmaking. Although she painted with her father when she was a child, she was not drawn to the social realist style or message that he espoused. She studied with Moses Soyer and also at Olivet College in Michigan, and received a bachelor's degree in anthropology and archaeology at Mexico City College in 1949. She did graduate work in art history at the Institute of Fine Arts at New York University.

Judith was born in Paris, but lived in New York City most of her early adulthood. She spent many summers in Truro, in the house on Cape Cod that her parents bought in 1924, and, lived there year-round from 1969 on. Her love for this Cape Cod house was related to her happy early childhood there, when her father and Walker Evans were in Truro photographing the local scene.

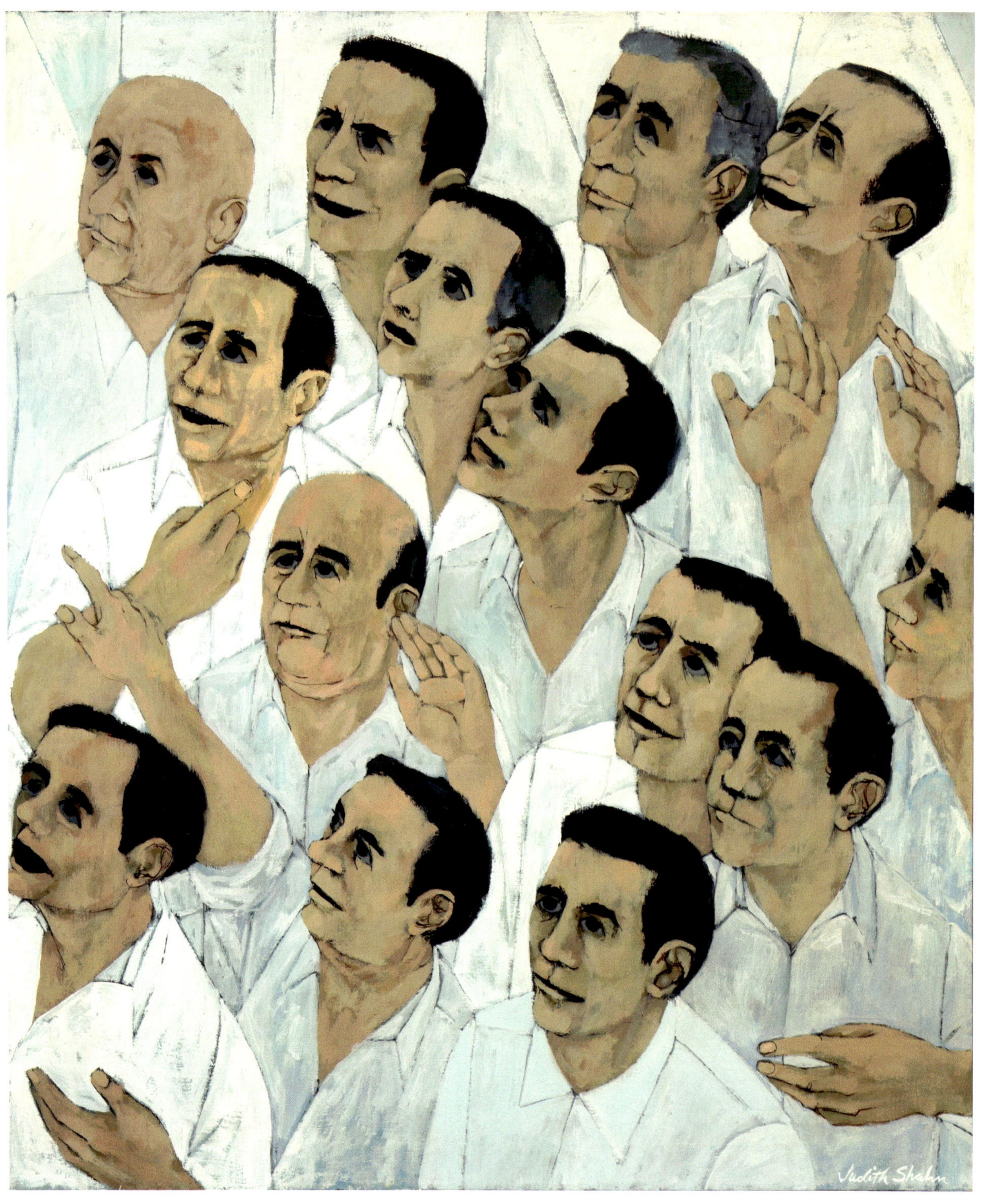

Judith Shahn, *Bleachers*, 1957. Oil on linen, 40 × 34 inches. *Gift of the Estate of Judith Shahn*, 2010.

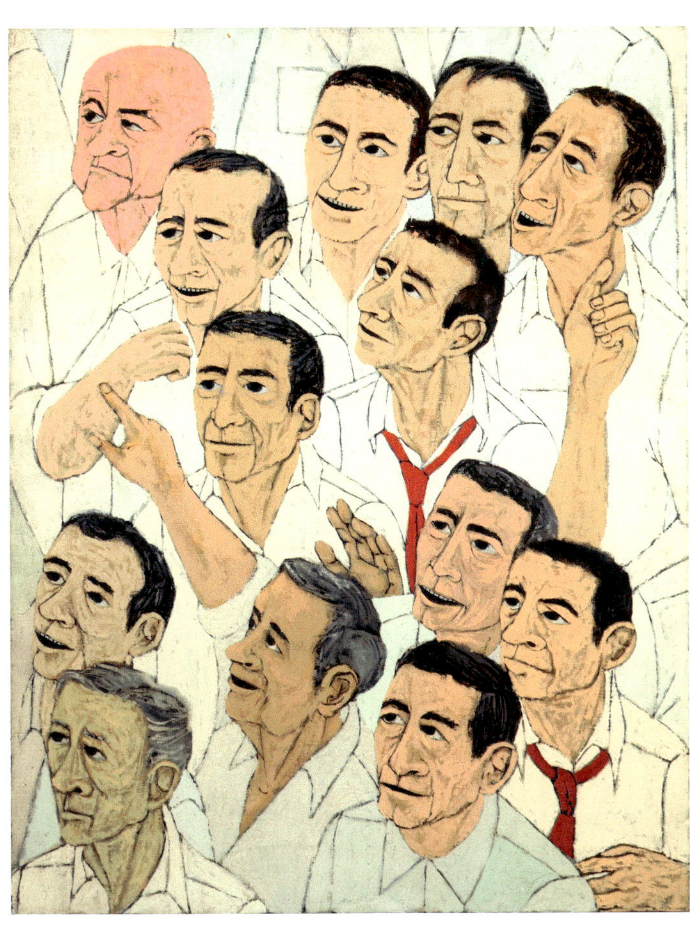

Judith Shahn, *Study for Bleachers*, n.d. Oil on Canvas, 28 × 22 inches. *Gift of the Estate of Judith Shahn,* 2011.

Although Shahn adopted her father's political persuasion, her work was not concerned with social or political commentary. Instead, her paintings are simple, straightforward images of ordinary life and include portraits, still lifes, city scenes, and landscapes.

That said, *Bleachers,* a 1957 oil painting (and its study) in the Cape Cod Museum of Art collection, depicts a dense group of men with differing facial expressions, reminiscent of her father's painting style and subject matter. If painted by the elder Shahn, these might be white-shirted socialists seemingly transfixed by a speaker, gazing out, yet responding with hand gestures at what they are hearing. For the daughter, they could be representing a political scene that she saw as a child, or they may merely be a group of men intensely viewing a sporting event. Although there are distinct personalities presented here, the painting style tends toward a flattening of forms, and the similarity of all the men's shirts create almost a flat, patterned backdrop for the faces.

Her silkscreen prints, more than two hundred of which are in the museum's collection, portray everyday people, settings, and objects flatly rendered, some simply composed, as in *Small Skiff* and *Still Life with Paints* and others neatly

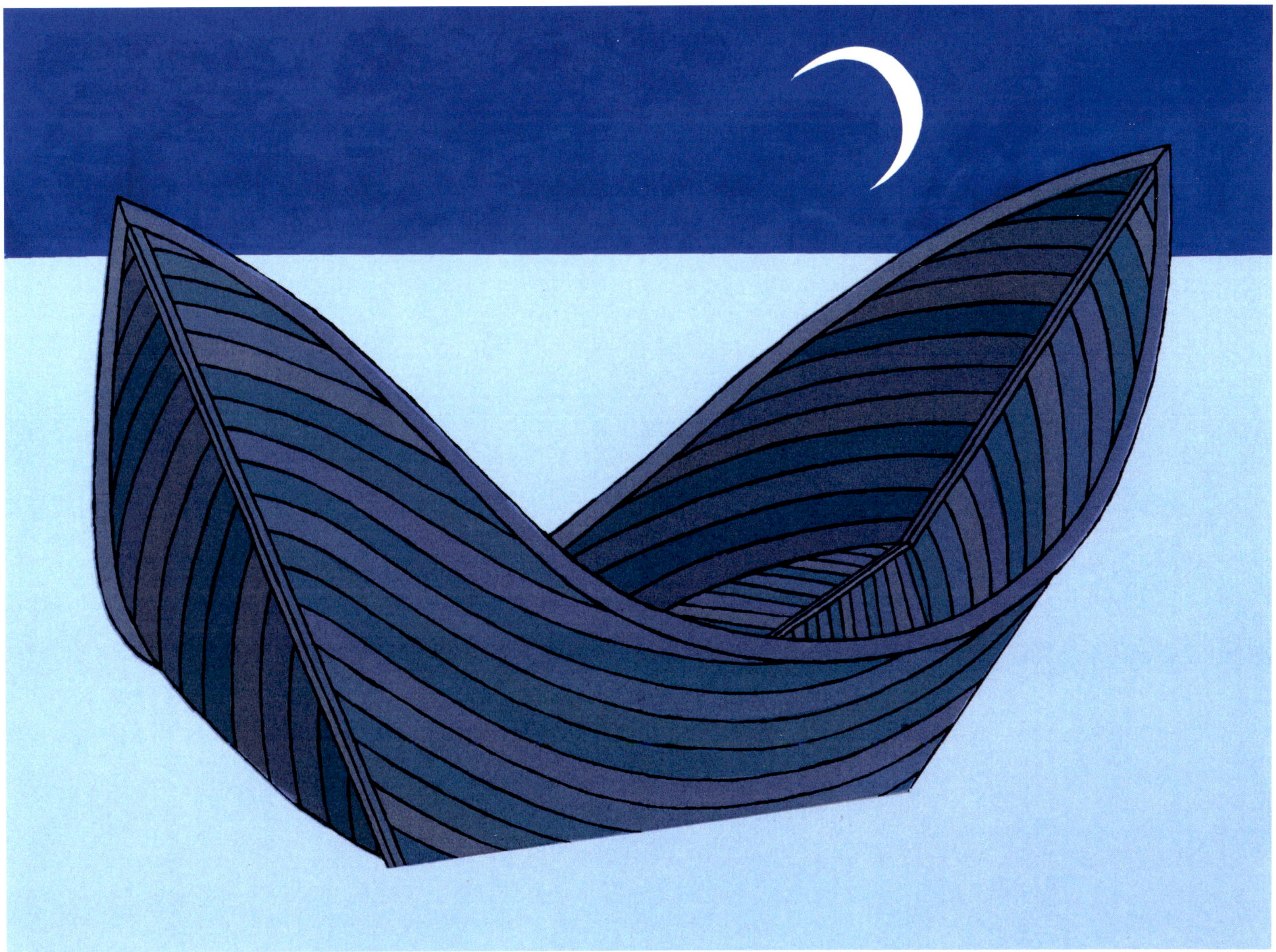

Judith Shahn, *Small Skiff* 82/90, n.d. Silkscreen on paper, 11 × 16 inches. *Bequest from the Estate of Judith Shahn*, 2011.

patterned. *Café* and *Woman & Cushions* show a reference to Will Barnet. Her subjects include houses decorated with flower boxes, gardens, a bucket of clams, vases of flowers, kitchen jugs and pitchers (*Kitchen Shelf*), and porches. *Striped Tablecloth* is a fine example of her porch views. There is a quiet about many of these images, a sense of time frozen. The graphic aspect of her precise draftsmanship is well suited to her prints. For years, she contributed drawings to the *New Yorker*, as well as *Harper's*, the *Nation*, and *Gourmet*.

Shahn's artwork may be found in several public collections, including the Newark Museum in New Jersey, Carnegie-Mellon University in Pittsburgh, and the Drackett Fine Art Collection in Cincinnati, Ohio.

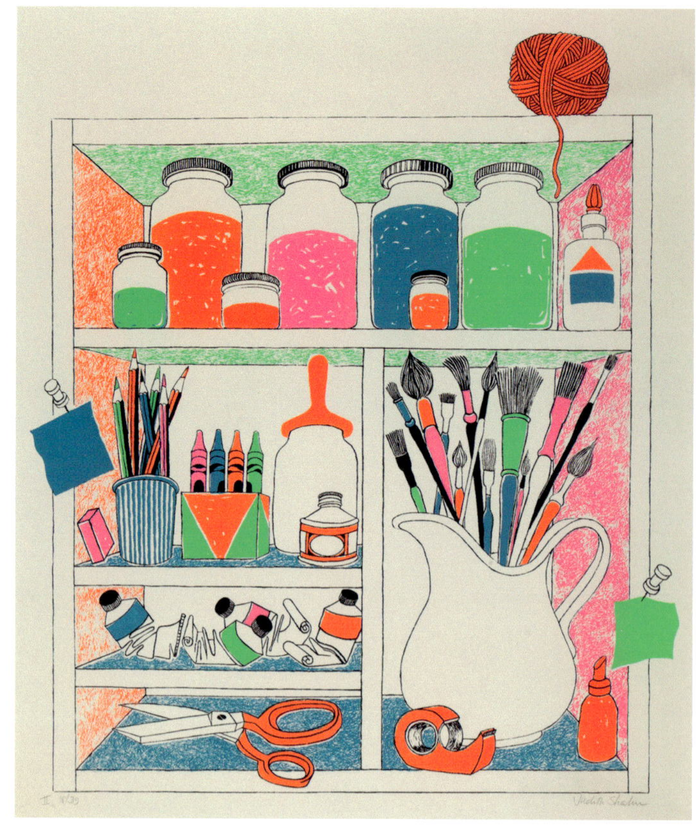

Judith Shahn, *Still Life with Paints II* 18/39, n.d. Silkscreen on paper, 23 × 20 inches. *Bequest from the Estate of Judith Shahn*, 2011.

Judith Shahn, *Woman & Cushions* 13/110, n.d. Silkscreen on paper, 4 × 6 inches. *Bequest from the Estate of Judith Shahn*, 2011.

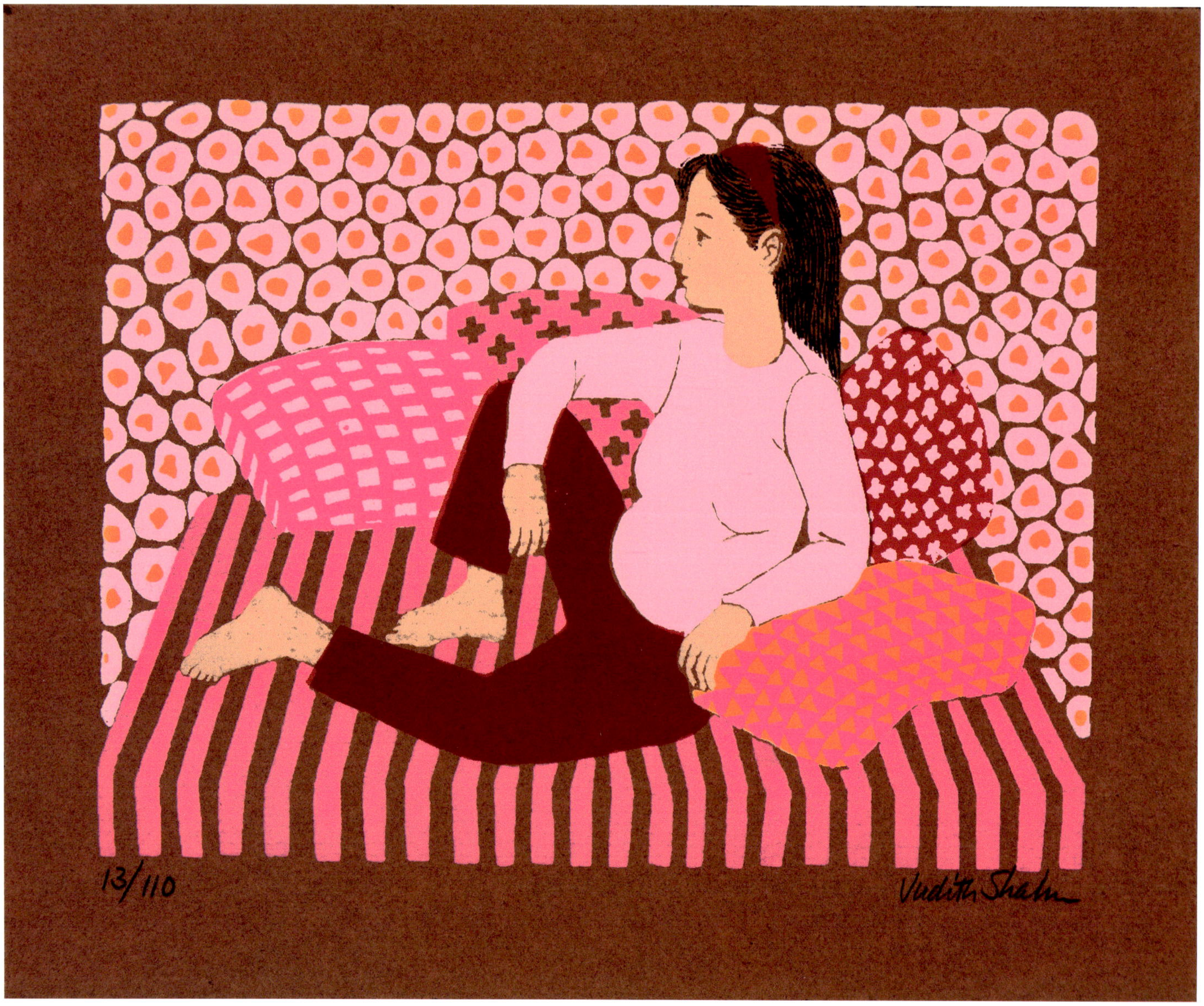

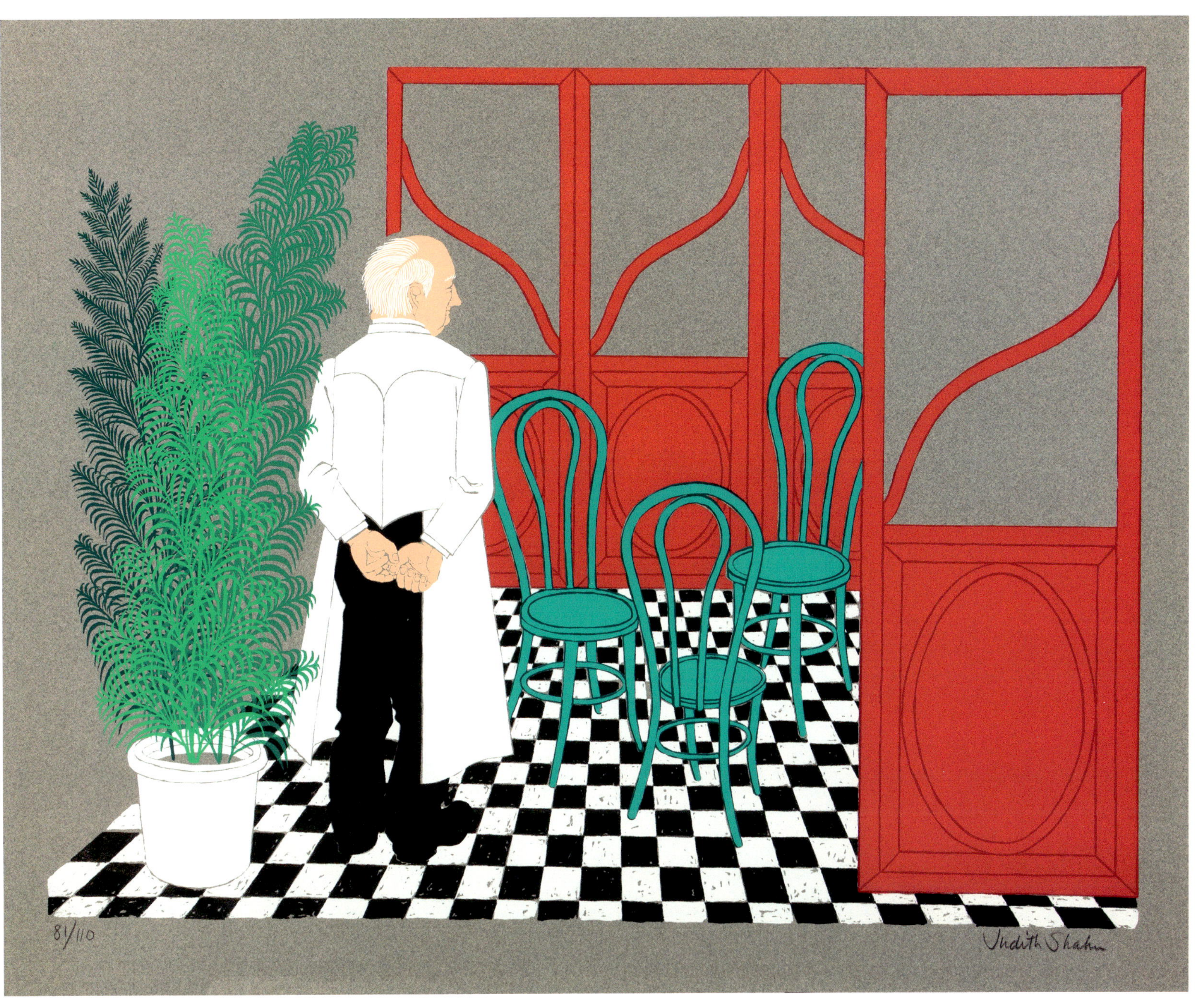

Judith Shahn, *Café* 81/110, n.d. Silkscreen on gray paper, 17 × 23 inches. *Bequest from the Estate of Judith Shahn*, 2011.

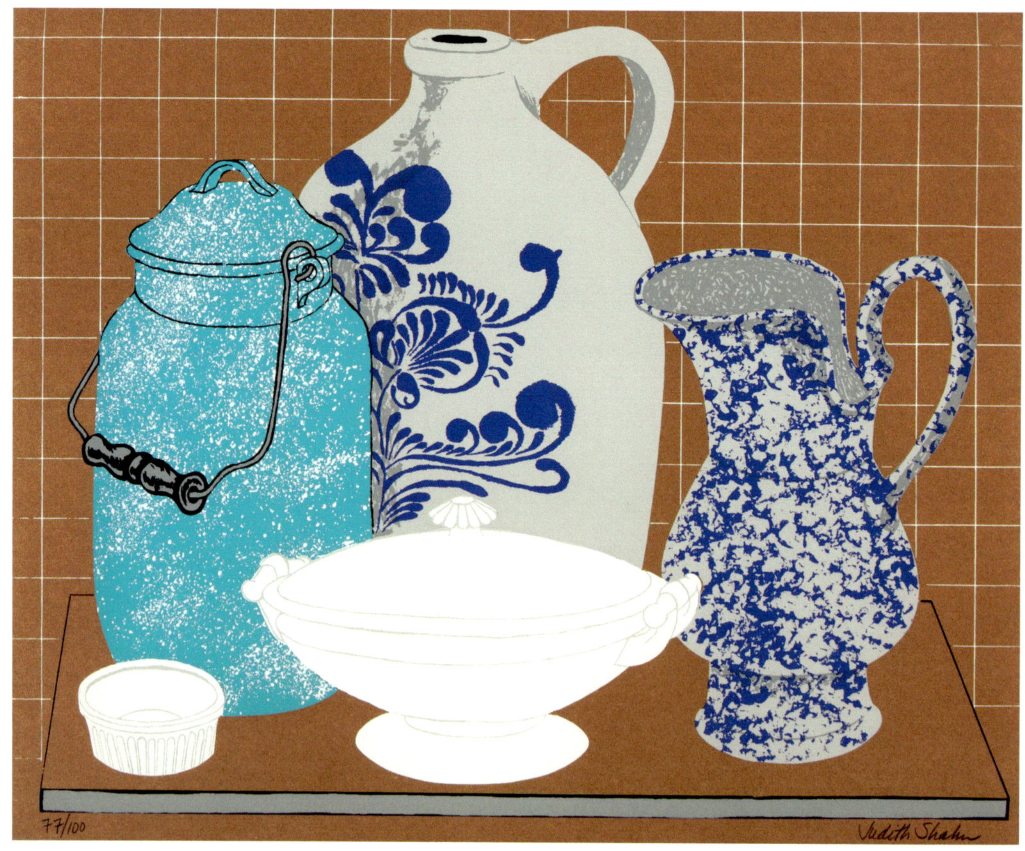

Judith Shahn, *Kitchen Shelf* 77/100, n.d. Silkscreen on paper, 14 × 17 inches. *Bequest from the Estate of Judith Shahn*, 2011.

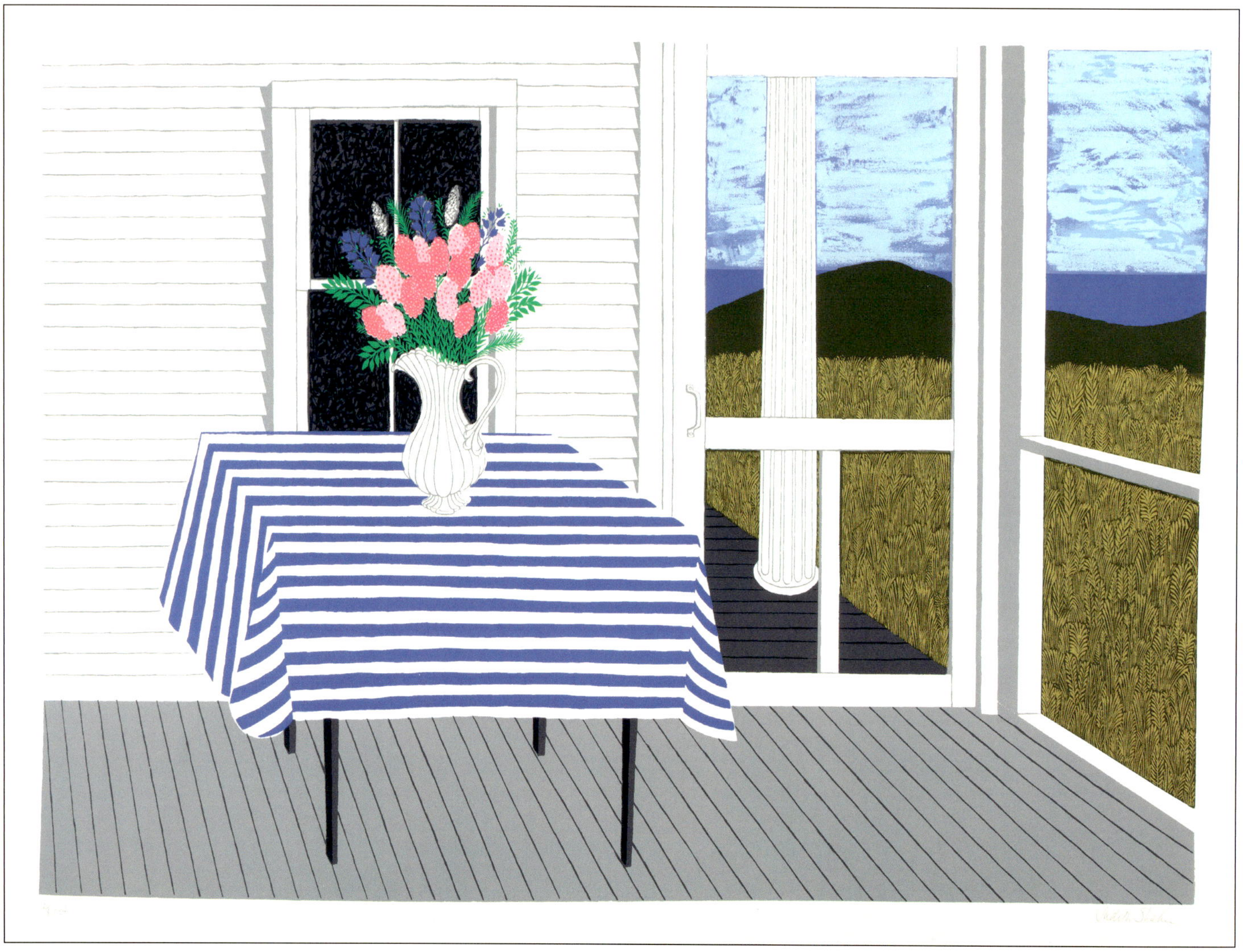

Judith Shahn, *Striped Tablecloth* AP, n.d. Silkscreen on paper, 22 × 30 inches. *Bequest from the Estate of Judith Shahn*, 2011.

ARTHUR BAUMAN
(1930–)

Although Arthur Bauman studied music at Columbia College, he ultimately found a career as a visual artist working with abstract shapes that lyrically move with rhythmic fluctuations. The sculpture of Alexander Calder inspired him to make mobiles in 1968 while he was in the Foreign Service at the US Embassy in Amman, Jordan. At first, he used anything he could find at hand: clothes hanger wire, tin can tops, and even yarn. Later, he graduated to aluminum sheet and spring steel wire for the mobiles he made while abroad.

In 1981, he left the Foreign Service to work full time on mobiles. He has continued to use aluminum sheet and stainless steel wire and he paints the objects with acrylic paint. Most of the shapes floating from the wire are abstract; however, he sometimes includes the shape of a fish, moon, sun, or star. Occasionally his shapes are hammered aluminum, bronze, or brass. The mobiles generally range in size from two to six feet in height. He also designs plate metal outdoor sculptures as large as eighteen feet tall.

His aluminum mobile *Once in a Blue Moon,* in lively colors, in the Cape Cod Museum of Art collection, hangs high in one of its arched galleries, a permanent fixture that animates the lofty space.

Although he acknowledges the influence of Calder, Bauman, who now lives on Cape Cod, has developed his own distinctive style. He is focused on balancing the structure to be viewed from all angles and on creating a moving, dancing element in space.

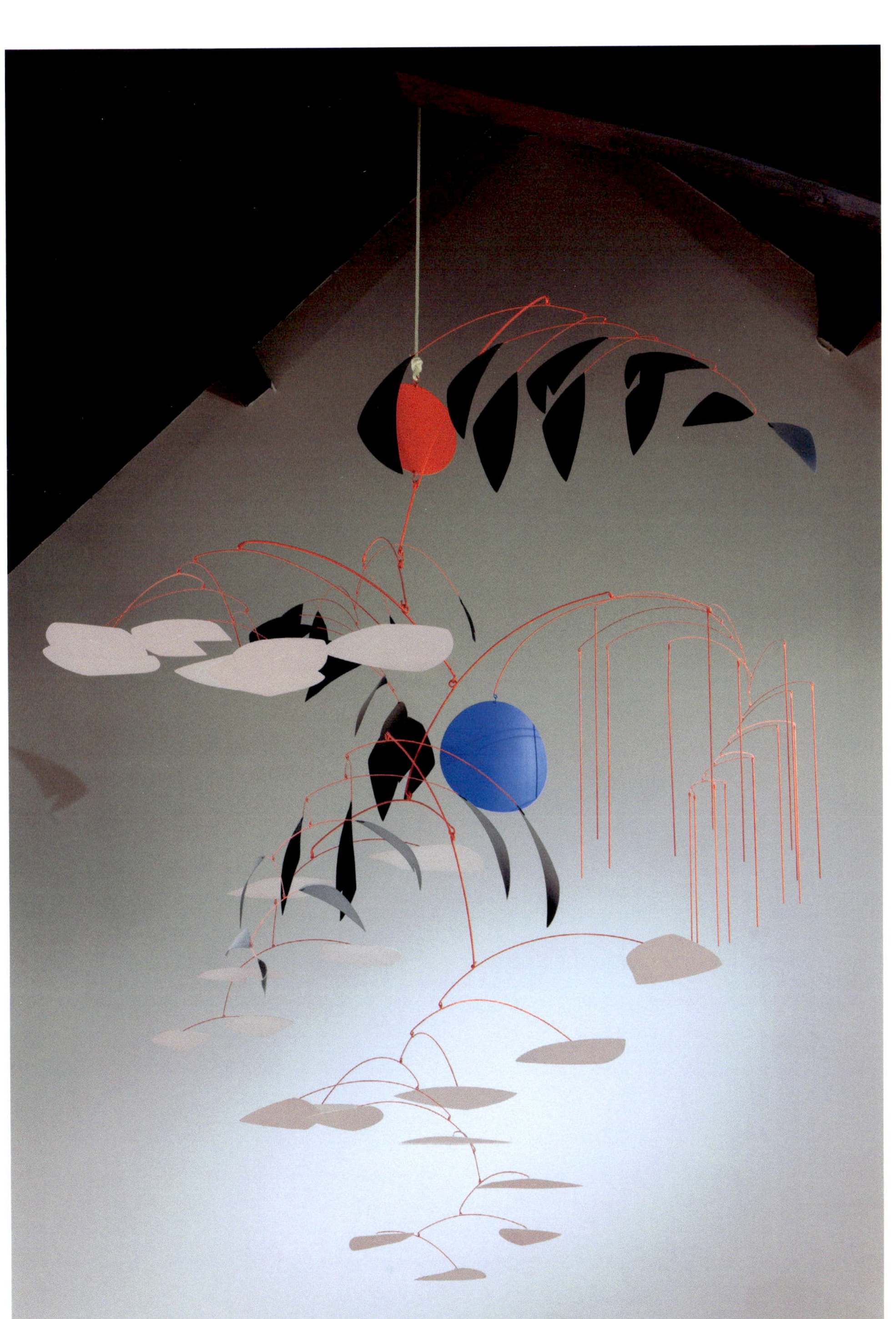

Arthur Bauman, *Once in a Blue Moon,* 1999. Aluminum mobile, 109 × 57 inches. *Gift of Arthur Bauman,* 1999.

JASPER JOHNS
(1930–)

Jasper Johns captured the fascination of the American public with art that contained familiar, popular images. When he entered the art arena in the 1950s, abstract expressionism reigned. However, pop art was soon to make a splash with representations of commonplace items and icons of mass culture. Johns was at the forefront of this new direction, with a cool, less emotional approach that straddled several movements: pop, minimalism, and conceptual art— all of which were moving away from individualistic, expressionistic abstraction.

Johns was born in Augusta, Georgia, and raised in South Carolina. He studied at the University of South Carolina and then moved to New York, where he briefly attended the Parsons School of Design. In New York, he also met composer John Cage, choreographer Merce Cunningham, and artist Robert Rauschenberg, who were challenging the cultural establishment with their new approaches. Johns also found inspiration from the early-twentieth-century dada movement with its "non-art" approach, and from the ideas of one of its leaders, Marcel Duchamp, known for his "readymades"—artworks constructed with found objects.

Johns's paintings of flags, targets, stenciled numbers, ale cans, and maps of the United States offered images that were recognizable and easily appreciated. His other subjects have included familiar shapes: handprints and footprints, body parts, and objects in his studio. He also is a sculptor and printmaker, working in silkscreen, lithography, and etching. Again he looks to everyday items: beer cans, light bulbs, and paint brushes. His lithograph *Gemini Edition,* in the Cape Cod Museum of Art collection, depicts, at first glance, a classically shaped vase in stark white, but, at a second glance, reveals two faces in black profile that form the vase. In this one image, Johns is playing with familiar objects, with visual ideas, and with negative and positive space.

Along with Andy Warhol and other artists connected with pop, Johns proposed that common commercialized objects, with manipulation, could be the subject of fine art. The pop art movement, celebrating America's consumerism, dominated the art world for a time, and influenced other important art movements, including performance art, during the last half of the twentieth century.

Johns's artworks have been collected by numerous museums, including the Metropolitan Museum of Art, the Museum of Modern Art, the Whitney Museum of American Art, and the Guggenheim Museum, in New York, and the Museum of Fine Arts in Boston.

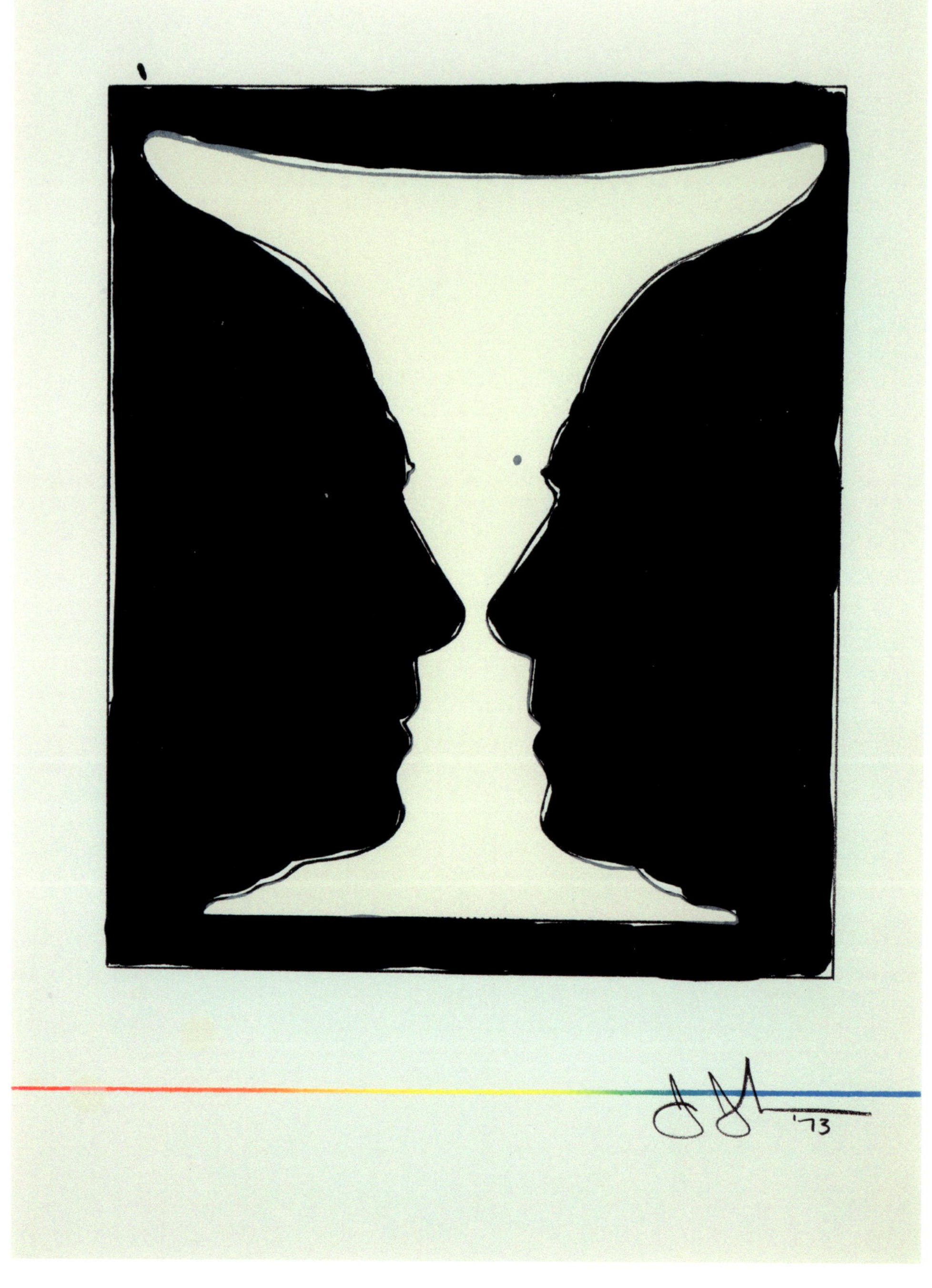

Jasper Johns, *Gemini Edition*, 1973. Lithograph on paper, 9½ × 8 inches. *Anonymous gift*, 2009.© *Jasper Johns and Gemini G.E.L./Licensed by VAGA, New York, New York.*

BUDD HOPKINS
(1931–2011)

When Budd Hopkins arrived in New York in the early 1950s, abstract expressionism was on its way to becoming the dominant art movement in the country. He felt its fever and his early art showed its influence. However, he was also drawn to the geometric abstraction of Piet Mondrian, which would later have an impact on him.

Hopkins was born and raised in Wheeling, West Virginia, and earned a degree in art history at Oberlin College in Ohio. After college, he moved to New York, where he became part of the circle of abstract expressionists, and was particularly influenced by Franz Kline and Mark Rothko. In the early 1960s, his abstract expressionist style evolved, and he began introducing hard-edge forms into his work, which showed the impact of Mondrian. By the late 1960s, geometric forms with flat planes of color defined his art. Working in this style, he produced collages, paintings, and architectural sculptures.

In 1977, Hopkins accidentally created his first *Guardian* collage. This "guardian," or sentinel image, would become part of an ongoing series in his work. This accidental first guardian came about through his use of left-over, variously colored circular fragments from previous collage studies, which he overlapped and supplemented with long stripes of different colors. With the circle as a head and the linear strips below, it became for Hopkins an abstract figure that seemed to be standing guard. That piece then became the inspiration for more than seventy works in vibrant contrasting colors that he made during the next few decades. His 1993 *Guardian Collage Study*, in the collection of the Cape Cod Museum of Art, is a representative example of this work, in which he contrasted the rounded forms with the linear lines in bold red and blue.

Hopkins had a home in Truro, was involved in the Provincetown art colony, and was a member of the prestigious Long Point Gallery there. His artworks are in the collections of major museums, including the Metropolitan Museum of Art, the Museum of Modern Art, the Whitney Museum of American Art, and the Guggenheim Museum in New York; the Hirshhorn Museum and Sculpture Garden in Washington, DC; the San Francisco Museum of Modern Art; and the Museum of Fine Arts in Boston.

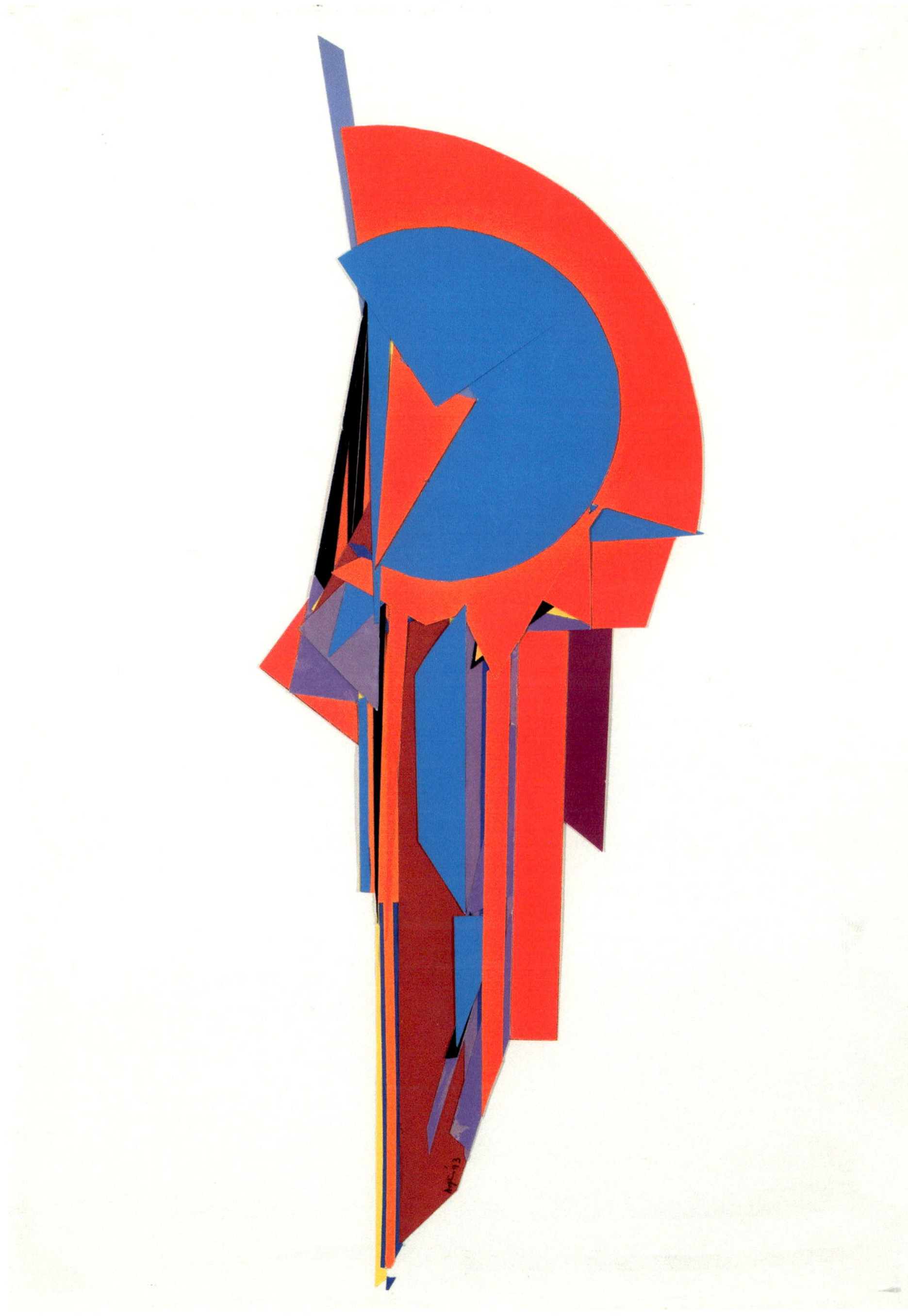

Budd Hopkins, *Untitled Guardian Collage,* 1993. Collage on paper, 14¾ × 5¼ inches. *Gift of Grace Hopkins*, 2015.

JACK COUGHLIN
(1932–)

A graphic artist and painter, Jack Coughlin is well known for his incisive portraits of literary figures and musicians. As a printmaker, he has worked in intaglio, including drypoint, aquatint, and engraving; lithography; and woodcut. In his printmaking and drawing, you can see the influence of Dutch and German Renaissance draftsmen, such as Hieronymus Bosch, Pieter Brueghel the Elder, Rembrandt van Rijn, and Albrecht Dürer.

Coughlin's choice of author portraits is determined by the ones he admires. He did a series of portraits of Irish writers, which includes James Joyce, George Bernard Shaw, and Sean O'Casey. His woodblock print *Samuel Beckett,* in the Cape Cod Museum of Art collection, depicts the lined face of Beckett and his questioning stare. Coughlin captured the dark side of the author whose absurdist *Waiting for Godot* continues to challenge audiences worldwide. American writers included in Coughlin's repertoire include Walt Whitman, Mark Twain, and Emily Dickinson.

In addition to his portraits, Coughlin made a series of etchings on the early whaling industry for the Whaling Museum of New Bedford in Massachusetts. As a sculptor, Coughlin has worked in bronze, producing figures that have been influenced by Rodin. He has produced additional imagery that is less naturalistic and includes dream-like subjects and imaginary interplays of human and animal forms.

Coughlin taught printmaking at the University of Massachusetts in Amherst for thirty-five years. His works are in many public collections, including the Metropolitan Museum of Art and the Museum of Modern Art in New York; the National Collection of Fine Arts in Washington, DC; the Norfolk Museum of Arts and Sciences in Virginia; the Worcester Art Museum in Massachusetts; the Philadelphia Free Public Library; Städelsches Kunstinstitut in Frankfort, Germany; and the British Museum in London, England.

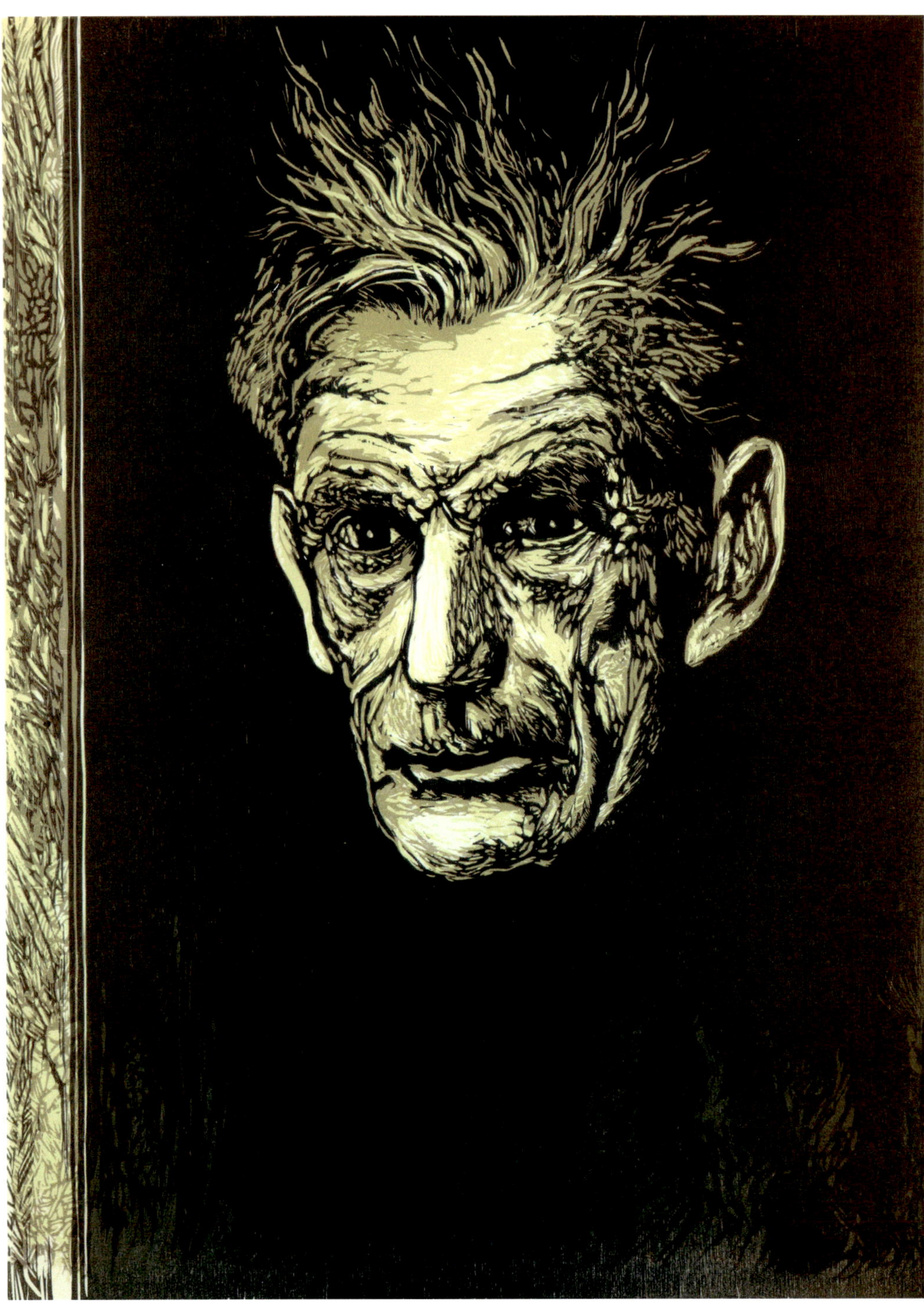

Jack Coughlin, *Samuel Beckett* 11/50, n.d. Woodblock on paper, 15¾ × 16½ inches. *Gift of Joan Hopkins Coughlin and Jack Coughlin*, 1987.

BRENDA HOROWITZ
(1932–)

Brenda Horowitz often dispenses with natural colors and does not hesitate to paint a sky, a field, or a body of water in a deep or fiery red. As for blue, even when she uses it in the sky, it is a deeper, richer hue than what is normally seen in nature. The emotional aspect of color is integral to Horowitz's work. The way she positions her colors in broad, flat shapes produces bold and dramatic landscapes of Cape Cod, which have a strong, colorful rhythm.

Horowitz has lived on the Cape in North Truro from May to September for many years, discovering the places that inspire her. When she returns to New York, the Cape summer stays with her all winter as she paints what she remembers with vibrant colors. Her continuing focus on the outer Cape landscape has allowed Horowitz to develop a deep understanding of the land, water, sky, and the relationships among them; and it is this relationship, and her own intense emotional response to the place, that Horowitz reveals.

She paints her landscapes with broad sweeps of color. There is no mistaking the subject, yet her dynamically placed large shapes indicate she is also guided by the abstract aspects of the composition. Looking at her paintings, it is not surprising to discover that Horowitz studied with Hans Hofmann, a supreme colorist and powerful influence on the modern American art scene. She earned a master's degree in art at the City University of New York and studied at Cooper Union School of Art. In the 1980s and '90s, Horowitz was a *plein-air* painter working in gouache and painting with colors true to nature. Her creative use of color came later.

Horowitz also has been influenced by the fauves, who dispensed with naturalistic colors. And she has great admiration for Henri Matisse and Paul Gauguin. Although her unusual colors are the first to demand attention, there is also a strong influence of cubism in her simple house shapes that have a place in most of her landscapes. *Orleans Night*, in the Cape Cod Museum of Art collection, is a dramatic example of her work with its cubist cottages set amid a dark night scene. Deep reds and blues play artfully along with acid greens in the foliage to form vibrating patterns that activate a landscape volleying between tranquil and dynamic.

Her work is in many private and corporate collections, including American Express, NYNEX Corporation, Rolls Royce, Citibank, and Colgate Corporation.

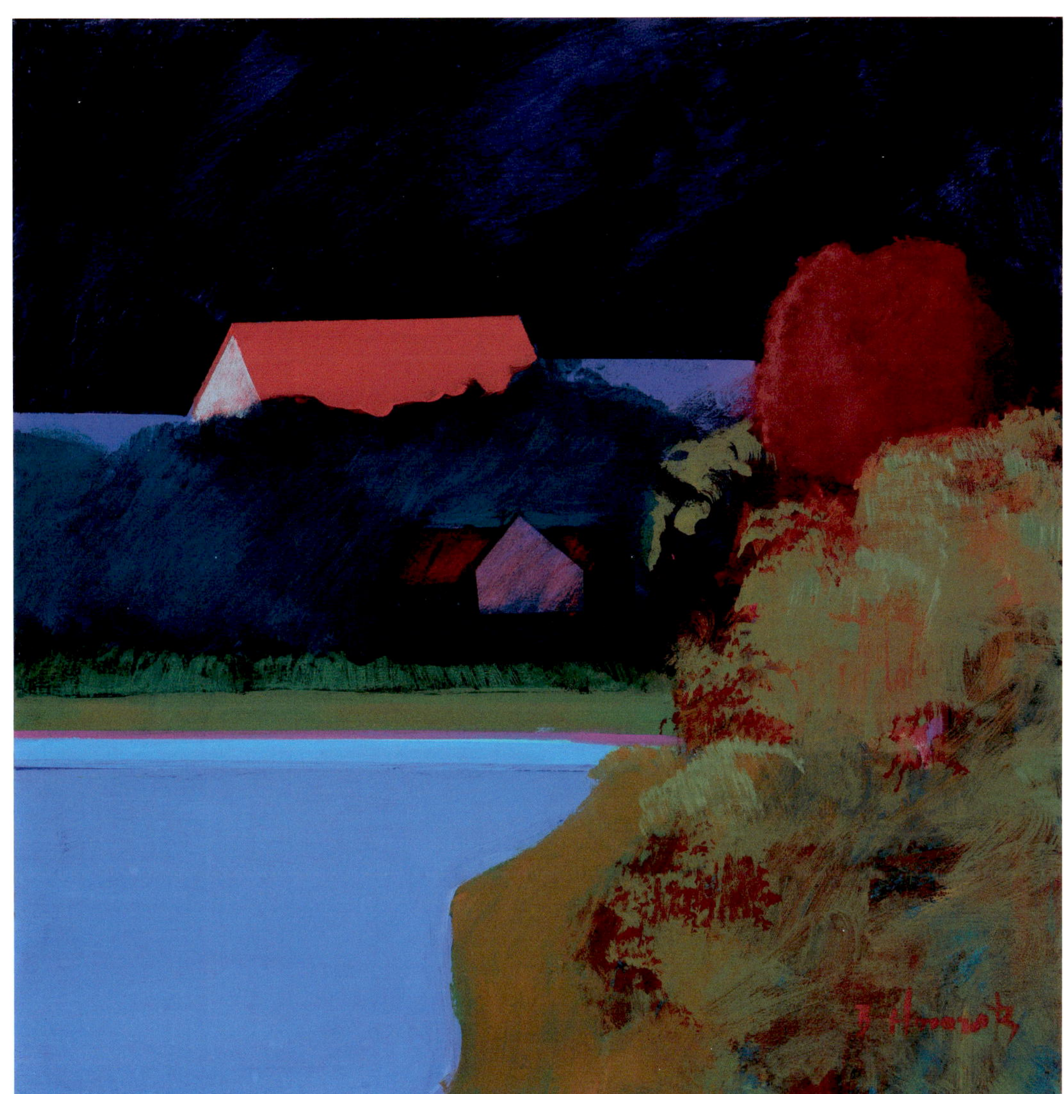

Brenda Horowitz, *Orleans Night*, 2008. Acrylic on canvas, 24 × 24 inches. *Gift of Brenda Horowitz*, 2015.

ROBERT HENRY
(1933–)

Robert Henry's paintings are always changing. He works both figuratively and abstractly because he does not see strong demarcations between the two types of imagery. In addition, his art is often narrative. He is telling a story that is defined with bold lines and strong colors. Those stories can be shrouded in mystery or wonder. This mysterious work is often intense, pondering, and dark. His colors are variegated and can be thick with texture. He depicts lonely figures or groups of people in dream-like and sometimes nightmare scenarios, which he seems to challenge the viewer to interpret.

Born in Brooklyn, Henry received a degree in art from Brooklyn College, studying with Ad Reinhardt and Kurt Seligman. He met artist Selina Trieff at college, and they were married for more than fifty years before she died in 2015.

In the early 1950s, Henry, along with Trieff, studied with Hans Hofmann in New York and Provincetown, and the influence remains, although, like so many of Hofmann's students, Henry found his own style. *Lillian 3,* his portrait of Lillian Orlowsky, in the Cape Cod Museum of Art collection, captures the robust character of an artist who was also a Hofmann student. And then there are bright moments, even sun-filled domestic scenes, such as *Selina and the Kids in 1972*, also in the museum collection.

Bravo, a series of eight works from the 1990s, one of which, *Surprise Bravo*, is in the museum collection, was sparked by a television show saluting Luciano Pavarotti. After the opera singer finished performing, he took a bow, and Henry was so impressed with that public recognition that he wanted to create a fantasy in which a visual artist is similarly applauded by an audience.

Henry taught at Brooklyn College for thirty years and he, along with Trieff, have been active in the Provincetown art colony for more than half a century. The couple's contributions to the art colony were celebrated in 2009 when the Provincetown Art Association and Museum honored them as "Distinguished Provincetown Artists for Their Lifelong Achievement." Henry still lives nearby in Wellfleet, where he and his wife have had a home for many years.

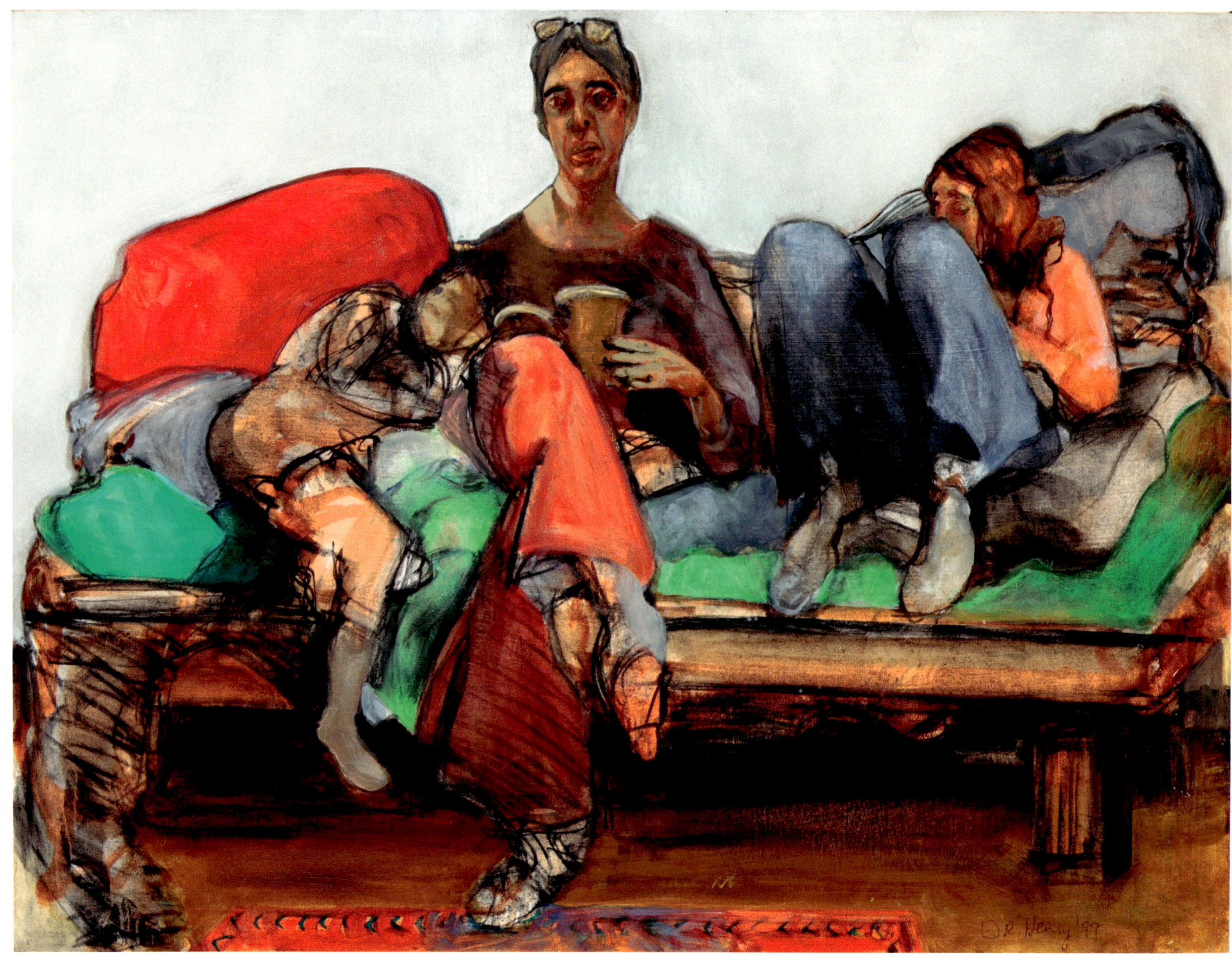

Robert Henry, *Selina and the Kids in 1972,* 1999. Oil on hypro mounted on canvas, 18 × 24 inches. *Gift of Kirby Veevers in honor of Jay Veevers*, 2010.

His works are in a number of public collections, including Columbia University, Pace University, and Queens College in New York; City University of New York; Brooklyn College; the Kresge Art Museum at Michigan State University in East Lansing; Mississippi Museum of Art in Jackson; the Neuberger Museum in Yonkers, New York; the Tucson Museum in Arizona; and the Amarillo Museum of Art in Texas.

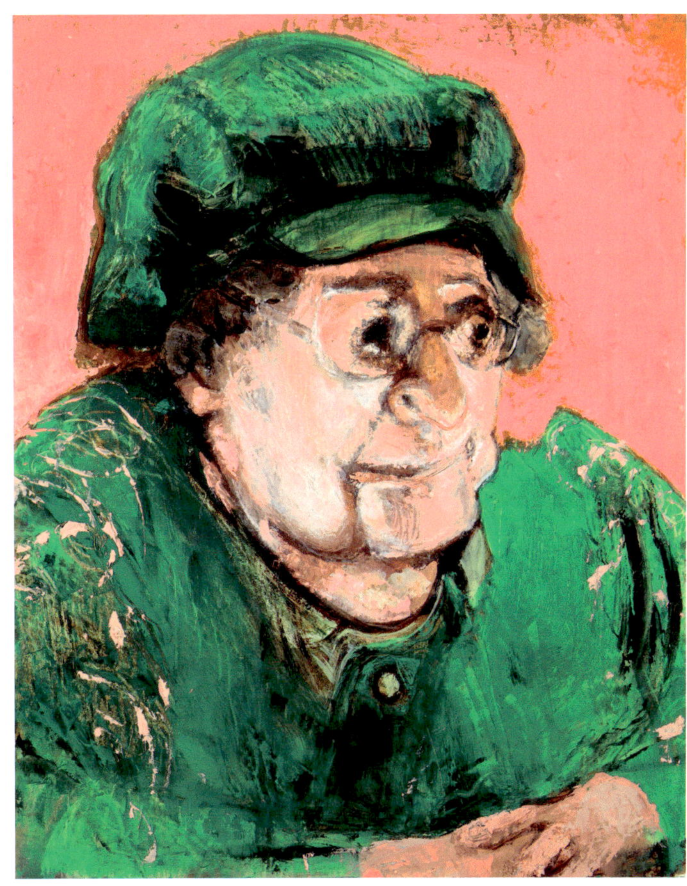

Robert Henry, *Lillian 3*, 2003. Oil on hypro mounted on canvas, 15 × 12 inches. *Gift of Robert Henry*, 2007

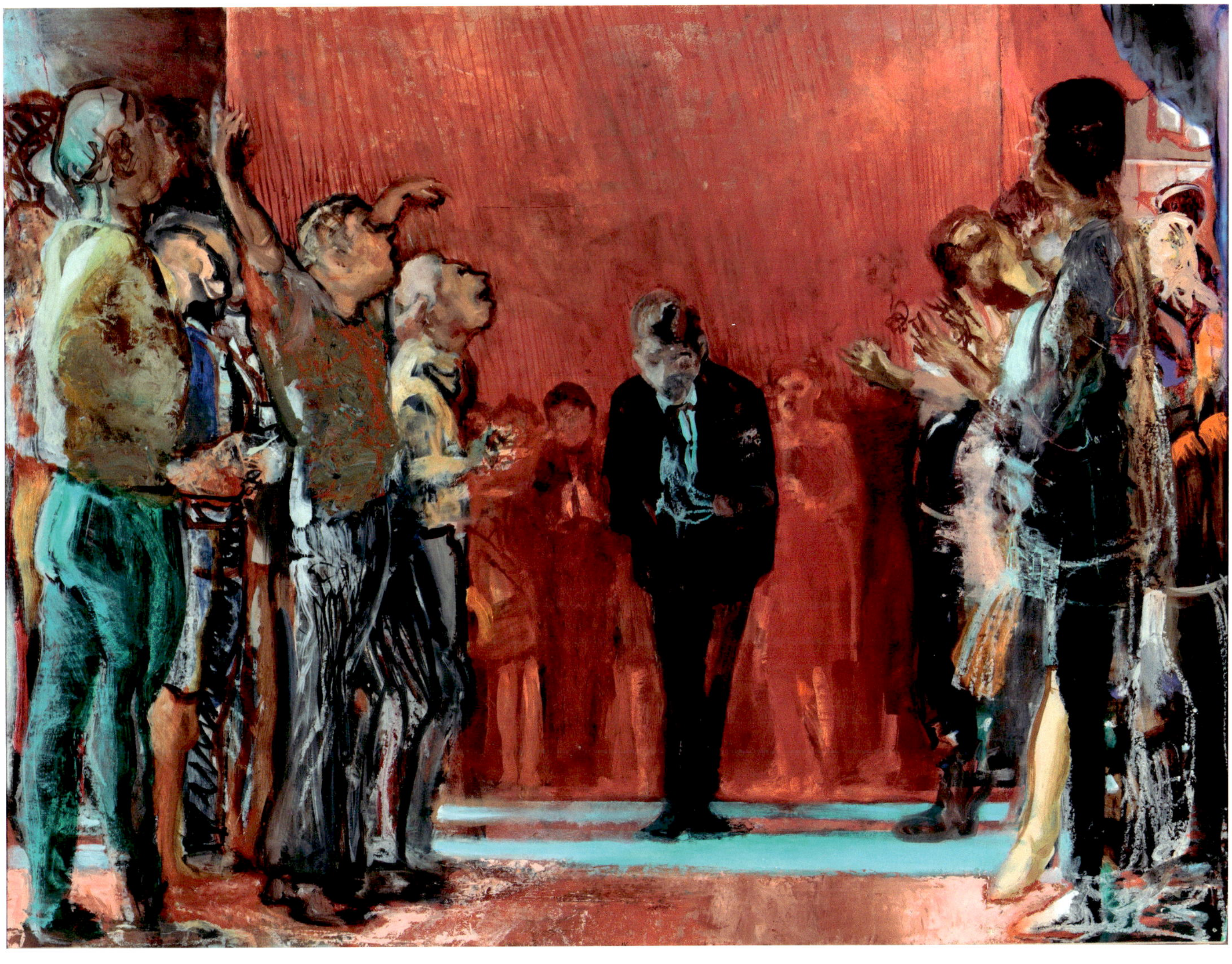

Robert Henry, *Surprise Bravo*, 1996. Oil on hypro mounted on canvas, 24½ × 32 inches. *Gift of Robert Henry*, 1999.

ANNE PACKARD
(1933–)

As was also the case with her grandfather, artist Max Bohm, Anne Packard has had a significant connection to the Provincetown art colony. Born and raised in Hyde Park, New York, she has been summering in Provincetown since she was an infant and began living in the town year-round in 1977. She studied with Philip Malicoat, who guided her early on, and although she never knew her grandfather, she has acknowledged that his work also has influenced her.

Packard mostly paints in her home right on the beach with a panoramic view of Cape Cod Bay, MacMillan Wharf, and the Pilgrim Monument. She has made a career of painting those long stretches of beach and calm waters, big skies, and dunes. Occasionally there's a solitary boat moored at low tide, a ramshackle cottage or lighthouse, or the stretch of buildings that line the Provincetown waterfront. Blues and beiges, the colors she sees every day, tend to be her colors of choice. For the most part, her work is reflective and peaceful, although she has, on occasion, painted a stormy sea.

Her images are an expression of how she sees herself and how she feels about the natural world that she paints. *Dory* and *A Summer Place,* both in the Cape Cod Museum of Art collection, show single boats seemingly lost on shore. The mood is quiet, still, with a feeling of solitude, and yet with a sense of expectation.

Her paintings always begin with a horizon line. She has an image in mind, from a sketch she made, a photograph she's taken, a memory—and, of course, the view from her window. Usually that horizon is low so she can paint those sometimes somber blue and gray skies; other times there is a gladdened blue sky with wispy clouds. When Packard tires of the horizon, she obscures it, but never totally loses it. So much of her work is a back and forth between beach, water, and sky.

Packard's art is in many private and public collections, including the Albrecht Museum in Ohio and the Oglethorpe University Museum in Atlanta, Georgia.

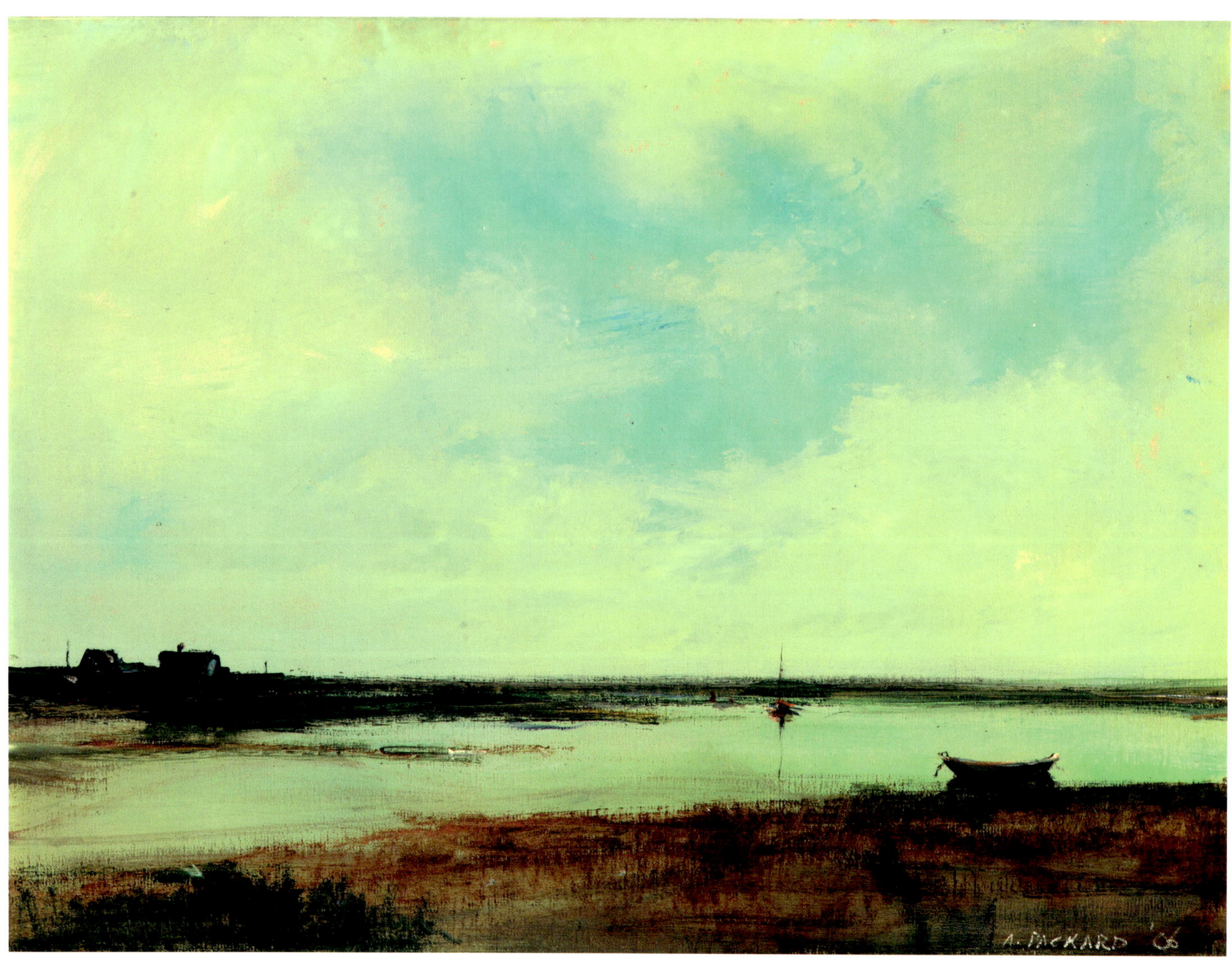

Anne Packard, *A Summer Place*, 2006. Oil on canvas, 18 × 24 inches. *Gift of Anne Packard*, 2006.

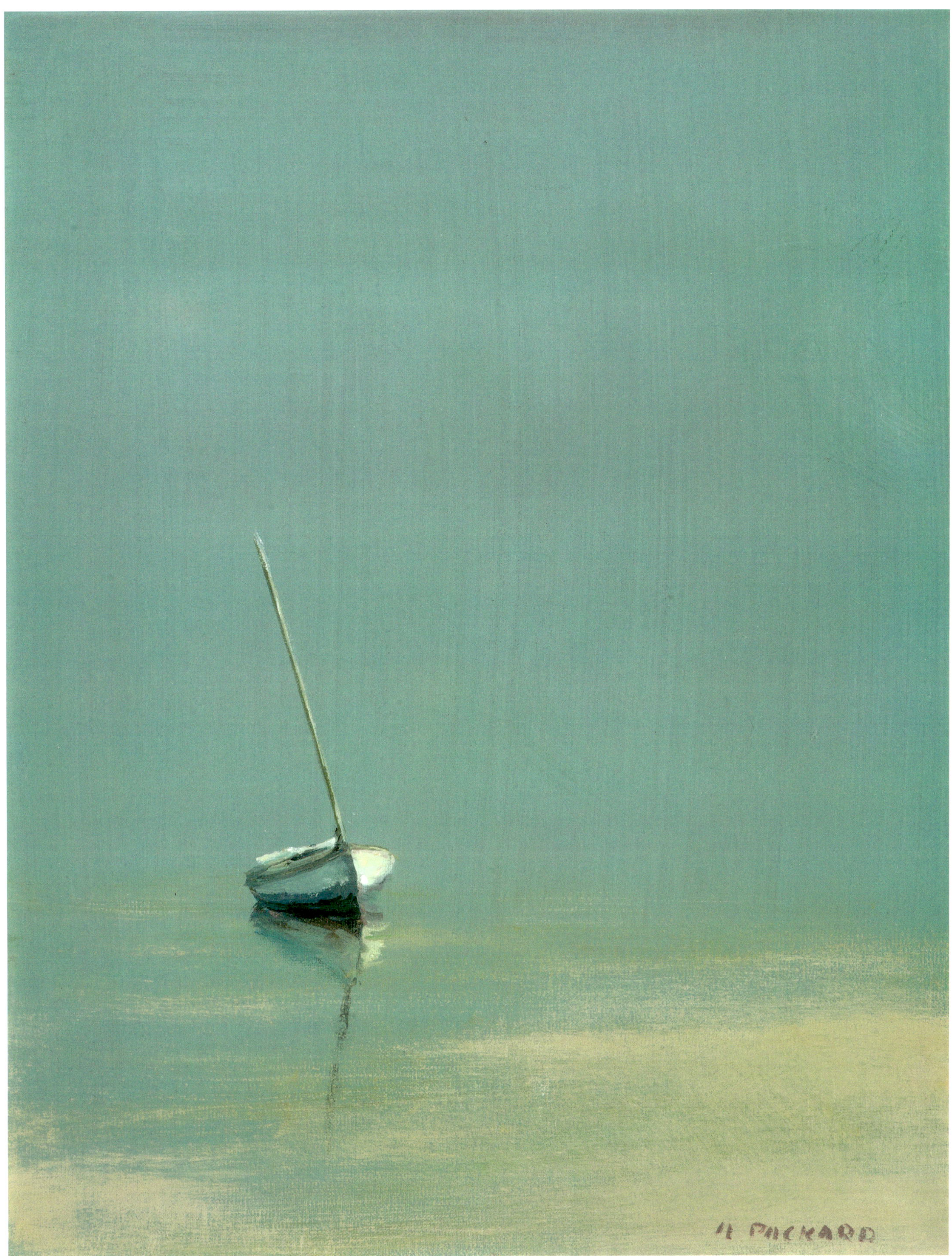

Anne Packard, *Dory,* 2001. Oil on canvas, 20 × 16 inches. *Anonymous gift*, 2009.

SELINA TRIEFF
(1934–2015)

For Selina Trieff, the world was a stage for her theatrical figures, played against a flat background of rich colors. Clowns and dancers, actors and pilgrims are dressed in leotards or robes, in tight hoods or wide-brimmed hats, all with disconcerting masklike faces. Her figures are painted in clear, fresh colors and often highlighted in gold leaf. The gold adds a rich and lustrous element to the work.

Her clowns reference the eighteenth-century *Gilles,* a painting by Jean-Antoine Watteau of a clown in a white costume. She was also influenced by the films of Ingmar Bergman, particularly the mystical *The Seventh Seal.* The faces in her paintings almost always look the same—large, staring eyes, a broad nose, and turned-down lips—as in *Head in Black*, in the Cape Cod Museum of Art collection. Her unusual *papier mâché Mask*, in the collection, seems to present a different persona than in her paintings; however, the colors are very similar, and if the viewer can imagine a large pair of dark eyes animating it from behind, it can be seen as a fitting companion for a work such as *Head on Black.*

Most of her faces may be similar, but the way she paints them, and the angles she creates in the compositions, give them a distinct personality. Her figures' costumes, whether black leotards or colorful robes, express an individuality that contrasts with their neutral faces. *Two Figures/Black and Red* and *Pink Bird on Her Shoulder*, in the museum collection, are vibrant examples of Trieff's work. Although her stylized paintings freeze her figures in a timeless framework, they are poised for a moment, as if ready to step off their stage, seemingly to reveal something profound and to engage us in a drama we are eager to see.

Goats, sheep, chickens, and dogs are also part of Trieff's repertoire. *Goat,* in the collection, is a bold, simplified image, typical of these works. Her paintings of animals are from drawings she made many years ago when her family was living on a farm in West Tisbury on Martha's Vineyard.

Born in Brooklyn, Trieff studied at the Art Students League and at Brooklyn College with Ad Reinhardt and Mark Rothko. It was at Brooklyn College where she met another art student, Robert Henry, whom she married. They both studied with Hans Hofmann, who drew them to Provincetown where they became very active in the art colony. In 2009 the Provincetown Art Association and Museum honored them as "Distinguished Provincetown Artists for Their Lifelong Achievement."

Although Trieff's paintings are clearly figurative, she saw them as abstract in their structure. It was a structure Hofmann taught. In addition to her bold colors, her line is distinctive. Whether slender or wide, it meanders around the face and figure in gentle curves. Her paintings range in size from several inches to as large as six feet tall.

Trieff's work is in a number of public collections, including the Brooklyn Museum of Art, the New York Public Library, and Provincetown Art Association and Museum.

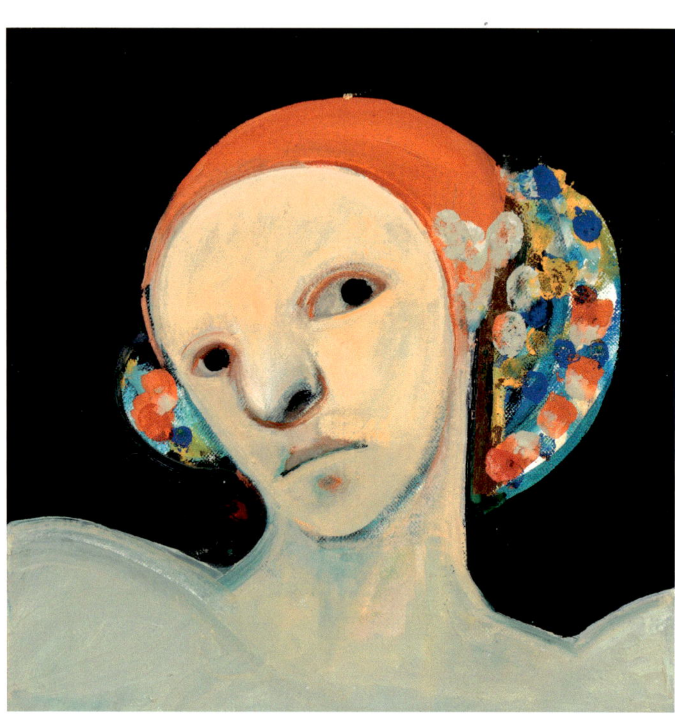

Selina Trieff, *Head on Black*, 1998. Oil and gold leaf on canvas, 12 × 12 inches. *Gift of Del Filardi and Harriet Rubin*, 2012.

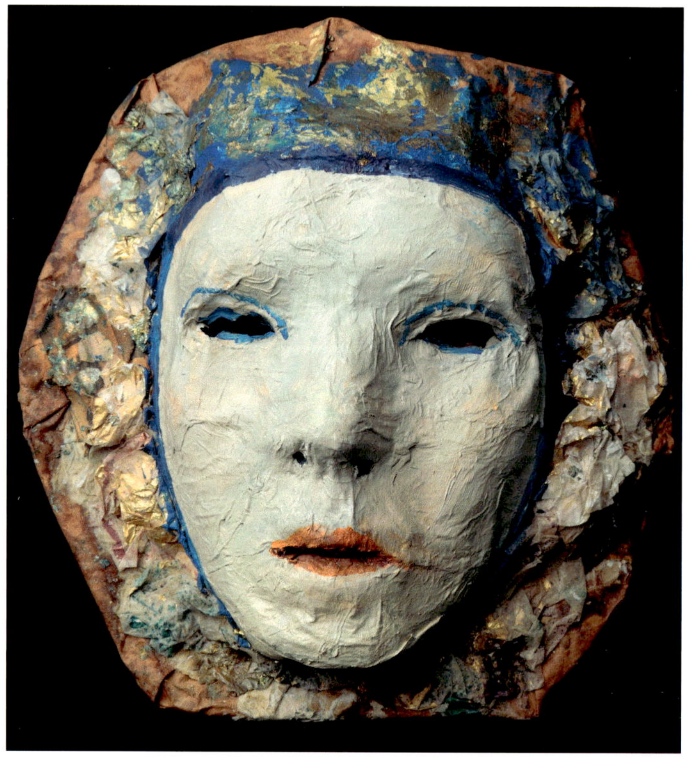

Selina Trieff, *Mask*, circa 1975. Papier mâché, 12 × 12 inches. *Gift of Del Filardi and Harriet Rubin,* 2012.

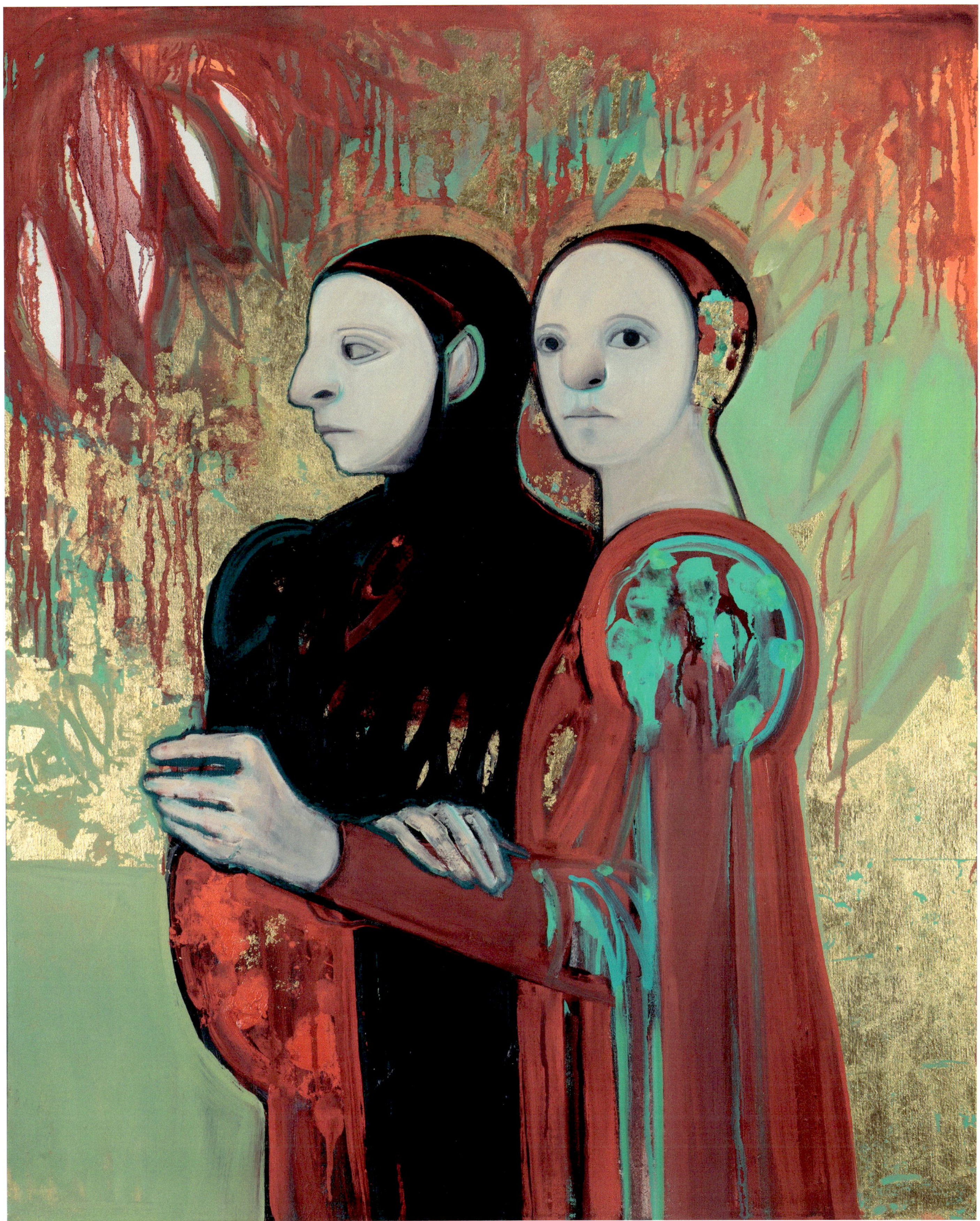

Selina Trieff, *Two Figures/Black and Red*, 1996. Oil and gold leaf on canvas, 36¼ × 30 inches. *Gift of Selina Trieff*, 1999.

Selina Trieff, *Pink Bird on Her Shoulder*, 1990. Oil and gold leaf on canvas, 72 × 60 inches. *Gift of Sanford and Carol Krieger*, 2010.

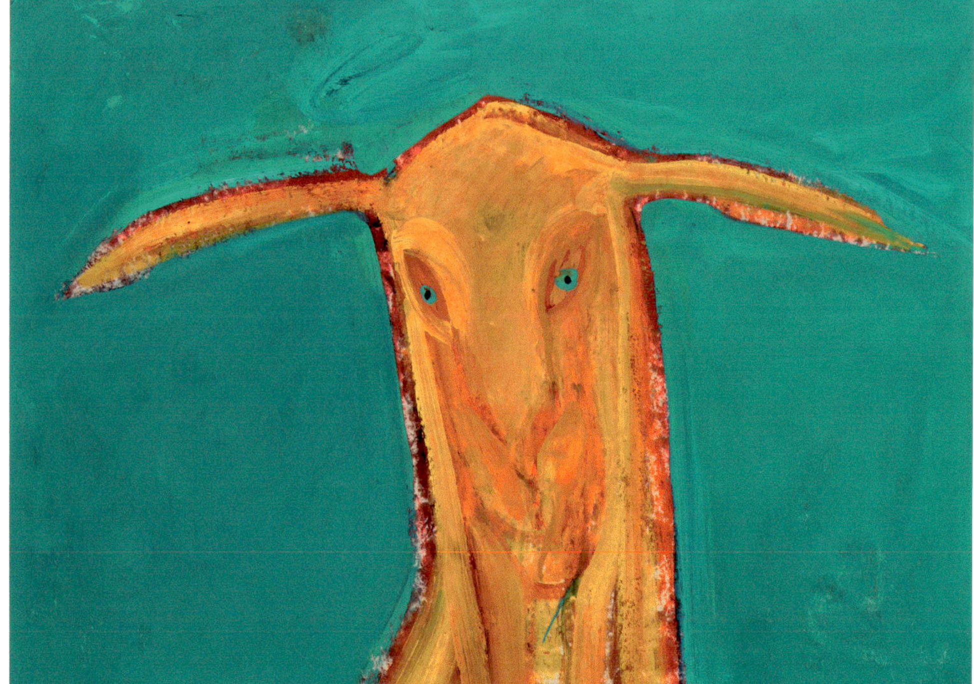

Selina Trieff, *Goat,* 1987. Oil on hypro paper, 17½ × 23½ inches. *Gift of Berta Walker*, 2005.

MEL LEIPZIG
(1935–)

Although Mel Leipzig paints real people in comfortable settings, his works are not exactly portraits. Rather they are paintings of a place, of the details of an environment, of a life and a story.

Most often the person or persons in one of his paintings is a relatively small element in the composition. The identity of his subjects resonates in their surroundings, beautifully delineated in rich details. The books, artwork, stacks of papers, benches, doors, windows looking out at a leafy summer day, fireplaces, easels, tables with all kinds of doodads, floorboards, and ceilings are vital elements of his unconventional portraits. In this way, his work is a lot about the space that contains the figure.

Despite the dominance of abstraction and all of the ideas he heard from the teachers in art schools where he studied, Leipzig was committed to realism from the beginning of his career. He kept true to his principles, all the while completing a degree from Yale University and an MFA from Pratt Institute.

Leipzig is interested in cluttered spaces that he can arrange and design to convey what he wants to communicate about the people he paints. He often includes reflections in mirrors and renditions of other artists' paintings, which demonstrate his technical skills. He paints family and friends, artists, writers, and people in the art world.

Although for the most part Leipzig uses linear perspective, he might record the scene from a few different angles, which tilt and distort, yet the effect isn't disorienting. *Cape Cod Museum of Art,* appropriately in the museum collection, depicts former director Elizabeth Ives Hunter and exhibitions curator Michael Giaquinto in the sculpture porch of the museum. The deep view of the long narrow space and fascinating distortions are striking elements, as important as the figures themselves.

He paints in acrylics and uses a limited palette, including primary colors, black, and white, to achieve the many colors that fill his paintings. His art has been influenced by the work of Édouard Manet, the master draftsman Edgar Degas, and the exquisite patterns of the room interiors by Henri Matisse and Édouard Vuillard.

Leipzig's home is in Trenton, New Jersey, and he spends his summers on Cape Cod, where he has the opportunity to paint a wide variety of artists and their environments. For more than forty years, he taught art and art history at Mercer County Community College in New Jersey. His works are in the collections of a number of museums, including the Whitney Museum of American Art and the Cooper-Hewitt Museum in New York City, the New Jersey State Museum in Trenton, the Montclair Art Museum in New Jersey, and the White House.

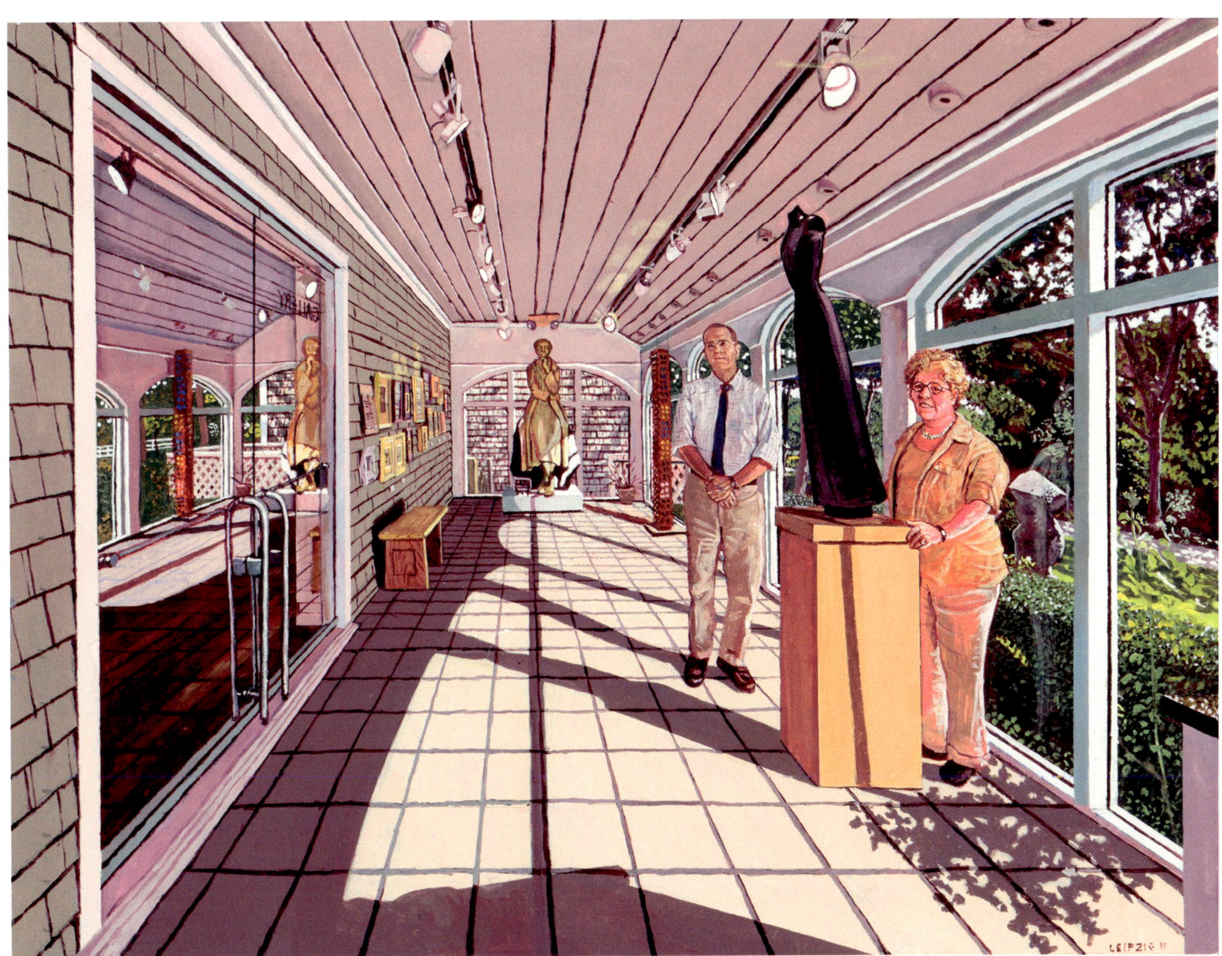

Mel Leipzig, *Cape Cod Museum of Art*, 2011. Acrylic on canvas, 38 × 50 inches.
Gift of Francesca Leipzig Picone and Joshua Leipzig, 2012.

PENELOPE JENCKS
(1936–)

Penelope Jencks's eight-foot bronze of Eleanor Roosevelt, situated on Riverside Drive and 72nd Street in New York City, leans against a rock in deep thought. A larger-than-life figure, Mrs. Roosevelt is an example of those giants Jencks creates in bronze, terra cotta, and plaster. However, Jencks's figures, scaled down to as small as several inches, also make an imposing statement in their own way. The dramatic swing in the scale of her sculpture is just one of the extraordinary aspects of her work.

Many of her sculptures are nudes— not idealized ones, but earthy, natural figures with the scars and inelegant shapes that are often what we see in the mirror in the privacy of our bedroom and bath. But Jencks puts them in full view to show us the unglamorous, the real, the everyday.

In the 1970s, despite her ongoing interest in the naked body, Jencks experimented with adding clothing. In the Cape Cod Museum of Art collection, *Pushing Forty* is a life-sized terra cotta sculpture of a woman in a long dress, her shoulders hunched with a frightened look on her face, a typical example of Jencks's work from this period.

By the 1980s, she was spending more time in Wellfleet, on Cape Cod. At this time, she returned to the nude and worked on life-sized terra cotta sculptures of nudes standing, sitting, and lying down. They are naturally positioned, the surface is smooth, and the elegant lines that shape the bodies have warmth and beauty.

In the subsequent *Beach Series II*, Jencks took a completely different approach. She abandoned models for these larger-than-life plaster figures; instead, they were created out of her childhood memories of summer days in the 1940s when her parents and their friends were on the beach *au naturel*. These six-to-ten-foot sculptures have pot bellies and sagging breasts and the plaster is mottled to depict imperfections of the skin.

Whether Jencks works big or small, from models or her imagination, she is constantly shaping a world she sees as natural. The exaggerations and distortions only emphasize aspects of a reality that are free from the artificially glamorous images so prevalent in popular culture.

Her works are in a number of public collections including the cities of Boston, New York, and Toledo, Ohio; Brandeis University in Waltham, Massachusetts; the Boston Public Library; and the White House. Her commissioned works include the Eleanor Roosevelt sculpture; one of Robert Frost at Amherst College in Amherst, Massachusetts; and the bronze statue of Samuel Eliot Morison, the maritime historian and Harvard professor, on Commonwealth Mall in Boston.

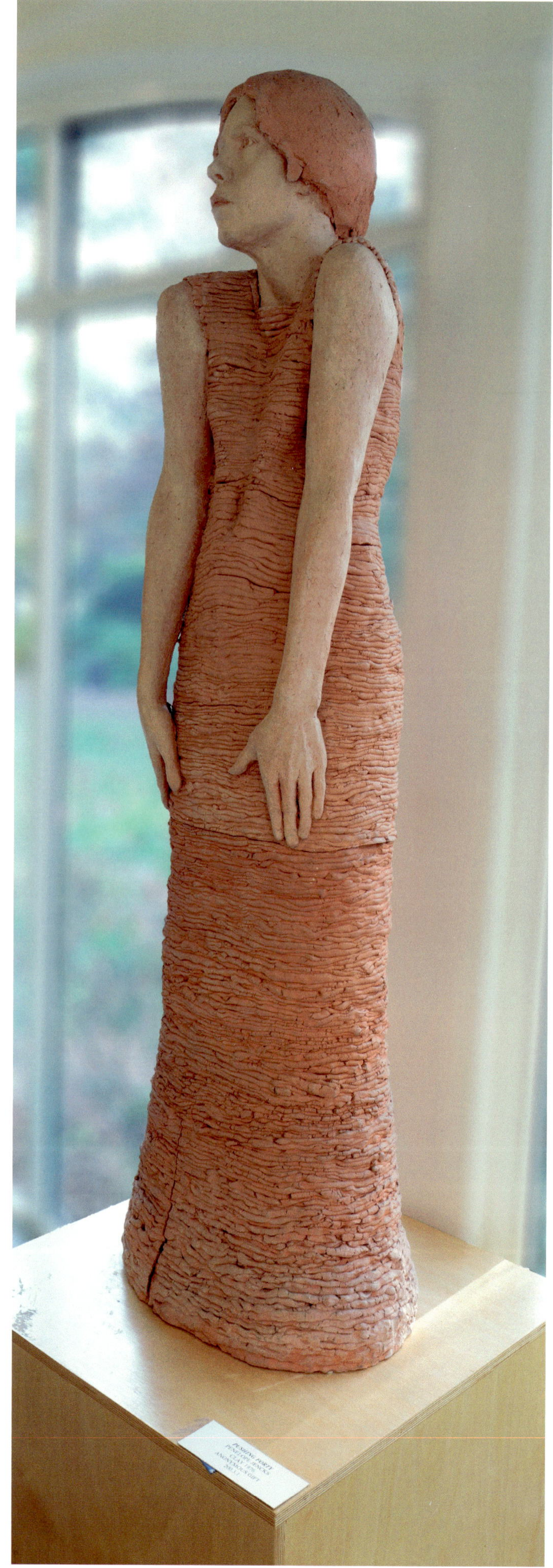

Penelope Jencks, *Pushing Forty*, 1976. Terra cotta sculpture, 5 feet tall. *Anonymous gift*, 2000.

CLAIRE FLANDERS
(1937–2003)

Claire Flanders (nee Altenburger) was born in Brussels and moved with her family to Lèves, southwest of Paris, at the beginning of World War II. She studied music and drama in France, married William Flanders, an American, and settled in the Washington, DC, area in 1959. It was then that she began taking photographs to send back to her family in Lèves.

Flanders's photographs are known for their skillful play of light and shadow, expert sense of composition, and eloquent simplicity. In her work, there are references to the work of Paul Strand, Berenice Abbott, and Eugene Atget, who are noted for their spare black-and-white images.

Flanders's work covers a broad spectrum of subjects, from an image of a fifteenth-century palace in Portugal to a photo of Edward Hopper's cottage and studio on Cape Cod, *World Apart*, in the Cape Cod Museum of Art collection. *Dune Shack Lunch*, also in the collection, is a simply composed still life of an extremely spare repast, with a pan of artist's colored oil sticks included that suggests her feelings about the important place and nourishment offered by a life in art. Flanders spent many summers on the Cape, which gave her the opportunity to become familiar with Hopper's environment and local scenes.

Flanders's other subjects include Mont Saint-Michel with its medieval abbey and the Chartres Cathedral in France; and a series titled *Rivers and Reflections*, depicting four rivers: the Potomac, the Pamet on Cape Cod, the Nile, and the Eure in France.

Her work has appeared in *Architectural Digest* and the British magazine *The World of Interiors*. She illustrated two books: *No Hidden Meanings* and *What Took You So Long?* by author Sheldon Kopp. Two series of her photographs are housed in the permanent collection of the Bibliothèque Nationale de France in Paris.

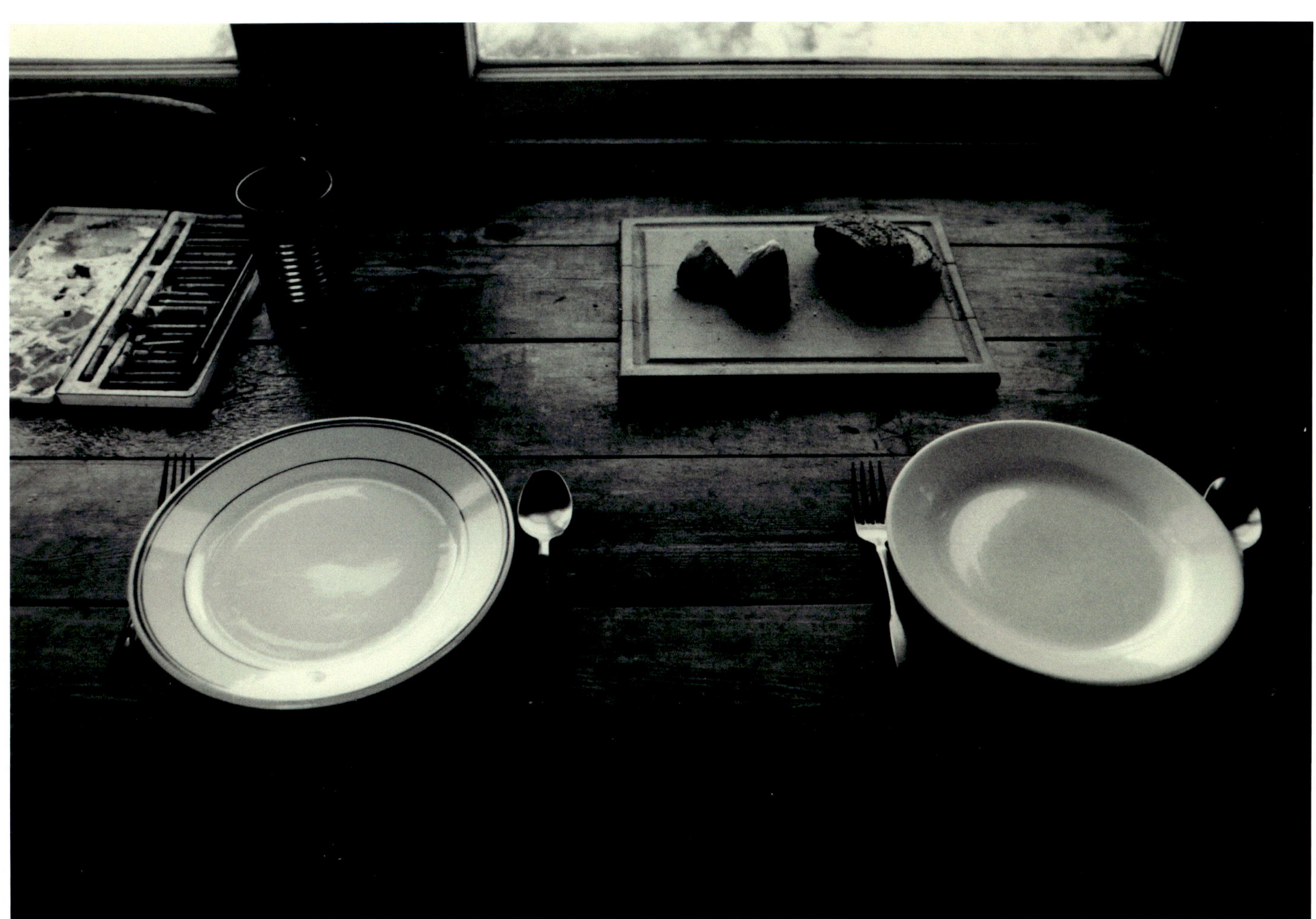

Claire Flanders, *Dune Shack Lunch,* 1997. Silver gelatin print on paper, 14 × 19 inches. *Gift of Claire Flanders,* 1997.

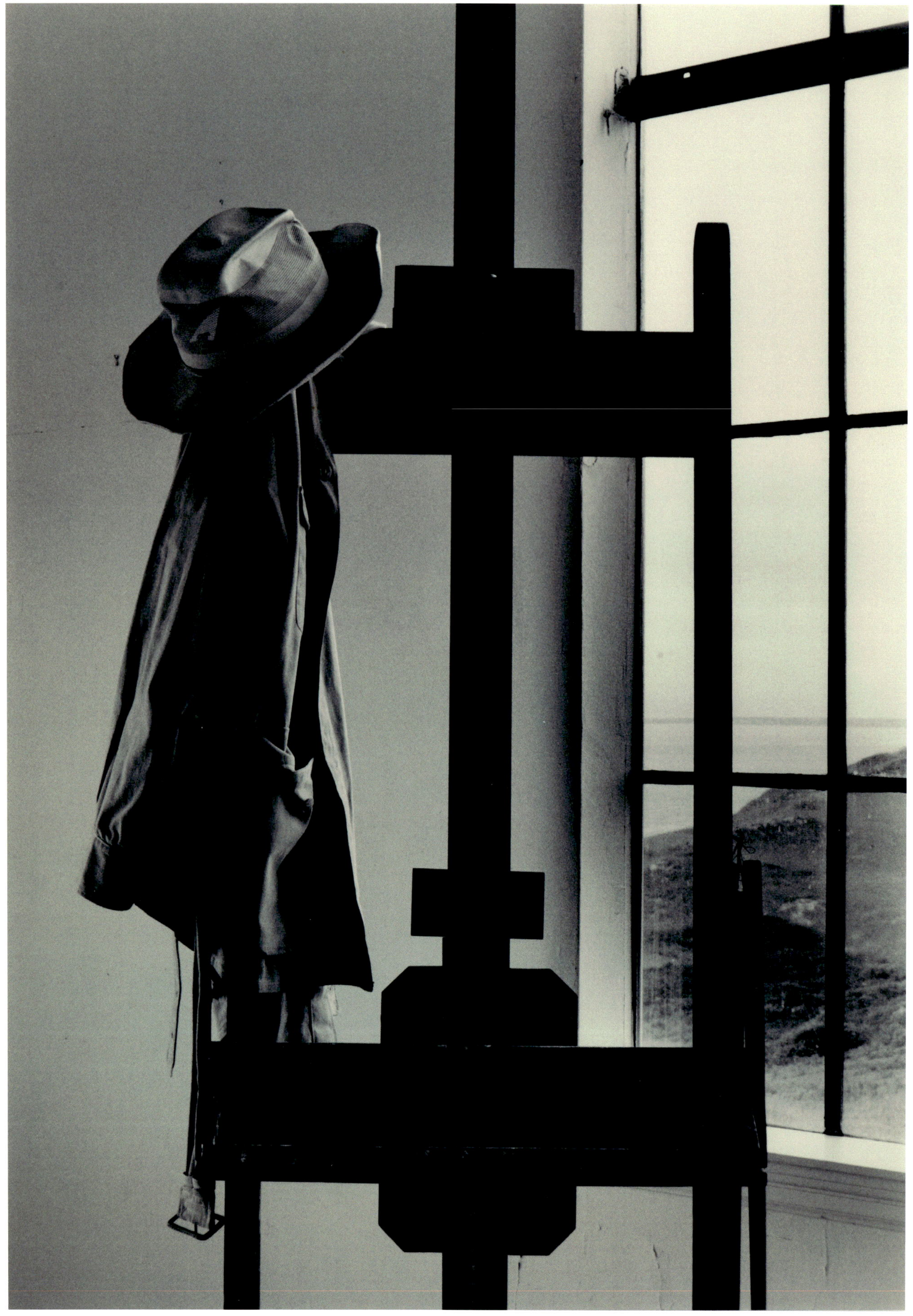

Claire Flanders, *World Apart 6/25*, 1997. Silver gelatin print, 19 × 14 inches. *Gift of Linda B. Miller*, 1997.

RED GROOMS
(1937–)

Charles Rogers Grooms, a twenty-year-old native of Tennessee, arrived in Provincetown in 1957 to study with Hans Hofmann. He wasn't "Red" Grooms then, but Provincetown changed that. Grooms found that Hofmann's classes were not for him, and he was washing dishes at the Moors restaurant that summer when he met Dominic Falcone, who was running the Sun Gallery. It was Falcone who dubbed him "Red" because of the color of his hair, and it stuck.

Provincetown's Sun Gallery was opened in 1955 by poet Falcone and artist Yvonne Andersen. Soon after, a group of artists leaning toward figurative art—Grooms, Claes Oldenburg, Alex Katz, Jan Müller, Bob Thompson, Lester Johnson, Tony Vevers and Alan Kaprow—came together to make this gallery space an exciting scene, a frothy mix of creativity and playfulness.

After Grooms's first summer in Provincetown, he returned to New York and lived in a loft with Andersen and Falcone. The next summer he was back in Provincetown washing dishes and installing his first solo exhibition at the Sun. In 1958, Grooms created the installation piece *The City,* which was a medley of painting, sculpture, drawing, photography, and poetry. A viewer could walk into and around the exhibit and become immersed in an environment.

By the summer of 1959 in Provincetown, Grooms had already found his place in art with collage and sculptural pieces. His pictures, assemblages, or walk-through environments— "sculpto-pictoramas," he called them—are raucous, rowdy, robust, and effervescing. These densely packed artworks are a great escape into a rollicking world.

Grooms's work often moves beyond simple fun into satire with his humorous depiction of modern life and especially urban living. His mixed-media assemblages of Manhattan are complex and crowded, bursting with a saucy style and frantic energy. He creates endless stories. He uses a variety of materials: plywood, two-by-fours, pine planks, fabric, Fiberglas, resins, styrofoam, and insulation foam.

His large works resemble stage sets, for which he even supplied the actors. Like a set designer, Grooms worked with a team. One of his assistants was his wife, artist Mimi Gross, daughter of sculptor Chaim Gross. They worked together on many of his large pieces until they separated in the mid-1970s and later divorced. Although he had lived in New York since he was twenty, Grooms presents a tourist's view. It's like he's still fresh from the Nashville suburbs, where he grew up, and can't get enough of the topsy-turvy world of New York.

As part of his satirical series depicting the major artists in history, the aquatint *To the Lighthouse*, in the collection of the Cape Cod Museum of Art, lightheartedly portrays Grooms admiring—or critiquing—the master realist artist Edward Hopper, who, in turn, is painting one of his iconic lighthouses. This work inserts humor into the picture of the serious Hopper being observed by Grooms, whose images so often are playful and almost cartoon-like.

Grooms's works are included in numerous museum collections, including the Whitney Museum of American Art, the Metropolitan Museum of Art, and the Museum of Modern Art in New York; the Art Institute of Chicago; the Hirshhorn Museum and Sculpture Garden in Washington, DC; the Museum of Contemporary Art in Los Angeles; Moderna Museet in Stockholm, Sweden; and the Nagoya City Museum, in Nagoya, Japan.

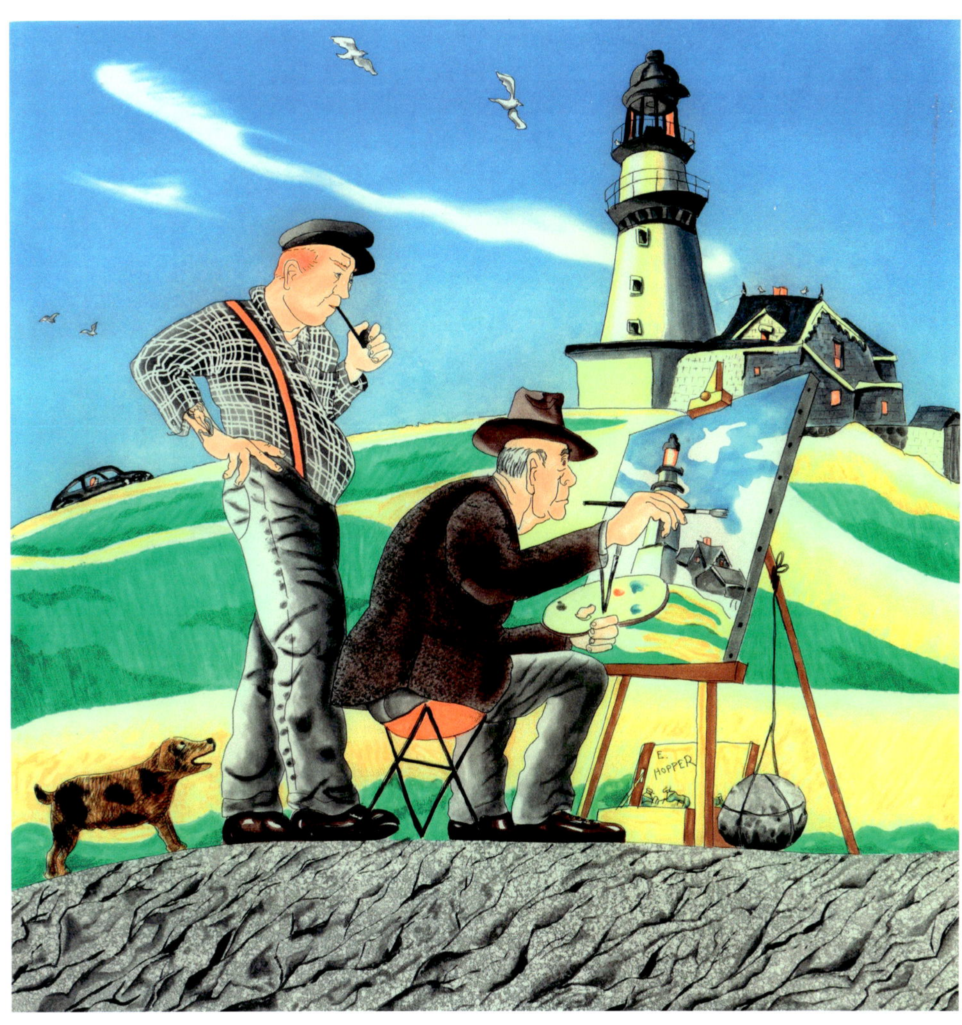

Red Grooms, *To The Lighthouse* 1/50, 1997. Aquatint etching on paper, 14 ¾ × 14¾ inches. *Museum purchase with funds from Jamie and Stephania McClennen,* 1997.© *Red Grooms/Artists Rights Society (ARS), New York.*

ROWLAND SCHERMAN
(1937–)

In 1958, Rowland Scherman began his career in photography working for *Life* magazine in New York, taking pictures and working in the darkroom. In 1961, he became a photographer for the Peace Corps and traveled extensively. He has photographed for *Life*, *Time*, *Newsweek*, *Paris Match*, *Playboy*, and *National Geographic*.

Scherman was born in New York and studied at Oberlin College. He photographed many of the musical, cultural, and political events of the 1960s, including: the 1963 Newport Folk Festival, where he had the opportunity to photograph a young Bob Dylan; the Beatles first concert in the United States in 1964; and the Woodstock festival. He won a Grammy Award in 1968 for his cover of *Bob Dylan's Greatest Hits*.

In 2000, Scherman settled in Orleans on Cape Cod, where he has found numerous subjects for his photography. *Cape Cinema*, in the museum collection, focuses on the rooftop of this historic building in a vigorous image that highlights the sharp angles of its architecture. *Jack's Beach, Wellfleet* and *Province Lands* are serene views of places near his home. *Mississippi John*, also in the Cape Cod Museum of Art collection, is a painterly photograph that relates to Scherman's interest in musicians.

In 1969, Scherman was voted Photographer of the Year by the Washington Art Director's Association. His book, *Timeless: Photography of Rowland Scherman*, edited by Michael E. Jones and Christine Jones, and published by Peter E. Randall in 2014, is a collection of his images and writings.

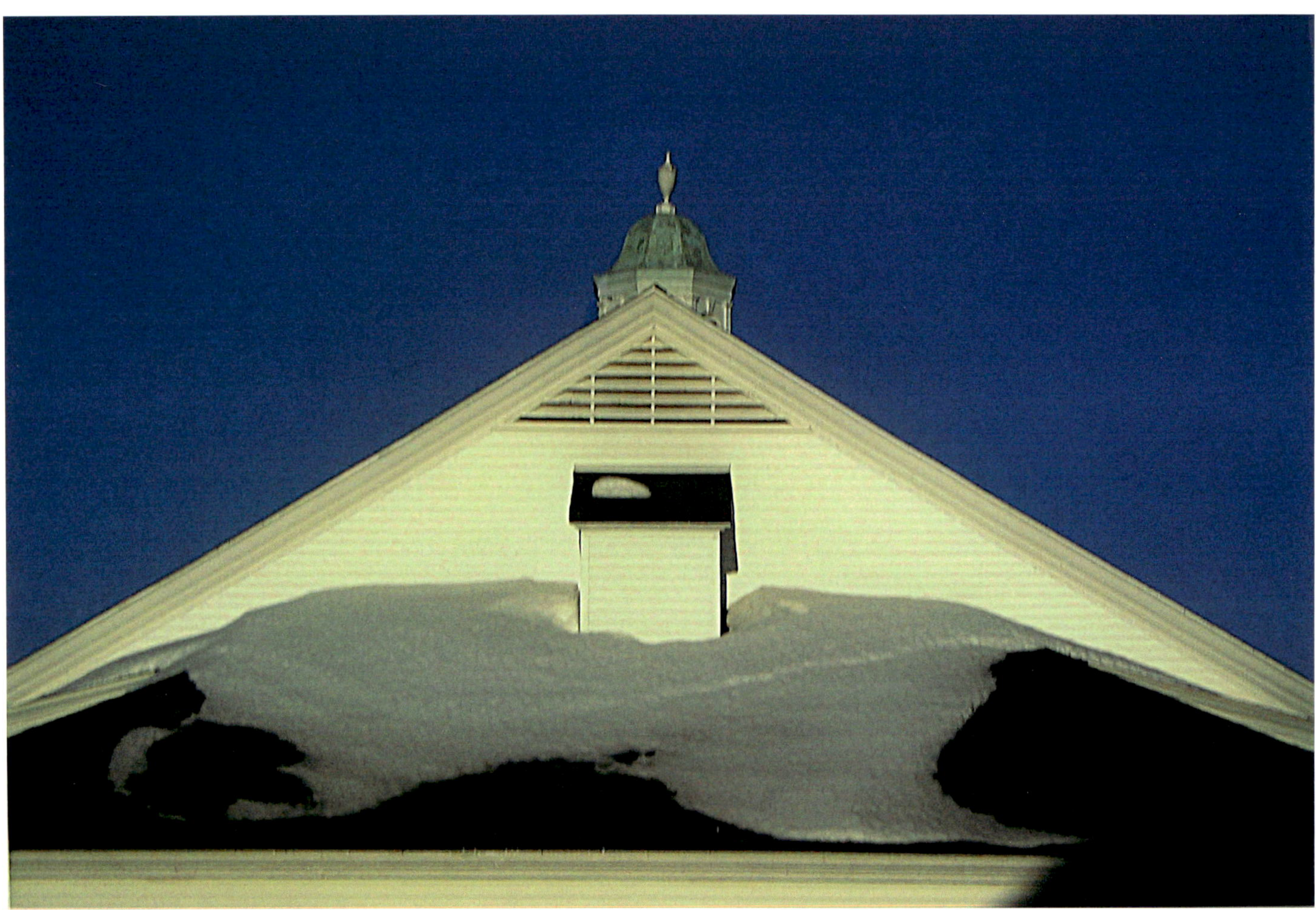

Rowland Scherman, *Cape Cinema*, 2000–2005. Archival pigment print, 11 × 16¾ inches. *Gift of Rowland Scherman*, 2005.

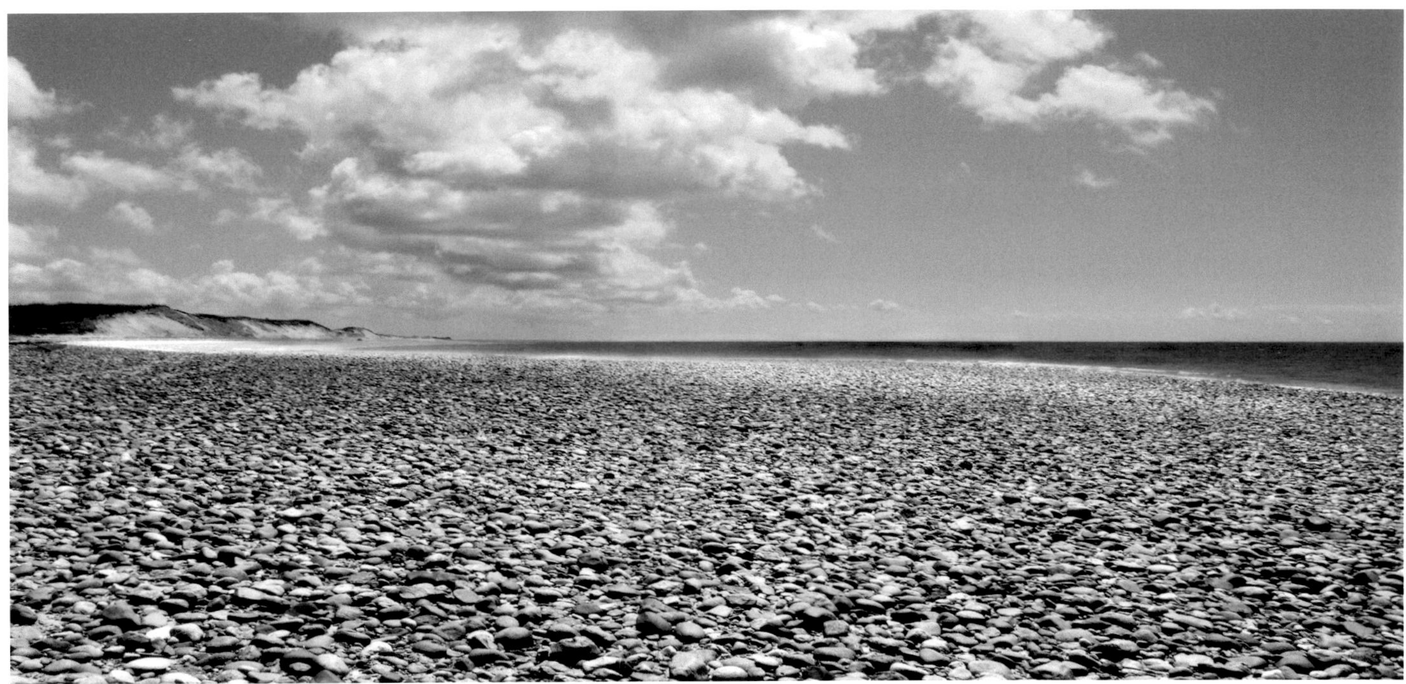

Rowland Scherman, *Jack's Beach, Wellfleet*, 2000–2005. Archival pigment print, 8½ × 17 inches. *Gift of Rowland Scherman*, 2005.

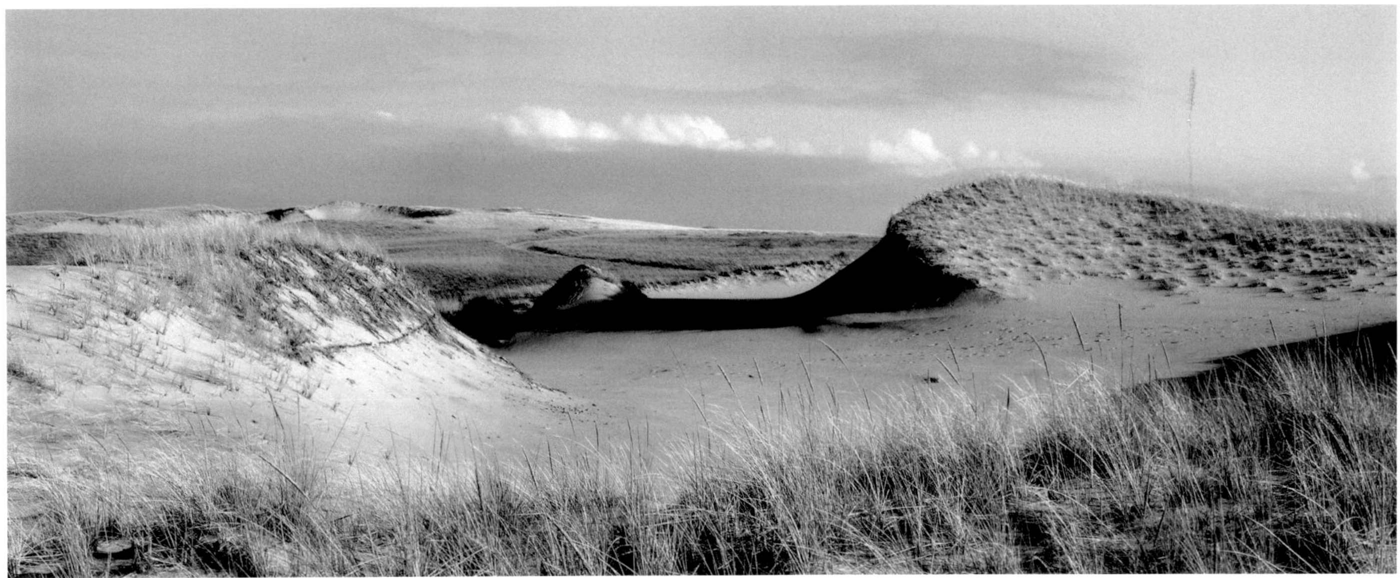

Rowland Scherman, *Province Lands*, 2000–2005. Archival pigment print, 6¾ × 17 inches. *Gift of Rowland Scherman*, 2005.

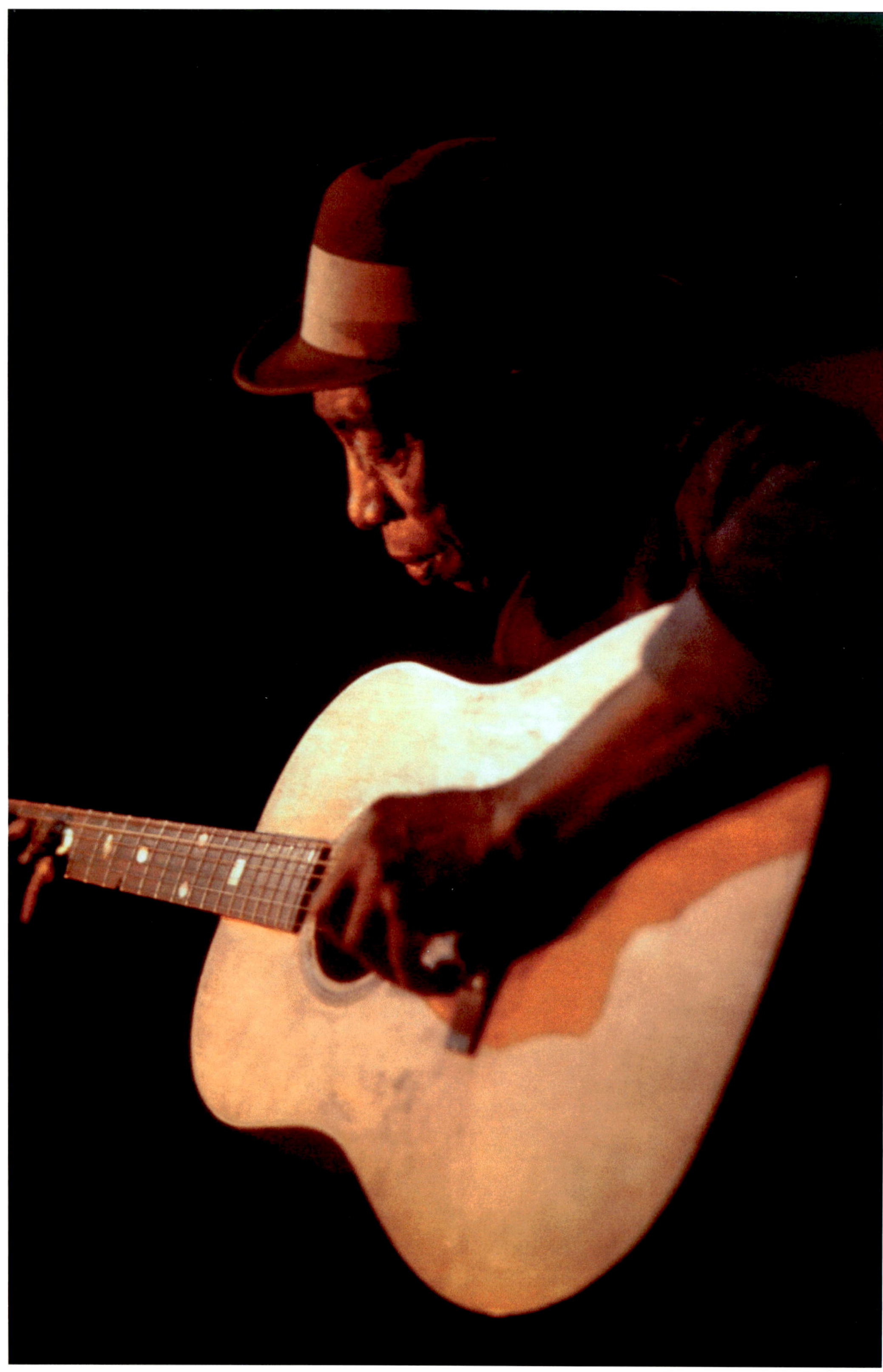

Rowland Scherman, *Mississippi John,* 2000–2005. Archival pigment print, 10¾ × 7¼ inches.
Gift of Rowland Scherman, 2005.

JOEL MEYEROWITZ
(1938–)

Joel Meyerowitz began his photography career on the streets of his native New York in the tradition of Henri Cartier-Bresson, the French photographer who pioneered an artful form of photojournalism.

After studying painting at Ohio State University, he worked as an art director for an ad agency. When he went out with photographer Robert Frank on an assignment and watched him work, he became inspired and quit his job. He loved street photography because he was thrilled by the crowds of people.

However, the first time he saw Cape Cod in 1976, he was enamored with the light. He photographed the Cape landscape and its houses, beaches, clotheslines, porches, and picket fences to produce a singular collection of color images, which were shown at the Museum of Fine Arts in Boston and published in *Cape Light*. The book is a collection of sensitive, atmospheric, carefully composed photographs taken in the 1970s. The porch scenes show changing effects of light and mood. His interior shots of artful compositions stop time. Lacking the mountains and grandeur of the American West, the Cape offered a simpler world that allowed Meyerowitz more creativity than just being a recorder of nature's spectacles. A simple row of cottages along Cape Cod Bay has the color, scale, and presence to spark his inventiveness. Other books of photographs related to Provincetown include *A Summer's Day* and *Bay/Sky*.

He was in Provincetown when the World Trade Center was attacked. When he heard the news, he couldn't wait to get back to New York City, where he began photographing the devastation and recording the mammoth cleanup. *Aftermath: World Trade Center Archive* was the result of that work.

The photographs from the museum collection are from the book *Legacy: The Preservation of Wilderness in New*

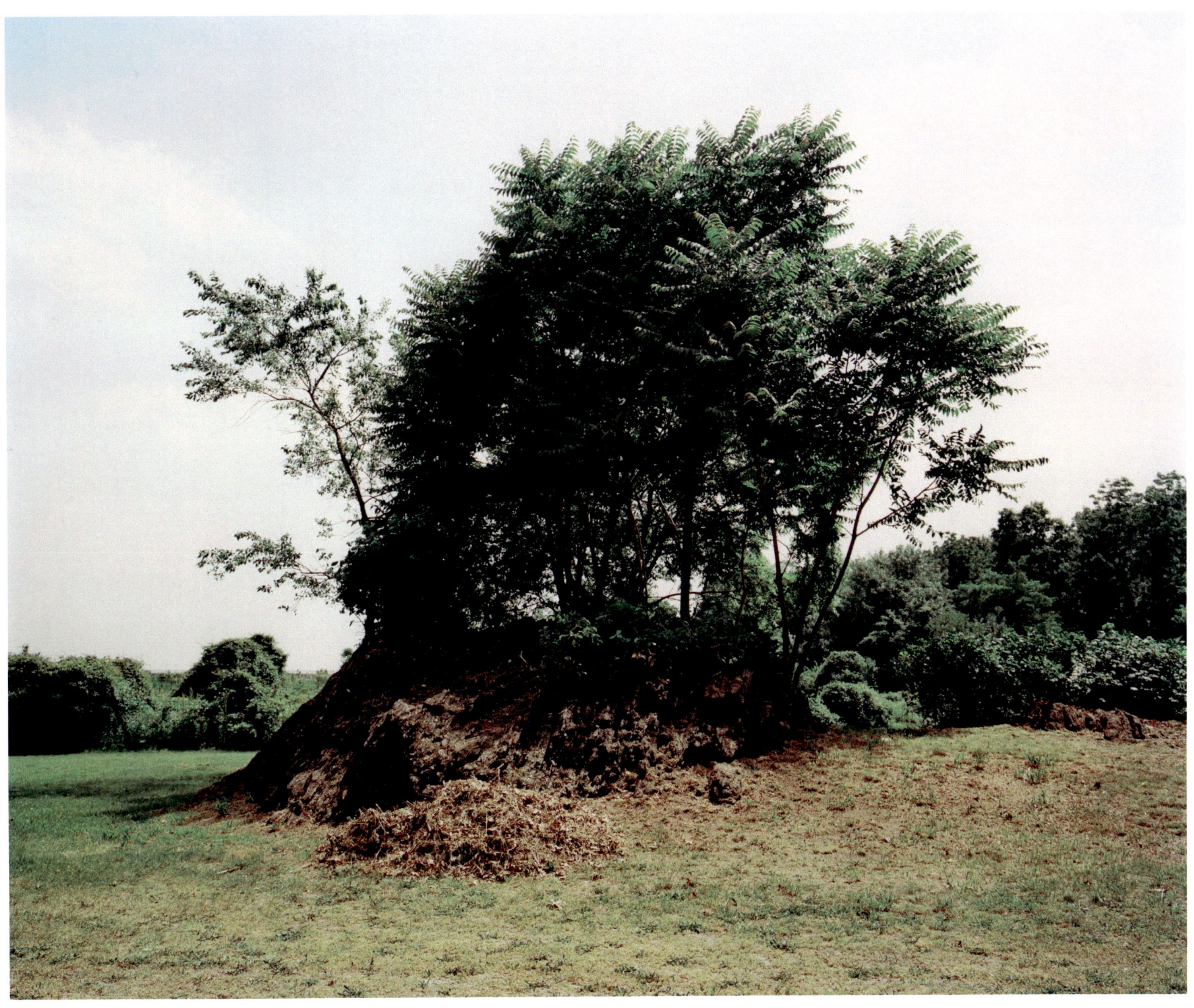

Joel Meyerowitz, *High Rock Park, Spring*, 2009. Archival pigment print, 14 9/16 × 16 inches. *Gift of the Aperture Foundation*, 2010.

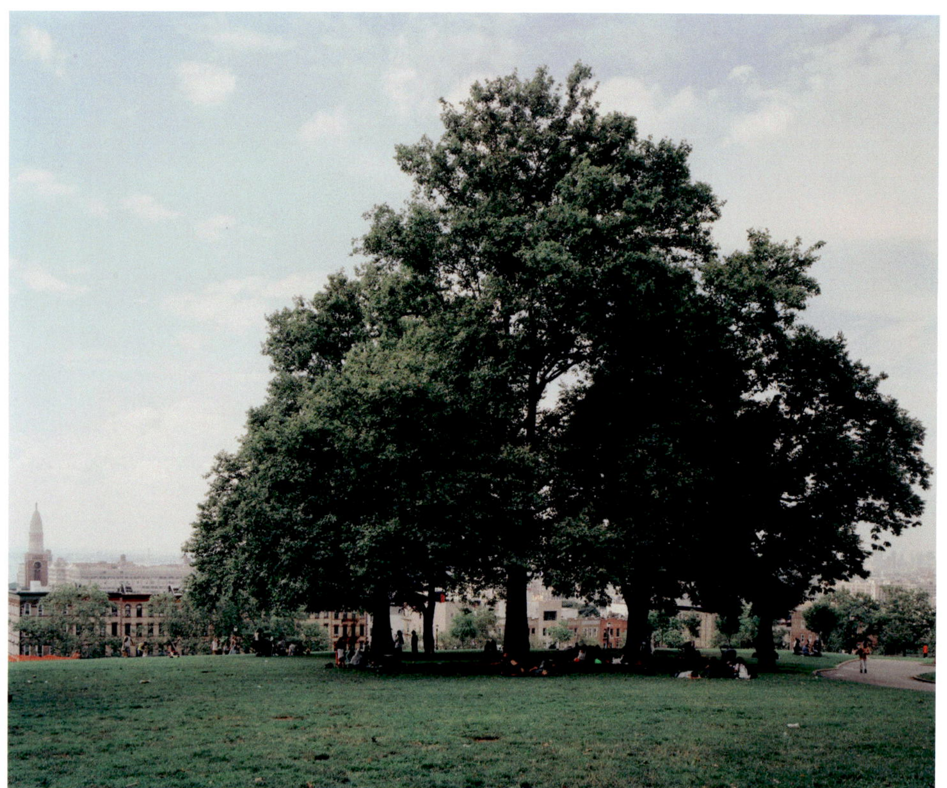

Left:
Joel Meyerowitz, *Sunset Park, Stand of Trees on the Western Side of the Park, Summer,* 2006. Archival pigment print, $14\frac{9}{16}$ × 16 inches, *Gift of the Aperture Foundation*, 2010.

Below:
Joel Meyerowitz, *Central Park, Magnolia Blossoms near Literacy Walk, Spring,* 2007. Archival pigment print, $14\frac{9}{16}$ × 16 inches. *Gift of the Aperture Foundation*, 2010.

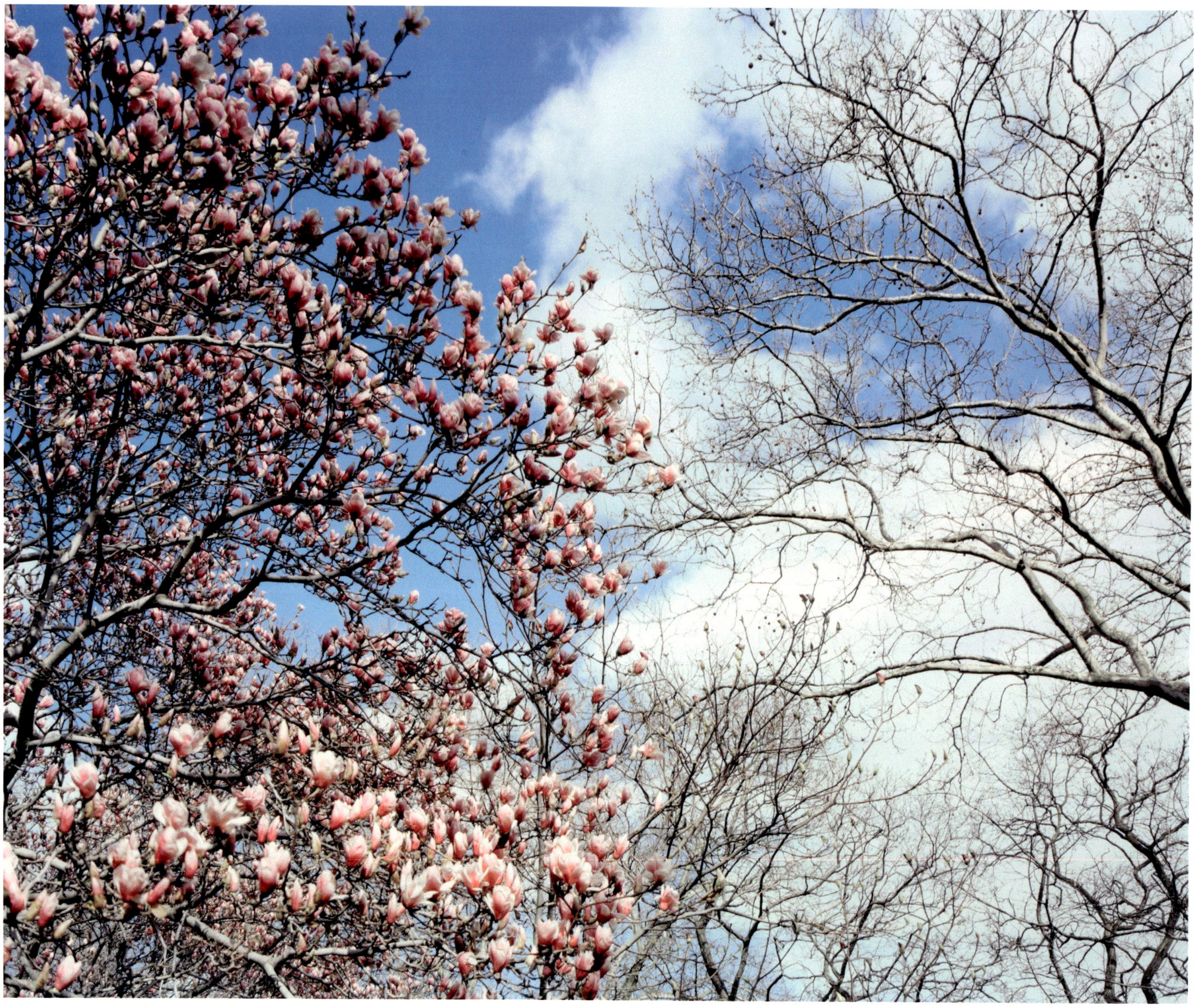

York City Parks, and include a burst of pink in *Central Park, Magnolia Blossoms Near Literary Walk, Spring*; the double image of reflections in water in *Pelham Bay Park; Orchard Beach Outcrop of Trees Behind Beach, Summer*, and trees covered in mist in *Udalls Park Preserve, Udalls Cove, Little Neck Bay, Spring.*

His work is held in many public collections, including the Museum of Fine Arts in Boston; the Metropolitan Museum of Art, the Whitney Museum of American Art, and the Museum of Modern Art in New York; the Philadelphia Museum of Art; the Chicago Art Institute; and the Centre Pompidou in France.

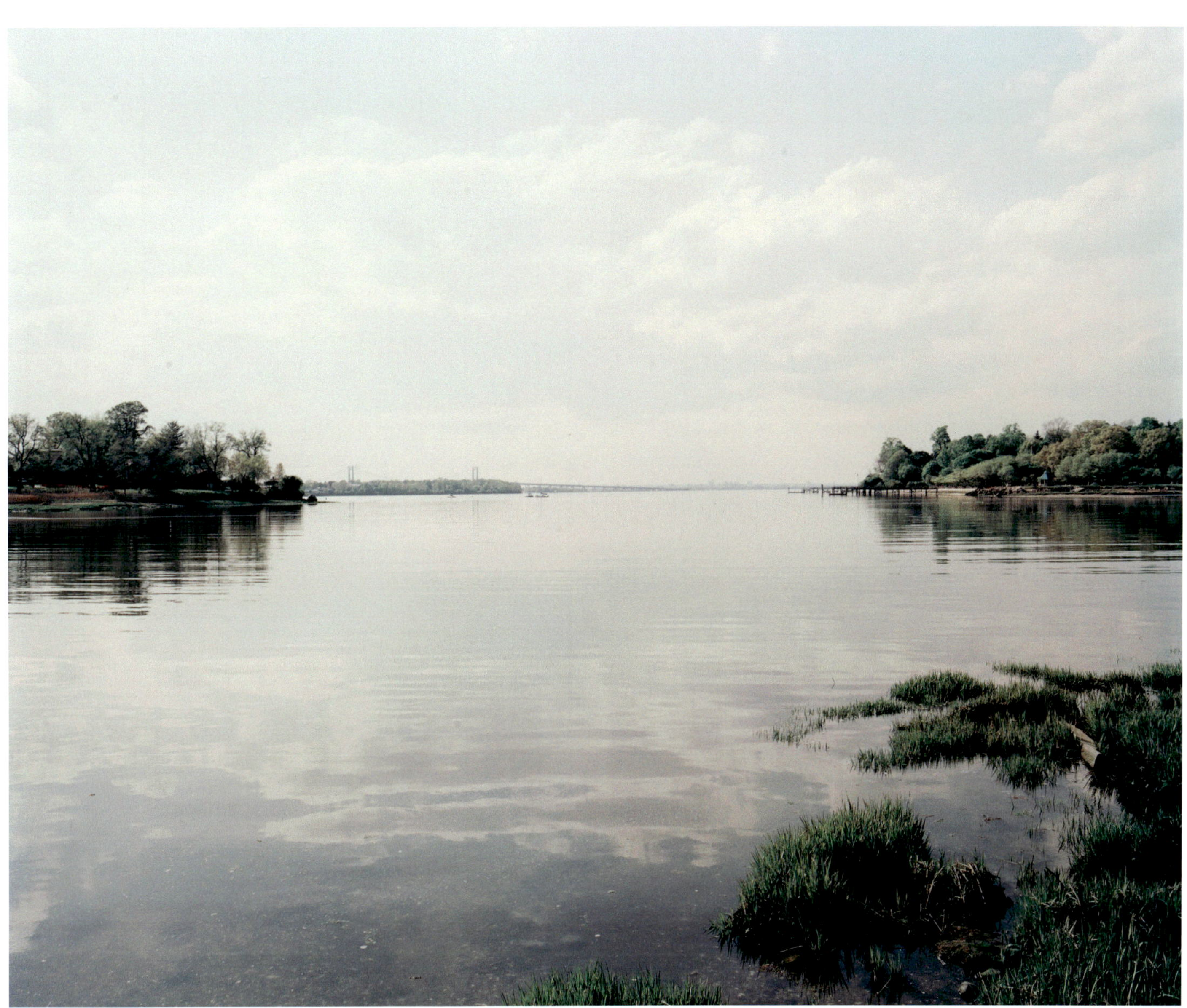

Joel Meyerowitz, *Pelham Bay Park, Orchard Beach Outcrop of Trees behind Beach, Summer*, 2006. Archival pigment print, 14⅝ × 16 inches. *Gift of the Aperture Foundation*, 2010.

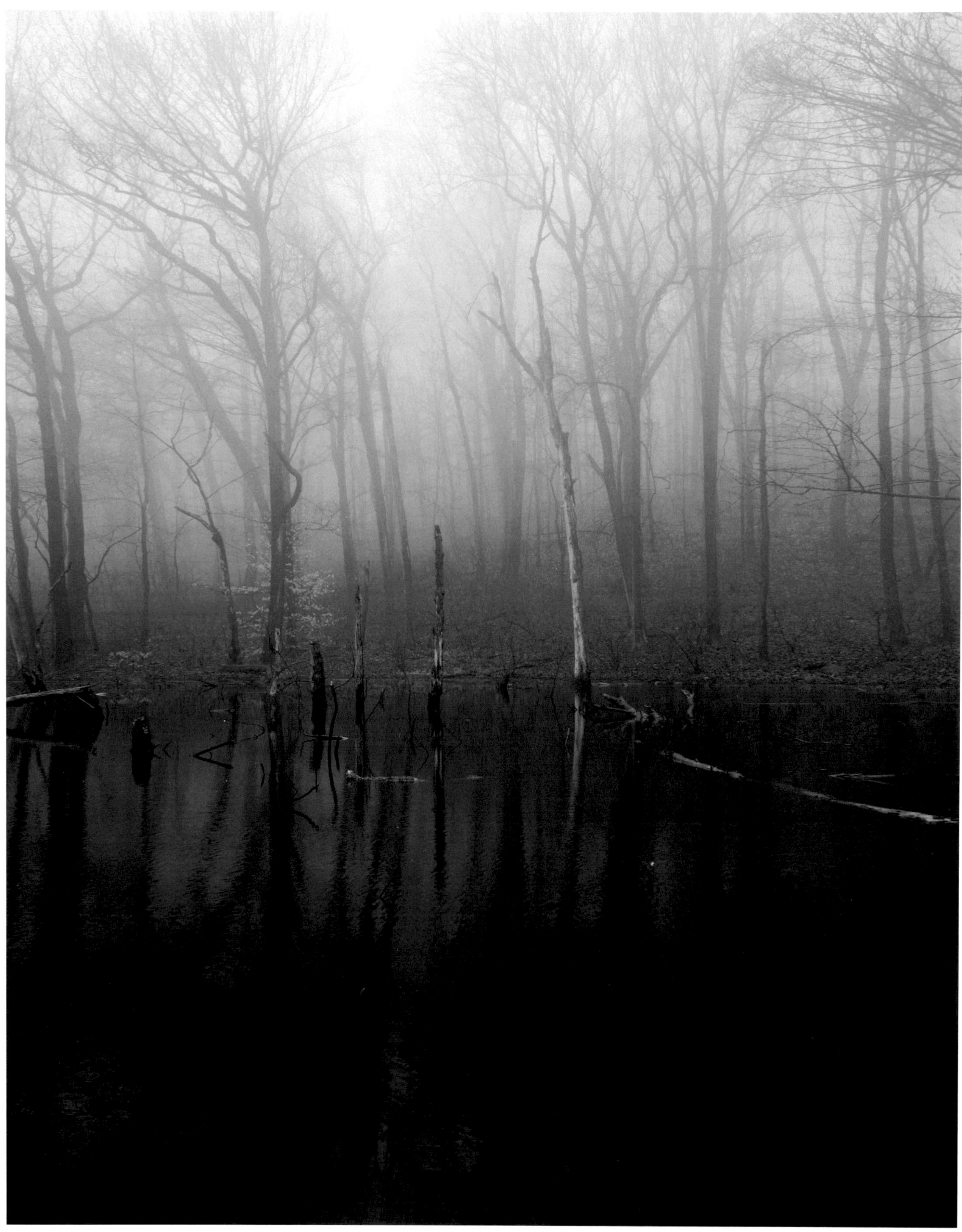

Joel Meyerowitz, *Udalls Park Preserve, Udall Cove, Little Neck Bay, Spring*, 2006. Archival pigment print, 16 × 14⁹⁄₁₆ inches.
Gift of the Aperture Foundation, 2010.

SAM BARBER
(1943–)

Sam Barber's paintings have been influenced by the work of the French impressionists, in particular Claude Monet and Edgar Degas, and by American impressionists Childe Hassam and Frank Benson. He is known for his light-infused landscapes with dappled, luminous colors and feathery brushwork. Born in Europe, Barber came to America when he was a child and grew up in New York. Barber studied at the Art Students League, the National Academy of Design, and in Provincetown with Henry Hensche, who was committed to impressionist color theories as an artist and a teacher.

Near his home on Cape Cod, Barber finds numerous subjects to activate his imagination. Quaint cottages lined along a quiet road, lily ponds, historic buildings. Provincetown rooftops, a sunlit day on Nantucket, a snowy scene in Wellfleet, a distant view of Sandwich village, and Brewster dunes in autumn are places he has captured. *Janie in the Garden*, in the Cape Cod Museum of Art collection, is a lustrous example of his interest in flower-filled gardens. Harbors with flickering light on the water intrigue Barber, and his *River Street, Bass River (Cape Cod)*, also in the museum collection, is typical of his impressionistic style. Sometimes he includes figures: a mother and child in a garden, a woman with a parasol. His still lifes have vases of flowers. Barber's world is quiet, glittering in the sunlight and even his winter scenes are lit like a summer day.

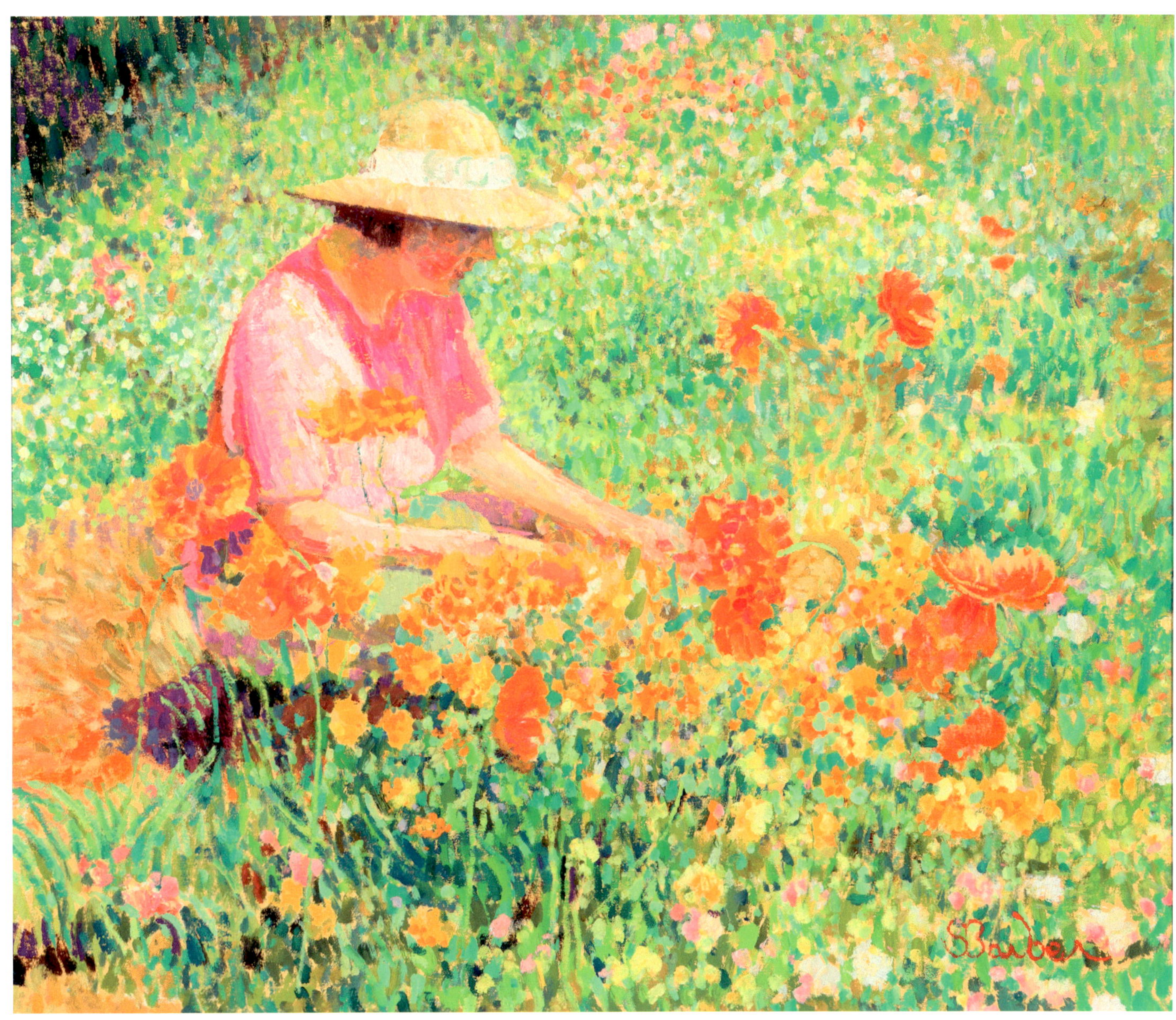

Sam Barber, *Janie in the Garden*, 2000. Oil on canvas, 30 × 36 inches. *Gift of Sam Barber*, 2003.

When he travels, he paints locations in France and Italy that engage him. He is a member of the Society of American Impressionists. His works are included in numerous museum collections, including the New Orleans Museum of Art; the University of Virginia Art Museum in Charlottesville; the Mississippi Museum of Art in Jackson; the Minnesota Museum of Art in St. Paul; the Museum of Fine Arts in St. Petersburg, Florida; the Mint Museum of Art in Charlotte, North Carolina; and the Memphis Brooks Museum of Art in Tennessee.

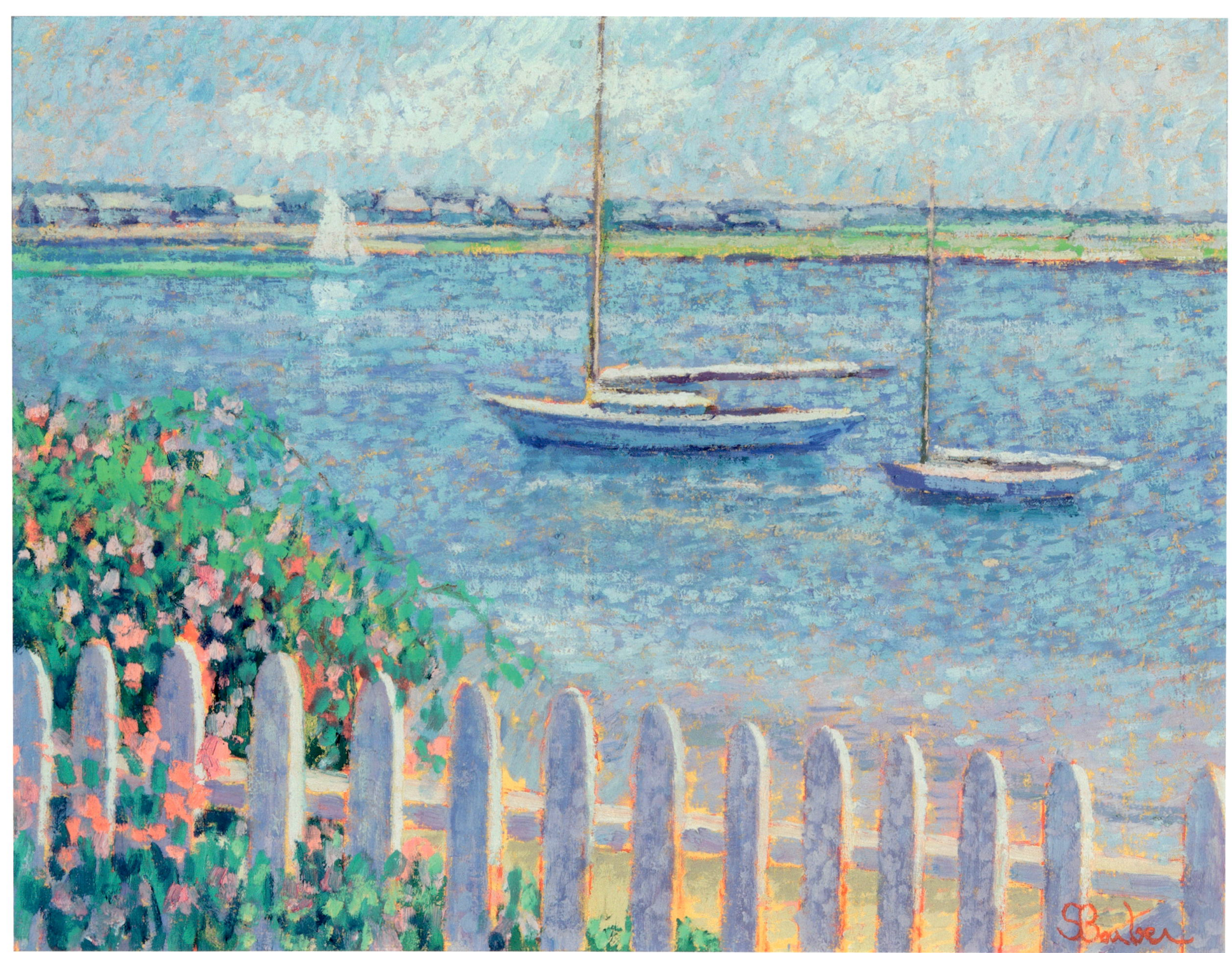

Sam Barber, *River Street, Bass River*, 1989. Oil on canvas, 18 × 24 inches. *Gift of Joan Gilson*, 2007.

JIM PETERS
(1945–)

Jim Peters's passion for painting the female figure has remained constant for years. His work has to do with the tension between a man and a woman in a confined space, and also the energy he creates on the canvas. His provocative images continue to capture the age-old dynamics between the sexes as they explore the intimacy and private lives of his subjects.

Peters was born in Syracuse, New York, and his first interest for a career was not in the arts but in nuclear physics. He has a bachelor's degree in atomic physics from the United States Naval Academy and earned a master's degree in nuclear engineering on an Atomic Energy Commission fellowship at the Massachusetts Institute of Technology.

When he decided he wanted to be an artist, he studied painting at the Maryland Institute College of Art and earned an MFA. He was a fellow at the Fine Arts Work Center in Provincetown from 1982 to 1984. In 1985, he was selected as one of nine artists out of a field of 2,000 for the Guggenheim's *New Horizons in American Art*.

Although he now lives in North Adams, Massachusetts, Peters lived for many years in Provincetown and Truro. He is still connected to Provincetown, where he teaches and exhibits his work.

There is a narrative aspect to Peters's art as the viewer is introduced to a scene that can trigger a variety of emotions and experiences related to loneliness, jealousy, companionship, separation, tenderness, and angst. *Alone with Mirror*, in the Cape Cod Museum of Art collection, depicts a solitary moment. The lines defining the figure are dynamic, the surfaces are erratic, scrubbed with texture and animated brushstrokes. He presents a private view, almost a voyeuristic one, an intrusion on an intimate act.

Peters's works are included in several public collections, including the Guggenheim Museum in New York; the William Benton Museum at the University of Connecticut; and the Flint Institute of Art in Flint, Michigan.

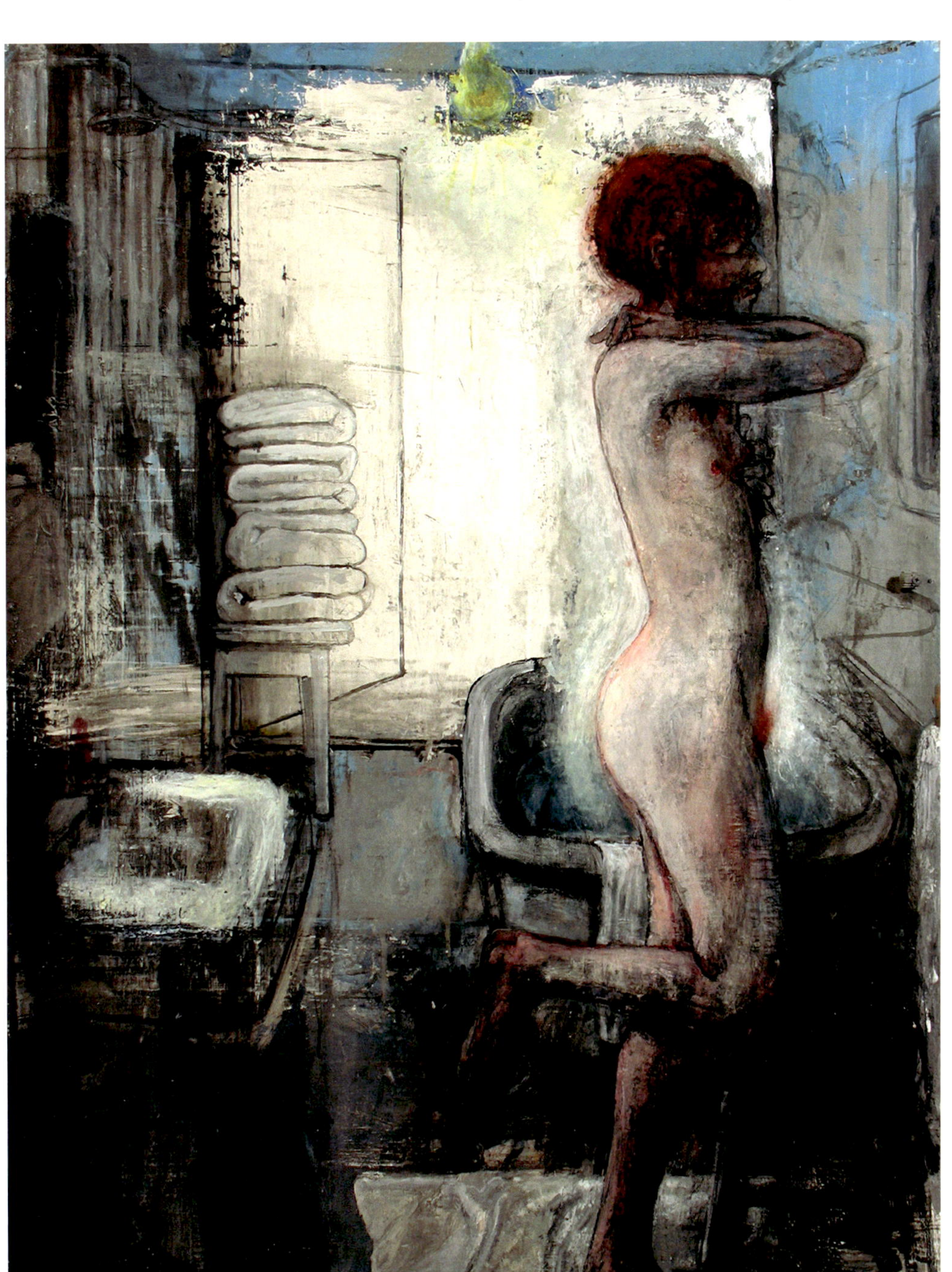

Jim Peters, *Alone with Mirror*, 2014. Oil on canvas, 48 × 36 inches. *Gift of Jim Peters*, 2016.

JAMIE WYETH
(1946–)

It is not surprising that Jamie Wyeth became an accomplished painter—just about everyone in his family paints or painted. The exception are their dogs, although occasionally some of them, such as Wyeth's golden Labrador retriever, Kleberg, have found a comfortable position in his work. Wyeth painted many images of Kleberg with the circle he drew around the dog's eye. He was taken with what he had done because it reminded him of Pete the Pup from *The Little Rascals*, and so this mark remained for the rest of Kleberg's life. A very appealing portrait of Kleberg and another one of his dogs, titled *Kleberg & Dozer*, is in the Cape Cod Museum of Art collection.

Jamie is the son of Andrew Wyeth and the grandson of N. C. Wyeth. Andrew depicted the world and people around him in subtle shades and with an approach that captures a reflective and often somber mood. He worked in the realistic tradition of his father N. C. (Newell Convers) Wyeth, who was well regarded as an illustrator. Jamie follows in that tradition, yet his more recent work has an expressionistic and bolder aspect, which departs from the quieter images of his father.

Nature and rural life are a large part of Wyeth's world. His work includes portraits; landscapes of the areas where he lives in the Brandywine River Valley (between Pennsylvania and Delaware) and the Southern and Monhegan islands in Maine; and paintings of animals and birds.

Jamie grew up in Chadds Ford, Pennsylvania, and now lives part of the year on a farm in Wilmington, Delaware, not far from his childhood home. His style of painting is subtle and sensitive, and involves a variety of mediums, including oil on canvas and panel, watercolor, pen and ink, etching, and lithography, as well as "combined mediums," which primarily consist of watercolor and gouache thickly painted. Wyeth's style has been influenced by American traditionalists John Singleton Copley, Thomas Eakins, and Rockwell Kent. When Wyeth spends time in Maine, he lives in a home Rockwell Kent built.

In the mid-1970s, Wyeth struck out for New York, and, oddly enough, spent time in Andy Warhol's Factory. These two artists were an unlikely duo, although they shared an interest in realism. Their styles, however, could not be more different. While in New York, Wyeth painted several portraits of Rudolph Nureyev, one of him nude and a dashing one as Don Quixote in a dramatic ballet position. However, the New York scene was just a passing one for Wyeth, who returned to his rural roots to continue painting the subjects that were his life in Brandywine and Maine.

Wyeth's paintings of architecture, especially the glittering white clapboards of lighthouses, are luminous and done from unusual perspectives. His pictures of dogs, chickens, ducks, owls, and roosters evoke the rural serenity of a bygone time. *The Seven Deadly Sins* paintings of ravenous and lustful gulls are fierce. His recent, often thickly painted images of the Maine coast, include turbulent waves, crashing against the shore.

Wyeth's works are included in many public collections, including the National Gallery of Art and National Portrait Gallery in Washington, DC; the John F. Kennedy Library in Boston; the Museum of Modern Art in New York; the Farnsworth Art Museum in Rockland, Maine; the Delaware Art Museum in Wilmington; and Brandywine River Museum of Art in Chadds Ford, Pennsylvania.

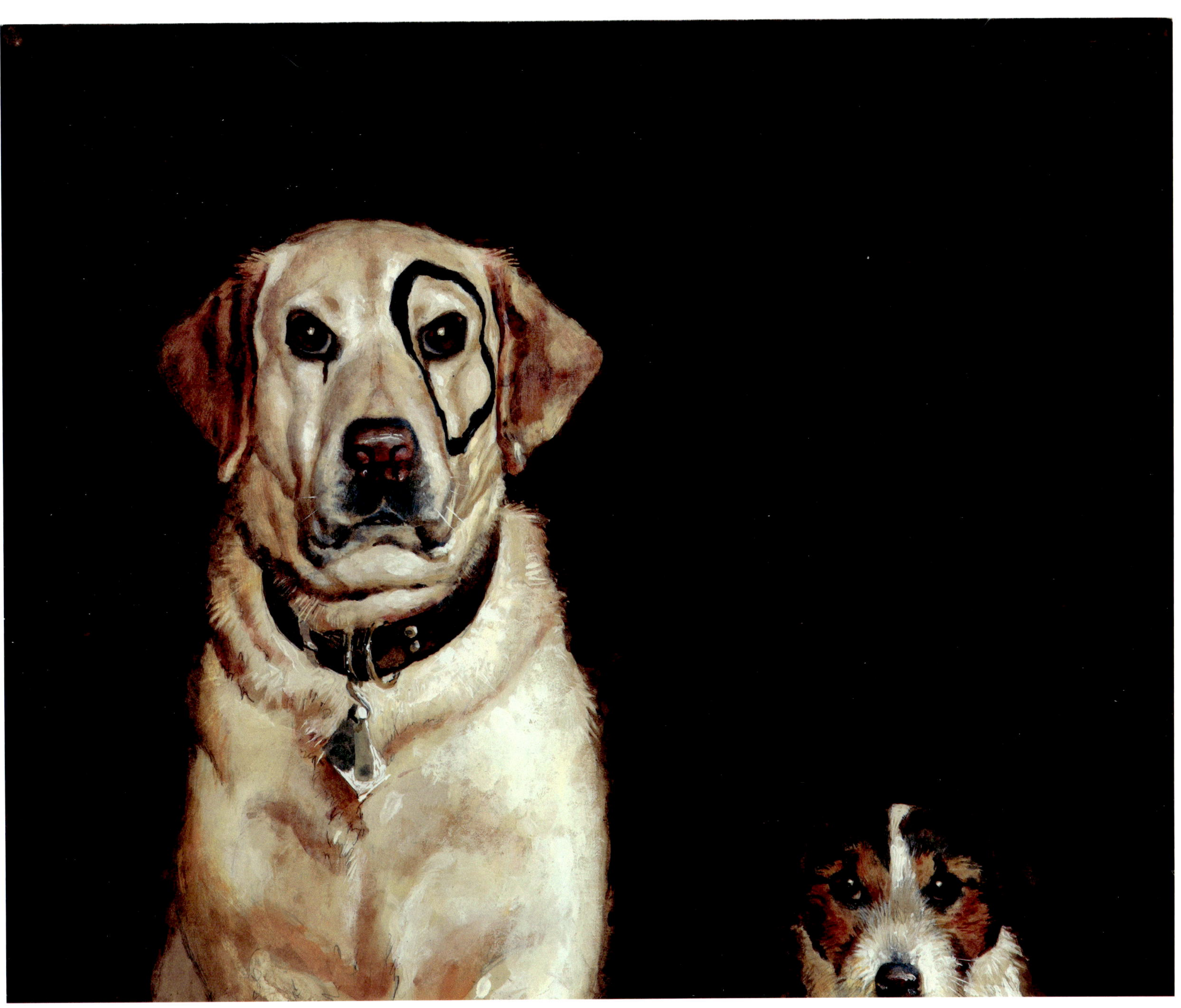

Jamie Wyeth, *Kleberg and Dozer*, 1987. Mixed media on canvas, 16 × 20 inches. *Gift of Mrs. Sarah B. Neal*, 2008.

MARIELUISE HUTCHINSON
(1947–)

Marieluise Hutchinson's paintings of solitary farmhouses and New England homes, set against stretches of spring grass or snow-covered lawns, take the viewer back to a gentler time, to the nineteenth, and maybe even the eighteenth century.

Hutchinson grew up in a nineteenth-century Federal Colonial house on eleven acres in Hanover, Massachusetts, which in the 1950s was still quite rural. Behind the house was a barn, where Hutchinson and her brother and sister used to play. Her affection for the older buildings she paints is related to these experiences of her childhood, and her respect for the hardiness of the people who inhabited them. A self-taught artist, Hutchinson divides her time between Yarmouth Port on Cape Cod and Cushing, Maine, which is Andrew Wyeth country. Wyeth spent summers there and his work has had a strong influence on her. The stoic quality of the architecture in her paintings can be compared to the spare character of the buildings in many of his images.

Hutchinson travels around Maine and sometimes ventures into New Hampshire and Vermont, searching for just the right structures to photograph. The painting is then designed and completed in her studio. She sometimes makes changes in the buildings to recapture an authenticity that may have been lost when the house was renovated or modernized.

Her carefully composed paintings, with intricate and precise details of pristine houses and barns, are highlighted by the sharp slant of roofs shown from various angles. *The Wonder of Winter,* in the Cape Cod Museum of Art collection, shows her interest in architecture and the value of those inclined roofs to the vitality of the composition. Her skies vary with the time of day and are of many colors—a glowing pink and blue light at sunset, as in *The Wonder of Winter*, or softer with winter clouds fading into mauve. In spring daylight, there's a cerulean, cloud-filled sky. And the heavens at night are deep blue with a cream-colored full moon shining among the stars.

Hutchinson is devoted to the rural New England image. Her work is all about creating serene images that evoke a gentler time: a red barn glowing against a white farmhouse, an immaculate snow-covered field, two children building a snowman, and a sense that all is right in the world.

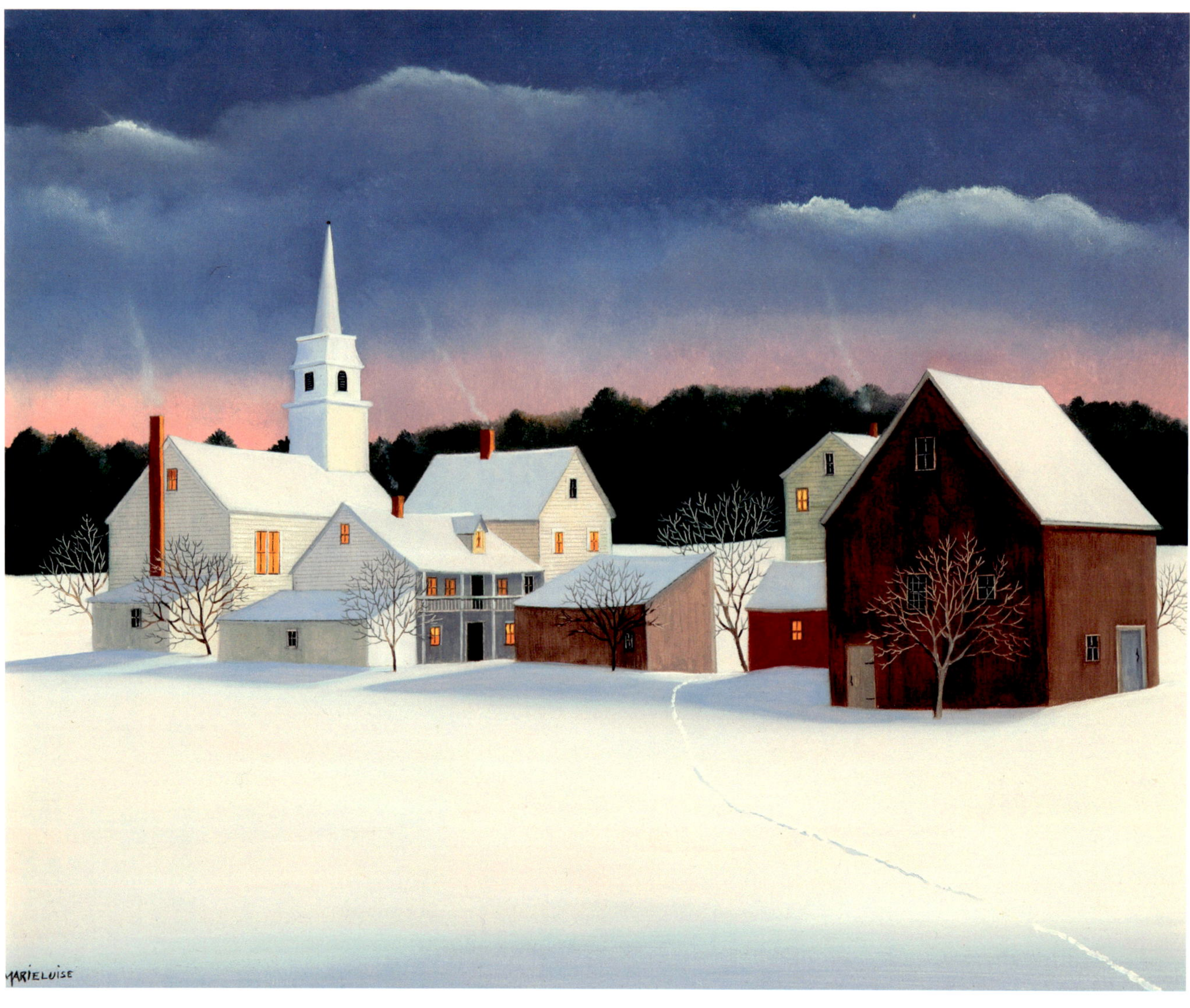

Marieluise Hutchinson, *The Wonder of Winter*, 2003. Oil on panel, 10 × 13 inches. *Gift of Marieluise Hutchinson,* 2003.

HILDA NEILY
(1947–)

Provincetown became Hilda Neily's home in the late 1960s and she has lived there ever since. Henry Hensche, who was running the Cape School of Art in the tradition of Charles Hawthorne, was the impetus for Neily's desire to study there and be part of the art colony.

Born and raised in Windsor, Vermont, Neily spent many hours drawing and painting in her early years, and later graduated from the Boston Art Institute. Growing up, she lived near the home of Maxfield Parrish and studied his paintings, which had an early influence on her. However, when she met Hensche, she recognized his skill as a colorist and found that his impressionistic approach was perfectly suited to her inclinations. She studied with him for fifteen years.

As a *plein-air* impressionist, Neily is committed to color and light, to the changing light conditions and the expression of those changes in color. As many artists have remarked, the light is special in Provincetown because it reflects off the water that surrounds it, as well as off the sand and dunes. Consequently, Neily has painted her luminous landscapes mostly in Provincetown, in the dunes, moors, and Beech Forest. She looks for quiet areas even in town, where she treasures the neat houses and streets near her home. Even her still lifes, such as *Ginger Jar in the Morning*, in the Cape Cod Museum of Art collection, capture a sparkling, reflected light.

Neily is a member of the Boston Society of Artists.

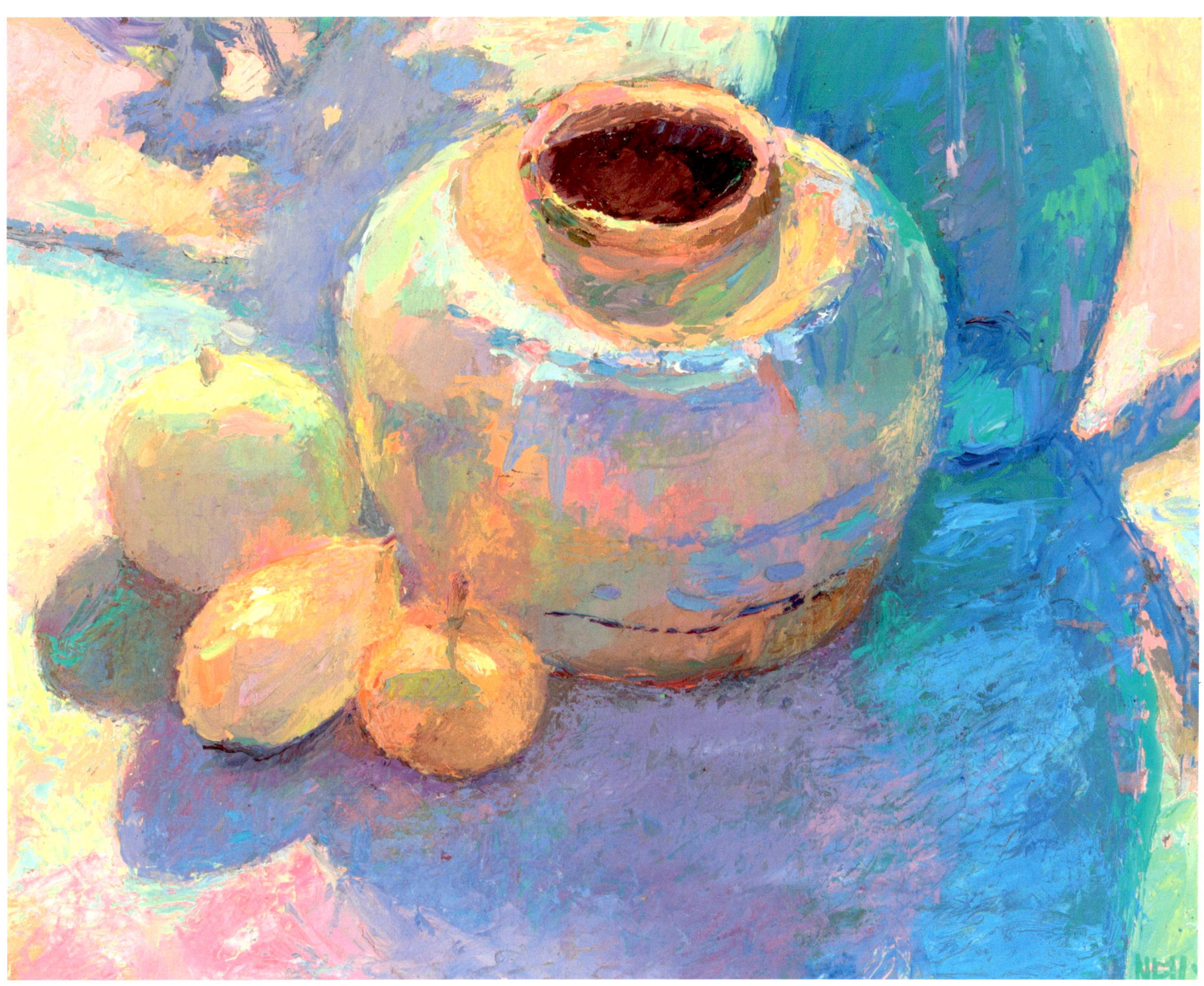

Hilda Neily, *Ginger Jar in the Morning*, 1981. Oil on board, 7½ × 10 inches. *Gift of Elizabeth and Robert Douglas Hunter*, 1991.

MIKE WRIGHT
(1949–)

Fragments of boats and the cast-offs Mike Wright finds on her walks on the Provincetown beaches and around town are the building blocks of her found-wood abstract sculpture.

Born in Baltimore, Wright received a bachelor's degree in art education from Towson University in Maryland. She taught art in an elementary school and worked as a graphic designer for a number of years before moving to Provincetown in 1984 to manage a bed and breakfast.

A class with Paul Bowen, who builds sculpture from wood fragments and other objects he often finds on the beaches, inspired Wright. She adopted his approach of scavenging for wood, dragging big, old pieces into her studio, and then finding ways to create something new from a piece of a boat or an old floor board.

Unlike Bowen's search, hers is only for painted wood. In her studio, at any time, she may have large orange boards from a wardrobe she found outside a home, painted wood she found washed up on the beach, or boat fragments, which are scarcer these days with the decline of the fishing industry in Provincetown. These elements may be cut or may be left exactly how she found them, as they are assembled into bold sculptures made up of dramatic shapes. Circles, rectilinear forms, and angled shapes are put together with a sharp eye for color relationships.

Her tools are simple: a jigsaw, drill, miter saw, an assortment of hand tools, nails, and screws. She is concerned with the dynamics, tension, and the balance of a piece, and for Wright, color is critical. The gritty fragments that make up Wright's sculpture can sometimes be identified as from a boat, an old floorboard, or a water ski, as is the case in *Fall Sunset* in the Cape Cod Museum of Art collection, composed of a yellow ski highlighted by pink fragments of wood, creating the abstraction of a sunset.

The abstract, constructed, and sometimes cubist character of her work is often directly influenced by the art of early modernists who worked in Provincetown: Blanche Lazzell, Karl Knaths, and Kenneth Stubbs. In her art, Wright is always aware of the town's rich history as she transforms remnants of the past into commanding modern constructions.

Wright has received a 2014 Pollock-Krasner Foundation Grant, was awarded a full fellowship to the Vermont Studio Center, won the Michael E. Deluty Outstanding Sculpture Prize at the CAA National Competition in 2007, and has exhibited in Japan, New York, Maryland, Florida, Louisiana, and Boston.

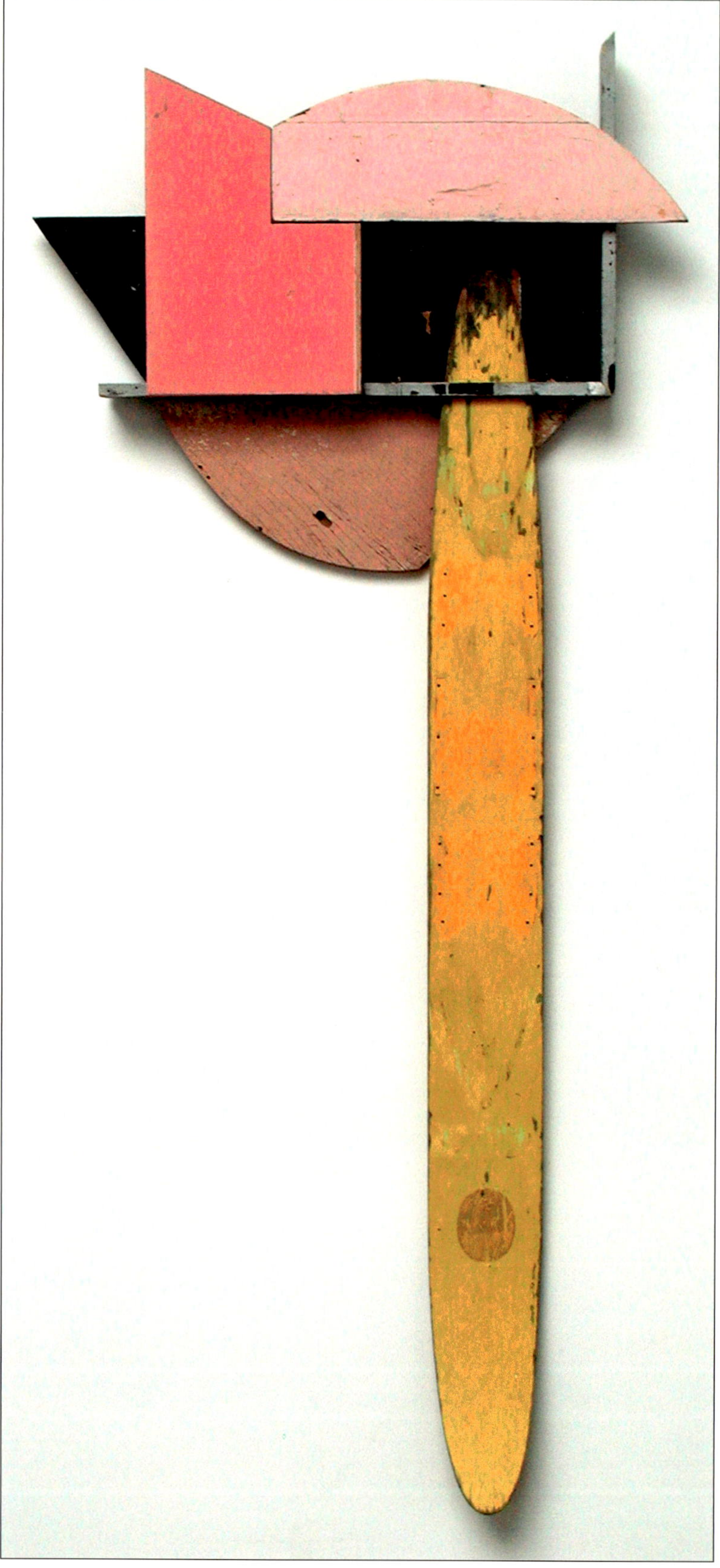

Mike Wright, *Fall Sunset*, 2002. Mixed media sculpture, 80 × 36 × 3½ inches. *Gift of Mike Wright,* 2015.

PAUL BOWEN
(1951–)

Growing up in the Victorian seaside resort Colwyn Bay, in Wales, Paul Bowen felt a special connection to the ocean, so when he came to Provincetown for a fellowship at the Fine Arts Work Center in 1977, he felt at home. And the sea has been a source for his abstract sculptures for years. He constructs these works, with references to cubism, with fragments of wood he has scavenged from the beaches in Provincetown and ones that are floating in the rivers of Vermont, where he now lives.

His sculptures, made up of the detritus that he collects, contain the echoes of the history that is part of each of his found elements. In many ways Bowen's background as his father's companion on exploration adventures has been a vital part of the work he does. His father was an architect and amateur historian, and together they explored the ancient land and history of Wales with its pre-Roman burial chambers, Roman roads, and megaliths.

Bowen lived in Provincetown until 2005 when he moved to Williamsville, Vermont. But he retains his ties to Provincetown, where he returns regularly as a member of the cooperative gallery artSTRAND and as a teacher at the Fine Arts Work Center.

Bowen searches for wood that shows signs of its previous use. The circular shape, which can take the form of a sphere, a disc, or a cylinder, is often found in his work. In *Untitled,* in the Cape Cod Museum of Art collection, the circle is replayed more than once with a woven ball erupting from a large wooden disc. The circular shape evolved, Bowen said, because he was finding on Provincetown beaches a lot of debris from cable drums used by the fishing fleets and the disc end of barrels. Often, however, Bowen builds the circular form with strips of wood boards that were once used to make fish boxes.

Bowen's 2002 *Windrush II*, installed outside the museum, is an immense circular form with boards extending from it, which add to the dimension and drama of the piece. It is made from redwood and mahogany. The redwood came from Narragansett Brewery beer vats; this was one of the rare occasions in which he bought wood. Some of Bowen's smaller wall pieces sit on shelves, and may have the curve of a tree branch or the bent wood from a rocking chair extending from a disc. In addition, Bowen's two-dimensional drawings and prints are imaginative images of fishing boats, as is *Untitled* in the museum collection.

His work is dynamic, built from materials that he manipulates and joins together. It is about shape and movement, yet his scavenged wood has a history, associated with the fishing industry, a dock that once was home to boats, or a house that before a storm stood firmly on land. This historical relationship gives his sculptures a dimension beyond their shape and texture, and reveals a deep connection to land and sea.

Bowen's works are part of major museum collections, including the Guggenheim Museum in New York and the Museum of Fine Arts in Boston.

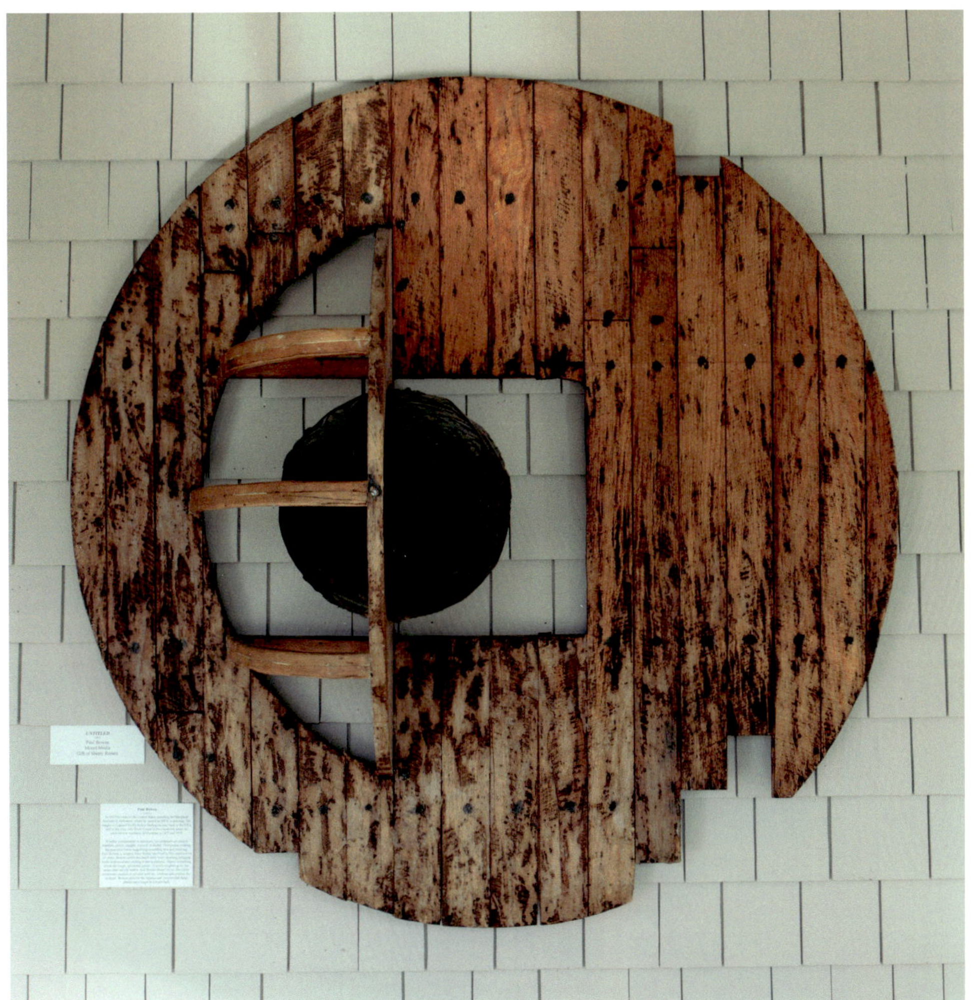

Paul Bowen, *Untitled,* 1985. Mixed media sculpture, 51 × 53 × 17 inches. *Gift of Sherry Remez*, 2001.

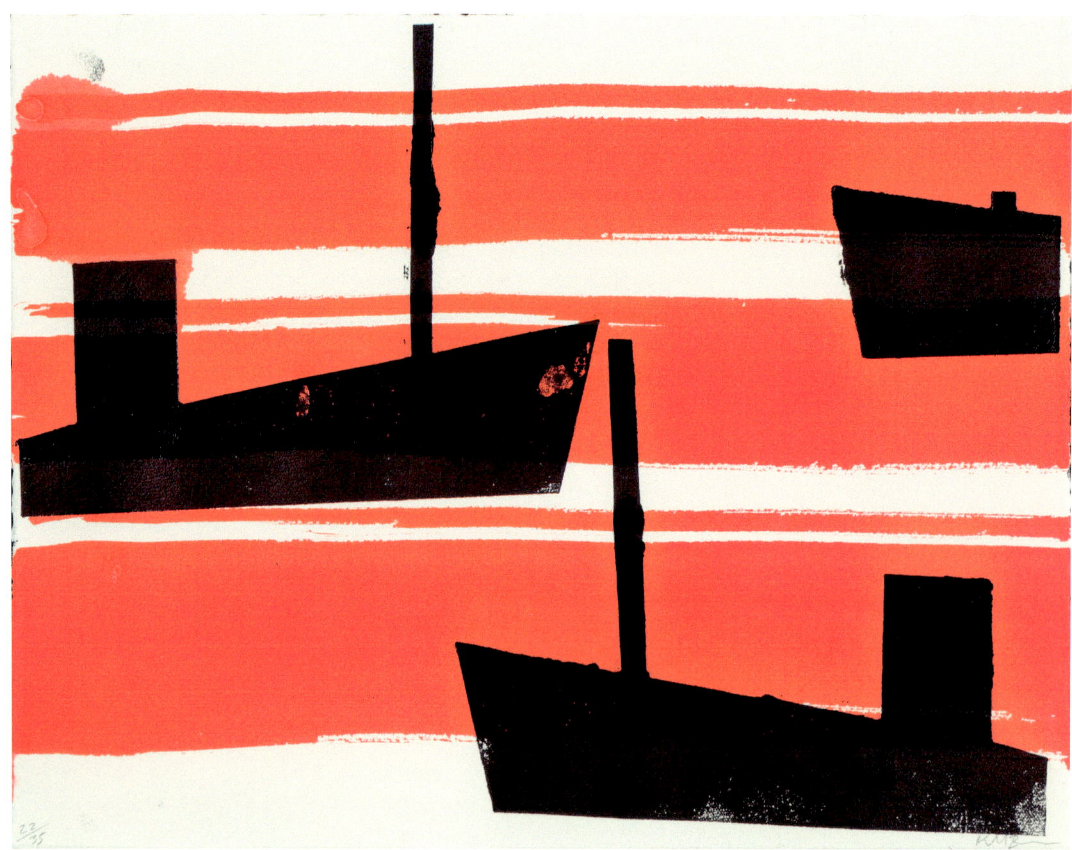

Paul Bowen, *Untitled* 22/35, n.d. Wood and lino-block on paper, 11 × 14 inches. *Gift of Chris and Sally Lutz,* 2005.

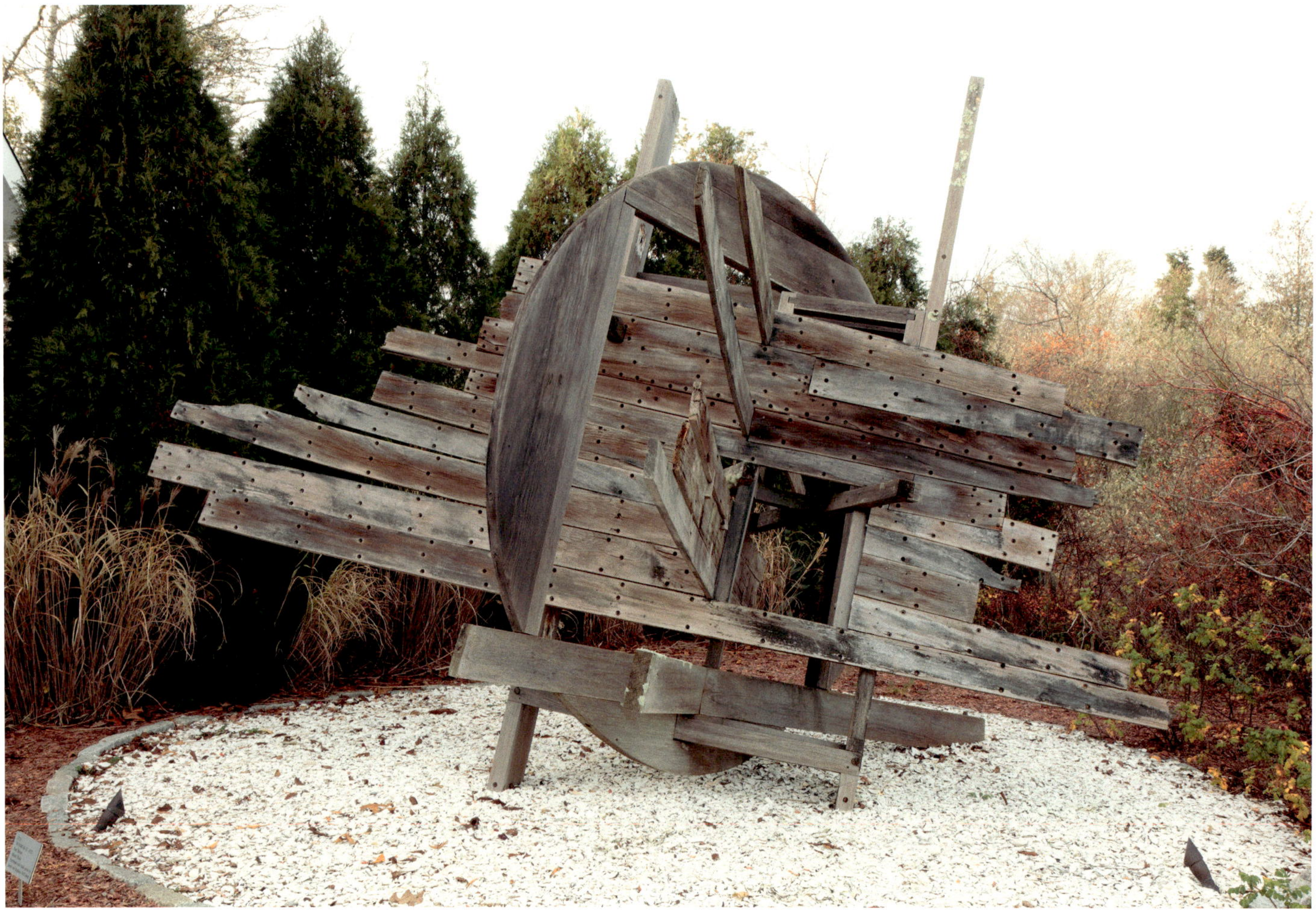

Paul Bowen, *Windrush II,* 2002. Redwood, 125 × 193 × 186 inches.
Museum purchase with funds from James C. A. and Stephania McClennen, 2002.

WILLIAM DAVIS
(1952–)

William Davis's marine art has a direct connection to his boyhood experiences when he took sailing lessons at the Hyannisport Yacht Club. He learned on Beetle Cats and other locally built wooden boats. The years of his youth go back to the 1960s, but Davis's paintings capture a much earlier time. *Summer Sailing, Nantucket*, in the Cape Cod Museum of Art collection, is a blissful painting that evokes the nostalgia of a century ago.

Essentially self-taught, Davis is enchanted with the late nineteenth century, when the seas were graced with elegant schooners in full sail. His paintings of square-riggers, clipper ships, steamboats, cutters, and catboats are often buoyant with bright blue skies. Davis also works in a tonalist palette, which can add a somber element to his work. The tonalist palette uses a color's middle values—warm hues of brown, soft greens, pale yellows, and muted grays—and avoids sharp contrasts and high colors. This approach emphasizes atmosphere and shadow, and reflects Davis's interest in the nineteenth-century painter George Inness. Other nineteenth-century landscape painters in the luminist tradition, such as Martin Johnson Heade and Fitz Hugh Lane, employed a similar color palette, and are an important influence on Davis's work.

Davis paints his marine pictures in the studio from memory, as well as referencing a large library of maritime books on the boats of yesteryear. His colors are imaginative. Sometimes his paintings are colored with the light of late in the day, so he can almost create a silhouette of one of those square-riggers by dramatizing the mellow colors of a sunset. Although best known as a marine artist, Davis does paint *plein-air* landscapes that are often completed in a few hours and have a softer, sketchier look, in contrast to his pristine marine works. In addition to his remarkable technical skills, mood–whether bright or somber–and nostalgia for an earlier, gentler time are always strong elements in Davis's paintings.

Davis's artwork has been chosen to be part of several publications, including *A Gallery of Marine Art*, by Rockport Publishers, and *Shipwrecks Around Boston*, written by William P. Quinn, and is also represented in numerous private and corporate collections.

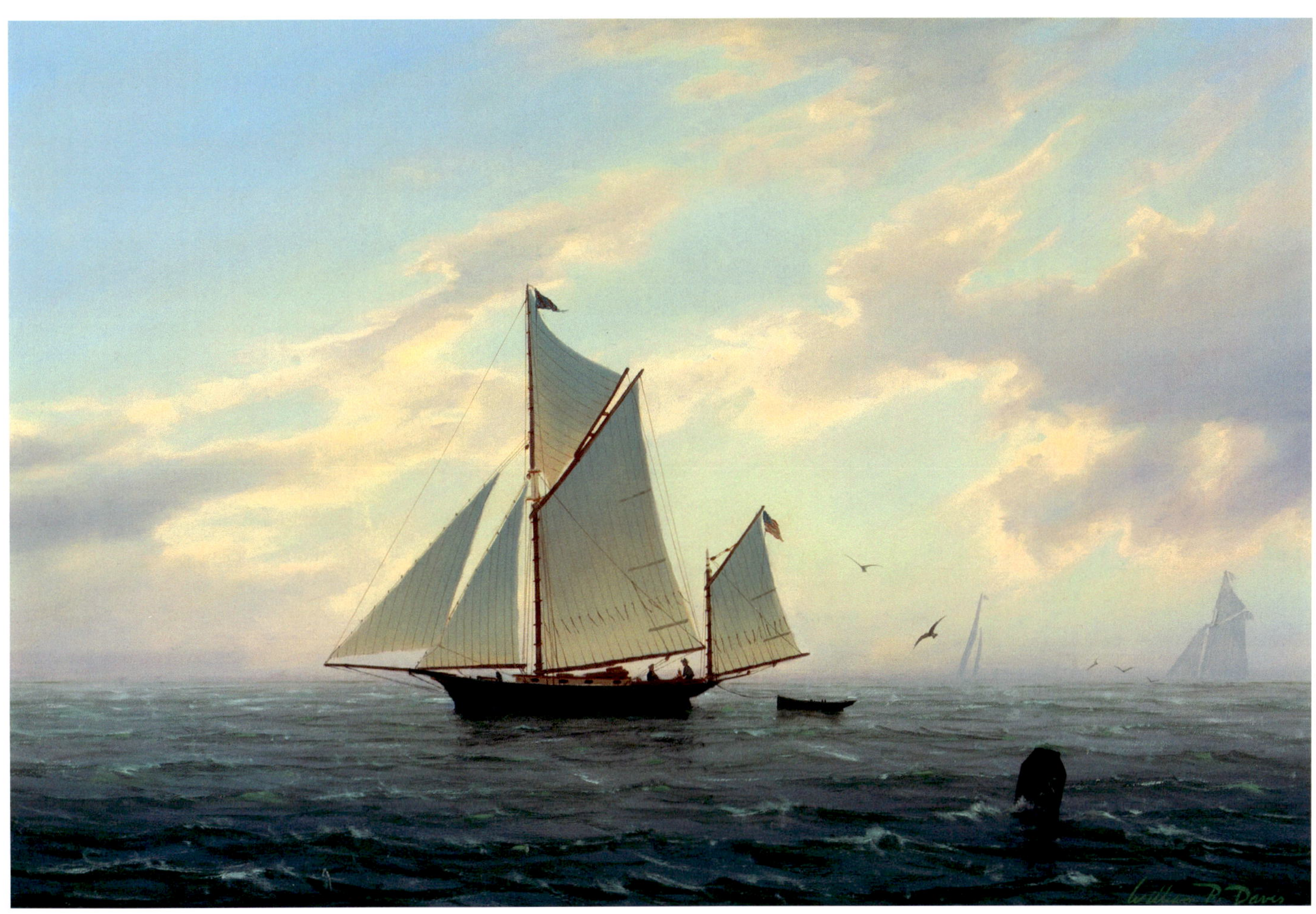

William Davis, *Summer Sailing, Nantucket*, 2001. Oil on panel, 18 × 22 inches. *Gift of Joseph McGurl*, 2003.

THOMAS BARBÈY
(1957–)

Thomas Barbèy's photographs may look like they come out of the real world because they are made up of familiar objects and scenes, but in combination they depict impossibilities. In his photomontages, he combines disparate images to create surreal situations. Unlike photographers using computer technology to create fantastical imagery, he uses only his imagination and traditional photographic techniques.

Barbèy was born in Connecticut, but when he was an infant his parents moved to Europe, and after a time living in Italy and Germany, they settled in Geneva, Switzerland. He began drawing when he was thirteen, which later led him to design posters for musical bands. He moved to Milan, Italy, and became a recording artist, lyricist, and fashion photographer before giving up commercial photography to step into a surreal world with his black-and-white photomontages, which are somewhat influenced by M. C. Escher and René Magritte.

The process for creating his dream-like images involves several techniques, including the sandwiching of negatives together and printing them simultaneously; taking a double-exposure with his camera; or rephotographing collaged photographs. He has built his world with photographs taken during his travels. As he peruses them, he finds various dissimilar images, either in scale or content, which when combined, develop into provocative and unlikely pictures. A gondola gliding down the aisle of a cathedral, surfers riding a wave in the middle of a city, skiers across a bank of snow that turns out to be a white cloth dropping off a table, are a few examples of his imaginative work.

Barbèy often plays with combining a variation in scale, as in *Tourist Trap,* in the Cape Cod Museum of Art collection, which shows a highway with buses, trolleys, and cars emerging out of a tunnel under a giant tree. People walk among the thick roots of the tree, which seems to reach out to enclose them, a bit ominously, thus the "tourist trap." Similar to many of his works, Barbèy has added a title that expands the meaning of the image in amusing ways, often using puns.

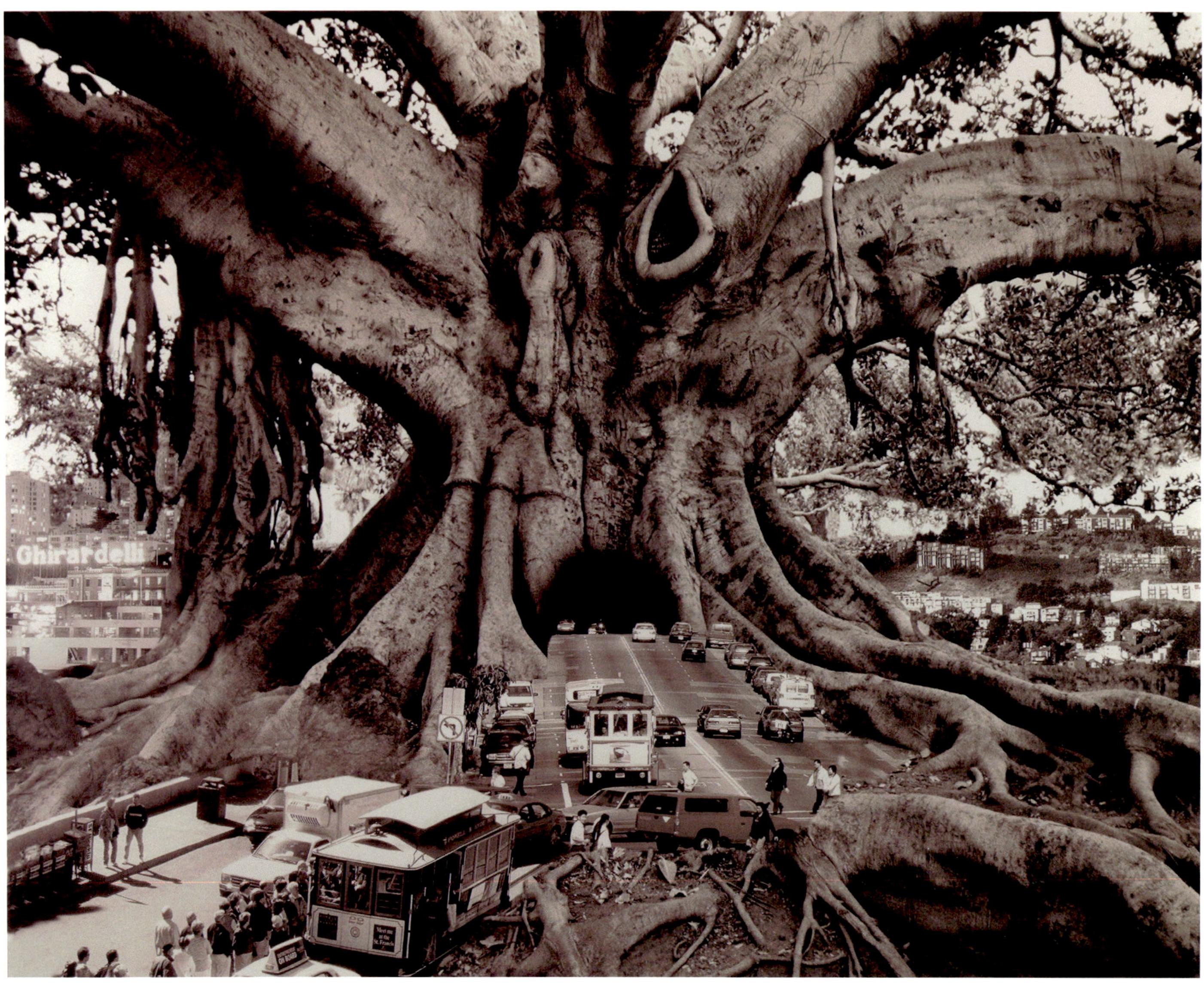

Thomas Barbèy, *Tourist Trap* AP, 2001–2005. Silver gelatin print, 23½ × 29¾ inches. *Gift of Thomas Barbèy in honor of Michael Giaquinto*, 2010.

Crash Course in Italian, also in the museum collection, depicts a canal in Venice dropping off in a waterfall with gondolas spilling over the side and landing on calm waters below. No "crash," but almost.

Barbèy's works are in the permanent collections of a number of museums, including the Madden Museum of Art in Colorado, the New Britain Museum of American Art in Connecticut, and the American Museum in Bath, England.

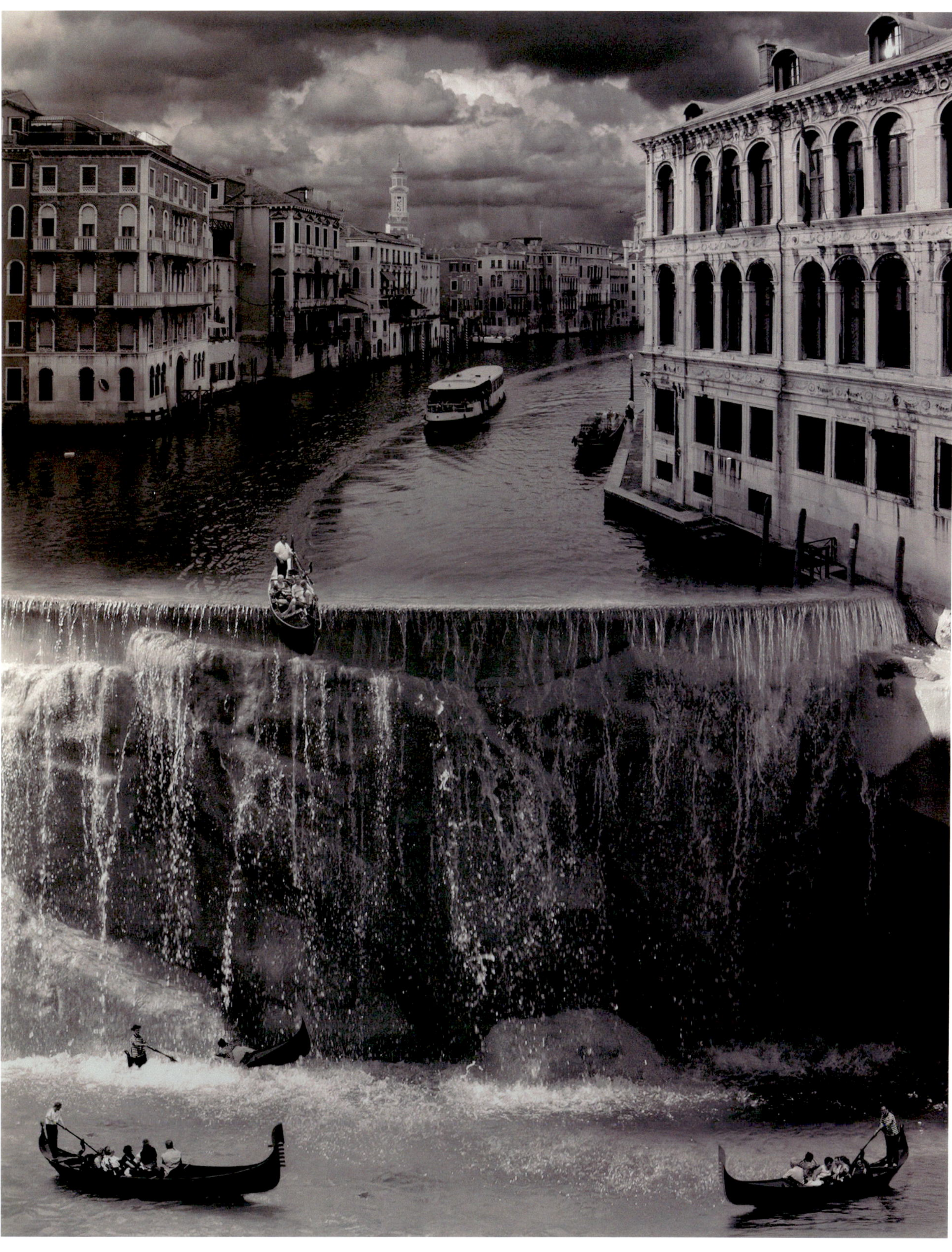

Thomas Barbèy, *Crash Course in Italian* AP, 2001-2005. Silver gelatin print, 29¾ × 23¾ inches.
Gift of Thomas Barbèy in honor of Michael Giaquinto, 2010.

TABITHA VEVERS
(1957–)

Tabitha Vevers, the daughter of artists Tony Vevers and Elspeth Halvorsen, spent many of her childhood summers in Provincetown where her parents had a home. And she still has a deep connection there, dividing her time between Wellfleet and Cambridge, Massachusetts. Born in New York, she received a BA from Yale University and studied at Skowhegan School of Painting & Sculpture.

Her work is often tied to the water and the beach, which were so much a part of her childhood. However, her art is not only about the place where she grew up, but also about evolution and life emerging from the sea. Her images, which include sensual nude figures in dream-like or even surreal situations, often in a seaside environment, deals in explicit ways with her various social concerns, including violence toward women, fertility, feminism, global warming, evolution, and war.

Vevers's work is small, some painted on seashells, as she did as a child, but the themes are large, full of references to the environment and to women's issues. Created in meticulous detail, her paintings are provocative, often sexually explicit and fraught with allegory. The small scale of Vevers's work enhances the intimacy of her connection with viewers, because it forces them to look closely at her pieces.

At one point, Vevers explored the world of nonobjective art but found it could not help her express the emotional content that was important to her. She does acknowledge her parents' influence on her work, although her artistic style is very different from theirs. She saw her father's early figurative paintings as narratives. The social and political concerns of her mother's box constructions have influenced that aspect of her art.

The narrative aspect of Vevers's paintings are clothed in mystery and fantasy, as is *David in Memoriam* from her *Flying Dreams* series, in the Cape Cod Museum of Art collection. Her paintings contrast her elegant and meticulous brushwork with often disturbing images, which come together to challenge the viewer to decipher a meaning. Her themes and strong social concerns are graphically expressed in the small, delicate arenas that make up her painting world.

Her artwork is in a number of public collections, including the Ballinglen Archive, Ballycastle, County Mayo, Ireland; the deCordova Sculpture Park and Museum in Lincoln, Massachusetts; the LaSalle University Art Museum in Philadelphia; the New Britain Museum of American Art in Connecticut; and Yale University Art Gallery in New Haven, Connecticut.

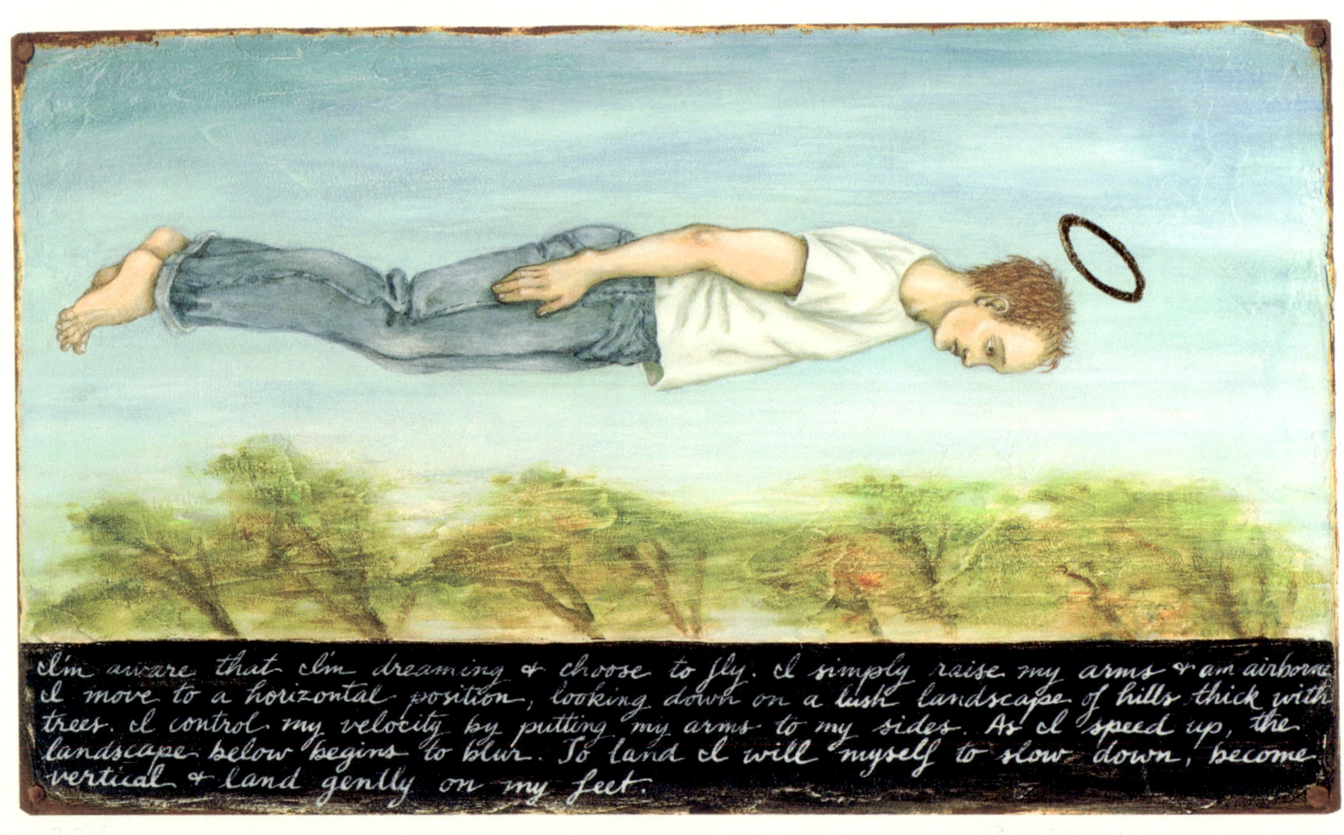

Tabitha Vevers, *David in Memoriam,* 2005. Archival inkjet print with gold leaf, 11 × 14 inches. *Gift of Chris and Sally Lutz,* 2005.

JOSEPH MCGURL
(1958–)

Joseph McGurl's awe for nature's wonders is expressed in his serene paintings of the shoreline as well as his more dramatic works of the mountains and grandeur of the American West. As a *plein-air* painter, his passion for being involved with nature—living, breathing, and painting it—is evident.

McGurl's colors range from muted to bold, and his forms can be gently undulating or stark and rugged, but the scenes he paints appear quiet and reflective. *Bleach*, in the Cape Cod Museum of Art collection, is an example of one of his subtly colored serene images with a not-so-subtle message. For him, painting a landscape is about trying to re-create a three-dimensional space and the sense of distance on a two-dimensional surface.

Born and raised in Massachusetts, McGurl learned his art from his father, James McGurl, who painted murals in churches and public places. The older McGurl also did decorative painting and architectural renderings. It is not surprising, then, that the son wanted to be an artist since he was five. He studied at Boston's School of the Museum of Fine Arts and the Massachusetts College of Art and continued his studies in England and Italy. McGurl lives on Cape Cod and has painted many scenes close to home. But he also travels to Maine, the western states, and to Italy and France to look for inspiration. He is influenced by the nineteenth-century luminists, the Hudson River School, Winslow Homer, and Edward Hopper.

McGurl has a commitment to spending hours outdoors on his oil sketches in order to connect deeply with the landscape and the immediate time and place in which he is working. Sometimes the studio painting comes close to what is represented in the sketches, and other times, it does not. But he continues to be devoted to the process of painting and the life that a work of art can have on its own.

He has received numerous awards, including the Guild of Boston Artists Gold Medallion, The Art Renewal Center First Place Landscape and Purchase Award, and the John Singleton Copley Award for Artistic Achievement.

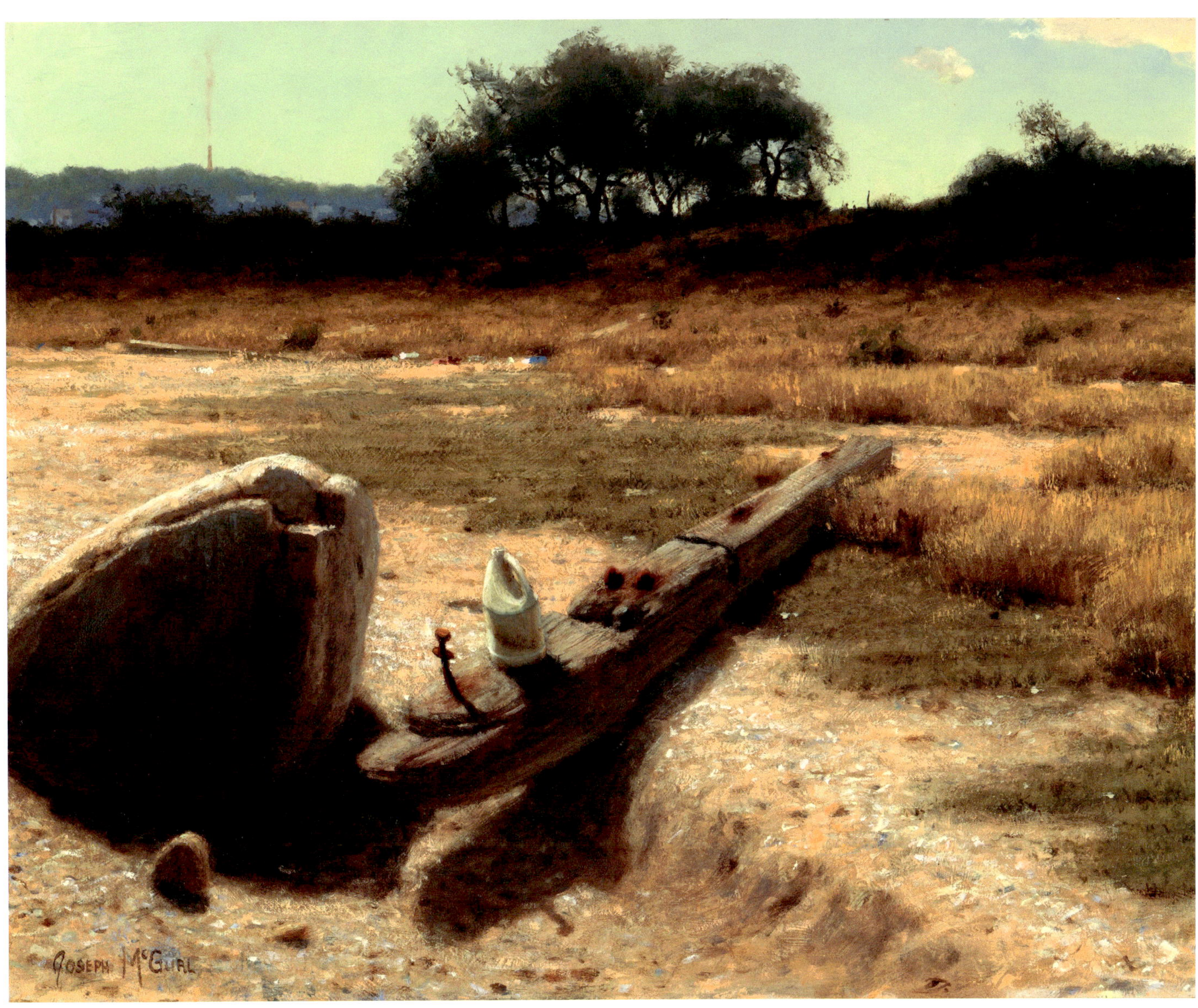

Joseph McGurl, *Bleach,* 2000. Oil on panel, 18 × 22 inches. *Gift of William R. Davis*, 2003.

DONALD BEAL
(1959–)

The landscapes that erupt onto Donald Beal's canvases relate to Provincetown, right outside his door, and northern Maine, where his family spent summer vacations when he was a child. That latter area was the home of his ancestors dating back to pre-Revolutionary War times. Born in Syracuse, New York, Beal grew up in Westford, Massachusetts, and memories of these places nourish his painting. He received a BFA from the Swain School of Design in New Bedford, Massachusetts, studied at Brooklyn College, and received an MFA from Parsons School of Design in 1983.

Beal works spontaneously on a canvas, and begins with making marks. He does not start with sketches or a plan. The painting grows from those spontaneous marks, building relationships between shapes and color.

As have many artists before him, Beal began by painting images of the harbor when he first arrived in Provincetown. He later became interested in finding a more complex subject, so he went into nearby Beech Forest. He found in these dense areas a fascination with the way the light, shapes, and colors change, even though there are still times when

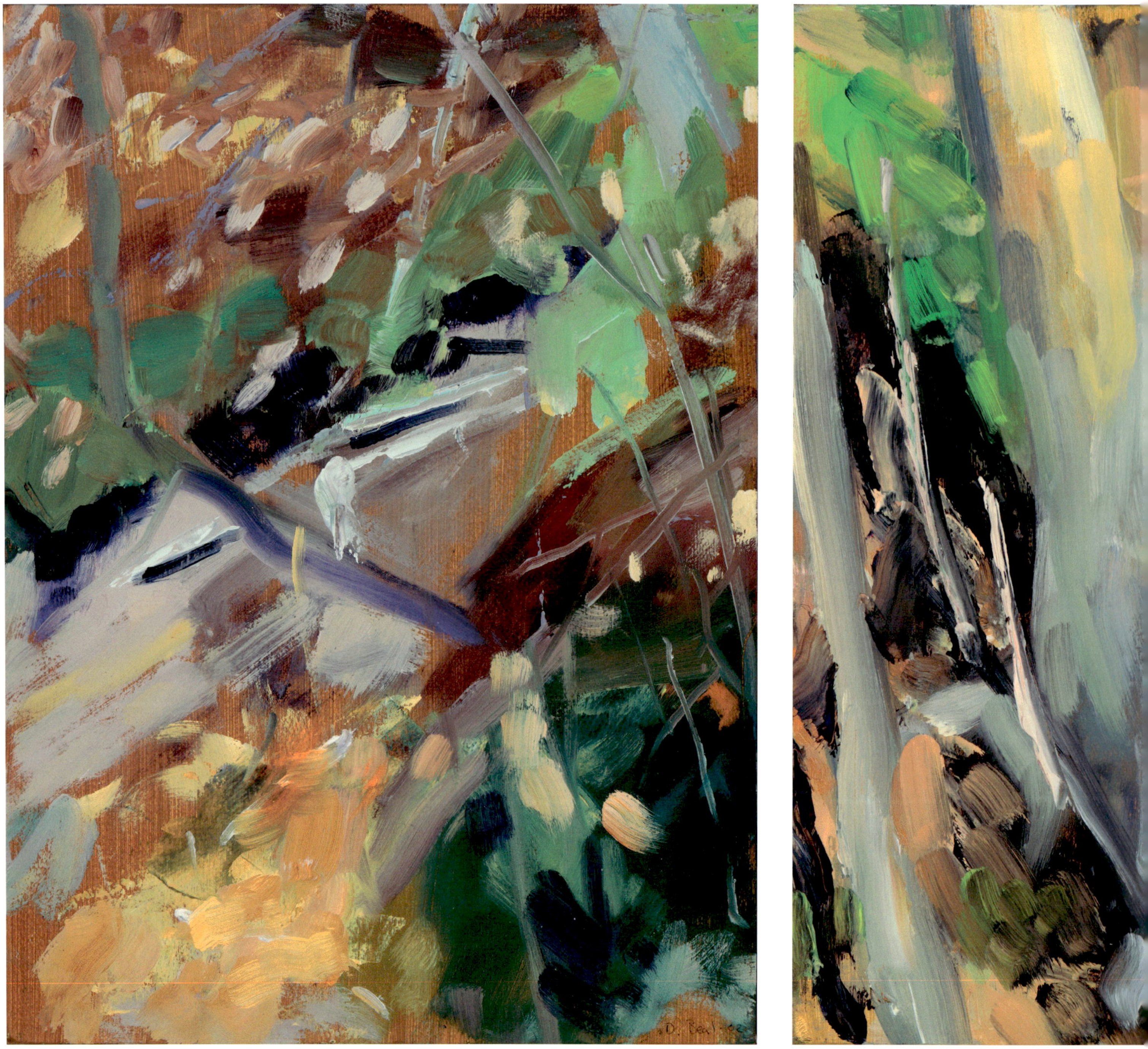

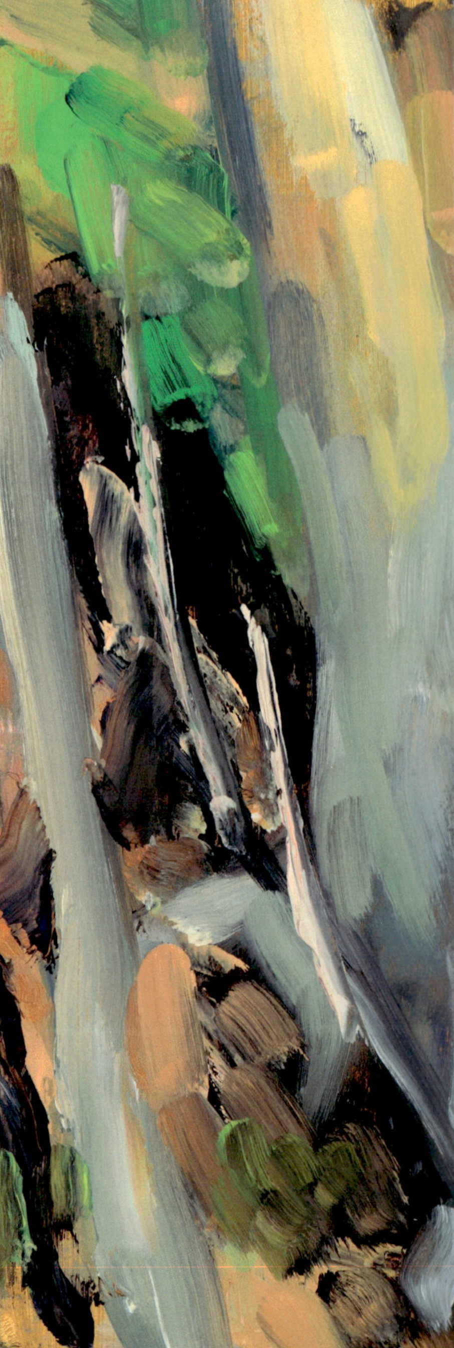

Donald Beal, *Hillside #1-#3* (Triptych), 2002. Oil on panel, 12 × 9 inches each. *Gift of Donald Beal*, 2004.

Provincetown's dunes and undulating land areas make their way into his work. In much of Beal's painting, the viewer can see the gestural approach that defined abstract expressionism. The forest pictures, such as his triptych, *Hillside,* in the Cape Cod Museum of Art collection, involve brushstrokes that bring with them a riot of color and create an almost abstract image, as is especially evident in the first and third paintings of this triptych.

Beal's work is sometimes fierce, compelling, and demanding of a strong emotional response. Other times, his paintings are quieter, made up of broad sweeps of colors, of a pile of rocks in Maine, or a patchwork sky over a vista of land and water. He also paints figures and flowers and even in these more sedate works, the stroke of the brush plays an evocative role.

Beal has lived in Provincetown since the mid-1980s. He has been professor of fine arts at the University of Massachusetts in North Dartmouth since 1999.

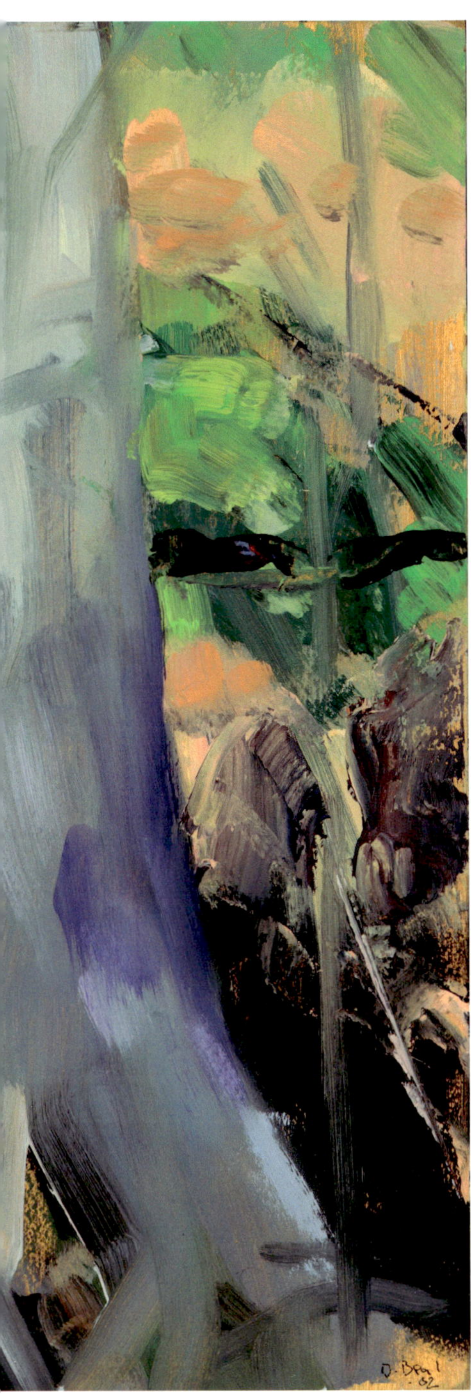

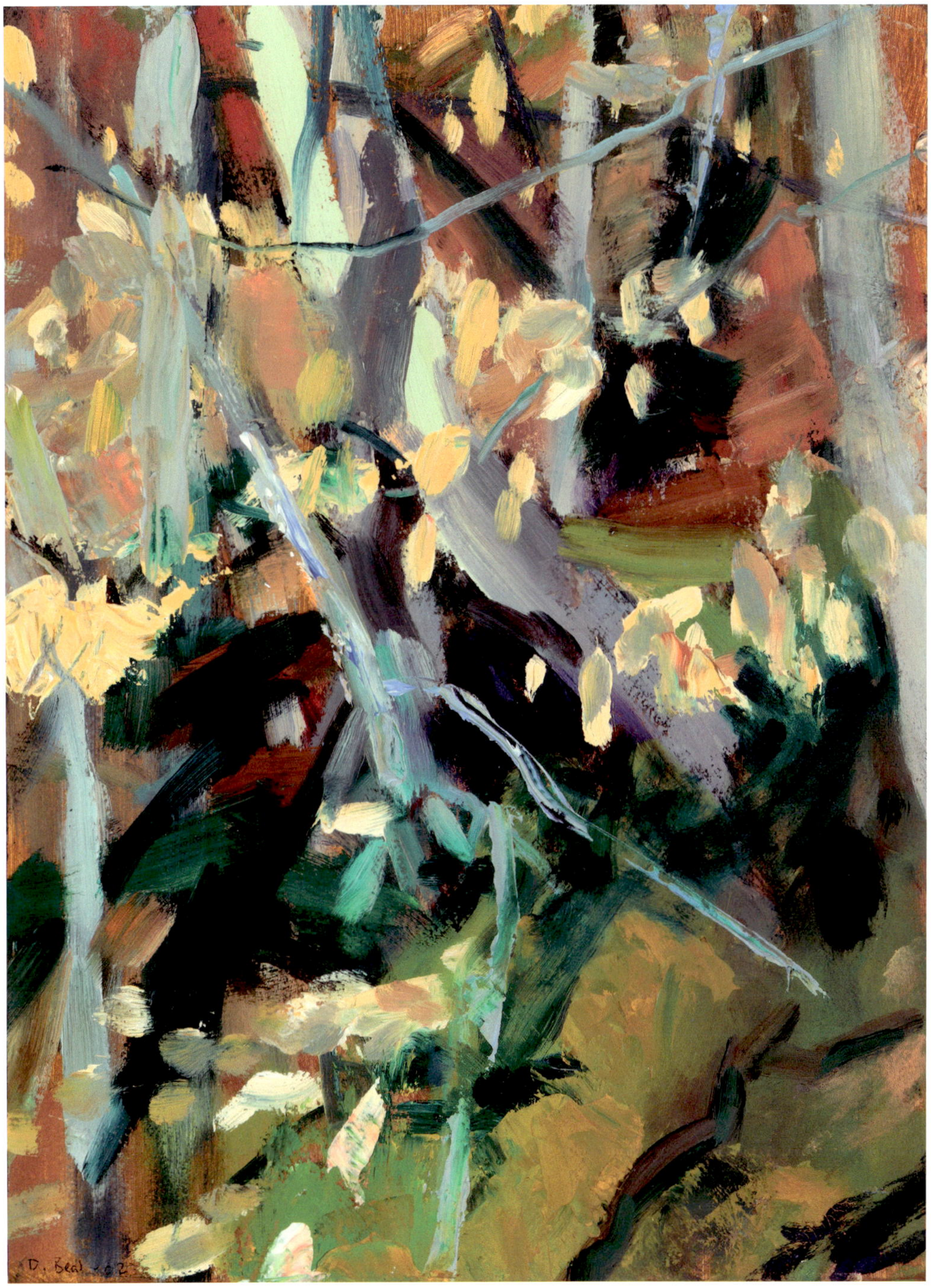

NICHOLAS KAHN
(1964–)

RICHARD SELESNICK
(1964–)

Nicholas Kahn and Richard Selesnick like to tell stories, but they do not use words. Since 1988 they have been collaborating on a series of complex "narrative photo-novellas" and sculptural installations. They specialize in fictitious histories set in the past and future.

Selesnick was born in New York City and Kahn in London. They met at Washington University in St. Louis, where they worked together from 1982 to 1986 as photography majors.

They eventually came to Cape Cod to work on a series of narrative projects, in painting, photography, and sculpture, which had fictional references. Between 1988 and 1995 they created installations combining painted portraits on plaster panels with bread, honey, and wax sculptures, displayed in wooden ritual architecture. During a residency at the Fine Arts Work Center in Provincetown, they created a full-scale oaken chapel, *Der Ruteloft des Bet'ubten Bienenkaisers* (*The Rood-Loft of the Drunken Beekeeper*) with 120 painted panels, all of heads in profile sprouting psychoactive plants from their mouths.

Ultimately they found staged photography was the best way to tell their stories. This photographic work combines fiction and false history, usually presented as large-scale immersive installations featuring a wide variety of media and various costumes and props. The 1997 *The Pavilion of the Greenman* was first shown at the deCordova Museum in Lincoln, Massachussetts. The *Greenman*, which includes a series of profile portraits of the artists as "Greenmen," was constructed as an internally illuminated chapel roofed with leaves and walled with twenty-seven silver photographs printed on vellum. When blown up into four-foot square silver prints, the artists' faces, masked by flowers and leaves glued on with honey, were dramatic, mysterious, and enigmatic. Two works, *Lemon Leaf Man* and *Celandine/Poppy Man*, from the series, are included in the Cape Cod Museum of Art collection. Rather than being the usual archival images that are produced to survive pristinely for hundreds of years, they are purposely intended to slowly age and obtain what the artists call a "patina."

Selesnick's and Kahn's works are in major museum collections, including the Brooklyn Museum of Art, the Philadelphia Museum of Art, the Museum of Fine Arts, Houston, the Los Angeles County Museum of Art, and the National Portrait Gallery in Washington, DC. The artists have also published three books with Aperture Press: *Scotlandfuturebog*, *City of Salt*, and *The Apollo Prophecies*.

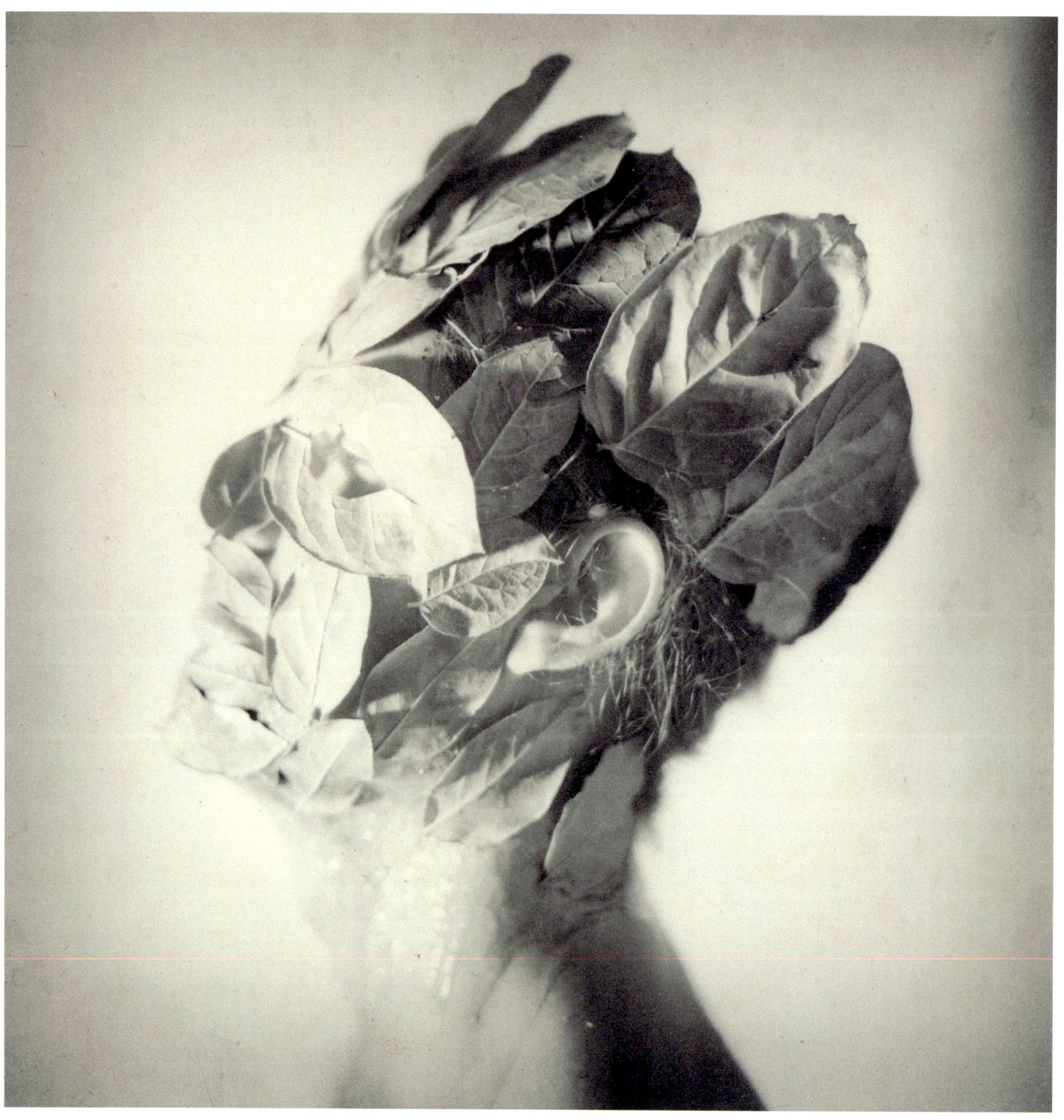

Nicholas Kahn and Richard Selesnik, *Lemon Leaf Man* AP (*Greenman* series), 1997. Silver gelatin print, 12 × 12 inches. *Anonymous gift*, 2009.

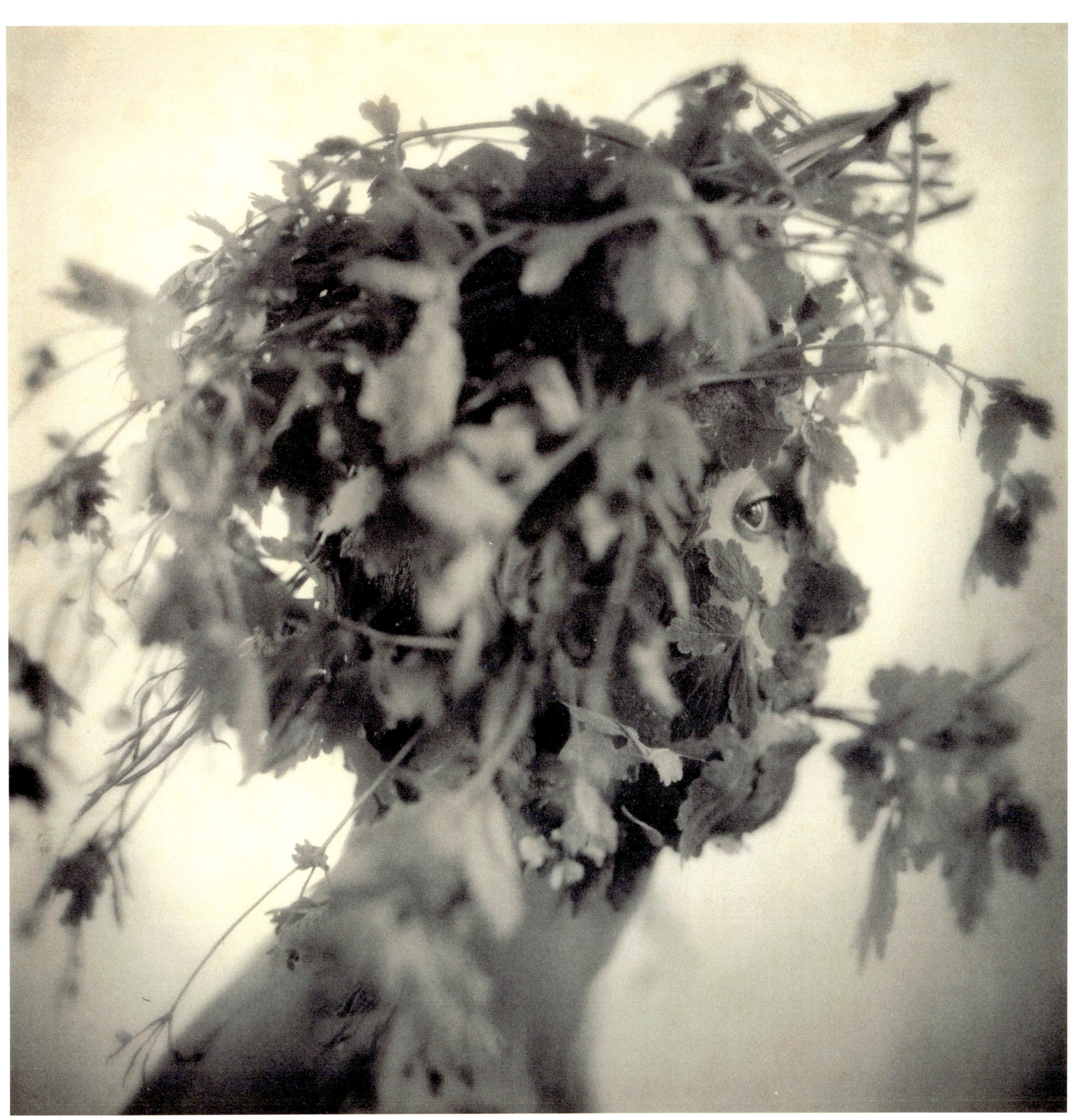

Nicholas Kahn and Richard Selesnik, *Celandine/Poppy Man* AP (*Greenman* series), 1997. Silver gelatin print, 12 × 12 inches. *Anonymous gift,* 2009.

Appendix

Complete List of Artists in the CCMoA Collection with Number of Works

A'Lee Heyerdahl, Jane – 2
Abeles, Sigmund – 1
Alessandra, Dominic – 3
Allen, Mary Cecil – 1
Anderson, BJ – 1
Armstrong, Bill – 1
Audubon, John James – 7
Babineau, John – 2
Backus, Yvonne – 1
Bailey, Bailey Bob – 1
Baker, Susan – 1
Bakker, James R. – 1
Baksa, Teresa – 1
Banks, Alan – 1
Barber, Sam – 2
Barbèy, Thomas – 2
Barnard, Edward Herbert – 1
Barnet, Will – 4
Bartlett, Richard – 3
Basile, Rose – 1
Baskin, Leonard – 15
Bauman, Arthur – 1
Beal, Donald – 3
Beal, Gifford – 3
Beal, Reynolds – 1
Beardsley, Susan – 2
Beauchamp, Robert – 5
Bennett, Betsy – 2
Bennett, Bruce – 1
Benson, Frank W. – 3
Benton, Thomas Hart – 1
Benzer, Sheila – 1
Berlin, Nancy – 3
Berry, Ruthe – 1
Blackwell, Patrick – 1
Blume, Heather – 2
Bodian, Betty – 1
Boghosian, Varujan – 19
Bohm, Max – 1
Boogar, William F. – 2
Boss, Martha – 1
Bourne, Evelyn Bodfish – 4
Bowen, Paul – 3
Bradford, Naomi E. – 2
Brodt, Craig – 2
Broe, Vern – 1
Brophy, Sally – 1
Brown, Harold Haven – 1
Browne, Byron – 1
Browne, George Elmer – 3
Bruckman, Lodewijk – 1
Bultman, Fritz – 1
Burkert, Robert – 1
Burlingame, Sheila – 1
Burliuk, David – 1
Burner, Janet – 1
Busa, Peter – 2
Cahoon, Charles Drew – 4
Cahoon, Martha – 2
Calder, Alexander – 1
Calhoun, Jean – 1
Camino, Denny – 3
Carter, B. Shirley – 4
Chaffee, Oliver Newberry – 2
Chamberlain, Roger – 1
Charron, T. A. – 1
Chater, Elizabeth – 2
Chester, Mark – 1
Christopher, LaVerne – 1
Cicero, Carmen – 3
Cipriani, Robert – 2
Clayton, John – 1
Cobb, Ruth – 1
Coes, Peter – 1
Cohen, Arthur – 7
Cohen, Barbara – 1
Coleman, Vernon – 2
Cormier, Robert – 2
Corti, Costantino – 1
Costa, Robert – 1
Coughlin, Jack – 2
Coughlin, Joan Hopkins – 1
Couper, Charles Alexander – 2
Critchley, Jay – 1
Crockett, W. – 1
Croney, Claude – 4
Crowell, Francis B. – 1
Cummings, Robert Homer – 1
Dahlstrom, Shawn Nelson – 1
Dangelo, Michele – 1
Davis, William R. – 1
Day, Arthur – 1

de Groot, Nanno – 3
de Nagy, Lazlo – 1
De Quattro, Richard – 1
Dearborn, Georgia – 1
Del Deo, Salvatore – 2
Dennis, Morgan – 1
Devita, Nancy – 1
Dicke, Scott – 1
Dickerson, Gay – 5
Dickinson, Edwin Walter – 1
Diehl, Arthur – 3
Dobkin, Alex – 1
Dodd, D. Cary – 1
Donahue, Beth – 1
Donnelly, Helen – 2
Dorfman, Gladys Winn – 4
Dowd, John – 1
Dubin, Ralph – 2
Dunbar, Harold – 1
Dunigan, Breon – 1
Dunn, Howard – 3
Eastwood, Evelyn – 2
Eastwood, Thomas – 79
Eaton, Thomas – 2
Eccles, Jane – 2
Eddy, Alan S. – 1
Edel, Albert – 3
Edwards, Ethel – 6
Edwards, Herb – 1
Edwards, S. – 1
Edwards, Sylvia – 1
Egelson, Polly Seliger – 6
Eldridge, Barbara Ann – 1
Engel, Harry – 1
Enneking, John Joseph – 24
Enneking, Joseph Eliot – 8
Ernst, Mike – 4
Euler, Edwin Reeves – 3
Evaul, William – 1
Falconer, Marguerite E. – 2
Fanelli, Joseph – 2
Farnham, Emily – 2
Farruggio, Remo – 2
Federoff, George – 1
Feeney, Loretta – 2
Feinstein, Samuel L. – 3
Fieux, Robert – 2
Filardi, Del – 10
Firman, Lisbeth – 1
Fisher, Robert M. – 5
Fitsch, Eugene C. 6
Flanders, Claire – 2
Fleury, Rick – 3
Florsheim, Richard – 26
Forman, Debbie – 1
Foster, Stephanie – 1
Frank, Robert – 1
Franklin, Gilbert – 6
Frantin, Lillia – 1
Freed, Roy N. – 7
Freed, William – 5
Freedman, Maurice – 1
Fried, Miriam – 3
Fried, Seymour (Cy) – 6
Fromboluti, Sideo – 1
Gahagan, James – 2
Gammell, R.H. Ives – 7
Garver, Jack – 2
Garvey, Carole Chisholm – 1
Geissbuhler, Arnold – 48
Giaquinto, Michael A. – 1
Gibbs, Howard – 66
Gibran, Kahlil – 3
Gieberich, Oscar – 1
Gilmartin, Garry – 1
Gilmore, Ada – 1
Ginandes, Carol – 1
Giobbi, Edward – 1
Glover, Alfred – 4
Goetz, Richard Vernon – 1
Goff, Emery – 1
Goldberg, Ida – 1
Golden, Franny – 1
Goldman, Virginia – 1
Gonzalez, Ronald – 2
Gonzalez, Xavier – 24
Goodman, Bertram – 1
Gorey, Edward – 1
Graham, Linda Ohlson – 1
Gregory, Dorothy Lake – 4
Griffel, Lois – 2
Grillo, John – 2
Grimaldi, Vince – 1
Grooms, Red – 1
Groshans, Walter – 5
Gross, Chaim – 4
Gross, Mimi – 1
Grosz, George – 1
Guiliani, Ann – 2
Gurr, Lena – 1
Hablanian, Ann – 1
Halberstadt, Ernst – 6
Halvorsen, Elspeth – 1
Hansen, Gordon – 64
Hansen, Hans Peter – 3
Hare, John C. – 4
Harmon, Lily – 1
Harrington, Andrea – 1
Harrington, James – 3
Harris, Harold – 4
Harrison, Myrna – 2
Hart, Sarah – 2
Hartley, Katherine Ann – 1
Hawthorne, Charles – 3

Hawthorne, Marion C. – 4
Hearle, Debbie – 1
Heinz, Charles 6
Heller, Amy – 1
Henry, Robert – 5
Hensche, Henry – 9
Heus, Ray – 3
Hinton, Megan – 1
Hofmann, Hans – 2
Hogan, Ruth – 3
Holden, Martha – 2
Holl, Harry – 12
Holl, Sarah – 1
Holt, William Lee – 1
Hondius, Gerrit – 3
Hopkins, Budd – 1
Horch, Nancy Sirkis – 1
Horowitz, Brenda – 2
Horrocks, Joan E. – 1
Howard, Richard E. (Ric) – 1
Howe, Marcia – 5
Hughes, Daisy Marguerite – 1
Hunt, Peter – 8
Hunter, Robert Douglas – 9
Hurlbert, Roberta – 1
Hutchinson, Marieluise – 1
Hyland, Christopher – 1
Ikeda, Eisen (Eisen) – 1
Jackson, Ella 7
Jackson, Eugene – 15
Jackson, Leslie Gillette – 1
Jacobs, Ted Seth – 1
Jencks, Penelope – 1
Jensen, Hank – 2
Johns, Jasper – 1
Johnson, Doug – 3
Johnson, Joyce – 3
Johnson, Renita – 2
Johnston, Maryalice – 1
Jones, Benton – 1
Jones, Eleanor Ferri – 11
Jones, Michael E. – 1
Joyce, Marshall – 1
Jules, Mervin – 1
Kaeselau, Charles – 2
Kahn, Nicholas & Selesnik, Richard – 2
Kalman, Bela – 1
Kamarck, Margaret – 2
Kaplan, Joseph – 7
Kapp – 1
Kashem, Cate Hunter – 1
Kass, Mary – 1
Katz, RJ – 1
Kaufman, Rachel – 15
Kelly, Ellsworth – 1
Kemble, Richard – 37
Kennedy, Steven – 1
Kent, Sister Mary Corita – 2
Kent, H. L. – 1
Kent, Rockwell – 12
Kimball, Yeffee – 1
Kingsland, James – 1
Kirk, Jerome – 1
Knaths, Karl – 6
Koch, Erik – 2
Koch, Philip – 2
Kornsand, Luisa – 1
Krenik, John – 1
Kriesberg, Irving – 2
Krohn, Don – 3
Kunichika, Toyohara (Kunichika) – 1
Kupferman, David – 5
Kupferman, Lawrence – 2
L'Engle, Lucy – 3
Laasko, David – 1
LaFleur Pieper, Karen – 1
Lambert, Jackson – 1
Lamont, Fraces Kent – 1
Lane, Betty – 20
LaPointe, Lorraine – 1
Larned, Jack – 2
LaSelle, Toni – 1
Lawson, Andrea – 1
Lazell, Blanche – 2
LeBow, Ellen – 3
Lechay, James – 7
Lee-Smith, Katherine – 1
Leighton, Clare – 20
Leipzig, Mel – 1
Levin, Dana – 1
Liebeskind, William – 2
Lincoln, E. F. – 1
Lincoln, Jane – 1
Lindenmuth, Tod – 2
Lipton, Irene – 1
Littlefield, William H. – 36
Loeb, Dorothy – 4
Lovell, May and Alexander – 2
Lundgren, Carl – 2
Lutz, Sarah – 1
MacKenzie, Pia – 3
Mainelli, Lorraine – 1
Malicoat, Philip C. – 1
Maloney, William J. – 1
Manso, Leo – 1
Margo, Boris – 32
Maril, Herman – 7
Marsh, Reginald – 2
Martin, Charles J. – 3
Maxim, Ora Hinge – 1
Mazer, Mike – 1
McDarrah, Fred W. – 15
McGurl, Joseph – 1
McKain, Bruce – 3

McLaughlin, Frances Louise – 1
McLean, Susan O'Brien – 2
McMurtry, Arthur – 3
McNeil, George – 2
Meeser, Lillian Burk – 1
Melcher, Barbara – 1
Meyer, Frederick – 1
Meyerowitz, Joel – 5
Milby, Frank – 1
Miller, Gustaf – 1
Moffett, Ross – 4
Mongeau, Alice – 3
Motherwell, Renate Ponsold – 14
Motherwell, Robert – 2
Movitz, Edward – 1
Mulcahy, John – 2
Mulhaupt, Frederick – 1
Mumford, Elizabeth – 1
Murphy, John F. – 1
Müller, Jan – 1
Nadeau, Rosalie Stambler – 1
Natale, Nancy – 1
Natale, Pasquale – 1
Neal, Richard – 1
Neill, Ben – 1
Neily, Hilda – 1
Neubauer, John Daniel – 1
Nicholas, Frank Cardozo – 2
Nisbet, Robert – 1
Nolan, Kevin – 1
Noyes, George L. – 1
Odell, Carol – 2
Odell, Tom – 1
Orlowsky, Lillian – 3
Orr, Elliot – 2
Orr, Joan – 1
Osmond, Susan – 1
Ownby, Haynes – 8
Packard, Anne – 3
Packard, Cynthia – 1
Packer, Suzanne M. – 1
Pairpoint Glass Company – 1
Parent, Neal – 2
Patten, Nick –6
Patterson, Margaret J. – 1
Paxton, William McGregor – 2
Pearson, Celia – 1
Pepitone, Richard – 7
Perry, Richard O. – 3
Peters, Jim – 2
Pfeiffer, Heinrich – 2
Pfeufer, Reed Champion – 2
Pieper, Philip – 3
Pierce, Earl – 1
Pimenta, Rosa – 1
Pissarenko, Miroslava – 1
Pluhar, Andrea – 1
Polak, Richard – 1
Polansky, Dorothy – 2
Pontbriand, Roger – 4
Poor, Anna – 1
Pratt, Elizabeth Hayes – 5
Preston, Malcolm – 1
Principato, Ernest – 3
Prior, Scott – 4
Purwin, Sig – 10
Ranalli, Daniel – 1
Randolph, Francie – 1
Rann, Vollian Burr – 2
Rayen, James Wilson – 4
Rayner, Ada – 2
Reed, Gladys – 1
Resika, Paul – 3
Rich, Sylvia G. – 1
Richert, Charles H. – 1
Ripley, Aiden Lassell – 2
Rizk, Romanos – 5
Roark, Robert – 2
Rockefeller, Barbara 7
Rogers, Robert B. – 1
Romano, Claire Camille – 1
Romano, Umberto – 1
Rosenblum, Richard – 3
Rosenthal, Karin – 1
Rosenthal, Margot – 1
Rosser, Curt – 6
Rourke, Richard White – 2
Ruhl, L.W. – 29
Rupe, Dan – 2
Salas, Anne – 1
Samuelson, Rose Ann – 1
Sandman, Jo – 2
Schaefer, Taf Lebel – 2
Scherman, Rowland – 4
Schlem, Betty Lou – 2
Schmidt, Hans – 1
Schulenberg, Paul – 1
Schulz, Matthew – 1
Scull, Nancy C. – 1
Searle, William Ross – 2
Sears, Olga – 1
Segalman, Richard – 1
Selman, Jan Collins – 25
Shackelford, Shelby – 5
Shahn, Judith – 231
Simon, Sidney – 3
Simon, Suzanne – 1
Simons, Charles W. – 1
Sitbon, David – 1
Slack, Chester – 1
Slade, C. Arnold – 1
Smith, David Loeffler – 1
Smith, Edward – 1
Smith, Geoffrey – 1

Index

Selected Artists from the Collection of the Cape Cod Museum of Art